THIRD EDITION

JUVENILE DELINQUENCY AND ANTISOCIAL BEHAVIOR: A DEVELOPMENTAL PERSPECTIVE

Curt R. Bartol & Anne M. Bartol

PEARSON

Prentice
Hall

Upper Saddle River, New Jersey
Columbus, Ohio

Library of Congress Cataloging-in-Publication Data

Bartol, Curt R., 1940-
   Juvenile delinquency and antisocial behavior : a developmental perspective / Curt R. Bartol &
Anne M. Bartol. —3rd ed.
      p. cm.
   Rev. ed. of: Delinquency and justice. 2nd ed. cl998.
   Includes bibliographical references and indexes.
   ISBN-13: 978-0-13-159925-3
   ISBN-10: 0-13-159925-9
   1. Juvenile delinquency—United States. 2. Juvenile delinquents—United states—Psychology.
3. Developmental psychology—United States. 4. Juvenile delinquents—Rehabilitation—United
States. I. Bartol, Anne M, II. Bartol, Curt R., 1940-Delinquency and justice. III. Title.
   HV9104.B344 2009
   364.360973—dc22   2007029551

Vice President and Executive Publisher: Vernon Anthony
Acquisitions Editor: Tim Peyton
Editorial Assistant: Alicia Kelly
Project Manager: Alicia Ritchey
Design Coordinator: Diane Ernsberger
Cover Designer: Kellyn Donnelly
Cover Art: Corbis
Senior Operations Supervisor: Pat Tonneman
Director of Marketing: David Gesell
Marketing Manager: Adam Kioza
Marketing Coordinator: Alicia Dysert

This book was set in by TexTech Inc. It was printed and bound by R.R. Donnelly & Sons Comp. was
printed by R.R. Donnelley & Sons Company.

Pearson Education Ltd.   Pearson Education Australia Pty. Limited
Pearson Education Singapore Pte Ltd.   Pearson Education North Asia Ltd.
Pearson Education Canada, Ltd.   Pearson Education de Mexico, S.A. de C.V.
Pearson Education—Japan   Pearson Education Malaysia Pte. Ltd.

10 9 8 7 6 5 4 3 2 1
ISBN-13: 978-0-13-159925-3
ISBN-10:   0-13-159925-9

To Darya,
Bright, loving, and spirited. . .
May your future be the same.

CONTENTS

PREFACE

A major difference between *Juvenile Delinquency and Antisocial Behavior: A Developmental Perspective* and the many other juvenile delinquency texts is the *psychological* orientation of this one. A psychological approach does not mean that delinquents or juvenile offenders are seen as mentally disturbed or in need of clinical treatment. Some do have serious emotional problems and need considerable treatment, but most are not clinically disturbed and do not require traditional forms of treatment. Contemporary psychology has moved away from seeing people, including juvenile offenders, as broken and needing to be fixed and toward seeing them as active problem solvers immersed in a wide variety of influences, ranging from their own cognitions to the economic and social systems around them. This new edition includes a significant increase in the contemporary research on the genetic, biological, and neuropsychological influences on development and delinquency.

This text has several major objectives. First, we hope to cultivate in readers a patience to see the world from multiple perspectives and to provide the necessary concepts with which to refine these perspectives. Perspectives on behavior, including delinquent behavior, are strongly influenced by political, economic, and social climates. In the 1980s, when juvenile crime rates were rising rapidly in the United States, many people responded with recommendations that we "get tough" with juveniles. In the 1990s, these no-nonsense approaches were seen as simplistic and were seriously questioned. Today, the nation's attention seems focused more on our economic situation and on political developments in the Middle East, and we hear very little about juvenile crime. Concurrently, social programs intended to provide support for children and their families are getting short-changed.

Our second major objective is to emphasize not only what can go wrong but—perhaps more importantly—what can go right. Rather than focusing exclusively on the factors and influences that may to lead to antisocial behavior, we give considerable attention to human capabilities and adaptive behaviors that promote healthy development and functioning. Research on delinquency has traditionally focused on risk factors that lead to antisocial behavior, violence, and chronic offending. Although we comprehensively review the research and theories on risk factors, we also give significant attention to individual adaptation and resilience factors, which prevent or reduce participation in antisocial behavior. *Resilience* refers to the ability to overcome risk factors and to function adaptively in spite of being exposed to serious threats and negative circumstances, such as neglect or poverty. Research on resilience underscores the perspective that children have different vulnerabilities and protective systems at different ages and points in their development. Many children do not display antisocial behavior even though they have been exposed to many of the risk factors that are believed to contribute to antisocial and delinquent behavior. Social and interpersonal skills, coping strategies, cognitive and self-regulation skills, motivation, positive opportunities, and self-confidence are all likely to reduce the influence of these risk factors. If society is to find better ways of preventing, intervening in, and treating delinquency and antisocial behavior, a focus on children's coping strategies and adaptive mechanisms is warranted. The book begins with a discussion of risk factors (Chapters 2 and 3), and quickly move, on to protective factors and the resilience that they promote.

Our third major objective is to have the reader understand that juvenile delinquency, as well as antisocial behavior in general, has multiple causes, manifestations, and developmental pathways. Consequently, we identify the many social, biological, and psychological influences during preadolescent and adolescent development that lead to chronic, persistent, and violent offending.

Our fourth goal is to recognize the multicultural perspectives that play critical roles in the development of delinquency. For example, well-trained professionals who work with juvenile offenders recognize that ethnic and racial sensitivity is critical to successful work with child and adolescent offenders, and these professionals know they must be constantly vigilant against the injustice that can result from a monocultural perspective. We try to pay close attention to the issue of cultural diversity throughout the text. Likewise, research and theory on gender and sexual identity are interwoven in the text as they are relevant.

The subtitle of the book, *A Developmental Perspective*, is significant because we concentrate on the rapidly expanding research on the relationship between development and antisocial behavior. We emphasize that developmental trajectories differ not only across individuals but also across cultures, subcultures, and sociodemographic environments. The developmental pathways approach to delinquency represents some of the most cutting-edge research available in this area, and we spend some time considering the longitudinal research method on which it is based and which many developmental psychologists and criminologists have embraced. Juveniles arrive at delinquency and antisocial behavior through a variety of paths, or trajectories. Some take the road very early in their development, while others do not embark on it until they reach adolescence. If we are able to identify the developmental trajectories of early antisocial or delinquent behavior, we will gain invaluable information about important targets and appropriate timing for intervention.

This book is designed to be a core text in undergraduate and graduate courses in juvenile delinquency, juvenile antisocial behavior, juvenile crime, or child and adolescent offending. Students majoring in psychology, social work, public policy, or criminal justice, as well as students with only limited exposure to these fields, should be equally comfortable with the material discussed. The text is substantially different from the second edition, entitled *Delinquency and Justice: A Psychosocial Approach*. We have chosen not to include an extensive review of juvenile justice, which deserves a separate book with a very different focus. This books content has been completely reorganized, rewritten, and refocused. The material is strongly research based, and we have tried to include the most current data and information available.

ONLINE INSTRUCTOR'S RESOURCES

To access supplementary materials online, instructors need to request an instructors access code. Go to **www.prenhall.com**, click the **Instructor Resource Center** link, and then click **Register Today** for an instructor access code. Within 48 hours after

Instructor Resource Center

Register today at www.prenhall.com to access instructor resources digitally.

registering you will receive a confirming e-mail including an instructor access code. Once you have received your code, go to the site and log on for full instructions on downloading the materials you wish to use.

ACKNOWLEDGEMENTS

Thank you to the many good people associated with Prentice-Hall. Once again, an extremely talented group of professionals offered guidance and assistance along the way. Senior Acquisitions Editor Tim Peyton has encouraged and supported us at every step, and we are grateful that he had the faith and vision needed to produce this third edition. Project Manager Alicia Ritchey guided the manuscript through its final stages. She has been helpful, efficient, and unflappable—as only she knows. Copyeditor Mary Benis surely ranks among the best in her profession; she was perceptive, organized, knowledgeable, and far more patient than we deserved. From the moment of our first contact with her, we knew our manuscript was in good hands. Many individuals behind the scenes at Prentice-Hall should be recognized for their careful work, and we thank them sincerely. They include: Editorial assistant Alicia Kelly, Proofreader Marianne L'Abbate, Senior Managing Editor JoEllen Gohr, Associate Managing Editor Alex Wolf, Art Director Diane Ernsberger, Art Cover Designer Kellyn Donnelly, and Senior Operations Supervisor Pat Tonneman.

The manuscript was reviewed by Fred A. Sams, Canyon College, and Anthony Walsh, Boise State University. Their comments and suggestions were invaluable to us, and we hope we have produced a better book as a result of their input.

Finally, and as always, we are appreciative of the love in our lives and the life we share with our children, their spouses, and our grandchildren: Gina, Ian, Soraya, Jim, Kai, Maddie, Darya, and Shannon. They are what matters.

CHAPTER 1

INTRODUCTION TO DELINQUENCY AND ANTISOCIAL BEHAVIOR

CHAPTER OBJECTIVES

◆ Introduce and define the concept *juvenile delinquency*

◆ Highlight a developmental perspective

◆ Introduce and define the terms used to classify antisocial behavior in children

◆ Introduce common research methods used in the study of juvenile delinquency

Year after year, approximately 1.8 to 2.2 million juveniles under the age of 18 are arrested by law enforcement officers in the United States. Although juvenile crime has declined in recent years, these statistics still represent an enormous amount of offending by American youth. In 2000 more than 30 million youth were under juvenile court jurisdiction (Puzzanchera, Stahl, Finnegan, Tierney, & Snyder, 2004), and 80% of these youth were between the ages of 10 and 15. In 2000, courts with juvenile jurisdiction handled an estimated 1.6 million delinquency cases, and in any day the juvenile courts processed roughly 4,500 cases (Puzzanchera et al., 2004). Nearly two-thirds of the cases involved youths aged 15 or younger at the time of referral. Although most juvenile offending is nonviolent in nature, many of the cases involved sex offending or other violent crime.

THE MANY CAUSES OF DELINQUENCY

Over the past three decades, research has increasingly indicated that juvenile delinquency has multiple causes. Furthermore, these multiple causes interact in a very complicated way for the individual, the family, the school, peers, the community, and the cultural context within which the child or adolescent resides. In order to be effective, delinquency prevention and intervention must not only be tailored to the individual's developmental level but must also address the significant influences of that individual's social environment. "To successfully reduce youth violence, prevention strategies must engage the entire spectrum of individuals and community systems impacting a young person's life, including families, schools, peers, and other adults in the community" (Coordinating Council, 1996, p. 8).

One mission of this text is to examine what is currently known about the many causes of delinquency and what can be done to reduce or eliminate these causes. We often hear from the media and other sources that certain children are "at risk" of becoming delinquent. *At risk* means that certain influences in the lives of many children make them good candidates for developing antisocial behaviors. In this text, we will describe these **risk factors**, those influences that increase the tendency to become delinquent. Examples of risk factors are socioeconomic disadvantages, inept parenting, maltreatment, parental psychopathology (especially depression), and an adverse psychosocial environment, such as antisocial peers (Rutter, 2003). Other risk factors are more individualized to the child, such as language deficiencies, inadequate self-control and self-regulation, and a strong tendency to be physically aggressive toward the social environment. Less widely recognized risk factors are biologically related, such as hereditary and prenatal influences, postnatal diseases, and inadequate nutrition. Recent research literature has given increasing attention to the role of these biological factors in the development of antisocial behavior.

Risk factors are only part of the picture, however. In the presence of considerable risk factors, many children continue to function without difficulty and display healthy, normal development. These children do not display violent or persistent antisocial behavior even though they have been exposed to a variety of significant risk factors that contribute to antisocial behavior in others. In essence, they seem to be adaptable and resilient. It will be important, then, to examine very carefully the research literature on protective or resilience factors. **Protective factors** are those life experiences, abilities, and events that help a child resist engaging in chronic, serious antisocial behavior. An adult mentor (such as a teacher or coach), the motivation to pursue a professional career (e.g., dancer, doctor, therapist), or an emotionally strong single parent are all examples of protective factors. Children who adapt and show no ill effects in their development after exposure to a series or a combination of risk factors are said to be resilient. The recognition and study of these resilient children have overturned the negative assumptions about the development of children growing up under the threat of disadvantage and adversity (Masten, 2001). Research indicates that there is nothing extraordinary about these children and thus supports a far more optimistic outlook for helping all children adapt to adverse conditions. "Resilience does not come from rare and special qualities, but from the everyday magic of ordinary, normative human resources in the minds, brains, and bodies of children, in their families and relationships, and in their communities" (Masten, 2001, p. 235).

We will focus more on resilience in Chapter 4, but for now it is important to note that psychological research traditionally has concentrated almost exclusively on risk factors that lead to maladjustment and problem behavior and has neglected the study of human adaptation and development. More recently, there has been a major shift toward the study of competence and resilience, especially pertaining to children. **Competence**

> refers to a pattern of effective adaptation in the environment, either broadly defined
> in terms of reasonable success with major developmental tasks expected for a person
> of a given age and gender in the context of his or her culture, society, and time, or more
> narrowly defined in terms of specific domains of achievement, such as academics,
> peer acceptance, or athletics. (Masten & Coatsworth, 1998, p. 206)

Competence results from a complex interaction between a person and his or her environment. Both the individual's capabilities and the nature of the contexts in which the individual lives will influence competence. Many people are competent in some areas and not in others.

TABLE 1–1: Summary of Key Concepts

Concept	Definition
Risk factors	Experiences and influences that increase the tendency to become antisocial and delinquent
Protective factors	Experiences and abilities that help people adjust and cope with negative and adverse events
Competence	Ability to exert control over one's life and to adjust to problems effectively
Resilience	Ability to overcome risk factors and to function adaptively despite being exposed to serious threats and negative experiences

Resilience refers specifically to the ability to overcome risk factors and to function adaptively in spite of being exposed to serious threats and negative circumstances. (Table 1–1 summarizes these key concepts.) Children, adolescents, and adults who have been exposed to few, if any, risk factors cannot then be called resilient, but they may very well be competent. "Resilience has been studied in a wide variety of situations throughout the world, including war, living with parents who have a severe mental illness, family violence, poverty, natural disasters, and in situations with many other risk factors and stressors" (Masten & Coatsworth, 1998). Research on resilience underscores the perspective that children have different vulnerabilities and protective systems at different ages and points in development (Masten & Coatsworth, 1998). This text will give considerable attention to the research on why many children and adolescents overcome adversity and achieve good developmental outcomes. Recent research on resilience is likely to change the nature of the frameworks, goals, assessments, strategies, and evaluation in the fields of prevention and treatment of antisocial behavior.

THE MANY FACES OF DELINQUENCY

Juvenile delinquency—as well as antisocial behavior—has multiple manifestations and can range in frequency and severity. Michael Lorber (2004) points out that "not all antisocial behavior is equivalent, and not all antisocial behavior is aggressive" (p. 532). Merely saying that someone is antisocial or delinquent does not capture the extreme diversity within the categories or the variation in offending (see Table 1–2). First, engaging in some antisocial behavior is a rite of passage for many youngsters. In fact, males who abstain completely from antisocial conduct and minor delinquency are rare and outside the norm for male adolescence (Moffitt, Caspi, Dickson, Silva, & Stanton, 1996). Second, children and adolescents who engage in serious, chronic delinquency do not specialize in any one type of behavior but display a wide range of different offenses, ranging from theft and vandalism to violence and sexual assault (Dodge & Pettit, 2003). However, the majority of adolescent violent and serious offending is committed by only 6% of the adolescent population (Dodge & Pettit, 2003; Elliott, 1994; Wolfgang, Figlio, & Sellin, 1972). In other words, a very small proportion of young people are responsible for over half of all serious juvenile crime. Finally, not only does delinquency have many causes and take many forms, but there are also many developmental pathways or trajectories associated with it. We address this last point in more detail, because it represents a major focus in contemporary research on juvenile delinquency.

TABLE 1–2: The Nature and Extent of Juvenile Offending

Unlawful Acts by Juveniles	*Definition*
Unlawful acts against persons	Violent crimes, similar to those crimes committed by adults
Unlawful acts against property	Property crimes, similar to those crimes committed by adults
Drug offenses	Possession, distribution, selling, manufacture of drugs
Public order offenses	Nuisance crimes against society, such as noise violations
Status offenses	Acts only juveniles can commit: violation of curfew, running away, school truancy

THE DIFFERENT DEVELOPMENTAL PATHWAYS TO DELINQUENCY AND CRIME

This book relies heavily on a **developmental perspective** to provide the most comprehensive explanation of delinquency. The blending of developmental psychology and criminology over the past 15 years has put more focus on individual development and the life course of offending (Loeber, Lacourse, & Homish, 2005). *Developmental perspective*, in this context, refers to the scientific study of the conditions and variables that influence the neurological, biological, mental, emotional, and social development of children. Early learning experiences, parental influences, peer relationships, and hereditary predispositions are all examples of these conditions.

Because it focuses on the various changes that occur during development, the developmental perspective requires a close examination of **developmental pathways**. Think of a developmental pathway as a path lined with risk and protective factors that have the potential to strongly influence how a child develops and adjusts to the world. The risk factors predispose the child toward delinquency, while resilience or protective factors steer the child away from delinquency. At certain points the path may be particularly treacherous, and the child may be more vulnerable to negative influences. When children are asserting their independence from parents or guardians, for example, these youth may be particularly vulnerable to the influence of antisocial peers.

The developmental pathways (also commonly referred to as **developmental trajectories**) not only differ across individuals but also may differ across cultures, subcultures, and sociodemographic environments. In this book we are particularly interested in the developmental pathways that begin in childhood with aggression and disruptiveness and culminate in persistent delinquency and adult criminality. If we are able to delineate the developmental trajectories of early antisocial or delinquent behavior, we can gain invaluable information about important targets and appropriate timing for intervention. This result is particularly likely if the mapping of trajectories is accompanied by identification of risk factors associated with the divergent pathways (Shaw, Gilliom, Ingoldsby, & Nagin, 2003).

There are two primary perspectives on developmental pathways to crime (Walters, 2002b). According to Walters, a generalist approach holds that there is one pathway with a common set of causes that all people who commit crime follow. The other approach embraces multiple pathways. Although research can be summoned in support of each position, contemporary and cutting-edge research strongly supports multiple developmental pathways, which we will cover in detail in Chapter 6.

DEFINITIONS

Research psychologists and mental health professionals often use some terms interchangeably, a fact that lends confusion to any attempt to discuss the general topic of juvenile offending (Tremblay, 2003). Consider terms like *juvenile delinquency*, *antisocial behavior*, *conduct disorder*, and *externalizing problem behavior*, which are often used interchangeably. In reality, many delinquents do not have conduct disorder or even externalizing problem behaviors, and many youth with serious disorders or antisocial behaviors are never adjudicated delinquent. Other professionals associated with the juvenile justice system—police officers, detention workers, probation officers, juvenile court judges, and attorneys, for example—have their own sometimes-conflicting terminology. And members of the public have still other versions of who should and should not be labeled a delinquent.

In order to prepare for the material that will be covered throughout this book, we must try to disentangle the semantic jungle of various terms that are often used by professionals and researchers to refer to basically the same behaviors. We begin with the most obvious label, *juvenile delinquency*, but then we tackle the triad of terms just mentioned, which are commonly used interchangeably to refer to behavior that violates social norms: *antisocial behavior*, *externalizing problem behavior*, and *conduct disorder*. We will also refer briefly to other diagnostic labels that often appear in the literature on juvenile delinquency and that will be discussed in greater detail in later chapters.

JUVENILE DELINQUENCY

Although the term *juvenile delinquency* appears to be straightforward and easy to understand, it becomes an imprecise and ambiguous term when examined more closely. Basically, it is a legal classification that is assigned by the court, and at first, a simple legal definition seems to suffice: *Delinquency is behavior against the criminal code, committed by an individual who has not reached adulthood, as defined by state or federal law.* But juvenile delinquency has multiple definitions and meanings beyond this one sentence. In some states, for example, the legal definition also includes status offending, behavior that is not against the criminal code but is prohibited *only* for juveniles. Examples include running away, curfew violations, incorrigibility, underage drinking of alcohol, underage sexual activity, and truancy. The most common status offenses in recent years are incorrigibility, followed by running away (Sickmund, 2004). The status offense that has increased substantially in frequency in recent years is underage drinking.

Even age is not a simple issue in the definition of *delinquency*. Although no state considers anyone above 18 a delinquent, some have provisions for "youthful offenders," who are older, and some use 16 as the cut-off age. At this time, four states give criminal courts, rather than juvenile courts, automatic jurisdiction over juveniles at the age of 16, and eight states, at the age of 17. Several other states are considering changes. Furthermore, all states allow juveniles—some as young as 7—to be tried as adults in criminal courts under certain conditions and for certain offenses. Under federal law, juveniles may be prosecuted under the criminal law at age 15. Increasingly more and more young offenders are moved to adult court in this manner. Under the legal definition of *delinquency*, the youths transferred to criminal courts are not delinquents. Nonetheless, their behavior, although not technically "delinquent," is clearly within the scope of this text.

Many states do not have a legally defined age of criminal responsibility, that is, a minimum age of arrest for children (H. N. Snyder, Espiritu, Huizinga, Loeber, & Petechuk, 2003). The minimum age also indicates at which point a child may be brought before a juvenile court for delinquency proceedings. When the minimum *is* specified, it varies from age 6 in North Carolina to age 10 in Arkansas, Colorado, Kansas, Pennsylvania, and Wisconsin. Canada stipulates a minimum age of 12. Another interesting and rarely mentioned issue is that of developmental disabilities. A shoplifter or exhibitionist with a mental age of 10 and a chronological age of 33 is not eligible for delinquency status, yet the mental abilities of such an individual resemble those of a child far more than those of an adult. On the other hand, an 8-year-old "genius" with a mental age of 25 could presumably not be tried in criminal court simply because of his or her mental age.

In recent years, the term *child delinquent* has come into vogue. **Child delinquents** are juveniles between the ages of 7 and 12 who have committed a delinquent act according to criminal law (Loeber, Farrington, & Petechuk, 2003). Child delinquents often attract the attention of the mass media and public officials, especially after an especially violent incident involving a very young offender. During the past decade, the number of child delinquents handled by juvenile courts has increased 33%, generating some concern in criminal justice circles and society in general. Overall, children younger than 13 make up about 7% of all juvenile arrests (H. N. Snyder, Espiritu, et al., 2003; see Table 1–3). Although their offenses are not necessarily serious, the early age of onset does not bode well for their futures. According to Loeber et al. (2003), child

TABLE 1–3: Arrest Estimates of Juveniles Younger Than Age 13 (2005)

	Younger Than 10	*Ages 10–12*	*Younger Than 13*
Violent Crime	**642**	**4,743**	**5,385**
Murder	0	10	10
Forcible rape	12	284	296
Robbery	73	751	824
Aggravated assault	557	3,698	4,255
Property Crime	**3,103**	**24,200**	**27,303**
Burglary	697	4,343	5,040
Larceny-theft	2,014	18,052	20,066
Motor vehicle theft	79	699	778
Arson	313	1,106	1,419
Other Offenses (e.g., vandalism, drug abuse violations)	**9,965**	**72,808**	**82,773**
TOTAL	**13,710**	**101,751**	**115,461**

Source: Data from *Crime in the United States—2005* by Federal Bureau of Investigation, 2006, Washington, DC: U. S. Department of Justice, Author.

delinquents are two to three times more likely to become serious, violent, and chronic offenders than are adolescents who begin offending in their teens.

Thus far, we have discussed the legal definition of *delinquency*, but the delinquency literature does not necessarily use *delinquent* in the strictly legal sense. Technically speaking, a child cannot be a delinquent unless he or she has been so adjudicated by a juvenile court, yet the term is often used to refer to children who are taken into custody by police or are detained before their court appearances. Furthermore, the public often has its own version of *delinquency*, which has led to the phrase "social delinquent." Children who steal flags, engage in underage drinking, get into fistfights, get suspended or expelled from school, torture animals, or sexually molest other children may all be referred to as delinquents even when they do not come to police or court attention. On the other hand, society may resist calling the 12-year-old boy who kills his classmate a delinquent, even if he does not qualify for transfer to a criminal court.

It will become obvious as we proceed through this text that the measurement of delinquency and the determination of who is delinquent are difficult. Delinquency is not a distinct entity easily located and studied. Whether defined legally or socially, delinquency is an artifact, ever changing and conceptually slippery. It is an imprecise, nebulous label for a wide variety of law- and norm-violating behaviors. *Delinquency*, then, may be considered a socio-legal term, used in different ways by criminologists, lawyers, judges, juvenile justice professionals, legal scholars, and members of the public.

In this context, care should also be exercised to distinguish between a delinquent and a delinquent act. The act—delinquency—is the behavior that violates the criminal code, whereas *delinquent* is the legal label we assign to a youngster who deviates from pre-scribed social standards. But even in the strict legal sense, a youth charged with committing a legally defined delinquent act is not automatically a delinquent. The youth becomes a delinquent only after pleading guilty to the offense (or failing to contest the charges) or after all elements of the offense have been proved beyond a reasonable doubt (similar to a criminal conviction). Furthermore, the juvenile system generally resists applying the label unless the behavior is serious or there are a number of delinquent acts. In most states, juveniles get diverted from court if they are charged with a first, nonviolent offense.

Given the numerous inconsistencies associated with the labels *delinquent* and *delinquency*, it is not surprising that many writers and researchers shy away from these terms. Tremblay (2003), for example, suggests that researchers stop using the legal term *juvenile delinquency* in developmental studies in favor of the more appropriate term *antisocial behavior*. This suggestion should especially be followed if researchers are focusing on theoretical issues, such as looking for causes. The term *juvenile delinquency* should be used only for studies specifically designed to address legal issues. In this book we will show a preference for the term *antisocial behavior*, particularly when discussing developmental research, and will try to reserve *delinquent* for a youth who has been adjudicated as such by the courts.

ANTISOCIAL BEHAVIOR

The term *antisocial behavior* is most frequently used by psychologists and other mental health professionals to refer to the more serious habitual actions that violate personal rights, laws, and/or widely held social norms. The term includes both the legal designation of delinquency and the antisocial behaviors that are undetected by law enforcement.

Although arrest *may* be a valid indicator of antisocial behavior, it isn't enough. Many antisocial behaviors—probably most—go undetected or escape the attention of law enforcement. And, of course, arrest is not necessarily an indicator of antisocial behavior, because police may be taking into custody the wrong individual.

In this text, **antisocial behavior** is best defined as "recurrent problem behaviors that lead to injury to others or arrest" (Dodge & Pettit, 2003, p. 350). The injury may be physical or emotional. Thus, included in this definition is a wide assortment of behaviors ranging from homicide and sexual assault to verbal assault and vandalism, not all of which qualify as delinquent acts. Furthermore, the antisocial behaviors we are most concerned about in this book are directed at others and their property, although we do give considerable attention to the self-destructive behavior of substance abuse.

EXTERNALIZING PROBLEM BEHAVIORS

Many research and developmental psychologists prefer to divide childhood problems into two very broad categories: (1) internalizing disorders and (2) externalizing disorders, or problem behaviors. **Internalizing disorders** are characterized by mood problems, such as depression, or by behavior featuring anxiety, social withdrawal and isolation, hypersensitivity, low self-esteem, and eating disorders. Externalizing disorders, on the other hand, cause problems for others and society in general. They include such behaviors as stealing, lying, physical aggression, fire setting, and cheating. Research consistently reveals that externalizing problem behaviors are the most common and persistent forms of childhood maladjustment (Bongers, Koot, van der Ende, & Verhulst, 2004; Campbell, 1995).

Externalizing problem behaviors are usually represented by three broad diagnoses: conduct disorder, oppositional defiant disorder (ODD), and attention-deficit/hyperactivity disorder (ADHD; Farmer et al., 2002). Externalizing problems are particularly relevant in this text because of their characteristic antisocial symptoms (e.g., aggression, fighting, theft, school behavioral problems) and their relatively high prevalence among children. After discussing externalizing problem behaviors as a group, we will touch on conduct disorder because it is a frequent diagnosis associated with adjudicated delinquents. Both ODD and ADHD will be discussed again later in the text, specifically in Chapter 3. For the moment, though, we must emphasize that—although these behaviors have relevance to delinquency—children and adolescents with these problem behaviors do not necessarily engage in delinquent acts.

Recent research shows that serious externalizing problems can be identified as early as the toddler and preschool years (Keenan & Wakeschlag, 2000; Olson, Semeroff, Kerr, Lopez, & Wellman, 2005). However, a lack of control of aggression and impulses is very common in early childhood (Tremblay, 2000) and is not necessarily predictive of a similar lack of control as the child gets older. Therefore, it is important that developmental psychologists and child clinicians distinguish between chronic and temporary patterns of externalizing behavior early on (Olson et al., 2005).

Researchers who have examined the factors influencing or contributing to externalizing behavioral problems have focused on three things: (1) characteristics of the child, such as temperament, gender, cognitive processes; (2) socialization forces that emerge within a child's social interactions and relationships, such as parenting styles, peer interactions, attachment characteristics; and (3) other external forces, such as socioeconomic status and family characteristics (Rubin, Burgess, Dwyer, & Hastings, 2003). Some studies, for example, have revealed that male toddlers with a high level of externalizing problem behaviors often come from troubled families characterized by considerable parent–child conflict and family adversity (Belsky, Woodworth, & Crnic, 1996). Other studies report that externalizing behavior problems, especially aggressive behavior, increase in situations in which there are signs of negative parental behaviors (such as little warmth, much physical or verbal punishment, much directiveness) combined with the child's "difficult" temperament (Rubin, Hastings, Chea, Stewart, & McNichol, 1998). Overall, children who demonstrate externalizing behavioral problems share a range of risk factors, including sociodemographic disadvantages and chaotic/disruptive family patterns, such as child abuse or neglect, marital conflict, and parental alcoholism or drug abuse (Burt, Krueger, McGue, & Iacono, 2001; Fergusson, 1998; Kuperman, Schlosser, Lidral, & Reich, 1999).

Taking a slightly different approach, Frick and his colleagues (1994) identified four types of externalizing behaviors, based on studies of 28,000 youths: (1) oppositional behavior, (2) aggression, (3) property violations, and (4) status violations. Each of these behaviors appears to follow a different developmental trajectory. For example, research by Lahey et al. (2000) indicates that levels of oppositional behavior were higher at young ages, aggression peaked at about 13 years of age, property violations appeared to be steady across all age groups, and status violations were more prevalent at older ages (16 to 18). **Oppositional behavior** is the tendency to be disobedient and hostile to authority figures, including parents. In another study, Bongers, Koot, van der Ende, & Verhulst (2003) discovered that aggressive behaviors and externalizing problems decline for most children as they get older (i.e., third or fourth grade). However, research also indicates that externalizing problems that become established usually become chronic, "placing children at risk for a wide range of negative adaptational outcomes including academic failure, rejection by peers, conflicted interactions with parents, siblings, peers, and teachers, and delinquent behavior" (Olson et al., 2005, p. 25).

The externalizing behaviors most closely associated with delinquency and antisocial behavior are conduct disorders. Before we proceed to a detailed discussion of these disorders, however, it should be pointed out that some *internalizing* problems often go hand in hand with delinquency and conduct disorders. In other words, some internalizing and externalizing problems may be closely related. For example, it is fairly well established that the co-occurrence of conduct disorders (and delinquency) and depression is a common phenomenon in adolescence (Wiesner & Kim, 2006). "Studies with both clinical and community samples have provided substantial evidence that adolescents with high levels of delinquency are also at risk for depressive symptoms, and vice versa" (Wiesner & Kim, 2006, p. 1220). In addition, research suggests that the coexistence of depressive symptoms and delinquency appears to follow different developmental paths for adolescent boys and girls (Wiesner & Kim, 2006).

CONDUCT DISORDERS

Conduct disorder (CD) is a *diagnostic* term often used by mental health professionals to encompass a group of behaviors characterized by habitual misbehavior, such as aggression toward people or animals, destruction of property (including fire setting), frequent deceitfulness, stealing, serious violation of rules, and hostile or defiant behavior.

As noted previously, it is often considered within the category of externalizing behaviors (Farmer, Compton, Burns, & Robertson, 2002). It is primarily a clinical label used to describe a child or adolescent who *repetitively* and *persistently* violates the basic rights of others. Conduct disorders account for the majority of referrals to outpatient child and adolescent mental health clinics in America (Dodge & Pettit, 2003; Loeber, Burke, Lahey, Winters, & Zera, 2000). Overall, between 2% and 6% of children and adolescents in the United States show behavioral patterns that may be diagnosed as a CD (Eddy, 2003). Boys are diagnosed with the disorder more frequently than girls by a ratio of roughly four to one (Bongers et al., 2004; McDermott, 1996). CD is found to be more common in lower-socioeconomic-class families, among boys with a biological parent known to be antisocial, and among boys with attention-deficit/hyperactivity disorder (ADHD; Lahey et al., 1995). And as we learned earlier, it may be more common in depressed adolescents.

Conduct disorder is the diagnostic label most often placed on youths who appear before juvenile courts, when a diagnosis is included in the record (Lahey et al., 1995). CD is generally considered to be the primary precursor to chronic and serious antisocial behavior during adulthood, and unless treatment is started very early, the behavioral pattern is difficult to change (Lahey et al., 1995). Court records consistently reveal that 50% to 70% of the youths arrested for antisocial behaviors during childhood or adolescence are arrested again in adulthood (Lahey et al., 1995).

The term *conduct disorder* is more fully described in the American Psychiatric Association's *Diagnostic and Statistical Manual* (fourth edition, 1994), commonly abbreviated as *DSM-IV*. The *DSM-IV*—now in a slightly revised edition referred to as the *DSM-IV-R* (2000)—divides conduct disorder into two categories, depending on when the habitual misbehavior begins. If the misbehavior begins in childhood (before age 10), it is called conduct disorder: childhood-onset type. If the misbehavior begins in adolescence, it is called conduct disorder: adolescent-onset type. According to the *DSM-IV*, at least 3 of the 15 criteria must be met to qualify as CD. Unfortunately, the criteria are so diverse that CD cases vary widely in specific offending characteristics. According to the *DSM-IV*, poor frustration tolerance, irritability, temper outbursts, and recklessness are frequent accompanying features.

The *DSM-IV* identifies four major behavioral groupings to help in the diagnosis of a conduct disorder. The first group refers to "aggressive conduct that causes or threatens physical harm to other people or animals" (American Psychiatric Association, 1994, p. 85). The second group refers to "nonaggressive conduct that causes property loss or damage" (APA, 1994, p. 85). Behavioral patterns characterized by deceitfulness or theft make up the third group, and the fourth group refers to behavior that demonstrates serious violations of rules, such as the rules set by the school or parents. An example of the fourth group would be truancy or running away from home. Remember that the key words in these behavioral patterns are *repetitive* and *persistent*; the behaviors must be committed repeatedly and across many different situations, such as at home, in the school, and in the community. The *DSM-IV* posits that at least three of these behaviors must be present during the past 12 months to qualify as a CD.

Behavioral signs of CD can be observed in the context of interaction with parents well before school entry (Reid, 1993). For example, children who are aggressive, difficult to manage, and generally noncompliant in the home at the age of 3 continue to have similar problems when entering school (Reid, 1993). These behaviors show remarkable

TABLE 1–4: Summary of Key Terms

Term	*Definition*
Delinquent behavior	Illegal behavior by a minor who has not yet attained the age at which he or she is treated as an adult for purposes of criminal law (usually under age 18)
Juvenile delinquency	A legal designation indicating that a minor, who falls under a statutory age limit, has participated in illegal behavior
Antisocial behavior	A clinical term reserved for adults or youths who frequently violate developmental or customary social norms and who jeopardize the rights and safety of others
Externalizing behavior	A broad clinical term characterized primarily as actions against the social environment, such as acting out with hostility and aggression; usually encompassing conduct disorders, oppositional disorders, and ADHD
Oppositional behavior	The tendency to be disobedient to authority figures, including parents
Conduct disorder	A diagnostic label from the DSM-IV-R used to identify children who exhibit habitual misbehavior

continuity right into adolescence and beyond. In addition, CD children often have significant problems in academic performance. And as we shall learn, aggressive CD youth are at high risk for quick and decisive rejection by their peers (Reid, 1993). This rejection lasts throughout the school years and is difficult to change (Reid, 1993). Children who are consistently rejected obviously miss out on opportunities to develop normal interpersonal and social skills.

Preliminary research suggests that conduct problems are more likely to emerge in homes characterized by hostility and conflict, lack of parental monitoring of children's activities, inconsistent discipline, coercive interchange between parents and children, and more generally low parental competence (Jester et al., 2005). Research by Jester et al. (2005) found that low emotional support and lower intellectual stimulation by parents in early childhood predicted a propensity toward delinquency in later development. Table 1–4 summarizes the definitions of these various behavioral categories.

RESEARCH METHODS

In order to advance our knowledge about the juvenile offender, various research strategies and methods are necessary. Schwartz and Jacobs (1979) have outlined some of the differences among the various scientific methods used in the social sciences, including criminology and the study of deviant behavior. One of the most relevant distinctions is that between quantitative and qualitative methods.

QUANTITATIVE AND QUALITATIVE METHODS

Quantitative methods assign numbers to observations and thus allow researchers to analyze data systematically and to detect patterns and differences. Typically, quantitative methods collect measurements on variables and apply various statistical techniques to these measurements. Researchers using quantitative approaches might collect arrest and victimization data describing the distribution of delinquency in a particular city.

Armed with these data, the researchers might do a statistical analysis to discover where delinquency is most heavily concentrated, what types of crimes are being committed, and who is most likely to be victimized. Quantitative methodology also allows us to gather data on the number of juveniles held in detention, processed through juvenile courts, or transferred to criminal courts. In addition, quantitative methods allow researchers to assess relationships among variables and test the strength of variables. The most sophisticated quantitative methods, for example, would allow a researcher to compare the relative influence of parents and peers on a juvenile's decision to use illegal drugs. Psychologists also rely heavily on quantitative methods to examine the reliability and validity of various assessment measures, such as measures of juvenile psychopathic tendencies. And through quantitative research, we are able to evaluate the effectiveness of rehabilitative strategies, such as juvenile sex offender treatment programs.

Qualitative methods are quite different. Researchers using a qualitative approach minimize the use of numbers or statistics in their research observations. Instead, "qualitative methodology refers to those research strategies, such as participant observation, in-depth interviewing, total participation in the activity being investigated, field work, etc., which allow the researcher to obtain first-hand knowledge about the empirical social world in question" (Filstead, 1970, p. 6). Researchers using qualitative methods most generally describe their observations in the "natural language" at hand. For example, some researchers try to gain the trust of a group of youths by interacting with their gang, hoping to acquire an "inside" view of how these youths perceive and construct their world. In this case, natural language would include the jargon, speech patterns, and symbols of the youths themselves, instead of the artificial categories and concepts imposed on them by the researcher. From a qualitative perspective, if we want to understand delinquents, we must know what they know, see what they see, and understand what they understand.

A good illustration of the qualitative approach is the now-classic research conducted by Anne Campbell (1984a) on the role of girls in New York City street gangs. She "wanted to observe and interact with girl gang members and to represent their own views of their situations" (p. 1). After researching nearly 400 known gangs in New York City, she selected 3 that seemed to represent the diversity of gang life: a street gang, a biker gang, and a religion–cultural gang. One was racially mixed, one was Puerto Rican, and one was African-American. Campbell was introduced to the gangs by a police officer who knew them well or by agencies and youth project members who worked with them. She spent several months with the gang members, getting to know them and building their trust, never disguising her identity or purpose. Data collection was through either field note taking or a tape recorder. Much of her book, *The Girls in the Gang*, is written in the girls' own words.

Another excellent illustration of qualitative research pertaining to juveniles can be found in the work of Paul Cromwell (1994), who conducted extensive interviews (310 hours) with 30 active burglars over a 16-month period in a southwestern metropolitan area. Cromwell's study was concerned with the decision-making processes and situational cues relied on in selecting burglary targets. The participants were also asked about their initiation into crime, their drug use, co-offenders, techniques for breaking and entering, and marketing of stolen property. Although they were young offenders past the age of delinquency, the study is relevant to us because most indicated they had begun their criminal activity in their midteens with one or more older acquaintances.

TABLE 1–5: Primary Differences Between Quantitative and Qualitative Research Methods	
Concept	*Approach*
Quantitative research method	Relies primarily on measurement and statistical analysis
Qualitative research method	Relies on descriptions of behavior and experiences, much less on numerical measurement and analysis

Both qualitative and quantitative approaches are highly useful in the study of delinquency and antisocial behavior. According to Schwartz and Jacobs (1979),

> Quantitative methods are best for conducting a "positive science"; that is, they allow for the clear, rigorous, and reliable collection of data and permit the testing of empirical hypotheses in a logically consistent manner. . . . qualitative methods, which use natural language, are best at gaining access to the life-world of other individuals in a short time. (p. 5)

Qualitative methods allow us to examine the motives, meanings, emotions, and other subjective aspects in the lives of delinquents. In short, they add life to our statistical, empirical knowledge. One method does not necessarily have to be chosen over the other; as David Silverman (1985) asserts, "It is not simply a choice between polar opposites that face us, but a decision about balance and intellectual breath and rigour" (p. 17). Table 1–5 summarizes the differences between these two methods.

LONGITUDINAL RESEARCH

Earlier in this chapter we introduced the topic of development pathways or trajectories to delinquency. Research on these pathways represents some of the most vibrant, cutting-edge work in the study of juvenile delinquency. In order to conduct this research, investigators typically conduct longitudinal studies, following youths through a number of developmental milestones in an effort to identify features (such as risk factors) that explain eventual delinquency or features (such as protective factors) that discourage it. Longitudinal studies can be retrospective or prospective. **Retrospective studies** focus on children or adolescents who are identified after the events of interest have already taken place. For example, the research identifies a group of delinquents in an institutional setting and tries to determine what life experiences, events, or circumstances may have influenced their current antisocial behavior. Unfortunately, most researchers must rely on parental reports, the child's or adolescent's self-reports, and records describing the individual's development, such as school or social service records. Accuracy of recall, as well as adequacy of record keeping, becomes a critical issue in this retrospective method. Although human memory has an incredibly extensive storage capacity, it is also replete with distortions, misrepresentations, and biases, and record keeping is rarely consistent or complete. Moreover, any researcher who has sought archival data has probably been faced with the problem of missing records.

In **prospective longitudinal research**, subjects are identified before the events or developmental milestones occur, and the data are collected as incidents and life experiences happen. For example, researchers might follow newborns all the way through high school graduation with extensive observations and notations about their development. The prospective method is generally preferred over the retrospective, because of its reliance on very recent events and memory in contrast to "old memory" or records, but it is also far more expensive and time-consuming.

The longitudinal method did not begin with a focus on developmental milestones, however. Before discussing the method's current strengths and weaknesses, it will be instructive to review its origins in classic cohort studies, which enabled criminologists to gain valuable information about the prevalence of offending among juvenile populations.

Cohort Studies

In the last quarter of the twentieth century, Wolfgang and his colleagues (Wolfgang et al., 1972; Wolfgang, 1983) carried out two massive cohort studies. The term *cohort* refers to a group of participants having one or more characteristics in common. In the two Wolfgang projects, the participants were born in the same year. The first birth cohort consisted of 9,945 males born in 1945 who resided in Philadelphia from their 10th to their 18th birthdays. The second birth cohort consisted of 13,160 males and 14,000 females born in 1958 who also lived in Philadelphia from their 10th to their 18th birthdays. The researchers also conducted an important third study in which they followed 10% of the 1945 cohort until age 30. Note that because Wolfgang and his fellow researchers conducted their research in the 1970s and 1980s, they were looking back in time to collect data and thus were conducting retrospective longitudinal studies.

Wolfgang followed the members of these cohorts through their adolescent years to discover who became delinquent and who did not. He collected data about their personal backgrounds and delinquency history from three sources: schools, police, and juvenile courts. Background data pertaining to race, sex, date of birth, and residential history were obtained from school records. Delinquency involvement was checked through the records of the Juvenile Aid Division of the Philadelphia Police Department. These data consisted of all recorded police contacts, whether or not the contact resulted in an official arrest. In Philadelphia, as in most jurisdictions, a police officer who had contact with a juvenile had the option of handling the offender informally or making an arrest. Delinquency, in the Wolfgang studies, was defined exclusively by the number of police contacts, although the records of the Juvenile Court Division of the Court of Common Pleas for Philadelphia were also examined to determine how a case was handled.

Of the 13,160 males in the 1958 cohort, 4,315, or 33%, had at least one police contact before reaching their 18th birthday, a proportion very close to that of the 1945 cohort, which was 34%. Females were not included in the 1945 cohort analysis, but the 1958 data revealed that male adolescents were two-and-one-half times more likely to have a police contact than were female adolescents. Of the 14,000 females, 1,972, or about 14%, had at least one police contact.

In both studies, Wolfgang differentiated three groups of offenders based on the frequency of police contacts: one-time offenders, nonchronic recidivists (two to four police contacts), and chronic recidivists (five or more police contacts). Because a recidivist is technically a person who reoffends after being convicted of a crime, Wolfgang took some liberty with the term. Subsequent researchers must be careful to recognize this small but important deviation in terminology. Wolfgang's recidivists did not necessarily have prior juvenile records.

In the 1958 cohort, the distribution of delinquents was 42% one-time offenders, 35% nonchronic recidivists, and 23% chronic recidivists. In the 1945 cohort, 46% were one-time offenders, 35% nonchronic recidivists, and 18% chronic recidivists. Thus, in both studies, the distributions were similar. Female delinquents in the 1958 cohort were 60% one-time offenders, 33% nonchronic recidivists, and 7% chronic recidivists.

One of the most important findings of both cohort studies pertains to the chronic recidivists, a group that qualifies as serious delinquents. In the 1945 cohort analysis, male chronic recidivists constituted only 18% of the delinquent sample, yet they were responsible for over 52% of all juvenile offenses. Even more striking, these chronic offenders accounted for 71% of the homicides, 73% of the rapes, 82% of the robberies, and 69% of the aggravated assaults. Similar statistics were found for the 1958 cohort. While 1958 male chronics constituted only 23% of the delinquent group, they were responsible for 61% of all juvenile offenses. They were also involved in 61% of the juvenile homicides, 75% of the rapes, 73% of the robberies, and 65% of the aggravated assaults. In sum, a relatively small number of males seemed to be responsible for the bulk of the serious, violent delinquency. Wolfgang's research served as the impetus for subsequent research on the "career criminal," an individual likely to pursue a life of crime.

Donna M. Hamparian and her colleagues (1978, 1982) conducted a retrospective longitudinal cohort analysis of 1,222 males and females born between the years 1956 and 1960 and arrested, as juveniles, for at least one violent offense. The researchers found that violent offenders accounted for just over 30% of all the juvenile arrests. However, nearly one-third of the cohort qualified as chronic offenders (five or more arrests), and these chronic offenders accounted for two-thirds of all reported juvenile arrests in the birth cohort.

The Hamparian project found that individuals in the cohort did not specialize in the types of crimes they committed. Few of the violent offenders became repeat violent offenders, for example. Rather, multiple offenders engaged in a variety of illegal acts, ranging from violence to petty larceny. Like Wolfgang and his colleagues, these researchers also tracked the offenders into their adult years to determine whether they continued their criminal activity. The researchers learned that approximately 60% of the males and fewer than one-third of the females were arrested for felonies as adults. Those who went on to be arrested as adults tended to have more arrests as juveniles, to have begun their delinquent careers at an earlier age, and to have been involved in the more serious types of violent offenses as juveniles. Significantly, three-fourths of those juveniles who had qualified as chronic offenders continued their criminal activity into adulthood. Thus, there appears to be a clear continuity between juvenile and adult criminal careers for some individuals.

While both the Wolfgang and the Hamparian projects were impressive in the sizes of the cohorts and their unique approaches, the data they gathered were obtained primarily from official records (including police, school, and court records). The longitudinal research that is widely conducted today—and that will be discussed throughout the book—is much more broad, often involving not only record checks but also observations and interviews with juveniles and significant adults in their lives. Furthermore, the focus on developmental milestones means that researchers seek to identify a wide variety of factors that may impinge on a child's or adolescent's development.

Desirable Features of Longitudinal Studies

David P. Farrington, Lloyd E. Ohlin, and James Q. Wilson (1986) recommend four features that should be part of any longitudinal design. First, they argue that ideally the study should be prospective. If we wished to design a longitudinal study to explore the effects of parental abuse on frequent, persistent delinquency, obviously, we would want to design a study that allowed us to sample subjects randomly, without exercising too much bias in the selection process. We would hope, also, to select our subjects before there was evidence of child abuse or before they demonstrated delinquent patterns. In addition, we would want to keep close tabs on the subjects as they grew up. In short, we would want a prospective design.

Secondly, Farrington et al. (1986) recommend that the longitudinal investigation collect data from a number of different sources, such as self-report questionnaires, court or police records, and interviews with teachers, peers, and parents. Material from different sources provides checks on the accuracy of the information and helps fill gaps in information. A high agreement among various sources offers consensual validation of the data.

A third desirable feature is that the sample size (i.e., the number of participants in the study) is large—at least 100 but preferably much more than that. In our proposed study, if we were to select only 50 youths, we might find ourselves with very few frequent, persistent delinquents—perhaps none. Similarly, we might also find little evidence of child abuse. Our research, then, would run the risk of having limited applicability to the study of delinquency. When a study can be generalized to other similar populations (e.g., serious delinquents), researchers say it has high external validity. Low external validity indicates that the data are not representative. Consequently, a longitudinal design should include as large a percentage of the relevant population as time and money will allow.

A fourth desirable feature is that the longitudinal project covers a significant amount of time in the life course of the subjects—the longer the better. Farrington et al. (1986) recommend that the project cover at least 5 years of development. Presumably, short longitudinal studies do not allow researchers to discover satisfactorily what is contributing to delinquency. David Magnusson and Vernon Allen (1983) believe that for any longitudinal study to be effective, it must (a) cover the total critical periods of development for the behaviors of concern (in this case, delinquency) and (b) make observations frequently enough so as not to miss any of these critical periods of development. In essence, longitudinal studies must continue over rather long periods of time. It is not very meaningful, for example, to begin examining the effects of child abuse during early adolescence without knowing how much earlier in the child's development the abuse began and how it affected that development.

Examples of Modern Longitudinal Studies

An ambitious longitudinal study sponsored by the Office of Juvenile Justice and Delinquency Prevention (OJJDP) began in 1986. Substantial grants were awarded to the State University of New York at Albany, the University of Pittsburgh, and the University of Colorado to track seventh and eighth graders (ages 11–13) in three American cities—Rochester, Pittsburgh, and Denver—over a period of 4 years.

The Rochester Youth Development Study is a longitudinal study of 1,000 urban adolescents living in Rochester, New York. The findings of the Rochester study highlighted the fact that children who were more attached to and involved with their parents were less involved in delinquency (Browning, Thornberry, & Porter, 1999). The study also found that the relationship between family-process factors and delinquency was bidirectional—poor parenting increased the probability of delinquent behavior, and delinquent behavior further weakened the relationship between parent and child. However, the impact of family variables seems to fade as the child grows into adolescence; peer relationships appear to take precedence then. In fact, the study found that associating with delinquent peers was strongly and consistently related to delinquency.

The Pittsburgh Youth Study involved 1,517 inner-city boys from Pittsburgh. One of the more important findings was that boys generally developed delinquent behavior in an orderly, progressive fashion, with less serious antisocial behavior preceding the more serious (Browning & Loeber, 1999). In addition, the study was able to identify three developmental pathways that displayed progressively more serious problem behavior. These pathways will be discussed more comprehensively in Chapter 6.

The Colorado project, known as the Denver Youth Survey, has been following 1,527 boys and girls from high-risk neighborhoods in Denver who ranged in age from 7 to 15 years old. The primary mission of the study is to identify social conditions, personal characteristics, and developmental patterns linked to sustained involvement in delinquency and drug use (Browning & Huizinga, 1999). The Denver study has found that the best predictors of avoiding serious delinquency are having conventional friends, having a stable family and good parental monitoring, having positive expectations for the future, and not having delinquent peers.

Although we have discussed only American studies up to this point, the reader should be aware that longitudinal research is a hallmark of criminology in Great Britain and the Scandinavian countries. Among the best-known British studies are those directed by Donald West and David Farrington (1973, 1977) and the National Survey of Health and Development, formulated by Douglas, Ross, and Simpson (1968) and carried on by M. E. J. Wadsworth (1975, 1979).

Perhaps one of the most informative international research investigations is the Dunedin Multidisciplinary Health and Development Study (Silva, 1990). This project is a longitudinal study of the health, development, and behavior of children born between April 1, 1972, and March 31, 1973, in Dunedin, New Zealand, a city of approximately 120,000. The Dunedin sample, consisting of 1,037 males and females, has been continually evaluated through a diverse battery of psychological, medical, and sociological measures about every 2 or 3 years since the subjects were born.

A cautionary note is necessary before we proceed. While most criminologists probably endorse the prospective longitudinal method, some are very critical of it. Michael Gottfredson and Travis Hirschi (1987), for example, argue that longitudinal research is not a necessary or even a valuable procedure to use in the study of crime and delinquency. They are convinced that cross-sectional procedures are more efficient and equally effective in gathering data about crime and delinquency because, as research consistently indicates, most individuals "age out" of crime. A **cross-sectional study** gathers information about individuals at one point in time. For example, a researcher might select groups of 10- and 14-year-old delinquents and compare them to nondelinquents on such factors as school performance and family structure (e.g., two-parent vs. one-parent family). The significant factors associated with delinquency can thus be identified and preventive steps taken to reduce it. Other criminologists accept the value of longitudinal research but do not agree with Farrington et al. (1986) on the requirements for data collection and quantification. Instead, these criminologists believe that verbal descriptions and other qualitative data offer as many insights about delinquency as numerical data do. In other words, they contend that research designs that allow researchers to talk informally with and perhaps even live among their subjects over a period of time without collecting extensive numerical data—or at least in addition to doing so—also supply valuable material.

A Summary of Findings of Longitudinal Studies

What do existing longitudinal studies tell us about delinquency? According to Farrington and his colleagues (1986), longitudinal research indicates that juveniles involved in a high rate of offending represent a small proportion of the entire juvenile population. Furthermore, frequent offenders do not seem to specialize in any one particular kind of offending, such as theft or larceny. Instead, they tend to be involved in a wide assortment of offenses, ranging from minor property crimes to violent actions. Longitudinal research suggests also that these persistent offenders are unusually troublesome in school, earn poor grades, have inadequate or inappropriate social skills, come from adverse family backgrounds, and receive poor parenting and supervision. Moreover, these troublesome behaviors begin at an early age (usually by age 3), and the more persistent and violent the offender, the earlier the childhood patterns appear. There is strong evidence, for instance, that aggressive and violent behavior is well developed at approximately 8 years of age (Eron, Huesmann, & Zelli, 1991).

The patterns of going "against the environment" extend into adolescence, frequently resulting in a youth's dropping out of school and being unable to maintain steady employment. And these offenders very often use drugs and alcohol regularly.

In sum, longitudinal research has consistently shown that a very small number of males engage in high rates of delinquent behavior across time and place. The research also confirms that another very large group of males engages in delinquency, sometimes engaging in frequent or even violent delinquent actions, but only during their teenage years. Before their teen years, and after, these youth are not involved in antisocial or criminal behaviors.

PSYCHOLOGICAL PERSPECTIVES ON DELINQUENCY

As our discussion of developmental pathways suggests, more than ever before, psychologists have been actively engaged in research on the causes of antisocial behavior and delinquency. This expanding research literature demonstrates a discernible trend toward integrating theories as the most meaningful approach toward the understanding of delinquency. Although this book recognizes the biological, social learning, and cognitive perspectives, as well as the influences of broader social systems (e.g., the educational system, the structure of society), these perspectives in isolation fail to present a cohesive approach for understanding. Furthermore, despite the material on childhood disorders (e.g., conduct disorders) presented earlier in the chapter, a psychological approach does not necessarily mean that delinquents are seen as mentally disturbed or needing clinical treatment. Some are mentally disturbed and some need clinical treatment, but the majority do not. As we shall see, contemporary psychology has moved away from seeing people, including delinquents, as broken and needing to be fixed and toward seeing children and adolescents as active problem solvers immersed in a wide variety of influences, ranging from their own cognitions to the economic and social systems around them.

This text is mostly concerned with serious, persistent, chronic juvenile delinquency and, more broadly, with antisocial behavior. In order to better understand these behaviors, we will need to put the pieces of research together to form a meaningful image. The first piece of the puzzle is the biological *predispositions* that are present at or near birth. We emphasize predispositions because it is highly unlikely that biological influences directly cause any form of antisocial behavior; they are more likely to influence some aspects of that behavior. For example, impulsivity or ADHD—both thought to have significant biological bases—probably, over the life course, have some influence on antisocial behavior. A child who cannot sit still for any length of time is likely to have some difficulty learning in a structured school environment, and difficulty learning frequently leads to early school failure, which in turn is often associated with delinquency (Roeser & Eccles, 2000).

Biological predispositions are influenced by genetics as well as by the prenatal environment. As pointed out by Dodge and Pettit (2003), "The genetic base for most problem behaviors likely reflects combinations of genes that are expressed in different ways at different points of life" (p. 351). In other words, genes influence different behaviors at different developmental stages of a child's or adolescent's life cycle. Risks to the health of the fetus include the mother's exposure to toxic substances (such as lead paint and other chemical toxins), physical abuse, lack of prenatal care, diseases, poor nutrition, or use of drugs, alcohol, or tobacco. These and other genetic and biological factors of antisocial behavior will be covered in Chapter 3.

Most researchers and theorists believe that the sociocultural environment also plays a significant role in the development of antisocial or delinquent behavior. The sociocultural environment consists of the cultural customs and expectations a child experiences during development, especially early development. This environment includes parents, caretakers, other family members, friends, peers, and social institutions, such as school and preschool or day care centers. Research has discovered, for example, that the amount of exposure that a child has to aggressive peers in day care or preschool is closely related to how aggressive the child eventually becomes (Sinclair, Pettit, Harrist, Dodge, & Bates, 1994). Research has also indicated that a young child's experience of physical abuse increases the risk for antisocial behavior and delinquency (Dodge & Pettit, 2003; Mayfield & Widom, 1996). In addition, poverty exposes youth to adverse environmental conditions that elevate risk for antisocial behavior. Moreover, rates of violent offending vary with handgun availability and media exposure to violence, with the size and nature of the community, and with cultural attitudes toward violence (Dodge & Pettit, 2003). These are all sociocultural influences that play prominent roles in the trajectory to serious crime in adulthood.

Summary and Conclusions

This book has several major objectives. We hope to cultivate in readers a patience to see the world from multiple perspectives and to provide the necessary concepts with which to refine these perspectives. We also emphasize not only what can go wrong in a child's life, but also what can go right. In other words, it is important to focus on the protective factors that can encourage resilience. Many children do not display antisocial behavior even though they have been exposed to risk factors such as poverty or dysfunctional families that are believed to contribute to antisocial and delinquent behavior. For these resilient children, protective factors such as positive role models or their own cognitive and self-regulation skills have reduced the influence of multiple risk factors. Finally, because juvenile delinquency has multiple causes, manifestations, and developmental pathways, an objective of the book is to take all of these into consideration.

This is a juvenile delinquency text, but much of what we are discussing is better considered antisocial behavior, a term often preferred by psychologists. *Juvenile delinquent* is a legal term that, technically speaking, should not be used unless a child or adolescent has been found by a juvenile court to have committed an offense. However, the term is used loosely to cover juveniles who violate the norms of society; thus, we are really referring to social delinquents. In recent years, *child delinquent* has been used to refer to children between the ages of 7 and 12 who have violated the criminal law.

Psychologists also use *internalizing* and *externalizing behaviors* in discussing problem behaviors among juveniles. Examples of internalizing behaviors are mood problems, anxiety, low self-esteem, and eating disorders. Externalizing behaviors are more likely to cause problems for others. Examples include stealing, fire setting, and bullying. As noted in this chapter, however, antisocial behavior sometimes reflects a combination of internalizing and externalizing problem behaviors, as when depression accompanies violent behavior.

It is not unusual to see diagnostic terms used in the literature on delinquency and antisocial behavior. The most common diagnoses accompanying externalizing behaviors are conduct disorder (CD), oppositional defiant disorder (ODD), and attention-deficit/hyperactivity disorder (ADHD). This chapter focused on definitions, prevalence, and features of CD, which accounts for the majority of referrals to child and adolescent mental health clinics. Conduct disorder is also a frequent diagnosis in juvenile court records. We must caution, though, against overuse of diagnostic labels, particularly when they suggest a mental disorder. Although a proportion of juvenile offenders do have mental disorders, it should not be assumed that all—or even a significant proportion—do. We return to this point when we discuss treatment issues later in the book.

The developmental-pathways approach to delinquency represents some of the most cutting-edge research available in this area. Many developmental psychologists and criminologists have embraced longitudinal study as a fruitful method of studying juvenile offending. After discussing classic examples of this research, we highlighted desirable features. Longitudinal research should be prospective, include data from different sources, have large sample sizes, and cover a significant amount of time in the life course of participants. Developmental research also has led to the conclusion that juveniles arrive at delinquency and antisocial behavior through a variety of paths or trajectories. Some take the road very early in their development, while others do not embark on it until they reach adolescence.

Key Terms and Concepts

antisocial behavior
child delinquents
competence
conduct disorder (CD)
cross-sectional study
developmental pathways
developmental perspective
developmental trajectories
externalizing problem behaviors

internalizing disorders
oppositional behavior
prospective longitudinal research
protective factors
qualitative methods
quantitative methods
resilience
retrospective studies
risk factors

CHAPTER 2
EXTRAFAMILIAL AND FAMILY RISK FACTORS

CHAPTER OBJECTIVES

◆ Introduce social risk factors that are believed to contribute to the development of delinquent behavior

◆ Present the very broad and devastating effects of risk factors that operate on the child and adolescent outside the family (extrafamilial)

◆ Discuss in some detail the powerful influence of early peer rejection on the lives of children and adolescents

◆ Briefly sketch some of the risk features of preschool, after-school experiences, and school failure and retention

◆ Introduce the many risk factors characteristic of families and caregivers, including parental styles and practices, supervision and monitoring, and other features of family psychopathology and dysfunction

This chapter will examine the known risk factors that are believed to play prominent roles in the development of antisocial and delinquent behavior in childhood and adolescence. Broadly defined, **risks** are "processes that predispose individuals to specific negative or unwanted outcomes" (McKnight & Loper, 2002, p. 188).

Risk factors, for our purposes, are individual attributes and developmental experiences that are believed to increase the probability that a person will engage in persistent antisocial behavior. Identifying risk factors that contribute to delinquency and measuring their overall impact can increase the effectiveness of prevention and intervention programs designed to reduce the overall severity and frequency of delinquency across all age groups and cultures. Negative life events are generally assumed to be risk factors (Stouthamer-Loeber, Wei, Loeber, & Masten, 2004).

Precisely *how* risk factors directly contribute to the development of antisocial behavior is largely unknown. Most risk factors have not been convincingly shown to be a *cause* of antisocial or delinquent behavior. Rather, most studies identify risk factors as possibly being *associated* with the development of antisocial behavior. A direct link is rarely demonstrated. As Moffitt (2005) has stated, "A variable is called a *risk* factor if it has a documented predictive relation with antisocial outcomes, whether or not the association is causal"(p. 534). She asserts further that the causal status of most risk factors is unknown. Therefore, it is important to keep in mind that although many studies reviewed in this text find that certain factors appear to be related to the development of antisocial behavior, it is often not known how or why.

The influence or impact of risk factors will probably vary with the developmental status of an individual. For example, child abuse may have far more impact during early childhood than during adolescence. Some researchers also believe that the more risk factors a child is exposed to, the more likely that child will become delinquent or antisocial (Coie et al., 1993). Herrenkohl and his colleagues (2000) conclude that a 10-year-old exposed to six or more risk factors is ten times as likely to commit a violent act by 18 as a 10-year-old exposed to only one risk factor. However, it should be emphasized that many youths exposed to multiple risk factors never commit delinquent or violent acts. These resilient youth seem able to overcome the adverse conditions that some of their peers have found insurmountable.

Another thing to keep in mind about risk factors is the social and cultural context within which they occur. What may be evaluated as a serious risk for a child within a certain culture may not present the same danger in another culture. Harsh parental punishment during childhood may be associated with eventual behavioral problems in children growing up within a European-American family but may not be in children growing up in African-American families (Deater-Deckard, Lansford, Dodge, Pettit, & Bates, 2003). We will explain this seemingly controversial statement shortly.

In this and the next chapter, we will review the research on the connection between risk factors and antisocial behavior from four different domains: (1) extrafamilial influences, (2) family characteristics, (3) individual attributes, and (4) psychobiological and health factors. **Extrafamilial risk factors** consist of such things as antisocial peers, peer rejection, inadequate schools, inadequate social networks and support systems, and dangerous neighborhoods. Extrafamilial factors also involve such things as poverty and its concomitant malnutrition, lead poisoning, low birth weight, conditions of chronic violence, and the many other influences of socioeconomic disadvantage. **Family risk factors** include faulty or inept parenting, parental psychopathology (especially depression), and various kinds of child maltreatment and abuse. **Individual risk factors** include inadequate cognitive and language ability, a troublesome temperament, poor self-regulation skills, low motivation, inadequate interpersonal and social skills, low self-esteem, and a negative self-concept. **Psychobiological** and **health risk factors** include hereditary influences, prenatal influences, postnatal diseases, and inadequate nutrition and medical care. Although for the most part these categories are mutually exclusive, the risk factors sometimes influence one another. For example, child abuse—a family risk factor—may produce a negative self-concept, an individual risk factor.

This chapter will examine the first two risk categories: extrafamilial and family. Chapter 3 will focus on individual factors and psychobiological and health factors.

EXTRAFAMILIAL RISK FACTORS

We begin this section with the many risks inherent in the extrafamilial factor of poverty, which sets the stage for all further discussions of the potential risk and protective factors in the developmental trajectories of antisocial/delinquent youth. Nevertheless, this focus on poverty must be approached with caution. The juvenile justice system—including police, juvenile courts, and correctional agencies—have long been accused of unfairly targeting the poor. Furthermore, researchers often place the poor under the research microscope and/or target them for intervention while ignoring the more privileged members of society. Juvenile crime is not limited to the poor; indeed, some of the most heinous juvenile crimes have been committed by youth from upper economic strata.

In addition, we must emphasize again that the developmental pathways to delinquency are "believed to be multifactorial and transactional, reflecting processes of continuous dynamic interplay between qualities children bring to their social interactions (such as temperamental dispositions) and characteristics of the immediate caregiving environment and its social-ecological context" (Olson et al., 2005, p. 27). And research clearly demonstrates that there are many pathways to delinquency (Sameroff, Peck, & Eccles, 2004). Nevertheless, we cannot ignore the fact that poverty creates conditions that place many children at risk of becoming involved in antisocial behavior.

GROWING UP POOR

In 2003 there were 73 million children aged 0 to 17 in the United States, representing about 25% of the population (Federal Interagency Forum on Child and Family Statistics, 2005). Also in 2003, 18% of all children in the United States lived in poverty (Federal Interagency Forum on Child and Family Statistics, 2005). The racial and ethnic diversity of the child population is increasing at a rapid rate, which suggests that poverty may increase substantially in the near future.

Poverty stands out as one of the most frequently identified risk factors associated with child development (Barbarin, 1993). According to Barbarin (1993), "The degradation of the human spirit and decrements of emotional adjustment are undeniably experienced by many children and adolescents living in poverty" (p. 479). Demographic data also suggest that one in five American children living in poverty is disproportionately exposed to significant adverse social and physical environments, including family turmoil, violence, separation from families, limited cognitive enrichment opportunities, and suboptimal physical living arrangements (Evans, 2004). Chronic poverty and instability of family life in childhood together significantly increase the risk of psychological, social, and academic impairment in adolescence and early adulthood. For the young children living in poor communities, inadequate housing, deficient medical care, faulty nutrition, and the lack of safe environments in which to play all compromise a healthy development (Barbarin, 1993). Moreover, as a rule, the schools these children attend have fewer resources and lower academic expectations. Children in low-income schools are also less likely to have well-qualified teachers. And even teachers with the necessary academic credentials are often not properly trained to deal with the specific challenges posed by this environment.

Poverty further diminishes a parent's capacity for supportive, consistent, and involved parenting. Unresponsive and harsher, more punitive parenting occurs more often among low-income families, often beginning in infancy (Evans, 2004). In comparison to middle-income children, low-income children are exposed to greater levels of violence, family disruption, and separation from their families. In addition, low-income American households have smaller and more limited social networks and social support systems for financial and emotional help and for child care. Research has also uncovered greater instability in peer relationships from preschool through third grade among lower-income children (Evans, 2004).

Poverty also affects parent–child interaction.

> Low-income children experience substantially less cognitive stimulation and enrichment in comparison to wealthier children. Low-income compared with middle-income parents speak less often and in less sophisticated ways to their young children, and as the children grow older, low-income parents are less likely than middle-income parents to engage jointly with their children in literary activities, such as reading aloud or visiting the library. (Evans, 2004, p. 80)

The quantity, quality, and responsiveness of parental speech to children vary strongly by social class. For instance, in a nationwide study of American kindergarten children, 36% of parents in the lowest-income levels read to their children on a daily basis, compared with 62% of parents from the highest-income brackets (Coley, 2002). Children in low-income families also watch far more television than their more affluent counterparts (Larson & Verma, 1999).

In addition, parental involvement in school activities seems to be strongly linked to income. For instance, higher-income parents are more likely to know their child's teachers by name, can more accurately identify their child's best and worst subjects, and more often know how well their child is performing in classes. Furthermore, in low-income day-care centers, caregivers show less warmth, responsiveness, and sensitivity to children's needs (Phillips, Voran, Kisker, Howes, & Whitbook, 1994). In-depth qualitative work has revealed that staff in low-income centers speak to children in more authoritarian and less cognitively complex ways than do staff in middle-income centers (Evans, 2004). For example, staff in predominantly low-income centers use verbal commands more often and are less likely to direct questions to toddlers that encourage answers beyond yes or no. Furthermore, the ratio of children to caregivers is higher in predominantly low-income centers.

Low-income families are also more likely to live closer to toxic-waste dumping sites, and their children carry a heavier body burden of toxins (Bullard & Wright, 1993). Unsafe lead levels, which are usually found in older houses, are four times higher in low-income families (Brody et al., 1994). During the years 1999 to 2002, approximately 2% of children aged 1 to 5 had blood-lead levels above 10 micrograms per deciliter, which is considered elevated according to federal safety standards (Federal Interagency Forum on Child and Family Statistics, 2005). Children in this age group are particularly affected because of frequent hand-to-mouth behavior, and significant and troubling behavioral and health effects have been shown to occur at even lower levels (Federal Interagency Forum on Child and Family Statistics, 2005). Childhood exposure to chips or dust from lead-based paint has contributed to learning and cognitive development problems, which increase the risk for antisocial and delinquent behavior. Fortunately, since the 1970s, lead exposure has declined primarily because of the removal of lead from gasoline and the drastic reduction in the use of lead-based paint.

However, even today, about 19% of African-American and 7% of Mexican-American children have blood-lead levels at or above 5µg/dl, and these children are predominantly in homes where incomes are below poverty (Dietrich, Ris, Succop, Berger, & Bornschein, 2001; Needleman, McFarland, Ness, Fienberg, & Tobin, 2002). Bone-lead levels have also been shown to be closely related to antisocial behavior in adolescents (Dietrich et al., 2001; Needleman et al., 2002).

In addition, pesticide exposure and air pollution are common in low-income families, including exposure to cigarette smoking. Although we cannot say that low-income parents are more likely to smoke, it does appear that population density and/or more confined spaces account for this exposure. Low-income homes also reportedly have higher levels of nitrogen dioxide, carbon monoxide, and radon, all of which have been shown to be associated with health and development problems.

Poverty does even more to a family than has been identified thus far. It also produces a sense of **social exclusion**, or alienation, and a sense of rejection from mainstream society (Clements, Althouse, Ax, Magaletta, Fagan, & Wormith, 2007). Contemporary research consistently demonstrates that socially excluded individuals.

> Exhibit increased aggression, poorer intellectual performance, a loss of prosocial behavior, and a susceptibility to self-defeating behavior patterns. . . . At the societal level, and at multiple points in history, groups and categories of people who have felt excluded by dominant culture have shown sadly similar patterns as reflected in high crime rates, underperformance in schools and intellectual life, withdrawal from positive contributions to the general societal good, and elevated rates of substance abuse, suicide, and other self-destructive patterns. (Baumeister, DeWall, Ciarocco, & Twenge, 2005, p. 603)

Persons who are sufficiently situated economically can also feel socially excluded.

PEER REJECTION

Peer rejection is a form of social exclusion that has significant impact and devastating effects on the lives of children and adolescents. School shootings, for example, have demonstrated that young people who feel socially rejected sometimes turn violent (Twenge, Baumeister, Tice, & Stucke, 2001). Very few, if any, school shooters were economically disadvantaged, yet virtually all perceived themselves as being rejected by peers as well as by others in the community. Consequently, it is important that we examine what is known about the effects of peer rejection on aggressive and violent behavior.

Developmental researchers have continually found that children's peer relations make unique and essential contributions to their social and emotional development (Bagwell, 2004; Newcomb, Bukowksi, & Pattee, 1993). During adolescence, there is an increase in susceptibility to peer influence and a decline in susceptibility to parental influence (Mounts, 2002). In addition, numerous investigators have found that peer influence is a strong predictor of adolescent substance use and delinquent behavior (Coie & Miller-Johnson, 2001; Mounts, 2002). Not surprisingly, many members of many societies find this connection to be obvious. Consequently, the folk wisdom to avoid "bad companions" has long been the traditional admonishment from parents and other concerned adults. The link between childhood peer *rejection* and antisocial behavior and delinquency is not so obvious, however.

One of the strongest predictors of later involvement in persistent antisocial behavior is early rejection by peers (Dodge, 2003; Parker & Asher, 1987). In elementary school, being liked and accepted by the peer group is a crucial developmental task and generally leads to healthy psychological and social development (Rubin, Bukowski, & Parker, 1998). Social rejection by peers in the elementary school grades, on the other hand, presents a very powerful risk factor for delinquency in adolescence and antisocial behavior throughout the life course (Laird, Jordan, Dodge, Pettit, & Bates, 2001). For example, rejection by first-grade peers appears to strongly predict the development of antisocial behavior by the fourth grade (Cowan & Cowan, 2004; Miller-Johnson et al., 2002). Furthermore, those children who had been rejected for at least 2 or 3 years by second grade had a 50% chance of displaying clinically significant antisocial behavior later in adolescence, in contrast with just a 9% chance for those children who managed to avoid early peer rejection (Dodge & Pettit, 2003). Consistent with our observation that risk factors sometimes influence one another, the quality of parent–child and marital relationships also seems to play a significant role in whether a child is rejected by peers early in life. Research by Cowan and Cowan (2004) demonstrates that "negative qualities in marital and parent–child relationships in both prekindergarten and kindergarten are risk factors for low social skills, aggressive behavior, and rejection in the early years of elementary school" (p. 173).

Peer-rejected children frequently interact with one another or gravitate to antisocial peers (Laird, Pettit, Dodge, & Bates, 2005). During the adolescent years, involvement with antisocial peers shows a robust and consistent relationship to delinquency, drug use, and a range of other problematic behaviors (Laird et al., 2005). Consequently, we would expect that both peer rejection and involvement with antisocial peers would be characteristic of those youngsters exhibiting antisocial or delinquent behavior early in their social development.

Children are often rejected by their peers for a variety of reasons, but aggressive behavior appears to be a prominent reason. Children tend to reject those peers who frequently use forms of physical and verbal aggression as their preferred way of dealing with others (Dodge, Coie, Pettit, & Price, 1990). These findings have prompted many social scientists to conclude that aggressive children are more likely than nonaggressive children to be rejected by peers. Interestingly, however, ongoing research indicates that the relationship may not be that straightforward. First, peers also reject peers whom they perceive as shy and socially withdrawn (a point we return to shortly). Second, not all aggressive children are rejected by peers; some are liked, accepted, and sought as friends. In fact, research finds that many popular youngsters are often dominant, arrogant, and physically and relationally aggressive (Cillessen & Mayeux, 2004; Rose, Swenson, & Waller, 2004). Thus, if children are rejected, it is not *always* because they are aggressive.

Nonetheless, aggression *combined with* peer rejection predicts serious antisocial or delinquent behavior. Children who are both physically aggressive and socially rejected by their peers have a high probability of becoming serious delinquents during adolescence and violent offenders during early adulthood. Researchers Coie and Miller-Johnson (2001), for example, conclude from their extensive review of the research literature that "those aggressive children who are rejected by peers are at a significantly greater risk for chronic antisocial behavior than those who are not rejected" (p. 201).

But an important question still remains: Why are certain aggressive children rejected in the first place? Coie (2004) points out that there are three important differences between peer-rejected boys and nonrejected boys. First, peer-rejected, aggressive boys are more impulsive and have problems sustaining attention and staying on task. In short, they are deficient in the capacity to control or alter their behavior, a pattern known as poor self-regulation. Consequently, they are more likely to be disruptive of ongoing activities in the classroom or during group play. Second, peer-rejected, aggressive boys are aroused to anger more readily and probably have more difficulty calming down. This emotional rage is more likely to result in physical and verbal attacks on peers, which in turn encourage peers to avoid these children altogether. Third, rejected, aggressive youngsters have fewer social and interpersonal skills for making friends and maintaining positive relationships with peers. They probably have acquired fewer social and interpersonal skills because they have had limited opportunities to practice these skills on nonrejected peers.

In summary, peer-rejected children often, though not invariably, are aggressive; but they also tend to be more argumentative, inattentive, and disruptive than others and generally have poorer social skills (Bierman, Smoot, & Aumiller, 1993; Bierman & Wargo, 1995; Coie, 2004).

The observation that peer-rejected boys demonstrate inattentive, impulsive, disruptive behavior brings into play the role that attention-deficit/hyperactivity disorder (ADHD) may contribute to peer rejection. A study by Erhardt and Hinshaw (1994) underscores this point. The study involved 25 boys with ADHD and 24 other boys who participated in a summer school program, none of whom knew one another at the beginning of the program. The boys ranged in ages from 6 to 12 years old. As early as the first day of social interactions between the two groups, the ADHD and the comparison boys showed clear differences in social behaviors, with the ADHD youngsters displaying socially noxious and noncompliant-disruptive behaviors. More importantly, within the first day, the ADHD youngsters were overwhelmingly rejected by their peers. Other studies have found similar results, with ADHD symptoms and aggression showing a close link to eventual antisocial behavioral patterns (S.B. Campbell, 2000; Coie, 2004; Miller-Johnson et al., 2002). ADHD will be discussed more fully in the next chapter.

Research also finds that boys who are both rejected and aggressive display a variety of behavioral, social, and cognitive deficits, as well as low levels of prosocial behavior in general (Coie & Miller-Johnson, 2001). Peer rejection has been closely associated with school problems, including negative school attitudes, school avoidance, and the likelihood of being disruptive and uncooperative in the learning process. Such behavior is likely to lead to considerable negative attention from teachers and eventual academic and school difficulties (Coie, 2004). "In time, some of these negative opinions of peers and teachers will come to be internalized by the boy and undermine whatever social confidence he has in himself" (Coie, 2004, p. 254). This development of a negative personal identity and a self-image as a "bad kid" sounds highly similar to the self-labeling process summarized many years ago by Edwin Lemert (1951) in his classic *Social Pathology* (discussed in Chapter 5).

Being rejected by peers encourages a child to behave less competently in social situations, creating a self-fulfilling prophecy cycle (Coie, 2004). Rejected children develop negative expectations about the way peers will react and behave in ways that fulfill their own expectations and those of the rejecting peers. Positive peer relations, on the other hand, have been shown to contribute to the development of empathy and also reinforce and model self-regulation and prosocial behavior (Eisenberg, 1998; Waaktaar, Christie, Borge, & Torgerson, 2004). In addition, positive peer relations are believed to reduce significantly the tendency to display hostile attribution bias.

It should be noted that, to date, almost all the research and theoretical work examining the effects of peer rejection, aggression, and delinquent behavior have focused on boys. Little is known about the combined effects of aggression and peer rejection on girls (Prinstein & La Greca, 2004). In one of the few studies focusing on girls, Prinstein and La Greca (2004) found that the development of antisocial and delinquent behavior in girls, as in boys, can be predicted by early involvement in aggressive behavior with peers. There is also some evidence to suggest that relationally aggressive behavior in girls, as in boys, can be predicted by early involvement in aggressive behavior with peers. Moreover, there is some evidence to suggest that relationally aggressive girls are more likely than nonaggressive girls to be peer-rejected (Crick, 1995). Girls usually use relationship aggression to hurt and diminish the social status of others rather than relying on the physical aggression typically used by boys. Prinstein and La Greca discovered—as did Crick—that peer rejection among girls in elementary school increased aggression but also was associated with increased substance abuse and other delinquent behaviors during adolescence. On the other hand, peer acceptance reduced and even eliminated the risk of aggression and other delinquent behaviors later on.

Some Caveats

Although research has focused primarily on the aggressive behavior of rejected children (Coie, 1990), particularly boys, a growing body of research indicates that not all peer-rejected children display discernible signs of aggressive behavior. As noted earlier, peer rejection may be directed at both aggressive and nonaggressive children (Bierman et al., 1993; Cillessen, Van IJzendoorn, Van Lieshout, & Hartup, 1992; Haselager, Cillessen, Van Lieshout, Riksen-Walraven, & Hartup, 2002). Nonaggressive, peer-rejected children often lack social, interpersonal, and cognitive skills and are described as shy, atypical, socially insensitive, and deficient in prosocial behaviors (i.e., internalizing behaviors; Haselager et al., 2002). Aggressive, peer-rejected children, on the other hand, exhibit behaviors that are against the social environment (i.e., externalizing behaviors). Peer rejection of withdrawn children often results in their feelings of loneliness, social anxiety, depression, and low self-esteem (Sandstrom & Zakriski, 2004).

It should also be recognized that some children display changing (decreasing or increasing) levels of antisocial behavior as they get older (Haselager et al., 2002). Haselager et al. (2002) found a stable antisocial group of boys (about two-thirds of the sample) who were consistently rejected and highly aggressive and who could be described as "persistors" in antisocial behavior, following the developmental pathway identified as "aggressive/versatile" by Loeber (1988), and as "life-course-persistent" offenders by Moffitt (1993). But Haselager et al. (2002) also discovered that some boys were initially rejected and highly aggressive but became less aggressive and less rejected over time. This finding suggests that, in addition to adolescence-limited antisocial behavior outlined by Moffitt (1993), there is also "early-childhood-limited" antisocial behavior, as exemplified by children who are highly aggressive with peers at an early age but desist from their antisocial behavior orientation before they reach early adolescence (Haselager et al., 2002). Haselager et al. (2002) also identified another group of rejected boys who were never very aggressive (actually they were shy and withdrawn) but who also became less rejected and more accepted over time. The researchers speculated that this was a group of initially withdrawn and rejected boys whose status improved because they became less compliant or more assertive with their peers. About one-third of the rejected boys changed their behavioral and rejection patterns as they grew older.

Rejected children are not necessarily without social networks and friends. However, several studies find that the friendships of serious male delinquent offenders may be simply relationships of convenience (Bagwell & Coie, 1999; Coie & Miller-Johnson, 2001). In addition, the relationships appear to lack trust of or respect for both participants (Dishion, Andrews, & Crosby, 1995) and are of lower quality than the friendships of less antisocial boys (Coie & Miller-Johnson, 2001). These findings may be relevant to the study of gang delinquency, discussed in Chapter 11.

Another important caveat concerning the relationship between aggression and peer rejection is that not all aggressive youths are perceived as unpopular by peers, a point made earlier in this section. Research suggests that acceptance by peers depends, in part, on the type of aggression used. Most of the research has emphasized overt (physical) aggression (Rose et al., 2004). However, recent studies of relational aggression have demonstrated the importance of this form of aggression in the developmental trajectories of children (Crick, Casa, & Mosher, 1997). **Relational aggression** "is aimed at damaging relationships or feelings of inclusion and involves such acts such as ignoring, excluding, spreading rumors, and threatening to end a friendship" (Rose et al., 2004, p. 179). Several studies of aggression among young children have shown that, as demonstrated for school-age children, relational aggression is a relatively frequent, hostile event in many preschool classrooms (Crick, Casa, & Ku, 1999). These studies have provided further evidence that relationally aggressive behaviors can be highly aversive and potentially damaging to the self-esteem of children (Crick et al., 1997). Also, both boys and girls who frequently use relational aggression toward their peers are at high risk of being rejected by their peers (Crick & Grotpeter, 1995; Grotpeter & Crick, 1996).

When preschoolers engage in relationally aggressive acts, they tend to do so in relatively simple, direct ways that typically involve a current situation or provocation—for example, telling a peer that the speaker will not be the peer's friend unless the peer gives him or her a crayon (Crick et al., 1999). In contrast, older children are more adept at using more complex and subtle forms of relational aggression, which may reflect a response to a situation or transgression that occurred in the past—for example, purposely excluding a peer from a party because the peer did not invite this child to the peer's party last month.

A study by Crick et al. (1997) provides the first evidence that relationally aggressive behaviors appear in children's behavioral repertoires at relatively young ages (3 to 5 years of age). In addition, the study found that teachers rate preschool girls as significantly more relationally aggressive and less physically aggressive than preschool boys, findings that are consistent with past research conducted on school-age children.

PEER GROUP AND GANG INFLUENCES ON REJECTED YOUTH

There are three major perspectives on the influence of peer groups on antisocial and delinquent behavior. One perspective argues that youngsters become delinquent as a direct result of association with deviant peer groups. According to this view, any child may become associated with a deviant peer group. A second perspective contends that antisocial, peer-rejected youths seek out greater contact with similar peer-rejected and socially unskillful peers. In other words, socially excluded youths tend to seek out other socially excluded youths. A third perspective lies somewhat between these two positions: Peer-rejected, antisocial children are drawn to deviant groups with members similar to themselves, thus encouraging and amplifying already-existing antisocial tendencies.

The research evidence favors the third perspective. It appears that childhood peer rejection encourages children to participate in deviant peer groups that then amplify tendencies to become more deviant and antisocial. Put another way, deviant group membership or gangs encourage and increase the already-existing antisocial patterns in children and adolescents. As noted by Coie (2004), "The impact of deviant peer group influences on the crystallization of an antisocial developmental trajectory has been solidly documented" (p. 257).

Although the overwhelming evidence supports the third perspective, there is some evidence that deviant group membership encourages some nondelinquent children to participate in *minor* delinquent actions rather than in more serious acts of violence. For example, while following the social development of youngsters aged 11 to 17, Elliott and Menard (1996) discovered that nondelinquent youths were more inclined to engage in minor delinquent activity after joining a deviant peer group. And Thornberry, Krohn, Lizotte, and Chard-Wierschem (1993) reported that youth who joined gangs increased their level of delinquent behavior, but they decreased their delinquent behavior when they left the group. These three perspectives are discussed in more detail in Chapter 11.

Bagwell (2004) makes the observation that many youths during middle childhood and adolescence engage in what she calls "temptation talk." Temptation talk refers to peer group discussions of potential rule violations and deviant behavior, and it serves as a way for youths to explore their thoughts and ideas about rule-breaking behaviors with their friends (Bagwell, 2004). Temptation talk may lead individuals to join a deviant peer group, even if temporarily. Although it appears both nondelinquents and delinquent youth participate in temptation talk with some regularity, delinquents are more likely to go beyond the talk and actually commit deviant acts.

DAY CARE AND PRESCHOOL EXPERIENCES

Today, more American children are cared for by paid providers than by relatives (Scarr, 1998). In recent years, the percentage of children who receive regular child care prior to school entry has increased from about 25% to over 80% (NICHD Early Child Care Research Network, 2006). A large number of these preschool children begin to experience regular child care in their first year or two of life (West, Denton, & Germino-Hausken, 2000).

Child care in the United States is, on average, mediocre. The quality, amount, and type of child care provided by day-care centers are highly variable. Quality in this context is defined as "sensitive and responsive caregiving as well as by cognitive and language stimulation" (NICHD Early Child Care Research Network, 2006, p. 111). High-quality child care is related to advanced levels of cognitive, language, and preacademic (school readiness) outcomes (NICHD Early Child Care Research Network, 2006). High-quality child care also appears to improve the social and emotional skills in most children. Children from more advantaged families tend to experience higher-quality child-care environments and, interestingly, are also in child care for more hours per week.

Poor-quality child care, on the other hand, has been reported to put children's development at risk for poorer language and cognitive development and lower ratings of social and emotional adjustment. Unfortunately, children from families with single employed mothers and low incomes were more likely to be found in lower-quality care (Howes & Olenick, 1986), although there have been some serious attempts to correct this problem.

Low-income children who experience high-quality infant and preschool care show better school achievement and socialized behavior in later years than do similar children cared for in lower-quality environments. For low-income children, quality child care offers learning opportunities and social and emotional supports that many would not experience at home.

According to Goldstein, Arnold, Rosenberg, Stowe, and Ortiz (2001), day-care teachers worry about aggression in their toddlers more than any other behavioral problem, and they report disruptive behavior as their greatest classroom challenge. These concerns may be important as persistent aggressive tendencies at 3 years of age predict persistent aggressive behavior later in life (Goldstein et al., 2001). Accumulating evidence indicates that the amount of exposure that a child has to aggressive peers in day care or preschool is predictive of the child's later aggressive behavior, perhaps because of modeling effects (Sinclair, Pettit, Harrist, Dodge, & Bates, 1994). There is further evidence that substantial hours in child care (more than 45 hours per week), beginning in infancy and combined with less sensitive mother–child interactions, may be related to disruptive and antisocial behavioral problems in later childhood (Vandell, 2004).

AFTER-SCHOOL CARE AND SUPERVISION

The quality of after-school care and supervision has also been associated with the development of antisocial behavior (Flannery, Williams, & Vazsonyi, 1999; Posner & Vandell, 1999; Vandell & Posner, 1999). In the 1990s, the term latchkey was applied to children who returned from school to an empty house and remained on their own until their parents or guardians finished their own work day. Children who spend fairly large amounts of time in unsupervised after-school self-care in the early elementary grades are at elevated risk for behavior problems and antisocial behavior in early adolescence (Goldstein, Davis-Kean, & Eccles, 2005; Pettit, Laird, Bates, & Dodge, 1997). Moreover, such children are more likely to spend time in unsupervised activity with peers in early adolescence (Colwell, Pettit, Meece, Bates, & Dodge, 2001). Antisocial children seek out niches that involve association with antisocial peers and environments with minimal adult supervision (Snyder, Reid, & Patterson, 2003). Thus, there tends to be negative mutual influence. Adolescents who engage in antisocial actions tend to be drawn to other antisocial peers, and antisocial peers further the development of risk behaviors (Goldstein et al., 2005). We will return to this topic when we discuss parental monitoring and supervision under family risk factors.

SCHOOL FAILURE

Research suggests that retention in kindergarten and in the early grades has long-term detrimental effects on behavior outcomes, in spite of its immediate academic benefits (Holmes, 1989; Sameroff, et al., 2004). On the other hand, delaying entry into kindergarten has *not* been shown to have the same adverse effects. Retained children are often viewed negatively and socially rejected by peers (Plummer & Graziano, 1987), which as we learned previously may promote antisocial development. Children's first experiences of failure with competitive academic tasks predict later antisocial problems (Moffitt, Gabrielli, Mednick, & Schulsinger, 1981).

In fact, early school failure itself seems to be more strongly predictive of delinquency than low intelligence (Hinshaw, 1992). For example, within the juvenile justice system, 70% suffer from learning disabilities, and 33% read below the fourth-grade level (Wald & Losen, 2003). Although some of these deficiencies could be the result of low intelligence, many other factors could also be involved. Approximately two-thirds of state prison inmates have not completed high school. Moreover, one of the strongest predictors of offending by adolescent females is having been suspended, expelled, or held back during the middle school years (Wald & Losen, 2003).

Researchers have discovered that grade retention of problem children, placement into special education, and negative feedback from teachers all serve to encourage conduct problems in the children (Dodge & Pettit, 2003; Holmes, 1989). Essentially, school failure may be interpreted by the child as a form of social rejection. Loeber, Farrington, Stouthamer-Loeber, and Van Kammen (1998) found that the odds of severe delinquent behavior in 8-year-old male children who were failing in school were nearly double those of other male children. At age 11, the odds of severe delinquency among the low school achievers were more than two-and-a-half times greater than those of other 11-year-old boys. Herrenkohl, Hawkins, Chung, Hill, and Battin-Pearson (2001) conclude from their review of the extant research that "children with low academic performance, low commitment to school, and low educational aspirations during the elementary and middle school grades are at higher risk for child delinquency than are other children" (p. 223).

Although school failure is likely to have negative effects on all children, it appears to be especially problematic for African-American children in the United States. African-American children receive more negative feedback for their school behavior and performance than do Caucasian children (Alexander & Entwisle, 1988). By age 13, 40% of black children have been retained a grade in school, in contrast with 25% of white children (Meisels, 1992). Furthermore, African-Americans have been disproportionately placed in special education classes for emotional disturbance, as compared with other minority children (Wang, Reynolds, & Walberg, 1986). It also should be noted that, in 2004, 10% of black youth dropped out of school or were not attending (Federal Interagency Forum on Child and Family Statistics, 2005). These observations suggest that social forces selectively operate across development to channel African-American adolescent males toward school failure, arrest, and recidivism (Dodge & Pettit, 2003).

Regardless of race or ethnic background, reading achievement appears to play a prominent role in school failure. In fact, poor reading achievement not only is closely associated with school failure, but also predicts later arrest and criminal activity in boys (Petras et al., 2004). On the other hand, a high level of reading achievement seems to prevent at-risk youth from engaging in later antisocial behavior. Specifically, a high level of reading achievement brings more acceptance from mainstream peers, greater attachment to school, enhanced job prospects in young adulthood, and better cognitive resources for anticipating the negative consequences of engaging in criminal activity (Petras et al., 2004). Figure 2–1 identifies multiple examples of extrafamilial risk factors.

FIGURE 2–1   Examples of Extrafamilial Risk Factors

- Poverty
- Social exclusion
- Availability of drugs and firearms
- Exposure to violence and racial prejudice
- Peer rejection
- Delinquent peers
- Gang membership
- Poor-quality day care and preschool experiences
- School failure
- Truancy and dropping out of school

FAMILY RISK FACTORS

Numerous family characteristics are risk factors linked to juvenile delinquency.

PARENTAL PRACTICES AND STYLES

Parenting practices are among the most powerful predictors of early antisocial behavior (Wasserman & Seracini, 2001). Inconsistent discipline and harsh discipline seem to be particularly strong factors, and certain types of parenting are connected to a child's lack of control. **Parental practices** are to be distinguished from parental styles. Practices are strategies employed by parents to achieve specific academic, social, or athletic goals across different contexts and situations (C. H. Hart, Nelson, Robinson, Olsen, & McNeilly-Choque, 1998). That is, parenting practices focus on affecting some particular aspect of a child (Mounts, 2002). Giving children a weekly allowance with the hope of teaching them to manage money is an example of a practice. Reading with children, attending their games, or serving as room parents in school are other examples. Parenting practices have a direct effect on the development of specific child behaviors (from table manners to academic performance) and characteristics (such as acquisition of particular values or high self-esteem; Darling & Steinberg, 1993).

Parental styles, on the other hand, refer to parent–child interactions characterized by parental attitudes toward the child and by the emotional climate of the parent–child relationship (Baumrind, 1991; Mounts, 2002). Non-goal-directed parental behaviors—such as gestures, changes in tone of voice, or the spontaneous expression of emotion—provide examples of parental style. For instance, *responsive* parent–child interactions are described as warm, playful, accepting, and engaging. Studies reveal that, generally speaking, a responsive parenting style leads to social competence, peer acceptance, and less antisocial behavior (Hart et al., 1998). However, a warm and accepting parent may also be permissive and lax.

Diana Baumrind (1971) identified three types of parental styles: (1) authoritarian, (2) permissive, and (3) authoritative. Those parents who use an **authoritarian parenting** style try to shape, control, and evaluate the behavior of their children in accordance with some preestablished, absolute standard. The authoritarian household has numerous rules and regulations that must be rigidly observed, often without question or explanation. Authoritarian parents expect their children to be obedient and unquestioningly respectful of authority. These parents are often referred to as "running a tight ship." Deviations and transgressions are met with punitive, forceful measures, which may or may not include physical punishment. The authoritarian parent discourages any verbal exchanges that imply equality between parent and child; the parent is the authority in all important matters as well as in many unimportant ones.

The **permissive parent** adopts a tolerant, nonpunitive, accepting attitude toward children's behavior, which may include expressions of aggressive and sexual impulses. Permissive parents generally avoid asserting authority or imposing social controls or restrictions. In this type of family, parents see themselves as resource persons to be consulted if needed. Permissive parents allow children to set their own schedule for eating, sleeping, watching television, playing video games, leaving the home, and meeting with friends, and they employ little parental monitoring. They are, in essence, ineffectual in their socializing roles.

Authoritative parents try to direct their children's activities in a rational, issue-oriented manner. There are frequent decision-making exchanges and a general spirit of open communication between parents and children. The hallmark of a family led by authoritative parents is reasoned discussion punctuated with social controls. Authoritative parents expect age-related behavior from their child, and they firmly and consistently enforce family rules and standards. At the same time, they encourage independence and individuality. Table 2–1 summarizes these three parenting styles.

Baumrind's types are not without their problems. Many parents, for example, vacillate between permissiveness and authoritativeness, and some vary their styles according to the age of the child. Authoritative parents may allow their children to set their own eating and sleeping schedules and choose their own modes of dress but may demand extensive input into decisions related to school, careers, or work. Likewise, some parents may be generally permissive in style but may suddenly erupt in anger and demand that their children abide by a newly announced rule. Nonetheless, despite its many shortcomings, "research based on Baumrind's conceptualization of parenting style has produced a remarkably consistent picture of the type of parenting conducive to the successful socialization of children into the dominant culture of the United States" (Darling & Steinberg, 1993, p. 487). The authoritative style—characterized by emotional support, high standards, appropriate individuality, and bidirectional communication between parent and child—has been shown to help children and adolescents develop a social competence characterized by academic success and the balancing of societal and individual needs and responsibilities.

Mounts and Steinberg (1995) reported that adolescents who said that their parents used a nonauthoritative style were more likely to be influenced by their peers to use

TABLE 2–1: Summary of Baumrind's Parental Styles

Style	*Intent*
Authoritarian	To shape and control the child's behavior
Permissive	To allow the child to make his/her own decisions, with the parent serving as a resource
Authoritative	To apply rational, reasonable restrictions to the child's behavior

drugs. Fuligni and Eccles (1993) discovered that adolescents who thought their parents were restrictive and asserted too much control reported far more deviant involvement with peers than did adolescents exposed to other parental styles.

Darling and Steinberg (1993) recommend that, in order to understand the long-term effects of parenting on children, both parenting styles and practices must be studied. In short, they suggest that parenting styles moderate the effects that parenting practices have on children's development; that is, parenting styles alter the parents' capacity to socialize their children by changing the effectiveness of their parenting practices. Recall the illustration of the parent who gives a child a weekly allowance (a parenting practice). The authoritarian parent may require that all but 10% of the allowance be banked; the permissive parent may allow the child to purchase whatever is desired; the authoritative parent may discuss with the child various options for spending and saving the money. Darling and Steinberg hypothesize that a parenting style influences parenting practices in at least two ways: (1) by transforming the nature of the parent–child interaction and thus moderating the influence of the practice on the child and (2) by influencing the child's openness to parental influence. Darling and Steinberg also emphasize that the prevalence of different styles of parenting varies markedly among ethnic groups in contemporary America and from one historical period to the next.

After an extensive review of the research literature, James Snyder and Gerald Patterson (1987) conclude that there are two parental styles that contribute directly or indirectly to delinquency. They label the two styles *enmeshed* and lax (similar to Baumrind's authoritarian and permissive styles). In the **enmeshed style,** parents see an unusually large number of minor behaviors as problematic, and they use ineffective, authoritarian strategies to deal with them. "These parents don't ignore even very trivial excessive behaviors. They issue more and poorer commands, use verbal threats, disapproval, and cajoling more frequently, but fail to consistently and effectively back up these verbal reprimands with nonviolent, nonphysical punishment" (J. Snyder & Patterson, 1987, p. 221). The ineffective use of coercive punishment sets up a reverberating pattern of family interactions, "which elicits, maintains, and exacerbates the aggressive behavior of all family members" (p. 221). When one family member in this coercive interaction acts aversively, other family members react the same way, escalating the exchange. For example, Cathy reacts strongly to her brother's loud music by suddenly screaming to him to turn it off. He screams back at her to "stick it." Cathy then bangs violently on his door. He screams louder. The father then screams at both of them, telling them to "shut up or else." Cathy screams louder and proceeds to kick in her brother's door. She throws a vase at him, just missing. He runs after her, throwing a book. The child sometimes "wins" this escalating confrontation when parents give in to demands, reinforcing this highly aversive interpersonal strategy. For example, if Cathy's father orders her brother to turn the loud music off, parent and child will have "taught" each other that this harsh tactic works in social interactions, a pattern that soon will extend to members outside the family.

Enmeshed parents also sometimes dispense authoritarian, harsh punishment, although it is inconsistent and ineffective. They probably do not have the energy to apply punishments to each and every behavior they perceive as problematic. Consequently, there are many instances of aversive behavior that go unpunished, such as in the preceding example. This pattern results in an intermittent, inconsistent punishment schedule that, in the long run, does little to discourage antisocial behavior.

Some research suggests that overcontrolling parental behaviors—those associated with enmeshed and authoritarian styles—are closely connected to the development of aggression and antisocial behavior in children and adolescents (Blitstein, Murray, Lytle, Birnbaum, & Perry, 2005; Ruchkin, 2002). By contrast, an authoritative style has the opposite effect. Blitstein et al. (2005) report evidence that violent behavior and antisocial behavior among girls may be buffered by the presence of warm, responsive (i.e., authoritative) mothers, although the same result was not found for boys. In short, authoritative mothers seem to play a more significant role in the prevention of antisocial behavior in girls than in boys (Hollister-Wagner, Foshee, & Jackson, 2001).

The parental style most strongly tied to delinquency, though, appears to be the permissive, or **lax style**. Baumrind (1967), for example, suggests that parental permissiveness may have a significant impact on children's antisocial behavior. The lax parents in her sample displayed warmth toward their children, but their failure to provide control and structure appeared to promote impulsive and antisocial behavior in their offspring. Recall the discussion about responsive parenting, which suggests that warmth and acceptance may not be enough. The children of permissive parents in Baumrind's research exhibited very low levels of self-reliance and had great difficulty controlling their impulses. Permissive parents have long been faulted for both lack of discipline and lack of supervision. According to Snyder and Patterson (1987), lax parents are not sufficiently attuned to what constitutes problematic or antisocial behavior in children. Consequently, they allow much of it to slip by without disciplinary actions. For a variety of reasons, they fail to recognize or accept the fact that their children are involved in deviant, antisocial, or even violent actions. They simply do not believe it is happening, or they convince themselves that there is very little they can do about it. "As a result, very few antisocial behaviors are punished. These parents, especially fathers, use punishment very infrequently, and when punishment is used, it has minimal deterrent effect" (J. Snyder & Patterson, 1987, p. 223).

Across a wide range of studies, parental coercion, **harsh punishment**, and hostility—which are most likely to go hand in hand with an authoritarian style—are associated with risk for children's antisocial behavior (Patterson, Reid, & Dishion, 1992). According to Bennett, Bendersky, and Lewis (2002), harsh punishment is closely associated with antisocial and disruptive behaviors in children as young as age 4, and these behaviors appear to continue at a high level throughout the elementary school years (Ackerman, Brown, & Izard, 2003). However, within certain cultural contexts, the effects of harsh punishment on delinquency remain unclear. For example, some scholars and researchers (e.g., Kilgore, Snyder, & Lentz, 2000) have pointed out that harsh punishment or discipline by parents is usually not associated with antisocial behavior when such parental styles and practices are normative and socially accepted in a particular ethnic, racial, or cultural group. Approval and use of more physical forms of discipline are more common among parents who have fewer socioeconomic resources and who are members of ethnic minority groups (Deater-Deckard et al., 2003). For example, in a troubling finding, Deater-Deckard, Dodge, Bates, and Pettit (1996) report that while the relationship between harsh and coercive punishment and delinquency holds up for European-Americans, it does not seem to hold for African-American children. The researchers found no relation between teacher-and peer-rated externalizing (antisocial) problems and the harshness of physical discipline for African-American children. In fact, there was even a trend whereby African-American children receiving harsh physical punishment demonstrated less aggression in school. However, it should be emphasized that the harsh punishment must be perceived by the child as fair and reasonable. Punishment intended to hurt a child emotionally is ineffective and ultimately destructive to the well-being and self-esteem of the child.

Punishment may also have different impacts depending on a child's age (Wasserman & Seracini, 2001) and the emotional tone of the parent administering it. In addition, there is evidence of a strong link between parenting styles and children's capacities for emotional regulation (Chang, Schawartz, Dodge, & McBride-Chang, 2003; Deater-Deckard & Dodge, 1997). These researchers have pointed out that the association between harsh parenting and child aggression and antisocial behavior depends on whether parental disciplinary actions are carried out in an emotionally controlled or an emotionally charged manner. Specifically, the lack of emotional control displayed by parents through harsh punishment affects the ability of their children to regulate their own emotions (Chang et al., 2003; Eisenberg et al., 1999). A parent who has a consistent pattern of lashing out in anger at a child's behavior is not helping the child learn self-regulation. Furthermore, it appears that children transfer some of the negative emotions and poor regulation strategies that they have learned from parent–child interactions to their own interactions with peers, resulting in poor peer relations and eventual peer rejection. In essence, parents who exhibit hurtful and hostile negative emotions provide models of aggressive and out-of-control behavior for children to imitate (Chang et al., 2003; Eisenberg et al., 2001). Aggressive physical and emotional interactions between parents and children form the basis for how children interact with others.

PARENTAL MONITORING

Closely related to parental styles and antisocial behavior is the issue of parental supervision or monitoring. **Monitoring** "refers to parents' awareness of their child's peer associates, free time activities, and physical whereabouts when outside the home" (J. Snyder & Patterson, 1987, pp. 225–226). The amount and quality of parental monitoring are influenced by a number of things. For example, divorce, serious financial distress, loss of job, parental psychological disorders, substance abuse, or death may significantly affect family dynamics and parental or caregiver monitoring. Monitoring appears to be especially important from the ages of 9 and 10 through midadolescence, an observation that has received substantial support from longitudinal studies (Laird, Pettit, Bates, & Dodge, 2003; J. Snyder & Patterson, 1987).

The bulk of the available research has concluded that the amount and quality of parental monitoring are a strong predictor of antisocial behavior during later childhood and adolescence (Kilgore et al., 2000). In the Pittsburgh Youth Study, for example, poor parental monitoring and supervision was the best explanatory variable for delinquency, increasing the risk of delinquency two-and-a-half times over that of youth who experienced better supervision (Browning & Loeber, 1999). Empirical studies continually report that poor parental monitoring is related to higher levels of antisocial behavior and violence (Singer et al., 1999; Webb, Bray, Getz, & Adams, 2002). Little parental monitoring is associated with earlier initiation of substance use (Chilcoat, Dishion, & Anthony, 1995; Steinberg, Fletcher, & Darling, 1994) and with drug use and drug trafficking among low-income African-American children and adolescents (Li, Stanton, & Feigelman, 2000).

Effective monitoring appears to be particularly critical in preventing delinquency in children from disadvantaged backgrounds. "In poor, high-crime neighborhoods, good parental monitoring reduces children's exposure to violence, illegal activity, inappropriate sexual activity, and drug use" (Kilgore et al., 2000, p. 837). In addition, a study of African-American children by Kilgore et al. (2000) suggests that good parental monitoring may minimize children's risk for antisocial behavior earlier in development than has been previously estimated. Ramirez et al. (2004) report that good parental monitoring significantly reduces drug abuse among European-American and Hispanic-American adolescents.

Two important aspects of parental monitoring and supervision should be mentioned. First, Kerns, Aspelmeier, Gentzler, and Grabill (2001) note that some children and adolescents are easier to monitor than others, largely because of their willingness to cooperate in the monitoring process. Kerns and her colleagues did find that a secure and responsive relationship between parent and child facilitated the monitoring process. Second, parents can put their adolescents at risk if the parents are perceived as being too protective or intrusive (Goldstein et al., 2005). Consequently, parents face a difficult balance in deciding how much control they should exercise over the social lives of their young adolescents. Either too much or too little can result in problem behavior.

INFLUENCE OF SIBLINGS

Siblings imitate each other, and most often younger children imitate their older siblings rather than the reverse (Garcia, Shaw, Winslow, & Taggi, 2000). Since siblings generally spend so much time together, it is reasonable to assume that they play a role in shaping the development of aggression and antisocial behavior. This area has not been researched as heavily as other peer influences have, but the few studies available indicate that adolescents with high rates of delinquency are more likely to have siblings with high rates (Coie & Miller-Johnson, 2001). In addition, the risk of delinquency is higher when a delinquent sibling is closer in age than when siblings have been spaced further apart (Rowe, Rodgers, & Meseck-Bushey, 1992). Rowe and Gulley (1992) also suggest that older siblings who engage in delinquent behavior reinforce antisocial behavior in younger siblings when there is a close and warm relationship between the youths. Although it has yet to be documented, it could be that the opposite effect occurs if siblings are not close. That is, a nonaggressive younger sibling may make it a point not to be like an older aggressive or antisocial sibling.

Because of sibling influence, "delinquent families" contribute disproportionately to the delinquency rate. For example, Harriet Wilson (1975) found in her study of disadvantaged inner-city British families that 16% of the families produced 62% of the delinquent children. Similarly, Farrington, Gundry and West (1975) reported that about 4% of the families from a working-class neighborhood in London produced 47% of the convicted delinquents. Loeber and Stouthamer-Loeber (1986) found that siblings engage in pretty much the same delinquent activities, such as substance abuse, burglary, and shoplifting.

PARENTAL PSYCHOPATHOLOGY

Various forms of parental psychopathology have been studied with respect to their influence on the behavior of children. Researchers have looked especially at antisocial personality disorders, depression, alcoholism, and the aggressive behavior exhibited in domestic violence.

In adults, antisocial personality disorder (APD) is a catch-all diagnostic category that encompasses a range of behaviors displaying "a pervasive pattern of disregard for, and violation of, the rights of others" (American Psychiatric Association. 1994, p. 645). As noted by Wasserman and Seracini (2001), high rates (45%) of parental APD are consistently reported in parents of boys referred for conduct problems and delinquency. This observation should not be surprising since there appears to be a strong correlation between familial criminality and antisocial behavior in family offspring (Murray, Janson, & Farrington, 2007; West & Farrington, 1977).

Depressive symptoms, particularly in mothers, appear to be related to increased levels of antisocial behavior and other adjustment problems (Bennett et al., 2002). Children of mothers who are clinically depressed are at increased risk for a range of socioemotional and behavioral problems, including antisocial behavior, emotion dysregulation, and poor cognitive development (Mazulis, Hyde, & Clark, 2004). As they grow older, children whose mothers were depressed during the children's infancy continue to display behavioral problems. Some researchers (e.g., Nelson, Hammen, Brennan, & Ullman, 2003) find that adolescents who display antisocial behaviors and other behavioral problems are more likely to have mothers with a history of depression. The risk for developing problem behaviors appears to be magnified if both parents are depressed during the child's early childhood. On the other hand, the absence of paternal depression may be a protective factor in the context of maternal depression for some children (Mazulis et al., 2004).

Parental alcoholism also elevates risk for a variety of negative child outcomes, including behavioral difficulties, antisocial behavior, and subsequent alcoholism (Loukas, Zucker, Fitzgerald, & Krull, 2003; Zucker et al., 2000). Interestingly, Loukas and her colleagues (2003) found that the presence of paternal alcoholism in the family may be more important than maternal alcoholism in contributing to a son's antisocial behavior and maladjustment.

The aggressive behavior that is demonstrated in domestic violence is clearly a form of parental psychopathology. In this case we are referring to violence perpetrated by one adult against another; maltreatment of children will be discussed separately. It should be noted at the outset that families in which domestic violence occurs are likely to experience higher levels of general stress, including lower income and more frequent moves. The couple is likely to be younger and less educated than the general population and to have more alcohol-related problems (Kitzmann, Gaylord, Holt, & Kenny, 2003). Furthermore, children in domestic violence situations are at higher risk of experiencing multiple forms of abuse, especially physical abuse. The clinical literature underscores the point that husband-to-wife violence presents a strong risk for mother-to-child violence (Slep & O'Leary, 2005). According to Slep and O'Leary (2005), "The stress of being victimized by one's partner could reduce a mother's ability to deal effectively and appropriately with child misbehavior and could contribute to overreacting and possibly being abusive when confronted with challenging child behavior" (p. 436).

A number of forces act on a child's development in such a context. Research clearly suggests that witnessing domestic violence during childhood may impair a person's interpersonal and psychological functioning during adulthood (Diamond & Muller, 2004). In fact, a meta-analysis by Kitzmann et al. (2003) discovered that the effects on children of witnessing interparental violence may be even greater than the effects of witnessing other forms of violence or conflict.

Some research in this area also indicates that witnessing domestic violence as a child places a person at risk for either using physical aggression in one's subsequent adult relationships or being the victim of physical aggression during adulthood (Holtzworth-Munroe, Smulter, & Sandin, 1997). Interestingly, Diamond and Muller (2004) point out, on the basis of their study, that witnessing interspousal aggression of a nonviolent nature (such as verbal abuse) may be just as harmful as witnessing physical violence. That is, children experience negative effects from both violent and nonviolent aggression in the home.

CHILD MALTREATMENT

In the United States, child maltreatment occurs in 138 per 1,000 children, or about 1 in 7 (Finkelhor, Ormrod, Turner, & Hamby, 2005). **Child maltreatment** refers to all forms of abuse and/or neglect and can be divided into five types: physical abuse, sexual abuse, emotional abuse, neglect, and family abduction (see Table 2–2). In a national survey of over 2,000 children, Finkelhor and his associates discovered that emotional abuse (e.g., name calling or denigration by an adult) was the most frequent of the five types. Boys and girls experienced similar rates of maltreatment with the exception of sexual abuse; girls are four times more likely to be sexually abused (Bartol & Bartol, 2005).

The observation that maltreated children have a higher prevalence of engaging in delinquent behavior is fairly well established (Stouthamer-Loeber, Loeber, Homish, & Wei,

TABLE 2–2: Definitions of Child Abuse and Neglect

Type of Abuse	*Definition*
Physical abuse	Willfully injuring causing injury to, or allowing a child to be injured, tortured, or maimed as a result of cruelty or excessive punishment
Sexual abuse	Exploitation of a child or adolescent for another person's sexual or control gratification
Emotional abuse	Chronic pattern of behavior in which a child is belittled, denied love to promote specific behavior, or subjected to extreme and inappropriate punishment
Emotional neglect	Failure to provide a child with appropriate support, attention, and affection
Child neglect	Chronic failure of a parent or caretaker to provide a child with basic needs such as food, clothing, shelter, medical care, educational opportunity, protection, and supervision
Abduction or exploitation	Kidnapping of a child from a custodial parent, child abduction by strangers, or sexual exploitation for child pornography, child prostitution

Source: Based on "Child Victimization" by D. Whitcomb, (2001), in G. Coleman, M. Gaboury, M. Murray, and A. Seymour (Eds.), *National Victim Assistance Academy*, Washington, DC: U. S. Department of Justice.

2001). Being a victim of childhood maltreatment increases the odds of future delinquency, substance abuse, violence, and adult criminality in boys by 40% (Bartol & Bartol, 2005). More specifically, being maltreated as a child increases the likelihood of arrest as a juvenile by over 50%, arrest as an adult by 38%, and arrest for a violent crime by 38% (Widom, 2000). The developmental link between *physical* child abuse and youth violence appears to be especially strong (Herrenkohl, Huang, Tajima, & Whitney, 2003; Keiley, Howe, Dodge, Bates, & Pettit, 2001). Maltreatment is also reported to increase the likelihood of being a gang member (Thompson & Braaten-Antrim, 1998).

The age at which maltreatment takes place appears to be especially important. Children who are physically maltreated during the first few years of life are likely to show more long-term effects and are more likely to participate in criminal activities later in life than are those children who are abused later in childhood or not at all (Keiley et al., 2001). But this statement may need to be qualified somewhat. Thornberry, Ireland, and Smith (2001) conclude from data of the Rochester Youth Development Study that persistent maltreatment has stronger and more consistent negative consequences during adolescence than does maltreatment experienced *only* in childhood. That is, they found that childhood-only maltreatment was generally not a significant risk factor for delinquency and other behavioral problems *unless* the maltreatment continued into adolescence. If the maltreatment stopped during childhood, its effects were not as strong on the problem behaviors displayed by youngsters during adolescence.

Thornberry et al. (2001) suggest two possible explanations for these results. One is that the consequences of maltreatment may fade with time if the maltreatment is not repeated. They point out that children and families can be very resourceful and resilient and may eventually be able to right themselves after a finite set of stressful events. The second explanation is that the absence of long-term effects may be due to successful interventions and counseling. Thornberry and his colleagues note that only substantiated cases of maltreatment were measured in the analysis, and "all of them received services, some of them quite intensive" (p. 976). Consequently, it is entirely possible that the interventions were effective in correcting the long-term effects of childhood maltreatment. This point underscores the need for early intervention in maltreatment cases.

Although studies are fairly consistent in showing that maltreatment raises the risk of later delinquency, it should be emphasized that many other risk factors play a major role as well, probably in combination with maltreatment in many cases. It is difficult, for example, to disentangle the effects of child maltreatment from other family risk factors, such as mental health problems, alcoholism, poverty, inadequate educational backgrounds, domestic violence, and faulty parenting and interpersonal skills. For instance, research has clearly identified a reoccurring connection between domestic violence with adult victims and child maltreatment (Hartley, 2002; Slep & O'Leary, 2005). In a review of 31 studies by Edleson (1999), the overlap of domestic violence and child maltreatment reported a co-occurrence rate of between 30% and 60% in the majority of studies analyzed. That is, where there is domestic violence, there is often child maltreatment also. And as noted earlier, it is sometimes at the hands of the adult who is the victim of the domestic violence.

Certainly, not all maltreated children become antisocial, and many show considerable adaptation to abuse and maltreatment (Jaffee et al., 2005; McGloin & Widom, 2001). Therefore, it is critically important to study why a significant proportion of maltreated children escape the adverse outcomes. However, as noted by Jaffee et al. (2005), "Very little systematic evidence is available to explain why children show such marked variations in their response to maltreatment" (pp. 67–68).

MULTIASSAULTIVE FAMILIES

Some years ago, Hotaling and Straus (1989) reported that at least 7% of all intact families are **multiassaultive** (Hotaling & Straus, 1989). That is, some families are characterized by continual cycles of intrafamilial physical aggression and violence. Some recent data, however, suggest that 7% may be a gross underestimation of the level of violence in families. Slep and O'Leary (2005) conducted a study in which they randomly selected 453 young couples living in New York State. Families were randomly contacted by phone and, if willing to participate, completed a brief demographic questionnaire via the phone. In order to be eligible for the study, the couple had to be able to complete the questionnaire in English, had to have been living together for at least 1 year, and had to be parenting a 3- to 7-year-old child who was the biological offspring of at least one of the parents. Initially, eligible participants then completed a slightly longer phone interview about family functioning. Then, eligible respondents were contacted by one of the researchers, who described the project in more detail and scheduled appointments for interested respondents to participate in the main study. The couples were paid $250 to participate in a 6-hour interview/questionnaire session.

The researchers found that physical aggression was fairly pervasive in these representative families with young children, with some form of aggression reported by 90% of the families. Over 30% of the families reported that a form of "severe aggression" had occurred; this included such acts as being beaten up, burned or scalded on purpose, kicked, slammed against a wall, choked, punched or hit with an object that could hurt, or harmed with a knife or gun. The researchers collected data completely anonymously. Participants were told that no would read their written responses to questions while they were in the office and that completed information would remain completely anonymous. In addition, the couples were separated when completing the two questionnaires—*Conflict Tactics Scale—Revised* and *Parent—Child Conflict Tactics Scale.* These scales asked the couples to indicate both being victimized and engaging in abuse themselves.

Severe partner aggression was reported by 24% of the families, with nearly half of those (10%) reporting severe aggression by both partners. As reported by the parents, 87% of the children experienced physical aggression from their parents, and 59% experienced it from both parents. Thirteen percent of the children experienced severe aggression from one parent, and 1.5% experienced it from both parents. Most revealing was the finding that 92% of the families characterized by severe aggression tended to be multiassaultive, with both partners severely aggressing against each other and at least one partner severely aggressing against a child. Slep and O'Leary (2005) concluded that both minor and severe violence may be much more widespread in young children's families than is currently believed.

Males who have witnessed, participated in, or been victimized by violence in their own families are five times more likely to have assaulted a nonfamily person than are men in nonassaultive families. A similar pattern holds for women from multiassaultive families, although the relationship is not as strong. Sibling violence is particularly high in families in which child assault and spousal assault are present, with boys displaying significantly more assaultive behavior (Hotaling & Straus, 1989). Furthermore, children from multiassaultive families have an inordinately high rate of assault against nonfamily members. These children are also more likely to be involved in property crime, to have adjustment problems in school, and to be more involved with the police (Hotaling & Straus, 1989). We will return to this important topic in Chapter 9.

DIVORCE, SEPARATION, AND DESERTION

Children from homes in which there has been a divorce, separation, or desertion are often believed to have higher rates of delinquency than children from "intact" homes. In the research literature, the terms *broken home* or *nonintact homes* are usually used to indicate the three types of family disruption described in this section.

Homes in which the original adult couple was split by something other than death are more likely than intact homes to produce antisocial children, according to a meta-analysis by Price and Kunz (2003). The meta-analysis included 72 studies on the relationship between divorce and delinquency rates. The form of the breakup sometimes makes a difference. For example, boys in the desertion category seem to commit more frequent and serious offenses than do boys who have experienced family divorce, separation, or death (Heck & Walsh, 2000).

Some research on official delinquency (e.g., Toby, 1957; Wadsworth, 1979) also has suggested that the earlier the parental breakup occurs in the developmental history of the child, the greater its impact on the development of delinquency (Wells & Rankin, 1985). This finding is compatible with studies in child development that suggest that the age at the time of parental discord and separation is a relevant factor in determining the effect on the child. Because they have formulated friendships with peers and have achieved some degree of personal autonomy from parents, older children appear to find separation less traumatic than younger children (Kellam, Adams, Brown, & Ensminger, 1982). Younger children experiencing divorce not only have fewer experiences outside the home, but also lack the cognitive and social competencies to understand and deal with the dissolution of their parents' marital relationship (Belsky, Lerner, & Spanier, 1984).

Indeed, child development research suggests that the coping styles of children of different ages vary as a function of their cognitive and social competencies. Young children, for example, may blame themselves for causing the separation and may otherwise be unable to evaluate the divorce situation accurately (Belsky et al., 1984). However, the few self-report studies conducted on the topic are at odds with the official studies; the self-report research does not support this age-at-divorce hypothesis (e.g., Nye, 1958; Rankin, 1983). Children's temperament and genetic makeup may also be a factor in how they react to a divorce situation. In a study by Hetherington, Cox, and Cox (1979), children who exhibited the highest level of behavioral problems as a result of divorce or marital discord were those who (1) had a prevalence of fussiness and crying during their infancies (according to their mothers), (2) adapted slowly to new situations and showed distress under those conditions, and (3) displayed biological irregularities in sleeping, feeding, and eliminating. Possibly some combination of marital disharmony and individual temperament produced a high-risk environment for the development of delinquency.

One frequent observation in the early literature was that delinquent girls came from broken homes more often than delinquent boys did (Rodman & Grams, 1967), suggesting that parental discord and separation may have a greater negative impact on girls. Jackson Toby (1957) argued that this difference was due to the greater control parents maintained over girls; when separation occurred, the contrast effects (from control to much less control) had a stronger impact on girls. Most of these earlier studies finding gender effects were based on official delinquency records (Wells & Rankin, 1985), leading some investigators (e.g., Datesman & Scarpitti, 1975; Rankin, 1983) to suggest that the gender difference was due to the family-related bias in official processing of female delinquents. Girls are more likely than boys to be referred to juvenile authorities and to receive official sanctions for such "ungovernable" behaviors as sexual misconduct, running away, and truancy, all of which are likely to be affected by the family situation (Wells & Rankin, 1985). Nevertheless, there was also evidence that boys were more strongly affected by divorce than girls were (Emery, 1982) and that family conflict was as important in male as in female delinquency (Norland, Shover, Thornton, & James 1979).

Self-report studies in general, however, were far less supportive of gender differences than were the studies based on official records. Wells and Rankin (1985, p. 256) summarized the empirical research with this comment: "The simple proposition that family break up has a greater negative effect on girls than on boys is too simple to be meaningful" (p. 256). They added that the broken home–delinquency relationship may itself be nothing but an artifact of official processing procedures. Indeed, the term *broken home* is so broad that it may be virtually meaningless for research purposes yet research does clearly suggest that more serious childhood problems are present in homes broken by divorce, separation, or desertion than in homes broken by death (Emery, 1982). However, it is still not justifiable to treat divorce, separation, and desertion as part of a unitary concept or even to treat them separately but still unitarily. We cannot assume that all divorces, all separations, all desertions affect families in the same way.

For this reason some researchers prefer to examine process variables rather than structural variables in family research, even though this is not easily done. Research on the effects of divorce in general often fails to acknowledge that the legal formality of divorce usually follows long after alienation (both psychological and physical) between the spouses (Lamb, 1977). Although there are exceptions, the research does not tell whether these exceptions are significant. Furthermore, although the stresses and strains of divorce generally occur gradually and include the psychological separation between children and parents, this is not invariably the case. The absent parent may continue to maintain a significant relationship with both the separated spouse and the child or children, with or without a shared custody arrangement. It is also not unusual for parental conflict to continue unabated after the home has been formally "broken." Some research indicates that children of divorced parents who remain in conflict after the divorce decree are more likely to be delinquent than children from low-conflict divorces (Hetherington, et al., 1979). Structural research—which focuses simply on whether the family is broken or intact—does not address these fine points.

In addition, broken homes are invariably defined from the reference point of children vis-à-vis their relationship with their parents, whereas siblings and extended family members who might be living in the household (e.g., grandparents, aunts, and uncles) are ignored (Wells & Rankin, 1986). Some research is beginning to pay attention to some of these factors. Neilsen and Gerber (1979) found that brothers and sisters of chronic truants tended also to be truant. G. R. Patterson (1986) concluded from a review of the literature that the evidence so far suggests that siblings are similar across a considerable range of behaviors, including involvement in delinquency.

Even the word *parent* is not sufficiently defined in much of the existing literature. Some researchers study only homes of biological parents, while others discount the primacy of biological ties, counting as parents any adults who effectively carry out parental tasks and perform the necessary caregiving functions (Wells & Rankin, 1986). The most frequent version of a broken home defines parents in biological terms (Wells & Rankin, 1986; West, 1982; Wilgosh & Paitich, 1982), but noteworthy studies have expanded the definition to include anyone considered to be a parent by the children in the home (e.g., Gove & Crutchfield, 1982; Matsueda, 1982; Blechman, 1982).

Investigators have also too often treated intact families as though they are a homogeneous collection when they are not. Some children live with both of their natural parents; others live in restructured nuclear families, in which a stepparent has entered the family, or in blended families, in which two adults have each brought offspring into the new nuclear group. Some studies (e.g., Johnson, 1986; Dornbusch et al., 1985) suggest a strong link between the presence of a stepfather and delinquency.

"Parental absence" is also a condition that encompasses a wide variety of situations. The absence may be due to occupational demands, military service, hospitalization, or incarceration. It may be total or partial (e.g., shared custody, visitation privileges, correspondence), temporary or long-term, voluntary or involuntary (Wells & Rankin, 1986). In addition, research rarely considers distinctions between father-absent and mother-absent homes, although the implicit assumption is that broken homes are generally father-absent households. Such variations in absence may have differential effects on a child's development and possible misconduct.

Some time ago, Emery (1982) and Gove and Crutchfield (1982) concluded after extensive literature reviews that it is parental conflict rather than separation per se that results in delinquency. Children from broken but conflict-free homes are less likely to be delinquent than are children from conflict-ridden but intact homes.

FAMILY SIZE AND BIRTH ORDER

Twenty years ago, a sizable amount of evidence suggested that both family size and birth order were linked to delinquency (Ernst & Angst, 1983). Family size refers to the number of siblings within one family; birth order refers to the ordinal position in the birth sequence among siblings (e.g., first born, second born, last born, only born). In their classic studies, Sheldon and Eleanor Glueck (1950) found that their delinquent group was more likely to come from a large family than was their nondelinquent group. Hirschi (1969) concluded from his self-report study of delinquency that "children from large families are more likely than children from small families to have committed delinquent acts" (pp. 239–240). West and Farrington (1973) reported similar findings. In their very extensive review of the research literature, Rolf Loeber and Magda Stouthamer-Loeber (1986) also concluded that delinquents often come from large families, but they could not locate a single study that tried to investigate why this relationship exists. They were unaware of any study that had concentrated on the familial *processes* that contribute to the connection between family size and delinquency.

- Poor family management practices and styles
- Low levels of parental involvement and monitoring
- Delinquent siblings
- Parental psychopathology, especially depression
- Parental substance abuse
- Parental criminality
- Family violence
- Child maltreatment
- Parent–child separation
- Large family size

The early evidence for birth-order effect was also quite robust, but little current research documents it. Middle-born boys were found to be overrepresented in delinquency (Ernst & Angst, 1983; West & Farrington, 1973; Glueck & Glueck, 1950; Lees & Newson, 1954). McCord, McCord, and Zola (1959) also found that middle-born boys were more likely to be delinquent. These researchers speculated that middle-born children were forgotten during times of heavy family burden. Others speculated about the many possible reasons for the birth-order effect, but research has yet to examine the processes through which middle-born children are potentially more prone toward delinquent behavior. We also do not know from the available research whether birth order was related to serious delinquency, nonserious delinquency, or both.

Again, we have a reported significant relationship between family structure and delinquency but little empirical evidence as to why it exists. Until further research focuses more on the family process involved, we can only speculate on what these connections mean. The causal chain, however, is unlikely to be as simple or direct as family size or birth order causing delinquency. M. Wadsworth (1979), for example, found that family size appears to be most strongly associated with delinquency in disadvantaged families (measured by income and father's occupation) and only weakly associated in middle-class families. There are likely to be many other contributing, codetermining variables in the equation. Figure 2–2 identifies numerous examples of family risk factors.

Summary and Conclusions

This chapter began to focus on those individual attributes, developmental experiences, and social experiences that increase the probability of antisocial or delinquent behavior. These risk factors may affect children differently at different stages in development. Peer influences, for example, are stronger during adolescence than during early childhood or middle childhood, whereas separation and divorce may be more difficult for young children than for adolescents. It is important to emphasize that, even given a host of risk factors, a child will not necessarily engage in antisocial behavior or delinquency. Resilient children, discussed again in Chapter 4, are able to overcome these barriers to socially accepted behavior. Risk factors are associated with delinquency but do not cause it.

Economic factors, specifically those associated with poverty, are among the most widely cited risk factors for delinquency and antisocial conduct. Although we emphasize repeatedly that most children who grow up poor do not engage in serious delinquency, we cannot deny that poverty creates a multitude of barriers to healthy development. Economically struggling communities, for example, often are characterized by inadequate educational and health care systems and a disproportionate number of families experiencing the disruption brought about by unemployment, underemployment, or family discord. Teachers can be overwhelmed by the multitude of problems faced by their students. And levels of lead and other toxic substances have been found to be higher in economically deprived areas than in middle-or upper-income communities. Even the quality of day-care services may be lower. Some research has found, for example, that in day-care centers located in poor neighborhoods, caretaker comments to children are more critical and there is less use of direct questions that encourage creative or expansive answers.

Peer rejection—another extrafamilial risk factor—appears regularly in the literature on delinquency. Children who are not accepted by their peers often form bonds with similar children and participate in illegal activity. Rejection is usually prompted by the child's own behavior, characteristics, or family circumstances, but the connection between aggression and rejection is not as clear-cut as it might appear. The aggressive child may be imitated and joined rather than rejected. However, a combination of aggression and rejection is related to later involvement in delinquency. For example, aggressive children who are also more impulsive, quick to anger, and limited in social skills are likely to be rejected and, subsequently, to engage in antisocial behavior. As noted throughout the chapter, risk factors often influence one another, in a sense intensifying their impact on the individual.

Family risk factors include parental skills, practices, and styles, including the monitoring of children's behavior. Parental maltreatment of children, violence within the family, and parental psychopathology, such as depression or alcoholism, are other examples of risk factors. Several different parental styles have been identified in the literature, most prominently Baumrind's authoritarian, permissive, and authoritative styles and Snyder and Patterson's enmeshed and lax styles. Research indicates that an authoritative style—whereby children are provided with structure and direction but are also encouraged to make decisions—is most conducive to healthy development. By contrast, permissive or lax styles—whereby children receive little direction and monitoring—are most conducive to delinquency. Lack of adequate monitoring has been consistently found to be a major contributor to delinquency in adolescents.

Child maltreatment and, generally, violence in the family have been linked to delinquency in a wide range of studies. However, we caution that children who are maltreated are not necessarily destined for delinquency. Research demonstrates, for example, that abuse that continues into adolescence is particularly problematic; the connection between delinquency and abuse that stops during childhood is not as strong. (Of course, child abuse has no redeeming qualities and should be eradicated, whether or not its connection to antisocial behavior is demonstrated.) Other forms of family violence, such as sibling-to-sibling violence and child-to-parent abuse, suggest that some children are learning, early in their development, that physical confrontation is normative, expected, and accepted.

Early research demonstrated connections between families broken by divorce, separation, or desertion and delinquency, at least as documented in official records. Self-report studies were far less definitive. Family research also found associations between antisocial behavior and parental absence (defined in many different ways), family size, and birth order. Although this early research found positive associations with delinquency, process variables were seldom studied sufficiently. Today, the research on family practices and styles has displaced much of the earlier research on broken versus intact homes. This research suggests that lax, permissive parenting places children and adolescents at particular risk for antisocial behavior.

The many risk factors identified in this chapter often accompany and interact with the individual and environmental factors discussed in Chapter 3. Even though efforts to confront and diminish risk factors must continue, we could easily become discouraged if we were to consider only that multitude of influences. However, we must constantly remind ourselves that promoting resilience in children, as well as establishing protective factors, may be the most effective approach to preventing, intervening in, and treating delinquency.

Key Terms and Concepts

authoritarian parenting
authoritative parenting
child maltreatment
enmeshed parenting style
extrafamilial risk factors
family risk factors
harsh punishment
health risk factors
individual risk factors
lax parenting style

monitoring
multiassaultive families
parental practices
parental styles
permissive parenting
psychobiological risk factors
relational aggression
risks
social exclusion

CHAPTER 3
INDIVIDUAL RISK FACTORS

CHAPTER OBJECTIVES

◆ Introduce individual social factors that predict delinquent behavior, such as aggression

◆ Introduce cognitive and language risk factors, such as hostile attribution bias

◆ Introduce emotional risk factors, such as poor anger control, lack of empathy, and cruelty to animals

◆ Identify biological risk factors, such as physical development, temperament, psychophysiological characteristics, and brain development

◆ Provide an overview of genetic and twin studies of the development of antisocial behavior

◆ Explore the link between ADHD and antisocial behavior

In the previous chapter we learned that serious delinquent behaviors can develop in response to a combination of risk factors that include a family history of antisocial behavior, early family conflicts and disorganization, inconsistent and harsh or lax discipline, deficient parental monitoring, peer rejection, inclusion in antisocial peer groups, failure to succeed in traditional education, and the loss of hope and opportunity in the mainstream culture due to poverty, inadequate social support systems, and unsafe neighborhoods. These risk factors can all be classified roughly as *contextual* factors that influence development. But individual risk factors also play a significant role in the complex interaction of factors influencing the development of delinquent or antisocial behavior. For example, more than 100 studies have addressed the question of genetic influence on antisocial behavior and have generally concluded that genes influence about 40% to 50% of the variation in the population (Moffit & Caspi, 2006). That is, almost half of the differences among individuals can be explained by genetic factors.

A wide range of individual risk factors have been identified in the literature. They include inadequate cognitive and language ability, impulsivity, inadequate interpersonal and social skills, a troublesome temperament, heredity, a negative self-concept, low self-esteem, a tendency toward aggressive behavior, and certain psychological diagnoses, such as conduct disorder (CD), oppositional defiant disorder (ODD), or attention-deficit/hyperactivity disorder (ADHD). When we take a developmental perspective, we quickly learn that all of these factors are influenced by various dynamic interactions with the social environment discussed in the previous chapter. In fact, none of the individual factors discussed in this chapter work independently of contextual or social factors. A child who is bullied and rejected by peers may develop low self-esteem, be diagnosed with an externalizing problem behavior, and ultimately engage in serious delinquency. Furthermore, the interactions between the environment and individual risk factors that exist during early childhood are unlikely to be the same during adolescence. For example, parents or caregivers play prominent roles during early childhood, but the role of peers becomes prominent during adolescence.

Individual risk factors can be divided into the social, cognitive, emotional, and biological characteristics of an individual at a given point in time (Tremblay & LeMarquand, 2001). Although these are useful divisions for the purposes of organization and discussion, we emphasize that some factors can easily be placed in more than one category. Aggressiveness and hostile attribution bias, for example—which we place in the social characteristics category—could easily be placed in the biological category. Also, as Tremblay and LeMarquand (2001) emphasize, there are numerous mutual influences among individual risk factors. For instance, the tendency to be impulsive (an emotional risk factor) often accompanies aggressive behavior (a social risk factor), and children who are impulsive often tend to have deficits in cognitive processing abilities. Furthermore, different risk factors may be relevant at various ages and may be associated with different offense trajectories. For example, youngsters who follow an early onset of persistent antisocial behavior may have certain biological/neurological risk factors, such as attention-deficit disorders, whereas late-onset offending is influenced more by social factors (Moffitt, Lynam, & Silva, 1994; Rutter, 1997; Rutter, Giller, & Hagell, 1998).

SOCIAL RISK FACTORS

AGGRESSIVE BEHAVIOR

One of the strongest social risk factors related to delinquency is the amount of aggressiveness a child demonstrates at the end of the kindergarten year. In Chapter 2 we discussed aggression in the context of peer rejection, because aggressive children are often rejected. Here we focus more on the specifics of aggression as a behavioral indicator. *Aggression* has many definitions, but we will use it primarily to mean physical attacks on another person. "Aggressive behavior measured from age 6 through age 13 has been shown consistently to predict later violence among males across studies" (Hawkins et al., 1998, p. 113). Tremblay and LeMarquand (2001) add this:

> Physical aggression rated by kindergarten teachers appears to be the best social behavior characteristic to predict early male delinquent behavior of any type, and prosocial behavior rated by kindergarten teachers appears to be a protective factor, specifically for those at risk for violent and property crimes before age 13 years. (p. 141)

It should be emphasized that physical aggression is a *normal* developmental behavior during early childhood, usually beginning before 24 months of age, and is no cause for concern (Tremblay, 2006). Recent data from large longitudinal investigations reveal that most children increase the frequency of physical aggression from 9 to 48 months of age (Tremblay, 2004; Tremblay et al., 2004). Behaviors such as pushing and shoving, taking something away from another child, or even biting, kicking, and slapping are not unusual for the very young. In fact, some research (e.g., Peterson & Flanders, 2005) suggests that play-fighting may be an important behavior for normal development.

The end of the second year of life, according to Tremblay and LeMarquand (2001), is the age at which the tendency to be physically aggressive is at its highest peak for most children. Many, if not most, children still exhibit high levels of physical aggression in preschool or kindergarten, but in most cases they show significant reductions in these behaviors during the early school years (Bongers et al., 2003; Séguin, Nagin, Asaad, & Tremblay, 2004). Through the influences of the psychosocial environment (e.g., parents, caregivers, and teachers), physical aggression is expected to subside substantially from the preschool years to preadolescence in a majority of children. Approximately 97% of boys show decreasing levels of physical aggression as they grow older (Tremblay & LeMarquand, 2001). The few children (5% to 10%) who continue to show various forms of physical aggression across a wide variety of social contexts well into middle childhood are those children most likely to engage in antisocial or delinquent behavior during adolescence and criminal behavior during young adulthood (Côté, Vaillancourt, Barker, Nagin, & Tremblay, 2007). Interestingly, this observation does not apply simply to violent crimes but extends to property crimes as well (Haapassalo & Tremblay, 1994).

There is mounting evidence, however, that children's aggressive behavior includes more than physical harm. Children and adolescents can hurt their peers through more subtle and covert or indirect forms of aggression, such as social exclusion, rumors, threats, and harassment (Vitaro, Brendgen, & Barker, 2006). In many instances, these forms of aggression may be more harmful to the victim than physical aggression, resulting in anxiety, constant fear, depression, and even suicide ideation (Owens, Slee, & Shute, 2000; Vitaro et al., 2006). Côté et al. (2007) report that most aggressive children use both physical and indirect forms of aggression, although girls are more likely to rely on indirect aggression.

TROUBLESOME BEHAVIOR

Although not necessarily aggressive, some children may be described by both adults and peers as "troublesome" or difficult to manage. This behavioral pattern appears to be another individual risk factor closely connected to delinquency. According to Tremblay and LeMarquand (2001), the best predictor of convictions for violent behavior during adolescence and young adulthood is teacher and peer ratings of troublesome behavior from ages 8 to 10. These findings pertain primarily to boys, but some cases involved girls as well. Another study (White, Moffitt, Earls, Robins, & Silva, 1990) found that children rated by their mothers as difficult to manage at age 3 were likely to display antisocial behavior during middle childhood and early adolescence. This does not mean that all children rated difficult to manage by their mothers become delinquents, but it does indicate that many children who engage in antisocial and delinquent behavior probably were considered by their parents to be difficult to manage at an early age. During the early school years, teacher ratings of disruptiveness and aggressive behavior are also strong predictors of later antisocial and delinquent behavior.

COGNITIVE RISK FACTORS

Practitioners and researchers have thought for some time that as young children learn more cognitive, language, and self-regulation skills, they are better able to cope with developmental challenges and avoid a lifetime of antisocial behavior and crime (Hill, Degnan, Calkins, & Keane, 2006).

LANGUAGE DELAY AND IMPAIRMENT

Delayed language development is believed to increase stress and frustration for many children and impede normal socialization (Keenan & Shaw, 2003). Even when socio-economic status (SES) and test motivation are controlled, researchers have found that language development for boys aged 6 months, 18 months, and 24 months predicts later delinquency and antisocial behavior (Nigg & Huang-Pollack, 2003; Stattin & Klackenberg-Larsson, 1993). Similarly, Stowe, Arnold, and Ortiz (2000) found that delayed language functioning was associated with observed disruptive behaviors in male preschoolers. The current research pertaining to girls is sparse and inconclusive.

Unfortunately, there appears to be a connection between poverty and language development. Investigators continually report that by the age of 3, children in poverty are already significantly behind their more affluent peers in the use of vocabulary and oral language skills (B. Hart & Risley, 1995; Wasik, Bond, & Hindman, 2006). Although these language deficits may be due in part to biological and genetic influences, they appear to be due principally to the parents' limited use of communication and literacy skills and to the absence of books and magazines in the home. Shared book reading encourages a dialogue and communication exchange between child and parent or care-taker (or teacher) and contributes substantially to vocabulary development. B. Hart and T. R. Risley (1995, 1999) estimate that, on average, a child in a professional family hears about 2,150 words per hour from parents or caretakers, a child in a working-class family hears about 1,250 words per hour, and a child in a family with unemployed parents hears about 620 words per hour. These differences in language exposure have a significant impact on a child's language development (Bono, Sheinberg, Scott, & Claussen, 2007). In fact, Hart and Risley (1999) discovered that by age 3, children's talk matched their parents' talk in quantity and quality. Their vocabulary was not as extensive, but the amount of time talking and the structure of their sentences were comparable.

Children who have infrequent communication exchanges with their parents or caregivers are likely to have language deficiencies that often lead to a life of limited opportunity and a developmental pathway of antisocial behavior. Language problems and a lack of communication skills increase frustration levels in children, who conse-quently have difficulty expressing their points of view, which are so necessary for rea-sonable resolution of conflicts and unmet needs. This frustration, if not self-regulated, is likely to lead to aggressive and disruptive behavior at home and at school.

Delay in language development may also be accompanied by language impair-ment, which usually refers specifically to problems expressing or understanding lan-guage. **Expressive language** refers to language produced by the speaker, as opposed to language received by a listener (receptive language). Expressive language problems pertain to inadequacies in the production of speech in reference to vocabulary, sen-tence structure, and other rules of language. For example, a 5-year-old child with very limited vocabulary and an inability to speak in sentences of more than three words might be considered to have an expressive language disorder. Male children who dis-play disruptive behaviors during the preschool years and antisocial behavior during the school years have been found to have a high incidence of problems with expressive language (Dionne, Tremblay, Boivin, Laplante, & Pérusse, 2003).

Brownlie et al. (2004) found that boys diagnosed with a language impairment at age 5 were far more likely to exhibit delinquent behavior at age 19 than were boys without indications of a language impairment. This relationship held even when verbal IQ and demographic and family variables were controlled. The researchers speculated that the association might be largely due to the negative impact that language impairments have on a child's schooling and academic performance in general. Language-impaired children are often rejected by peers and are frequently viewed negatively by their teachers (Brownlie et al., 2004). In essence, language deficiency—whether a delay or an impairment—often makes school a painful and unappealing enterprise, leading to poor or disinterested performance on academic tasks. Not surprisingly, according to Tremblay and LeMarquand (2001), "When children are followed from elementary school to high school, academic failure clearly predates adolescent delinquency" (p. 150).

The literature is clear that language-impaired children have poorly developed social skills and are at considerable risk of developing a variety of academic, behavioral, and social problems (Horowitz, Jannson, Ljungberg, & Hedenbro, 2005). There is strong evidence that language impairment increases the risk of antisocial behavior, at least in boys (Brownlie et al., 2004; Stansbury & Zimmermann, 1999). In addition, a high percentage of children and adolescents diagnosed with and treated for antisocial behavior and conduct disorders demonstrate language impairments (Cohen et al., 1998; Giddan, Milling, & Campbell, 1996).

To explain this strong association between language and delinquency or antisocial behavior, researchers theorize that when language deficits limit general communication, children may use disruptive behavior to compensate for limited communication skills (Dionne et al., 2003). Basically, early language delay and limited communication skills may predispose a child to employ more physically aggressive tactics for dealing with the social environment. Frustrated about not getting their needs met through normal communication and social strategies, these children are drawn to more physical, demonstrative behavior to get their way. There is a circular effect at work, however, since aggressive and disruptive behaviors interfere with a social or academic environment conducive to learning and may thus, in turn, curtail language development.

LIMITED COGNITIVE CONSTRUCTS

Some people seem to possess more structure about the world than others—in other words, some people are more **cognitively complex**. People with many sophisticated structures, or constructs, evaluate behavior and world events in more complex ways than people with a few, crude structures. Constructs are mental representations of the environment; they are our mental summaries of what we know and understand about the world. Children's constructs vary with age. As experiences with the environment accumulate, the number, quality, and organization of these constructs change.

Our thinking processes are structured by the properties of the language we speak. The language habits of our community, culture, or subculture predispose us to what we see, hear, or otherwise experience. Thus, language is the human guide to social reality. One's language, cultural background, cognitive sophistication and, more generally, one's version of the world are all likely to have an extremely important connection to delinquency. For example, some years ago King (1975) published a qualitative study of ten adolescent murderers (average age of 14 years). The nine boys and one girl committed unusually brutal murders that appear senseless to an outsider (e.g., a machete dismembering, a gasoline burning). To the consternation of authorities, none of the teenagers expressed any guilt or remorse. Their families, while intact, were characterized by turmoil, conflict, and excessive drinking; the parents and caretakers exhibited unpredictable mood swings and physical violence, especially when drinking.

On the basis of interview data, King determined that these youngsters were "confused" about their environment, viewing it as chronically hostile and largely unpredictable. Most surprising, however, were the psychological evaluations. Although these adolescents had average IQ scores, each one was "most severely retarded in reading, and drastically stunted in language skills" (p. 136). This finding led King to conclude that a lack of language skills and cognitive constructs may have interfered with the youths' ability to interpret and interface adequately with the world. Such cognitive deficits, he believed, contributed to poor judgment and little realization of the consequences of their actions. Furthermore, these youngsters seemed to be unable to conceptualize their victims as persons. To the offenders, the victims were merely nonperson objects or targets. King maintains that the poverty of language may have directly contributed to the adolescents' actions. Their versions of the world seemed to be simplistic, black-and-white conceptions, in which hostility reigned and compassion was for "suckers."

This study illustrates the potential value of studying the language development and construct systems of serious delinquents. Far-reaching generalizations from a single study are, of course, unwarranted. Furthermore, we are not implying that "intelligent" people or people with sophisticated language development do not commit crimes. Rather, individuals with limited cognitive constructs and language skills may be less able to mediate and get along in their social worlds, as compared to others with a richer cognitive structure and process.

HOSTILE ATTRIBUTION BIAS

For some time, investigators have found that many aggressive behaviors are in reaction to provocation. As noted by Dodge (2006), "The tendency to retaliate when one has been intentionally and maliciously provoked seems to be a human inclination" (p. 794). However, it appears that some persons have a tendency to constantly see hostile intentions when there are none. This tendency to infer hostile intent in response to ambiguous or accidental provocations decreases between the ages of 3 and 7 years, primarily as a result of cognitive development and maturation (Dodge, 2006). Some children, however, fail to develop the ability to differentiate hostile from nonhostile intent.

Children who demonstrate high aggression and who are rejected by their peers (recall the importance of this factor, discussed in the previous chapter) often have **hostile attribution bias** (Dodge et al., 2003). This characteristic leads them to process social information in maladaptive ways, such as making attributions of hostile intent that lead to aggressive behavior toward peers (Dodge et al., 2003). Research indicates that this bias begins to develop during the preschool years (Dodge et al., 2002; Nigg & Huang-Pollock, 2003). For example, a 4-year-old may believe that his playmate deliberately smashed his Bob the Builder wrench, when in reality the playmate stepped on it accidentally. The tendency to attribute hostile intention seems to carry throughout life. Dodge (1993) reports that when children were followed from elementary school to middle school, those with a tendency to attribute hostile intentions to others were rejected by peers during elementary school and were increasingly aggressive during middle school.

According to Nigg and Huang-Pollock (2003), the term *hostile attribution bias* was first used by Nasby, Hayden, and DePaulo (1979) to describe the tendency of many aggressive children to routinely attribute hostile intent to other children, even if the other children have no such intentions. For example, in elementary school, a foot casually and innocently positioned near a school desk may be interpreted as a deliberate attempt to trip. Children with a hostile attribution bias are twice as likely as other children to see aggressive intentions and actions where there are none (Hubbard, Dodge, Cillessen, Coie, & Schwartz, 2001). Some aggressive and peer-rejected children are hyperalert to any actions that could be remotely interpreted as aggressive.

A growing body of evidence supports hostile attribution bias and finds that violent youth "typically define social problems in hostile ways, adopt hostile goals, and seek few additional facts, generate few alternative solutions, anticipate few consequences for aggression, and give higher priority to their aggressive solutions" (Eron & Slaby, 1994, p. 10). Similarly, Serin and Preston (2001) conclude,

> Aggressive juvenile offenders have been found to be deficient in social problem-solving skills and to espouse many beliefs supporting aggression. Specifically, they tend to define problems in hostile ways, adopt hostile goals, seek less confirmatory information, generate fewer alternative solutions, anticipate fewer consequences for aggressive solutions, and choose less effective solutions. (p. 259)

And Coie (2004) adds,

> The fact that rejected, aggressive males show persistently higher tendencies toward hostile attribution biases, as well as other social cognitive deficits related to aggression, fits with their pattern of higher involvement in violent delinquent acts in adolescence and their tendency to persist in violent behavior into the early adult years. (p. 255)

Further research suggests that some children are especially primed to develop hostile expectations of peers because of earlier exposure to family abuse and maltreatment (Dodge, Bates, & Pettit, 1990; Hubbard et al., 2001). These studies have revealed that children exposed to maltreatment early in their lives become "hypervigilant toward hostile social cues, perceptually ready to perceive hostility in others' intentions, and quick to generate aggressive retaliatory responses to even mild provocations" (Dodge, 2001, p. 65). In addition, peer-rejected children with hostile attribution bias are frequently targets of physical assault by others, prompting them to be more suspicious of the motives of others (Coie & Miller-Johnson, 2001). These children appear to be especially quick to develop hostile attribution biases against a wide range of peers, including new acquaintances. "These children come to have a generalized set of social cognitions that dispose them to draw hostile inferences from the behavior of new peer acquaintances more quickly than their peers do" (Hubbard et al., 2001, p. 277). Some other children, although prone to hostile attribution bias, tend to be specific in whom they identify as hostile, probably because of certain behavioral patterns or interests they find threatening.

Being rejected by peers encourages a child to behave less competently in social situations, creating a self-fulfilling-prophecy cycle (Coie, 2004). The rejected child develops negative expectations about the way peers will react and then behaves in a way that fulfills the child's own expectations and those of the rejecting peers. Positive peer relations, on the other hand, have been shown to contribute to the development of empathy, as well as reinforcing and modeling self-regulation and prosocial behavior (Eisenberg, 1998; Waaktaar et al., 2004). Positive peer relations are also believed to reduce significantly the tendency to display hostile attribution bias. We discuss these positive peer relationships in Chapter 4.

EMOTIONAL RISK FACTORS

Every parent or caregiver knows that emotional expression is apparent even in early infancy; babies express joy, surprise, sadness, disgust, anger, and fear during the first 6 months after birth (M. Lewis, 1993). Such emotions have been identified as major determinants of behavior, including delinquent and antisocial behavior, for several reasons: (1) Emotions are generally considered the major motivational system for behavior; (2) they have an impact on perceptions, cognitions, and actions; (3) they develop early; (4) they remain stable over time; and (5) they lead to the individual differences we call personality (Tremblay & LeMarquand, 2001). The single emotion that has been most frequently associated with problem behaviors in children and adolescents is anger. In recent years, considerable attention has also been given to the role of empathy, or the lack of it.

ANGER

Learning to control one's anger is one of the first important steps in the socialization process (Tremblay & LeMarquand, 2001). Practitioners and researchers refer to this control as **emotional control**. Anger is typically expressed when a goal is not achieved or when activity toward a goal is blocked. Clear expressions of anger following frustration have been observed as early as 8 weeks after birth (Tremblay, 2004). For example, an infant might cry fiercely when a rattle she is grasping is taken away. Although such expressions of anger are normal, children prone to become angry *easily* seem to be at risk for later delinquency. For both boys and girls, the inability to control anger as early as ages 3 and 5 is linked to antisocial and aggressive behavior at ages 9 and 11 (Offord, Lipman, & Duku, 2001).

Lack of anger control, impulsivity (Lynam, 1997), and excessive stimulation seeking (Caspi & Silva, 1995; Tremblay & LeMarquand, 2001) all appear to be strong predictors of delinquency and adult criminal behavior. (Impulsivity and stimulation seeking are discussed shortly.) Childhood lack of anger control is not only associated with antisocial behavior but is also linked to problems in relating socially to others and developing interpersonal skills (J. Snyder, Reid, & Patterson, 2003). Self-regulation, on the other hand, is closely associated with prosocial behavior and social competence.

LACK OF EMPATHY

Empathy is "an emotional response characterized by feelings of concern for another and a desire to alleviate that person's distress" (Young, Fox, & Zahn-Waxler, 1999,

p. 1189). **Empathy** refers to the ability to understand a person from his or her frame of reference or point of view rather than simply from one's own point of view. Also defined as understanding and sharing in another's emotional state or context (Eisenberg & Strayer, 1987), empathy has been deemed critical to all social processes, including morality, caring, and general positive growth and development (Lovett & Sheffield, 2007). Deficiencies in empathy have long been considered characteristic of aggressive and antisocial individuals (Cohen & Strayer, 1996; Hastings, Zahn-Waxler, Usher, Robinson, & Bridges, 2000). The relationship between a lack of empathy and aggressive or disruptive behavior becomes discernible in children during the early to middle elementary school years (Hastings et al., 2000; Tremblay, Vitaro, Gagnon, Piche, & Royer, 1992) and seems to get stronger with age (P. A. Miller & Eisenberg, 1988). Children who do not seem to display empathy in third grade seem to display even less in eighth grade.

The systematic study of empathy and prosocial behavior in young children is a relatively recent phenomenon (Young et al., 1999). Studies have discovered that the development of empathy appears to start early. Between 20 and 24 months of age, the average child undergoes a developmental transition in which behaviors that signify some forms of empathy and a desire to alleviate another's distress can be observed (Kiang, Moreno, & Robinson, 2004; Robinson, Zahn-Waxler, & Emde, 1994). Girls appear to show more concern for others than boys do, beginning at the second year of life and continuing on through adolescence (Eisenberg & Fabes, 1998; Hastings et al., 2000). Specifically, females have been found to be generally more emotionally expressive than males, exhibiting greater prosocial behaviors and concern and less indifference toward a victim in distress.

Infants and young children convey empathy through several channels of expression. That is, young children may express both empathic concern and inquisitiveness in response to a distressed individual, or they may be initially inquisitive—suggesting concern—but then convey indifference by reengaging in play or ignoring the distressed person. Parents with more positive and adaptive parenting attitudes express greater empathy toward their children, which, in turn, develops empathetic responding in their children.

CRUELTY TO ANIMALS

One childhood behavior that is demonstrative of a lack of empathy is cruelty to animals, which may be defined as "socially unacceptable behavior that intentionally causes unnecessary pain, suffering, or distress to and/or death of an animal" (Guymer, Mellor, Luk, & Pearse, 2001, p. 1057). Normally, this definition does not include the swatting of flies or the destruction of insects (although torture of insects may qualify), but cruelty to dogs, cats, or other household pets is usually considered significant. Cruelty here does not refer to chasing the family cat and playfully pulling its tail, but setting the cat's whiskers on fire is another matter. Several studies have found a strong link between animal cruelty and antisocial or violent behavior toward humans. Stouthamer-Loeber and her associates (2004) followed young male participants of the Pittsburgh Youth Study from the ages of 13 to 25 and found that cruelty to animals and people was one of the strongest predictors of serious, violent criminal behavior.

Merz-Perez, Heide, and Silverman (2001) investigated whether cruelty to animals in childhood might serve as an early warning sign of future violence against humans. One of the major drawbacks of the study is that the participants were inmates who were incarcerated in a maximum security facility and who self-reported their cruel behavior. (A more powerful approach would be a longitudinal study that follows participants from their early childhood to adulthood.) The study found that violent offenders were far more likely than nonviolent offenders to have committed childhood acts of cruelty against animals in general and against pet and stray animals in particular. Earlier investigations of incarcerated adults have shown similar results (Felthous & Kellert, 1986, 1987; Kellert & Felthous, 1985).

Hensley and Tallichet (2005), who also used inmates as participants, report support for the findings of Merz-Perez et al. but added evidence that those who abused animals had earlier witnessed someone else—particularly family members—hurt or kill animals. "Inmates who witnessed a family member hurt or kill animals were more likely to commit animal cruelty with greater frequency" (Hensley & Tallichet, 2005, p. 44). Those inmates who said they witnessed animal cruelty at an early age were even more abusive to animals as they got older than those who witnessed animal cruelty at a later age.

Arluke, Levin, Luke, and Ascione (1999) used the official records of the Massachusetts Society for the Prevention of Cruelty to Animals to identify those who intentionally and criminally harmed an animal, including pets, strays, or wild animals. They found that animal abusers were more likely than nonabusers to be interpersonally violent, but they were also more likely to commit property offenses, drug offenses, and public disorder offenses. In other words, the link between animal abuse and violence is not a simple one; it involves a wide assortment of antisocial behavior beyond just violence.

Interestingly, studies have further revealed that pet abuse often accompanies child abuse (Arkow, 1998). That is, caregivers and parents who abuse children also tend to abuse the family pet, which is usually a treasured companion of an abused child. Abusers often threaten to harm or kill a pet to frighten a child into secrecy about the abuse, particularly sexual abuse. A robust relationship also exists between pet cruelty and spousal abuse (Bartol & Bartol, 2004).

Based on parental reports, the prevalence of cruelty to animals in 12- to 16-year-olds is estimated to be about 2% (Guymer, Meller, Luk, & Pearse, 2001). For children aged 4 to 11 years, the prevalence appears to be less than 2% if we rely on parental reports. However, if we rely on self-reports from the children themselves, the prevalence is around 10% (Offord, Boyle, & Racine, 1991). In contrast, in children who demonstrate serious antisocial behavior, the animal cruelty rate is closer to 28%, based on combined parental and child reports (Luk, Staiger, Wong, & Mathai, 1999). In other words, more than one-fourth of children with serious antisocial behavior problems have demonstrated cruelty to animals.

Researchers investigating animal abuse seem to get bogged down with issues of motivation and definition, which has generally detracted from the critical need for studies in this area. Nonetheless, it is clear that a youth who consistently tortures and harms pets or other animals—setting a dog on fire, strangling or stabbing a neighbor's cat, breaking the neck of a kitten—is on the developmental pathway for serious violent and antisocial behavior. Figure 3–1 lists examples of individual risk factors.

> **FIGURE 3–1**   Examples of Individual Risk Factors
>
> - Aggressiveness
> - Inadequate language skills
> - Limited cognitive constructs
> - Signs of hostile attribution bias
> - Tendency to become angry easily
> - Lack of empathy
> - Cruelty to animals
> - Poor self-regulation skills
> - Early signs of antisocial behavior

BIOLOGICAL RISK FACTORS

Children are born with a range of genetic influences, neurological predispositions, and temperamental characteristics. During the past 20 years, significant progress has been made in uncovering biological risk factors that predispose individuals to antisocial behavior (Raine, 2002), but it is clear that early psychosocial and physical environments can significantly shape and modify these innate biological influences. For example, the general consensus is that a lack of physical contact, verbal stimulation, and responsiveness from parents and caregivers can drastically alter the rate of intellectual, emotional, and social growth in children (Dahlberg & Potter, 2001). Dalhberg and Potter (2001) further note: "Even though parents can never completely determine the course of development for their children, many critical dimensions of self—attitudes, beliefs, prejudices, behaviors—are acquired within the family" (p. 7). Ever mindful of these psychosocial influences, this section briefly covers those psychobiological proclivities that may, if not handled effectively by the psychosocial environment, *predispose* children to engage in a variety of violent and antisocial behaviors across their lifetimes.

PHYSICAL DEVELOPMENT

We begin our discussion of biological risk factors with physical development but caution that much of the research in this area is both dated and questionable. The belief that personality and criminal tendencies are somehow closely related to bodily size and appearance has been expressed in a variety of forums for at least 2,000 years (Montemayor, 1978). Tremblay and LeMarquand (2001) note: "Because the external appearance of our bodies is the product of their development from conception, it makes sense that some physical characteristics could be markers of complex physiological processes that affect social behavior" (p. 153).

In criminology this view is associated primarily with the early work of W. H. Sheldon, a physician who theorized that body structure and delinquency are closely linked. Sheldon developed a classification system based on the shape of the body and related these body "types" directly to a genetic propensity to engage in delinquency. After extensively and painstakingly collecting physical measurements and documenting them with photographs, Sheldon delineated three basic body builds in both males and females (see Figure 3–2): **ectomorphic** (thin and fragile), **mesomorphic** (muscular and hard), and

FIGURE 3–2   Sheldon's Somatotypes in Relation to Physique and Temperament

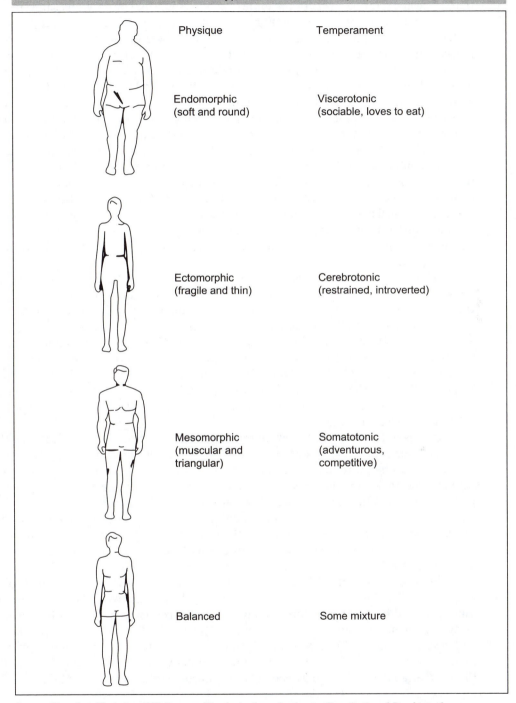

Physique	Temperament
Endomorphic (soft and round)	Viscerotonic (sociable, loves to eat)
Ectomorphic (fragile and thin)	Cerebrotonic (restrained, introverted)
Mesomorphic (muscular and triangular)	Somatotonic (adventurous, competitive)
Balanced	Some mixture

Source: Based on *Varieties of Delinquent Youth: An Introduction to Constitutional Psychiatry* by W. H. Sheldon, E. M. Hertl, and E. McDermott, 1949, New York: Harper.

endomorphic (fat and soft). A reader with some background in embryology will recognize that the terms refer to layers of the embryo. The ectodermal layer evolves into the nervous system; the *ectomorphic*, then, has a well-developed brain and central nervous system within a tall and thin body. The mesodermal layer of the embryo develops into muscle; therefore, the muscular body that is tough and well equipped for strenuous activity is labeled the *mesomorph*. The endodermal embryonic layer develops primarily into the digestive tract; thus, individuals who are flabby and fat (*endomorphs*) are associated with the digestive system. Sheldon did not make sharp, abrupt distinctions between the body types; rarely does a person's body structure fall exclusively into one of the three "pure" types. Rather, most people have features of all three to varying degrees. However, most people fall roughly into one of the three primary categories.

Sheldon believed there is a significant connection between body type and temperament and personality. He argued that the ectomorph is inhibited, reserved, self-conscious, and afraid of people. A mesomorph, on the other hand, seeks muscular and vigorous physical activity, risks, and adventure. A person with this temperament is likely to be aggressive, ruthless, and callous in relationships with others. The endomorph is one who loves comfort, food, affection, and people and is usually even-tempered and easy to get along with.

Sheldon did extensive research to test his theory as it relates to delinquency. In his book *Varieties of Delinquent Youth* (Sheldon, Hartl, & McDermott, 1949), he discussed the research on the body structures of 200 delinquent boys, as compared to those of male college students. As predicted, Sheldon found a preponderance of mesomorphs and very few ectomorphs in his delinquent sample. Other studies conducted during that time also indicated that delinquent boys tended to be more mesomorphic than the general population (Cortes & Gatti, 1972; Glueck & Glueck, 1950, 1956). Similarly, Epps and Parnell (1952) compared the physiques of 177 female delinquents with those of 123 Oxford undergraduates and found the delinquents to be more mesomorphic than the undergraduates.

Reviews of the research literature (e.g., Eysenck & Gudjonsson, 1989; Raine, 1993; Wilson & Herrnstein, 1985) continue to suggest that adult criminals and juvenile delinquents tend to be more mesomorphic and, to a lesser extent, more endomorphic than ectomorphic. Following their review of the extant research, Tremblay and LeMarquand (2001) conclude: "In summary, height, weight, and body bulk appear to be associated with early-onset aggression in both boys and girls" (p. 154). Longitudinal studies have revealed similar trends: Children rated by their parents as physically and verbally aggressive at age 11 years were taller, weighed more, and were more muscular at age 3 than their nonaggressive peers (Raine, Reynolds, Mednick, Venables, & Farrington, 1999; Raine, Reynolds, Venables, Mednick, & Farrington, 1998). These scholars reasoned that larger and taller children probably learn quickly and early in development that they can intimidate and bully other children because of their size. They conclude, therefore, that body size might be a small but meaningful risk factor for later antisocial behavior and violence. Tremblay and LeMarquand (2001) also speculate that early aggression based on size and muscle density may develop into an effective strategy for winning social conflicts and attaining desired goals. Raine (1993) advances a similar observation:

> For example, body build may be linked to delinquency because having a larger, more muscular body build allows bullying to be an effective strategy in winning

social conflicts in the playground setting. Early reinforcement of this behavior may encourage the use of force and violence later in life. (p. 203)

TEMPERAMENT

A child's temperament—defined very loosely for the moment as a "natural" mood and behavioral disposition—may offer important clues about delinquency. How we approach and interact with our social environment influences how that environment will interact with us. This is true even of very young children. Parents, caretakers, teachers, and physicians know very well that infants and young children differ in activity, emotionality, and general sensitivity to stimuli. A smiling, relaxed, interactive child is apt to initiate and maintain a different social response than a fussy, tense, and withdrawn child does.

One of the most influential perspectives on temperament has been advanced by Thomas and Chess (1977). They argue that temperament is an innate readiness to respond across a variety of situations; it is continually evolving and is strongly influenced by family and extrafamilial environments. Thomas and Chess systematically studied temperament by asking parents to report on nine characteristics of their infants: (1) rhythmicity of biological functions, such as regularity of bowel movements, sleep cycles, and feeding times; (2) activity level; (3) approach toward or withdrawal from new stimuli; (4) adaptability; (5) sensory thresholds; (6) predominant quality of mood; (7) intensity of mood expression; (8) distractibility; and (9) attention span or persistence. The researchers then classified infant temperament into three temperamental styles: (1) the easy child, (2) the difficult child, and (3) the slow-to-warm-up child.

Table 3–1 summarizes the characteristics of each style. The easy child is characterized by high rhythmicity, positive moods, high approachability, high adaptability, and low intensity of mood expression. The difficult child shows the opposite patterns: irregular biological functioning, initial aversion and slow adaptability to environmental changes, high intensity of emotional expression, and more generally a negative mood. The slow-to-warm-up child displays high activity, withdrawal from new stimuli and people, low adaptability, negative mood, and low intensity. Difficult children, according to Thomas and Chess, represent a specific cluster of inborn temperamental attributes that make child rearing more challenging for many parents. Such children may be at higher risk for developing a consistent pattern of antisocial behavior and other behavioral problems.

As it is currently used in the research and scholarly literature, **temperament** is assumed to (a) have a constitutional or biological basis, (b) appear in infancy and

TABLE 3–1: Examples of Child Temperaments

	Easy Child	*Difficult Child*	*Slow-to-Warm-Up Child*
Rhythmicity	Regular	Irregular	Regular
Approachability	High	Low	Low
Adaptability	Rapid	Slow	Slow
Mood	Positive	Negative	Negative
Intensity of expression	Low	High	Low

Source: Based on *Temperament and Development* by A. Thomas and S. Chess, 1977, New York: Brunner/Mazel.

continue throughout life, and (c) be influenced by the environment (Bates, 1980; Else-Quest, Hyde, Goldsmith, & Van Hulle, 2006). Most experts today believe that temperament has biological underpinnings that are best discerned at birth (Bates et al., 1998; Dodge & Pettit, 2003; Else-Quest et al., 2006; Lahey & Waldman, 2003). Most of the contemporary research on temperament, therefore, focuses on infants, because the connection between temperament and behavior seems uncomplicated at this stage but becomes more complex as children mature and interact with their psychosocial environments.

Among researchers, there is no universally accepted definition of *temperament*; it is generally operationally defined by identifying the behaviors commonly associated with it. However, there is little disagreement that activity and emotionality are two of those behaviors. Activity, the most widely studied, refers to gross motor movement across a variety of settings and times—for example, the movement of arms and legs, squirming, crawling, or walking. Children who exhibit an *inordinate* amount of movement compared to that of their peers may be labeled hyperactive or as having an attention-deficit/hyperactivity disorder. Emotionality refers to such features as irritability, sensitivity, soothability, and general intensity of emotional reactions. Researchers disagree as to what other behaviors should be included in descriptions of temperament, and some argue that temperament should not be defined according to demonstrated behaviors in the first place.

Despite the difficulty in defining *temperament*, an understanding of it is important because it encourages us to consider the possibility that heritable, or biological, individual differences may be critical in the early formation of delinquency and crime. Failure to acknowledge these dispositional or temperamental variables might leave us with an incomplete picture of the etiology of antisocial behavior. Even if the label comes strictly from subjective parental perceptions, "difficult children" may be at higher risk to engage in antisocial behavior than "easy children" are. Recent research does suggest that a difficult temperament in early childhood predisposes a child to become aggressive and delinquent in later childhood (Dodge & Pettit, 2003; Pepler & Slaby, 1994). The temperamental attribute most closely associated with antisocial behavior is a lack of self-regulation or impulsivity. Highly impulsive, unmanageable, and poorly self-regulated children move into (and often against) their environments at a more rapid pace and more aggressively than less impulsive children do. Henry, Caspi, Moffitt, and Silva (1996), using data from the Dunedin (New Zealand) Multidisciplinary Health and Development Study, found that children considered temperamentally explosive and lacking in self-control were more likely to become violent adolescents, as compared to their more temperamentally stable peers.

Thus, investigators have continually discovered strong links between children's difficult temperament and the concurrent and subsequent occurrence of persistent antisocial behavior (e.g., Bates, Pettit, Dodge, & Ridge, 1998; Rubin et al., 2003; Rubin, Hastings, Chen, Stewart, & McNichol, 1998; Shaw, Owens, Giovannelli, & Winslow, 2001). However, *links* is the key word, not "causes." As Robert Hogan and Warren Jones (1983) write,

> It is easy to imagine that a child who is very emotional, active, unsociable, and impulsive might be constantly in trouble with his or her adult caretakers and perhaps predisposed

to delinquency. . . . [The temperament model] is interactional in the best sense of the word; it does not maintain that certain temperaments cause delinquency, but rather that the concurrence of these temperaments and certain kinds of family environments may lead to delinquent outcomes. (pp. 6–7)

Bates et al. (1998) also note that "in theory, temperament does not lead to behavior problems by itself; it does so only in conjunction with particular environments" (p. 982).

The overwhelming consensus among experts is that parental responsiveness, nurturance, and warmth are critical core dimensions of the early parent–child relationship (Kochanska et al., 2004). Research has clearly indicated that parental responsiveness enhances child security and other adaptive developmental outcomes (Belsky, 1999). But research has further suggested with some regularity that poor parent–child relationships and considerable tension and conflict in the home are common, although not inevitable, ingredients in antisocial behavior. In essence, both parent and child are active agents who cocreate their emerging relationship by continuous transactions (Kochanska, Friesenborg, Lange, & Martel, 2004). Temperament alone may increase or decrease the *probability* of antisocial behavior, but it does not determine whether an individual will or will not engage in antisocial behavior.

A study by Rubin et al. (2003) examined the longitudinal relations of temperament, initiations of conflict and aggressive behavior at age 2, and maternal negative control with aggressive and antisocial problems at age 4. The researchers hypothesized that a difficult temperament interacting with certain parenting styles promotes the development of aggressive behavior in preschool children. They discovered that male toddlers (2-year-olds) and 4-year-olds exhibited significantly higher frequencies of aggressive behaviors—such as taking objects away from an unfamiliar peer or pushing, shoving, or hitting the other play partner—than did same-age female children. Moreover, and consistent with other studies, children who were aggressive as toddlers also tended to be aggressive as preschoolers. Changes in this pattern were associated with parental styles. In other words, a warm and firm parenting style could dampen the child's aggressive tendencies. On the other hand, parenting styles characterized by hostility, rejection, and intrusion were more likely to place young children who were already prone to behave aggressively on a developmental trajectory toward antisocial behavioral patterns. More precisely, impulsive, poorly self-regulated children whose parents provide little support and warmth but do provide hostility and negative control are likely to become aggressive. Parents who respond to their impulsive toddlers with warmth, sensitivity, and guidance are more likely to help their children avoid the developmental trajectory to aggressive behavior. Overall, this longitudinal investigation illustrates the collective importance of individual and social risk factors and the interaction of temperament and parenting.

In summary, although temperament is present at birth, its manifestations can be modified by the social environment, especially by competent parents and significant caregivers. Difficult temperaments can be challenging, but a nurturing and warm environment in which rules are firmly laid out can prevent, change, or eliminate antisocial behavior in children (Moffitt, 2005).

Furthermore, the temperament of parents must be considered as a possible component in the development of the delinquent child. Moffitt (1993) suggests that parents and their offspring often resemble each other in temperament and personality. An irritable, temperamental child may have a high probability of being born to highly irritable, temperamental parents. Thus, parents of difficult children may lack the necessary psychological and physical resources to cope effectively with a difficult child.

ATTENTION-DEFICIT/HYPERACTIVITY DISORDER

The terms *hyperactivity* and *attention-deficit/hyperactivity disorder* **(ADHD)** have been used interchangeably to refer to children who demonstrate a heterogeneity of problem behaviors. The three central behaviors have traditionally been (1) inattention (not listening, being easily distracted); (2) impulsivity (acting before thinking, shifting quickly from one activity to another); and (3) excessive motor activity (being unable to sit still, fidgeting, running about, being talkative and noisy). ADHD is most commonly diagnosed when children start to attend school, because they are faced with more complex and structured tasks that require focused attention. Educators note that ADHD children have difficulty staying on task, remaining cognitively organized, sustaining academic achievement in the school setting, and maintaining control over their behavior.

ADHD is the most commonly diagnosed childhood disorder of all externalizing problem behaviors, affecting an estimated 3% to 5% of school-age children (K. R. Stern, 2001). It occurs more often in boys than in girls, usually in a ratio of five to one. Furthermore, ADHD is diagnosed more frequently in children who have a close biological relative with ADHD, suggesting a significant biological component in the cause (K. R. Stern, 2001). Boys with ADHD are at increased risk for engaging in delinquent and antisocial behavior. "As they grow older, children with untreated ADHD—often in combination with oppositional-defiant and conduct disorders—may abuse drugs or alcohol, engage in antisocial behavior, and suffer physical injury at higher rates than the general population" (K. R. Stern, 2001, p. 1).

ADHD is a puzzling problem that some scientists argue is closely related to temperament. They contend that some ADHD children are born with the tendency, making this a temperamental as well as a neurological factor. Other children are exposed to environmental events that damage the nervous system. Loeber (1990) illustrates that exposure to toxic substances during the preschool years often retards or negatively influences children's neurological development, potentially engendering symptoms of ADHD. For example, Loeber noted, children exposed to low levels of lead toxicity (from certain paints) were more distractible, hyperactive, impulsive, and easily frustrated and had difficulty following simple instructions. Despite the general consensus that ADHD has a neurological component, very little research has focused on understanding the family context within which it develops (Jester et al., 2005).

Some researchers argue that the cognitive constructs of ADHD children have been hampered in their development. ADHD youth, it seems, do not possess effective strategies and cognitive organization to deal with the daily demands of both school and work. They often have particular difficulty in abstract thinking. ADHD children also do not seem to possess cognitively organized ways of dealing with new knowledge; thus, they seem destined to fail in the academic environment. Other investigators (e.g., Barkley, 1999; Pennington & Ozonoff, 1996) have discovered that ADHD is associated with impaired **executive functions** and with cognitive difficulty in controlling behavior. Executive functions refer to the higher levels of cognitive processes that organize and plan behavior, including reasoning, logic, and abstract thinking.

Children and adolescents with ADHD have particular problems in the area of language and communication that are persistent and are associated with social and academic difficulties (Clark, Prior, & Kinsella, 2002). These language and communication difficulties appear to be closely linked to executive functioning deficits (Clark, Prior, & Kinsella, 2000, 2002).

Although many behaviors have been identified as accompanying ADHD, the overriding theme is that ADHD children are perceived as annoying and aversive by those around them. While children with ADHD are socially busy, continually seeking and prolonging interpersonal contacts, they manage to irritate and frustrate the people with whom they interact (Henker & Whalen, 1989). More often than not, ADHD children, especially if they are aggressive, are rejected by peers (Henker & Whalen, 1989). Over half of children with ADHD are rejected by their peers, compared to 15% of comparison children (Hoza, Mrug, Gerdes, Bukowski, Kraemer, Wigal, et al., 2005; Mikami & Hinshaw, 2006). This peer rejection appears to be consistent and ongoing throughout the developmental years (Reid, 1993). The combination of peer rejection *and* ADHD in childhood often leads to a wide range of negative adolescent outcomes for both boys and girls, including antisocial behavior, substance abuse, poor academic achievement, and (in girls) eating disorders (Mikami & Hinshaw, 2006).

In recent years it has become apparent that ADHD is not so much a disorder of activity as it is a disorder of interpersonal relationships. Even those individuals who are not aggressive and who manage to control some of their hyperactivity still have problems in their social interactions. "Children with ADHD have difficulty taking turns, often interrupt and intrude on others in games, in conversations and classroom discussions, talk excessively, and often appear not to be listening when spoken to" (Clark et al., 2002, p. 785). As noted by Henker and Whalen (1989), they seem to lack friendship and intimacy. This observation is especially true for boys (S. B. Campbell, 1994; Erhardt & Hinshaw, 1994; Melnick & Hinshaw, 1996). Interestingly, it takes non-ADHD children about 30 minutes and a few social exchanges to identify an ADHD child (De Boo & Prins, 2007). Figure 3–3 lists common ADHD characteristics.

FIGURE 3–3   Representative ADHD Characteristics

- Fails to attend to details or makes careless mistakes
- Has difficulty sustaining attention
- Avoids and dislikes tasks requiring sustained mental effort
- Is easily distracted by extraneous stimuli
- Does not seem to listen when spoken to
- Does not follow instructions
- Is forgetful
- Has difficulty with abstract thinking
- Is seen as annoying and aversive
- Is often rejected by peers
- Interrupts or intrudes on others
- Has difficulty taking turns
- Fidgets with hands or feet
- Talks incessantly
- Has executive function deficits

The most common problem associated with ADHD is not an emotional or psychological disorder, such as serious depression or schizophrenia, but delinquency and substance abuse. It is estimated that about one-fourth to one-half of all children with ADHD engage in serious antisocial behavior during childhood and adolescence and in criminal behavior as adults (Pfiffner, McBurnett, Rathouz, & Judice, 2005). Terrie Moffitt (Moffitt & Silva, 1988; Moffitt, 1993) states that a large proportion of ADHD children report delinquent behaviors in early adolescence. She has also found that children aged 5 to 7 who demonstrate the characteristics of both ADHD and antisocial behavior not only have special difficulty with social relationships but also have a high probability of consistent serious delinquency in adolescence and beyond (Moffitt, 1990). The data suggest that youth with a combined ADHD-antisocial symptomology are at very high risk for developing the most lengthy and serious criminal careers (Moffitt, 1990; Satterfield, Swanson, Schell, & Lee, 1994). Pfiffner et al. (2005) note that "children having both ADHD and CD have more learning problems, neuropsychological deficits, and poorer prognosis with high rates of antisocial outcomes" (p. 551). The combination of ADHD and CD leads to more persistent and serious antisocial behavior throughout the child's life course. David Farrington (1991) found that violent offenders often have a history of hyperactivity, impulsivity, and attention problems.

For some unknown reason, Canadian ADHD youth seem to be less prone toward delinquency than their American counterparts (Henker & Whalen, 1989). This suggests that the social and parental reactions to ADHD, rather than the disorder itself, may be the key to understanding the relationship. Recall that very little research has focused on understanding the family context within which ADHD develops (Jester et al., 2005).

The common psychopharmacological method of treatment for ADHD is stimulant medication (e.g., methylphenidate, or Ritalin). However, this approach is marked by limited success and a myriad of side effects, some of them severe. Because social incompetence is a serious debilitating condition for the ADHD child, social skills training (SST) has become a widely accepted and effective treatment program for many ADHD youths who are highly aggressive and antisocial (De Boo & Prins, 2007). However, it has also been found that SST does not generalize to homes with negative parenting (e.g., maternal criticism or physical force; Webster-Stratton, Reid, & Hammond, 2001). Other forms of treatment have been tried, including counseling and psychotherapy, but they too have had limited success with this puzzling phenomenon, especially over the long term. As noted previously, ADHD children demonstrate multiple social problems that require a treatment strategy encompassing all the systems within the children's social world. A multicomponent, multisystemic approach offers the best hope for helping ADHD youngsters in their social development and education. Promising interventions of this nature are discussed in more detail in Chapter 12.

GENETICS

Robert Plomin (2004) has observed that "one of the most dramatic shifts in developmental psychology during the past 50 years has been toward acceptance of a more balanced view that recognizes the importance of genetics as well as environment" (p. 342). Genetic factors seem to play a more prominent role in the development of *persistent* aggressive and violent behavior than in other forms of nonaggressive delinquent behaviors (Eley, Lichtenstein, & Moffitt, 2003; Rhee & Waldman, 2002; van Goozen, Fairchild, Snoek, & Harold, 2007).

The study of twins is commonly used to determine the relative contributions of genetic and environmental influences on development. **Dizygotic twins** (DZ), also called fraternal twins, develop from two different fertilized eggs and share an average of 50% of their genes by descent (Ehringer, Rhee, Young, Corley, & Hewitt, 2006). **Monozygotic twins** (MZ), or identical twins, develop from a single egg; they are always the same sex and share all the same genes. Presumably, then, if genes are determinative, identical twins should display highly similar behavior. Because MZ twins share 100% of their genes, it can be inferred that a child's genetic risk for antisocial behavior is high if his or her MZ twin shows antisocial behavior and low if the MZ twin does not exhibit antisocial behavior.

According to Raine (2002), "There is now clear evidence from twin studies, adoption studies, twins reared apart, and molecular genetic studies to support the notion that there are genetic influences on antisocial and aggressive behavior" (p. 312). He notes that the more challenging issues now are to determine if and how genetic processes interact with environmental factors in predisposing individuals to antisocial and violent behavior. So far, twin studies provide more support for the heritability of antisocial behavior than adoption studies do, which look for similarities and differences between the behavior of children and that of their biological parents. For example, Jaffee and her colleagues (2005) used MZ and DZ twin pairs to study the interplay between genetic and environmental risks in the development of antisocial behavior in a representative sample of over 1,000 5-year-old British twin pairs and their families.

The Jaffee researchers ascertained the children's antisocial behavior through parent and teacher interviews. The environmental risk factor in the study was the amount of maltreatment the child reportedly received from parents. Maltreatment was used as the environmental risk factor because research shows that early maltreatment often leads to antisocial behavior, as suggested in Chapter 2 (Langsford, Dodge, Pettit, Bates, Crozier, & Kaplow, 2002). Not surprisingly, Jaffee et al. (2005) discovered that the effect of maltreatment on the risk for antisocial behavior was strongest among those at higher genetic risk.

In their study of 1,162 male and female adolescent twin pairs (570 MZ pairs, 592 DZ pairs) and 426 siblings of these twins, Ehringer et al. (2006) discovered that genetic influences play a significant role in the development of serious antisocial (externalizing) behaviors. These findings and the findings of many other studies support the general consensus that environmental changes turn genetic influences on and off across the life span and that biological factors and environmental influences do interact (Raine, 2002).

PSYCHOPHYSIOLOGY

Psychophysiology refers to the study of the dynamic interactions between behavior and the autonomic nervous system. Emotions, such as fear or anger, influence the autonomic nervous system by arousing or activating it. Heart rates (cardiovascular activity) and electrical conductance in the skin (electrodermal activity, or skin conductance) are the usual measures of psychophysiological investigations examining the relationship between antisocial behavior and autonomic activity. The autonomic **arousal theory of**

crime (Raine, 1993, 1996) stipulates that persistent, chronic offenders—compared to those with no or little offending history—exhibit low levels of autonomic arousal (lower heart rates and lower electrodermal activity) across a wide variety of situations and conditions. Presumably, low levels of arousal predispose a person to crime because such a condition produces some degree of fearlessness and also encourages the seeking of antisocial stimulation, or excitement (Raine, 2002). That is, persistent offenders experience little anxiety and fear and are not troubled about getting caught and punished. Furthermore, they find certain aspects of crime exciting and challenging. On the other hand, high levels of autonomic arousal, which produce anxiety and fear of disapproval, encourage childhood socialization. As we discovered earlier in this chapter, fearlessness and an uninhibited temperament in infancy and childhood is closely associated with antisocial behavior.

Some studies reveal that antisocial boys do appear to have lower levels of physiological arousal than their nonantisocial counterparts (Brennan, Mednick, & Raine, 1997; Raine, 2002; Raine, Venables, & Williams, 1995, 1996). In fact, there is some evidence to suggest that lower heart rates may be the strongest psychophysiological predictor of antisocial behavior in children (Ortiz & Raine, 2004; van Goozen et al., 2007).

HEALTH

The genetic and psychophysiological factors just discussed are controversial, and criminologists often devaluate or de-emphasize their importance. However, criminologists are far more likely to accept that health factors can contribute to antisocial behaviors.

Prenatal and Perinatal Factors

It is commonly assumed that **prenatal factors** (i.e., those before birth) can directly and indirectly alter brain structure and function, and brain dysfunction has been linked to later violence and delinquency (Liu & Wuerker, 2005). **Perinatal factors** (i.e., those 5 months before birth and 1 month after birth) are also likely to influence brain development. During pregnancy the fetus is exposed to various influences that may adversely affect development and lead to potential risks for serious antisocial behaviors later in life. Studies have examined the influence on child development of maternal exposure to alcohol, tobacco, and drugs, pregnancy/birth complications, and malnutrition. According to Raine (2002, p. 317), "The effects of fetal exposure to alcohol in increasing risk for conduct disorders is well known, but recently a spate of studies has established beyond reasonable doubt a significant link between smoking during pregnancy and later conduct disorder and violent offending." One study (Brennan, Grekin, & Mednick, 1999), using a birth cohort of 4,169 males, found a strong connection between violent offending in adults and smoking by their mothers during their pregnancy. On average, the mothers smoked 20 cigarettes a day. This relationship was especially strong (increasing by fivefold) when the offspring were exposed to *both* nicotine and birth complications. In another study using a large sample from the general population of Finland, Räsänen et al. (1999) found that, compared to the sons of mothers who did not smoke, the sons of mothers who smoked during pregnancy had more than a twofold greater risk of having committed a violent crime or having repeatedly committed crimes. This finding held even when other biopsychological risk factors were controlled for. The available evidence suggests that smoking during pregnancy may contribute to fetal brain deficits and altered brain development, which have been found to be related to antisocial behavior (Raine, 2002).

Fetal alcohol exposure has long been known to alter brain development (Liu & Wuerker, 2005), and heavy alcohol ingestion during pregnancy is associated with antisocial behavior in young children (Delaney-Black et al., 2000; Roebuck, Mattson, & Riley, 1999). However, the effects of other drugs of abuse (e.g., maternal cocaine use) on fetal and child development is not that clear cut, and conclusions will have to wait for further study and evaluation. Preliminary investigations suggest that children exposed to cocaine in utero do not show significant damage from their prenatal exposure, and there is little evidence to confirm the crack baby syndrome (Bono, Sheinberg, Scott, & Claussen, 2007; Frank, Augustyn, Grant Knight, Pell, & Zuckerman, 2001; Messinger & Lester, 2007). On the other hand, a few studies (e.g., Bandstra et al., 2002, 2004) have reported that cocaine exposure in utero does affect language development and sustained attention processing during early childhood. Bono et al. (2007) argue, however, that these children are at high developmental risk, particularly in language development, not because of cocaine exposure in utero but because of the social environmental factors that are associated with parental substance abuse. They point out that mothers who use cocaine during pregnancy are less likely to receive adequate nutrition and prenatal care, are more likely to use alcohol and tobacco during pregnancy, and often provide a deprived postnatal environment, characterized by poor parent–child interactions and inadequate caregiving. Bono et al. (2007) further assert that recent studies have found that the quality of the home environment is a much better predictor of cognitive and language development than is prenatal cocaine exposure. In summary, research results suggest that many of the negative outcomes of observed problems in children of cocaine users may result from the quality of caregiving during infancy rather than from the direct effects of the cocaine.

A growing body of data indicates that prenatal, perinatal, and neonatal (newborn) complications are related to a wide range of child maladjustment and behavioral problems later in life (Laucht et al., 2000). In addition, these problems—particularly aggressive and antisocial behavior—appear to be exacerbated in children growing up in disadvantaged family environments (Laucht et al., 2000), in families that use rigid and coercive parenting techniques (Granic & Patterson, 2006), in families with a depressed mother (Bennett, Bendersky, & Lewis, 2002; Mazulis et al., 2004), or in families with abusive parents (Stouthamer-Loeber et al., 2001).

Birth and Neonatal Complications

Based on his review of the research literature, Raine (2002) concludes that "babies who suffer birth complications are more likely to develop conduct disorder, delinquency, and commit impulsive crime and violence in adulthood when other psychosocial risk factors are present" (p. 317). The psychosocial risks most commonly related are maternal separation, maternal rejection, marital discord, parental mental health problems, and paternal absence. For example, Raine, Brennan, and Mednick (1997) followed the criminal offending history of over 4,000 Danish babies to age 34. It was found that birth complications, when combined with early maternal rejection, predicted careers of violent crime. The relationship did not hold for nonviolent criminal careers.

The relationship between birth or pregnancy complications and a disadvantaged familial environment found in the Denmark study has also been replicated in four other countries—Sweden, Finland, Canada, and the United States (Raine, 2002). It should be emphasized that birth or pregnancy complications by themselves are not enough to trigger violent crime and serious antisocial behavior. The relationship seems to require the presence of negative environmental circumstances and heightened psychosocial risks in general. For example, one study (Arseneault, Tremblay, Boulerice, & Saucier, 2002) found that obstetrical complications (preeclampsia, chronic fetal hypoxia, placenta problems, umbilical cord prolapse, and induced labor) increased the risk of being violent at both 6 and 17 years of age among boys who grew up in highly adverse familial environments (early maternal rejection or a disadvantaged familial environment).

In sum, birth and pregnancy complications in combination with a faulty psychosocial environment are most likely to have a negative impact on children's abilities to learn to control their behavior. Neurological deficits (such as brain damage) due to birth and pregnancy problems, if not modified and buffered by a stable home environment, are apt to lead to antisocial behaviors characterized by poor impulse or self-control. It is these antisocial behaviors that may develop into delinquency.

Minor Physical Anomalies

During the past three decades, there has been a renewed interest in the relationship among certain physical attributes, temperament, and antisocial behavior. Specifically, some researchers have focused on **minor physical anomalies** (MPAs). MPAs have been associated with disorders of pregnancy and are thought to be a marker for problems in fetal neural development during the first 3 months of pregnancy (Raine, 2002). While the specific origin of MPAs is not fully understood, some experts believe that they may be indirect signs of abnormal brain development and later behavioral problems.

MPAs are subtle abnormalities that are generally not noticed by people who have them or by others. They are discernible only to trained observers and usually do not significantly interfere with attractiveness. Observable physical indicators of MPAs in children include asymmetrical ears, soft and pliable ears, curved fifth finger, ocular hypertelorism (widely spaced eyes), multiple hair whorls, webbed toes, and a furrowed tongue. MPAs seem to be related to some temperamental, neurological, and behavioral attributes in children. But it should be emphasized that it is the *total number* of MPAs rather than any specific physical anomaly that seems to be most closely connected to antisocial behavior or violence.

At least six studies have discovered an association between increased MPAs and increased antisocial behavior in children (Raine, 1993, 2002). For example, Pine, Shaffer, Schonfeld, and Davies (1997) found high numbers of MPAs in boys demonstrating conduct disorders. In a study conducted by Mednick and Kandel (1988), an experienced pediatrician assessed MPAs in 129 12-year-old boys; the researchers then followed the boys' development until they were 21 years old. They discovered that MPAs were related to violent offending, but only if the boys were from unstable, non-intact homes. Boys from stable homes with high MPAs did not show the relationship, demonstrating once again the importance of the home environment. Interestingly, though, Mednick and Kandel did not find an MPA relationship for nonviolent or property crimes, only for violent crimes. In another study, Brennan, Mednick, and Kandel (1993) found that subjects who had delivery complications at birth and a high number of MPAs were more likely to be adult violent offenders than individuals who had only one of these conditions or neither of them. These findings underscore the importance of considering the interactions of the psychosocial environment and biological factors in any explanations of antisocial behavior involving biological factors.

However, not all studies have reported the interactions between the psychosocial environment and MPAs as the best predictors of violent and/or antisocial behavior. Arseneault, Tremblay, Boulerice, Séguin, and Saucier (2000) discovered that higher counts of MPAs in boys evaluated at age 14 predicted violent delinquency at age 17. The MPAs most closely associated with violence were anomalies of the mouth, such as a high steepled palate, rough spots, or a furrowed tongue. But unlike previous studies (e.g., Mednick & Kandel, 1988; Brennan et al., 1993), the *interaction* between MPAs and family adversity as a predictor of violence was not found. In other words, the number of MPAs, especially those pertaining to the mouth, was significantly connected to violent delinquency, independent of the psychosocial environmental conditions.

Anomalies of the mouth, the authors point out, have been found in individuals with neurological deficits and may be associated with neurological problems that increase the risk for violent delinquency. The critical period for the development of both anomalies of the mouth and certain neurological structures starts at the 9th week of gestation. "It is then plausible," Arseneault et al. (2000) write, "that insults occurring at specific periods during gestation increase the risks for the development of violent delinquency as a result of atypical brain development" (p. 921).

Malnutrition and Cognitive Deficits

Neuropsychological deficits, especially those associated with executive functions, are reasonably well-established risk factors for antisocial behavior in children, adolescents, and adults (Raine, 2002). Moffitt (1993) has argued that neuropsychological deficits in combination with certain family risk factors are often found in persistent, serious, violent offenders. Liu, Raine, Venables, and Mednick (2004) report from their investigations that malnutrition at age 3 predisposes a child to neurocognitive deficits, which in turn predispose a child to persistent antisocial behaviors throughout childhood and adolescence. The authors believe that early malnutrition negatively affects brain growth and development and that the brain impairments may promote antisocial and violent behavior by affecting cognitive executive functions. Morgan and Lilienfeld (2000), after their extensive review of the research literature, concluded that there is a robust and statistically significant relationship between antisocial behavior and executive function deficits.

BRAIN DEVELOPMENT

Neurological and brain dysfunction due to faulty brain development is clearly linked to serious and violent antisocial behavior (Ishikawa & Raine, 2004). The link is especially strong if the brain dysfunction is located in the frontal lobes or cortices (the front of the brain). After their careful review of the research literature, Ishikawa and Raine (2004) concluded that "in all likelihood . . . both prefrontal cortices play a role in the onset and persistence of antisocial behavior" (p. 290).

The quality of the prenatal environment is clearly important in brain development. The brain is highly vulnerable to intrinsic hazards (cell development gone wrong) and to external insults resulting from malnutrition, viral infection, drug or alcohol exposure, or other teratogens. Nutritional adequacy is a crucial prenatal and postnatal influence on brain development because of the growing brain's reliance on folic acid, iron, vitamins, and other nutrients. Thus, malnutrition is a biological hazard to which the developing brain is especially vulnerable. Other hazards include fetal exposure to maternal viruses like HIV and rubella, illicit drugs such as cocaine and heroin, alcohol ingestion, environmental toxins (e.g., DDI, lead, mercury, and PCB), and other teratogens. Moreover, the vulnerability of the developing brain to many of these hazards continues throughout the early years after birth.

After birth, early experiences are crucial in shaping the cultivation and pruning of neural synapses that underlie the functional capabilities of the developing brain (Thompson & Nelson, 2001). Recent studies of humans and other species have made it clear that the developing brain is profoundly responsive to experience (Nelson & Bloom, 1997). Both structure and function are affected by experience, a phenomenon known as plasticity.

Among the most important of these early experiences is warm, sensitive care. Although there are few relevant neuroscientific data, parents and caregivers are encouraged to talk and sing to, play with, and sensitively nurture young children because of the ways these contingent sensory experiences provide stimulation for the brain (Thompson & Nelson, 2001). When caregivers are unable to provide these multisensory stimulations, brain development is likely to be delayed, either temporarily or permanently depending on the timing and quality of any intervention.

The first 3 years of life are significant in the prevention of antisocial behavior and persistent, serious criminal behavior throughout life, but other periods are also important. Research demonstrates that the brain retains its capacity to grow throughout life (Thompson & Nelson, 2001). Thus, brain development can be facilitated not only during the first 3 years, but also at other developmental stages, meaning early deprivation and harm can be treated in later years, especially with carefully designed interventions.

Summary and Conclusions

Individual risk factors are those that are specific to a certain child or adolescent. Whereas children from a single family are likely to experience the same extrafamilial and family risk factors, they may well have different individual risk factors. Individual risk factors often overlap with each other but, for organizational purposes, can be placed in four categories: social, cognitive, emotional, and biological.

The predominant social risk factor discussed in the literature is aggression. Aggressive behavior, even in early childhood, is often predictive of serious delinquency as the child grows older. Very early aggression in children is not unusual; during the second year, for example, most toddlers display some aggressive behavior, such as hitting parents, pets, toys, or other young children. By age 3 that behavior should begin to diminish. Aggressive behavior in children 8 to 10 years old is clearly linked with serious delinquency, displayed in all types of offending, not only violence. Serious delinquents are typically described by their parents or caretakers as having been difficult to manage at early ages.

Hostile attribution bias often goes hand in hand with aggression. Children who attribute hostile intentions to others—both children and adults—frequently engage in antisocial behavior. Some research suggests that children who have experienced abuse in the home are especially prone to hostile attribution bias; they are hypervigilant to cues that are perceived as leading to their maltreatment. The emotional factor of anger is closely connected with both aggression and hostile attribution bias.

Psychologists have conducted extensive research on empathy, a positive emotion that is believed to contribute significantly to healthy development. Its opposite, the lack of empathy, is a risk factor that seems highly predictive of antisocial behavior. Researchers have found deficiencies in empathy in many delinquents, but it is not clear why these deficiencies exist. They are likely to be more apparent in children and adolescents who commit violent acts rather than property or drug offenses. Research has also found a lack of empathy in children who display cruelty to animals, which is itself often found in the backgrounds of serious delinquents and adult violent offenders. Research has not sufficiently explored the connection between empathy and various types of antisocial behavior, but researchers have identified gender differences in the display of empathy, with girls more likely to show empathy.

Biological risk factors include body size and build and temperament, as well as numerous others. Research on body structure is quite dated, hearkening back to the studies of William Sheldon and his followers in the 1930s through 1950s. However, some contemporary researchers have noted that delinquents, particularly those who engage in aggressive behaviors, are often larger and more muscular than their peers. In light of all other risk factors, however, body structure is unlikely to be a significant predictor of antisocial conduct.

Temperament may have more to do with delinquency and other antisocial conduct than previously acknowledged. Children's temperament influences both their own behavior and the behavior of others toward them. Researchers have concluded that temperament (a) is constitutionally and biologically based, (b) is evident in infancy and continues throughout a person's lifetime, and (c) is influenced by the environment. Adjectives like *easygoing, calm, difficult,* and *touchy* all describe temperamental features. The critical aspect to keep in mind is that nurturing and warm parents or other caretakers can modulate the effects of a difficult temperament in an infant or older child.

One of the most puzzling individual risk factors for antisocial conduct is ADHD, a diagnosis that has been both overused and misunderstood. It is estimated that about one-fourth of children diagnosed with ADHD engage in serious delinquency. On the other hand, many creative, successful adults of today were diagnosed with ADHD as children, so we must be careful not to overemphasize its connection to antisocial behavior. ADHD appears to have a biological basis and may have a connection with exposure to toxic substances. It is found in boys more than in girls (by a 5:1 ratio). Clinicians warn that if it is untreated, ADHD may be accompanied by ODD and conduct disorders, and untreated children are susceptible to abusing alcohol or other drugs and engaging in antisocial behavior. ADHD and ODD occur so often together that there is some debate as to whether they are truly distinct behavioral patterns.

Some researchers find that children with ADHD do not possess effective strategies or skills in cognitive organization for dealing with the demands of school work. ADHD children often have trouble with abstract thinking. Increasingly, though, ADHD is recognized as a problem in social relationships. ADHD children are socially busy, constantly seeking interpersonal contacts, and become irritating to others. If ADHD children are also aggressive, they are rejected by their peers. The predominant method of treating ADHD is through drugs.

Several risk factors are genetic or psychobiological in nature. Adrian Raine (2002), a prominent researcher in this area, maintains that there is clear evidence from twin and adoption studies that genetics influence antisocial and aggressive behavior. He, as well as other theorists and researchers, emphasizes the role of the environment interacting with genetic factors, however. For example, twin research has suggested that identical twins are more likely than fraternal twins to be similar, including having similar antisocial tendencies. But recent research implicates maltreatment in this phenomenon. That is, maltreatment has particularly strong negative effects on children who are genetically at risk.

The role of the autonomic nervous system in facilitating antisocial behavior is also a consideration. People experience different levels of autonomic arousal. The higher the level, the more anxious one is and the more concerned about disapproval from others. Low arousal both produces some fearlessness and encourages stimulation seeking. According to those who espouse psychobiological theories, persistent offenders experience little anxiety, are not concerned about getting caught, and often seek the excitement and challenge of committing crimes. Research with adolescents who are persistent juvenile offenders does document the lower levels of arousal. However, we do not know whether this phenomenon preceded their involvement in delinquency or whether they learned to be fearless and "cool" as a result of other childhood experiences.

Complications associated with pregnancy and birth have also been linked to later antisocial behavior. These complications include minor physical anomalies (MPAs), which are unusual but barely noticeable physical features traced to early pregnancy. Research has found that a high number of these anomalies are predictive of delinquency in boys and crime in adult males. The anomalies most closely related to violence, however, are also likely to be accompanied by neurological deficits, which already have been linked with violent behavior. Research on MPAs is quite new and far too tentative to identify MPAs as strong risk factors for delinquency.

Fetal exposure to nicotine, alcohol, and illegal drugs is another matter, because an increasing number of studies link this exposure with later conduct disorder and violent offending. It appears that these substances have effects on brain development, producing cognitive deficits. Psychobiological researchers highlight the importance of healthy brain development in the prenatal stages and in a child's early years following birth. Good prenatal care, including adequate nutrition and a healthy living environment, are crucial to this development. Complications at birth can be a risk factor, but only if combined with psychosocial risks like maternal separation or rejection, parental mental health problems, or marital discord.

The numerous individual risk factors discussed in this chapter should be kept in perspective. Nearly all children are faced with some of these factors in their lives, and it would be foolhardy to state that, because one's mother used nicotine while she was pregnant or because one is quick to anger, one is likely to be a serious delinquent. The effects of risk factors on antisocial behavior are additive; and like the extrafamilial risk factors discussed in Chapter 2, some present a greater danger than others. Early, persistent aggressive behavior and lack of empathy, for example, are certainly of more concern than body build. Furthermore, as we noted in Chapter 1, even in the face of numerous risk factors and apparent adversity, some children and adolescents do not engage in serious delinquency or other antisocial conduct. We meet these children and adolescents in the following chapter.

Key Terms and Concepts

ADHD
arousal theory of crime
cognitive complexity
dizygotic twins
ectomorphic
emotional control
empathy
endomorphic
executive functions

expressive language
hostile attribution bias
mesomorphic
minor physical anomalies
monozygotic twins
perinatal factors
prenatal factors
psychophysiology
temperament

CHAPTER 4
PROTECTIVE FACTORS
❧

CHAPTER OBJECTIVES

◆ Introduce those factors and experiences that moderate, buffer, or insulate against risk for delinquency

◆ Discuss in detail the important concept of resilience

◆ Explore the contributions of the family and peers to the development of resilience

◆ Identify the many personal or individual factors that contribute to the development of resilience

The risk factors discussed in the previous two chapters clearly place an individual at elevated risk for involvement in antisocial behavior. Nonetheless, a significant number of children who are considered at risk do not engage in serious, persistent antisocial behavior but rather develop into prosocial and productive adults (Doll & Lyon, 1998). That is, despite experiencing a stressful, disadvantaged, or abusive childhood, many children do not engage in serious delinquency and, indeed, mature successfully (Masten & Coatsworth, 1998). A growing body of research on human development "challenges the conventional wisdom that growing up in oppressive conditions inevitably damages individuals and thwarts development" (Waller, 2001, p. 290). In fact, studies (e.g., Buckner, Mezzacappa, & Beardslee, 2003) suggest that between 22% and 29% of children exposed to high-risk factors demonstrate significant coping skills. Research has further found that these children possess certain strengths and benefit significantly from protective influences that help them overcome adverse conditions and thrive (Alvord & Grados, 2005). Clearly, it makes sense for researchers to study this phenomenon in order to facilitate its broader prevalence.

Interest in identifying and studying protective factors emerged initially from work in developmental psychopathology (Jessor, Van den Bos, Vanderryn, Costa, & Turbin, 1995). **Protective factors**—which are sometimes called *promotive factors*—are those cognitive, social, or emotional influences and experiences that serve to moderate, buffer, or insulate against risk. Garmezy (1985) organized protection variables into three categories: (1) dispositional or personality attributes, such as competence, cognitive abilities, self-regulation; (2) family attributes, such as parental support, skillful guidance, and affection; and (3) extrafamilial circumstances, such as support from other adults or peers. Thus, protective factors have both genetic predispositions and environmental elements (Kim-Cohen, Moffitt, Caspi, & Taylor, 2004). For example, certain genetically transmitted abilities (e.g., intelligence, temperament) may provide a protection from adverse and disadvantaged environments; on the other hand, positive features of one's environment—for example, an emotionally close family—are protective. In this book, protective factors are conceptualized as decreasing the likelihood of engaging in persistent antisocial behavior, especially of a violent nature.

Researchers and scholars refer to the ability to develop healthily despite adverse and stressful conditions as **resilience** (Garmezy, 1991; Werner, 1987). Thus, although risk factors remain a major concern in the development of delinquency and criminal behavior, their conceptual opposites—protective factors—are now considered equally important. Knowledge about the personal attributes of resilient children and the environmental influences they experience can help greatly in the prevention and treatment of delinquent and antisocial behavior among at-risk populations.

RESILIENCE

Resilience is generally defined as "successful coping with or overcoming risk and adversity, the development of competence in the face of severe stress and hardship, and success in developmental tasks or meeting societal expectations" (McKnight & Loper, 2002, p. 188). Masten, Best, and Garmezy (1990) define the concept as "the process of, capacity for, or outcome of successful adaptation despite challenging or threatening circumstances" (p. 426). Resilience is the ability to bounce back from negative emotional experiences by flexible adaptation to the changing demands of stressful experiences and adversity (Tugade & Frederickson, 2004). Although resilience can be developed at any point during the life span, most of the study in the area has focused on children (Tedeschi & Kilmer, 2005).

EARLY RESEARCH ON RESILIENCE

The study of resilience arose from the study of risk as pioneering investigators realized that there were many children who flourish in the midst of extreme adversity and stressful conditions (Masten & Coatsworth, 1998). Prior to the current resilience research, the conventional wisdom was that growing up in oppressive and adverse conditions inevitably damages children and thwarts normal development (Waller, 2001). It was also assumed that children who survived and emerged psychologically healthy from severe adversity were very unusual or special. However, well-designed research on resilience in children soon revealed that the original assumptions about the dire and irrevocable effects of growing up under adverse conditions were wrong or misleading (Masten, 2001) and that resilience in children is far more common than originally supposed (Bonanno, 2004). According to Masten (2001), "The great surprise of resilience research is the ordinariness of the phenomenon" (p. 227). The accumulating evidence strongly implies that resilience in children and adolescents is far more common than was traditionally believed (Bonanno, 2004; Masten, 2001). "Resilience does not come from rare and special qualities, but from the everyday magic of ordinary, normative human resources in the minds, brains, and bodies of children" (Masten, 2001, p. 235).

The study of resilience in children at risk began in earnest during the 1970s (Masten, 2001). Having originated in the disciplines of psychiatry and developmental psychology, this study has tended to focus on the individual, often to the exclusion of the psychosocial environment (Waller, 2001). Resilience was initially conceptualized as the result of personality traits or coping styles that allowed some children to progress along a relatively normal developmental trajectory, even when confronted with considerable and long-lasting adversity. However, the social environment (especially the family) is also critical in the development of resilience in most children.

One of the earliest studies on resilience was Emmy Werner's (1987) longitudinal research, known as the Kauai study. Werner and her collaborators (Werner, Bierman, & French, 1971; Werner & Smith, 1977, 1982; Werner, 1987) followed a cohort of 698 children living on the Hawaiian Island of Kauai, from birth to adulthood. This prospective longitudinal study spanned the years 1954 to 1986 and included data from pediatricians, psychologists, public health personnel, and social workers. The project identified a number of personality, constitutional, and environmental variables that presumably distinguish children who become delinquent from those who do not. The Werner measure of delinquency is problematic, however. Of the 698 children, 102 were labeled "delinquent" based solely on official records or police and family court files. A vast majority of these 102 "juvenile offenders" (both males and females) committed relatively minor offense violations, such as traffic violations or running away. This word of caution should be kept in mind as we review the findings of the study.

Werner (1987) stated that a combination of about a dozen variables provided the best prediction for eventual delinquency. For example, children with a history of a difficult temperament, hyperactivity, substandard living conditions, low IQ, and unstable, conflictful home life were more likely to be delinquent than children without these background variables. However, a significant number of these children (a total of 72) with four or more of these features in their background did not become delinquent, indicating that predictions of delinquency on the basis of background variables alone is unwarranted.

Werner divided those children with four or more high-risk variables into a "resilient" group (those who did not become delinquent) and a "vulnerable" group (those who became delinquent). She reports that one of the strongest differences between the two groups was the mother's perception of the child's temperament. Mothers of the resilient children perceived them as affectionate, cuddly, good-natured, and easy to handle. Furthermore, these children demonstrated a positive social orientation toward others. The study found that resilient children were more skilled at engaging others and recruiting care, help, and support from siblings, peers, grandparents, neighborhood adults, and teachers. In addition, the families of the resilient children had fairly extensive social support systems. That is, they had many supportive adults and caretakers available to them when problems arose. "A social support network entails a functional collection of persons providing or making available to individual members opportunities for security, recognition, affirmation, instrumental assistance, emotional comfort, personal growth, and social control" (Harrison-Hale, McLoyd, & Smedley, 2004, p. 276).

On the other hand, mothers of vulnerable children perceived them as being difficult to handle. These mothers believed their children exhibited more temper tantrums and eating and sleeping problems. Furthermore, the children's orientation toward others was negative and aggressive. Overall, the families of the vulnerable children seemed to have meager support systems.

CONTEMPORARY RESEARCH

Interest in resilience has continued, with researchers attempting to focus more on fine-tuning the concept and identifying common characteristics of resilient children. Furthermore, the concept has been expanded to include resilient families and communities.

Some experts argue that, at a minimum, two critical conditions must be met before a child can be called resilient. First, the child must have been exposed to significant threats or severe adversity, ranging from a single stressful event, such as war, to an accumulation of ongoing negative experiences, such as abuse. As was mentioned earlier, children who show positive outcomes and adjustment without having experienced significant hardship of one sort or another can be considered *competent* but not resilient (Buckner et al., 2003). Second, the child must demonstrate the achievement of positive adaptation despite major assaults on the developmental process (Luthar, Cicchetti, & Becker, 2000). Resilience has been conceptualized as an outcome or process that does not eradicate risk but allows an individual to compensate for it successfully. Thus, resilient children do not simply evade the negative outcomes associated with risk but are able to take risk head on and adapt in the face of such adversity.

Some experts (e.g., Cicchetti & Rogosch, 1997) have also recommended that, in order to qualify as resilient, a person should show positive outcomes and adaptation across several aspects of life over periods of time. In other words, resilience is not a straightforward, one-dimensional attribute that a person either has or does not have (Alvord & Grados, 2005; Reivich & Shatté, 2002). "Rather, resilience implies the possession of multiple skills, in varying degrees, that help individuals to cope" (Alvord & Grados, 2005, p. 239). At-risk children may be resilient in one domain of functioning but not in others.

In an effort to emphasize the ongoing and changing developmental nature of resilience, some professionals define the concept as "a dynamic process encompassing positive adaptation within the context of significant adversity" (Luthar et al., 2000, p. 543). Other investigators try to distinguish between the terms *resilience* and *resiliency*. For them, *resilience* refers to a dynamic developmental process, while *resiliency* refers to a personality trait or attribute that is relatively stable over the course of a lifetime (Masten, 1994). However, there is increasing evidence that, although resilience may be subjected to developmental fluctuations, at-risk children who show resilience at one stage of their lives tend to show resilience across their entire life span (Luthar et al., 2000). Consequently, it becomes difficult to make the fine distinction between resilience and resiliency with any kind of precision. To avoid confusion, the term *resilience* will be used broadly here to encompass both the process and the personality aspects of the concept.

Studies on resilience underscore the perspective that children have different vulnerabilities and protective systems at different ages and points during their development (Masten & Coatsworth, 1998). For example, because of their total dependence on parents or caregivers, infants are highly vulnerable to the consequences of mistreatment by these adult figures. Adolescents, on the other hand, tend to be more vulnerable to the experiences they have with friends and school, which would be well beyond the understanding of young children (Masten & Coatsworth, 1998).

However, even infants have considerable power to elicit assistance from parents and caregivers, especially from parents and caregivers who are sensitive to their needs (Masten & Coatsworth, 1998). Maternal warmth appears to be especially important (Kim-Cohen et al., 2004); the quality of this relationship has predictive significance for success on later developmental tasks, such as problem solving in toddlers and peer relations in middle childhood. Caregivers help infants regulate their emotions until the children learn to self-regulate, and caregivers provide a secure environment for further exploration (Masten & Coatsworth, 1998).

In recent years, developmental psychologists have been able to identify some common characteristics of resilient children and adolescents. For children who have experienced high levels of risk factors, protective factors appear to be related to personal qualities, such as reflectiveness, self-efficacy, a good-natured temperament, self-esteem, and high levels of cognitive and interpersonal skills. These abilities equip children to make adaptive responses to challenges and to access the environmental resources that facilitate healthy and normal development.

In general, the accumulating evidence reveals that resilient children exhibit positive social, interpersonal, and cognitive competencies that help them survive and succeed even under high stress and in adverse environments. A good-natured, sociable temperament helps substantially in developing resilience. In addition, research consistently "indicates that resilient individuals have optimistic, zestful, and energetic approaches to life, are curious and open to new experiences, and are characterized by high positive emotionality" (Tugade & Frederickson, 2004, p. 320). High positive emotionality includes a great sense of humor and optimistic thinking. Children and adolescents who participate in serious, violent behaviors or chronic delinquency rarely display these qualities. In fact, research suggests that resilient youth not only do not engage in serious or violent delinquency, but they usually do not participate in delinquent gangs or use illegal drugs either (Tiêt & Huizinga, 2002).

Interestingly, recent studies highlight the possibility of "late-emerging resilience" (Masten et al., 2004). It appears that it is never too late to develop resilience and coping skills for life's stresses and challenges, even into late adulthood. This observation has -significant implications for prevention and intervention strategies for antisocial and criminally prone adults.

FAMILY RESILIENCE

Although resilience is most often thought of as being a feature of an individual, more recent thinking has extended the concept to the family, peers, and the community (Simon, Murphy, & Smith, 2005; Walsh, 1998, 2003). Thus, **family resilience** is defined as "the ability of a family to respond positively to an adverse situation and emerge from the situation feeling strengthened, more resourceful, and more confident than its prior state" (Simon et al., 2005, p. 427). Family resilience is more than the *sum* of the characteristics of its individual members; it is the result of the *interaction* "between the characteristics of the individuals within the family and the characteristics of the family unit" (Simon et al., 2005, p. 429).

There is growing recognition, then, that resilience is a multidimensional and multidetermined concept that can best be understood as the result of transactions within and between multiple systemic levels over time (Waller, 2001). For example, family resilience researchers recognize three dimensions as key components in resilience (Simon et al., 2005). The first is the length of time the family (or child) experiences the adversity. If the time is short-term, the adversity may be referred to as a "challenge." If long-term, it may be referred to as a "crisis." A second dimension is the life stage (or for the child the developmental stage) during which the challenge or crisis is experienced.

Families with preschoolers may face financial difficulties with child care, employment strains, or difficulties associated with pregnancy. Families may use certain strengths to effectively overcome challenges during one life stage, but the same strengths may not be effective with challenging situations at other stages of life (Simon et al., 2005). A third dimension of resilience is associated with the internal or external sources of support that a family has available during challenges or crises (Simon et al., 2005). That is, a family may rely exclusively on the strengths of its immediate members or seek the support of the extended family, a religious organization, or the community. As noted by Simon et al., studies indicate that greater resilience is found in families that reach out to others in their social environment, such as extended family, friends, and community agencies, including providers of health care and mental health services. What all of this means in relation to antisocial behavior and delinquency is that prevention and treatment strategies must be directed at strengthening the resilience of *both* the child and the family. (Of course, when children emerge resilient in life, despite growing up in dysfunctional, ineffective, or abusive families, we direct our attention to the resilience characteristics of the individual child.)

Not surprisingly, when a family is resilient, the likelihood is greater that the individual children within it will also be resilient. Families are considered resilient if they focus on family accord, communication, finances, and family-focused events (Simon et al., 2005). "The nurturing of supportive relationships with one another can assist family members in improving the ability to grow, learn, and challenge each other in positive and growth-enhancing ways" (Simon et al., 2005, p. 429). But it is more than simply spending time together. Parents must provide social support, warmth, responsiveness, and stimulating activities to optimize resilience in their children.

RECOVERY-TO-NORMAL TRAJECTORIES

Some research has focused on youth resilience after the youth has left an institutional setting that was characterized by extreme deprivation. Studies of Romanian adoptees provide dramatic documentation of developmental catch-up in many of the children, both physically and cognitively. In fact, the degree of catch-up by the age of 4 was spectacular (Rutter & ERA Study Team, 1998). "As observed in many other situations of extraordinary adversity, the capacity for developmental recovery when normative rearing conditions are restored is amazing" (Masten, 2001, p. 233). However, not all children recover well. Some develop serious and chronic problems, including antisocial behavior, partly as a result of their earlier experiences with adversity. Systematic investigations of why some children responded adaptively while others did not should offer a promising framework for intervention.

ENVIRONMENTAL FACTORS

Studies continually corroborate the importance of four broad factors in resilient children: (1) connections to competent and caring adults in the family and community, (2) cognitive and self-regulation skills, (3) positive views of self, and (4) motivation to be effective in the environment (Masten, 2001). The first factor involves the social environment, especially the family, peers, and the school. The other three broad factors primarily involve individual attributes. Our discussion begins with the social environmental factors and then moves on to the individual attributes later in the chapter.

Although much of the theoretical and research work has tended to view resilience as a quality of the individual, a strong argument can be made that it is also a quality of the social context in which the child develops. Many developmental theorists have argued that resilience in aversive childhood contexts results from a cumulative and interactive mix of risk and protective factors—genetic (e.g., disposition), personal (e.g., family interaction), and environmental (e.g., community support systems; Moffitt, 2005; Rutter, 1999; Werner, 1995).

> Therefore, resilience is not only a quality of individuals but also of social contexts that have embedded within them factors that offer protection against forces that might affect development adversely. Protective factors within the environment or social context include family functioning characterized by warmth, cohesion, enlightened discipline, culture and ethnic identification, and supportive extrafamilial relationships and community structure, such as churches, neighborhood organizations, and schools that effectively promote competence in social and cognitive domains. (Barbarin, 1993, pp. 482–483)

The research associating resilience with neighborhood factors is sparse, but it does indicate that neighborhoods supplement the other environmental and individual factors associated with resilience by providing a context in which children can be exposed to positive influences (Wandersman & Nation, 1998). Early investigators of resilience (e.g., Garmezy, 1983; Rutter, 1979; Werner & Smith, 1982) all underscored the ameliorative role of social support systems in the community, especially for disadvantaged families. Werner and Smith discovered that resilient adolescents made extensive use of the assistance of peers, older friends, ministers, and teachers. Based on their extensive review of the relevant literature on the topic, Lösel and Bender (2003) conclude: "The availability and use of social support from family members, relatives, teachers, educators, ministers of religion, and friends . . . contribute to resilience" (p. 164).

Interestingly, but perhaps not surprisingly, youth are mentally and physically healthier in neighborhoods where adults talk to each other and get along (Wandersman & Nation, 1998). A repetitive theme that emerges from the research literature is that resilience is developed from close relations with supportive, loving caregivers, effective schools, and connections with competent, caring adults in the wider community (Luthar et al., 2000). Resilient youths "often join clubs, teams, and other groups and frequently find mentors such as coaches, teachers, scout leaders and other prosocial adults in their communities" (Alvord & Grados, 2005, p. 241). Religious and spiritual organizations can also serve as protective influences, providing social services and support within the community (Alvord & Grados, 2005).

Several studies (e.g., Garbarino & Kostelny, 1992; Garbarino, Kostelny, & Dubrow, 1991) highlight the importance of good social networks in preventing child abuse and child antisocial behavior and violence, even in areas of concentrated poverty (Wandersman & Nation, 1998). In fact, we have discovered that supportive peers and a nonpunitive community are among the *most* important network factors contributing not only to resilience in children and adolescents but also to the prevention and significant reduction of antisocial and delinquent behavior (Waaktaar et al., 2004).

FAMILY INFLUENCES

For many decades, research has shown that good parental functioning in at least one parent or an adequate and stable caregiver is critical in the development of resilience and healthy functioning (G. Smith, 1999; Waaktaar et al., 2004). "Children with at least one warm, loving parent or surrogate caregiver (grandparent, foster parent) who provides firm limits and boundaries are more likely to be resilient" (Alvord & Grados, 2005, p. 240). A caregiver environment that is characterized as emotionally warm, supportive, communicative, and responsive to the child's needs is most likely to be associated with resilience in children. The caregiver or parental environment should also include firm and consistent control, balanced discipline, and reasonable monitoring of children's activity. Far too often, caregivers and adults impede the development of resilience in children, and as a consequence too many children feel vulnerable, helpless, unaccepted, or sad.

Resilience is a key factor in a child's ability to adapt to parental divorce (Chen & George, 2005). Studies on divorce consistently indicate that the quality of the parent–child relationship and the child's perception and understanding of the divorce are major influences on how children adapt to the divorce of their parents (J. D. Chen & George, 2005). Children who have a positive and supportive relationship with at least one of their parents are more resilient to the negative emotions that often accompany parental divorces.

More directly relevant to the topic of this book, investigations have consistently shown that effective parenting provides a strong protective environment in preventing antisocial or delinquent behavior (Dubrow, Edwards, & Ippolito, 1997; Masten, 2001). In fact, there are compelling studies that suggest that the quality of parental care can even alter gene expression in offspring (Meany, 2001; Moffitt, 2005). Good parenting can apparently neutralize a genetic propensity to be difficult and antisocial. Furthermore, parents' optimism and their perceptions of themselves as capable of coping successfully with life's problems are positively associated with children's social and academic functioning. Recent research indicates that sibling support is also a strong protective factor in the development of resilience (Ozer, 2005).

Good family communication contributes to resilience and competence by providing a model for a child's development of cognitive abilities, such as attending, focusing, and sustaining task orientation. Supportive, understanding, and stimulating communication by parents and siblings appears to be highly predictive of cognitive and social-emotional competence, as identified in teacher and peer ratings. In addition, in homes that provide a cognitively stimulating environment (e.g., one with books and toys that teach color, size, and shape and that encourage creativity), children are far more advanced cognitively in the early school years than are children growing up in homes without those resources (Evans, 2004; Linver, Brooks-Guan, & Kohen, 2002; McLoyd, 1998). Young children who are read to on a regular basis generally demonstrate better cognitive abilities and skills than children who are rarely or never read to. Similarly, the cognitive development of adopted children placed in stimulating homes appears to be significantly greater than that of children left behind (van IJzendoorn, Juffer, & Klein Poelhuis, 2005). In fact, "in a cognitively richer and emotionally safer environment, on average, adopted children may recover and nearly get back on a normal track" (van IJzendoorn et al., 2005, p. 313). A preadoptive or foster home placement can also provide the emotional warmth and cognitive stimulation so crucial in early development.

An understanding of resilience can be further facilitated by consideration of cultural and ethnic factors. Some noted characteristics of resilient families include family celebrations, family time and routines, and family cultural traditions (Simon et al., 2005). Examples are numerous—family meals, game nights, trips, meetings, and family traditions associated with holidays and religious events.

In recent years, systematic, empirical study of resilience has expanded to many countries and cultures. Loth and Heggen (2003) found that having hope and finding meaning and purpose in life were the strongest sources of resilience in young Ethiopian famine survivors. Religious beliefs and spirituality played key roles in the maintenance of that hope. Hernández (2002) discovered that hope and solidarity with family and community were key sources of resilience in Latin American countries under conditions of racism, poverty, terrorism, and war. Research on the resilience of Native American children and adolescents indicates that the strong traditions and values gained from the family and the social support received from peers are among the major determinants of resilience within that culture (Montgomery, Miville, Winterowd, Jeffires, & Baysden, 2000). In addition, Native American college students relied heavily on contact and relationship with other Native American students for support in getting through tough times and challenges.

PEER INFLUENCES

As we noted in Chapter 2, one of the strongest predictors of later involvement in antisocial behavior is early rejection by peers (Dodge, 2003; Laird et al., 2001; Parker & Asher, 1987). Those children who had been peer rejected for at least 2 or 3 years by the time they reached second grade had a 50% chance of displaying significant antisocial behavior later in adolescence, in contrast with just a 9% chance for those children who managed to avoid early peer rejection (Dodge & Pettit, 2003). Studies find that peer-rejected and aggressive children are deficient in being able to emotionally and cognitively put themselves in the place of others (Pepler, Byrd, & King, 1991). As a result, these youths, with increasing age, become less concerned about the consequences of violence, including the suffering of the victim.

Recent studies have also discovered that supportive, prosocial peers are among the most important factors contributing to resilience in children and adolescents and to the prevention of antisocial behavior (Stouthamer-Loeber et al., 2004; Waaktaar et al., 2004). Positive peer relations have been thought to contribute to the development of empathy and also reinforce and model self-regulation and prosocial behavior (Eisenberg, 1998; Waaktaar et al., 2004). Interestingly, resilient children—particularly as they get older—seem to have a knack for attaining these positive relationships with their peers. Resilient youth appear to place themselves in healthier contexts, generating opportunities for success or raising the odds of connecting with prosocial mentors in a manner consistent with the concept of "niche seeking." In other words, resilient children and adolescents select and create social environments that enable them to grow and thrive. They also learn from one another and reinforce each other's positive attributes.

INDIVIDUAL FACTORS

INTELLIGENCE

Cognitive factors contribute substantially to resilience. Intelligence, language skills, reasoning, attentiveness, and various personal attributes, such as self-efficacy, self-regulation, and talent, have been studied extensively (Olsson, Bond, Burns, Vella-Broderick, & Sawyer, 2003). A nearly universal finding is that children with a higher level of intelligence are more likely to be resilient (Aldwin, 1994; Curtis & Cicchetti, 2003). Overall, good intelligence appears to have specific and important protective functions. Intelligent children are more likely to develop better and more realistic coping strategies. Further, such children may function well at school and thus acquire a source of self-esteem, which can buffer other stressors. Good intelligence also contributes substantially to language development. Not surprisingly, more intelligent children receive greater levels of social reinforcement from the general social environment (e.g., teachers and other significant adults) than less intelligent children do (Born, Chevalier, & Humblet, 1997).

This relationship holds true in the reverse as well. Nigg and Huang-Pollock (2003) find strong links between problems in cognitive ability and antisocial behavior in children and adolescents. Cognitive problems "may contribute to difficult interactions with caretakers, interfere with socialization, and leave the child unprepared to adapt to the greater diversity he or she faces in a high-risk environment" (Nigg & Huang-Pollock, 2003, p. 237). As early as 1977 criminologists Travis Hirschi and Michael Hindelang took social scientists to task for ignoring a persistent and statistically significant negative correlation between IQ scores and delinquency. After reviewing major official and self-report studies (e.g., Hirschi, 1969; Reiss & Rhodes, 1961; West & Farrington, 1973; Wolfgang et al., 1972), Hirschi and Hindelang concluded that IQ was a strong predictor of delinquency. Throughout their literature search, they continually uncovered a negative correlation: the lower the IQ, the higher the incidence of delinquency, whether official or self-reported. In their article, Hirschi and Hindelang hypothesized that an indirect causal relationship exists between IQ and delinquency. By "indirect" they meant that a low IQ leads to poor performance and attitudes toward school, which in turn leads to delinquency. A high IQ leads to good performance and attitudes toward school, which in turn leads to conformity (or at least nondelinquency).

Recent research supports this connection, particularly with reference to verbal intelligence.

> Early specific weakness in verbal-learning and verbal-reasoning modestly but reliably predicts later persistent offending, conduct disorder, and antisocial outcomes, whereas nonverbal intelligence does not do so.... Weakness in verbal intelligence is associated with the subgroup of delinquent youth with early onset and chronic patterns of anti-social behavior ... even though not all of those youth have antisocial outcomes."
> (Nigg & Huang-Pollock, 2003, p. 231)

Although the term *intelligence* is subject to competing interpretations and multiple definitions, the relationship between intelligence test scores and school performance is strong and consistent. "Wherever it has been studied, children with high scores on tests of intelligence tend to learn more of what is taught in school than their lower-scoring peers" (Neisser, Boodoo, Bouchard, Boykin, Brody, Ceci, et al., 1996, p. 82). There is also a relationship between intelligence and years of education and, to a lesser extent, social status and income.

Assessing Intelligence

Intelligence is generally defined as the ability to adapt, learn, and engage in abstract thought (Nigg & Huang-Pollock, 2003). Although research has shown that juvenile delinquents as a group do not do well on standardized test scores, people who work with them often find them "intelligent" in other areas, especially in those activities that interest them. Brazilian street children, for example, are capable of doing the math required for survival in their street business even though they have failed mathematics in school (Neisser et al., 1996; Carraher, Carraher, & Schliemann, 1985).

It is widely accepted that standardized intelligence tests do not sample all forms of intelligence, such as creativity, wisdom, practical sense, social sensitivity, or musical ability. Most psychologists today would agree that intelligence test scores are strongly influenced by social, educational, and general cultural background (Neisser et al., 1996). Intelligence test scores, then, are "culture biased," in spite of recurring efforts to develop culture-free instruments. Furthermore, intelligence test scores typically are crude indices of mainstream language skills, which are strongly influenced by academic and language-development experiences. In general, rich and varied experiences increase test scores, and limited experiences decrease them (Neisser et al., 1996; Garbarino & Asp, 1981). School experiences, if positive, may increase language skills and, if negative, may stagnate, or even decrease, language skills.

Multiple Forms of Intelligence

Intelligence exists in multiple forms and relates to a wide assortment of abilities. It is likely that resilient people have a variety of intelligences and abilities. Howard Gardner describes nine different types of intelligences or cognitive styles (see Table 4–1), and there are probably many more—such as wisdom, spirituality, synthesizing ability, intuition, metaphoric capacities, humor, and good judgment (Gardner, 1983, 1998, 2000). Many of these have been used to describe resilient persons. Gardner considered two of the nine types—insight into oneself and the understanding of others—to be features of **emotional intelligence**, which is the ability to know how people are feeling and the capacity to use that information to guide thoughts and actions. A deficiency in this form of intelligence may play a prominent role in human violence. Individuals who continually engage in violence may lack significant insight into their own behavior and may possess little sensitivity or empathy toward others.

Another theory of intelligence was proposed by Robert Sternberg (1985), whose **triarchic theory** identifies three fundamental aspects of intelligence: analytic, creative, and practical (see Table 4–2). Whereas Gardner considered the nine intelligences to be largely independent, Sternberg emphasizes the extent to which these three aspects work together, as well as how prior experience affects them. Of the three, only the first—analytic or academic intelligence—has been tested to any great extent by mainstream assessments of intelligence. The second aspect is the capacity to use problem-solving skills that require creative thinking, the ability to deal with new situations, and the ability to learn from experience. The third aspect is the capacity to use practical thinking skills that help people adjust to, and cope with, their social and cultural environments.

TABLE 4–1: Summary of Gardner's Different Intelligences

Intelligence	Definition
Linguistic	• Reflected in good vocabulary and reading comprehension
Visual/spatial	• Ability to visualize objects, find one's orientation in space, navigate from one location to another
Logical-mathematical	• Ability to think logically, reason deductively, detect patterns, carry out mathematical operations
Interpersonal	• Ability to understand and interact with others effectively
Intrapersonal	• Ability to understand oneself
Existential	• Tendency to ponder the meaning of life, death, the nature of reality
Kinesthetic	• Ability to dance well, handle objects skillfully, be competent in sports
Musical	• Ability to hear, recognize, and manipulate patterns in music
Naturalistic	• Ability to see patterns in nature and discriminate among living things (plants and animals)

Source: Based on H. Gardner, *Frames of Mind: The Theory of Multiple Intelligences,* 1983, New York: Basic Books; "Are There Additional Intelligences: The Case for Naturalist, Spiritual, and Existential Intelligences," 1998, in K. Kane (Ed.), *Education, Information, and Transformation,* Englewood Cliffs, N.J: Prentice Hall; and *Intelligence Reframed: Multiple Intelligences for the 21st Century*, 2000, New York: Basic Books.

Although a large amount of research links cognitive deficits to antisocial behavior in children and adolescents (Nigg & Huang-Pollock (2003), considerable research has also shown that youth with high or above-average intelligence are far less likely to participate in serious or chronic delinquency (Lösel & Bender, 2003). "Intelligent children may be more capable of planning their behaviour, anticipating negative outcomes, settling conflicts verbally, developing alternatives to aggressive reactions, and making better decisions" (Lösel & Bender, 2003, p. 155). Resilient children are more likely to develop better and more realistic coping strategies and, because of their cognitive skills, are more likely to learn nonaggressive problem-solving capabilities at an early age.

Good intelligence may also reflect the central importance of cognition and language to adaptation during early development, and it appears to have specific and very

TABLE 4–2: Summary of Sternberg's Triarchic Theory of Intelligence

Intelligence	Definition
Componential	• Ability to think abstractly and process information effectively; useful in learning how to solve problems; frequently referred to as analytical intelligence
Experiential	• Ability to formulate new ideas and use different kinds of information; capacity to deal with new situations by drawing on prior knowledge and existing skills; sometimes referred to as creative intelligence
Contextual	• Ability to adapt to whatever comes one's way and to change the environment to maximize one's abilities; very similar to "street smarts"; often referred to as practical intelligence

Source: Based on R. J. Sternberg, *Beyond IQ,* 1985, New York: Cambridge University Press, and *The Triarchic Mind: A New Theory of Human Intelligence,* 1988, New York: Viking.

important protective functions (Masten & Coatsworth, 1998). Interestingly, the verbal and language aspects of intelligence seem to be some of the more important components of the relationship between intelligence and delinquency. Nigg and Huang-Pollock (2003) affirm: "Early specific weakness in verbal-learning and verbal-reasoning modestly but reliably predicts later persistent offending, conduct disorder, and antisocial outcomes, whereas nonverbal intelligence does not do so. . . . Weakness in verbal intelligence is associated with the subgroup of delinquent youth with early onset and chronic patterns of antisocial behavior . . . even though not all of those youth [with poor verbal skills] have antisocial outcomes" (Nigg & Huang-Pollock, 2003, p. 231). Perhaps more importantly, good verbal intelligence contributes substantially to language development.

LANGUAGE DEVELOPMENT

Language is a powerful tool for transmitting and expressing social expectations and values. It is also the primary means by which children can communicate their needs, frustrations, and concerns. Language "facilitates the rehearsal of rules, the ability to consider and to modify ongoing behavior with respect to its consequences, and the ability to form appropriate plans for future action" (Brownlie et al., 2004, p. 461). Therefore, language serves both as a form of external communication and as the basic internal ingredient for thinking and self-regulation. In essence, language plays a major constructive role in the growth of all cognitive processes. According to Keenan and Shaw (2003), language is the "primary means by which children learn to solve problems nonaggressively and effectively decrease negative emotions such as anger, fear, and sadness" (p. 163). Toddlers with better communication skills are easier to socialize because they comprehend parental instructions better, are more able to develop internal control of their emotions and behaviors, and can communicate their wishes better (Lahey & Waldman, 2003). Hence, these children are less likely to become highly frustrated during interactions with their parents.

On average, children utter their first word between 8 and 14 months of age (Ganger & Brent, 2004). During this time, they add words to their repertoire at a relatively slow rate. For the average child, there is a substantial amount of growth in language during the second year of life (Keenan & Shaw, 2003); at 24 months, children have an average vocabulary of 300 words (Ganger & Brent, 2004). It is widely held that children's rate of vocabulary acquisition does not simply increase but undergoes a discrete transition at approximately 50 words. At this stage, children presumably switch from an initial stage of slow vocabulary growth to a subsequent stage of faster growth (Ganger & Brent, 2004). Although the reasons for this transition remain debatable, it is often called the **vocabulary spurt**, the *vocabulary burst*, or the **naming explosion** in the developmental research literature. By the end of the preschool period, the average child has internalized—primarily through the use of language—rules that are linked to the ability to inhibit behavior, follow rules, and manage negative emotions (Keenan & Shaw, 2003; Kochanska, Murray, & Coy, 1997). In addition, children demonstrate more empathy and prosocial behavior toward others as a result of language development (Keenan & Shaw, 2003). Thus, verbally advantaged children may benefit from their verbal skills by developing prosocial behaviors and may, as a result, steer away from antisocial trajectories (Dionne et al., 2003).

In general, the research literature suggests that girls are more likely than boys to use language to form and maintain relationships and social connections, whereas boys are more likely to use language to assert their independence and to achieve utilitarian goals (Leaper & Smith, 2004). Girls also tend to develop language earlier than boys (Gleason & Ely, 2002) and are less likely to use hostile attribution in their perceptions of the social environment (Dodge, 2003).

SELF-REGULATION SKILLS

Self-regulation appears to be one of the most important skills in the development of resilience and ultimately in the prevention of antisocial behavior. "Effective self-regulation allows individuals to control and alter their behavior so as to resist temptations, stifle socially undesirable impulses, follow rules, pursue enlightened self-interest despite short-term costs, and make positive contributions to society" (Baumeister, Dewall, Ciarocco, & Twenge, 2005, p. 603).

Self-regulation is defined as the capacity to control and alter one's behavior and emotions. But self-regulation is more than control. Regulation includes the ability to activate and change behavior, as well as the ability to shift attention (Eisenberg et al., 2004). Note also that the definition includes *both* behavioral and emotional regulation. Regulating emotions, especially anger, is a crucial skill in getting along with others and with society in general. Research finds that, not only are poor behavioral and emotional self-regulation related to aggression and serious delinquency, but they are also related to the early onset of substance use and the escalation of use during adolescence (Wills & Stoolmiller, 2002; Wills, Walker, Mendoza, & Ainette, 2006). Although most research has focused on behavioral self-control, emotional self-control is becoming a prominent partner in the prediction of persistent and serious antisocial behavior.

A common observation is that children differ in the intensity, frequency, and duration of emotional and behavioral reactions and in the strategies they use to manage such reactions. One of the most important protective factors against antisocial behavior is success in developing self-regulation or self-control of these emotions, impulses, and behavioral reactions (Alvord & Grados, 2005). In fact, "the development of self-regulatory skills is a defining feature in the emergence of competence and resilience among younger children" (Buckner et al., 2003, p. 141). And Posner and Rothbart (2000) argue that understanding self-regulation is the single most crucial goal for advancing knowledge about development and psychopathology.

Resilient youth do not usually possess an extraordinary or special skill but simply appear more adept in regulating their emotions and behavior. Children who can control their emotions and behavior and calm themselves will most likely draw positive attention from others and develop healthy relationships. Even at the age of 3, some toddlers walk away when other toddlers try to engage them in an altercation, such as by taking away a toy. Still another toddler recognizes that something upsets her and is able to take some time out by herself until she feels better. By contrast, the child with difficulty regulating negative emotions and behavior is at risk of developing aggressive tendencies, possibly violence, later in life. Self-regulatory skills developed in childhood form the basic foundation of positive coping, interpersonal success, and academic achievement throughout life. Therefore, preventive interventions designed to promote self-regulations skills in young children go a long way in preventing antisocial behavior as the children get older.

In their relationships with adults, children begin to acquire in numerous ways the tools that enable them to control their behavior and emotions. Although self-regulation skills may reflect some temperamental qualities with a genetic component, it is clear that self-regulation skills are malleable and can be taught or improved upon by the social environment (Buckner et al., 2003). An infant's success at regulation depends considerably on the caregiver's awareness of, flexibility, and responsiveness to the child's emotional expressions (Calkins & Fox, 2002). Sensitive and consistent caregiving and warm but firm parenting styles have been associated with the development of self-control and compliance with social rules. Fundamentally, child compliance is associated with a parental disciplinary style that is responsive to child cues, places warm and consistent limits, minimizes the use of power, and encourages concern for others (Feldman & Klein, 2003). Kochanska, Aksan, and Carlson (2005) found that highly difficult and anger-prone children became far more cooperative with responsive mothers who provided warm control, as compared to mothers who were not responsive. "With highly responsive mothers, angry infants became highly cooperative, but with unresponsive mothers, they were strikingly uncooperative at 15 months" (Kochanska et al., 2005, p. 655). Cooperation was defined by the researchers as the child's social responsiveness and harmonious interaction with the parent in multiple settings.

Clear signs of self-control begin to emerge in the second year, as does the concern for others. During the third year of life, children are expected to become reasonably compliant with parental requests and to internalize the family standards and values for behavior. Girls, on average, tend to show more self-regulated compliance and are more socially involved in free play than are boys (Feldman & Klein, 2003; Kochanska, Coy, & Murray, 2001). The research by Kochanska and colleagues (e.g., Kochanska & Aksan, 1995; Kochanska et al., 2001) underscores child compliance as the first marker of socialization (Feldman & Klein, 2003) and a critical variable in the development of resilience.

The work on self-regulation as a whole strongly suggests that these skills are extremely important for the development of competence and resilience. Self-regulation skills begin to emerge in early childhood and are strongly influenced by learning experiences and support from the psychosocial environment. As noted by Buckner et al. (2003), "Preventive interventions designed either to promote environments that foster children's self-regulation or directly teach them these skills could test the hypothesis that self-regulation skills are a proximal cause of children's resilience" (p. 157).

Effortful Control

Similar to the self-regulation concept, the term **effortful control** has been introduced (Rothbart, 1989; Rothbart & Bates, 1998, Rothbart, Derryberry, & Posner, 1994) to describe the level of a child's capacity to inhibit impulsive behavior and to pay attention. Effortful control appears to be an acquired skill that emerges during the latter half of the first year of life and, in most children, develops rapidly during the toddler and preschool years, ages 2 to 6 (Olson et al., 2005; Posner & Rothbart, 2000). The development of effortful control is considered an important milestone in the developmental trajectory toward delinquent behavior. Recent research (Olson et al., 2005) has shown a strong connection between low effortful control skills and antisocial behavior across different social situations. Deficient effortful control of impulsive behavior is clearly a major step on the road to antisocial behavior.

Bates and his colleagues (1998) investigated the interaction of toddlers' impulsivity–unmanageability (which they called "resistance to control") and parental attempts at controlling the behavior. These researchers argue that the core behavior in resistance to control is the child's failure to comply with parental attempts to stop or redirect the child's action. In other words, when the parent admonishes a child not to touch a breakable object, the unmanageable child does so anyway. The researchers hypothesized that very young children's differences in response to caregivers' attempts to regulate the children's actions are strongly related to antisocial behavior and other problems in older children and adolescents. The researchers observed that a socially unresponsive, dominating, or impulsive child did not respond well to a caregiver who was relatively weak in communicating prohibitions, warnings, or scoldings. The toddler challenged the caregiver every step of the way. On the other hand, a caregiver who demonstrated reasonable and responsible control over the toddler's early resistance actions was more effective in controlling the child's actions as he or she got older. Highly resistant children with very controlling parents turned out better behaved than their counterparts with less-controlling parents, whether the behavior was reported by the parents or teachers. These results underscore the importance of a favorable social environment in controlling or moderating certain biological/genetic dispositions that, left unchecked, could result in a long career of antisocial behavior.

Although not extensively studied, spontaneity and its relationship to resilience deserve some mention. **Spontaneity** refers to the ability to act naturally and automatically in real-life situations. Eisenberg et al. (2004) discovered that children low in spontaneity were also low in resilience. These investigators report that resilience appears to require some degree of spontaneity in order to test new ways of dealing with stressful and unanticipated circumstances. However, resilient people apparently know when to be spontaneous and when not to be.

Gender Differences in Self-Regulation

Although the research on gender differences in temperament in general is not extensive, it seems that there are gender differences in infant expressive and self-regulatory behavior during the first year of life. Furthermore, some of these differences are already present in newborns (Else-Quest et al., 2006; Weinberg, Tronick, Cohn, & Olson, 1999); gender differences in social responsiveness and self-regulatory capacity have been documented within hours of delivery. Infant boys, compared to infant girls, appear to have a more limited capacity for self-regulation and for making their needs explicit to their mothers; the boys use a narrower range of both positive and negative expressions (Weinberg et al., 1999). Else-Quest et al. (2006) found consistent evidence that girls have greater ability to self-regulate their impulses and attention.

However, in assessing gender differences in infant behavior, gender-related differences in caregiver response to infants must be considered. As noted by Weinberg et al. (1999), several studies have reported that parents hold different expectations and stereotypes about girls than about boys (Rubin, Provenzano, & Luria, 1974; Stern & Karaker, 1989) and they interact differently with male and female infants. For instance, some research indicates that mothers are more likely to talk to and engage in face-to-face interaction with their daughters than with their sons and to hold and touch their male infants longer than their female infants. On the basis of their investigation, Weinberg et al. (1999) conclude that "it remains unclear whether the gender differences in self-regulation and expressivity observed in this study are attributable to biological factors or socialization forces or, as is most likely, a combination of these factors" (p. 186).

Olson and her colleagues (2005) and Conway (2005) note that before age 4, boys and girls show few differences in disruptive, aggressive, or antisocial behavior. After age 4, however, discernible differences emerge. Boys are more likely than girls to be diagnosed with conduct disorders, and they demonstrate less ability to self-regulate (Hinshaw & Anderson, 1996). Although the reasons for these differences are not clear, Keenan and Shaw (1997) suggest that toddler and preschool-age girls are more mature than boys in developmental, cognitive, and language skills, which contribute to the control of aggression and impulsivity. Another strong possibility is that toddler and preschool-age girls appear to demonstrate more advanced effortful control than boys do (Olson et al., 2005).

EXECUTIVE FUNCTIONS

Closely related to self-regulation is the concept of **executive functions**, which refer to deliberate problem solving and the regulation of one's thoughts and actions (Tremblay, 2003; Zelazo, Carter, Reznick, & Frye, 1997). The concept is largely based on complex neuropsychological functions and includes such components as set shifting, interference control, inhibition planning, and working memory (Nigg & Huang-Pollock, 2003). Not only do executive functions recognize and inhibit inappropriate behavior, but they also direct focus and attention to external events and organize information for higher-order reasoning. They also prioritize the steps necessary for solving problems.

Children with good executive functions are well-organized, diligent, focused on completing tasks, and skillful in their approach to resolving problems (Buckner et al., 2003). They are adept at focusing attention, able to concentrate well, and flexible in their thinking. In short, they are apt to be resilient. On the other hand, several studies of school-age children and adolescents have demonstrated a relationship between different aspects of executive functions and antisocial behavior (Morgan & Lilienfeld, 2000; Nigg, Quamma, Greenberg, & Kusche, 1999; Séguin, Tremblay, Boulerice, Pihl, & Harden, 1999; Tremblay, 2003). Deficits in executive functions have also been shown for disruptive preschoolers (Hughes, Dunn, & White, 1998; Hughes, White, Sharpen, & Dunn, 2000; Speltz, DeKlyen, Calderon, Greenberg, & Fisher, 1999; Tremblay, 2003).

POSITIVE EMOTIONS

Emotions influence how we perceive and respond to people and events. They inspire us to take action or discourage us from doing so, and they contribute to or disrupt our interpersonal bonds (Lagattuta & Wellman, 2002). **Positive emotions** include joy, interest, contentment, pride, and love; all share the ability to build a person's enduring personal resources (Frederickson, 2001). **Negative emotions** include hostility, anger, anxiety, sadness, and despair. Positive emotions and positive beliefs seem to build psychological resilience. Even though highly resilient individuals may experience high levels of anxiety and frustration in stressful situations, their reliance on positive emotions to adapt to these conditions appears to be very effective in their long-term coping ability (Tugade & Frederickson, 2004).

One way people experience positive emotions in the face of adversity is by finding positive meaning in ordinary events and even within the adversity itself (Folkman & Moskowitz, 2000; Frederickson, 2001). The belief and the emotion are reciprocal. That is, not only does finding positive meaning trigger positive emotions, but positive emotions, because they broaden thinking, increase the likelihood of finding positive meaning in subsequent events (Frederickson, 2001). Individuals who experience more positive emotions become more resilient to adversity over time, as indexed by increases in broad-minded coping. Research shows that happy people experience and react to events and circumstances in relatively more positive and more adaptive ways (Lyubomirsky, 2001). Happier and more satisfied people are more likely to employ optimistic strategies in response to life's victories and defeats. That is, they tend to perceive and frame life circumstances in positive ways, to expect favorable life circumstances in the future, to feel control over outcomes, and to possess confidence about their abilities and skills.

Davidson (2000) hypothesizes that **affective style** is closely linked to resilience. Affective style "refers to consistent individual differences in emotional reactivity and regulation" (p. 1196). Davidson believes that the capacity for emotional self-regulation and rapid recovery after negative or stressful events is an important ingredient in resilience. In addition, resilient individuals have a heightened ability to learn from the experience of negative affect. These abilities appear to be partly determined by brain and nervous system structures and functioning and partly by the social environment and caregiving during development.

Negative emotions and poor emotional self-regulation, on the other hand, are associated with antisocial and delinquent behavior (Bates, 2000; Lahey & Waldman, 2003; H. N. Snyder et al., 2003). Children and adolescents who frequently overreact with anger when upset or frustrated often resort to high levels of aggressive or antisocial behavior. Violence is often the result of uncontrolled negative emotions in older children or adolescents. In addition, a chronically complaining person who perceives negative aspects to almost all situations is most likely to be socially isolated and not well liked by peers.

SELF-ESTEEM

Self-esteem refers to the positive beliefs that people have about their personality and qualities. Research findings have refuted the idea that a person's level of self-esteem is established in early childhood and remains stable throughout life (American Psychological Association, 1996). This is a critically important point, because most of us experience a lack of self-esteem at some point in our lives; during the transition to junior high school, high school, or college, for example, the self-esteem of many students plummets. Some no longer feel competent scholastically, and others fail to gain the support of their new peer group.

Self-esteem may be the most important trait in resilient adolescents (Davey, Eaker, & Walters, 2003), despite temporary lapses in this area. Youths with generally high self-esteem have positive feelings about themselves, their social environment, and their ability to deal with life's challenges and to control what happens to them. Individuals with a high self-esteem, a strong sense of purpose, and a positive outlook on life have a greater capacity to transcend life's challenges, as compared to that of less-optimistic people (Simon et al., 2005). More importantly for our purposes, they are far less likely to engage in antisocial and criminal activities throughout their lives.

Researchers have studied self-esteem from a variety of perspectives and have concluded that, contrary to intuition, individuals have not one but several self views, encompassing many domains of life. For example, a young girl may have low self-esteem within her neighborhood peer group but view herself very highly among her drama-group friends. Self-esteem is often affected by social comparisons (American Psychological Association, 1996). In our example, the neighborhood peer group may value participation in competitive sports very highly, but this girl may typically be the last to be picked for various teams. There is also a complex relationship of ethnicity and culture to self-esteem. Although one's ethnicity per se bears no natural relation to one's self-esteem, psychological factors associated with the experience as a member of a particular ethnic or cultural group can influence self-esteem.

MOTIVATIONAL FACTORS

Psychologists have long distinguished between intrinsic and extrinsic motivation. Intrinsic motivation refers to behavior prompted by pleasure and enjoyment, whereas extrinsic motivation refers to behavior encouraged by external pressures or constraints (Henderlong & Lepper, 2002). **Intrinsic motivation** prompts someone to do something because the activity is enjoyed for its own sake, such as solving a puzzle or painting. With extrinsic motivation, someone does something to receive rewards from others, such as a gift or money. Resilient children tend to demonstrate significant amounts of intrinsic motivation.

According to research on resilience, intrinsic motivation is most effectively encouraged and developed through praise that encourages competence and self-efficacy. Thus, parents and caretakers should make effective use of praise to encourage intrinsic motivation, but the key word here is *effective*–the kind and quality of the praise is very important (Henderlong & Lepper, 2002). The child should be praised for attempts at mastery over something, such as puzzle solving, language development, or reading. By contrast, praise that is based primarily on social comparisons—ranking a child or making comparisons to the performance or abilities of others—is problematic. "Tina, you're so much better at this than Jack is" is not an effective approach. Neither is "Good for you! You're the best in the class." In the classroom, an emphasis on social comparison necessitates that some children receive positive feedback while others receive negative feedback (Henderlong & Lepper, 2002). However, resilience researchers emphasize that praise based solely on social comparison may, in the long run, not be helpful to the children who are praised, because it may leave them unprepared for the eventual, inevitable negative feedback they are bound to experience at some time as they progress through school.

Intrinsic motivation appears in many forms, including a desire for academic success or, in sports, a desire to achieve one's personal best. In combination with other resilience factors, it can be a strong deterrent to antisocial behavior. For example, McKnight and Loper (2002) found that the most prominent resilience factors in adolescent girls at risk for delinquency were academic motivation, a desire to go to college, absence of substance abuse, feeling loved and wanted, a belief that teachers treat students fairly, parental trust of adolescent children, and religiosity. Other studies also

FIGURE 4–1   Factors That Help Develop Resilience
• Connections to competent, emotionally warm, caring adults   • Social experiences with supportive, prosocial peers   • Good language skills and cognitive ability   • Self-regulation skills   • Good interpersonal skills   • Good attention and focus skills   • Positive attitude and emotions   • Positive views of self and abilities   • Intrinsic motivation to be effective

have reported that students who perceived religion (or a belief in a higher power) as important were less likely to be delinquent. Religiosity provides some adolescents with a sense of purpose and thus has been associated with intrinsic motivation and resilience (Perkins, Luster, & Jank, 2002). Despite hard times, some adolescents draw on their faith for a sense of confidence that things will work out. Figure 4–1 lists numerous factors that contribute to resilience.

BIOLOGICAL FACTORS

The study of resilience from an individual perspective has focused almost exclusively on behavioral and psychological aspects and, until very recently, has not examined possible biological or genetic aspects or contributions (Curtis & Cicchetti, 2003). However, some researchers believe that biology and brain development can help us understand how and why resilience develops in some children but not in others. Curtis and Cicchetti (2003) view resilience as a dynamic process that is influenced by brain and neurological development and by interactions with the environment. "Biological factors influence psychological processes; however, social and psychological experiences also exert actions on the brain by feeding back upon it to modify gene expression and brain structure, function, and organization "(Curtis & Cicchetti, 2003, p. 777). Although guided and controlled to some extent by genetics, brain development is a malleable process strongly influenced by social and psychological exchanges the individual experiences by interacting with the environment. Basically, each individual follows a unique and "partly self-determined pathway of brain building that we believe may have important consequences for the development of resilient adaptation" (Curtis & Cicchetti, 2003, p. 777).

Kim-Cohen et al. (2004) examined genetic and environmental conditions as they might affect young children's resilience and vulnerability to poverty and its accompanying risks. The participants in the study were 1,116 5-year-old twin pairs. The results of the study supported the view that maternal warmth, stimulating activities, and children's outgoing temperament improved resilience in children exposed to socioeconomic deprivation. Note that maternal warmth and stimulating activities are both environmental protective factors, whereas temperament is an individual factor. The researchers report that approximately 46% of the variation in resilience was accounted for by genetic factors; the rest of the variation was attributed to environmental influences.

The relative influence of genetic, neurological, and biological factors in the development and maintenance of resilience is largely unknown at this point. Research on the relationship between resilience and genetic/biological aspects is still in its infancy, but many exciting discoveries will likely be forthcoming within the next few years.

ASSESSMENT OF RESILIENCE

How do we know whether a child or an adolescent is resilient and, if so, how resilient? Assessment of resilience has become a popular and influential topic in recent years. In her comprehensive review of the clinical and research literature on resilience and strength-based counseling, Elsie Smith (2006) recommends that assessments of resilience in youth examine the possession of eight core competencies. These elements provide an excellent beginning for evaluating, developing, and enhancing resilience in children, adolescents, and adults (Kaczmarek, 2006):

- Critical support in the family, school, and community
- Positive self-identity, self-esteem, and self-efficacy
- Academic achievement and school bonding skills
- Secure ethnic identity, with achievement of cultural competence and acceptance within at least one ethnic group
- Coping skills and self-control
- Communication and social competence skills
- A sense of purpose that is based on a positive outlook on life
- Religious faith (or an alternative value system) that provides moral guidance for one's actions and decision making

An increasing number of instruments have been developed to assess resilience within the school setting, and most incorporate some aspect of these competencies. The instruments include the *Behavioral and Emotional Rating Scale* (Epstein & Sharma, 1998), *California Healthy Kids Survey—Resilience Module* (Constantine, Benard, & Diaz, 1999), *Child and Adolescent Strengths Assessment Scale* (Lyons, Uziel-Miller, Reyes, & Sokol, 2000), and the *Strengths and Difficulties Questionnaire* (Goodman, 1999). The focus of these measures is to identify the positive attributes and protective factors possessed and experienced by each child or adolescent. The extent to which these instruments are being used in either school or clinical settings is not known.

Summary and Conclusions

Until recently, it was assumed that growing up under adverse and oppressive conditions would thwart human development; some theorists also assumed that such a situation would almost inevitably lead to delinquency and other antisocial behavior. We now recognize that even under highly adverse situations, children can be psychologically healthy and delinquency free. These children, who overcome the risk factors identified in the previous two chapters and demonstrate successful coping, are called resilient. There are numerous protective factors that may shield at-risk youngsters from the onset of antisocial behavior and help them develop resilience.

"Resilience is one of the most important and challenging terms in contemporary psychology. Understanding resilience is important because it may pave the way to intervention and prevention of undesired outcomes of adverse conditions" (von Eye & Schuster, 2000, p. 563).

Much of the contemporary research on resilience and delinquency can be traced to the longitudinal study conducted by Werner and her colleagues (1971) on Kauai, Hawaii. In that study involving 698 children, the researchers identified many of the risk factors that were discussed in Chapters 2 and 3, such as substandard living, hyperactivity, and unstable home environments. However, they also found a group of children exposed to those risk factors who had adapted positively and did not display antisocial conduct. These resilient children lived in families with extensive social support systems. The children themselves were described as affectionate, good natured, and engaging. Since then, numerous researchers have succeeded in identifying additional protective factors associated with resilient children. It appears that four broad factors are crucial: (1) connections to competent and caring adults (social environment), (2) cognitive and self-regulation skills, (3) a positive self-concept, and (4) motivation to be effective. Resilience can also be a feature of families and neighborhoods as well as of individuals.

Competent and caring adults are found in both the family and the surrounding neighborhood or community. Children who have at least one warm, loving parent or caretaker who sets firm limits and boundaries are far more likely to develop resilience than are those without such an adult in their lives. Quality of communication and a stimulating environment (e.g., being read to on a regular basis) are also important. Cultural experiences and the opportunity to participate in community activities are other aspects of this positive social environment. Thus, family traditions, celebrations, and group activities encourage resilience, even when many risk factors are present. In addition, positive relationships with prosocial peers encourage children to develop empathy and to feel a sense of belonging.

Intelligence has long been a controversial concept in delinquency literature. Early theories of delinquency suggested that antisocial juveniles were cognitively deficient, based on standardized IQ tests. More recently, multiple forms of intelligence have been recognized, and developmental psychologists, as well as educators and parents, recognize the limitations of IQ tests. Nevertheless, some aspects of cognitive development continue to be linked with delinquency and with the development of resilience. For example, resilient children, compared with those who do not display this characteristic, have more advanced language development skills and more complex cognitive constructs. This is not to say that resilient children are exceptional in these areas; rather, children who are *below average* on these measures are less likely to be resilient. Delayed language development, even at 6 to 18 months of age, has been predictive of later delinquency, suggesting that problems associated with communication deficits may follow some children through childhood and adolescence.

Resilient children also have good self-regulation skills and display positive emotions, such as joy, interest, or pride in a task completed. They are able to control their behavior to achieve positive responses from others.

The research on resilient children and adolescents has truly excited many developmental psychologists and mental health clinicians in recent years. The discovery that exposure to persistent and seemingly overwhelming risk factors does not necessarily consign a child to serious delinquency has led to shifts in delinquency research. For example, instruments to measure resilience in children have been developed, and core resilience competencies have been identified—for instance, a positive self-image, secure ethnic identity, academic achievement, a religious faith or other alternative that provides moral values. The identification of protective factors has contributed to prevention and intervention programs as well as to individual treatment offered by mental health professionals.

Key Terms and Concepts

affective style

effortful control

emotional intelligence

executive functions

family resilience

intelligence

intrinsic motivation

naming explosion

negative emotions

positive emotions

protective factors

resilience

self-esteem

self-regulation

spontaneity

triarchic theory of intelligence

vocabulary spurt

CHAPTER 5
CLASSICAL THEORIES OF JUVENILE DELINQUENCY AND THEIR UPDATES

❧

CHAPTER OBJECTIVES

◆ Introduce the early and most viable theories of juvenile delinquency

◆ Focus on those classical theories of delinquency that are most closely related to psychological perspectives

◆ Provide some recent updates on those theories

One of the main tasks of a criminologist is to try to "explain" crime rates or the criminal behavior of an adult or juvenile. Why are juvenile crime rates so high in X City? What could have prompted that person to commit such horrendous acts? Why are two siblings, raised in similar circumstances, so different in their behavior—one a model citizen and the other a felon? Criminologists from both sociological and psychological perspectives have proposed numerous theories in search of answers to these elusive questions and have devised scientific research methods to test the theories. Presumably, a strong theory—one with much empirical support—will help us to prevent crime as well as to change both society and the individuals who have engaged in crime.

In this chapter we review some of the dominant theories proposed, none of which is perfect. Each has engendered significant criticism as well as significant support. We focus on those that are called "classic" because they have stood the test of time in the criminological literature. A good theory rarely dies; it reappears over the years, often in modified form, but still retaining its basic assumptions.

In keeping with the theme of this book, we focus further on theories that have the clearest relationship to psychology, although many were proposed by sociologists or sociologically oriented criminologists. In other words, these theories rely considerably on psychological concepts such as learning, stress, frustration, or self-concept. Some are considered **structure-based theories** in the sense that they highlight the importance of a person's or a group's place in the social system, or the structure of society. Others are **process-based** in that they describe the process of becoming criminal. For the most part we omit conflict theories, which presume that abuses of power, power struggles between and among groups, and social ills such as discrimination and violation of human rights are the best explanations for the crime problem. We do this not because these theories are unimportant but because their nexus with psychology is not strong; they have not been sufficiently incorporated into psychological research.

SOCIAL STRUCTURE THEORIES

THE CONCEPT OF SOCIAL DISORGANIZATION

Social disorganization was and continues to be an elusive concept (Carey, 1975). Despite its ambiguity, it has been used extensively in the formulation of many theories of juvenile delinquency and has been often cited as an implicit or explicit cause of delinquency. The term *social disorganization* was probably first used by William Thomas in his classic book *The Polish Peasant in Europe and America*, which he coauthored with F. Znaniecki in 1927. The concept was later adapted and applied in the research of Clifford Shaw and Henry McKay, who, like Thomas, were part of the well-known Chicago School of Criminology.

To Thomas, **social disorganization** referred to a breakdown in the influence of existing rules of conduct on individual members of a group. It was the result of an erosion of standards and values as a particular subculture encountered a new and strange social environment to which it was ill adapted. With reference to the Polish culture that Thomas studied, social disorganization reflected the disrupting influence of an urban, industrial environment. The nuclear family's control over its members was greatly reduced, and children were thus deprived of an effective guide to behavior. Delinquency, then, was the result of ineffective socialization by the family; it was random and "wild" behavior without parental or social control. Reflecting Thomas's interest in psychological principles, delinquency was also seen as behavior instigated by temperamental tendencies and swayed by momentary moods (Finestone, 1976).

From his observations of the Polish peasant family, as well as other families he studied, Thomas concluded that social disorganization in the broader subculture had led to decreased control of the family unit over children's behavior. However, disorganization was not inevitable when old world values clashed with those of the new world; it occurred only if the old world subculture lost its force with exposure to the American urban environment. If the subculture could retain its identity, it could achieve the best of both worlds. If not, delinquency within the subculture was one by-product of this decrease in social control. This refusal to consider disorganization and delinquency inevitable within a subculture is reflected today in many programs and approaches that seek to strengthen and recognize a child's cultural background.

SHAW AND McKAY

Shortly after Thomas's discussion of social disorganization, Clifford Shaw and Henry McKay became keenly interested in the **ecological distribution of delinquency** in Chicago. In a report written for the 1929 Illinois Crime Survey, Shaw, McKay, and their colleagues offered a comprehensive interpretation of the nature of the delinquency problem, its causes, and the shortcomings of existing treatment methods, which were psychologically based and typically considered delinquents intellectually or emotionally flawed. Delinquency, they declared, was clearly a product of the social situation. Its roots could be found in community characteristics, the family situation, and peer companionship, including gang membership.

Using an elaborate system for plotting the home addresses of over 100,000 juveniles who had been processed by the Juvenile Court of Cook County between 1900 and

1927, the Shaw group found that the regions having the highest rates of delinquency corresponded roughly to a theory of concentric zones, which had been proposed by Park and Burgess, with McKenzie (1928). Specifically, areas of high delinquency were characterized by deteriorating buildings, widespread poverty, and residences interspersed with industry and commerce. These areas not only had the highest rates of delinquency, but the highest rates of adult crime as well.

Expanding on Park and Burgess's ideas, Shaw and his colleagues posited that criminal adults were deviant models for the young and that delinquency was especially high in areas with high concentrations of recent immigrants. As the economic status of these immigrants improved, they often moved to more attractive outlying regions. And once a family moved to better surroundings, the children apparently did not continue their previous behavior, since rates of delinquency in the new areas were not high. However, the "hot beds" of delinquency—areas of high poverty—remained the same. This recurring pattern of high delinquency even in areas of high resident mobility suggested to Shaw and McKay that delinquency was not due primarily to cultural or ethnic background or to individual pathology, but rather to a "delinquency tradition" transmitted from older to younger youths within a specific geographical area, year after year.

Shaw and McKay compared features of two living areas: the "better" residential areas and the rent areas where residential mobility was high. In the better residential neighborhoods, they found similarities in attitudes among families. These families adopted conventional values, such as the desirability of a general health program, education, and the promotion of constructive use of leisure time. There were also subtle pressures throughout the community to keep the children engaged in conventional activities, as well as some blatant condemnation directed at those who violated the community's standards of conduct. Furthermore, the youth were generally insulated from direct contact with deviant forms of behavior engaged in by older models. In other words, the delinquency tradition was absent. By contrast, in sections with high delinquency rates, attitudes and values varied widely. Although families may have valued health and education, because of economic pressures, these were not easily attainable. Delinquent and adult criminal models abounded, however.

Shaw and McKay believed that many of the relationships between delinquency and social factors were too complex to be unraveled strictly by statistical data, however. Clearly, not all youths living in delinquency-prone areas became delinquent, and for those who did, the developmental path was often different from person to person. Shaw, in particular, became an advocate of the **life-history method**, which was a way of recording detailed information about a person's life. Therefore, in addition to compiling maps and official data, Shaw and his colleagues asked some youths—almost invariably boys—to tell about various experiences of their lives. The information was often reported in a youth's own words in the form of an autobiography or a diary, or it was presented in the format of an interview. According to Shaw and McKay (1942), the life-history or own-story method revealed important information on several aspects of delinquent behavior: (a) the point of view of the delinquent, (b) the social and cultural situation within which he lived, and (c) the relevant experiences in his life that had an extended impact on his point of view. Three classic books by Shaw illustrate the life-history method: *The Jack-Roller: A Delinquent Boy's Own Story* (1930), *The Natural History of a Delinquent Career* (1931), and *Brothers in Crime* (1938), the last written with McKay and James F. McDonald.

The Jack-Roller, an example of qualitative research, is perhaps one of the best-known case studies in criminology. (*Jack-roller* was the term for a person who robbed intoxicated persons or individuals sleeping on city streets.) The book is biographical of "Stanley," an adolescent boy who grew up in a poor neighborhood near the Chicago stockyards. Interestingly, Stanley's story is continued in the book *The Jack-Roller at Seventy*, written by Jon Snodgrass (1982). The author located Stanley more than 50 years after his young life had been chronicled by Shaw. Stanley had continued his life on the margins of society, holding some menial jobs and being incarcerated periodically for property offenses.

The life-history approach easily falls prey to criticisms about objectivity, particularly because the researcher chooses which events to recount and how to tell them. For the most part, the work of the Chicago School did not include middle- or upper-class delinquents; Shaw's case studies focused on delinquents residing in areas characterized by social disorganization. Nor did he include life histories of youths who did not become delinquent but yet were exposed to many of the same life events. Nevertheless, despite questions about its ability to produce generalizable data, the life history can provide valuable insights into how particular individuals perceive and mentally construct their worlds.

The extensive and carefully accumulated data from Shaw and McKay supported Park and Burgess's earlier conclusions that the distribution of juvenile delinquency corresponded to the physical layout and social organization of the American city. Delinquency, the researchers found, was concentrated near the center of the city, where physical deterioration and social disorganization were most in evidence. Dilapidated housing, proximity to railroad yards, crowded neighborhoods, and industry characterized the physical structure. Adult crime, poverty, disease, suicide, mental disorders, and family instability characterized the social disorganization element. As one moved away from the city's core, the rate of delinquency decreased until it almost vanished in the residential areas with better physical environments and less social disorganization.

The idea that a disorganized social environment is conducive to crime—particularly violent crime and property crimes like burglary and vandalism—is a core feature of modern criminology theories that are updates of the ecological approaches that came out of the Chicago School. There has been much recent research on the determinants of community differences in crime rates: some communities are more criminogenic than others, and some are even said to have "criminal careers." Social disorganization theories dominate the explanations for these differences (Agnew, 1999). Research by Delbert Elliott (Elliott et al., 1996), Robert Sampson (Sampson, Raudenbush, & Earls, 1997), and William Wilson (Wilson, 1996) clearly illustrate this focus, which has led in turn to delinquency prevention programs that focus on providing increased resources to residents of socially disorganized communities.

STRAIN AND ANOMIE THEORIES

Another group of theories emphasizes the effects of social structure without focusing on social disorganization. Instead, these theories focus on the strain that is produced by society's values. Strain theories were initially applied predominantly to crime committed in lower-class environments—and by members of the lower-socioeconomic class.

More recently, these theories have been adapted to explain criminal behavior across a range of social classes.

MERTON'S STRAIN THEORY

Robert Merton (1938), considered one of the foremost sociological theorists in criminology, was drawn to the concept of **anomie** first described by the French sociologist Emile Durkheim. Durkheim believed that humans are born with intense biological desires that must be held in check by society. He was convinced that people are incapable of controlling or limiting their biological needs without society's help and controls; without social controls, an individual's desires expand until he or she aspires to everything and is satisfied with nothing. Thus, when social controls are weak or nonexistent, individual needs run rampant, resulting in chaos and normlessness in a given society. Durkheim labeled this state of affairs *anomie*, which was a feature of society, not of an individual.

While Merton liked some aspects of the concept of anomie, he rejected Durkheim's view of human nature. He did not accept the view that people are driven by innate impulses and desires but believed that one's wants and goals in life are acquired as a result of living in a given society. Thus, culture, not biology, determines an individual's motivation; culture sets the individual's goals and designates the appropriate means of achieving them. Merton posited that deviance (including crime and delinquency) occurs when there is a discrepancy between the values and goals cherished by a society and the legitimate means of reaching these cultural goals. If a society communicates to its members that the accumulation of wealth is paramount but offers few acceptable ways for most people to achieve it, strain would develop. Groups experiencing this strain would be inclined to violate norms and thus contribute to anomie.

Probably ever mindful of his own childhood experiences in an economically deprived neighborhood, Merton was disenchanted with American culture, its emphasis on economic success, and its persuasive communication that all the symbols representing wealth should be valued. Merton believed that while American society myopically and fanatically pushed economic success, it failed to put much emphasis on the norms regulating the means to reach that goal. In short, he found a troubling discrepancy in American society between cultural goals and the available means for reaching these goals. For some who accepted the importance of wealth, only illegitimate conduct could bring economic success.

One of the more interesting and most discussed aspects of Merton's strain theory was his suggestion that individuals differed in their acceptance of society's view of what is important and the means for reaching what is important. According to Merton, there were five possible strategies, or **modes of adaptation**, to strain: conformity, retreatism, ritualism, rebellion, and innovation.

Merton believed that most individuals accept, and therefore conform to, both the goals advocated by society (e.g., wealth, status) and the means to achieve them (e.g., hard work, education). Merton suggested that the stability and continuity of society would be threatened if this conformity did not occur. Conformity, then, is the rule rather than the exception. Retreatism, the rejection of both goals and means, is the least common strategy. Individuals who rely on this form of adaptation are considered "drop-outs" within a given society. Merton believed that the emotionally disturbed, vagrants, alcoholics, and drug addicts all illustrate retreatism. Ritualism occurs when a person accepts the means but rejects the goals because they are beyond reach. In Merton's view, many law-abiding citizens go through the motions: they work hard but believe that certain goal attainment is impossible. Rebellion occurs when a person rejects both the means and the goals of the social mainstream and replaces them with new ones. "Rebels" deviate from the social mainstream perspective and try to introduce a new social order. Ecoterrorists and political terrorists are good illustrations of this mode of adaptation.

The fifth mode of adaptation, innovation, represents individuals who have accepted the cultural emphasis on success, but not the prescribed norms for reaching it. An innovative person rejects institutional or approved practices but retains the culturally induced goals. This approach is most likely to occur when a person has little access to conventional means for attaining such success. Innovative individuals, therefore, adopt unapproved means, such as theft, burglary, or robbery.

For the most part, Merton's theory is considered a better explanation of property offenses and substance abuse than of violent offenses like aggravated assault or rape. However, it can be argued that violence often occurs as a result of anger and frustration over a lack of opportunity to achieve the American dream. Persons who engage in violence are angry about being blocked from attaining widely prized goals by the existing structure of society. In effect, angry, frustrated individuals can constitute any of the modes of adaptation outlined by Merton and may express these emotions through violent actions.

Merton's theory did not focus on juveniles, but in the 1950s and 1960s other theorists (e.g., Cohen, 1955; Cloward & Ohlin, 1960) and their followers used versions of strain theory to do just that, specifically studying juvenile gangs. Albert Cohen suggested that juveniles, particularly boys, learned delinquent behaviors from one another and sought peer approval. Their strain was achieving status among their peers. Cloward and Ohlin proposed a **differential opportunity theory**, which reflected the frustrations faced by juveniles when their avenues to socially valued goals were blocked. Thus, they adopted illegitimate means to achieve their goals. Cloward and Ohlin also identified different gang subcultures based on their members' desired goals and the forms of antisocial behavior they adopted.

AGNEW'S GENERAL STRAIN THEORY

With few exceptions, empirical support for traditional strain theory and its early modifications has not been strong. As alternative theories emerged, interest in strain theory as an explanation of crime and delinquency waned (Paternoster & Mazerolle, 1994). In the 1960s, for example, criminologists became increasingly uncomfortable about supporting a theory that focused almost exclusively on lower-class offending and seemingly ignored crimes committed by the economically privileged. In response to this weakness as well as to the lack of research support for the theory, Robert Agnew (1992) developed a more comprehensive version called **general strain theory** (GST), which is an extremely well-cited theory in criminology today.

Agnew believed that traditional strain theory was too narrow in its conceptualization of the sources of strain. Like Merton's strain theory, GST maintains that strain or stress is a major source of criminal motivation (Agnew, 1999). However, GST builds on previous strain theories in four ways. First, it identifies several new categories of strain, including the loss of positive stimuli (e.g., loss of a romantic partner, death of a friend), the presentation of negative stimuli (e.g., physical assaults, verbal insults), and new categories of goal blockage (Agnew, 2001). Second, Agnew offers a more general explanation of criminal activity among all groups in society rather than restricting his views to lower-class or class-based crime. Third, GST posits that exposure to strain often produces negative emotional states, such as anger. If the strain engenders these angry emotional states, the tendency to engage in delinquent behavior increases (Mazerolle, Piquero, & Capowich, 2003). And fourth, Agnew maintains that not all strain is equally disagreeable. Strain, he argues, varies in its magnitude (how much discomfort is inflicted), its recency (recent events are more stressful and unpleasant than more distant ones), its duration (strain experienced over longer periods is more stressful), and its clustering (many stressful events experienced over a short period of time are more unpleasant (Pasternoster & Mazerolle, 1994).

According to Agnew (1992), strain refers to "relationships in which others are not treating the individual as he or she would like to be treated" (p. 48). Strain is most likely to lead to crime when individuals lack the skills and resources to cope with the strain in a legitimate manner. In order to be more sensitive to individual differences in interpretations of and reactions to strain, Agnew (2001) subdivides strain into two major categories: objective and subjective. Objective strains "refer to events or conditions that are disliked by most members of a given group" (Agnew, 2001, p. 320). Therefore, persons experiencing objective strain are being subjected to an event or condition that is usually disliked by most members of their group. Examples include physical and verbal assaults, lack of adequate food and shelter, limited job opportunities, and prejudice. Subjective strains, on the other hand, refer to "events or conditions that are disliked by the people who are experiencing (or have experienced) them" (Agnew, 2001, p. 321). Subjective strains involve specific events or conditions that a *particular* individual interprets as a strain or a stressor. This approach recognizes that people differ in their expectations and interpretations of events or conditions. For example, people differ in how they evaluate such events and circumstances as a move to a new home, a family wedding, or poverty.

According to Agnew, certain types of strain, either objective or subjective, are more likely to result in crime than other types are. Strains are most likely to result in crime when they (a) are seen as unjust, (2) are seen as high in magnitude, (3) are associated with low social control, and (4) create some pressure or incentive to engage in criminal coping. In the context of delinquency, low social control refers largely to parenting styles, such as erratic parental discipline, inadequate parental monitoring, or parental rejection. However, it may also refer to lack of social support for effective parenting, such as budget cuts for needed social service programs in a community.

GST argues that strains or stressors—particularly subjective strains—increase the likelihood of negative emotions, like anger and frustration (Agnew, 2001). These negative emotional states create pressures to take action, with one of the prominent actions being crime and delinquency. Anger, according to GST, is a critical component in the processes because it increases perceived injury and generates the need for adaptive responses, including delinquency and crime (Mazerolle et al., 2003).

Not all individuals who experience strain engage in delinquent behavior. Many find or have the resources to cope and adapt to the strain or stress. However, when certain factors are present (e.g., exposure to deviant peers, weak moral constraints against delinquent conduct), the probabilities increase that a child is likely to become delinquent. In what can be considered a radical departure from traditional strain theory, Agnew (1992) further suggests that delinquent behavior is more likely in some children because of certain temperamental dispositions, such as problems with self-control and impulsivity, while in other children strain does not result in delinquency because stress and consequent negative affective states can be effectively handled or managed by the child (Paternoster & Mazerolle, 1994).

More recently, Agnew (2003) has proposed an "integrated strain theory" to explain the well-known adolescent peak of delinquent or criminal offending. Official crime data have continually shown that property crimes peak at around age 16 and then show a sharp drop after age 20. As age increases, the property crime arrest rate shows a continual decline. As an explanation for the increase and peak, strain theories in general argue that adolescents develop an increased desire for adult privileges but are unable to obtain such privileges through legitimate channels (Agnew, 2003). They are thought to desire such privileges because of biological changes associated with puberty, cognitive changes that make adolescents more aware of and feel more entitled to adult privileges, and the desire for popularity in a peer-oriented social world (Agnew, 2003). However, adolescents are often denied such privileges and, in their frustration, resort to delinquent and antisocial behaviors as a way to achieve autonomy, enhance status, obtain money, punish those who deny them privileges, and adapt to stressors of imposed restrictions. The subsequent decline in offending is believed to occur because the adolescents have matured, both biologically and cognitively, and have gained more opportunities to attain the goals they have desired.

Agnew takes a slightly different tack in explaining the adolescent peak in property offending. He suggests that adolescents are given some, but not all, of the privileges and responsibilities of adults. This granting of only some adult privileges and responsibilities has five important effects on juvenile offending: It (1) reduces parental supervision and monitoring; (2) increases social, academic, and occupational demands; (3) encourages participation in a larger, more diverse, peer-oriented social world; (4) increases the desire for even more adult privileges; and (5) increases the opportunity to participate in criminal activity.

SOCIAL LEARNING THEORIES

Social learning theories comprise a large group of theories that are based on the common assumption that behavior, including delinquent behavior, is learned. The process of that learning is what differentiates one theory from another. The many variants of social learning theory can be divided into two categories: those based on social reinforcement, derived from principles articulated by Burrhus Frederick (B. F.) Skinner, and those based on social imitation. However, both positions have their roots in classical behaviorism, as articulated by John B. Watson and later by Skinner. Gerwirtz (1961) and Bijou and Baer (1961) adapted Skinner's classical behaviorism to emphasize the influence of social reinforcement on child development, especially prosocial and deviant behavior. The social imitation school of thought was led by

Albert Bandura and Richard Walters (1963), who emphasized—as Baldwin had earlier—the important element of modeling the behavior of significant others in the social environment.

Social learning theory can be traced as far back as the late nineteenth century to the writings of child psychologist James Mark Baldwin and social psychologist Gabriel Tarde. The fundamental principle of social learning is that people learn their behavior from their social environment: parents, peers, teachers, and significant others. Theories based on social reinforcement and social imitation were stated most explicitly by psychologists during the early 1960s (Cairns, 1983), but they were also implicit in the work of sociologist Edwin Sutherland, whose theory began with the proposition that all criminal behavior is learned. (We discuss Sutherland's theory later in this section.) Today, no single discipline can claim exclusive guardianship of the basic ideas of social learning; theorists in both psychologically based and sociologically based criminology have tried to reformulate or expand various aspects of earlier approaches. All of these social learning theorists see humans as active problem solvers who perceive, encode, interpret, and make decisions on the basis on what their environment has to offer. To understand delinquency, social learning theorists tell us we must examine perceptions, thoughts, expectancies, competencies, and values.

REINFORCEMENT PRINCIPLES

All reinforcement theories are based on the work of B. F. Skinner, who could be called the single most influential psychologist in the United States in the twentieth century. Skinner believed that all human behavior is predictable and thus ultimately can be controlled. Environmental, or external, stimuli are the primary, if not the sole, determinants of that behavior. Skinner accepted the basic premise of classical conditioning as outlined by the psychologist Ivan Pavlov: a stimulus elicits a response (sometimes called S-R psychology). All students in general psychology classes are told of Pavlov's experiments with dogs: Repeated exposures to a stimulus (bell) followed by food "taught" the dogs to salivate at the sound of the bell. Skinner, however, focused on the concept of reinforcement, believing that humans would learn to respond to stimuli only if they were rewarded or could avoid punishment—in other words, if they were reinforced.

Skinner was a strong situationist; he believed that individuals have no control or self-determination. Independent thought and free will are myths that humans use to delude themselves into thinking that they are under their own control. In truth, both animals and humans react, like complicated robots, to their environments. For Skinner, crime and delinquency are exclusively the result of forces within the environment and are not due to any personal predisposition or personality trait.

If people do things simply to get rewards and avoid punishment, they are operating on their environment for this purpose; thus, Skinner's theory is referred to as *operant conditioning*. Skinner referred to the rewards as **reinforcements**, defined as anything that increases the probability of future responding. In **positive reinforcement**, one gains something desired as a consequence of certain behavior. Nicole disciplines herself to train faithfully for the track team and is rewarded with a varsity position. In **negative reinforcement**, one avoids an unpleasant event, or stimulus, as a consequence of certain behavior. Fred successfully avoids what he anticipates will be an unpleasant day at school by feigning illness. The behaviors of both Nicole and Fred—hard training and feigning illness—were reinforced and thus are likely to be used again, in one case to gain a reward and in the other to avoid an aversive situation.

Negative reinforcement must be distinguished from punishment and extinction. In **punishment**, a person receives noxious or painful stimuli as a consequence of something he or she has done. In **extinction**, a person receives nothing, neither reinforcement nor pain. Skinner argues that punishment is an ineffective way to eliminate or change behavior, because it merely suppresses the behavior temporarily. Extinction is a far better procedure for the elimination or alteration of behavior. Once a person learns that a particular behavior brings no reinforcement, that behavior will drop out of the repertoire of possible responses for that set of circumstances. Once 6-year-old Darryl realizes that temper tantrums at the checkout counter of the local supermarket do not gain the anticipated chewing gum, the behavior should drop out of his response pattern.

The premise that operant conditioning is the basis of delinquency is deceptively simple: Delinquent behavior is learned behavior, which has been learned through the principles of operant conditioning. It is behavior that brings rewards for the respondent. According to Skinner, human beings are born neutral, neither bad nor good. Culture, society, peers, parents, and the whole social environment reward and shape our behavior. Delinquent behavior is the result of reinforcement—both positive and negative—received from the social environment.

IMITATIONAL ASPECTS

The term *social learning* reflects the theory's strong assumption that we learn primarily by observing and listening to people around us—our social environment. In fact, social learning theorists believe that the social environment is the most important factor in the acquisition of most human behavior. Like Skinner, they accept the necessity of reinforcement for the maintenance of behavior. Delinquent behavior, for example, may be initially acquired through association and observation; however, whether or not it is maintained will depend primarily on reinforcement for the behavior.

According to Albert Bandura (1977), an individual can acquire behavior simply by watching others in action, as opposed to actually receiving direct reinforcement. Bandura calls this process **observational learning**, or **modeling**. Thus, Bandura belongs to the social imitation variety of social learning. He contends that much of our behavior is initially acquired by watching others, who are our models. For example, children may learn how to shoot a gun by imitating TV characters. They may rehearse and fine-tune this behavioral pattern by practicing with toy guns. They then watch the models again for confirmation about their behavior, which is likely to be maintained if peers also play with guns and reinforce one another for doing so. Some children may learn to be aggressive by modeling the aggressive behavior of antisocial peers.

According to Bandura, the more respected the models, the greater their impact on behavior. Relevant models include parents, teachers, siblings, friends, and peers, as well as symbolic models like literary characters or, more likely, media heroes. Rock stars, entertainment celebrities, and famous athletes are modeled by many young people, which is one reason our society is exposed to so many public figures touting everything from cosmetics to a drug-free life.

Reinforcement also has its place in Bandura's version of social learning. The observed behavior of the model is more likely to be imitated if the observer thinks the model is rewarded for the behavior. Conversely, a model is less likely to be imitated if the model is punished. Bandura believes that once a person has made the decision to use a newly acquired behavior, whether it is actually performed and maintained will depend on the situation and the expectancies for potential gain (reinforcement). This gain may come from the outside in the form of praise from others or perhaps financial profit or from within in the form of self-satisfaction.

Television, the Mass Media, and Violence

An ever-present source of aggressive models is television. Surveys show that approximately 98% of households in the United States have television and that many of these homes have multiple sets (Donnerstein, Slaby, & Eron, 1994; Huston, Donnerstein, Fairchild, Feshbach, Katz, & Muray, 1992). Furthermore, in homes with television, watching averaged about 28 hours per week for children aged 2 to 11 years and 23 hours for teens. Television viewing occupies more time for children than any other non-school activity. More importantly, many of the poorest and potentially most vulnerable children are the heaviest viewers of television because of a lack of alternative activities (Donnerstein et al., 1994; Kuby & Csikszentmihalyi, 1990). Research has found that by the end of elementary school, the average child has watched over 8,000 TV murders and 100,000 other violent acts (Huston et al., 1992). By the time youth near the end of their teen years, it is estimated that they have viewed over 200,000 violent acts in the media. And today, rapidly developing technologies allow individuals to carry their media with them in the form of cell phones, portable DVD players, and iPods.

Does all of this exposure to various media influence the development of aggressive and violent behavior in children and adolescents? Are children likely to model the violence they witness? Many years ago, Bandura (1965) conducted what is now considered a classic study in psychology: 66 nursery school children were divided into three groups and shown one of three 5-minute films. All three films depicted an adult verbally and physically assaulting a BoBo, a large inflatable doll with a sand base—a common household toy in the 1950s and early 1960s. One group saw the adult model being rewarded with candy and a soft drink after displaying the aggressive behavior. A second group observed the model being spanked and reprimanded verbally. A third group witnessed a situation in which the model received neither punishment nor reward.

After the children saw the film, they were permitted to free-play for 10 minutes in a playroom of toys, including a BoBo doll. The group that had witnessed the adult model being rewarded for aggressive behavior exhibited more aggression than the other two groups. In addition, boys were more aggressive than girls. The group that saw the adult model being punished exhibited the lowest amount of aggression in the playroom.

Bandura's subsequent research, which included variations on this basic study design, consistently demonstrated this modeling effect. Furthermore, numerous follow-up studies not only replicated his findings but also suggested that media violence may have a strong influence on real-life violence in many situations (Baron, 1977).

The relationship between viewing aggression and committing violent acts is a complicated one and is certainly dependent upon other factors that may also predispose a child to violence (e.g., conduct disorders, temperament, victimization). However, social learning theorists believe that, as some children become less popular at school with peers and teachers and begin to fail academically, they begin to drop out of the school scene and become more regular viewers and users of television and other media. Researchers have found that aggressive children do watch television more regularly than nonaggressive children, do watch more media violence, do identify more with violent characters, and do believe more that the violence they observe reflects real life (Huesmann, 1988; Huesmann & Eron, 1986).

In general, experimental studies clearly reveal that television violence has a significant impact on the frequency and type of aggressive and antisocial behavior expressed by some adults and some children. Repeatedly, numerous well-designed research projects over the past 25 years have found that the mass media are significant contributors to the aggressive and antisocial attitudes of many children, adolescents, and adults (Donnerstein et al., 1994; Surgeon General, 1972; National Institute of Mental Health, 1982; Huston et al., 1992).

Repeated exposure to violence on television may also habituate more-frequent viewers to violence and distort their perception of the world. More-frequent television viewers respond to violence with less physiological arousal than do less-frequent viewers, suggesting that repeated exposure has desensitized them to violent effects. Furthermore, television is heavily populated with villainous and unscrupulous people, portrayals that may give more-frequent viewers a jaded view of the world. There is some evidence that more-frequent viewers, compared to less-frequent viewers, are less trustful of others and overestimate their chances of being criminally victimized (Gerbner & Gross, 1976).

Although television and the mass media do not directly cause aggression and violence, they contribute to these behaviors by reinforcing certain values and beliefs. Television and the media show people being aggressive and violent and being rewarded. They also demonstrate that aggressive behavior is a quick and easy way to solve problems.

DIFFERENTIAL ASSOCIATION THEORY

Edwin H. Sutherland is regarded by many scholars and students as one of the great masters of theory in American criminology. In some circles, he is considered the Father of Criminology. Sutherland's major contributions include both the earliest published research on white collar crime and a comprehensive statement on the formation of crime known as differential association theory. Sutherland stated his own general theory in a series of propositions that were designed to have universal application across culture and time. Sutherland did not believe it was useful to distinguish between juvenile and adult criminal conduct; he believed juvenile and adult offenders followed the same principles of development. Both juvenile and adult criminal behavior, he believed, was learned by exposure to events and persons conducive to the development of antisocial action.

Sutherland strongly endorsed the idea that criminal behavior is learned, not inherited, and is not due to psychopathology. Criminal behavior is learned in interactions with other persons. The social influences of associations with others dictate what one believes and does, according to Sutherland. The decision-making ability, thoughts, and unique cognitive features of an individual were irrelevant to Sutherland: "If a person is self-determinative, science is impossible and criminal behavior cannot be explained" (Sutherland, 1973, p. 43).

Sutherland called his theory the **differential association theory**. It was originally set forth in seven propositions but was later refined and extended to nine propositions. The core of the theory can be found in Proposition 6: "A person becomes delinquent because of an excess of definitions favorable to violations of law over definitions unfavorable to violation of law. This is the principle of differential association" (Sutherland & Cressey, 1974). The term *association* signifies the critical importance that intimate contacts with others have in determining one's behavior. The term *differential* was introduced to emphasize the importance of a ratio, specifically of favorable to unfavorable *definitions* that result from these associations. Some criminologists prefer to conceive of the definitions as messages that are received, some favorable to violating the law and some unfavorable. For example, a father telling his son, "There's a sucker in every crowd," is giving a message that is favorable to law violation; "treat others as you would like to be treated" is a message unfavorable to law violation.

Sutherland's theory suggests that adolescents become delinquents or adults become criminals because their pro–law violating definitions outnumber their anti–law violating definitions. Sutherland did not believe that persons engage in criminal conduct simply because they are exposed to criminal behavior or to ideas that promote it. Individuals become criminals because of an overabundance of such exposure. If the ratio is in reverse (in favor of noncriminal activity), the person will not be criminal. It is important to note that Sutherland's theory does not suggest that persons become delinquent simply because of excessive associations with delinquents. The critical aspect lies in the *definitions* (or internalized messages) received from those associations. Adolescents can get procriminal definitions—and thus learn antisocial conduct— from persons who are not criminals or delinquents (even from well-meaning parents) and can likewise learn anticriminal patterns from criminals and hard-core delinquents. Parents may verbalize that it is wrong to break the law but may display a reckless disregard for the property of others. On the other hand, an individual labeled "delinquent" may demonstrate honesty and integrity in most situations and may generally be a "good" model except for his rare transgressions.

As Sutherland refined his theory, he also added a level of complexity that made the theory very difficult to test. He proposed that the definitions vary in their frequency, duration, intensity, and priority. Frequency and duration are self-explanatory, although still not easy to measure. Intensity refers to the prestige and significance of the models with which one associates; the more significant the models, the more intense the impact of the definitions (or messages) they transmit. Priority refers to Sutherland's belief that behavior learned in early childhood has more impact on a person's overall conduct than does behavior learned later in life. Since Sutherland had already stressed the importance of learning in small, intimate groups, this suggests that definitions obtained in early childhood and in the family circle are crucial.

To illustrate the complexity of Sutherland's theory, consider the case of 6-year-old Preston, who had an excess of definitions favorable to fire-setting behavior. For example, an older brother is a fire-setter, and Preston's best friend taught him to build small forts with matches and then burn them down. Presumably, Preston would learn more from these associations than from associations with the firefighter who visited his classroom last week. But to test Sutherland's theory, we would have to be able to detect and assess Preston's definitions. Do we try to measure those that have to do with law breaking in general but not fire setting in particular? We could easily complicate this scenario by supposing that Preston's uncle, to whom he has recently been introduced and whom he idolizes, happens to be a firefighter. Can this new association, providing intense definitions unfavorable to fire setting, outweigh the earlier, frequent, intense definitions? What appeared to be intuitively sensible has now become a Gordian knot.

Critics have identified many vague areas in Sutherland's theory. Its lack of clarity and precision makes empirical investigations nearly impossible to carry out, although researchers have attempted to test it. Even the later spokesperson for the theory, Donald R. Cressey (1960), admitted that "the current statement of the theory of differential association is neither precise nor clear" (p. 3). Although the proposition that criminal behavior is learned has appeal, researchers have been at a loss to measure frequency, duration, intensity, and priority of definitions. Furthermore, the theory presents the individual as a passive recipient of definitions received from associations with others. Later social learning theorists decided that a more active process was at work, prompting them to develop a role for reinforcement.

DIFFERENTIAL ASSOCIATION–REINFORCEMENT THEORY

When psychologists discuss social learning theory, they invariably cite Albert Bandura and Julian Rotter. When sociologists and sociologically oriented criminologists discuss social learning theory, they generally cite Ronald Akers (1977, 1985; Burgess & Akers, 1966). Akers proposed a social learning theory of deviance that tries to integrate core ingredients of Skinnerian behaviorism, the social learning theory outlined by Bandura, and the differential association theory of Edwin Sutherland. Akers called his theory **differential association–reinforcement** (DAR). He postulates that people learn to commit deviant acts through experiences with significant others.

Burgess and Akers (1966) and ultimately Akers alone (1977, 1985) tried to correct some of the problems other researchers and theorists had identified in Sutherland's approach by reformulating the differential association theory. Akers proposed that most deviant behavior is learned according to principles outlined in classical behaviorism. Furthermore, the strength of the deviant behavior is a direct function of the amount, frequency, and probability of reinforcement the individual has experienced by performing the behavior in the past. The reinforcement may be positive or negative, in the Skinnerian meanings of the terms.

Critical to the Akers position is the role played by social reinforcement, in contrast to other forms of reinforcement: "Most of the learning relevant to deviant behavior is the result of social interactions or exchanges in which the words, responses, presence, and behavior of other persons make reinforcers available, and provide the setting for reinforcement" (Akers, 1977, p. 47). It is important to note that most of these social reinforcements are symbolic; very often they are verbal rewards for participating in or for agreeing with group norms and expectations. For example, Dalton longs for acceptance by his deviant peers. He burglarizes his neighbor's home, a behavior in accordance with their norms, and is rewarded by their admiration and by entry into their social circle.

Deviant behavior, then, is most likely to develop as a result of social reinforcement given by significant others, usually within one's peer group. The group first adopts normative definitions about what conduct is good or bad, right or wrong, justified or unjustified. These normative definitions become internal, cognitive guides to what is appropriate and will most likely be reinforced by the group. In this sense, normative definitions operate as discriminative stimuli—social signals transmitted by subcultural or peer groups to indicate whether certain kinds of behavior will be rewarded or punished within a particular social context.

According to Akers, two classes of discriminative stimuli operate in promoting deviant behavior. First, **positive discriminative stimuli** are the signals (verbal and nonverbal) that communicate appropriate behaviors, as determined by the subgroup. Not surprisingly, positive discriminative stimuli follow the principle of positive reinforcement: the individual engaging in them gains social rewards from the group. Akers' second type, **neutralizing**, or **justifying, discriminative stimuli**, neutralize society's warnings that certain behaviors are inappropriate or unlawful. According to Akers, they "make the behavior, which others condemn and which the person himself may initially define as bad, seem all right, justified, excusable, necessary, the lesser of two evils, or not 'really' deviant after all" (Akers, 1977, p. 521). Statements like "Society gave us a bum rap," "Cops are on the take; we just want our fair share," or "She deserved it" reflect the influence of neutralizing stimuli.

The more that people define their behavior as positive or justified, the more likely they are to engage in it. If the deviant activity (as defined by society at large) has been reinforced more than the conforming behavior (also defined by society) and if it has been justified, it is likely that the deviant behavior will be maintained. In essence, behavior is guided by the norms that have been internalized and that are expected to be socially reinforced by significant others. Akers agrees with Bandura that modeling is a crucial factor in the initial acquisition of deviant behavior. Its continuation, however, depends greatly on the frequency and personal significance of social reinforcement, which comes from association with others.

Akers' theory has received its share of criticism. Some sociologists consider it tautological: the behavior occurs because it is reinforced, but it is reinforced because it occurs. Kornhauser (1978) declared that the theory was not empirically supported, and Akers himself stressed the need for longitudinal research to test it. During the 1980s and 1990s he and his colleagues published a number of studies that supported the strength of his theory, particularly with respect to drug use (Akers & Cochran, 1985; Akers & Lee, 1996; Krohn, Akers, Radosevich, & Lanza-Kaduce, 1982).

SOCIAL REACTION THEORY: LABELING

Criminologists who espouse social reaction theory believe that the feedback individuals receive from society is essentially what explains their deviant behavior. More commonly referred to as the labeling perspective, this approach holds considerable appeal for many professionals who work day to day with juvenile delinquents. It was Frank Tannenbaum's 1938 book, *Crime and the Community*, that contained the seeds of the labeling perspective. In his book he argues that the proper study of crime and delinquency is not the behavior itself but society's reaction to it. Tannenbaum maintains that once individuals are "tagged" or labeled deviants or delinquents, others begin to see them as such and treat them accordingly; thus, the reactions of others become the primary source of the individual's conduct.

> The process of making the criminal, therefore, is a process of tagging, defining, identifying, segregating, describing, emphasizing, making conscious and self-conscious;

it becomes a way of stimulating, suggesting, emphasizing, and evoking the very traits that are complained of. . . . [T]he person becomes the thing he is described as being. (Tannenbaum, 1938, pp. 19–20)

Tannenbaum believed that, initially, children are usually involved in mere mischief, but some are labeled "bad" as a result. These children then come to see themselves as bad and take on the role and behaviors associated with badness. This process, which he called the "the dramatization of evil," is a slow and gradual one and represents the transformation of an offender's self-identity from a doer of mischief to a doer of evil. As the community's definition of a youth changes from one who occasionally misbehaves to one who is a delinquent, so the youth's own self-definition changes. Eventually the youth comes to believe that he or she is basically evil, quite possibly beyond salvation.

Edwin M. Lemert was one of the earliest to outline in detail the labeling perspective, which he preferred to call the "societal reaction perspective" in his book *Social Pathology* (1951). That book was not taken seriously by criminologists and sociologists in general until 10 years after its publication. During the 1960s, the labeling perspective gained favor under the influence of Howard S. Becker, Erving Goffman, John Kitsuse, Kai T. Erikson, and Edwin Schur.

In *Social Pathology* Lemert distinguishes between two kinds of deviant behavior, primary and secondary deviation. **Primary deviance** is neither identified nor punished by anyone in authority; in a sense, it is hidden or secret. Even though the behavior violates a norm, it remains undetected and thus escapes the reactions of others. In Lemert's view, deviant behavior in society is ubiquitous and secret, since most forbidden behavior goes unobserved and unsanctioned. Not even the offenders may consider the behavior representative of their inner selves. Consider Kingston, who regularly and skillfully lifts videos from an unattended counter in a chain store and has never been apprehended. According to Lemert, Kingston may not see himself as a thief. His "violations" are really just occasional bouts of forgetfulness, reactions to boredom, or an adventure peripheral to his cognitive constructs, that is, his perceptions of himself. These incidents are, in essence, behaviors largely foreign to Kingston's "true self."

Rule-breaking behavior profoundly changes an individual when it receives negative recognition from the outside world. Detection of Kingston's conduct by the store detective begins to change his self-image. The unpleasant identity of "thief" or "delinquent," even if not officially imposed by a juvenile court, prompts Kingston to defend his actions as nothing serious or not in character: "I am not a thief!" However, with continued societal reactions to the transgressions—notification of police and/or parents, contact with a court diversion program or a juvenile court judge—Kingston gradually comes to believe that he is, in fact, a thief. Slowly Kingston incorporates these societal reactions into his existing cognitive structure, and at this point, according to Lemert, Kingston may begin to do the things and play the role that others associate with him. He may enter into a pattern of additional violations of the norms, which Lemert calls **secondary deviance**. "When a person begins to employ his deviant behavior or a role based upon it as a means of defense, attack, or adjustment to the . . . problems created by the consequent societal reaction, his deviation is secondary" (Lemert, 1951, p. 76).

There is, then, a significant difference between the experience of one who shoplifts and is not caught and one who is certified a thief. Secondary deviance affects the self-concept or inner belief system as well as the performance of social roles. Lemert stressed, however, that secondary deviance does not follow from a single reaction to an individual, but rather after a long and sustained process. Kingston becomes a good candidate when his parents do not let him forget what happened. Lemert believed we tend to see ourselves as others see us and tend to act on this self-definition. Thus, labeling leads to "symbolic reorganization," or construct rearrangement. But primary deviation, which is not detected, usually does not affect one's self-concept or social role, nor does it initiate symbolic reorganization.

Being publicly or officially labeled a deviant is socially stigmatizing, adversely affecting social relationships and opportunities. Kingston may find his circle of friends dwindling, since parents may warn their children not to associate with him. In addition, employers rarely hire known deviants or delinquents. Thus, according to Lemert, the initial societal reactions precipitate a chain of events, perceptions, identities, and actions that call forth new interactions that reinforce the delinquent label. **Labeling interactions** underscore the complicated interplay of the deviance process. They transform deviance from a simple cause-and-effect relationship—you steal; therefore you are a thief—to a complex process that continually feeds on the individual's own cognitive constructs, along with those of others.

Lemert believed the societal reaction process is affected by many factors, including age, gender, socioeconomic status, race, manner of dress, and neighborhood, each of which may influence the responses of legal authorities to a young offender. The police officer who realizes that a youth is a member of one of the influential families in the community may be more likely to ignore his behavior. Youths from less powerful families, perceived as "continually breeding trouble," will not have that advantage.

In 1979 Lemert credited Howard Becker as the real initiator of the labeling perspective. "Becker's ideas of labeling took precedence over mine so far as popular acceptance and recognition were concerned. At the same time his writings seem to have been the target for more criticism than mine" (Lemert, 1983, p. 125). Lemert also admitted that he became disinterested in the societal reaction approach because "it was becoming too psychological" (Lemert, 1983, p. 126). The theory was never developed to its full potential to show the reciprocal effects of the labeling process, Lemert said. Instead, it focused too much on the self-concept issue and not enough on the interplay with the labelers. "Without looking at this—the way the labeled persons respond, and problems created for the agents of social control by their responses—it is difficult to study changes in patterns of deviance, policy, and social control" (Lemert, 1983, p. 126).

Lemert's observation concerning the popularity and influence of Becker's writings was probably an accurate one. Becker's book *The Outsiders* (1963) was one of the two most frequently cited criminology books of the period between 1945 and 1972 (Downes & Rock, 1982). The term **outsiders** refers to those people who are judged deviant by others and therefore stand outside the circle of "normal" members of a group. Becker, more than Lemert, succeeded in moving deviance far outside the individual, treating it not as a quality of the person but as a social problem. The police, the courts, correctional and residential personnel, and welfare agencies are the principal culprits; their labeling and dehumanizing produce deviance in those they consider outside mainstream society. These stigmatizing social labels placed on the rule violator by institutional powers push the offender into additional deviant behavior, a deviant way of life, and, basically, a deviant identity. While Lemert delineated two categories of deviants, primary and secondary, Becker (1963) outlined four: (1) those who have violated a rule and have been sanctioned, or the **pure deviants**; (2) those who have violated a rule but have escaped notice of or sanction for the violation, the so-called **secret deviants**; (3) those who have not violated a rule but who have been negatively sanctioned anyway (i.e., the falsely accused, such as a girl labeled a delinquent because her two best friends have a record of police contacts); and (4) those who have neither violated a rule nor been negatively sanctioned. This last category represents conforming behavior, which Becker recognized could be deviant behavior under certain conditions. For a subordinate might take it upon himself to do things he thinks his commander wants done, even though the commander did not have that intention.

The most controversial of Becker's types is the secret deviant, who differs from the primary deviant described by Lemert. According to Becker, secret deviants have so labeled themselves, even though others are unaware of their behavior. For example, Becker describes the sado-masochistic fetish market that publishes expensive, high-quality catalogs, and has a large clientele. Although a person who is detected using fetishes for sexual pleasure is commonly labelled a sexual deviant, the thousands of undetected individuals who browse the catalog and purchase items are examples of secret deviants.

Becker also makes a distinction between a **master status** and a **subordinate status** to emphasize that some statuses in a society override all others and have a certain priority in their influence over behavior. Race is an example of a master status, as are actor, pro-football player, mother, and gay activist. An actor may be a parent, member of a Lutheran church, brown-haired, and diabetic, but the status of being a well-known actor can override all other statuses. As Becker notes, this same master status may develop for deviants. If one receives the status of deviant as a result of breaking rules, this self-identification may develop to be more important in one's daily life than other subordinate statuses combined.

Becker's approach suggests that people lack a sure knowledge of what they are and what they can accomplish. Individuals are assumed to follow almost blindly the dicta of social groups and institutions. Becker does not allow a person to resist or reject a label assigned by some social group, although he does recognize that deviants form social groups with other deviants for support. In addition, Becker's perspective—along with that of other labeling theorists—seems to suggest that deviant behavior does not occur as a result of individual choice or lack of opportunity but rather as a result of differential applications of rules and labels. However, like Lemert, Becker emphasized that the labeling perspective was not a causal theory, but rather a way of looking at a general area of human activity.

George Vold (1979) notes that the labeling perspective has been criticized on three additional fronts. First, it overemphasizes the importance of the official labeling process. Second, it assumes that deviants resent the deviant label. Actually, particularly in the case of juveniles, deviance may allow the person to gain status or approval from peers or even significant adults. Third, reducing the labeling process might create more crime than it would eliminate, since it would water down the effect of general deterrence. In other words, some juveniles and adults may need the threat of being negatively labeled as an incentive not to commit crime. This criticism of the labeling perspective assumes that most people do not commit crime because they fear the stigma that would result. As we noted earlier, though, many professionals who work day to day with juveniles believe that the labeling perspective is an important one to consider in delinquency prevention programs. Typical juveniles in an institutional setting have been labeled negatively throughout their young lives, not only as delinquent but also as "stupid," "feeble," "loser," "slut," "crazy," or other similar terms. It is not unreasonable to believe that such negative labels have some effect on a child's or adolescent's self-concept, and it is clearly worthwhile to urge caretakers and other adults to resist using them. Explaining delinquency is not that simple, however.

COGNITIVE CONSTRAINTS AND NEUTRALIZATION THEORIES

Under normal circumstances, we perceive, interpret, compare, and act on the basis of cognitive constructs, which we will also refer to as personal standards. **Cognitive constructs**, you may recall from Chapter 4, are mental representations of the world, including ourselves. If we do not like what we are doing, we can change our behavior, justify it, or try to stop thinking about it. We can also reward and punish ourselves for our conduct. Self-punishment is expressed as guilt or remorse following actions we consider alien to our standards. In most instances, however, we prefer self-reinforcement to self-punishment; therefore, we behave in ways that correspond to our cognitive constructs. We anticipate the feelings of guilt we will experience for "bad" actions and thus restrain ourselves. In the process, each of us develops personal standards or codes of conduct that are maintained by self-reinforcement or self-punishment, as well as by external reinforcement and punishment. Walter C. Reckless's containment theory addresses the balance between internal (cognitive) and external controls of behavior, and Sykes and Matza talk about psychological neutralizations of internal controls.

CONTAINMENT THEORY

Walter C. Reckless (1961, 1973) describes delinquent and nondelinquent behavior as functions of personality and social/family influences, both of which serve to "contain" the individual. This **containment theory** is based on two sources of constraints. One source originates from within the person, a kind of self-regulatory mechanism that prevents us from acting out our impulses or desires. This source is called **inner containment**. A second source originates from outside the person and is found within the social institutions of the family, friends, church, school, and generally the community. This source, which represents informal social control, is termed **outer containment**.

Reckless assumes that strength in one source of containment compensates for weaknesses in the other. For example, a youngster with strong inner containment—which Reckless describes variously as self-concept, goal orientation, frustration tolerance, sense responsibility, and resistance to distractions—will be prevented from engaging in delinquent behavior, even under circumstances of weak external containment. Outer containment, in order to be strong, must offer effective supervision and discipline, a reasonable set of social expectations and activities, and good social role models. If inner containment is weak, a strong outer containment can compensate and hold the adolescent in check.

Reckless acknowledges that in our mobile society, with external circumstances changing frequently, an individual is forced to rely on internal standards more than ever. Hence, Reckless affirms, the most important prevention of delinquency in contemporary society is the development of strong inner constraints, or **self-regulation**. Of greatest importance in inner containment, Reckless tells us, is a solid self-concept, a product of favorable socialization by parents.

Reckless and Dinitz (1967) tested the role of self-concept in delinquency using a group of predominantly white boys living in high delinquency areas of Columbus, Ohio. Reckless and Dinitz found that, over a 4-year period, boys with a good self-concept, as measured by an inventory of self-concept developed by the investigators, had significantly fewer contacts with the juvenile court system than did boys with a poor self-concept. Reckless and Dinitz concluded that a good self-concept is "indicative of a residual favorable socialization and a strong inner self, which in turn steers the individual away from bad companions and street corner society, toward middle class values, and to awareness of the possibility of upward movement in the opportunity structure" (p. 196).

Containment theory does offer a plausible explanation for some delinquent behavior. For example, it is reasonable to assume that some juveniles resist serious and even minor delinquent behavior, even when given ample opportunity in a high-crime area, because of strong inner containment, or self-regulation. But why do some juveniles with strong outer containment or informal social controls, such as those found in middle- and upper-class cohesive, stable families and neighborhoods, engage in delinquent behavior? According to containment theory, the strong outer constraints provided by such environments should override a weaker inner containment, and delinquency should not occur. Likewise, why do some juveniles in high-delinquency areas (i.e., weak outer containment) with weak inner containment (i.e., poor self-concept, lack of goals, etc.) remain uninvolved in delinquent acts?

Containment theory is also weak in clearly defining inner and outer containment. Reckless throws in an armory of vague terms to describe each, but direct measurement of them is nearly impossible. This may be one reason that this theory, while often cited, has prompted exceedingly little research.

TECHNIQUES OF NEUTRALIZATION

Criminologists Gresham Sykes and David Matza (1957) enumerated five major strategies that people use to avoid self-blame and blame from others. These are common methods used alone or in combination to separate or disjoin our construct systems from our actions. Sykes and Matza called these personal strategies **techniques of neutralization** and applied them specifically to delinquents. They are denial of injury, denial of the victim, denial of responsibility, condemnation of the condemners, and appeal to higher loyalties. Sykes and Matza believed delinquents are at least partially committed to the dominant social order and are therefore susceptible to experiencing guilt or shame when they engage in deviant acts. However, they protect themselves from these unpleasant feelings by rationalizing that their violations are acceptable. According to Sykes and Matza, each delinquent has a preferred strategy that is applied across situations. A youth may excuse her act of vandalism, for example, by convincing herself (and others) that she "didn't really hurt anybody"; it was just a "prank" or "mischief." Or she might conclude that the person whose property she destroyed can well afford it. Both reactions illustrate **denial of injury**. The **denial of the victim** technique is usually expressed in the form of rightful retaliation or punishment. The victim is transformed into one deserving injury: "He had it coming to him." Alternately, delinquents might convince themselves that their theft was from "crooked" chain stores.

Denial of responsibility involves such perceptions as "I couldn't help myself" or "I didn't mean to do it." Delinquents who use this strategy see themselves as billiard balls—or better yet, soccer balls—helplessly propelled or kicked from event to event. They are not actors as much as they are acted upon. **Condemnation of the condemners** includes the belief that "the cops are out to get me" or "society gave me a bum rap." These delinquents shift attention away from their own deviant acts to the motives and behavior of those who disapprove of their violation. The condemners are often seen as hypocrites and violators of the law themselves. Finally, the delinquent using an **appeal to higher loyalties** convinces himself of a positive motive: "I didn't do it for myself" or "I did it because me and my buddies are all in this together," or "My mother needed the money."

Sykes and Matza's theory has similarities to strain theory, discussed earlier, because it assumes that society has dominant values that have been internalized. In fact, these values may be internalized to such an extent that the techniques of neutralization are not effective enough to shield juveniles completely from the force of those values or from the reactions of others who conform to those values. Therefore, many, if not most, will suffer some shame and guilt about violating the rules of the dominant social order.

In Sykes and Matza's view, the learning of the techniques is a crucial step, because it allows juveniles to become delinquent in the first place. They have accepted the validity of the dominant value system and have internalized it to a large extent, but they then rationalize to suspend the adopted values temporarily. However, although the theory regards learning as important, it does not explain how the techniques are learned.

The Sykes and Matza position has some appeal, but it may not apply to many situations. Moreover, it has not been tested to any great extent. In order to confirm the strength of the neutralization, one would have to demonstrate that the techniques are used prior to committing the deviant act rather than as justification after the fact. Practicing psychologists, however, have long observed that we do use strategies of neutralization both in planning and in justifying our everyday actions. Thus, an important component of some treatment programs is to encourage individuals to confront these neutralizing tactics. For example, a juvenile burglar who believes "nobody got hurt" may learn of the fear created in the children of the family whose home was burglarized.

CONTROL THEORIES

There are other ways by which we become disengaged from our codes of conduct. High levels of emotional arousal can take our attention away from our internal mechanisms of control. When we become extremely angry, for example, we often say and do things we later regret. We feel upset, remorseful, and guilty and wish we could take back our words and actions. If we had carefully considered and evaluated the consequences of our behavior, we would probably have acted differently. But in the heat of emotion, our self-regulatory system, with all its standards and values, is sometimes held in abeyance. The assertion that we are all capable of violence is one reason laws are needed. Most people learn from experience to pay closer attention to their internal control mechanisms.

As a group, control theories assume that individuals need "something" to keep in check their tendency to deviate from acceptable rules and norms. In that sense, control theories begin with a relatively negative view of human nature: We would all commit crime if we could. The most well-known representative of control theory is Hirschi's classic theory, formulated and tested with juveniles, particularly juvenile boys.

HIRSCHI'S SOCIAL CONTROL THEORY

In 1969 Travis Hirschi published *Causes of Delinquency*, in which he outlined his theory and reported on the research he had conducted to test it. Social control theory, also called social bonding theory, contends that delinquency occurs when a child's ties to the conventional order are weakened or broken. The control or bonding begins within the family system and then branches out to include others within the neighborhood and community. When delinquency occurs, it is primarily because the appropriate socialization process has not occurred. More specifically, it is because the necessary socialization process within the family has not taken place. Delinquency—and deviance in general—occurs when people have not been adequately indoctrinated with the rules and expectations of a given society and when external social constraints are lacking.

Hirschi proposed four basic elements of the social bond: (1) attachment to parents, teachers, and peers; (2) commitment to conventional lines of activity, such as educational and occupational achievement; (3) involvement in that conventional activity; and (4) belief in the legitimacy and morality of the social rules and laws. Hirschi speculated that these elements had an additive effect: the more attachment, commitment, involvement, and belief an individual had, the more likely that individual would be bonded to society—and less likely to engage in delinquent activity. Hirschi also posited that the more a person was tied or bonded to conventional society by one element, the more likely he or she would be bonded by the other elements, too.

Attachment refers to the degree of sensitivity a person has to the opinions of others. According to Hirschi, the most important persons within a child's social environment are parents, peers, and school officials, with parents being the most critical. "The fact that delinquents are less likely than non-delinquents to be closely tied to their parents is one of the best documented findings of delinquency research" (Hirschi, 1969, p.85). Insensitivity to what these groups think and feel is a sign of weakened or nonexistent bonds to the conventional social order.

Commitment refers to the physical and emotional investment a person puts into the normative, conventional way of life. It includes such activities as studying, building up a business, saving money, acquiring a reputation for virtue and honesty, and generally doing those things encouraged and expected by conventional others. The more a person commits to these activities, the less likely that person will engage in acts that ultimately jeopardize his or her position in the social order. "The person becomes committed to a conventional line of action, and he is therefore committed to conformity" (Hirschi, 1969. p. 21).

Involvement refers to the amount of time and energy expended in the pursuit of conventional activities. According to Hirschi, a person heavily involved in conventional endeavors has neither the time nor the energy to engage in deviant behavior.

> The person involved in conventional activities is tied to appointments, deadlines, working hours, plans, and the like, so the opportunity to commit deviant acts rarely arises. To the extent that he is engrossed in conventional activities, he cannot even think about deviant acts, let alone act out his inclinations. (Hirschi, 1969, p. 22)

Thus, the juvenile involved in recreational, social, religious, and school endeavors has little time to engage in delinquent acts, underscoring the adage "An idle mind is the devil's workshop." In some ways, Hirschi sees delinquents as members of a leisure class, plagued with free time and characterized by "a search for kicks, disdain for work, a desire for the big score, and the acceptance of aggressive toughness as proof of masculinity" (Hirschi, 1969, pp. 22–23).

Belief is the degree to which a person internalizes and accepts the common value system of the society or group. The value system includes sharing, sensitivity to the rights of others, respect for and acceptance of laws and rules, and concern for the plight of others. Hirschi proposed that there were many variations in the extent to which people believe they should obey the rules of society; beliefs exist on continua, ranging in degrees of conviction. According to Hirschi, the less committed a person is to the rules (i.e., the weaker the bonds), the more likely that person is to violate them.

Hirschi tested his control theory in 1964 in a study of 1,300 junior high and high school boys living in an urban California county. He used data from both official and self-report sources. The boys completed questionnaires in which they were asked about their involvement in delinquency. In addition, Hirschi included a number of questions designed to measure the four elements of their bond to society. For example, attachment was measured by such questions as "Would you like to be the kind of person your father is?" Commitment was measured primarily by the importance they placed on grades; involvement, by the amount of time the boys devoted to school activities; and belief, by the degree of their respect for police and the law.

The most striking finding of Hirschi's study was the importance of identification with the male parent. Boys who reported that they discussed their future plans and shared their thoughts and feelings with their fathers were much less likely to engage in delinquent acts than were the boys who reported less intimate communication. The amount of communication was less significant than the closeness or the intimacy as perceived by the boys.

The Hirschi data suggested that the relationship with the father was possibly the most important factor in the development of male delinquency. A close and intimate relationship between father and son was correlated with nondelinquency, regardless of the relationship with the mother. A similar finding was reported by Alayne Yates and colleagues (1983). These researchers discovered that a vast majority of the 339 young offenders reviewed (aged 18–20) described the early relationships with their fathers as more important than the early relationships with their mothers. Interestingly, in Hirschi's study, boys whose parents themselves engaged in criminal behavior were no more likely to be delinquent than were those boys whose parents were noncriminal. Hirschi explained this by speculating that all parents—criminal and noncriminal—communicate allegiance to societal norms, even though they may not conform to them personally.

The Hirschi survey also uncovered a complex relationship among parents, the child, the school, and peers. Boys who did poorly in school tended to lack intimate communication with their parents. Hirschi disagreed with theorists who concluded that dislike of school was a source of motivation for delinquency or that delinquency was a means of relieving frustration generated by unpleasant school experiences. Success in school, Hirschi said, depended on how competent the boy believed himself to be. These perceptions of competence stemmed partly from the parents' perceptions of his competence, as they were communicated to him. If parents communicated that the boy was competent and should do his best, then school became tolerable and even pleasant. Although teachers and peers played significant roles, parental influences were paramount.

In sum, attachment to parents became a central tenet in Hirschi's control theory: strong attachment essentially precluded delinquency. Furthermore, attachment to parents was associated with other relationships, both within and away from home. Attachment to parents was often associated with attachment to peers, for example. And Hirschi found that the closer the boy was to his peers, the less delinquent he tended to be. Importantly, though, Hirschi later recognized that delinquents could be attached to parents and to peers who were not law-abiding; consequently, he modified his approach to indicate that attachment must be to "conventional" others. Hirschi also found a negative relationship between ambition and delinquency. The more ambitious a boy was, the less likely he would become delinquent.

Michael J. Hindelang (1973) conducted a "quasi-replicative" study of Hirschi's survey, using both male and female adolescents in a rural New York State community. Hindelang's project was quasi-replicative because some of his questions were worded slightly differently, and the resources available to Hindelang were not nearly as extensive as Hirschi's. Even so, and despite the fact that the surveys were conducted nearly 10 years apart and in different parts of the country, Hindelang's results were remarkably similar to Hirschi's. It was this research, though, that prompted Hirschi to recognize the distinction between conventional and nonconventional others. Hindelang found that attachment to conventional parents and peers, teachers, and school officials; commitment to "adult" activities and conventional activities; involvement in school-related activities; and conventional beliefs produced results very similar to Hirschi's.

Today, Hirschi's social control theory remains *among* the leading explanations of juvenile delinquency among criminologists (Akers, 1997; Junger & Marshall, 1997; Longshore, Chang, Hsieh, & Messina, 2004). The assumption that delinquents have a weakened social bond has led to support for many delinquency prevention programs, such as after-school activities, parent training, and mentoring. However, as is typical for many theories in criminology, research support for the theory has been mixed (Greenberg, 1999; Kempf, 1993), and the theory has received considerable criticism (Taylor, 2001; D. Smith, 1995). Many criminologists believe it is more effective in explaining property crime and relatively minor offending than violent crime. Interestingly, Hirschi eventually rejected or modified many aspects of his original social control theory and, along with his colleague Michael Gottfredson, developed a different theory, which they called a **general theory of crime**.

GENERAL THEORY OF CRIME

Whereas in social control theory the major factors for delinquency are the elements of a weak social bond, the general theory of crime (GTC) explains criminal behavior by relying primarily on individual differences in self-control. Gottfredson and Hirschi (1990) defined *self-control* as the extent to which a person is "vulnerable to the temptations of the moment" (p. 87). "In sum, people who lack self-control will tend to be impulsive, insensitive, physical (as opposed to mental), risk taking, short-sighted, and non-verbal, and they will tend therefore to engage in criminal and analogous acts" (Gottfredson & Hirschi, 1990, p. 90). Elsewhere, Hirschi and Gottfredson (1993) write, "In our version, self-control is the (general) cause of crime: many apparent traits of personality may also be its byproducts" (p. 49). Examples of these byproducts include temper and "cautiousness." Individuals high in self-control, by contrast, are able to evaluate and avoid the long-term consequences of any criminal or deviant action. Hirschi and Gottfredson (1993) hasten to add that the GTC does not claim that a lack of or defects in self-control are the *only* cause of crime, but are the major one. Their theory assumes that self-control is set in early childhood and remains stable over a lifetime. Low self-control is an enduring criminal predisposition, which is strongly influenced by biological, inherited factors and early social influences, such as poor or faulty parenting.

Whereas Hirschi's social bonding theory was a theory of delinquency, the GTC was developed to explain a broad range of major and minor forms of crime and deviance, such as reckless or drunken driving, smoking, gambling, having children out of wedlock, and even engaging in illicit sex, along with violent crime and white-collar offending. In this sense, the theory really is a *general* theory of criminal and deviant behavior.

In addition to self-control, the GTC also points out that the link between self-control and crime is conditional on **criminal opportunity**, which is a function of the fortuitous circumstances encountered by a person (Longshore & Turner, 1998). Apparently in opposition to social learning theory, the GTC posits that opportunity refers to the availability of a target and the possibility of taking advantage of that target through criminal means. The opportunity to steal and engage in criminal action is essentially limitless; opportunities to commit a particular crime, on the other hand, may be severely limited (Hirschi & Gottfredson, 1993). Self-control and opportunity may therefore interact for specific crimes but are independent in general. "For example, driving under the influence presupposes access to alcohol and a car, but these conditions are generally available. Therefore, driving under the influence (DUI) should be largely a function of self-control. But not entirely" (Hirschi & Gottfredson, 1993, p. 50). Legal restrictions on the availability of alcohol (opportunity) may play a significant role, as well as the availability of a motor vehicle. An example of self-control and opportunity being dependent would be bank embezzlement. In order to embezzle from a bank, a person would have to first be employed by the bank.

Longshore et al. (2004) draw a connection between the GTC and Hirschi's social control theory. According to Longshore et al., low self-control may have negative effects on the development of social bonds later in life. They note that a person with low self-control may be less likely to form and maintain stable friendships, more likely to associate with others who lack self-control, and less able to adjust to the demands of school and the workplace. In this sense, Longshore et al. believe that an integration of self-control and its long-term effects on social bonds may be a very useful approach for explanations of delinquency and long-term criminal careers.

As noted by Longshore and Turner (1998), Hirschi and Gottfredson advanced their theory in explicit opposition to other, long-standing criminological perspectives, including strain theory and a classical theory of crime that views crime as simply a result of the exercise of free will. Developmental theories of crime (discussed in the following chapter) are, according to Hirschi and Gottfredson, of questionable value. Furthermore, Hirschi and Gottfredson questioned the tendency of many of their fellow criminologists to place great importance on the point at which an individual first engages in criminal activity. For example, the age-of-onset hypothesis predicts that the earlier the child begins to offend, the more serious and persistent the criminal career will be. David Farrington (1979) writes that boys first convicted at the earliest ages tended to become the most persistent offenders as adults. But Hirschi and Gottfredson charge that there is very little value in developing theories based on this age-of-onset hypothesis because all individuals and groups of individuals share a common age/crime distribution, regardless of when they begin to offend. In other words, according to the GTC, a youth who begins criminal activity at age 13 will peak between ages 16 and 18; a youth who begins at age 8 will still peak at ages 16 to 18.

In support of the GTC, many recent studies have found a significant relationship between low self-control and adult crime and juvenile delinquency (Burton, Evans, Cullen, Olivares, & Dunaway, 1999; Longshore et al., 2004; Wood, Pfefferbaum, & Arneklev, 1993; Wright, Caspi, Moffitt, & Silva, 1999). The relationship seems to be a moderate one, however (B. Marcus, 2004); and like virtually every other theory of crime or delinquency, the GTC has its critics (Akers, 1997; Geis, 2000; Greenberg, 1985, 1991, 1992; B. Marcus, 2004). B. Marcus (2004), for example, argues that the concept of self-control, as defined by the GTC, has never been adequately measured, and thus, the theory itself has not been adequately tested. Taylor (2001) posits that if we follow the Hirschi-Gottfredson argument to its logical conclusion, attempts to rehabilitate and reform offenders become pointless. In fact, Gottfredson and Hirschi (1990) themselves assert that "the search for personality correlates of crime other than self-control is unlikely to bear fruit, that short-term institutional experiences (e.g., treatment programs, jobs, jail) are incapable of producing meaningful change in criminality" (p. 232).

CONTROL BALANCE THEORY

The word *control* is used in a different sense in control balance theory (Tittle, 1995). Although not yet popular or well-known, this theory has attracted some research interest in recent years (Piquero & Hickman, 2003). It is considered by some to be one of the more important theoretical contributions in explaining deviance (Braithwaite, 1997). The theory assumes that all people can be characterized by **control ratios**, which represent the total amount of control they are subject to by the situation, relative to the amount of control they can exercise on their own (Tittle, 2004). These ratios influence both the probability and the type of criminal behavior a person will engage in. A person's control ratio can be balanced or unbalanced. When balanced, a person is inclined to conform and refrain from deviant behavior. "Control balance theory interprets deviant behavior as a way of managing relative control, a way of altering a control imbalance" (Tittle, 2004, p. 406). When the control ratio is unbalanced, the person is predisposed to become deviant or delinquent.

Twelve-year-old Tabitha has a highly regimented life in which she is seldom allowed to make choices, even in the clothes she wears to school each day. She must help care for three younger siblings, attends a highly structured school, was sexually abused by an uncle who has now just moved in with the family, and has been enrolled in many after-school and weekend activities, most of which she detests. She has recently begun to take money and items of value from parents, teachers, and friends. While other theorists might discuss strain, a weakened social bond, or social learning, control balance theorists would see her deviant behavior as a way of trying to achieve some balance in a life in which she seems otherwise powerless. She may, for example, plan to accumulate enough money to run away, or she may hope that she will be discovered and have attention brought to her untenable living situation.

When a person has the ability to exercise more control than she or he is subjected to, it is called a control surplus (Piquero & Hickman, 2003; Tittle, 2004). This might occur in the case of a juvenile who is given too much freedom by his parents, such as with no monitoring of his activities. On the other hand, when a person is subjected to more control then she or he can exercise (such as in the case of Tabitha), this is called a control deficit. Both are examples of cognitive imbalance and have the potential to lead to delinquent behavior. Tittle stipulates that the greater the imbalance, the greater the chances for delinquency.

Other control theories usually ignore the motivation for criminal behavior, assuming that everyone, in the absence of control, is sufficiently inclined toward crime (Tittle, 2004). Control *balance* theory is unique in that it takes into account the motivation for deviant and delinquent behavior. Basically, the theory postulates that deviance and delinquency result when motivation is triggered by provocation and enabled by the presence of opportunity and absence of constraint (Braithwaite, 1997). Provocations are "contextual features that cause people to become more keenly cognizant of their control ratios and the possibilities of altering them through deviant behavior" (Tittle, 1995, p. 163). In Tabitha's case, perhaps her uncle's moving into the house or a particularly difficult day caring for her siblings provoked her to realize how little control she had over her life.

Although Tittle has continually refined his theory (e.g., Tittle, 2004), it has received some incisive criticism for its conceptual ambiguity and its one-sided view of human nature (Jensen, 1999; Savelsberg, 1999). Still, control balance theory represents one of the more provocative control theories to arrive on the scene in recent years and should be followed in the years to come.

BRONFENBRENNER'S SYSTEMS THEORY

Bronfenbrenner's theory is not considered a classic theory of crime or delinquency. It is, rather, a general theory of how individuals, groups, and even institutions operate and are influenced by one another. As such, it has clear relevance to the mission of this text, which is to encourage a critical perspective of the different ways of understanding criminal behavior. In addition, we believe that the theory has powerful ramifications for the prevention of delinquent and criminal behavior.

Systems theory has adherents in a variety of disciplines spanning the natural and social sciences. The biologist Ludwig von Bertalanffy (1968) is credited with developing the most comprehensive systems approach. Currently, social systems theory is particularly well articulated by the late developmental psychologist Urie Bronfenbrenner. The systems model is highly compatible with interactionism, a perspective that *is* found in criminology literature and that describes the mutual and ongoing influence of the psychosocial environment on the individual, as well as the individual's influence on the environment.

Bronfenbrenner (1979, 1986b) has outlined a social systems theory that has considerable relevance for the study of delinquency; he specifically applied his ideas to research in child development. Thus, psychological explanations that view delinquency within a developmental context seem most obviously in tune with Bronfenbrenner. However, his theory is relevant to all human behavior within any social environment, as well as to the social environments themselves. Systems theory can comfortably accommodate a wide range of perspectives, from those that see delinquency as a result of unique, individual factors to those that indict the structure of society as a whole.

Bronfenbrenner conceives of society as a set of nested structures, which are called *systems* because they involve interrelationships and mutual, ongoing influences. The nested systems exist at different levels of abstraction, from the concrete and specific to the abstract and general. Each requires a different level of analysis. Families, schools, neighborhoods, cities, nations, and the world all exist at increasingly larger or more abstract levels of description.

MICROSYSTEMS

The immediate setting, which contains the person, is called a **microsystem**. It is, to Bronfenbrenner, the smallest unit for social analysis. Microsystems are patterns of activities, roles, and interpersonal relations that take place within settings directly experienced by an individual. Each person is an active participant in his or her microsystems, which might be as varied as a family, an anthropology class, a juvenile gang, or a poker group. The microsystem consists of how the person acts and reacts to others within these groups. Microsystems also contain subsystems, such as how Lucia reacts to her twin brother or how Larson reacts to his teacher. Therefore, while the immediate family as a whole represents a microsystem, this social system also has marital, parent–child, and sibling components, or subsystems. Of these three family subsystems, the relationship between parents is regarded by many as the core of family solidarity and the key element in determining the quality of family life (Erel & Burman, 1995).

An important phrase contained in the definition of a microsystem is "experienced by an individual." As Bronfenbrenner (1979) states,

> The term [*experienced*] is used to indicate that the scientifically relevant features of any environment include not only its objective properties but also the way in which these properties are perceived by the persons in that environment.... Very few of the external influences significantly affecting human behavior and development can be described solely in terms of objective physical conditions and events; the aspects of environment that are most powerful in shaping the course of psychological growth are overwhelmingly those that have meaning to the person in a given situation. (p. 22)

By implication, if we are to understand delinquent behavior, or any human behavior, we must appreciate how different people perceive, interpret, and reconstruct their environments. While social pressures and influences are critically important, so, too, are the personal interpretations of those pressures and influences.

MESOSYSTEMS

Also important in Bronfenbrenner's theory are interrelationships among microsystems. The child does not remain within the family microsystem but goes to school, to the homes of relatives and friends, to grocery stories, to amusement parks. Each of these settings influences the child, and each is, in turn, influenced by him or her.

Bronfenbrenner calls these interrelationships between microsystems **mesosystems**. Thus, a wider social environment must always be kept in mind when considering a child and his or her family, since what goes on beyond its immediate boundaries invariably affects and is affected by what transpires within it. Consider how the safety of a neighborhood playground can influence the freedom parents grant their children in playing there, away from their careful supervision. Child-rearing practices, in turn, affect how the child approaches other children at the neighborhood playground.

Mesosystem models take into account the joint effects of processes occurring within and between two or more settings—in each of which the developing person is an active participant (Bronfenbrenner, 1986b). In essence, a mesosystem is a system of microsystems, or a network of relationships among microsystems. Bronfenbrenner argues that researchers interested in child development have concentrated on microsystems without commenting on the relationships among them.

EXOSYSTEMS

Bronfenbrenner notes that systems beyond the micro- and mesosystems also affect a person's development, feelings, thoughts, and actions, even though he or she may not directly participate in them. These **exosystems** include at least one setting that does not directly involve the person as an active participant. For example, what happens at a parent's place of work has considerable impact on the child at home, even if the child never visits that workplace or has direct contact with it. Recent research indicates that there is often a robust spillover effect from one situation to another; that is, there is a direct transfer of mood, affect, or behavior from one setting to another. Examples of this effect include a troubled marital relationship spilling over and negatively affecting the parent–child relationship (Erel & Burman, 1995) or a parent bringing home all the negative moods accumulated during a conflict-filled day at work. This latter situation includes a setting that only one member of the family experiences directly and thus represents an exosystem. Research by Melvin L. Kohn (1977) indicates that the type of work engaged in by a parent may strongly influence the development of everyone within the home. For example, Kohn found that occupations allowing considerable freedom and personal autonomy seem to have a significantly different impact on parenting styles than occupations requiring conformity and personal constraints. Kohn found that working-class men whose jobs involved compliance with authority tended to demand unquestioning obedience on the part of their children. On the other hand, middle-class fathers who held jobs encouraging self-direction and independence expected similar behaviors in their children. This is a good illustration of the influence of an exosystem on lower-level systems, particularly the family. Of course, the fathers here may have done some self-selection of their own by choosing the nature of the work, independent of any major influences of the job on the father's personality or family style. However, the work situation is more likely to be bidirectional: The father does some selection and influencing, and the work system influences the father and his role at home. Although Kohn's research was limited to fathers, similar principles might apply in the case of mothers.

The family's outside social supports (such as friends, relatives, adequate health care, social guidance) also strongly influence the home microsystem. A child may never meet the members of his parent's Alcoholics Anonymous group, but what happens to the parent there ultimately affects the parent–child relationship. James Garbarino (1976) suggests an association between maternal child abuse and the degree to which mothers receive adequate social support in parenting—the less adequate the social support, the higher the probability of abuse. The Garbarino research is intriguing for those who believe that child abuse is a predictor of delinquency and crime. In addition, findings like Garbarino's lend support to the many social programs that seek to provide emotional, financial, and child-care support to families.

Neighborhoods may also qualify as exosystems (as well as a microsystem) according to Bronfenbrenner's scheme. The neighborhood as a whole, with its many clusters of groups, represents the larger exosystem. However, peer groups or gangs within a neighborhood—say, the Neighborhood Watch Group or the group that gathers to play basketball every weekend—represent microsystems to their participants. Ever since the pioneering work of Burgess and Shaw and McKay discussed earlier in the chapter, social scientists have recognized the importance of the neighborhood in the development of crime and delinquency. The ecological perspective points to a robust relationship between deteriorated residential areas and rates of delinquency. Therefore, we must also consider the neighborhood when explaining delinquency.

MACROSYSTEMS

At an even higher level of analysis, Bronfenbrenner suggests clusters of interrelated exosystems that form **macrosystems**. In Bronfenbrenner's scheme, macrosystems are the belief systems, expectations, customs, attitudes, and associated ideologies that pervade a subculture or culture. Latino, African-American, Native American, Pacific Islander, and Asian cultures all represent macrosystems, as do their numerous and heterogeneous subcultures. For example, cultures differ in their expectations of boys and girls. For many, if not most, cultures, little boys are expected to start acting "masculine" (as defined by their culture) within the first 2 years of life. Little girls are expected to act "feminine." In the United States, despite contemporary emphases on gender equality, these expectations are well established, as a walk down the aisles of a toy store will document. Gender stereotypes of accepted behavior, as an aggregate variable across American culture, represent a component of the macrosystem. Socioeconomic status (SES) is also a component of the macrosystem. However, gender and SES data are useful but hardly sufficient; by themselves, they provide only hints at the underlying processes operating on people.

CHRONOSYSTEMS

In 1986 Bronfenbrenner (1986a) revised his model to add the chronosystem. The **chronosystem** accounts for changes across time. He found this concept necessary in order to account for the obvious changes that occur in time across all four systems just outlined. Historically, developmental psychologists have treated the passage of time as synonymous with chronological age. As we will emphasize throughout this text, the developmental sequence of a child is extremely critical in understanding delinquency. Fire setting by a curious 4-year-old is likely to represent very different behavior when compared to fire setting by a 16-year-old. In current research designs, time appears not merely as an attribute of the developing person but also as a property of the surrounding environment (Bronfenbrenner, 1986b). Neighborhoods change, communities change, cities change, and cultures change. The school environment is different in September than it is in June. Firstborns experience a different home environment when later children are born. A child's adjustment to school may be affected by several factors, including apprehension about the first day (microsystem), the death of her mother (mesosystem, representing the relationship between home and school), the fact that her father suddenly becomes unemployed (exosystem), or the society that becomes torn by racial tension (macrosystem). Each person's life course involves numerous transitions that accumulate and interact to affect his or her emotions, cognitions, behaviors, and overall perceptions of the social world at any given point in time.

Bronfenbrenner distinguishes between two types of chronosystems, those that most people experience (normative) and those that are rare or unexpected (nonnormative). Examples of normative chronosystems are school entry, puberty, entering the labor force, marriage, and retirement; examples of nonnormative chronosystems are death, a severe illness in the family, divorce, sexual assault, and winning the sweepstakes. Nonnormative events may have decidedly different effects on one's life in that they typically cannot be planned for and may involve physical and/or emotional trauma. Furthermore, persons experiencing them may feel isolated from others who have not experienced or are not experiencing the same event.

It is important to keep in mind that controversy in theory and empirical research on delinquency often stems from the confusion surrounding what system is being defined or explained. Seemingly contradictory findings may be due to differences in data across systems. For example, delinquency patterns gleaned from large collections of aggregate data across one nation or different countries—macrosystems—are apt to provide a different picture than delinquency patterns gathered at the neighborhood or exosystem level. Macrosystem analysis offers different clues about delinquency than microsystem analysis does. As another example, consider the debate over the relative merits of the self-report method and official statistics. As we will learn in Chapter 8, self-report data are gathered at the individual level, by asking individuals about their own involvement in crime. Official statistics are collected from agencies and large organizations over a wide cross section of society. These methods approach the issue from two different levels, requiring different perspectives. In this sense, whether self-report data support official data may not be all that important. Neither one can present a "true" picture of crime; they are most helpful in what they reveal about the respondents.

INDIVIDUAL SYSTEMS

Bronfenbrenner's basic framework does not conceptualize the individual as a system within him- or herself. This is a significant omission. We have adjusted his theory, therefore, adding an **infrasystem**, where personal constructs, beliefs, or schema (organized mental information about a particular topic) interact with temperament and genes to form a personality. "Whatever else personality may be, it has the properties of a system" (Allport, 1961, p. 109). The personal system changes and continually interacts with higher-level systems, particularly the microsystems and mesosystems. It is sometimes tempting to conclude that social environments dictate who we are or what we do. Yet it is not wise to overlook the fact that each person has a personal version of the world, conceptualized and organized in a unique way. The environment provides us with information and experience, but how these are integrated and stored is itself a system. It is premature, then, to attribute most behavior to either social or individual factors.

In summary, in order to understand and effectively prevent delinquency, we must approach its study in a way that recognizes the multiple social systems impinging on each human life. Sociologist Albert J. Reiss, Jr. (1986) writes: "If our understanding of crime and criminal behavior and its control is to advance, governmental data collection and scholarly research must be designed to collect individual, organizational, and community-level information" (p. 27). Elsewhere, Charles Wellford (1987) asserts: "We must develop theories of criminal behavior that take seriously the notion that there are biophysical effects on criminal behavior, psychological effects, social effects, cultural effects or any other organized effects that we wish to identify through our specification of the appropriate categories or levels of analysis" (p. 7).

INTERACTIONISM

One of the most productive strategies for explaining, preventing, and treating delinquency may lie in interactionism, which has many parallels to social systems theory. Interactionism is not a new approach; its many variants were utilized in the first half of the twentieth century by James Mark Baldwin, George Herbert Mead, C. H. Cooley, Herbert Blumer, William James, Kurt Lewin, and John Dewey—to mention only a few. The concept of interaction between an individual or a group and the society was also critical to the labeling perspective, discussed earlier in the chapter. Later, the principles of interactionism were expressed most clearly by David Magnusson and his colleagues (1981; Magnusson & Allen, 1983).

Interactionism refers to the continuously ongoing, bidirectional influence that occurs between systems. The most obvious illustration is the interactionism between the individual system (the person) and the microsystem (the immediate environment). Magnusson and Allen (1983) state that "the person-environment interaction process is an open system that consists of a dynamic process in which mutual influence and change are taking place continuously" (p. 370). The person influences the microsystem and the microsystem influences the person in a continuous stream of influences across time. The individual and the environment are inseparable; they form an indivisible whole or totality. Therefore, to illustrate interactionism correctly, we need more than a linear, static, two-way interaction. We need a series of causal loops connected across time. In this sense, the development of delinquency can be conceptualized as a spiral or helix.

"The process of person-environment interaction is a system, as we have noted; but it must be remembered that this system is embedded within a hierarchy of other systems, some of which are at a higher, and others at a lower, level than the person-environment system itself" (Magnusson & Allen, 1983, p. 370). Thus, the development of delinquency is best conceptualized as spirals within spirals (like funnel clouds of tornadoes within increasingly larger funnel clouds), each influencing the other. The larger, more powerful funnel clouds (e.g., macrosystems) influence the inner funnels more than the inner funnels influence the outer. In order to understand delinquency development adequately, "we need to know as much as possible about the degree and frequency of penetration from other systems at different levels into the systems being studied" (Magnusson & Allen, 1983, pp. 370–371).

As we have described, the family, school, and peer systems interact with each other and with the larger systems (the community) and the smaller systems (the person), forming a rich tapestry of mesosystems. The delinquent is not an isolated entity of deviance, but rather is embedded among swirls of other systems. The delinquent is a totality who views the world from a certain perspective, functions as an ongoing system, and interacts with other systems.

Terence Thornberry (1987) ties interactionism to theory and research on delinquency. Thornberry asserts that most theories of delinquency, classical and contemporary, are plagued by three fundamental limitations. First, they tend to be unidirectional in their explanations rather than reciprocal. They describe adolescents as being propelled along a single, one-way path. Early factors affect later ones in a single direction. Falling into the company of bad peers or limited opportunity, for instance, pushes the child toward a life of delinquency and crime. Second, most theories of delinquency do not recognize the important developmental changes that occur over the life course. They fail to consider that, "as the developmental process unfolds, life circumstances change, developmental milestones are met (or, for some, missed), new social roles are created, and new networks of attachments and commitments emerge" (Thornberry, 1987, p. 881). Third, most theories assume uniform causal effects throughout the social structure (such as race, class, and community of residence). In other words, most theories ignore the person's position in a given society and "fail to provide an understanding of the sources of initial variation in both delinquency and its presumed causes" (p. 864). Youngsters from lower SES, for example, may be at a decidedly greater disadvantage in relation to commitment to family, school, and conventional beliefs than those from the working and middle classes. But we cannot *assume* this is the case; there are multiple exceptions. Thornberry argues that many theories are not sensitive to the initial systems network within which one begins life.

According to Thornberry (1987), a viable theory of delinquency must take into consideration the concept of reciprocity, developmental changes across time, and the initial setting for a person's developmental sequence. Two concepts are emphasized in the model: the concept of **reciprocity** and the initial starting place to begin describing this reciprocity or interactionism. Reciprocity refers to the process whereby individuals and social environments mutually influence one another in an ongoing process. For example, peers may be a contributing cause to delinquency, but it is equally plausible that delinquent behavior causes certain individuals to seek each other out. In other words, delinquency-prone adolescents may look for the company of other delinquency-prone adolescents, and when they get together, their delinquent behavior is likely to increase.

Thornberry's interactional theory further asserts,

> The fundamental cause of delinquency lies in the weakening of social constraints over the conduct of the individual. . . . The weakening of controls simply allows for a much

> wider array of behavior, including the continued conventional action, failure
> as indicated by school dropout and sporadic employment histories, alcoholism,
> mental illness, delinquent and criminal careers, or some combination of these
> outcomes. (p. 865)

Thus, weakened social controls reduce the behavioral restrictions, encouraging the individual to experiment with any variety of nondeviant and deviant behaviors. For delinquency to occur, the individual must find him- or herself in an "interactive setting in which delinquency is learned, performed, and reinforced" (p. 865). In this sense, Thornberry is including both control and Aker's social learning in his model. But he is careful to emphasize that he is not integrating the two theories; he is simply engaging in "theoretical elaboration." That is, Thornberry is extending the theories to fit with empirical findings.

Thornberry focuses on the interrelationships among six concepts: (1) attachment to parents; (2) commitment to school; (3) belief in conventional values; (4) associations with delinquent peers; (5) adoption of delinquent values; and (6) engaging in delinquent behavior. The first three are from Hirschi's social control theory; the next two are from Akers' social learning theory. When attachment to parents, commitment to school, and belief in conventional values are strong, the person's behavior is channeled toward conventional society. When one or more of these bonds are weakened, behavioral freedom increases, and the probability of delinquent involvement increases correspondingly. Involvement in delinquency, in turn, reduces the bonds to parents, school, and conventional society. Thus, while weakening of bonds initially causes engagement in delinquency, delinquency eventually becomes its own indirect cause because it influences (weakens further) the individual's bonds to family, school, and conventional beliefs. Unless this causal loop is interrupted, higher and higher rates of delinquent involvement are likely.

Thornberry also suggests that parental influences have their greatest impact during the early formative years and become less as the child grows older. "The family declines in relative importance as the adolescent's own world of school and peers takes on increasing significance" (p. 879). In other words, the social systems of the child change, and the networks and microsystems grow larger, more complicated, and more influential with age. This observation has the substantial support of many developmental psychologists (e.g., Bronfenbrenner, 1979; Garbarino, 1982; Hartup, 1983).

Finally, theories must consider where each person begins his or her developmental journey.

> Youths from middle-class families, given their greater stability and economic security,
> are likely to start with a stronger family structure, greater stakes in conformity, and
> higher chances of success, and all of these factors are likely to reduce the likelihood
> of initial delinquent involvement. In brief, the initial values of the interactional
> variables are systematically related to the social class of origin. (Thornberry,
> 1987, p. 885)

Children deprived of family stability, a decent and comfortable physical environment, a caring social network, adequate nutrition and medical care, and a neighborhood where crime is held in check begin the interactional course at a decidedly different place than children who have these advantages. This interactive model illustrates well some of the points made in this chapter and appears to hold great promise in understanding, preventing, and treating delinquency.

Summary and Conclusions

Theories in criminology are offered in an attempt to make some sense out of what is often inexplicable. When confronted with evidence of a particularly heinous juvenile crime or with a pattern of persistent, antisocial behavior, we seek explanations. In this chapter we have reviewed some of the classic explanations that have been offered by both sociologically oriented and psychologically oriented criminologists. In addition to understanding, however, psychologists believe that a major goal of theory is to predict (and thus ultimately prevent) behavior. If we can predict with a high degree of certainty that a given individual will be antisocial, we should be able to eliminate or diminish the risk factors and establish or strengthen the protective factors in that individual's life. As we have seen, and will continue to see throughout this text, this is a complex undertaking.

The most influential early theories in juvenile delinquency were proposed by sociologists, often reacting against the view that delinquents were somehow intellectually or emotionally deficient. Representatives of the Chicago School, for example, believed that social conditions, particularly in urban areas, promoted antisocial behavior. Such factors as poverty, high mobility, and conflicts in values and norms among various cultures all led to social disorganization, which was reflected in a breakdown in the family's control over its children. Representatives of strain theory believed that normlessness in society, as well as society's emphasis on material goods without providing the means to attain them, led children (and adults) to seek illegal avenues. Although these early theories focused on crime among those in the lower class, later adaptations—particularly of strain theory—expanded to include crimes and delinquent acts committed by individuals in the middle and upper classes. Thus, Agnew's general strain theory acknowledges that such factors as loss of valued goals can occur within any economic level.

Learning theories have taken a decidedly different approach, focusing on how individuals or groups learn criminal behavior, rather than on their place in the social structure. In psychology these theories have their roots in behaviorism, including Pavlovian classical conditioning. Even more influential, though, is Skinnerian behaviorism, which emphasizes the importance of reinforcement if behavior is to be learned. Humans operate on their environment in order to achieve positive and negative reinforcements; behaviors that bring about these reinforcements are maintained. To Skinner, punishment (or noxious stimuli) was ineffective; extinction of undesirable behavior could best be achieved by withholding reinforcement. Social learning theorists saw individuals as learning more from other individuals, who serve as models for their behavior.

Learning theory in sociology is most apparent in the differential association theory of Sutherland and in the differential association–reinforcement theory of Akers. Sutherland, who had considerable antipathy toward psychology and its individualistic theory, nonetheless saw criminal behavior as learned in intimate groups. Akers added the element of reinforcement to Sutherland's theory.

Other theories that rely heavily on psychological concepts are labeling, cognitive constraint theories, control theories, and the general theory of crime. Sociologists associated with the labeling perspective blamed society for its placement of negative tags, either through social censure or through the court process. The outcome was a negative self-concept and the individual's internalization of the deviant label. Hirschi's social control theory emphasizes the need for individuals to be bonded to society through such elements as attachment and belief. In the contemporary general theory of crime, proposed by Hirschi and Gottfredson, the psychological concept of self-control is dominant.

We ended the chapter with a discussion of Bronfenbrenner's systems theory and interactionism. The former is rarely considered a theory in criminology, even though Bronfenbrenner's delineation of the various systems in which individuals are embedded is clearly relevant to the study of delinquency. Those who seek explanations for antisocial behavior cannot ignore these multiple influences on a child's or adolescent's life. Interactionism is compatible with Bronfenbrenner's systems approach, because it appreciates the social systems and networks in a child's world. An interactionist approach also tries to integrate key ideas from various theories (e.g., the bonding associated with social control and the learning associated with social learning) in order to explain a broader range of behavior.

Key Terms and Concepts

anomie
appeal to higher loyalties
attachment
belief
chronosystem
cognitive constructs
commitment
condemnation of the condemners
containment theory
control ratios
criminal opportunity
denial of injury
denial of responsibility
denial of the victim
differential association theory
differential association–
  reinforcement
differential opportunity theory
ecological distribution of
  delinquency
exosystems
extinction
general strain theory
general theory of crime
infrasystems
inner containment
interactionism
involvement
justifying discriminative stimuli

labeling interactions
life-history method
macrosystems
master status
mesosystem
microsystem
modeling
modes of adaptation
negative reinforcement
neutralizing discriminative
  stimuli
observational learning
outer containment
outsiders
positive discriminative stimuli
positive reinforcement
primary deviance
process-based theories
punishment
pure deviants
reciprocity
reinforcements
secondary deviance
secret deviance
self-regulation
social disorganization
structure-based theories
subordinate status
techniques of neutralization

CHAPTER 6

DEVELOPMENTAL THEORIES AND MODELS OF DELINQUENCY

❧

CHAPTER OBJECTIVES

◆ Identify and define key concepts in developmental perspectives of delinquency, including developmental norms and age of onset

◆ Present the major developmental theories of delinquency

◆ Describe in some detail Moffitt's developmental theory, the most researched and discussed developmental theory of delinquency

◆ Examine the coercion developmental theory, one of the most frequently discussed in prevention and treatment of delinquency

◆ Outline the Loeber and Stouthamer-Loeber developmental theory, a well-researched and carefully hypothesized theory of delinquency

◆ Sketch other developmental theories of delinquency that have solid research support and approach developmental models differently

Over the past three decades, the psychological study of crime has shifted away from personality traits as the sole or even the major determinants of criminal and delinquent behavior and toward a more interactive cognitive and developmental focus. A considerable amount of more contemporary research has focused on understanding the *developmental processes* leading to aggression, antisocial behavior, and delinquency during the elementary school years and into adolescence. Contemporary research has consistently demonstrated that the offender population consists of various subgroups, each one following an identifiable developmental pathway that is associated with different risks and outcomes (Wiesner & Windle, 2004).

Studying the developmental process of individuals requires an examination of the trajectory of that development. A **developmental trajectory**, or **developmental pathway**, reflects the course of an individual's cognitive, emotional, biological, and social growth, maturation, and overall change over time. In a sense, we are examining the chronosystems of the individual. Investigating the differences in the developmental trajectories of individuals is more informative and more predictive of delinquency than focusing on the differences among individuals at any one point in time. Theories that use developmental trajectories as models can examine several influences at once and can integrate these into a sequential chain to suggest how antisocial behavior is shaped and sustained (Kazdin, 1989).

Research has led to the striking consensus that children and adolescents follow different developmental pathways in their offending or nonoffending careers. Some children engage in stubborn, defiant, and disobedient behavior at very young ages, progressing to mild and then more-severe forms of violence and criminal behavior during adolescence and young adulthood (Dahlberg & Potter, 2001). Some children exhibit cruelty to animals, aggressive behavior toward peers, bullying, and substance abuse at a very early age and continue this antisocial pathway far into adulthood. Other children show very few signs of antisocial behavior at very young ages but during adolescence engage in various forms of delinquent behavior. Still others avoid engaging in any significant antisocial behavior over their lifetimes.

There is good evidence that most serious, persistent delinquency patterns usually begin early and worsen with age. Researchers have noted early childhood differences in impulsiveness, social skills, and feelings for others among those children who become seriously antisocial, as compared to those children who stay on a prosocial life course. Contemporary developmental psychologists have begun targeting the development of antisocial behavior even during the preschool years.

A host of questions about delinquency have been investigated by developmental psychologists in recent years, but the two questions drawing the most attention have been these: (1) To what extent does the development of antisocial behavior demonstrate stability over time? and (2) Does a single pathway or do multiple pathways best capture individuals' development of antisocial behavior (Loeber & Stouthamer-Loeber, 1998)?

The first question asks if antisocial behavior follows a predictable developmental sequence, rather than being continually shifted by subsequent experiences. This issue is often referred to as the continuity question in developmental psychology. If aggression and other antisocial behaviors follow a discernible, relatively stable pathway, then it is possible to not only predict future behaviors but also develop preventive measures to reduce future antisocial behaviors. Abnormally high levels of aggressive behavior, for example, do appear to remain stable over time. Research in the emerging field of developmental psychopathology clearly demonstrates that *some* individuals—even as toddlers—exhibit aggressive behaviors that carry on through a life course of violent crime. For example, Wicks-Nelson and Israel (2003) note that one of the most important features of conduct disorder, which typically includes the component of aggression, is its stability over time: "Considerable evidence exists that the presence of early conduct-disordered behavior appears to be related to later aggressive and antisocial behavior and to a range of adverse psychological and social-emotional outcomes" (p. 206).

As noted in Chapter 3, almost all "normal" children display physical aggression early, usually beginning before 24 months of age and reaching a peak at around 6 years of age. A vast majority of children, however, decrease the frequency of physical aggression during the early school years as a result of socialization. As described in Chapter 4, even children living under dire and adverse risk conditions, ranging from maltreatment to poor neighborhoods, are able to adopt a prosocial behavioral pattern. The challenge, then, is to identify how and why most children outgrow their aggression but a small minority (3% to 5%) do not.

The second question that intrigues developmental psychologists relates to whether there are several developmental pathways that lead to similar delinquent and criminal behaviors in the long run. As noted by Lahey and Waldman (2003), "Although it is generally agreed that antisocial behavior has a multifactorial origin that involves both genetic and environmental factors (and probably multiple types of each), much less attention has been paid to what this might mean in terms of causal pathways" (p. 6). As the research results come in, it is becoming increasingly apparent that there are multiple developmental pathways on a trajectory toward delinquency and antisocial behavior (Lahey & Waldman, 2003). The question now becomes, How many meaningful developmental pathways can be identified? Two? Three? More? In this chapter we try to answer that question.

HISTORICAL ROOTS OF THE DEVELOPMENTAL PERSPECTIVE ON DELINQUENCY

Much of the early work on a developmental theory of antisocial behavior was inspired by **social learning theory** (Tremblay, 2000). As discussed in Chapter 5, this theory posits that all behavior is learned through a process involving imitation of models or significant others in one's environment, as well as reinforcement. For example, the work of Patterson and his colleagues at the Oregon Social Learning Center (Patterson, 1982; Patterson, Dishion, & Bank, 1984) concentrated on understanding how family interactions and peer relationships influence the development of antisocial behavior. Researchers observed the interactions among family members in the families of preadolescents and adolescents with behavioral problems. In the 1980s, the social learning perspective and cognitive theories were merged to create social-information-processing models of antisocial behavior (Dodge, 1986; Huesmann, 1988; Tremblay, 2000). The focus of this perspective was on how the brain operates in making decisions and drawing conclusions.

Another major influence on developmental perspectives was **systems theory**, as outlined by developmental psychologist Urie Bronfennbrenner (1979). Also discussed in Chapter 5, Bronfennbrenner's theory emphasized the social ecology of development, which considers the multiple influences of various social settings (i.e., family, peers, schools, and neighborhoods) and their interactions. Systems theory led the way in pointing out that the relative impact of parenting, peer, and neighborhood behavior may vary in different environments or at different points of development (Ingoldsby & Shaw, 2002; Sameroff et al., 2004). Sameroff et al. (2004) cogently demonstrated the importance of the various social contexts that work together in making unique contributions to the development of antisocial behavior. They demonstrated, also, that there are many routes to delinquency, depending on the interactions of these contextual factors. Furthermore, their study made it clear that one of the most important determinants of behavior is the social contexts in which it occurs. This is one of the key tenets of the developmental perspective.

A third influence on the developmental perspective on juvenile delinquency has been the emergence of **developmental psychopathology**, which refers to the study of behavioral disorders within the context of developmental influences. This field of study seeks to unify and integrate knowledge from different developmental and clinical perspectives (Cicchetti & Rogosch, 2002). Although developmental psychopathology views disordered behavior in relation to normal behavior (Wicks-Nelson & Israel, 2003), it argues that there are *multiple* contributors to the development of maladaptive and adaptive behaviors (Calkins & Fox, 2002). The issue of change and continuity of behavior is the central concern of developmental psychopathology, as well as of developmental psychology.

BASIC CONCEPTS

Three important points will become clear during the course of this chapter. One, as noted by Schaeffer and her colleagues (2003), is that despite the differences in terminology and emphasis, each development theory or model of antisocial behavior identifies from two to five distinct groups of antisocial youth with different behavioral patterns, risk factors, and prognoses for desistence. Each theory or model identifies one or two chronic, serious, persistent offender groups whose early and serious aggressive behavior may be related to biological or genetic vulnerability exacerbated by problems in parenting or the social environment. Each theory or model also proposes one or two groups whose antisocial behavior starts later in development, is usually less violent, and generally stems from later experiences with the social environment. In addition, each theory or model notes that there is at least one other group of youths who do not show serious antisocial behavior while growing up.

The second important point reflected in this chapter is that the developmental theories and models of antisocial behavior have focused almost exclusively on boys, to the exclusion of girls. Basically, the early course of female antisocial behavior remains unknown (Schaeffer, Petras, Ialongo, Poduska, & Kellam, 2003). What *is* known suggests that boys and girls may follow very different developmental trajectories on the way to antisocial behavior.

The third point is that although the prediction of later antisocial behavior based on these early pathways is not perfect, it is exceptionally accurate in many cases (Petras et al., 2004; Schaeffer et al., 2003). But as we noted in earlier chapters, resilience and protective factors may come into play at any time during development and across the life span. Consequently, developmental trajectories provide only rough estimates of the life course; rarely do early experiences automatically result in problem behaviors (or adjustment) later on.

In addition to these points of consensus, there are several concepts that occur frequently in the literature on pathways and deserve early definition: cumulation, equifinality, developmental norms, and age of onset.

CUMULATION AND EQUIFINALITY

Cumulation suggests that the probability of a violent or antisocial outcome builds, brick by brick, as risk factors are added to a child's life (Dodge, 2001). In other words, some scholars believe that risk factors operate in an additive or cumulative fashion. For instance, a significant amount of research suggests that youths exposed to multiple risks are more likely than others to engage in later violence (Herrenkohl et al., 2000). However, it is also believed that the multiple effects of risks can be lowered by prevention efforts designed to remove at least some of the risk factors (Dodge, 2001). This can be done at any given time during the life course by introducing protective factors known to alter the overall effects of certain risk factors (Dahlberg & Potter, 2001).

Equifinality refers to the frequent observation that there are multiple pathways to the same final outcome of violence and antisocial behavior (Dodge, 2001). For this text, it means that there are different ways of becoming delinquent, antisocial, or violent. Thus, prevention efforts that focus on certain risk factors will have an effect on some, but not nearly all, high-risk children.

DEVELOPMENTAL NORMS

Developmental norms serve as standards to evaluate a child's development and behavior. The average child is expected to roll over, sit up, stand, walk, and talk within a certain age range. Because children change so rapidly and there is such a wide spectrum of behavioral differences, norms are only rough estimations for comparison purposes. Delay or failure to demonstrate normative development *may* suggest some problems or deficiencies, but adults in a child's environment must guard against assuming that there is something wrong when there is a delay. Some infants do not roll over until they are almost ready to sit up; some produce many words before showing any interest in walking, others utter very few words but walk steadily well before they have reached their first birthday. However, significant delay in reaching these developmental milestones can be a cause for concern. Likewise, if a child continues to display childish or immature behavior beyond a typical age, developmental problems may be indicated. For example, noncompliance is a typical behavior that is common during the second year of life—hence the label "the terrible twos" (Keenan, 2001). However, for most children, there is a slow but steady decline in this behavior during the preschool-age period. Other studies have demonstrated that it is not unusual in our society for preschool children to lie to avoid punishment (Bussey, 1992; Ceci, Leichtman, & Putnick, 1992); approximately 20% of 4- to 5-year-old girls and boys engage in mild to frequent lying (Keenan, 2001). But unlike noncompliance, lying does not seem to change with age.

One of the hallmarks of developmental psychopathology is the idea that knowledge of normal development is necessary to fully understand psychopathology (Cicchetti & Rogosch, 2002). Thus, knowledge of the biological, cognitive, and social changes that occur during normal development can contribute toward an understanding of delinquency and serious antisocial behavior. More importantly, the identification of distortions, disturbances, or degeneration of normal functioning that leads to serious forms of antisocial behavior can provide important clues as to strategies that may be most effective in prevention and treatment.

Cultural and gender norms should also be considered in deciding what is normal or abnormal. Different cultures have different expectations about child behavior (Weisz, Chaiyasit, Weiss, Eastman, Eastman, & Jackson, 1995). In Japanese schools, for example, if an altercation occurs between young children, the children themselves are expected to resolve it, with minimal interference from the teacher. In American schools, the teacher is expected to intervene because the aggressive behavior might accelerate. In other words, the norm is not to tolerate such behavior. Norms are basically "pooled knowledge about child development that are culturally transmitted from one generation to the next" (Masten & Coatsworth, 1998, p. 206). While the milestones found in baby books are examples of norms, there are far more subtle behavioral patterns that are also expected in various cultures. In many societies, males are expected to be more physically aggressive, active, and stimulation seeking, whereas females are expected to be more passive, physically nonaggressive, dependent, and empathetic. Although there is some evidence of biological factors associated with these behaviors, normative expectations also encourage them.

AGE OF ONSET

Onset has become one of the most fashionable words in developmental theories of delinquency and crime (Tremblay, 2000). "From a developmental perspective the word 'onset' generally refers to the age at which an individual first starts to engage in a type of behaviour that will persist for a relatively long period of time" (Tremblay, 2000, p. 132). Usually, **age of onset** is measured by asking parents or others who know the child, such as teachers, to report the age at which a specific problem first occurred. Tremblay notes that many toddlers hit, kick, intentionally break things, take other children's toys, and resist the authority of adults from the time they can walk and talk (Lahey & Waldman, 2003; Tremblay, Japel, et al., 1999). Although not all toddlers display these behaviors, about 40% do. Thus, these behaviors are considered normative for this age. However, the prevalence of these behaviors declines significantly as the child grows older and becomes socialized. At the age of 5, for example, children generally acquire the social skills to play cooperatively. In general, physical aggression that is pervasive, frequent, and of a severe form after age 7 is considered unusual in American culture (Keenan, 2001). Consequently, if parents report aggressive behavior at age 3, it is not necessarily indicative of future problems (although in combination with other factors, it may be); however, if they report the same aggressive behavior at age 7, a significant behavior problem may be indicated. In a different example, the initial drinking of alcoholic beverages suggests very different qualitative processes of development at age 10 as compared to age 17. Although the 17-year-old is still under the legal drinking age, we would worry more about the 10-year-old.

The age of onset of aggression has been the focus of careful study in developmental criminology over the past two decades. Researchers have discovered that antisocial behavior changes so much in expression and frequency over the course of development that studies conducted at any single point in development provide only limited information (Bongers et al., 2004; Kraemer, Yesavage, Taylor, & Kupfer, 2000). As noted earlier, most children show elevated levels of physical aggression before age 5 and as early as age 2 but then show a significant reduction in that behavior as they get older (Bongers et al., 2003; Tremblay, Japel, et al., 1999). However, some children continue to display significant physical aggression throughout childhood and into adolescence (Nagin & Tremblay, 1999). Research has indicated that an early age of onset of antisocial behavior is related to more serious and persistent antisocial and delinquent behavior (Loeber & Farrington, 2000). In one study (Le Blanc, McDuff, Charlebois, & Gagnon, 1991), the age of onset of delinquency was assessed retrospectively through self-report. That study revealed that at least one act of serious delinquency—defined as theft of $100 or more, burglary, or fighting with a weapon—was committed by 21% of low-income boys as early as age 4 or 5.

Some offenders start in early childhood, while others begin offending in early adolescence or later. Some offenders show a gradual involvement in crime, while others display signs of violent behavior early on. Research indicates that early offenders may differ from late offenders in fundamental ways and that early offenders have more extensive and serious delinquent careers (Krohn, Thornberry, Rivera, & Le Blanc, 2001). According to the developmental perspective, antisocial behavior that begins at midadolescence is not qualitatively the same as antisocial behavior that begins during the preschool years. More importantly, these two types of behavior require different strategies for prevention, intervention, and treatment. Table 6–1 summarizes these important basic concepts.

TABLE 6–1: Summary of Basic Concepts

Concept	Definition
Cumulation	An additive process suggesting that the more risk factors a child experiences, the more likely he or she is to become antisocial or delinquent
Equifinality	The attainment of the same final outcome, such as serious delinquent behavior, by way of multiple pathways
Developmental norms	The typical skills and expected level of achievement associated with a particular stage of development
Age of onset	The chronological age at which a problem first occurs

MOFFITT'S DEVELOPMENTAL THEORY

Age of onset is a concept that appears in most of the developmental models of delinquency, including the well-known theory of Terrie Moffitt (1993a, 1997). In fact, in Moffitt's theory, age of onset is the primary feature that distinguishes two alternative pathways. In one, serious, persistent offenders begin offending during early childhood and continue throughout much of their lives; in the other, youth begin offending during early adolescence and stop, usually before they reach adulthood.

LIFE-COURSE-PERSISTENT OFFENDERS

The ongoing research of Moffitt and her colleagues (1993a, 1993b, 2003) has provided the major impetus for the developmental perspective offering an explanation for delinquency. On one path Moffitt identifies the child who begins a lifelong trajectory of delinquency and crime at a very early age, probably around age 3 or even younger. Moffitt (1993a) observes, "Across the life course, these individuals exhibit changing manifestations of antisocial behavior: biting and hitting at age four, shoplifting and truancy at age ten, selling drugs and stealing cars at age sixteen, robbery and rape at age twenty-two, and fraud and child abuse at age thirty" (p. 679). These individuals, whom Moffitt calls **life-course-persistent (LCP) offenders**, continue their antisocial ways across all kinds of conditions and situations.

Moffitt reports that many of these LCP offenders exhibit neurological problems during early childhood, such as difficult temperaments as infants, attention-deficit disorder and hyperactivity as children, and learning problems during their later school years. Judgment and problem-solving deficiencies are often apparent when these children reach adulthood. According to Moffitt (2003), "The child's risk emerges from inherited or acquired neuropsychological variation, initially manifested as subtle cognitive deficits, difficult temperaments, or hyperactivity" (p. 50). These neuropsychological problems are exacerbated by a high-risk social environment, such as inadequate parenting, disrupted family bonds, and poverty. The social-environment risks expand beyond the immediate family as the child ages, to include poor relations with peers, teachers, and other adults. LCP offenders generally commit a wide assortment of aggressive and violent crimes over their lifetimes.

LCPs as children miss opportunities to acquire and practice prosocial and interpersonal skills at each critical stage of development, partly because they are rejected and avoided by their childhood peers and partly because their parents, teachers, and caretakers become frustrated and give up on them (Coie, Belding, & Underwood, 1988; Coie, Dodge, & Kupersmith, 1990; Moffitt, 1993a). According to Moffitt (1993a), "If social and academic skills are not mastered in childhood, it is very difficult to later recover from lost opportunities" (p. 684). Furthermore, disadvantaged homes, inadequate schools, and violent, threatening neighborhoods are factors that are very likely to exacerbate the ongoing and developing antisocial behavior patterns.

Overall, LCPs are plagued by problems throughout their lifetimes. To paraphrase Jaffee et al. (2005), early-onset antisocial behavior appears to be associated with pervasive mental (Moffitt, Caspi, Harrington, & Milne 2002), physical (Farrington, 1995), economic (Caspi, Wright, Moffitt, & Silva, 1998), and interpersonal (Moffitt et al., 2002) problems across the life span. Wiesner, Kim, and Capaldi (2005) describe it like this: "Developmental theories posit that antisocial behavior that onsets early in childhood is likely to lead to a cascade of secondary problems, including academic failure, involvement with deviant peers, substance abuse, depressive symptoms, health-risk sexual behavior, and work failure" (p. 252). It appears as though LCPs become entrapped in a deviant lifestyle right out of the developmental gate, and they are embedded in a social context that further increases their risk status (van Lier, Vitaro, Wanner, Vuijk, & Crijnen, 2005). Other researchers, too, have consistently reported that a small minority of children (about 3% to 5%) follow a highly antisocial developmental trajectory (van Lier, Vuijk, & Crijen, 2005). They are almost exclusively males. In addition, the level of antisocial behavior of LCPs seems to diverge from their less antisocial counterparts across time (van Lier, Vitaro, et al., 2005). In other words, LCPs actually increase their offending as they grow older, perhaps in part because of their exposure to the learning, practicing, and reinforcement of antisocial behavior through affiliation with similarly diverging antisocial peers. Basically, antisocial youth progressively affiliate with similarly antisocial peers (van Lier, Vitaro, et al., 2005).

ADOLESCENT-LIMITED OFFENDERS

The great majority of delinquent offenders, however, are those individuals who follow a second developmental path. They typically begin offending during their adolescent years and stop offending sometime after their 18th birthday. Moffitt calls these individuals **adolescent-limited (AL) offenders**. Their developmental histories do not reflect the early and persistent antisocial problems that members of the LCP group manifest. However, the frequency—and in some cases the violence level—of offending during the teen years may be as high as that of the LCP youth. In effect, the teenage offending patterns of the ALs and LCPs may be highly similar (Moffitt et al., 1996). "The two types cannot be discriminated on most indicators of antisocial and problem behavior in adolescence; boys on the LCP and AL paths are similar on parent, self-, and official records of offending, peer delinquency, substance abuse, unsafe sex, and dangerous driving" (p. 400). That is, a professional could not easily identify the group classification (AL or LCP) *during the teen years* simply by examining juvenile arrest records, self-reports, or information provided by parents. Moffitt (2003) sums it up like this:

> Life-course-persistent offenders' antisocial behavior has its origins in neurodevelopmental processes, begins in childhood, and continues worsening thereafter. In contrast, adolescent-limited offenders' antisocial behavior has its origins in social processes, begins in adolescence, and desists in young adulthood. (p. 49)

The AL delinquent is most likely, during the teen years, to be involved in offenses that symbolize adult privilege and demonstrate autonomy from parental control. The antisocial behavior of these delinquents often stems from their dissatisfaction with their dependent status as children and their impatience to gain what they perceive as the privileges and rights of adulthood. Thus, they engage in vandalism, drug and alcohol offenses, and status offenses, such as running away or truancy. In addition, AL delinquents are likely to engage in crimes that are profitable or rewarding, like theft, but they also have the tendency to abandon these actions when prosocial styles become more rewarding. In other words, the onset of young adulthood brings opportunities not attainable during the teen years, such as leaving home for college, obtaining a full-time job, or entering a relationship with a prosocial person.

Interestingly, the evidence shows that in adolescence, teens that place high value on conforming to adults' rules and expectations are often unpopular with peers (Moffitt, 2003). In this sense, AL offenders are more strongly influenced by delinquent peers than are LCPs. It appears that ALs rely on peer support for delinquency and antisocial behavior, whereas LCPs are more willing to commit antisocial behavior independent of peer support. Table 6–2 compares some of the characteristics of LCPs and ALs.

In contrast to the LCP child, the AL youngster has learned to get along with others, and thus the AL delinquent tends to have a satisfactory repertoire of academic skills that enable him or her to "get ahead." Moffitt's theory hypothesizes that most young persons who become AL offenders desist from crime as they become mature, turning gradually to a more conventional lifestyle (Moffitt & Caspi, 2001). It is becoming increasingly apparent, though, that not all do.

In a follow-up study of AL offenders, Moffitt et al. (2002) discovered that many ALs were still showing some antisocial behavior at age 26. In addition, the researchers found that some men who were identified as AL offenders in adolescence accounted for twice their share of the property and drug convictions during adulthood, as compared to men without an offending history. It seems as though some former ALs relied on crime to supplement their incomes. To explain this finding, the researchers speculated that "emerging

TABLE 6–2: Comparison of LCPs and ALs

	Life-Course-Persistent (LCP)	*Adolescent-Limited (AL)*
Onset of crime or antisocial behavior	Early (perhaps as early as age 3)	Later (usually during the early adolescent years)
Duration of criminal behavior	Continuing throughout the offender's life	Usually stopping after early adulthood
Types of criminal behavior	Assorted	Assorted
Developmental background	Frequently exhibiting neurological problems, ADHD, conduct problems	Usually normal and without neurological problems
Academic skills	Usually below average	Usually average to above average
Interpersonal and social skills	Usually below average	Usually average to above average

adulthood"—which could be regarded as a new developmental state—prolongs the crime-promoting conditions of adolescence. "This state is characterized by roleless floundering, in which young people neither perceive themselves to be adults, nor choose to occupy any adult roles historically favored by people in their 20s (e.g., parenthood, marriage)" (p. 200).

GENDER DIFFERENCES

Moffitt's theory has been developed primarily on the developmental trajectories of males. Do females demonstrate a similar pattern? Moffitt and Caspi (2001) report that the developmental typology appears to fit both genders. However, the LCP pattern of behavior is far more likely to be followed by males than females (approximately 10 males to 1 female), whereas the gender difference is negligible for the AL pattern (approximately 1.5 males to 1 female). These findings are consistent with several other earlier studies (Kratzer & Hodgins, 1999; Mazerolle, Brame, Paternoster, Piquero, & Dean, 2000).

A growing body of research has been relatively consistent concerning gender differences in the age of onset of persistent physical aggression and antisocial behavior. It now appears that girls may be more vulnerable to early onset than was previously thought. Although early research suggested that early-onset persistent aggression might be exclusively a male phenomenon, Brennan, Hell, Bor, Najman, and Williams (2003) found that girls in their sample displayed the same pattern as boys. In the Brennan study, 9% of the boys and 7.4% of the girls in the high-risk sample were classified as displaying early-onset persistent aggressive behavior. In a study of 820 girls, Côté, Zoccolillo, Tremblay, Nagin, and Vitaro (2001) found that only 1.4% of the girls clearly fit the LCP profile, but 9.6% of the girls demonstrated disruptive behaviors in elementary school that might classify some of them as LCPs during adolescence. These data are somewhat similar to the pattern found by Nagin and Tremblay (1999) in boys. When the researchers combined these two groups and followed them 10 years later into adolescence, it was discovered that the disruptive girls were 4.46 times more likely to participate in serious antisocial behavior as adolescents, as compared to girls who engaged in few, if any, disruptive behaviors during elementary school.

McCabe, Rodgers, Yeh, and Hough (2004) offer some evidence that a high percentage of seriously antisocial girls began their antisocial behavior before the age of 10. Similar results were reported by Leve and Chamberlain (2004), who found that 23% of seriously antisocial girls were arrested before age 11, and 71% before age 14. These results suggest that a large portion of girls can be considered early-onset delinquents and may well follow the same developmental trajectory as early-onset boys. These researchers identified parental transitions (e.g., separation, divorce, death, incarceration) and biological-parent criminality as the strongest predictors of early-onset status in girls.

Similarly, Gorman-Smith and Loeber (2005) report, based on extensive data from the National Youth Survey, that girls tend to follow the same developmental pathways toward antisocial behavior and delinquency as boys do. Although fewer girls than boys engage in antisocial or delinquent behavior, the girls that do show similar pathways. In other words, serious antisocial and delinquent involvement in girls showed early-onset antisocial patterns just as it did in boys. However, Gorman-Smith and Loeber learned that the risk factors for girls may be somewhat different than they are for boys. For example, because girls are more invested in interpersonal relationships than boys are, they are more likely to get involved in or be affected by parental conflict and transitions, a finding similar to that reported by Leve and Chamberlain (2004). Peer influences may also be different for boys and girls. Delinquent peers appear to be a necessary social condition for the early-onset of delinquency among adolescent girls, suggesting that the indicators of neurological/biological problems found in boys may not be that prevalent in girls (Moffitt, 2003). In addition, an intimate relationship with an offender (usually a boyfriend) is closely connected to serious delinquency in adolescent girls (Moffitt, Caspi, Rutter, & Silva, 2001). Therefore, although the developmental pathways may be similar, the family and peer risk factors may be different for boys and girls, exemplifying the principle of equifinality.

Not all scholars agree that the age of onset of serious antisocial behavior is similar for boys and girls. For instance, Silverthorn and Frick (1999) maintain that girls, as compared to boys, tend to engage in serious antisocial behavior for the first time at later ages—generally in adolescence. According to Silverthorn and Frick, antisocial behavior in girls is delayed because of such factors as parental and school-based socialization practices, which encourage girls to restrict their outward aggressive tendencies during middle childhood.

RACIAL AND ETHNIC DIFFERENCES

Moffitt (1994) originally postulated that developmental theory would apply to ethnic minority groups in basically the same manner that it applied to the white population. Because ethnic minority children are often exposed to a wide variety of high-risk physical and social environments, the hypothesis predicted that ethnic minorities would demonstrate a higher incidence of LCPs. Recent evidence supports this hypothesis (Kim-Cohen et al., 2004). As we learned earlier, poverty is associated with lower levels of maternal warmth, responsivity, and less opportunity for cognitively stimulating activities. Furthermore, "among poor black families, prenatal care is less available, infant nutrition is poorer, and the incidence of exposure to toxic and infectious agents is greater, placing infants at risk for nervous system problems that research has shown to interfere with prosocial child development" (Moffitt, 1994, p. 39).

OTHER PATHWAYS

As the research on developmental pathways has progressed, it has become clear to many researchers, including Moffitt herself (e.g., Moffitt et al., 2002), that there may be more than two pathways to delinquency. Over the past 15 years, social scientists have developed more sophisticated statistical techniques for identifying developmental pathways that result in delinquent and criminal behavior (Chung, Hill, Hawkins, Gilchrist, & Nagin, 2002; Wiesner & Windle, 2004). These new techniques indicate that at least one and probably more developmental paths must be added to account more fully for delinquent behavior.

For example, one subgroup of offenders are the **low-level chronic delinquents**, so called because they tend to offend persistently at low rates from childhood to adolescence and into adulthood (D'Unger, Land, McCall, & Nagin, 1998; Fergusson, Horwood, & Nagin, 2000; Nagin, Farrington, & Moffitt, 1995). In her own research,

Moffitt and her colleagues (Moffitt et al., 1996) identified a small group of males who displayed pervasive and persistent antisocial behavior problems during childhood, but who participated in only low to moderate delinquency during adolescence. Their antisocial behavior during adolescence was not extreme enough to meet the criteria for LCP, but their numbers were apparently not large enough for Moffitt and her colleagues to give them their own developmental pathway at the time. These offenders showed extremely undercontrolled temperaments as 3-year-olds, suffered family adversity during childhood, and apparently had low intelligence (Moffitt, 2003). Thus, the low-level chronics comprise a group that should be submitted to continuing research.

COERCION DEVELOPMENTAL MODEL

Like Moffitt, Patterson and colleagues also believe that what they call **early starters** are at greater risk for more serious criminal offending. However, the major difference is that the Patterson group places greater emphasis on the role of parenting than on specific characteristics of the child. The coercion developmental model contends that poor parental monitoring of child activities, disruptive family transitions (e.g., divorce), and inconsistent parental discipline are major psychosocial contributors to early-onset delinquency (Brennan et al., 2003; Patterson, 1982). This model argues that the key predictor of early-onset offending is the family environment in which the child learns to use coercive behaviors (e.g., temper tantrums, whining) to escape aversive parental discipline and authority.

Coercion theory acknowledges that certain children (e.g., those with an irritable temperament) are more likely to elicit inept parenting strategies. In the coercive cycle, the parent and child each behave in a way that is aversive to the other, in an attempt to control the other's behavior. As the child's aversive behaviors increase in intensity and frequency, the parent eventually acquiesces, unwittingly reinforcing the child's behavior. But as the child becomes increasingly irritating, the parent escalates power-assertion techniques and, presumably, the level of hostility displayed toward the child.

> In its most basic form, coercion theory is a model of the behavioral contingencies that explain how parents and children mutually "train" each other to behave in ways that increase the probability that children will develop aggressive behavior problems and that parents' control over these aversive behaviors will decrease. (Granic & Patterson, 2006, p. 101)

Coercive exchanges between parents and children may emerge as early as 18 months of age (Granic & Patterson, 2006). At approximately 18 to 24 months, a normative developmental pattern for children is to become oppositional, saying "no" to about anything and throwing occasional attention-getting tantrums. For most children, these behaviors peak at the end of the second year. However, for some, coercive exchanges may be triggered by inappropriate parental responses to these oppositional patterns and outbursts.

Coercion then becomes the child's primary interpersonal strategy and generalizes to environments outside the home. According to coercive theory, antisocial and coercive behavior progresses from faulty parent–toddler interactions to similar interactions with teachers, peers, and others in the child's environment. "The unskilled and overly aggressive child enters school unable to cooperate, share, attend quietly, and flexibly regulate and inhibit his angry and distressing emotions when they arise" (Granic & Patterson, 2006, pp. 117–118). The socially inept child who uses coercive methods in dealing with others soon finds he is rejected by his peers.

The coercion developmental model is largely based on social learning theory. According to that theory, "developmental trajectories for antisocial behavior are initiated, maintained, and diversified as a result of cumulative daily social experiences with parents, siblings, and peers that are highly aversive, inconsistent, and unsupportive" (J. Snyder, Reid, & Patterson, 2003, p. 31).

The theory is developmental in that it identifies two developmental trajectories of antisocial behavior, each characterized by an orderly sequence of stages (Patterson & Yoerger, 2002). "One trajectory leads to early arrest (prior to age 14) and adult crime and the other to late-onset arrests and desistence from adult crime" (Patterson & Yoerger, 2002, p. 147). However, the model holds that both the early- and late-start trajectories represent variations of the same basic processes. That is, social-environmental influences—such as divorce, poverty, parental depression—work in combination with inept parenting and deviant peer socialization to engender different levels of delinquent and antisocial behavior. In this model, inept parenting refers to parents who use ineffective discipline practices and who themselves tend to be antisocial and unemployed, living under low-socioeconomic conditions, and plagued by frequent marital transitions and discord.

PRESPECIFIED CONSTRAINTS

According to coercion theory, the early-onset antisocial trajectory may begin as early as birth (or before). The child is born with a particular temperament and other genetic/biological predispositions that may contribute to a coercive parenting style. These early predispositions are called **prespecified constraints** (Granic & Patterson, 2006). Examples include a difficult temperament, ADHD, and significant impairments in executive functioning and language abilities. Basically, prespecified constraints are risk factors. According to the coercion theory, parents also have prespecified constraints, such as depression, limited cognitive abilities, and a tendency to participate in antisocial behavior. Depressed mothers, for example, make more negative appraisals of their children, believe they have little control over their children, tend to withdraw from their infants, and are more likely to engage in coercive parenting (Granic & Patterson, 2006). Similarly, impoverished environments are considered prespecified constraining environments.

CHARACTERISTICS OF EARLY- AND LATE-ONSET OFFENDERS

According to coercion theory, three variables distinguish early- from late-onset trajectories: (1) the early-onset process begins during the preschool years, whereas the late-onset begins in midadolescence; (2) the inept parenting is more severe for the early-onset, as compared to the late-onset; and (3) the levels of social incompetence are more pronounced for the early- as compared to the late-onset delinquency. Early-onset delinquents tend to demonstrate limited levels of social skills, more disruptive peer relations, and lower self-esteem. Late-onset delinquents exhibit similar deficiencies, but not to as great a degree as early-onsets do.

Late-onset delinquents (or late starters) are characterized by their marginal levels of antisocial behavior and social competency. Basically, they are less antisocial than the early starters but more antisocial than nondelinquents. Moreover, the deviant peer group is more important for the development and maintenance of antisocial and delinquent behavior in late starters than in early starters. Research also finds that the likelihood of arrest as a young adult is high for early onsets, whereas the likelihood for late onsets is relatively low (Patterson & Yoerger, 2002). For example, the majority (71%) of late-onset boys desisted from involvement in adult crime (Patterson & Yoerger, 2002), whereas 74% of early-onset offenders were arrested as young adults (aged 21 to 29; Stattin & Magnusson, 1991).

The coercion developmental model takes the position that growth in antisocial behavior is discontinuous rather than continuous (Patterson & Yoerger, 2002). That is, during the developmental process, some forms of behavior increase while others decrease. For example, there is evidence that the rates of aggression in children decrease significantly between ages 2 and 12 (Stanger, Achenbach, & Verhulst, 1997). Thus, a **quiescent hypothesis** suggests that there is very little growth in the frequency or severity of antisocial behavior during the period from about age 2 through 12 for most children. Antisocial children, however, often get worse during this quiescent interval. They continue to rely on coercive strategies for dealing with others, and they begin to demonstrate an arrested ability to get along with others. Academic difficulties become apparent by the second or third grade, and rejection by normal peers is evident within a few weeks of school entrance. It is at this time that the warning signs of juvenile forms of aggression lead teachers (who are twice as likely as parents to identify aggressive behavior) to refer a child for testing and possible placement in special classrooms or programs.

The coercion developmental model has received impressive research support, suggesting that process variables play a prominent role in the development of persistent antisocial behavior. For example, the research continually demonstrates that coercive parents tend to be deficient in cognitive skills (Patterson & Yoerger, 2002). An unskilled caregiver often reacts to a child in such a way as to develop deviant behaviors and is unlikely to help develop socially competent behaviors. Further, the caregiver's lack of skills is often amplified if accompanied by such stress-inducing factors as divorce, unemployment, illness, and poverty.

BIDIRECTIONAL ASPECT

Coercion development theory hypothesizes that the child is an active agent in the process and not a passive blank slate simply receiving demands and experiences from the social environment. The child also makes demands on the environment and participates in the social exchange. Furthermore, children's choice of environments is not random. They gravitate toward social settings, activities, and people that are compatible with their own background, characteristics, and behavior (J. Snyder, Reid, & Patterson, 2003). Thus, unskilled antisocial children seek out places that involve association with antisocial peers and environments with minimal adult supervision. The younger child selects settings and peers at school that serve as adjuncts to the basic training in antisocial behavior that is being carried out by parents, caregivers, and siblings at home. Unfortunately, the child's coercive interpersonal style—typically developed early in life in the family setting—leads to rejection by many noncoercive peers, which encourages the child to select other individuals to reward his or her coercive style. "Typically, this would consist of younger children and also children who reinforce his or her deviant behaviors, and, on the short term, ignore his or her coercive interpersonal style" (Patterson & Yoerger, 2002, p. 150). Even in the elementary school grades, deviant peers provide reinforcement and encouragement for deviant behaviors. However, since there is usually a limited amount of time given to unsupervised peer interaction, the effect on the overall deviant and antisocial behavior may be minimal and may serve mainly as support for the family influence (Patterson & Yoerger, 2002). During adolescence, though, large amounts of time are unsupervised by adults. Consequently, deviant peers are likely to have significant influence in the development and maintenance of antisocial behavior.

Coercion development theory hypothesizes that antisocial behavior undergoes a transformation from being overt and open to being increasingly covert and unobservable during the elementary school years. For example, the shoving or kicking that occurs in the presence of the teacher in first grade shifts to bullying behavior out of the sight of the hall monitor in middle school. Many of the coercive-style children become bullies and intimidators quite early in their development. As adults (especially teachers) discourage overt forms of antisocial behavior, such as physical aggression and fighting, antisocial behavior "goes underground" and is increasingly expressed in its more surreptitious forms, especially in playground and neighborhood settings where peer interaction is subject to minimal adult monitoring.

GENDER DIFFERENCES

According to the coercive development perspective, gender differences in aggression are well in place by age 5 and persist throughout childhood and adolescence (J. Snyder, Reid, et al., 2003). These early differences largely favor aggressiveness in boys. The coercive perspective posits that gender differences in antisocial behavior are largely the result of the different environmental experiences and reinforcements encountered by boys and girls. Because boys and girls evoke different responses from parents, each gender responds differently to the same parenting conditions. Mothers tend to be more coercive toward boys than toward girls, and this difference appears to be more pronounced for highly aggressive boys and girls (J. Snyder, Reid, et al., 2003). The coercive development model hypothesizes that girls display less antisocial behavior because they are less frequently involved in coercive parent–child interactions and are also less frequently reinforced for oppositional and countercoercive responding (J. Snyder, Reid, et al., 2003).

Peer socialization factors begin to play a significant role as a child moves into preschool and kindergarten. Boys and girls demonstrate a strong preference for interaction with same-gender children beginning at age 3. This may be especially apparent in the case of boys, who tend to ignore girls who try to enter their play groups. There are more physical challenges, noncompliance, and rough-and-tumble play among boys, whereas there tends to be more cooperation, verbal exchange, compliance, and mutual accommodation among girls. Unlike boys, girls find fewer highly antisocial, same-gender older peers with whom to associate, model, or exchange deviant talk. Consequently, when girls do begin to show antisocial behavior, it most often occurs during the adolescent years and appears to be somewhat tied to pubescence. During adolescence the preference for same-gender peers diminishes, and a broad array of peer affiliates becomes available, including antisocial ones.

TABLE 6–3: Highlights of the Coercion Developmental Model	
Major theoretical base	• Social learning theory
Primary contributor to delinquency	• Coercive exchanges between parent and child
Additional contributors to delinquency	• Inadequate parental monitoring
	Disruptive family transitions
	Inconsistent parental discipline
Key concepts	• Early and late starters
	Prespecified constraints
	Discontinuous growth in antisocial behavior
	Quiescent hypothesis
	Bidirectional influences between social environment and child
	Peer socialization factors

Research by Capaldi, Dishion, Stoolmiller, and Yoerger (2001) underscores evidence that male aggression toward females is part of a deviant socialization process rather than a normative process. Their study found that friendships between antisocial male adolescents are likely to include mutual expressions of hostile talk about females. This hostile socialization process undermines the quality of intimate relationships these males are able to have with females throughout their adolescent and into their adult years. Table 6–3 identifies the major aspects of the coercion developmental models.

LOEBER AND STOUTHAMER-LOEBER MODEL

Even though the two onset-related pathways are significant, it is clear that alternative trajectories are needed to encompass some offenders. Loeber and Stouthamer-Loeber (1998) proposed *five* distinct subtypes to account for the accumulating evidence on developmental pathways. However, one of the five groups pertains only marginally to juveniles.

First, Loeber and Stouthamer-Loeber identified two types of life-course-persistent offenders. Like other models, this scheme sees LCP offenders as developing aggression in childhood and continuing and accelerating their aggressive behavior into adulthood. But differences related to that aggression distinguish two subgroups: (1) whether the serious aggression begins in early childhood or later childhood–early adolescence and (2) whether ADHD symptoms are present. Specifically, one persistent subgroup exhibits preschool onset of aggression and qualifies for an ADHD diagnosis, while the other displays a middle-childhood onset of aggressive behavior without clinical indications of ADHD. The first subtype is called the **preschool-onset subtype**; the second is called **childhood-adolescent-onset subtype**.

The role of ADHD is an important one to consider. According to Loeber and Stouthamer-Loeber (1998), the role of ADHD in the preschool-onset subtype is three-fold: "(a) It is associated with poor cognitive and academic functioning; (b) it is implicated in the maintenance of oppositional behavior; and (c) it activates an early, accelerated development of aggressive behaviors, conduct problems, and substance abuse" (p. 246). The childhood-adolescent subtype usually does not show ADHD symptoms. Instead, these youth display persisting oppositional behavior early in life, which eventually spills over into serious aggression and other antisocial behavior.

Loeber and Stouthamer-Loeber also hypothesized that there may be two subgroups of offenders whose aggression and other antisocial activity is limited. The principal feature of the limited-duration type is that these individuals outgrow serious aggression. These researchers suggest that they outgrow it either during the preschool–elementary school age or during late adolescence to early adulthood. The limited-duration subtypes are similar to Moffitt's adolescent-limited offender, except that one of the subgroups identified by Loeber and Stouthamer-Loeber begins and reduces or eliminates its involvement in serious aggressive behavior during childhood. Moffitt, in contrast, described the AL group as largely beginning and stopping aggression and other forms of violent or antisocial behavior during late adolescence or early adulthood.

The final subgroup, **late-onset offenders**, is hypothesized to include those youth who show no early problems with serious aggression but who later develop serious forms of aggression and antisocial behavior during late adolescence or early adulthood. In their review of the research in this area, Loeber and Stouthamer-Loeber found several studies revealing that a minority of adult violent offenders did not exhibit serious aggression early in life, suggesting that it might be necessary to establish a separate category for these young adult offenders. Loeber and Stouthamer-Loeber (1998) write that "the data indicate that in a minority of male and female populations, the onset of violence takes place in adulthood" (p. 246). Note that this fifth subgroup is not really a category of *juvenile* offenders, however, with the exception of those offenders who began in late adolescence (e.g., age 17) rather than in early adulthood (e.g., ages 18–24). Thus, if we are discussing developmental pathways to *delinquency*, this last group applies only marginally.

GENDER DIFFERENCES

As noted by Loeber and Stouthamer-Loeber (1998), the degree to which pathways characterize the development of antisocial behavior in girls is unclear (Blitstein et al., 2005; Dahlberg & Potter, 2001). Loeber and Stouthamer-Loeber (1998) find that, as noted earlier, the empirical research generally concludes that there are major gender differences in aggression in terms of behavior patterns, age of onset, and development over time. Although the extant research is extremely limited, girls seem to develop antisocial behaviors mainly during adolescence rather than earlier. In addition, girls seem to engage in a broader array of antisocial behaviors, whereas boys tend to show a greater specialization (Blitstein et al., 2005; R. F. Marcus, 1999).

Loeber and Stouthamer-Loeber (1998), as well as Gorman-Smith and Loeber (2005) hypothesize that girls are probably exposed to very different risk factors than boys are. For example, some research suggests that abused or neglected girls are more likely than abused or neglected boys to become violent during adolescence (Rivera & Widom, 1990). Recent evidence also suggests that protective factors seem to be more important for girls than for boys, especially when it comes to the development of violent behavior (Blitstein et al., 2005; Hollister-Wagner et al., 2001; Marshal & Chassin, 2000). Although the reasons for this difference remain unknown, Loeber and Stouthamer-Loeber (1998) speculate that the protective factors for girls may be very different in kind and impact from the protective factors for boys. Perhaps, they suggest, those protective factors that prevent girls from engaging in violence could be used to prevent violence in both genders. They write, "This is a crucial area of inquiry, because protective mechanisms found for women may also shed some light on why protective influences against violence apply to some men but not to others" (p. 254). One prominent protective factor for girls is the presence of a warm, responsive mother. Unfortunately, this factor does not appear to protect boys from engaging in violence (Blitstein et al., 2005).

A particularly strong individual risk factor for girls appears to be ADHD. Loeber and Stouthamer-Loeber (1998) report that once girls qualify for ADHD, they are at a substantially higher risk than boys are of developing other serious problems, including serious antisocial behavior. For example, some research (Szatmari, Boyle, & Offord, 1989) indicates that girls with ADHD are 40 times more likely to develop conduct disorders than are girls who do not demonstrate symptoms of ADHD. In the same study, boys with ADHD were 14.7 times more likely than their non-ADHD peers to be diagnosed with conduct disorder. Loeber and Stouthamer-Loeber refer to this phenomenon as the **gender paradox**.

The Loeber and Stouthamer-Loeber model is not the last word in identifying alternative pathways to delinquency. Other researchers continue to explore this area, also. Although it is too early to make many definitive statements about the number of different trajectories that may be possible, one thing seems clear: there are more than the two pathways previously identified by Moffitt and her colleagues.

OTHER DEVELOPMENTAL MODELS

The major models discussed here have prompted some researchers to propose adaptations or revisions, based on their own discoveries. Typically, these researchers are identifying more than two developmental paths. Schaeffer et al. (2003) examined the developmental pathways of antisocial behavior within a sample of urban, primarily African-American boys. Teacher-rated aggression, measured longitudinally from first to seventh grade, was used to identify the antisocial trajectories in the sample. The researchers were able to distinguish *four* distinct trajectories of aggressive behavior, several of which were similar to those found in other developmental models, especially the Loeber and Stouthamer-Loebel model. Schaeffer et al. discovered that a substantial proportion of boys (32%) displayed low levels of aggression throughout development and had very low rates of antisocial behavior later in development (first trajectory). In addition, the researchers were able to identify a group of boys (9%) who exhibited consistently high levels of aggression early and who were at high risk for delinquency (second trajectory). In support of Loeber and Stouthamer-Loeber's model, attention and/or concentration problems in first grade were associated with this chronic high-aggression trajectory. This finding is also consistent with the notion that the aggression displayed by these boys may be linked to neuropsychological deficits that are usually associated with ADHD (as pointed out by Moffitt, 1993, and others). Furthermore, this group showed a much higher incidence of peer rejection as early as first grade.

Also in line with the Loeber and Stouthamer-Loeber hypothesis was the finding that a small group of boys (7%) exhibited an aggression trajectory that started low but increased throughout the elementary and middle school years (third trajectory). And finally, the researchers identified another large group of boys (52%) who demonstrated a moderate aggression trajectory, a pattern not usually identified in other models (fourth trajectory). In most cases, these boys showed a decline in aggression with no or little involvement in antisocial behavior as they got older, but some continued a pattern of moderate aggression across their early life span. The boys displaying this trajectory fell between the chronic high-aggression and nonaggressive groups in terms of later risk for delinquency, suggesting that researchers should take a closer look at this group as possible candidates for preventive services.

Daniel Nagin and Kenneth Land (1993) identified four development paths in British male youths: (1) the never-convicted, (2) the ALs, (3) the high-level chronics (HLCs), and (4) the low-level chronics (LLCs). The offending paths of the ALs followed the typical contour: Offending began late, reached a peak at age 16, and then showed a precipitous decline to zero by age 21 (Nagin et al., 1995). The LLC curve showed a rise through early adolescence, reached a plateau, and remained at the same level well past age 18. The HLC group (essentially the same as Moffitt's LCP) showed an early and frequent antisocial and offending pattern that continued through adolescence at a high rate and remained high well into adulthood.

Shaw et al. (2003) also found four developmental trajectories for antisocial behavior when they followed 284 lower-income boys from age 2 to 8. These paths were (1) a persistent-problem trajectory, (2) a high-level desister trajectory, (3) a moderate-level desister trajectory, and (4) a persistent-low trajectory. Three of the four groups showed a marked decrease in antisocial behavior from ages 2 to 8. The persistent-problem group (about 5.6% of the sample) exhibited a high rate of aggressive behavior through the preschool and early school-age periods.

Côté et al. (2001) studied the developmental trajectories of girls. They also identified four developmental trajectories, all showing decreasing numbers of problem behaviors with increasing age.

Chung et al. (2002) were able to identify *five* developmental trajectories, although only four involve offending. The identified groups were nonoffenders, late onsetters, desisters, escalators, and chronic offenders. Late onsetters were similar to AL offenders and late starters as described by Moffitt (1993) and Patterson and colleagues (1992). Interestingly, these late onsetters did not limit their offending to the adolescent period; many continued offending (e.g., using drugs, getting into fights, committing minor offenses) until at least age 32. This finding about late onsetters has also been reported by other researchers (e.g., Loeber & Stouthamer-Loeber, 1998). The desister group and the escalator group represented more than half (54.6%) of the total sample. Neither of these two groups was discussed in the original Moffitt or Patterson developmental formulations. Desisters engaged in only minor offending at age 13 and stopped offending at around age 21. Escalators were similar in seriousness of offending to the desisters at age 13 but continued to commit increasingly more serious offenses until at least age 21. Other features that distinguished this group from the desisters were having more antisocial peers, having less of a bond to school, and living in neighborhoods where drugs were readily available. Chung et al. suggest that this group may represent a subset of the chronic group, which was similar in their offending to LCP offenders and represented about 7% of the sample (Moffitt estimates 6% in the general population of male youths).

Chung et al. (2002) did not examine gender or ethnic differences in offending patterns. In addition, they looked only at general offending and did not distinguish among specific types of offenses committed during development (e.g., drug use, larceny, violence, or sexual assault). Still, their study offers considerable promise in refining developmentally based classification of offending patterns.

Finally, Wiesner and Windle (2004) report data that suggest the existence of *six* distinct developmental pathways: rare offenders, moderate late peakers, high late peakers, decreasers, moderate-level chronics, and high-level chronics. Their findings indicated the existence of two pathways with a late-onset of delinquency.

Other recent research has focused on the various trajectories that revolve around physical aggression. Nagin and Tremblay (1999) and Brame, Nagin, and Tremblay (2001) identified four developmental trajectories of physical aggression in high-risk boys in Canada. The aggressive behavior levels were rated by teachers and the boys themselves, beginning in kindergarten. Some boys (17% of the sample) displayed practically no disruptive or aggressive behaviors during childhood and continued this behavioral pattern at least until adolescence. Another group (nearly 30%) displayed a high level of physical aggression during childhood but showed a steady decline of such behavior throughout adolescence. The largest group (approximately 50% of the sample) demonstrated moderate aggression during childhood and virtually none in adolescence. One small group (4% of the sample) engaged in chronic levels of disruptive and physically aggressive behavior during childhood and continued into adolescence. According to Tremblay (2000),

> Results have generally indicated that children labeled aggressive, conduct disordered, antisocial, and delinquent are less attentive to most social cues, more attentive to aggressive social cues, they make more frequent hostile interpretations of others' intentions, they generate less alternative responses to a specific situation, their alternative responses are qualitatively different, they respond more impulsively, and they tend to give a more positive value to an aggressive response. (p. 137)

Broidy et al. (2003) used data involving approximately 7,500 children from six sites in three countries to examine the developmental course of physical aggression in childhood and to determine its connection to violent and nonviolent delinquency. Longitudinal data on disruptive behavior problems were collected on the children, beginning at ages 5 and 7 years and continuing until adolescence. The researchers found that a small group of children stood out as displaying more physically aggressive behavior than their peers throughout childhood. In addition, the study found that chronic physical aggression during the elementary school years substantially increased the risk for both violent and nonviolent forms of delinquency during adolescence, at least in boys. In girls, the results were not so clear. Table 6–4 lists the various pathways in the models we have described here.

AGE-OF-ONSET CONTINUUM THEORIES

Up to this point, the models and the research we have discussed place individuals into categories, based on such factors as their age of onset and persistence of offending. In this sense, the research has identified developmental typologies, or classification systems, in which individual juveniles may fall. A **typology** tries to put people (or things) into distinctive groups. Some critics of this approach maintain that such classification of separate groups of offenders based on their ages of onset and trajectories of offending is unwarranted. These critics propose instead that it might be more meaningful to place child and adolescent offenders on a continuum rather than in a classification

TABLE 6–4: Models of Developmental Pathways to Delinquency

Researchers	Developmental Pathways Identified
Moffitt and colleagues	• Life-course-persistent (LCP) offender Adolescent-limited (AL) offender
Patterson and colleagues	• Early-onset delinquent
Loeber & Stouthamer-Loeber	• Preschool-onset offender
	• Late-onset delinquent Childhood-adolescent-onset offender Limited-duration/preschool-elementary offender Limited-duration/late-adolescence offender Late-onset offender
Schaeffer, Petras, Ialongo, Poduska, & Kellam	• Low-level aggression Chronic high aggression Low to high aggression Moderate aggression
Nagin & Land	• Never convicted ALs High-level chronics (HLCs) Low-level chronics (LLCs)
Shaw, Gillion, Ingoldsky, & Nagin	• Persistent problems High-level desister Moderate-level desister Persistent low level
Chung, Hill, Hawkins, Gilchrist, & Nagin	• Nonoffenders Late onsetters Desisters Escalators Chronic offenders
Wiesner & Windle	• Rare offenders Moderate late peakers High late peakers Decreasers Moderate-level chronics High-level chronics

or typology. Lahey and Waldman (2003), for example, propose that differences in antisocial behavior and delinquency should be examined based on an age of onset that falls along a *continuum* of ages, rather than restricting explanations to some kind of developmental typology. Thus, Lahey and Waldman believe that Moffitt's theory may have unintentionally contributed to the neglect of children whose behavior improves over time because that theory places some children in the LCP category and implies that there is little hope for these offenders, especially once they reach adolescence. However, Lahey and Waldman note that nearly half of all children who engage in high levels of antisocial behavior early in their childhood show considerable improvement by early adolescence. Furthermore, as we will see in Chapter 12, some treatment approaches have been able to promote changes in youths who appear to follow the characteristics of LCP offenders.

DEVELOPMENTAL PROPENSITY MODEL

The developmental propensity model posits that causes and risk factors that contribute to crime (together referred to as *antisocial propensity*) can emerge at any age, but the strength and pattern of these causal influences vary with each individual. Included in antisocial propensity are factors such as lower intelligence, slow language development, higher levels of daring, impulsivity, difficult temperament, high activity level, and physical strength. The developmental propensity theory emphasizes that there are individual differences in this antisocial propensity and that some of the characteristics associated with that propensity are more important at certain ages than at others. For youth with earlier onset of antisocial behavior, Lahey and Waldman (2003) believe that a difficult temperament and low cognitive ability play significant roles during the preschool years. Then, parenting, temperament, and cognitive ability play significant roles in the development of antisocial behavior during the early- to midschool years. As the child enters adolescence, peer influence and other social factors play prominent roles in the formation of delinquency. "Thus, following the lead of Moffitt (1993), we posit differences in causal influences on earlier and later onset conduct problems, but we view these as reflecting a continuum of differences in age of onset" (p. 80).

THORNBERRY AND KROHN INTERACTION MODEL

Similar to the developmental propensity model, Thornberry and Krohn's (Thornberry, 1987; Thornberry & Krohn, 1997) interaction perspective views the onset of antisocial behavior as continuously distributed across the age span, at least from early childhood to young adulthood. Rather than classifying offenders as early or late, Thornberry and Krohn argue that antisocial behavior can begin anywhere along the continuum. What differentiates early starters from late starters is the intensity of the structural, psychological, and social deficits experienced by children and adolescents and their families. Thornberry and Krohn concur that many of the factors identified by Moffitt and Patterson contribute to antisocial behavior. Agreeing with Moffitt, they state that "individual deficits (e.g., negative temperamental qualities) contribute to, and are adversely affected by, parenting deficits (e.g., low affective ties, explosive physical disciplinary styles)" (Krohn et al., 2001, pp. 72–73). Agreeing with Patterson, they note that "over time, parents and children will develop a coercive interaction style, and children will develop persistent patterns of oppositional and aggressive behavior" (Krohn et al., 2001, p. 73). What distinguishes the Thornberry and Krohn position is its focus on structural adversity, "defined as the position in the social structure that leads to accumulated disadvantage" (Krohn et al., 2001, p. 73). Structural adversity—that is, low-socioeconomic status—increases parental stress and decreases opportunity, which in turn leads to poor family skills and faulty parenting. Structural adversity also leads to negative temperamental qualities in children. Thus, the starting point for delinquency is not the individual deficits of the parents or the children but rather the family's position in the broader society.

According to Thornberry and Krohn, the persistent antisocial behavior that results from these early factors and adverse conditions impedes the development of positive and effective relationships with parents, teachers, and peers. "Structural adversity reduces the children's ability to succeed in school, leading to weakened bonds of commitment to school and attachment to teachers as well as the erosion of social supports" (Krohn et al., 2001, p. 73). Thornberry and Krohn (2001) also maintain that peer influences are relatively weak during childhood but increase substantially in strength during adolescence.

Summary and Conclusions

Research on delinquency, its causes, prevention, and treatment has taken a decidedly developmental approach in recent years. This research has been strongly influenced by social learning theory, systems theory, and advances in developmental psychopathology. Many theorists now believe that following children through various developmental stages is more informative than looking at their conduct at any point in time or even at several different points in their development. As a result, longitudinal studies on delinquency have proliferated, and a number of developmental pathways have been identified. One of the main questions driving contemporary research relates to the number of different pathways that exist. Another question relates to the consistency of behavior over time.

The various developmental theories discussed in this chapter have several things in common, as Schaeffer et al. (2003) have observed. First, each one identifies from two to five separate groups of juveniles with distinctive pathways, or trajectories, to delinquency. Second, they focus heavily on boys. Although most theories do mention gender differences, they have been formulated predominantly with boys as research participants. No current developmental theory begins with girls and uses them as its main research participants. Historically, this has been the case with delinquency theories as a whole, whether sociologically or psychologically based, and it has led to criticisms that the theories do not adequately explain the behavior of girls. Third, the various developmental theories discussed in this chapter seem to do a decent job of predicting delinquency. For example, it is likely that a child demonstrating early-onset, persistent aggressive behavior—with many risk factors and few protective factors—will demonstrate serious antisocial conduct as an adolescent.

Developmental norms and the age of onset are critical concepts in all developmental theories. Norms provide some standards against which to measure a child's progress; significant delay in reaching some milestones can signal problems in the future. The age of onset of certain types of conduct (particularly aggression, but also behaviors like lying and stealing) is significant if the conduct does not decline. For example, most children display aggressive behavior in the preschool years, but that aggression gradually lessens as they approach school age. If a child is still highly aggressive at age 7, it is usually cause for concern.

Research has been inconsistent with regard to gender differences in the age of onset. Although it has been assumed that girls usually begin offending in adolescence, recent studies suggest that more girls are beginning to offend before age 10. Furthermore, the risk factors for girls and boys may be different. There is some indication that parental conflict and disruptive family transitions may be harder for girls and peer influences may be less important. On the other hand, the influences of older, antisocial men may be greater for girls than for boys.

The two-path theory of Terrie Moffitt and her colleagues has provided the major impetus for research on developmental perspectives on delinquency. Moffitt's delineation of life-course-persistent (LCP) and adolescent-limited (AL) offenders prompted extensive inquiry into whether these two paths satisfactorily classified delinquent offenders—or even whether such classifications or typologies were justified. Many developmental psychologists today, including Moffitt, believe that additional paths are needed because not all delinquents fall into those two groups.

Nonetheless, the concepts of LCP and AL offenders continue to be supported in the research. Early aggressive behavior, neurological problems, learning difficulties, and cognitive defects typify the LCP offender and are often accompanied by problems in the home. For these individuals, antisocial behavior continues across the life span. AL offenders, who constitute the great majority of juvenile offenders, begin their offending in adolescence but desist as they get older. However, they participate in a considerable amount of delinquency during those years. Moffitt has also identified low-level but chronic offenders, who display early conduct problems but only low-level offending in adolescence. More recently, she and her colleagues have encountered the AL offender who does not desist but rather continues antisocial behavior into early adulthood.

Patterson and his colleagues have advanced a two-path theory also focusing on early starters and late starters. They propose a coercion developmental model that suggests that children learn coercive behaviors in the home. The interactive process between parents and children in disruptive family environments is carried over into neighborhood, school, and community settings. For early starters, problems are apparent in the preschool years, parenting is more inept, and the child displays high levels of social incompetence. Late starters demonstrate marginal competence, their parenting is less inept but still coercive, and the influence of a deviant peer group is crucial.

Loeber and Stouthamer-Loeber accept the two-path approach (LCP and AL) but divide these pathways into additional subgroups. LCP offenders are divided according to whether aggression begins early or late and whether symptoms of ADHD are present. AL offenders are divided according to whether their limited offending occurs during childhood and then stops or during adolescence and then stops. The Loeber and Stouthamer-Loeber model also includes a fifth group: adult persistent offenders who showed no evidence of offending in childhood or adolescence.

Variations of these models demonstrate that research in this area is ongoing and that many questions remain to be answered. For example, the research on gender differences is both fascinating and equivocal. No theories have been formulated specifically with girls as the center of inquiry, and some researchers suggest that girls do follow different trajectories than boys (e.g., delayed onset). Recent research also suggests that risk and protective factors are different for the two groups and that protective factors seem to have more influence on girls, particularly in preventing violent behavior. Some research also suggests that ADHD in girls is a higher risk factor than it is in boys. For both genders, early drug and alcohol abuse are significant risk factors.

The chapter discusses two other contemporary models, the developmental propensity model and the Thornberry-Krohn interaction model. Rather than placing juveniles into typologies, or categories, based on age of onset (e.g., the LCP offender, the late starter, the early starter), the developmental propensity model places them on a developmental continuum and recognizes that even children who show early signs of conduct problems can stop offending as they grow older. Likewise, the interaction model notes that serious antisocial behavior can begin anywhere along the age continuum and can be affected by a wide range of contributing factors (risks). However, structural adversity, particularly low-socioeconomic status, is particularly problematic because it increases parental stress, limits opportunity, and leads to faulty parenting and negative qualities in children. Positive and effective relationships are thus impeded with teachers, peers, and others who could provide social supports.

Key Terms and Concepts

adolescent-limited (AL) offenders
age of onset
childhood-adolescent-onset subtype
cumulation
developmental norms
developmental pathway
developmental psychopathology
developmental trajectory
early starters
equifinality

gender paradox
late-onset offenders
life-course-persistent (LCP) offenders
low-level chronic delinquents
preschool-onset subtype
prespecified constraints
quiescent hypothesis
social learning theory
systems theory
typology

CHAPTER 7
CHILD AND ADOLESCENT PSYCHOPATHY

❧

CHAPTER OBJECTIVES

◆ Introduce the important and popular concept of psychopathy

◆ Review the evidence for juvenile psychopathy

◆ Review the various models and perspectives on juvenile psychopathy

◆ Identify the ethical dilemmas that the term *juvenile psychopathy* presents

◆ Examine the neurophysiological characteristics of psychopathy

◆ Review the various measures of juvenile psychopathy

In some ways, 14-year-old Rodge is not unlike many other teenagers. He does not care about school, he teases his younger siblings, he tends to hide his feelings, he cannot sit quietly and is constantly seeking stimulation, he does not take well to criticism, and he often acts without thinking or planning ahead. In other ways, though, Rodge is very different. He is a pathological liar, has a grandiose sense of his own worth, and is continually trying to con others, often relying on his superficial charm. When he broke his younger brother's arm during a backyard football game, he demonstrated no remorse. When the children's beloved grandfather died, Rodge expressed no emotion.

Some psychologists would suggest, although very cautiously, that Rodge has many of the characteristics of a psychopath. They would add, of course, that more information is needed, as well as some psychological testing, before they could arrive at a firm conclusion. Even if further tests indicated that Rodge is high on psychopathy scales, most psychologists would be concerned about how this information would be used. The label *psychopath* carries many negative connotations. A child so labeled might be treated very differently by teachers, parents, the juvenile justice system, and the community. For example, the juvenile justice system might engage in more punitive sentencing for a budding psychopath (Edens, Guy, & Fernandez, 2003; Petrila & Skeem, 2003). It is also entirely possible that any attempt to rehabilitate a child or adolescent psychopath would be thrown by the wayside, because in some circles the term *psychopathy* implies a stable, biologically determined personality pattern that is untreatable. Such a child might even be excluded from special educational services in school settings (Frick, 2004; Salekin & Frick, 2005).

Many experts question whether juvenile psychopaths—if they do exist—are really qualitatively the same as adult psychopaths. That is, do the behavioral, cognitive, and emotional features that occur with some regularity in adult psychopaths also occur with the same regularity and intensity in children and adolescents? We will review the research on that topic.

WHAT IS A PSYCHOPATH?

One of the earliest comprehensive descriptions of an adult psychopath is credited to Herve Cleckley (1941, 1976). In his well-cited book *The Mask of Sanity*, Cleckley, who was a professor of psychiatry and neurology, described psychopaths in great clinical detail, identifying 16 behavioral features that focused primarily on personality traits in adults. In another influential book, *The Psychopath: An Essay on the Criminal Mind*, McCord and McCord (1959/1964) emphasized the importance of identifying and treating psychopathy in youthful offenders, even before anyone seriously entertained the existence of psychopathy in children (Salekin & Frick, 2005). The McCords estimated that about 14% of delinquent youth demonstrated psychopathic traits.

Prompted by Cleckley's popular book and systematic descriptions, psychologist Herbert Quay (1965) and Robert Hare (1965a, 1965b, 1980) began conducting systematic studies dedicated to a deeper understanding of this intriguing phenomenon. Today, following decades of research in this area, Hare is arguably the foremost contemporary expert on the psychopath. He is especially noted for having developed the **Psychopathy Checklist** (PCL), designed initially to measure psychopathic characteristics of inmates in correctional institutions (Hare, 1980, 1985). The instrument was revised a decade later (Hare, 1991, 2003) and is now known as the **Psychopathy Checklist—Revised (PCL-R)**. The PCL-R has become the gold standard for assessing psychopathy in forensic and correctional settings (Edens, Skeem, Cruise, & Cauffman, 2001, p. 54).

BEHAVIORAL DESCRIPTIONS OF THE PSYCHOPATH

Cleckley's pioneering work focused on characteristics that were primarily behavioral, although several did have cognitive or emotional components. As was mentioned, he identified 16 behavioral features that best describe the typical psychopath (see Figure 7–1). The first characteristic is a combination of superficial charm and average to above-average intelligence. Although these may appear to be two distinct features, Cleckley believed they frequently occurred together as one trait, which was especially apparent during initial contacts. Adult psychopaths tend to impress others as friendly, outgoing, likable, and alert. The term "impression management" has replaced "glib" and "superficial charm" in more recent conceptions of psychopaths.

Psychopaths often seem well educated and knowledgeable, and they display many interests. They are verbally skillful and can talk themselves out of trouble. In fact, their vocabulary is sometimes so extensive that they can talk at length about anything (Hare, 1991). Careful attention to their conversation, though, reveals that they often jump

> from one topic to another and that much of their speech is empty of real substance, tending to be filled with stock phrases, repetitions of the same ideas, word approximations, abstract terms and jargon used in a superficial or inappropriate fashion, logically inconsistent statements and phrases, and half-formed sentences. (Hare, 1991, p. 57)

However, many psychopaths are so charming and manipulative that these language shortcomings are not readily apparent to the casual observer.

FIGURE 7–1 Cleckley's 16 Characteristics of Psychopathy

1. Superficial charm and good intelligence
2. Absence of delusions and other signs of irrational thinking
3. Absence of nervousness or psychoneurotic manifestations
4. Unreliability
5. Untruthfulness and insincerity
6. Lack of remorse or shame
7. Inadequately motivated antisocial behavior
8. Poor judgment and failure to learn by experience
9. Pathological egocentricity and incapacity for love
10. General poverty in major affective reactions
11. Specific lack of insight
12. Unresponsiveness in general interpersonal relations
13. Fantastic and uninviting behavior with drink and sometimes without
14. Suicide rarely carried out
15. Sex life impersonal, trivial, and poorly integrated
16. Failure to follow any life plan

Source: Based on *The Mask of Sanity* by H. Cleckley, 1941 and 1976, St. Louis, MO: C. V. Mosby.

Studies using standard psychological tests indicate that psychopaths often score higher on intelligence exams than the general population does (Hare, 1970, 1996). Some research (e.g., Ishikawa, Raine, Lencz, Bihrle, & Lacasse, 2001) has found that a useful dichotomy of criminal psychopaths is to divide them into "successful" psychopaths (those who have committed crimes but avoided arrest and conviction for their offenses) and "unsuccessful" psychopaths (those who have been convicted and imprisoned). Presumably, the successful ones are more intelligent than the unsuccessful group.

Other principal traits of the psychopath are selfishness and an inability to love or give genuine affection to others. According to Cleckley, egocentricity is *always* present in the psychopath and is essentially unmodifiable. Psychopaths may be likable, but they are seldom able to keep close friends, and they have great difficulty understanding love in others. They may be highly skillful at pretending deep affection, and they may effectively mimic appropriate emotions, but true loyalty, warmth, and compassion are foreign to them. Essentially, psychopaths are distinguished by "flat" emotional reaction and affect. And since psychopaths have so little need to receive or give love, as a group they have relatively little contact with their families and may change their residences frequently (Hare, 1991). In addition, they do not usually respond to acts of kindness. "No matter how well he is treated, no matter how long-suffering his family, his friends, the police, hospital attendants, and others may be, he shows no consistent reaction of appreciation except superficial and transparent protestations" (Cleckley, 1976, p. 354). Paradoxically, they may do small favors for and appear considerate toward someone one day and run off with the person's life savings the next day. In contemporary research, these egocentric characteristics are well documented. As Hare and Hervé (1999) write, psychopaths "drift through life, leaving a broad trail of broken hearts, shattered expectations, bloody bodies, and empty wallets" (p. 2).

Psychopaths have a remarkable disregard for the truth and are often called pathological liars. They seem to have no internalized moral or ethical sense and cannot understand the purpose of being honest, especially if dishonesty will bring some personal gain. They have a cunning ability to appear straightforward, honest, and sincere, but their claims to sincerity are without substance.

Psychopaths are unreliable, irresponsible, and unpredictable, regardless of the importance of the occasion or the consequences of their actions. These characteristics, too, are well documented. Impulsivity is a central, or core, feature of psychopathy (S. D. Hart & Dempster, 1997), although this pattern of impulsive actions is cyclical. Psychopaths may, for months on end, be responsible citizens, faithful spouses, and reliable employees. They may experience great successes, be promoted, and gain honors. But as skillfully as they have attained these socially desirable goals, they have an uncanny knack of suddenly unraveling their lives. They become irresponsible and may pass bad checks, sabotage the company computer, go on a drunken spree, or steal the boss's car. They also tend to have a bad temper that flares up quickly and leads to arguments and aggression. Psychopaths may later say they are sorry and plead for another chance—and most will probably get it.

Another cardinal fault of psychopaths is their absolute lack of remorse or guilt for anything they do, regardless of the severity or immorality of their actions and their traumatic effects on others. "They lack a normal sense of ethics, morality, duty, or fair play" (Hare & Hervé, 1999, p. 2). Since they do not anticipate personal consequences, psychopaths may take absurd risks and engage in destructive or antisocial behavior (such as forgery, theft, rape, brawls, fraud) for insignificant personal gain. When caught, they express no genuine remorse. They may readily admit culpability and may take considerable pleasure in the shock their confessions produce in others.

Psychopaths usually have little capacity to see themselves as others perceive them. Instead of accepting the facts that would normally lead to insight, they externalize blame and project it onto the community, acquaintances, and family. In addition, their poor judgment is usually not modified by experience. However, Cleckley (1976) writes, "Despite the extraordinary poor judgment demonstrated in behavior, in the actual living of his life the psychopath characteristically demonstrates unimpaired (sometimes excellent) judgment in appraising theoretical situations." That is, in complicated matters of judgment involving ethical, emotional, and even wise decisions or advice, the psychopath may not show any observable or noticeable problems. But when judgment issues are applied to the psychopath's own life, problems often emerge.

Interestingly, psychopaths seem to react differently than nonpsychopaths to alcohol. Even small amounts of alcohol prompt most psychopaths to become vulgar, domineering, loud, and boisterous and to engage in practical jokes and pranks. Cleckley noted that they choose pranks that have no appeal for most individuals and that seem bizarre, inappropriate, and cruel. Psychopaths lack genuine humor and, not surprisingly, the ability to laugh at themselves.

Psychopaths are found in all age groups, in both genders, and in every society, race, or ethnic group (Hare & Hervé, 1999). Many psychopaths are often on the "shady side" of the law. "Some are spouse and child abusers, mercenaries, corrupt politicians, unethical lawyers and doctors, cult leaders, high-pressure salespeople and promoters, and radical political activists" (Hare & Hervé, 1999, p. 2).

Although some mental health professionals contend that psychopathy is a form of mental disorder, most experts believe that psychopaths tend to be remarkably free from the usual mental or behavioral disorders found in the general population (except for personality disorders). According to Cleckley, a majority of psychopaths lack any symptoms of excessive worry, anxiety, psychotic thinking, delusions, severe or bipolar depression, or hallucinations. Even in high-pressure situations, they usually remain relaxed and calm. However, some evidence suggests that it is not uncommon to find some psychopaths who seem mentally disordered in maximum-security psychiatric units for highly violent and dangerous patients (Hare, 1996).

CONTEMPORARY RESEARCH

Research on the adult psychopath has been reviewed extensively elsewhere (Bartol & Bartol, 2005; Hare, 1991, 1996; Hemphill & Hare, 2004; Hemphill, Hare, & Wong, 1998; Salekin, 2002) and will only be summarized here. Today, psychologists recognize psychopathy in adults as consisting of emotional, interpersonal, and neurological characteristics, as well as antisocial behaviors that seem highly resistant to change. Although researchers would agree with the features outlined by Cleckley, they have added other components. Psychopaths are believed to have deficits in temperament (Lykken, 1995) and in conditionability (Hare, 1996), the latter presumably due to an underaroused nervous system. Measurements of psychopathy are widely believed to predict general and violent recidivism in adult offenders, as well as both violent and nonviolent recidivism in adolescents with psychopathic characteristics (Gretton, McBride, Hare, O'Shaughnessy, & Kumka, 2001). However, extending the construct to juveniles is controversial and, in the opinion of some researchers and theorists, unwarranted.

MODELS OF PSYCHOPATHY

Following Cleckley's listing of 16 features, researchers began to develop various psychological measures that would identify these traits or behavioral indicators, as well as place them in logical groups. The Psychopathy Checklist (Hare, 1991), for example, revealed that psychopathic behavioral characteristics could be grouped into two dominant categories, one reflecting emotional and interpersonal components (e.g., callousness, manipulation of others, shallowness) and another reflecting an unstable or deviant lifestyle (e.g., poor planning, lack of realistic goals; Hare, 1991; Hart, Hare, & Forth, 1993; S. D. Hart & Dempster, 1997; Seto & Barbaree, 1999). This became known as the **two-factor model of psychopathy**.

Although the two-factor model has been instrumental in advancing research on psychopathy, the increasing sophistication of statistical methods indicates that there may be at least three core behavioral or personality dimensions that best describe psychopathy (Cooke & Michie, 2001; Cooke, Michie, Hart, & Clark, 2004; Vitacco, Rogers, & Neumann, 2003). In an influential paper, Cooke and Michie (2001) challenged the traditional two-factor explanation of psychopathy and recommended that a more complete understanding of psychopathy must include these three core dimensions:

1. An arrogant and deceptive interpersonal style, which includes a grandiose sense of self-worth, glibness, superficial charm, lying, conning, manipulation, and deceitfulness (a dimension also referred to as impression management)

2. Deficient affective or emotional experience characterized by little remorse, little guilt, a weak conscience, an absence of anxiety, fearlessness, callousness, little empathy, and a failure to accept responsibility for personal actions

3. An impulsive and irresponsible behavioral style, including failure to think before acting, a lack of long-term goals, stimulation seeking, unsatisfactory work habits, and a parasitic lifestyle (living off others, including spouses, intimate partners, friends, and parents)

Some researchers (e.g., Hare, 2003; Neumann, Kosson, Forth, & Hare, 2006; Salekin, Brannen, Salot, Leistico, & Neumann, 2006; Vitacco, Neumann, & Jackson, 2005) have asserted that the definition of psychopathy should also include a fourth dimension: antisocial behavior (see Table 7–1). Their argument is based on the finding that individuals manifesting psychopathic traits often exhibit violence and a large collection of other antisocial behavioral patterns. Thus, a crucial element in the understanding of psychopathy is missing if measures of antisocial behavior are left out of the equation. It is also argued that much of the predictive power of psychopathy is enhanced if we take into consideration past criminal behavior (Salekin et al., 2006).

TABLE 7–1: Multifactor Models of Psychopathy with Examples of Associated Features

Two-Factor Model	*Three-Factor Model*	*Four-Factor Model*
Interpersonal/affective traits	**Arrogant, deceptive interpersonal style**	**Arrogant, deceptive interpersonal style**
Callousness	Grandiose sense of self-worth	Grandiose sense of self-worth
Manipulation of others	Superficial charm	Pathological lying
Shallowness	Pathological lying	Manipulation of others
Lack of remorse	Manipulation of others	
Failure to accept responsibility		**Deficient emotional experience**
	Deficient emotional experience	Lack of remorse
Unstable, deviant lifestyle	Lack of remorse	Lack of empathy
Poor planning	Lack of empathy	Fearlessness
Lack of realistic goals	Fearlessness	Callousness
Impulsivity	Callousness	Shallowness
Thrill seeking	Failure to accept responsibility	
Poor self-regulation		**Unstable, deviant lifestyle**
Parasitic lifestyle		Poor planning
	Impulsive, irresponsible behavior	Parasitic lifestyle
	Thrill seeking	Thrill seeking
	Failure to think before acting	Impulsivity
	Poor work habits	
	Lack of long-term goals	**Antisocial behavior**
	Parasitic lifestyle	Poor self-regulation
		Early behavior problems
		Criminal involvement
		Juvenile delinquency

When it comes to definitions of **juvenile psychopathy**, however, Farrington (2005) maintains that antisocial behavior should not be part of the equation: "To the extent that psychopathy might be used to explain delinquency, it is important that the definition of psychopathy should not include measures of offending or antisocial behavior" (p. 490). The basic argument is that antisocial behavior is a *result* rather than a definitional *antecedent* (Salekin et al., 2006). In other words, antisocial behavior is a result of being a psychopath and does little to explain the causes of psychopathy. In addition, childhood may be too early to begin applying labels of criminality. However, Salekin et al. (2006) point out that antisocial behavior (i.e., persistent and varied rule breaking) may be an important consideration in defining psychopathy in *certain* adolescents. That is, there may be different subtypes of juvenile psychopaths, some of which require the label *antisocial* and some of which do not. Identifying subtypes may help in establishing effective intervention and treatment methods designed for chronic juvenile offenders.

Overall, though, it may be that both the three- and four-factor models are justifiable in their application to delinquency at this point in our knowledge—or that neither may be. Even in adults, pychopathic behavior may be too diverse to be captured in only three or four dimensions. Psychopathy is a multidimensional concept that involves disturbances in interpersonal, affective, behavioral, genetic/biological, and antisocial domains.

PRIMARY PSYCHOPATHY VERSUS SECONDARY PSYCHOPATHY

Years ago, Hare (1970) proposed that a useful classification for psychopaths might include two categories: the primary and the secondary, or neurotic, psychopath. He pointed out that only the **primary psychopath** is a *true* psychopath and suggested that **secondary psychopaths** commit antisocial or violent acts because of severe emotional or neurotic problems. The latter are anxious, tense, and impulsive and have also been called acting-out neurotics, neurotic delinquents, or symptomatic psychopaths by other mental health professionals working with offenders. Lykken (1995) further describes secondary psychopaths as having inadequate intelligence, psychotic thinking, excessive neurotic anxiety, and an unusual sex drive (Newman, MacCoon, Vaughn, & Sadeh, 2005). Farrington (2005) notes that "the concept of secondary psychopathy has fallen into disuse in the past 20 years, and current definitions of psychopathy describe a fearless individual characterized by low guilt and low remorse" (p. 492). However, the recent research of Salekin (2002, 2006) does indicate that there may well be psychopaths who exhibit stress, anxiety, and guilt. That research again underscores the strong possibility that psychopathy—both adult and juvenile—is a heterogeneous concept that will eventually need to be divided into various subtypes.

One investigation reports that a meaningful distinction could be made between emotionally stable psychopaths and aggressive psychopaths (Hicks, Markon, Patrick, Krueger, & Newman, 2004). Emotionally stable psychopaths, the researchers reasoned, tend to be planful and act with forethought, demonstrate low emotional reactions to events, and have a high need for stimulation and excitement in their lives. Aggressive psychopaths, on the other hand, tend to exhibit impulsivity, high levels of aggression, ADHD, and various kinds of psychological maladjustment. More research is needed in this area, but it is possible that identifying different subtypes of psychopaths might help explain why the antisocial behavior of psychopaths appears to be so variable in terms of the frequency, nature, and intensity of the offenses committed.

THE CHILDHOOD OF PSYCHOPATHS

Many researchers in this area believe that psychopathy begins in childhood and continues throughout adulthood (Forth & Burke, 1998; Grehsam, Lane, & Lambros, 2000; Lynam, 1998), an idea that has led to intense interest in juvenile psychopathy. According to the research, the childhood of the psychopath is littered with signals that something is amiss. Marshall and Cooke (1999) found that psychopaths were more likely than nonpsychopaths to have experienced family difficulties such as parental neglect, abuse, antipathy, or indifference. They were also more likely to have experienced negative school experiences, such as peer rejection and academic failure. Inadequate parental monitoring and inconsistent discipline have also been identified in the backgrounds of many psychopaths (Tolan, Gorman-Smith, & Henry, 2003). As discussed earlier, Lynam (1998) reports that children with symptoms of hyperactivity, impulsivity, and attention problems *and* conduct problems closely resemble psychopathic adults. We hasten to add, however, that not all children with similar problems are necessarily fledgling psychopaths.

"Few researchers have tried to investigate early childhood risk factors that might predict, influence, or cause psychopathy" (Farrington, 2005, p. 493). And very few researchers have conducted **prospective longitudinal investigations** of those risk factors (Farrington, 2005). Some **retrospective studies** (Koivisto & Haapasalo, 1996; Patrick, Zempolich, & Levenston, 1997) and some longitudinal studies (Lang, af Klinteberg, & Alm, 2002; Weiler & Widom, 1996) have found that PCL-R scores appear to be related to early childhood abuse. One prospective longitudinal study of 400 London boys, aged 8 to 10 years, found that physical neglect, poor parental supervision, a disrupted family, large family size, a convicted parent, a depressed mother, and poverty predicted psychopathy scores at age 48 (Farrington, 2006).

A fruitful avenue for exploring the childhood of the psychopath would be close examination of the life-course-persistent offender described by developmental theorists, particularly Terrie Moffitt and her colleagues. Developmental theory postulates that LCP offenders manifest antisocial behaviors across all kinds of conditions and situations in their childhood. Neurologically, LCPs demonstrate a variety of minor neuropsychological disorders, such as difficult temperaments as infants, attention-deficit disorders or hyperactivity as children, and learning problems as adolescents. Socially, LCPs are rejected by peers during their preteen years and are annoying to adults. Emotionally, these children display virtually no empathy or concern for others, show very little bonding to family, and often are sadistic and manipulative. They are also highly impulsive and lack insight. A careful reading of LCPs' developmental histories often shows a striking resemblance to the symptomology of criminal psychopaths.

GENDER DIFFERENCES

Compared to that of male psychopathy, a limited amount of research has examined the nature of female psychopathy, although that research has increased significantly during the past 5 years. In general, research *suggests* that there are significantly fewer female than male psychopaths, both in the general population and among persons convicted of crime. Several national surveys of the general North American population estimate that psychopathy is found in males five to seven times more often than in females (Saltaris, 2002). Part of this disparity, however, might be due to the tendency of researchers to include violent and physically aggressive behaviors, which are less applicable to females, as prominent features of psychopathy. Salekin, Rogers, and Machin (2001) found that, according to child clinical psychologists, psychopathic boys are much more aggressive and violent, whereas psychopathic girls tend to be less aggressive but still defiant and antisocial. There are likely other gender differences as well.

Salekin, Rogers, and Sewell (1997) reported that the prevalence of psychopathy in female offenders in a jail setting is about 16%, as compared to 25% to 30% in male offenders. In another study, Salekin, Rogers, Ustad, and Sewell (1998) found that 12.9% of 78 female inmates qualified as psychopaths. Another investigation involving 528 adult women incarcerated in state prisons in Wisconsin documented that 9% of the participants could be classified as psychopaths (Vitale, Smith, Brinkley, & Newman, 2002).

Preliminary data also indicate that female psychopaths recidivate less often than male psychopaths (Salekin et al., 1998). The Salekin et al. data suggest, in fact, that psychopathic female inmates may have recidivism rates that are no different from those reported for nonpsychopathic female inmates.

GENETIC FACTORS AND PSYCHOPHYSIOLOGICAL CHARACTERISTICS

Contemporary research favors the perspective that psychopathic behavior results from a complex interaction between neuropsychological and learning and socialization factors. Although the research on psychopaths in recent years has focused on their psychometric and behavioral features, neuropsychological factors remain a critical component in understanding psychopathic behavior. Neuropsychological indicators (called **markers**) have been repeatedly found in psychopaths, reflected in brain wave patterns, electrodermal (skin conductance) measures, and cardiovascular and other nervous system indices (Fishbein, 2001; Herpertz et al., 2001). But beyond these neuropsychological markers is the question of temperament. As we learned in Chapter 3, temperament plays a major role in the formation of personality all through life. As noted by Saltaris (2002),

> Children's temperamental style and quality of their early relationships with their primary caregivers are known to exert a powerful and long-lasting influence on the emergence of their social skills, behavioral competence, and emotional well being. . . . The deficits in moral emotions that are characteristic of psychopaths are generally thought to develop partly as a function of a unique temperament style, low fearful inhibition, that makes a child difficult to socialize and resistant to emotional ties. (p. 733)

According to Blair et al. (2004), there are two main theoretical positions that try to explain why psychopaths show problems in emotional expression and poor socialization. One is the low-fear position, which hypothesizes that failed socialization in psychopaths is the result of a diminished ability to experience fear. If a child is fearless, then socialization of that child and the development of a conscience will not be easy. A second position revolves around the **violence inhibition mechanism** (VIM) model, which suggests that there is a neurocognitive system that responds preferentially to sad and fearful emotional displays in others (Blair, 1995, 2001). The VIM is hypothesized to be crucial for moral socialization. For example, individuals who have an effectively functioning VIM learn to avoid initiating behaviors that result in sadness and fear in others because displays of those emotions are aversive to them (Blair et al., 2004). The VIM model predicts that, because of significant impairment in neurological structures in the brain's limbic system and frontal lobe, adult and juvenile psychopaths will have particular difficulty processing sad and fearful expressions, whether facial or vocal. The neurological structure that appears to be especially involved in this impairment is the **amygdala**, a small, almond-shaped structure that is part of the complex circuitry of the limbic system, which governs emotion (Blair, Colledge, Murray, & Mitchell, 2001; Blair & Firth, 2000; Tiihonen et al., 2000).

Research by Hare and his colleagues (e.g., Hare, 1970, 1986; Hare, McPherson, & Forth, 1988; Harpur & Hare, 1994) has documented physiological differences between psychopaths and nonpsychopaths in terms of learning processes. Hare asserts that, because of differences in brain patterns—specifically **slow-wave activity**, or **immature brain-wave patterns**—psychopaths do not "condition" as easily as nonpsychopaths, a fact that presumably explains their not seeming to have a conscience or to be remorseful for their cruelty. Slow-wave brain activity in a person who is awake may indicate brain immaturity or delay in brain development. Psychopaths are often represented as unable to experience guilt or to appreciate the consequences of their actions. This *physiological* distinction, which is demonstrated in studies of EEG activity (e.g., Hare, 1970), may be critical to understanding what might account for some of the psychopath's behavioral characteristics. However, early research on EEG activity in psychopaths (as well as in nonpsychopathic criminals and delinquents) has been criticized for its methodological flaws, including failure to abide by strict criteria for psychopathy (Raine, 1993). In addition, even if psychopaths do exhibit "abnormal" brain-wave patterns, it is not clear whether the behavioral and cognitive characteristics that typify psychopathy influence these patterns, or vice versa.

Extensive research has also been collected on the psychopath's autonomic nervous system, which reacts or responds to stimuli in the environment. Essentially, the autonomic nervous system activates emotional behavior in response to stress and tension. Researchers have found that psychopaths have a comparatively underactive, underaroused autonomic nervous system, as measured by skin conductance and heart rate (Gottman, 2001; Hare, 1965a, 1965b; Lykken, 1957; Ogloff & Wong, 1990). This finding helps to explain why psychopaths often give the impression of being anxiety free, carefree, and cool and display a devil-may-care attitude (Bartol & Bartol, 2005). Some research suggests that if emotional arousal, such as fear, can be induced, psychopaths can learn from past experiences and avoid normally painful or aversive situations (Bartol & Bartol, 2005).

The neuropsychological features and neurocognitive impairments found in adult psychopaths also appear to exist in individuals identified by some researchers as juvenile psychopaths (Blair, 1997, 1999; Blair et al., 2001; O'Brien & Frick, 1996). For example, both adults and children with psychopathic tendencies have significant difficulty recognizing and responding appropriately to sad or fearful faces but not necessarily to angry, disgusted, surprised, or happy faces (Blair & Coles, 2000; Blair et al., 2001; Montagne et al., 2005; Stevens, Charman, & Blair, 2001). Because facial expressions are important for conveying feelings and thoughts, failure to recognize them can handicap a person in developing effective social and interpersonal skills.

PSYCHOPATHY AND CRIME

Psychopaths are believed to be responsible for a disproportionate amount of crime in society and are considered to be the most violent and persistent of offenders (Forth & Burke, 1998; S. D. Hart & Hare, 1997; Newman, Schmitt, & Voss, 1997; Saltaris, 2002). Psychopathic sex offenders are likely to be more violent, brutal, unemotional, and sadistic than are other sex offenders (Hare, Clark, Grann, & Thornton, 2000; Porter, Birt, & Boer, 2001; Woodworth & Porter, 2002). In addition, serial murderers described as excessively sadistic and brutal tend to have many psychopathic features (Hare et al., 2000; Stone, 1998). Porter et al. (2000) write, "Given its relation to crime and violence, psychopathy is arguably one of the most important psychological constructs in the criminal justice system" (p. 227). Specifically pertinent to juvenile delinquency, there is substantial evidence that psychopathic offenders start their criminal careers at a very early age (Rutter, 2005). "Youngsters with psychopathic traits have been found to differ from other antisocial youth in terms of the age of onset of their behavior problems, the number of violent acts committed, the seriousness of their offenses, as well as the likelihood of recidivism" (Saltaris, 2002, p. 734).

Two points should be emphasized: Many psychopaths, despite a probable history of antisocial behavior, have no history of violence or serious criminal behavior, and many individuals who exhibit chronic, violent antisocial behavior are not psychopaths (Cooke & Michie, 2001). Nonetheless, in general, psychopathy is a strong predictor of violence and violent recidivism and, as such, is increasingly assessed in criminal defendants and convicted offenders to inform legal decisions. These include pretrial release decisions (e.g., bail or pretrial detention), sentencing decisions (e.g., a prison term versus probation or a death sentence versus life without parole), and decisions involving classification of offenders (e.g., placement in custody or treatment programs). Psychopathy may also be assessed for the purpose of informing a parole decision. A diagnosis of psychopathy is not accepted in support of an insanity defense, however, and in some states cannot be taken into consideration in determining whether an individual should be sentenced to death.

JUVENILE PSYCHOPATHY

It is important to keep in mind that there is considerable debate about whether psychopathy can or should be applied to juveniles at all. Can features of adult psychopathy be found in children and adolescents in the first place? And even if psychopathy can be identified in juveniles, does the label have too many negative connotations? The label implies that the prognosis for treatment is poor, a high rate of offending and recidivism can be expected, and the intrinsic and biological basis of the disorder means that little can be done beyond biological interventions. However, some researchers (e.g., Salekin, 2002) have reported good results with treatment programs oriented toward juveniles with psychopathic characteristics.

Another major problem of identifying juvenile psychopaths is that psychopathy may be very difficult to measure reliably because of transient and constantly changing developmental patterns. Many clinicians and researchers have resisted any trend to search for psychopathy in juveniles, noting that features of the adult psychopath represent normal adolescent development. In other words, adolescents often appear callous and narcissistic, sometimes to hide their own fear and anxiety. They are also often impulsive and engage in sensation-seeking behaviors, display problems in judgment at critical times, and may not be particularly good at long-range planning. But these and other psychopathic-like characteristics may represent either a passing phase in the difficult transition to adulthood and/or an adolescent's "cover" to appear noncaring. For some children, psychopathic-like characteristics may be indicative of physical or sexual abuse. Children in abusive homes often demonstrate an abnormally restricted range of emotions, which are similar to the emotional characteristics of psychopathy, but these symptoms are a child's way of coping with a stressful home environment (Seagrave & Grisso, 2002). Furthermore, "some adolescent behavior may . . . appear psychopathic by way of poor anger control, lack of goals, and poor judgment, but is actually influenced by parallel developmental tasks encountered by most adolescents" (Seagrave & Grisso, 2002, p. 229). Moreover, going against the rules is part of many adolescents' attempts to gain autonomy from adult dominance.

Certain problem characteristics in children and adolescents—for example, conduct problems, hyperactivity, impulsivity, and attention difficulties—do resemble features of the adult psychopath and suggest that the term *juvenile psychopath* may have some validity. On the other hand, these characteristics may simply represent disorders, such as conduct disorder, which is distinct from psychopathy. As Cruise, Colwell, Lyons, and Baker (2003) have emphasized, to be useful the construct of juvenile psychopathy must be distinguished from other diagnoses. Thus, the issue of construct validity is paramount.

There is also considerable concern about the misuse of the psychopathy label by juvenile justice professionals, including judges, youth detention workers, and treatment providers. Because of the widespread assertion that psychopaths are highly resistant to treatment, an adolescent psychopath accused of a crime—or even a youth demonstrating psychopathic characteristics—is more likely to be transferred to the adult court system rather than kept in the juvenile system, where treatment is more likely to be available once the youth has been adjudicated delinquent. Until very recently, a 16- or 17-year-old juvenile labeled a psychopath was more likely to be sentenced to death in some states (Edens et al., 2003). However, in 2004 the U.S. Supreme Court ruled that juveniles who committed their crimes at these ages could not be sentenced to death (*Roper v. Simmons*). Nevertheless, juveniles who are tried in criminal courts continue to be subjected to punitive criminal sanctions, including life sentences.

Even when juveniles are kept in the juvenile system and placed in treatment centers, the label *psychopath* can become a self-fulfilling prophecy for treatment providers who may be unlikely to expend considerable effort on a seemingly hopeless case. However, supporters of the construct of juvenile psychopathy argue that treatment providers should have that information at their disposal, both to make management decisions regarding custody and programming and to fashion the type of treatment that could be effective. Indeed, researchers are beginning to identify such treatment (e.g., Spain, Douglas, Poythress, & Epstein, 2004), as we discuss in Chapter 12. Thus, if there is a distinct difference between psychopathic youth and nonpsychopathic youth, as supporters claim, it is critical that knowledge of this difference be communicated to those who work with those youth most closely. Supporters also believe there is wisdom in targeting for early intervention a subgroup of adolescents who otherwise might become career criminals (Skeem & Cauffman, 2003). This presumes, of course, that youth are correctly identified, which leads to the issue of reliability and validity.

Psychopathic assessment of youths must achieve a high level of confidence before it can be used in the criminal justice system, where individuals might face dire consequences (Seagrave & Grisso, 2002). The validity of a diagnosis becomes paramount. Cruise et al. (2003) note that most investigations of validity focus on **predictive validity**, which is a statistical index of how well an assessment procedure predicts future behavior. However, construct validity may be equally important. **Construct validity** refers to whether an instrument is actually measuring the construct it claims to measure. For example, if an assessment instrument is designed to measure juvenile psychopathy, then there must be considerable research to demonstrate that it does, in fact, measure juvenile psychopathy. A majority of experts (e.g., Seagrave & Grisso, 2002; Salekin, Rogers, & Machin, 2001) maintain that we are not near that point yet.

Even so, over the past 15 years, knowledge regarding the theoretical and empirical applicability of juvenile "psychopathy" has expanded at a fast pace (Salekin, Leistico, Trobst, Schrum, & Lochman, 2005). Research has demonstrated that the construct is linked to conduct disorder (Forth & Burke, 1998; Frick, 1998; Lynam, 1998) and higher levels of delinquency and police contacts (Corrado, Vincent, Hart, & Cohen, 2004; Falkenbach, Poythress, & Heide, 2003; Murrie, Cornell, Kaplan, McConville, & Levy-Elkon, 2004; O'Brien & Frick, 1996; Salekin, Ziegler, Larrea, Anthony, & Bennett, 2003). In addition, Forth and Burke (1998) report that children and adolescents with psychopathic traits differ from other antisocial youngsters in terms of the age of onset of their behavior problems, the number of violent acts committed, the seriousness of their offenses, and their recidivism rates. Thus, while many psychologists remain extremely skeptical, it is important to be aware of this continuing research activity.

PREVALENCE

Hare (1998; Hare & Hervé, 1999) believes that the number of adult psychopaths in the general population of any culture or society is about 1%. Among prisoners in North America, the psychopathic population is estimated at between 20% and 30% (Hare, 2003). In a study examining the prevalence rate of psychopathic tendencies in children, Skilling, Quinsey, and Craig (2001) found that 4.3% of a sample of over 1,000 boys in Grades 4 to 8 could be classified as psychopathic on every measure employed in the study. Dåderman and Kristiansson (2003) found that 59% of their sample of violent juvenile offenders qualified as psychopaths. Similarly, Brandt, Kennedy, Patrick, and Curtain (1997), using a sample of incarcerated adolescents with persistent violent offending histories, reported that they could identify 37% of the sample as psychopathic. By contrast, M. A. Campbell, Porter, and Santor (2004) found that only 9% of their sample of incarcerated adolescent offenders could be classified as psychopaths. Those authors note, though, that their sample was primarily nonviolent in nature, with only 15% having a history of violent offending. Clearly, the sample used in a study, as well as the measuring instrument itself, will strongly influence the number of psychopathic traits identified within a given group of adolescents.

RECENT THEORIES

Callous/Unemotional Temperament in Children

Frick and his colleagues (e.g., Frick, O'Brien, Wootton, & McBurnett, 1994; Frick, Barry, & Bodin, 2000) have concentrated on the presence of **callous and unemotional**

(CU) **traits** to define a subgroup of child–adolescent psychopaths who demonstrate a particularly severe and chronic pattern of antisocial behavior. These CU traits are characterized by a lack of empathy, lack of guilt, lack of conscience, and poverty in emotional expression. The CU traits, combined with certain clinical diagnoses, seem to be particularly problematic. For example, Frick and other scholars have discovered that children with both conduct disorders and CU traits exhibit behaviors that appear consistent with those demonstrated by adult psychopaths (Loney, Frick, Clements, Ellis, & Kerlin, 2003; Salekin & Frick, 2005). These youths with both conduct disorders and CU traits show a more severe, more aggressive, and more stable pattern of antisocial behavior (Frick & Dantagnan, 2005; Kruh, Frick, & Clements, 2005).

Several studies indicate that young offenders with CU traits do not typically respond well to treatment and intervention (Hawes & Dadds, 2005). Treatment may be effective for some, but it takes many intense approaches to be successful with young "psychopaths" showing CU traits. Some preliminary data suggest that young children with CU traits show evidence of a stronger *temperamental* contribution to the development of conduct problems than do children without these traits (Viding, 2004; Viding, Blair, Moffitt, & Plomin, 2004). Frick (1998) believes that a temperamental disposition (e.g., low fearfulness and low behavioral inhibition) in combination with emotional detachment may prevent these children from obtaining social support from significant others in their environment. On the other hand, Frick does not rule out the power of loving caregivers to develop prosocial behavior in their children.

In light of the apparent association between conduct disorder and juvenile psychopathy, some researchers have made the argument that the two are basically the same. Recent research is not supportive of this view, however. Only a small number of conduct-disordered children display the callous and unemotional traits associated with adult psychopathy (Barry et al., 2000; Salekin, 2006; Salekin, Brannen, Zalot, Leistico, & Neumann, 2006). Moreover, many juvenile psychopaths display lower levels of fearlessness and anxiety and higher levels of callous and unemotional traits than do those children with conduct disorders alone (Frick, Barry & Bodin, 2000; Frick & Dantagnan, 2005).

Psychopathy Constraint Model

According to Lynam (1996), children who show a combination of hyperactivity-impulsivity-attention (HIA or ADHD) and conduct problems from an early age are at an extremely high risk of becoming adult psychopaths. Specifically, Lynam (1996) asserts that the co-occurrence of ADHD and conduct problems identifies a child who could best be described as a "fledgling psychopath" (p. 211). He notes that children with a combination of ADHD and oppositional defiant disorder (ODD) and conduct disorder (CD) exhibit a particularly severe form of antisocial behavior and a number of neuropsychological features (e.g., absence of anxiety, low brain arousal, inability to self-regulate, and deficits in executive functions). **Oppositional defiant disorder** is a childhood behavioral disorder characterized by recurrent strong negativistic, disobedient, or hostile behavior toward authority figures. Lynam points out that the behavior of children with these features is remarkably similar to that of adult psychopaths. He further believes that psychopaths begin life with a deficiency in constraint, which hampers their ability to integrate feedback from the environment and to use this information to modulate responses while pursuing rewards. Someone high in constraint would be described as cautious and restrained, refraining from risky adventures, and accepting the expectations of conventional society. Someone low in constraint would be described as impulsive, adventurous, and inclined to reject conventional restrictions on behavior. Lynam argues that children with ADHD and conduct disorder would be low in constraint and high in impulsivity. Lynam suggests that this deficit leads to an inability to pause and empathize with others or to feel remorse and guilt, ultimately resulting in psychopathy. Lynam further speculates that children with both ADHD and conduct problems will require very different types of treatment than that required by children who show only ADHD or only a conduct problem.

Low-Fear Model of Psychopathy
Lykken (1995) argues that the main features of a psychopath are a reduced ability to experience fear, poor passive avoidance of negative stimuli, and weak electrodermal anticipation of punishment. Lykken makes a distinction between anxiety and fear, saying that psychopaths are not necessarily low in anxiety, but they are fundamentally fearless. Because of this low innate fearfulness, child psychopaths are more difficult to socialize using typical parenting methods, which rely on a child being motivated to avoid punishment. Children low in fearfulness generally respond better to reward-oriented parenting styles for socialization rather than parenting styles that rely primarily on the threat of punishment. This observation has important implications for developing prevention and treatment approaches for juveniles with psychopathic features.

MEASUREMENT OF JUVENILE PSYCHOPATHY

The avid interest in psychopathy, including juvenile psychopathy, has led to the development of a variety of instruments designed to measure it, or at least to measure psychopathic characteristics. Several instruments for measuring juvenile psychopathy have been developed in recent years, including the **Psychopathy Checklist: Youth Version**, or **PCL:YV** (Forth, Kosson, & Hare, 2003); the *Psychopathy Screening Device*, or PSD (Frick & Hare, 2001; Frick et al., 1994); the *Youth Psychopathic Traits Inventory*, or YPI (Andershed, Kerr, Stattin, & Levander, 2002); and the *Childhood Psychopathy Scale*, or CPS (Lynam, 1997). Although originally developed as research instruments rather than for diagnosis, they are rapidly becoming available to forensic clinical examiners for use in their private practice and their consulting work with the courts and the juvenile justice system. As Seagrave and Grisso (2002) point out, "It is not overstated to imagine that juvenile psychopathy measures will become one of the most frequently used instruments in forensic assessments of delinquency cases of any kind within a few years after they are made generally available to forensic clinical examiners" (p. 220).

All the measures have some difficulty because juveniles with psychopathic tendencies are unlikely to give accurate or honest self-reports about their emotions, thoughts, or behavior. The PCL:YV relies on an interview that has some specific questions to ask, plus collateral and other written data. Because of the interview and collateral data requirement, the PCL:YV requires extensive training to administer and is time-consuming. In addition, the PCL:YV is more research based and measures all three dimensions of psychopathy.

There have been several attempts to compare these measures of juvenile psychopathy in terms of their validity and reliability (Farrington, 2005). Preliminary research so far indicates that they do not have much in common, but considerably more research needs to be done before conclusions can be drawn. One interesting addition is the Hare P-Scan: Research Version (Hare & Herve, 1999), a 90-item scale apparently intended to serve as a screening device for use by nonclinicians. Although not a formal psychological test, it is nevertheless available for judges, counselors, probation officers, and other justice figures. According to Edens et al. (2001), the P-Scan is clearly intended for use with adolescents.

PCL:YV

The predominant instrument appears to be the Psychopathy Checklist: Youth Version, or PCL:YV (Forth, Kosson, & Hare, 1997). The PCL:YV became commercially available for clinical and forensic use in the early 2000s. Designed for use with adolescents 13 and older, it attempts to assess psychopathy across a youth's life span and focuses on peer, family, and school adjustment. Like the adult PCL-R, the youth version requires a lengthy clinical interview, as well as a review of records by a trained psychologist.

Some researchers and clinicians also use the Psychopathy Checklist: Screening Version (PCL:SV), a quick, 12-item measure of adult psychopathy that, with minor modification, has demonstrated excellent validity and reliability with adolescent offenders (Rogers, Salekin, Hill, Sewall, Murdock, & Neumann, 2000). Interview and record data are used to score the test. Similar to other screening measures, a high score on the PCL:SV (in this case greater than or equal to 17) suggests a need for further testing.

PSD/Now APSD

The name of the Psychopathy Screening Device was changed to the Antisocial Process Screening Device (APSD) when the instrument became commercially available to clinicians and juvenile justice professionals in 2001. (It is highly likely that the new name was more palatable to clinicians concerned about the labeling effects of psychopathy.) The APSD was developed by taking items from the PCL and rewriting them for use with children and adolescents. In contrast to the PCL:YV, the APSD does not require administration by a trained clinician. Parents and teachers fill out a 20-item questionnaire, responding "Not true," "Sometimes," or "Definitely true" to each item. The APSD can be used with children as young as 6. Sample items include "Teases other people," "Gets bored easily," "Does not show emotions," and "Is concerned about schoolwork." A self-report version, in which the juvenile rates him- or herself, is also available (Caputo, Frick, & Brodsky, 1999).

The APSD is based on a two-factor model: impulsive/conduct problems (I/CP) and callous/unemotional traits (CU). Recall that recent research supports a three-factor model as a more appropriate way of conceptualizing *adult* psychopathy. Likewise, Frick, Barry, and Bodin (2000) have proposed an alternate, three-factor model of juvenile psychopathy that includes narcissism. The APSD was validated on youth in the community, awaiting juvenile justice processing. In a recent study (Vitacco et al., 2003), researchers applied the APSD to incarcerated youth and found the two-factor model questionable but found support for the three-factor model. In general, the APSD has garnered substantial research support for its construct validity (Falkenbach et al., 2003).

YPI

The Youth Psychopathic Traits Inventory, or YPI, is another self-report measure. It was developed as a research instrument to identify children 12 and older who will persist in frequent and serious antisocial behavior into adulthood. Compared with the PCL:YV, the YPI focuses more narrowly on core features of psychopathy (i.e., interpersonal and affective traits such as remorselessness, grandiosity, and unemotionality). The YPI is also a self-report instrument, in which the items appear neutral so that the adolescent is less likely to expect a negative judgment (Skeem & Cauffman, 2003). A sample item in the YPI is "I usually feel calm when others are scared."

In a recent study comparing the YPI and the PCL:YV when administered to 160 serious juvenile offenders, Skeem and Cauffman (2003) found both tests reliable, but they questioned the construct validity of psychopathy applied to youth. The YPI was a good predictor of short-term institutional misbehavior, while the PCL:YV predicted disciplinary actions and violence. However, the authors considered these developmental markers rather than identification of a disorder that would remain stable during the transition period from adolescence to adulthood.

CPS

The Child Psychopathy Scale, or CPS, is a 41-item scale derived from other child personality measures. Lynam has recently modified the scale (mCPS) to a 55-item version (Falkenbach et al., 2003). The CPS can be completed by a parent/guardian or by the youth. Sample items include "Is he [or are you] a good liar?" "Does he have a quick temper?" "Does he try to act charming in order to get his way?" In his own research, Lynam found the scale a better predictor of serious delinquency than was socioeconomic status, previous delinquency, IQ, or impulsivity (Bartol & Bartol, 2005). Falkenbach et al. (2003) administered the CPS (as well as the APSD) to a sample of youths referred to diversion. They found that both scales had promise in predicting rearrests and failure to complete diversion contracts. However, like many other researchers, they cautioned against premature use of the scales in forensic practice.

ADAPTED TESTS AND SCALES

The instruments reviewed here were developed specifically for the measurement of psychopathic-like characteristics in youth. Taking a different approach, some researchers have used more general instruments and have modified them or identified subscales for the measurement of psychopathy. For example, both the adolescent version of the Minnesota Multiphasic Personality Inventory (MMPI-A), specifically its Pd scale, and the socialization scale of the California Personality Inventory (CPI) have been suggested as having relevance to juvenile psychopathy (see Cruise et al., 2003). Perhaps the best-known adapted instrument is the Psychopathy Content Scale (PCS; Murrie & Cornell, 2000, 2002), a 20-item self-report instrument derived from the Millon Adolescent Clinical Inventory (MACI). Like the APSD, the PCS is a screening instrument and was designed for use in clinical and correctional settings (Lexcen, Vincent, & Grisso, 2004).

In another attempt to develop a self-report screening instrument for psychopathy, Rogers and his colleagues (Rogers, Vitacco, Jackson, Martin, Collins, & Sewell, 2002) selected items from the Rogers (1996) Survey of Attitudes and Life Experiences (SALE). The original SALE, a clinical screen for antisocial attitudes in adolescents, was deliberately developed with low face validity, because deception is a common feature of delinquents, as Rogers et al. noted. Therefore, rather than asking youths to self-disclose their own antisocial behavior, the SALE gets at their attitudes via their appraisal of others. For example, rather than asking an adolescent to respond to "Teachers don't like me" or "Teachers are out to get me," a sample item reads, "Most teachers treat kids like they are stupid." Furthermore, because some juveniles want to make themselves look bad, the SALE attempts to detect the possibility of social nonconformity.

Rogers et al. (2002) developed two versions of a Psychopathy Screen Scale, one with 11 items and one with 24—PS-11 and PS-24, respectively—and found them moderately useful as a screen for juvenile psychopathy, identifying youths who needed further assessment. The items on the PS-11 and PS-24 assessed three major dimensions: unstable self-image and unstable relationships; manipulation and lack of guilt; and nonviolent delinquency. While the original SALE also measured aggressive behavior, the PS versions did not, presumably because of the researchers' emphasis that scores on juvenile psychopathy measures should not be used to predict violence. Nonetheless, the psychopathy construct is useful in treatment situations, because psychopathic characteristics can complicate treatment and make youth difficult to manage in juvenile facilities. The scales were also able to detect social noncomformity.

Each of these surveys, inventories, and scales has garnered some supportive research. Many studies indicate that there is considerable validity in measures of juvenile psychopathy (Edens et al., 2001; Kosson, Cyterski, Steverwald, Neuman, & Walker-Matthes, 2002: Murrie & Cornell, 2002; Murrie et al., 2004), but a vast majority of the researchers also believe that much more research needs to be done on this concept (see Johnstone & Cooke, 2004). Most researchers are extremely cautious about proclaiming the superiority of any one measure, as well as about endorsing the construct of juvenile psychopathy, without more documentation.

PERSONALITY DIMENSIONS

One of the more popular approaches to identifying personality traits in juvenile delinquents is known as the **five-factor model of personality** (FFM), commonly referred to as the "big five" (McCrae & Costa, 1990). This model contends that there are five universal dimensions of personality: (1) neuroticism, (2) extraversion, (3) openness, (4) agreeableness, and (5) conscientiousness. Briefly, neuroticism refers to emotional adjustment and stability. Individuals scoring high on this factor are prone to feeling anxious in many situations. They are also generally susceptible to a variety of other negative emotions—such as depression, anger, and sadness—and they tend to overreact to stress and pressure. High scores on this dimension suggest that the person has unrealistic ideas, excessive cravings or difficulty tolerating the frustration of not acting on urges, and maladaptive coping responses (Costa & Widiger, 2002). In contrast, persons scoring low on this factor tend to stay on an even keel, are generally optimistic, and do not overreact to stressful circumstances.

Extraversion pertains to the quantity and intensity of social interactions, activity level, and need for stimulation. High scorers on this dimension tend to be sociable, active, talkative, person oriented, optimistic, fun loving, and affectionate (Costa & Widiger, 2002). People low on the extraversion factor are described as aloof, sober, independent, and quiet.

Openness relates to a person's interest in culture and preference for new activities and new experiences. Persons high on this dimension are described as having active imaginations, being intellectually curious, and seeking challenges and new places, people, and events. They are willing to entertain novel ideas and unconventional values, and they experience the whole gamut of emotions more intensely than do those who score low on this dimension. Those persons who score low tend to be conventional in their beliefs and attitudes, are conservative in their approach to life, and are considered dogmatic and rigid in their beliefs. Overall, they are set in their ways and generally unresponsive emotionally.

A person high in agreeableness would be considered trusting, straightforward and empathic, good-natured, helpful, and softhearted. A person low in agreeableness would be described as arrogant, rude, uncooperative, vengeful, ruthless, manipulative, cynical, and unconcerned about others.

Finally, conscientiousness refers to the ability to plan, be self-directed and punctual, organize, control impulses, and complete tasks. Low scores on this dimension are associated with undependability, laxness, negligence, carelessness, hedonism, and aimlessness.

Because these five dimensions are depicted in just about every culture or society, they may reflect a universal core of human personality. Extensive research has shown that the five-factor model is valid in its application to children and adolescents (Lynam et al., 2005). In addition, theory and research link the five-factor model to psychopathy in adulthood (Lynam, 2002; J. D. Miller, Lynam, Widiger, & Leukefeld, 2001; Salekin et al., 2005). Lynam et al. (2005) report that "results are quite consistent in showing that adult psychopathy consists of a mixture of low agreeableness and conscientiousness, high extraversion, and a combination of low openness and high neuroticism" (p. 432). Similar results have been found for children (Lynam, 2002) and adolescents (Lynam et al., 2005; Salekin et al., 2005) who are prone to exhibit psychopathic traits. Salekin et al. (2005) discovered in their study of 114 male and female young offenders that adolescents with psychopathic tendencies exhibited some neurotic or anxiety-like characteristics. These findings are surprising, considering that previous research has consistently identified the *absence* of anxiety and neurotic symptoms as a hallmark of psychopathy. Clearly, additional research is needed. However, if juveniles with psychopathic tendencies do experience anxiety, they may be more responsive to traditional forms of treatment. In fact, Caldwell, Skeem, Salekin, and VanRybroeck (2006) report evidence that youths with psychopathic tendencies may be able to change if interventions are started early. Overall, these findings suggest that clinicians should be able to obtain considerable information on juvenile psychopathy by assessing general personality.

Summary and Conclusions

Despite many concerns about the implications of labeling a juvenile a psychopath, contemporary research strongly indicates that some juveniles do have psychopathic characteristics that resemble those of adult psychopaths. However, some of these characteristics—for example, lack of planning, self-centeredness, impulsivity—are not atypical of older children and adolescents as a group. It is important, therefore, that the psychopathic-like features in young people be distinguished from normal adolescent development. In addition, it is important that a construct like juvenile psychopathy not be confused with some of the more common clinical diagnoses, such as conduct disorder or oppositional defiant disorder.

The earliest research on adult psychopathy was conducted by Cleckley, who identified 16 behavioral features characteristic of a psychopath. Included are such traits as superficial charm, above-average intelligence, apparent inability to give genuine affection, disregard for truth, and lack of remorse. Later research (e.g., Hare, 2003) identified cognitive, emotional, and neuropsychological features, such as deficits in temperament and conditionability. This chapter reviewed these key features and discussed how they apply to juveniles. Although researchers have found that adult psychopaths and juveniles with psychopathic tendencies have many characteristics in common, the juveniles appear to have higher anxiety than the adults do. The typical adult psychopath demonstrates very little anxiety.

The childhood of a psychopath seems to be littered with negative experiences, including defects in parental monitoring, as well as parental neglect and/or abuse. As a child, a psychopath was often hyperactive and had attention problems, features that have led to concerns that hyperactive children are candidates for adult psychopathy. Research has not supported either hyperactivity or conduct disorders, in isolation, as predictors of psychopathy. However, a combination of hyperactivity and conduct disorder or ODD may place a child at a high risk of adult psychopathy.

Recent research also focuses on the presence of callous and unemotional traits (CU) in juveniles who have psychopathic tendencies. The combination of CU traits and conduct disorder appears to be particularly problematic. Young children with CU traits may appear emotionally detached, making it difficult for them to obtain social support from others in their environment.

In addition, contemporary research has focused on specifying the most efficient model for describing psychopathy. Until recently, the predominant model was a two-factor version, describing emotional and interpersonal features and a deviant lifestyle. Lately, a three-dimensional model has emerged describing an arrogant and deceptive style, deficient affective or emotional expression, and impulsive and irresponsible behavior. Still other researchers believe a fourth factor should be added, one representing antisocial behavior. These models should be subjected to considerable additional research before being applied to juveniles. The recent interest in juvenile psychopathy has also led to the development of a number of instruments designed to measure it: the PCL:YV, PCL:SV, APSD, YPI, and CPS.

Although not all psychopaths engage in criminal behavior, psychopaths as a group are responsible for a disproportionate amount of crime. Furthermore, the violent crimes of psychopaths are particularly heinous and brutal. This is a major reason for the intense interest in juvenile psychopathy among some psychologists. If juveniles with these characteristics can be identified and treated, perhaps some crimes can be prevented.

Until recently, much of the literature on adult psychopathy emphasized the psychopath's nonresponsivity to treatment. Because psychopaths were considered unlikely to change their behavior, many psychologists have resisted placing juveniles in this category. A poor prognosis virtually guarantees that society is giving up on them and encourages the juvenile justice system to give them over to the adult criminal justice system. Recent research suggests, though, that even adult psychopaths may respond to intensive treatment approaches. Thus, juveniles are even more likely to be successfully treated. Contemporary researchers note that, because juveniles with psychopathic characteristics do not respond to punishment or fear, interventions that offer rewards for acceptable behavior are more likely to be effective.

Key Terms and Concepts

amygdala
callous and unemotional traits
construct validity
five-factor model of personality
immature brain-wave patterns
juvenile psychopathy
markers
oppositional defiant disorder
predictive validity
primary psychopath
prospective longitudinal studies

Psychopathy Checklist
Psychopathy Checklist—Revised
 (PCL-R)
Psychopathy Checklist: Youth
 Version (PCL:YV)
retrospective studies
secondary psychopath
slow-wave activity
two-factor model of psychopathy
violence inhibition mechanism

CHAPTER 8
MEASUREMENT OF JUVENILE CRIME

❧

CHAPTER OBJECTIVES

◆ Introduce the various sources of measurement of criminal and delinquent behavior

◆ Review some research methods for measuring delinquency

◆ Present status offenses in detail, including runaways, school truancy, ungovernability, and liquor-law violations

◆ Review some of the common property crimes of juveniles, including larceny–theft, shoplifting, burglary, and motor vehicle theft

One of the primary uses of quantitative methodology is the accumulation of statistics on juvenile crime and victimization. Additionally, data are gathered on youths held in detention, processed in juvenile courts, placed on probation, and held in custody in private and public facilities after having been adjudicated delinquent. The quantitative methods used for these purposes can be divided into two major categories, official and unofficial. **Official statistics** refer to recorded data published or supervised by governmental agencies. **Unofficial statistics** refer to data published by private organizations or independent researchers, sometimes with the help of government grants. Some types of measurement may fall into both categories; for example, there are official as well as unofficial victimization studies. Because relying on any single type of quantitative data is likely to yield a limited perspective about delinquency, criminologists often prefer to classify delinquency data according to their source: agencies of the juvenile or criminal justice system, victims, or offenders themselves.

OFFICIAL DATA

The most widely cited form of official statistics is the FBI's **Uniform Crime Reports** (UCR), which includes crimes known to police, as well as law enforcement arrest data on adults and juveniles (defined as arrestees under age 18). Thus, the source of the UCR is the law enforcement community across the nation. It is widely acknowledged, however, that many crimes—adult and juvenile—are not reported to law enforcement. Moreover, if reported, they are not necessarily followed by an arrest. Therefore, although statistics suggest that roughly 1.5 to 2 million juvenile arrests are made each year, we must keep in mind that the figure underestimates juvenile offending. Furthermore, the figures provide some estimate of the incidence, but not the prevalence, of delinquency, a distinction that will be explained shortly.

In addition to the UCR, another useful data base is juvenile court records. These records do not help us to estimate the juvenile crime problem, however, because only about half of those arrested are referred to juvenile court. The others are not charged, or the charges against them are dropped. Juvenile court statistics do indicate the types of crimes for which juveniles are processed, as well as the dispositions they are given if found guilty of their offenses. While most juveniles reach juvenile court as the result of an arrest, some are referred by parents, school personnel, citizens, social agencies, or probation departments, usually for relatively minor offenses (Sickmund, 2004).

After referral to juvenile court, a decision is made as to whether to handle the case formally or informally (see Figure 8–1). Informal processing is considered when the decision makers believe accountability and rehabilitation can be achieved without the use of formal court intervention (H. N. Snyder & Sickmund, 1995). Of the total number of cases referred to juvenile court, about half are processed informally (Butts et al., 1995), without a delinquency petition being filed. Formal processing usually occurs when the juvenile is involved in more serious offenses, is older, and has a longer court record. Of the total cases in which a delinquency petition is filed, about three in five result in a juvenile being adjudicated "delinquent." Roughly, then, between 550,000 and 625,000 young people attain delinquency status each year (Puzzanchera et al., 2004). They may then be institutionalized, placed on probation, made to pay fines or make restitution, ordered to undergo counseling or to enroll in specified programs, or given some combination of these options (H. N. Snyder & Sickmund, 1995).

Many researchers argue that we lose valuable clues about delinquency if we define the delinquent population strictly according to legal rules or these sources of data, and they are, of course, correct. After all, most of those arrested never reach delinquency status, and as with adult crime, there is a "dark figure" representing young lawbreakers who never come to official attention at all. **Dark figure** is the term criminologists use for the amount of crime that is not reflected in statistics. Research by Elliott, Dunford, and Huizinga (1987) suggests that as many as 86% of American juvenile offenders escape detection, including more serious and repeat offenders.

The nonrandom sample designated "delinquent" severely misrepresents the population of true delinquents for other reasons as well. Widespread judicial discretion and differences in procedures mean that juveniles who have engaged in similar conduct are not necessarily treated similarly. Furthermore, some juveniles may have been diverted from the court either by specific programs intended for that very purpose, by the discretion of a police officer, or by the intervention of parents or guardians. Finally, some juveniles—because of their age or the heinousness of their crime—are processed in adult rather than juvenile court. In short, official figures from police and the courts represent a special population of people under special circumstances and *not* the whole population of individuals about whom we are concerned. It is primarily for this reason that legal definitions or official figures alone should be used with caution.

UNIFORM CRIME REPORTS

The FBI's Uniform Crime Reports (UCR), compiled since 1930, is the most-cited source of U.S. crime statistics. The UCR is an annual document, released to the public between late July and early September, containing information received on a voluntary

FIGURE 8–1 Key Decision Points in the Juvenile Justice System with Illustrative System Objectives and Decision Options

Arrest	Adjudication			Disposition	Postdisposition
System objectives: • Conducted initial assessment • De-escalate and stabilize • Refer accused for formal adjudication • Prevent further offending • Assure initial court appearance	*System objectives:* • Determine need for formal adjudication • Determine guilt or innocence • Evaluate the situation of the accused and his or her amenability to intervention • Maintain the accused and prevent further offending during case processing			*System objectives:* • Protect the community • Hold offenders accountable • Rehabilitate • Prevent future crime	*System objectives:* • Support successful reintegration into the community • Rehabilitate • Prevent future crime
Arrest/ Referral Intake/ Detention	Case Filing Pretrial Release or Detention	Trial/ Adjudication Sentencing/ Disposition		Sanction/Sentence Modification	Aftercare

Decision options:
 • Warn and release
 • Issue citation or summons
 • Refer to law enforcement diversion
 • Refer to services
 • Take youth into custody
   – Conduct intake and assessment
   – Provide crisis services
   – Detain pending court hearing
   – Release with or without conditions pending court hearing
	Decision options:
	 • File petition or divert from formal adjudication
	 • Determine need for continued detention during adjudication
	 • If eligible for release pending adjudication, set release conditions
	 • Refer to services (voluntary or as a condition of release)
		Decision Options:
		 • Determine guilt or innocence
		 • Determine need for pre-disposition evaluation
		 • Determine disposition
		   – No intervention
		   – Civil fine or penalty
		   – Probation with or without conditions
		   – Commitment to state custody
				Decision Options:
				 • Placement (ranging from home to secure setting)
				 • Supervision level
				 • Services required
				 • Progress in meeting court orders or case plan goals
				 • Revocation if court ordered conditions not met
				 • Discharge
					Decision Options:
					 • Reentry services required
					   – Placement
					   – Level of supervision
					   – Services required
					 • Progress in meeting aftercare goals
					 • Revocation if release conditions not met
					 • Discharge

Source: From *Planning Community-Based Facilities for Violent Juvenile Offenders as Part of a System of Graduated Sanctions,* by S. Zavlek, August 2005, Washington, DC: U.S. (p. 10) Department of Justice, OJJDP.

basis from law enforcement agencies throughout the country. While the first UCR was published with data from fewer than 1,000 law enforcement agencies, the 2004 UCR data collection was based on nearly 17,000 agencies, representing about 98% of the total U.S. population (Federal Bureau of Investigation, 2005). The UCR represents the only major data source permitting a comparison of national aggregate data, broken down by age, sex, race, and offense. The more recently developed FBI Supplementary Homicide Report contains data on victim and offender demographics, the offender–victim relationship, the weapon used, and the circumstances surrounding the homicide. Other special reports include those on hate crimes, campus crimes, and the events of September 11, 2001.

The UCR divides crime statistics in a number of ways, including by age, sex, race, city, and region of the country. Crimes are also categorized according to seriousness. Serious crimes are referred to as **index,** or **Part I, crimes**; nonserious, as **nonindex,** or **Part II, crimes**. Even this distinction is misleading, however. For example, larceny–theft is categorized as a Part I crime, whereas fraud and drug offenses are classified as Part II crimes. Table 8–1 contains definitions of some of the Part I and Part II crimes reported in the UCR, specifically those which will be discussed in the text.

According to the UCR, persons under 18 accounted for 15.8% of the arrests for violent crimes and 26.0% of the arrests for property crimes in 2005 (FBI, 2006). In order to be recorded in the UCR, a crime must be (at a minimum)

- perceived by the victim or by someone else
- defined as a crime by the victim or the observer
- in some way known to a law enforcement agency
- defined by that law enforcement agency as a crime
- accurately recorded by the law enforcement agency
- reported to the FBI compilation center

Figure 8–2 portrays the distribution of total arrests of juveniles in 2005. As it shows, larceny–theft led the arrests, followed by drug abuse and curfew violations. The lowest arrests were for murder and prostitution. Figure 8–3 illustrates the distribution of Part I arrests of juveniles under age 15.

NATIONAL INCIDENT-BASED REPORTING SYSTEM

During the late 1970s, the law enforcement community called for the expanded use of the UCR and developed new guidelines for reporting crime statistics. These guidelines formed the basis of the National Incident-Based Reporting System (NIBRS) under the Uniform Federal Crime Reporting Act, passed by the U.S. Congress in 1988 (Public Law No. 100-690, 102 Stat. 4181). Congress required all federal law enforcement agencies, including those within the Department of Defense, to collect and report data to the FBI on two categories of offenses—Group A and Group B. For Group A, reporting agencies must make incident reports for 22 offense categories, which include 46 specific crimes (see page 190 Figure 8–4). This new approach greatly expanded the traditional Part I categories found in the UCR.

The Group A incident reports include all aspects of a crime, including information about the victim, weapon, location of the crime, alcohol/drug influence, type of criminal activity, relationship of victim to offender, residences of victims and

TABLE 8–1: Definitions of Some Part I and Part II Crimes in the Uniform Crime Reports

Part I Crime	*Definition*
Murder and nonnegligent manslaughter	The willful (nonnegligent) killing of one human by another
Forcible rape	The carnal knowledge of a female forcibly and against her will
Robbery	The taking or attempting to take anything of value from the care, custody, or control of a person(s) by force or threat of force or violence and/or by putting the victim in fear
Aggravated assault	An unlawful attack by one person on another for the purpose of inflicting severe or aggravated bodily injury; includes attempts
Burglary	The unlawful entry of a structure to commit a felony or theft
Larceny–theft	The unlawful taking, carrying, leading, or riding away of property from the possession or constructive possession of another; includes shoplifting, pocket picking, purse snatching, thefts from motor vehicles, and bicycle thefts
Arson	Any willful or malicious burning or attempt to burn, with or without intent to defraud, a dwelling house, public building, motor vehicle or aircraft, or personal property of another

Common Part II Crimes	*Definition*
Simple assaults	Assaults and attempted assaults in which no weapon is used and no serious or aggravated injury to victim results
Forgery and counterfeiting	Making, altering, uttering, or possessing, with intent to defraud, anything false in the semblance of that which is true
Fraud	Fraudulent conversion and obtaining of money or property by false pretenses
Embezzlement	Misappropriation or misapplication of money entrusted to one's care, custody, or control
Stolen property	Buying, receiving, or possessing stolen property, including attempts
Offenses against the family and children	Nonsupport, neglect, desertion, or abuse of family or children
Drug abuse violations	State and/or local offenses relating to the unlawful possession, sale, use, growing, or manufacture of drugs
Gambling	Promoting, permitting, or engaging in illegal gambling
Vandalism	Willful or malicious destruction, injury, disfigurement, or defacement of any public or private property, real or personal, without the consent of the owner or persons having custody or control

Source: Based on *Crime in the United States—2005* by Federal Bureau of Investigation, 2006, Washington, DC: U.S. Department of Justice, Author.

arrestees, and a description of property and its value. Presumably, this added information is an indispensable tool for law enforcement agencies and researchers because it provides them with detailed data about when and where crime takes place, what form it takes, and what the characteristics of its victims and perpetrators are.

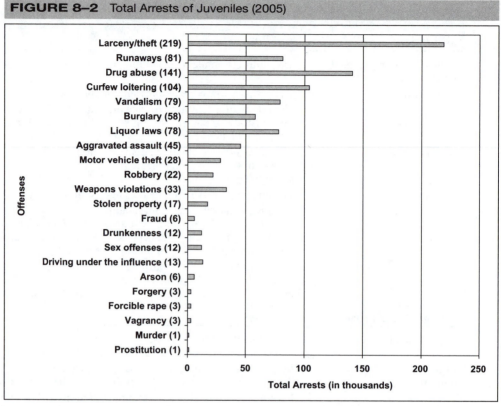

FIGURE 8–2   Total Arrests of Juveniles (2005)

Source: Data from *Crime in the United States—2005* by Federal Bureau of Investigation, 2006, Washington, DC: U.S. Department of Justice, Author.

For Group B offenses, reporting agencies must file arrest reports for such offenses as bad checks, driving under the influence of alcohol, disorderly conduct, drunkenness, nonviolent family offenses, liquor-law violations, Peeping-Tom activity, running away, trespass, and other offenses not specifically designated as Group A offenses. Group B arrest reports contain information about only the arrestee and the circumstances of the arrest.

State and federal agencies participating in the NIBRS use automated systems to report information on Group A and Group B offenses to the FBI on a monthly basis, much as they do in the UCR program. However, the NIBRS information is much more detailed, and the program has not yet been fully implemented across the United States. Data analyses based on NIBRS are just beginning to appear in the criminological literature. Therefore, much of the arrest and crime-rate data reported in this text will be based on information provided in the UCR.

JUVENILE COURT STATISTICS

A variety of sources provide information on juvenile courts. These include the Juvenile Court Statistics series, first published in 1929 by the Children's Bureau of the

FIGURE 8–3 Distribution of Part I Arrests of Juveniles Under Age 15 (2005)

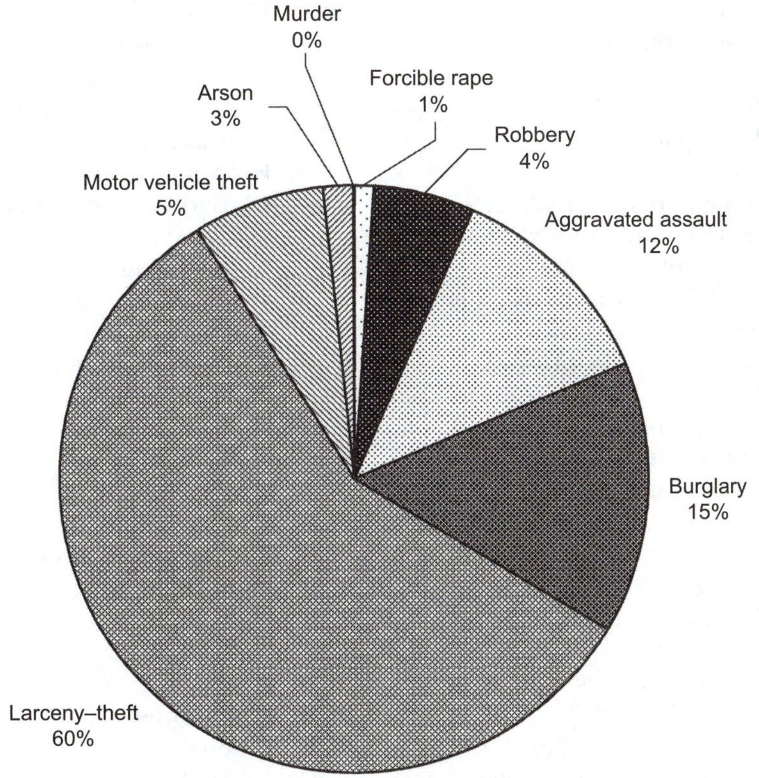

Source: Data from *Crime in the United States—2005* by Federal Bureau of Investigation, 2006, Washington, DC: U.S. Department of Justice, Author.

U. S. Department of Labor, which depends on the voluntary support of courts with juvenile jurisdiction. The series describes the number and characteristics of delinquency and status offenses that came before courts with juvenile jurisdiction. However, data reported in the document are not based on a nationally representative sample, and there is no way of determining their validity. The national figures for 2002 are based on case records from more than 2,100 juvenile courts and data on cases from more than 300 additional courts. Together, these courts had jurisdiction over 75% of the U.S juvenile population.

Juvenile courts in the United States processed an estimated 1.6 million delinquency cases in 2002 (Stahl, 2006). Figure 8–5 gives an overview of the processing of those cases. According to the most recent data, 624,900 of the cases handled by juvenile courts were property offenses, 409,800 cases were public order offenses, 387,000 of the cases concerned person offenses (violent offenses), and 193,200 cases dealt with drug-law violations. Public order offenses include obstruction of justice, disorderly conduct, weapons offenses, liquor-law offenses, and nonviolent sex offenses. Between 1997 and 2002, juvenile court cases decreased by 11% (Stahl, 2006).

FIGURE 8–4   NIBRS Group A Offenses

Arson
Assault offenses
  Aggravated assault
  Simple assault
  Intimidation
Bribery
Burglary/breaking and entering
Counterfeiting/forgery
Destruction/damage/
  vandalism to property
Drug/narcotic offenses
  Drug/narcotic violations
  Drug/equipment violations
Embezzlement
Extortion/blackmail
Fraud offenses
  False pretenses/swindle/confidence game
  Credit card/ATM fraud
  Impersonation
  Welfare fraud
  Wire fraud
Gambling offenses
  Betting/wagering
  Operating/promoting/assisting gambling
  Gambling equipment violations
  Sports tampering

Hate crimes
Homicide offenses
  Murder/nonnegligent manslaughter
  Negligent manslaughter
  Justifiable homicide
Kidnapping/abduction
Larceny–theft offenses
  Pocket picking
  Purse snatching
  Shoplifting
  Theft from building
  Theft from coin-operated
    machines
  Theft from motor vehicles
  Theft of motor vehicle parts/
    accessories
  Motor vehicle theft
Pornography/obscene materials
Prostitution offenses
  Prostitution
  Assisting or promoting prostitution
Robbery
Sex offenses, forcible
  Forcible rape
  Forcible sodomy
  Sexual assault with an object
  Forcible fondling
Sex offenses, nonforcible
Stolen property offenses
Terrorism
Weapons law violations

Source: Based on *National Incident-Based Reporting System* by Federal Bureau of Investigation, 2004, Washington, DC: U.S. Department of Justice.

PROBATION AND PAROLE STATISTICS

Juvenile probation refers to the conditional freedom granted by the court to a juvenile offender in place of incarceration, as long as he or she meets certain conditions of behavior. **Parole** is a status granted an offender upon release from a correctional facility if his or her sentence has not expired. Although juvenile probation is the most common disposition given to delinquents, the term *parole* has been rarely used until recently. Its equivalent is **aftercare**, which refers to the ongoing community supervision of juveniles who have been in some type of juvenile facility.

Statistics on probation, aftercare, and juvenile court processing in general can be found in the various reports published by the Office of Juvenile Justice and Delinquency

FIGURE 8–5 Processing of Delinquency Cases by Juvenile Courts (2002)

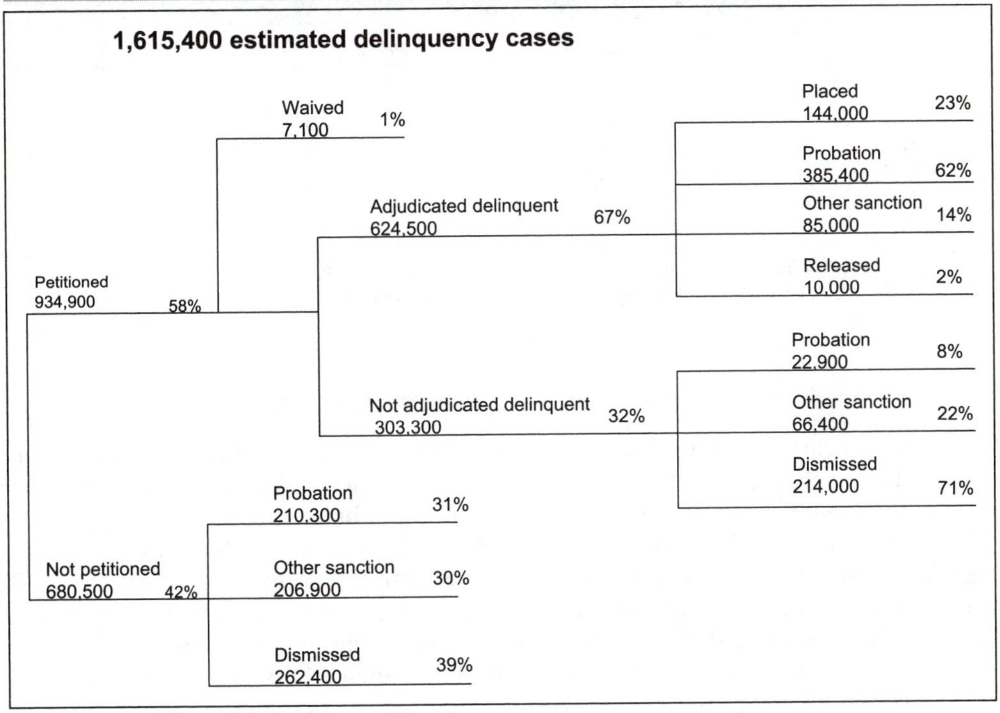

1,615,400 estimated delinquency cases

Petitioned
934,900 — 58%

   Waived
   7,100 — 1%

   Adjudicated delinquent
   624,500 — 67%

     Placed 144,000 — 23%
     Probation 385,400 — 62%
     Other sanction 85,000 — 14%
     Released 10,000 — 2%

   Not adjudicated delinquent
   303,300 — 32%

     Probation 22,900 — 8%
     Other sanction 66,400 — 22%
     Dismissed 214,000 — 71%

Not petitioned
680,500 — 42%

   Probation 210,300 — 31%
   Other sanction 206,900 — 30%
   Dismissed 262,400 — 39%

Note: Cases are categorized by their most severe or restrictive sanction. Detail may not add to totals because of rounding. Annual case-processing flow diagrams for 1985 through 2002 are available online at www.ojjdp.ncjrs.gov/ojstatbb/court/faqs.asp.

Source: From *Juvenile Court Statistics 2001–2002* (p. 53) by A. Stahl, C. Puzzanchera, A. Sladky, T. Finnegan, N. Tierney, and H. Snyder, December 2006, Washington, DC: OJJDP.

Prevention (OJJDP). National data on probation and aftercare indicate that probation was ordered in about 55% of the 1.1 million delinquency cases that received a juvenile court sanction in 2002 compared with about 14% that received placement in an out-of-home facility (OJJDP, 2005). Table 8–2 shows that property offenses accounted for the greatest percentage of juvenile probation cases in 2002 (38%), followed by public order offenses (25%; Stahl et al., 2006). Researchers estimate that the juvenile justice system affects the lives of between 8% and 10% of all American youths between the ages of 10 and 17 (Steinberg, Len Chung, & Little, 2004).

In addition to this formal type of probation—received by over half of adjudicated delinquents—juvenile courts also employ a system of **informal**, or **voluntary, probation**, in which youth who are not adjudicated delinquent agree to abide by certain probation conditions (Puzzanchera, 2003b). If they successfully complete their probationary period, their cases are terminated without formal processing and, consequently, a juvenile record. The advantage to the youth seems obvious, but it is also seen as advantageous to many communities, which are using this informal system as a way of monitoring at-risk youth, hoping to prevent them from engaging in more serious antisocial behavior.

TABLE 8–2: Offense Profile of Cases Adjudicated Delinquent That Resulted in Probation

	Percentage in 1985	Percentage in 2002
Personal	16	24
Property	61	38
Drugs	7	13
Public order	16	25
Total	100	100

Source: Data from *Juvenile Court Statistics 2001–2002* (p. 49) by A. Stahl, C. Puzzanchera, A. Sladky, T. Finnegan, N. Tierney, and H. Snyder, December 2006, Washington, DC: OJJDP.

CENSUS OF JUVENILES IN RESIDENTIAL PLACEMENT

The principal source of data on incarcerated juveniles is the biennial census on children in both public and private juvenile correctional facilities, including detention centers, throughout the 50 states and the District of Columbia. Formerly known as the Children in Custody (CIC) report, it is now called the **Census of Juveniles in Residential Placement** (CJRP) and is sponsored by the OJJDP in conjunction with the U.S. Bureau of Census. In 2002, the most recent data at this writing, the report analyzed data on 102,388 youths held in 2,964 public and private facilities across the country (Sickmund, 2006, see Table 8–3). Juveniles are more likely than adults to be held in settings operated by private groups or foundations, rather than in the equivalent of adult jails and prisons. For example, juveniles may be in boot camps, wilderness camps, group homes, or small private facilities specializing in the treatment of special offending, such as sex offending or arson. In 2002, 61% of the facilities holding juveniles were private but accounted for only 31% of all juveniles held (Sickmund, 2006).

The CJRP is conducted biennially and provides detailed information on all juveniles in residential placement facilities. The report includes data on each juvenile offender, such as gender, date of birth, race, placement authority, most serious offense charged, court adjudication status, and security status. The juveniles may be committed to a facility as part of a court-ordered disposition, or they may be detained prior to or after adjudication while awaiting disposition or placement elsewhere. A small number of juveniles may be admitted voluntarily in lieu of adjudication as part of a diversion agreement.

The CJRP does not collect data on juveniles held in adult prison or jails. However, a separate report, the Bureau of Justice Statistics' Annual Survey of Jails, estimates that 7,600 youths younger than 18 were held in the nation's jails in 2000. The Juvenile Justice and Delinquency Prevention Act of 2002 (JJDPA) states that "juveniles alleged to be or found to be delinquent," as well as status offenders and nonoffenders, "will not be detained or confined in any institution in which they have contact with adult inmates" (Sickmund, 2004, p. 18). This provision is commonly referred to as the sight and sound separation requirement.

In 1999 the vast majority of residents in juvenile facilities (78%) were there for offenses that would be considered criminal offenses for adults (Sickmund, 2004). Status offenders, which we will discuss shortly, accounted for another 4%, mostly for

TABLE 8–3: Numbers of Juvenile Facilities and Juvenile Offender by State (2002)

	Juvenile Facilities			Juvenile Offenders		
State	Total	Public	Private	Total	Public	Private
Alabama	48	12	36	1,539	827	712
Alaska	23	7	16	402	303	99
Arizona	51	16	32	1,892	1,488	320
Arkansas	35	9	26	733	211	522
California	286	122	164	17,294	15,561	1,733
Colorado	65	12	52	2,063	928	1,131
Connecticut	26	4	22	665	244	421
Delaware	6	4	2	271	243	28
Dist. of Columbia	13	2	11	280	183	97
Florida	181	53	128	8,508	3,043	5,465
Georgia	53	30	23	2,681	2,224	457
Hawaii	5	2	3	112	99	13
Idaho	22	14	8	466	402	64
Illinois	45	25	20	2,921	2,539	382
Indiana	95	42	53	3,433	2,386	1,047
Iowa	65	16	49	941	376	565
Kansas	56	17	39	1,114	809	305
Kentucky	50	32	18	985	814	171
Louisiana	62	21	41	2,363	1,830	533
Maine	14	2	12	278	242	36
Maryland	43	10	33	1,216	611	605
Massachusetts	68	18	50	1,400	452	948
Michigan	94	37	57	2,856	1,353	1,503
Minnesota	100	24	76	1,699	886	813
Mississippi	17	15	2	688	600	68
Missouri	72	60	12	1,559	1,332	227
Montana	24	7	15	308	177	99
Nebraska	19	5	14	732	513	219
Nevada	18	10	8	1,169	861	308
New Hampshire	8	2	6	234	137	97
New Jersey	49	42	7	2,043	1,972	71
New Mexico	27	18	9	803	698	105
New York	221	51	170	4,455	2,328	2,127
North Carolina	66	27	39	1,286	870	416
North Dakota	11	4	7	246	131	115
Ohio	97	66	31	4,480	4,023	457
Oklahoma	56	14	41	1,010	634	351
Oregon	45	26	19	1,473	1,262	211
Pennsylvania	179	33	146	5,080	1,262	3,818
Rhode Island	14	1	13	346	233	123

(*continued*)

TABLE 8–3: (Continued)

State	Juvenile Facilities			Juvenile Offenders		
	Total	*Public*	*Private*	*Total*	*Public*	*Private*
South Carolina	38	14	24	1,461	966	495
South Dakota	22	8	12	598	334	256
Tennessee	58	26	32	1,659	830	829
Texas	129	78	51	8,371	6,726	1,645
Utah	47	17	30	1,073	472	601
Vermont	5	1	4	61	27	34
Virginia	71	63	8	2,635	2,448	187
Washington	40	30	10	1,931	1,759	172
West Virginia	23	6	17	394	281	113
Wisconsin	81	25	56	1,784	1,182	602
Wyoming	21	2	19	417	141	276
U. S. total*	2,964	1,182	1,773	102,388	70,243	31,992

Source: From *Juvenile Residential Facility Census, 2002: Selected findings* by M. Sickmund, June 2006, Washington, DC: U.S. Department of Justice, OJJDP.

*U. S. total includes 153 offenders in 9 tribal facilities. These tribal facilities were located in Arizona, Colorado, Montana, Oklahoma, and South Oakota.

Note: State is the state where the facility is located. Offenders sent to out-of-state facilities are counted in the state where the facility is located, not the state where their offense occurred.

incorrigibility (39%). Some residents held in the facilities have not been charged with or adjudicated for an offense, representing about 19% of the total residential population.

The data reveal that minorities accounted for 7 in 10 juveniles held in custody for violent offenses. A large proportion of these were African-American. Females accounted for 13% of juveniles in residential placement. The small proportion of female juveniles in residential placement was greater for private facilities (16%) than for public facilities (12%) and greater for detained juveniles (18%) than committed juveniles (12%; Sickmund, 2004). However, the female proportion of those admitted to placement under a diversion agreement was large (40%). Furthermore, although the guiding principle is to house juvenile offenders in the least restrictive placement alternative, about 7 in 10 were confined by locked doors and/or gates within the facility and its grounds (Sickmund, 2004, p. 16). The proportion of juveniles held under locked arrangements increased with age. Juveniles held in residential placement for status offenses were more likely to be confined under staff-secure rather than locked arrangements.

NATIONAL CRIME VICTIMIZATION SURVEY

Another source of official statistics that provides useful information on juvenile crime is the **National Crime Victimization Survey** (NCVS). The Bureau of Census interviews, on a staggered schedule, a large national sample of households (approximately 60,000) representing 136,000 persons over the age of 12. Crimes committed against children below age 12 are not counted because of privacy reasons and because the designers of the survey believe that younger respondents are not as likely as adults to provide accurate information. However, a valuable supplement to the NCVS, a report on school victimization, does include these younger age groups.

The households sampled in the NCVS are asked about personal crimes experienced during the previous 6 months. The survey is currently designed to measure the extent to which persons and households have been victims of rape, robbery, assault, burglary, motor vehicle theft, and larceny.

NCVS researchers use a **panel design**, a method that involves examining the same selected sample or group repeatedly over a certain length of time. In this case, each household is contacted twice a year for 3 years. The interviewers return to addresses (places of residence) rather than to individuals. That is, they contact (in person or by phone) the same housing unit every 6 months. If the family contacted during the previous interview cycle has moved, the new occupants are interviewed. Housing units in the panel are visited a maximum of seven times, after which new units are selected.

The original impetus for the NCVS came from the President's Commission on Law Enforcement and Administration of Justice, which in 1966 commissioned the first national victimization survey. The commission wanted to supplement the annual UCR compiled by the FBI, because of widespread dissatisfaction with and distrust of the accuracy of the UCR. After considerable experimentation and a variety of pilot projects to test the method and its feasibility, the NCVS was fully implemented in 1973.

When respondents indicate that they have been victims of a crime, they are asked a series of detailed questions relating to the offense. Specifically, the NCVS interviewer wants to know the following:

1. Exactly what happened
2. When and where the offense occurred
3. Whether any injury or loss was suffered
4. Whether the crime was reported to the police
5. What the victim's perceptions were of the offender's sex, race, and age

In 2004, NCVS data revealed that 24 million U.S. residents aged 12 or older experienced violent or property offenses (Catalano, 2005). Victims aged 12 and older reported that the offender was a juvenile (under age 18) in one-fourth of personal (i.e., violent) crimes (Catalano, 2005). These victims also reported that a large majority (about 90%) of the offenders were male. Furthermore, the NCVS data revealed that more than half of the incidents in which persons reported being victimized by a juvenile in a violent crime involved a group of offenders.

These data, as very rough estimates of juvenile crime, are dependent on (a) the victim actually seeing the offender and (b) the victim's correct perceptions of the age of the offender. Unfortunately, these important potential shortcomings undermine the accuracy of the NCVS data to some extent. But more importantly, the omission of children under age 12 not only reflects a lack of sophistication about children's cognitive development, but also results in a large number of crimes committed by juveniles going unreported. Crimes committed by juveniles often have younger juveniles as victims. In addition, the omission of victims under 12 limits our information on the sensitive issue of intrafamily violence and child abuse.

UNOFFICIAL DATA

It is doubtful that any researcher believes that official statistics provide an accurate picture of crime and juvenile delinquency. As we noted earlier, a large amount of adult and juvenile offending is undetected or hidden from the police data reported in the UCR and consequently from court statistics. Official victimization studies offer additional information, but they are limited in a number of ways, including the willingness of victims to reveal what has happened to them. Some researchers maintain that a third procedure for estimating true delinquency, the self-report method, is better.

SELF-REPORT METHOD

The self-report method involves having juveniles in the general population simply reveal the extent of their own misconduct. Instead of relying on biased or incomplete official records, researchers ask a random sample of youth representative of segments of the population to report their own law-violating behavior. This procedure, called the **self-report method** (SR), is extremely important in the measurement (and definition) of delinquency. Currently, the SR method is a dominant method of measurement in studies focusing on the extent and cause of delinquency, particularly offenses associated with drug and alcohol use. The usual procedure is to prepare a list of questions asking about specific delinquent or criminal activities. The list is then presented to youths, most often in a written questionnaire form but occasionally in an interview setting. Very often, the youths are "captive" subjects in schools or detention facilities. The SR method is also used to evaluate the effectiveness of intervention or treatment programs. For example, youths who have gone through a program designed to provide them with alternatives to violence may be contacted 6 months or a year later to see if they have remained free of violent behavior.

In SR measures, subjects usually are asked to indicate whether they have engaged in any of the specified activities and, if so, how frequently. Some studies ask whether the activities resulted in police contacts. In most cases, anonymity is guaranteed, although Michael Hindelang and his colleagues (1981) found in their research that anonymity did not significantly increase the accuracy of the responses.

Gwynn Nettler (1984) noted that numerous international studies employing the SR procedure (with adults as well as juveniles) have consistently drawn the following three conclusions: (1) almost everyone, by his or her own admission, has violated some criminal law; (2) the amount of "hidden crime" (i.e., the dark figure) is huge; and (3) most of the infractions are minor. Current research continually emphasizes that the statistics collected through SR methods indicate that official measures, such as arrest records, reflect merely the tip of the massive iceberg of offending. Undetected rates of adolescent offending are enormous. As we learned in Chapter 6, they are so large that offending appears to be a normal part of being a teenager.

SR studies also continually show that the proportions of respondents involved in serious (defined primarily as violent) crimes are relatively small, but that the juveniles who do these crimes are quite busy. Jesness (1987) suggests that some offenders must be working overtime to accumulate the large numbers of offenses they report. In short, he finds some self-reports hard to believe and recommends that criminologists be cautious about accepting the validity of SR questionnaires. Nonetheless, it is clear that a majority of serious or violent juvenile crime is committed by a small portion of the juvenile population. Furthermore, contrary to common belief, the SR investigations indicate that there is not offense specialization among serious delinquents. That is, serious and chronic juvenile offenders do not concentrate on a specific criminal activity, such as robbery; they show considerable versatility in criminal involvement, committing a wide variety of offenses, violent as well as nonviolent.

SR data also underscore the observation that serious juvenile delinquency is not evenly distributed across the country, nor across cities or communities (Weis & Sederstrom, 1981). Youthful offenders are more prevalent in some communities and neighborhoods than in others. Certain communities, sectors of cities, and neighborhoods tend to have criminal careers of their own, even with turnovers of population. By inference, then, if we are to accept the information gleaned from SR studies, some neighborhoods and communities may play a key role in the development of crime and delinquency.

Although advocates of the SR method believe that SR measures are more accurate indices of delinquency than other methods are, we would be cautious about accepting this claim without further examination. For many years psychologists and sociologists have wrestled with the troubling problems of SR questionnaires. For at least a hundred years, for instance, psychologists attempting to measure personality via SR methods have encountered a myriad of problems. For one thing, individuals attach a wide range of interpretations to the wording of questions. For example, the word *often* is open to multiple interpretations. In addition, respondents enter a test situation displaying widely different attitudes about answering questions. These pretest attitudes are called **response sets**. An offender may misinterpret a question or may approach the questionnaire or the interview with suspicion, determined not to be honest. Sociologists, too, have recognized these dilemmas. They have examined the many pitfalls in survey research in general, realizing that the quality of this research depends on many things, including the content of the questions and the manner in which they are asked. Thus, images of delinquent conduct drawn from SR studies vary according to who is drawing them, with which methods, and from which population (Nettler, 1984).

A NEED FOR CAUTION

Because this chapter and the next cover trends in juvenile offending, they focus heavily on official statistics, surveys, and other measures of delinquency. Such measures are helpful but do not provide the complete picture. As was mentioned earlier, criminologists often refer to a dark figure, the amount of crime that never comes to the attention of police. Victimization and self-report studies make attempts to cut into this dark figure, but they have their own limitations. In reviewing statistical information, we caution against reading too much into these figures. For example, to say that 1.6 million juvenile arrests were made in 2005 is not the same as saying that 1.6 million *different* juveniles were arrested; some juveniles are arrested more than once a year. Or to say that 25 crimes were cleared by arrest—a term often used in crime data—is not to say that 25 different persons were arrested; one person could have been responsible for 10 of those crimes. Moreover, because juveniles often commit crimes in groups, some of those 25 crimes might have been committed by more than one person. Sources of official data are fraught with such fine distinctions. While the data themselves may be reasonably accurate (statisticians tell us that statistics don't *really* lie), we must be mindful of what they actually tell us and wary of making unwarranted interpretations.

JUVENILE OFFENDING TRENDS

In 2005, law enforcement agencies in the United States made an estimated 1.6 million arrests of persons under age 18 (FBI, 2006). Although this number seems large, it actually continues a 10-year decrease in the total number of juvenile arrests and in the juvenile arrest rate. (The arrest rate is the percentage of juveniles arrested per 1,000 juveniles in the population.) There was public concern when juvenile violent-crime arrests began to increase in the late 1980s, but since 1994 there has been a steady decline in juvenile violence (Snyder, 2006; see Figure 8–6). Juvenile violent offenses are those that involve physical harm or the threat of physical harm. The juvenile arrest rate for murder has declined 77% since its peak in 1993. Although juvenile violent crime moves in cycles, it has fallen 55% from its peak level in 1994. In addition, juvenile rapes and aggravated assaults have leveled off in recent years or have shown a slight decline. Some juvenile offenses have increased, however. Between 1980 and 2003, the juvenile arrest rate for simple assault increased 102% for males and 269% for females (H. N. Snyder, 2005).

Overall arrests for juvenile property crimes have also decreased significantly (H. N. Snyder, 2006; see Figure 8–7). Property offenses are crimes directed at physical property and do not involve physical harm, even though the victim may be present. A bicycle theft, for instance, is a property crime, as is a burglary. A robbery, on the other hand, is a violent offense because it involves the use of force or the threat of force. Other examples of property crimes are larceny–theft, shoplifting, and motor vehicle theft. In the UCR, arson is included as a property offense, but we will classify it in this text as a violent offense.

Crimes against public order and drug offenses round out the list of actual crimes for which juveniles are arrested. Examples include disturbing the peace, possession of

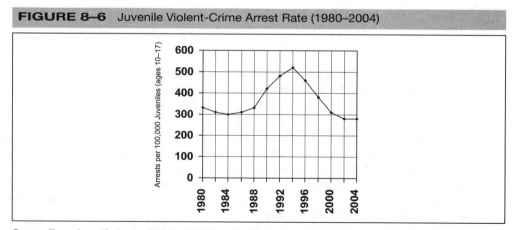

FIGURE 8–6 Juvenile Violent-Crime Arrest Rate (1980–2004)

Source: From *Juvenile Arrests 2004* by H. N. Snyder, December 2006, Washington, DC: U.S. Department of Justice, OJJDP.

marijuana, possession with intent to distribute, prostitution, and public intoxication. Recent trends indicate that the juvenile offenses in these categories have remained largely the same over the past decade (H. N. Snyder, 2005).

The term **child delinquent** has come into vogue in recent years. As mentioned in Chapter 1, child delinquents are juveniles between the ages of 7 and 12 who have committed a delinquent act according to criminal law (Loeber, Farrington, & Petechuk, 2003). The number of child delinquents handled in the juvenile court system has increased 33% over the past decade (Loeber et al., 2003; H. N. Snyder, 2001). Figure 8–8 shows the number of juvenile cases handled by juvenile courts by offense type. This situation has caused some societal concern, not only because these offense patterns reflect more serious crimes among this young group, but also because these offenders are more likely to continue their involvement in crime. Child delinquents are two to three times more likely to become serious, violent, and chronic offenders than are adolescents who begin their delinquent behavior in their teens (Loeber et al., 2003).

A final category of juvenile offenses has long troubled criminologists and juvenile justice officials. These are the **status offenses**: violations of the law specifically restricted to juveniles. Examples are running away, truancy, possession of malt beverage, and incorrigibility. "A status offender is a minor who engages in behavior that, although legal for an adult, is unlawful by reason of the 'status' of minority" (Costello, 2003, p. 234). Although status offenses are not technically crimes, police can take juveniles into custody for these violations, which are reported in arrest data. The enforcement of status offense laws is based on a blend of the doctrine of **parens patriae** and a police power rationale. *Parens patriae* is based on the belief that government has the right to intervene in the lives of children whose parents or guardians default in their caregiving duties. This intervention is presumably done in the best interest of the child. In addition, it is assumed that children must be protected from participating in more serious delinquent and criminal actions and provided with rehabilitative treatment (Costello, 2003). In recent years, there has been a trend toward a decrease in

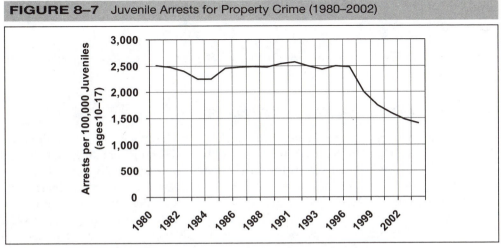

FIGURE 8–7   Juvenile Arrests for Property Crime (1980–2002)

Source: Data from *Juvenile Arrests 2004* by H. N. Snyder, December 2006, Washington, DC: U.S. Department of Justice, OJJDP.

FIGURE 8–8 Age at Referral to Juvenile Court by Offense (2002)

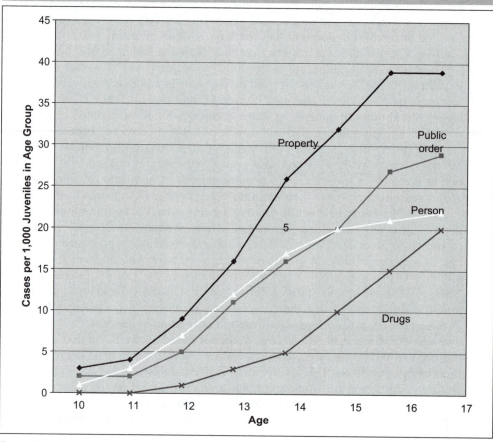

Source: Based on *Juvenile Court Statistics 2001–2002* (p. 10) by A. Stahl, C. Puzzanchera, A. Sladky, T. Finnegan, N. Tierney, and H. Snyder, December 2006, Washington, DC: OJJDP.

status offenses (H. N. Snyder, 2005). Status offenses are discussed in greater detail later in the chapter.

JUVENILE PROPERTY CRIMES

Most of the serious crimes committed in the United States are not violent crimes but are crimes against property. Annually, property crimes represent more than 75% of the total number of juvenile arrests for Part I crimes (see Figure 8–9). We will define property crimes here as including the offenses of larceny–theft, motor vehicle theft, and burglary. The UCR property crime category also includes arson because the offense involves the destruction of property, even though the offense may also involve the intentional or accidental loss of life. However, this text will include arson as a violent crime and consequently will focus in this section on larceny–theft, motor vehicle theft and burglary.

FIGURE 8–9   Distribution of Juvenile Part I Arrests (2005)

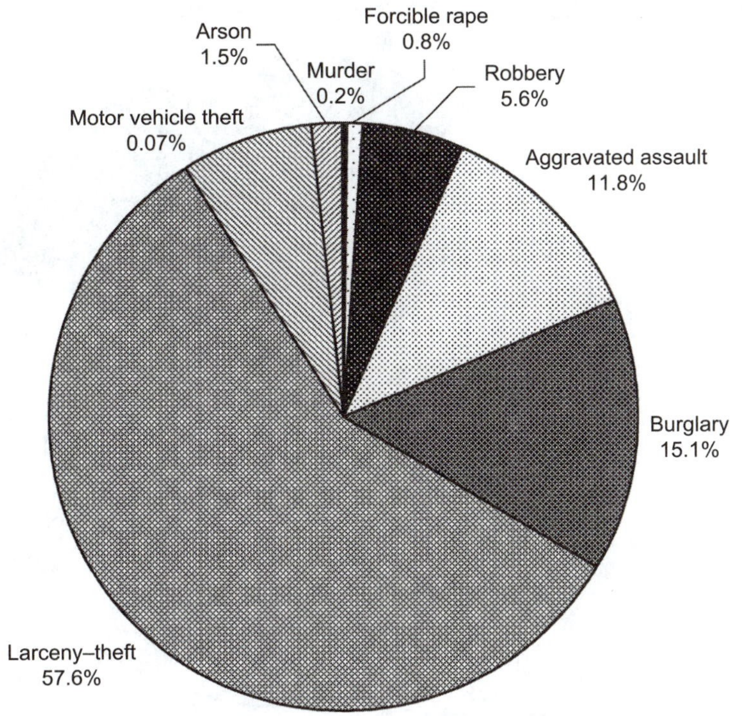

Source: Data from *Crime in the United States—2005* by Federal Bureau of Investigation, 2006, Washington, DC: U.S. Department of Justice, Author.

As mentioned earlier, of all individuals arrested for property crimes in 2005, 26% were juveniles (FBI, 2006). About two-thirds of all the individuals arrested were male, of whom 26.8% were juveniles. Of the female arrestees, 27.3% were juveniles. About 9% of the juvenile arrests were youths under the age of 15. Between 1994 and 2003, the juvenile property crime arrest rate dropped 46% to its lowest level since the 1970s (H. N. Snyder, 2005).

LARCENY–THEFT

The UCR defines **larceny–theft** as the unlawful taking, carrying, leading, or riding away of property from the possession or constructive possession of another. As with other index crimes, attempts to do these acts are also included in the definition. This crime category includes pickpocketing, purse snatching, shoplifting, stealing from vending machines, or taking things from motor vehicles. Theft of property left outdoors—such as bicycles, pedigreed dogs, and lawnmowers—is also included. Motor vehicle theft is placed in a separate category.

Larceny–theft constitutes approximately two-thirds of all property crimes reported to police and over 72% of all Part I crime arrests. It is the offense resulting in the most

FIGURE 8–10 Juvenile Property Arrests (2005)

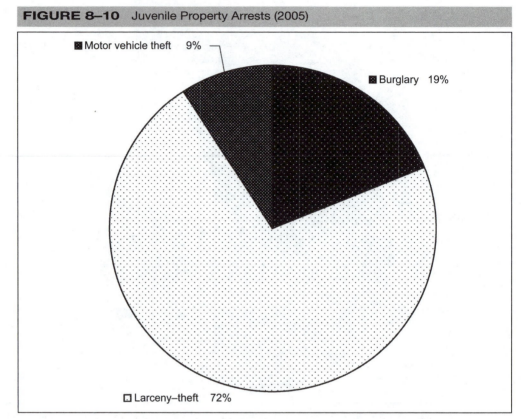

- Motor vehicle theft 9%
- Burglary 19%
- Larceny–theft 72%

Source: Data from *Crime in the United States—2005* by Federal Bureau of Investigation, 2006, Washington, DC: U.S. Department of Justice, Author.

arrests of persons under the age of 18. Figure 8–10 shows the large proportion of juvenile property arrests represented by larceny–theft in 2005; Figure 8–11 shows the range of ages of those juveniles arrested for larceny–theft in 2005. Of juvenile arrestees, 69.2% were white, 27.4% were black, and 2.4% were of other races. An analysis of arrests across all property crime categories reveals that females are arrested more often for larceny–theft than for other property crimes. Of all females arrested for larceny–theft, 30% were under age 18. Larceny–theft cases constituted 45% of all property cases referred to juvenile courts in 2002 (Stahl, 2006).

For most juveniles who commit theft, it is an isolated incident (or one of very few incidents) that is not serious or a cause for alarm. In many situations, theft is done on a dare or in response to a challenge put forth by a peer group, such as shoplifting from retail stores in a mall. For a few—especially girls—theft may be a symbolic cry for help because of depression, unhappiness, or insecurity (Puura et al., 1998). For a small percentage of delinquent youth, however, persistent theft is an early indicator of a developmental path toward more serious delinquency and a life of crime. In the early lives of LCP offenders, theft becomes a dominant part of their early offending and antisocial history. Stealing is also one of the

FIGURE 8–11   Juvenile Arrests for Larceny–Theft (2005)

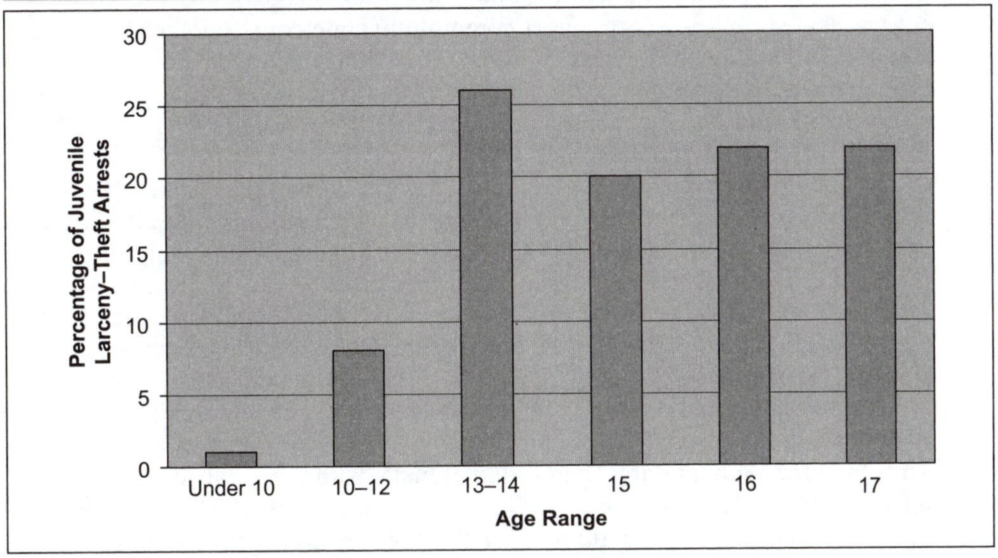

Source: Data from *Crime in the United States—2005* by Federal Bureau of Investigation, 2006, Washington, DC: U.S. Department of Justice, Author.

15 behavioral indicators used by the American Psychiatric Association (1994) in diagnosing conduct disorder. Early, persistent stealing is closely related to "impulsivity and acting out, focusing on immediate gratification without consideration of the consequences, and less social competence including poor social judgment and social problem solving skills" (E. R. Taylor et al., 2001, p. 348).

Based on their study of 200 juveniles in a Texas juvenile detention center, Taylor and her colleagues (2001) suggest that early serious stealing may be a "gateway" crime that leads to more extensive juvenile offending later. Their investigation found that serious delinquency was frequently characterized by persistent stealing before the age of 12, and a considerable proportion of that stealing took place in school. The researchers also report that the family situation most closely related to persistent stealing was poor and inadequate parental supervision and monitoring.

Shoplifting

Although shoplifting comprised about 13.9% of all arrests for larceny–theft in 2005, it is widely unreported. The data on all property crimes are difficult to obtain, but especially so for shoplifting offenses because store security and other personnel exercise wide discretion in reporting offenses. For instance, there is a tendency for store managers not to report young juvenile offenders to the police (Farrington & Burrows, 1993).

Based on self-report data, as many as 60% of American consumers have shoplifted at least once in their lives, and 30% to 40% of adolescents admit that they shoplift repeatedly (Krasnovsky & Lane, 1998). These data are surprising in light of the rapid improvement in security measures designed to discourage and prevent shoplifting; cameras now are ubiquitous in large retail stores, hidden in clocks, smoke alarms, and pushbars on fire-exit doors (Adler, 2002).

Roughly 40% of all apprehended shoplifters are adolescents (Cox, Cox, & Moschis, 1990). An analysis of 1 million juvenile court records across nearly 2,000 jurisdictions reveals that shoplifting is the most common juvenile court referral for youths under age 15 (Kelley, Kennedy, & Homant, 2003). Shoplifting appears to decline, however, both in the number of offenses and in the number of those engaging in this behavior, as offenders mature and move into early adulthood (Krasnovsky & Lane, 1998; Osgood, O'Malley, Bachman, & Johnstone, 1989).

In one of the first major studies on adolescent shoplifting, Klemke (1982) collected self-report data from students in four small-town high schools in the Pacific Northwest during the late 1970s. Klemke (1992) discovered that approximately three-fourths of the frequent shoplifters began shoplifting before the age of 10 but then stopped soon after their 18th birthday. Interestingly, data from college bookstores indicate that first-year students are more likely to be apprehended for shoplifting than are other college students (Klemke, 1992).

As described by Lo (1994), the shopping mall has become a part of life in North America and has also become a major hangout area for teenagers. Shoplifting represents the predominant crime committed at malls, with the greatest amount of shoplifting occurring at major anchor stores and large chain stores. Most of the mall shoplifters are teenagers, who often commit their theft in groups. At this writing, the most frequently confiscated item from juvenile shoplifters is clothing, especially prestigious brand name items (Forney et al., 2005).

The causes of juvenile shoplifting are multiple. It is influenced by economic factors, peer pressure, moral attitudes, and perceptions of low apprehension risk (Tonglet, 2002). A large proportion of shoplifters do not consider shoplifting to be immoral or dishonest (Tonglet, 2002). Furthermore, many (85%) view retail security as ineffective and believe that shoplifting is a low-risk crime. Lo (1994) reports that teenagers shoplift primarily for fun and thrills, often combined with peer pressure to commit the theft. Tonglet (2002) found in her self-report study that peer influence and encouragement was a powerful factor in the formation of shoplifting beliefs, attitudes, and intentions. Cox, Cox Anderson, and Moschis (1993) argue that teenagers shoplift because they wish to emulate peers who shoplift and/or they have inadequate attachment to caregivers in their lives. For reasons not yet fully understood, the presence of peers makes adolescents and youth, but not adults, more likely to take risks and to make risky decisions (Gardner & Steinberg, 2005).

Kleptomania, the irresistible urge and uncontrollable impulse to steal unneeded objects, has not been substantiated by the research literature. The irresistible or uncontrollable aspect of the behavior has been especially troublesome in verifying the disorder. However, it has been found that depression may be a symptom of juveniles who engage in "nonsensical shoplifting" (Lamontagne, Bayer, Hetu, & Lacerate-Lamontagne, 2000). It appears that some adolescents may engage in nonsensical shoplifting as a stimulating, exciting activity that moves them away from feelings of helplessness.

MOTOR VEHICLE THEFT

According to the UCR, motor vehicle theft includes the stealing of automobiles, trucks, buses, motorcycles, snowmobiles, and similar equipment. The taking of a motor vehicle for temporary use by persons having lawful access is excluded from this definition.

There were approximately 1.2 million thefts of motor vehicles reported in 2005, worth about $7.6 billion (FBI, 2006). These data represent a rate of 421.3 motor vehicles stolen for each 100,000 Americans. In 2004 automobiles were stolen at a rate of 320.5 cars per 100,000 in population; trucks and buses, at a rate of 81.1 vehicles per 100,000; and other types of vehicles, at a rate of 38.4 vehicles per 100,000. Automobiles were, by far, the most frequently stolen vehicle type, accounting for 72.8% of all vehicles stolen.

The 2004 arrest data indicate that juveniles made up 26.5% of the arrests for all motor vehicle thefts. Most of the juvenile arrestees were male (80%). Motor vehicle theft represents 10% of juvenile arrests for property crime, and since 1994 there has been a 52% decline in those arrests. The arrest rate is now the lowest it has been since the 1970s (H. N. Snyder, 2005). Motor vehicle theft by juveniles is largely a group activity done for fun and challenge. If the motive is profit, then the theft is usually done by gangs or is sponsored by older individuals who can quickly tear down and distribute the vehicle or vehicle parts.

BURGLARY

Burglary is the unlawful entry into a structure, with or without force, with the intent to commit a felony or theft. The FBI classifies burglary in three categories: forcible entry, unlawful entry without force, and attempted forcible entry. Approximately 2.2 million burglaries occurred in the United States during 2005, a figure that has been relatively consistent over the past 5 years (FBI, 2006). Nationwide, the residential burglary rate is 746.2 per 100,000 inhabitants.

About one-third of all burglaries in 2005 did not involve forced entry. That is, offenders entered through an unlatched window or unlocked door or used a key hidden in an obvious place, such as under a doormat or over the door frame. About another 6% were attempts at forcible entry. Consistently over the years, about two-thirds of burglaries are residential; the remaining involve unlawful entry into commercial properties. Furthermore, about two-thirds of residential burglaries occur during the day. The average dollar amount taken from a residence in 2005 was $1,725, whereas the average amount stolen from a nonresidential establishment was $1,708.

It is estimated that 9 out of 10 burglaries are committed by males. Of the total number of males arrested for burglaries in 2005, 28.6% were male juveniles. Females arrested for burglary constituted 14.3% of the total number of burglary arrests; 22.7% were juveniles. Criminologists interested in exploring gender differences in offending often note that girls and women rarely commit burglaries alone or in small female groups. Rather, these offenders are most likely to commit their crimes in the company of boys or men, and they generally play a less active role, such as serving as a lookout. The given arrest data do not allow us to make these distinctions, however.

Burglary seems to be a crime committed primarily by the young. Nearly two-thirds of those arrested in 2005 were under 25, with an average age of 22 (FBI, 2006). Juvenile burglars report that they began their criminal careers during their midteens with one or more older acquaintances (Cromwell, Olson, & Avary, 1994). These older youths served as mentors or tutors. Juvenile burglars also reported that they initially committed their offenses for excitement or fun or to obtain consumer goods or small sums of money. If the juveniles continued to commit burglaries for income, they either developed full membership in an older gang or established a new group with friends their own age. To become independent, these juvenile burglars found it necessary to locate and develop a business relationship with a "fence," who would provide a safe and reliable market for the stolen goods. According to Cromwell et al. (1994), finding a fence was difficult because fences do not usually like to do business with juveniles.

STATUS OFFENSES

Juvenile courts became inundated with status offense cases, beginning in the middle of the 20th century; and regardless of their attempts to "correct" status offenders' behavior, the courts have not been highly successful. The disposition of status offenders remains controversial in juvenile justice today. Many observers are concerned that the behavior of status offenders will accelerate, and they will commit more serious offenses. Others are concerned that status offenses are often indicative of victimization in the home (e.g., sexual abuse) and they leave children vulnerable to further victimization (e.g., runaways on the streets get assaulted). Studies have shown that for some offenders, early involvement in status offenses are stepping-stones to serious, violent, and chronic offending (Loeber, Slot, & Stouthamer-Loeber, 2006).

There are four major status offense categories: (1) **running away**, (2) **school truancy**, (3) **ungovernability** (sometimes called *incorrigibility* or being beyond the control of one's parents), and (4) **underage liquor-law violations** (e.g., a minor in possession of alcohol, underage drinking). A number of other behaviors may be considered status offenses (e.g., curfew violations, tobacco offenses), depending on the jurisdiction. We will pay some attention to curfew violations because curfew laws appear to be on the increase nationwide.

Status offenses are an elusive category for which to obtain data. Many cases escape police detection and thus are not reported in arrest data. And even when they are detected, a law enforcement officer in most jurisdictions can exercise wide discretion over whether or not to take a juvenile into custody. More importantly, though, status offenses are often handled informally by agencies other than the police. For example, in some communities social service agencies are responsible for processing status offenses. When status offenders are referred to juvenile court (either by police, community agencies, or parents), we obtain another source of data, either from the intake process or from statistics on court disposition (see Table 8–4 and Figure 8–12). In addition, we get data on status offenses from self-report research and from statistics on juvenile detention. The information provided in this section is gleaned from all of these sources.

TRENDS IN STATUS OFFENDING

Historically, one of the most disturbing trends in status offending has revolved around gender differences in processing juveniles for some violations. Adolescent girls, for example, have often been detained for incorrigibility or running away from home, when the same behavior in adolescent boys was ignored or tolerated. Until recently, about three times as many girls as boys were detained for status offenses (U.S. Department of Justice, 1988). In recent years, as a result of suits brought on behalf of juvenile girls, many courts have put authorities on notice that this discriminatory approach is unwarranted.

TABLE 8–4: Status Offenses Referred to Juvenile Court (2002): Percentage of age group within each category

Age	Runaway	Truancy	Ungovernability	Liquor	Total
10	0	1	1	0	1
11	1	3	3	0	1
12	4	6	7	0	4
13	11	14	14	2	10
14	21	24	22	7	18
15	29	30	26	16	25
16	25	16	20	32	24
17	9	7	8	42	18

Source: Data from *Juvenile Court Statistics 2001–2002* (p. 66) by A. Stahl, C. Puzzanchera, A. Sladky, T. Finnegan, N. Tierney, and H. Snyder, December 2006, Washington, DC: OJJDP.

FIGURE 8–12   Juvenile Court Decisions Pertaining to Status Offenses (2002)

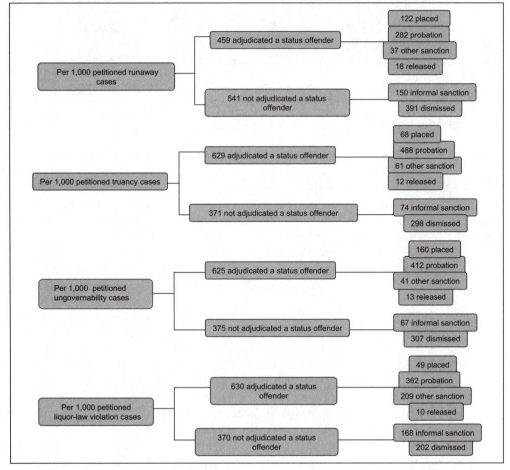

Source: From *Juvenile Court Statistics 2001–2002* (p. 72) by A. Stahl, C. Puzzanchera, A. Sladky, T. Finnegan, N. Tierney, and H. Snyder, December 2006, Washington, DC: OJJDP.

FIGURE 8–13 Percentage of Males and Females in Petitioned Status Offense Cases

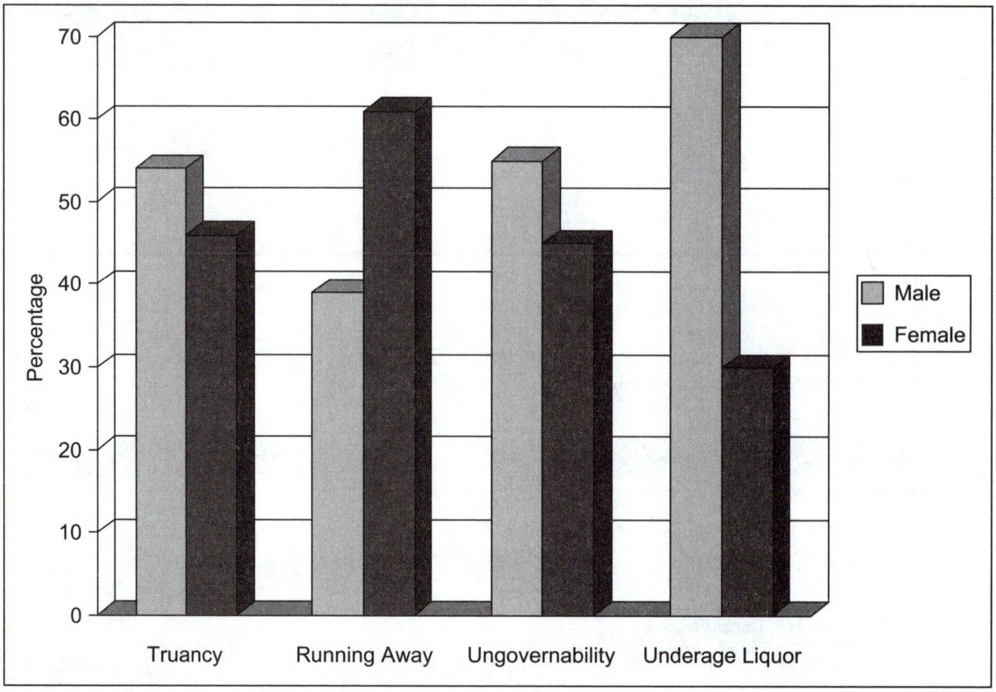

Source: Data from *Juvenile Court Statistics 2001–2002* by A. Stahl, C. Puzzanchera, A. Sladky, T. Finnegan, N. Tierney, and H. Snyder, December 2006, Washington, DC: OJJDP.

Recent figures indicate that girls are still more likely than boys to be "arrested" as runaways (National Center for Juvenile Justice, 2003; Snyder, 2000; see Figure 8–13). Approximately 60% of the arrests for runaways are female, despite the fact that self-report information from 11th- and 12th-grade students indicates that runaway incidents are equally distributed between males and females (Johnston, O'Malley, & Bachman, 2000; Kratcoski & Kratcoski, 1996). During the years 1985 through 2000, runaway cases processed by juvenile courts were consistently disproportionately female (61% versus 39%; Puzzanchera et al., 2004). Thus, police and court processing in the cases of runaways continues to be influenced by gender.

During the years 1985 through 2000, the male and female proportions of truancy and ungovernability cases processed by the courts were roughly similar to their representation in the general population (Puzzanchera et al., 2004). However, liquor-law violation cases were disproportionately male (71% versus 29%; Puzzanchera et al., 2004), which is a similar distribution to that found in arrest data. But self-report data show a more even distribution. This discrepancy may reflect the fact that male juveniles are more likely to violate liquor laws in public and thus are more likely to come to the attention of police.

Some states have tried to move away from classifying juveniles as status offenders because the offense category lends itself to so much subjectivity.

Although many states do not label status offenders delinquents, these states do allow their detention and/or supervision because they are presumed to be in need of protection, either from their own impulsivity or the behavior of others. The statutes allowing this response are usually referred to as **PINS** or **CHINS** laws (person or child in need of supervision). Under these laws, runaways or incorrigible youngsters are subject to juvenile or family court jurisdiction, often at the instigation of their parents, even though they may not have committed an act comparable to a crime. These statutes also allow juvenile or family courts to address the needs of neglected and dependent children.

Nevertheless, status offenders should not be kept in secure institutions. The JJDPA, first passed in 1974, mandated that states receiving federal funds make progress toward **deinstitutionalizing** all status offenders, both boys and girls. A number of amendments to this law have been passed over the years, many associated with this deinstitutionalization mandate, and the great majority of states were supposedly in full or substantial compliance by the mid-1990s. However, Costello (2003) reports that during the same time period, many laws were amended to allow the confinement of runaways, ungovernable children, and truants. Furthermore, some juvenile courts have found, and some states have allowed, alternative ways of confining status offenders (Chesney-Lind & Shelden, 1998; Costello, 2003). Costello (2003) reports the following tactics: (a) refer or commit them to secure mental health facilities; (b) allege a delinquent act rather than a status offense (e.g., trespass rather than runaway); (c) develop "semisecure" facilities that technically are not secure but operate as secure; and (d) hold status offenders in contempt for violating a court order, thereby "bootstrapping" them into delinquency. This last tactic would occur, for example, when a judge orders a truant to attend school or a runaway to remain at home and the truant or the runaway defies that order. Thus, although the JJDPA mandate may be honored on paper, the spirit of the mandate is often violated. Many status offenders—after being taken into custody by police and/or being referred to juvenile court—are then placed in secure detention. In other words, there has been a concerted effort to "reinstitutionalize" status offenders by legislatures and juvenile courts (Costello, 2003).

CURFEW VIOLATIONS

A curfew is usually a municipal ordinance that forbids a person under the age of 16 or 17 from being in a public place during late evening or nighttime hours. Curfew laws are usually established to control juvenile gangs and to deter juvenile crime (Steinhart, 1996), as well as to help combat juvenile victimization (Fried, 2001). Critics of curfew laws maintain that they are overly restrictive and deprive law-abiding juveniles of their liberty unnecessarily. Additionally, solid research data from various cities indicate that curfews are *not* effective in reducing juvenile crime or victimization (Fried, 2001; Males & Maccallair, 1999; McDowall, Loftin, & Wiersema, 2000; Reynolds, Seydlitz, & Jenkins, 2000). However, curfew violations do provide an indication of which youth may lack reasonable parental supervision and monitoring.

In 2005, 137,400 curfew violators were arrested, 75% of whom were male (H. N. Snyder, 2006; see Figure 8–14). Nearly 30% of all arrests for curfew violations were youths under the age of 15. Juvenile curfew ordinances have become increasingly

FIGURE 8–14 Juvenile Arrests for Curfew Violations (2005)

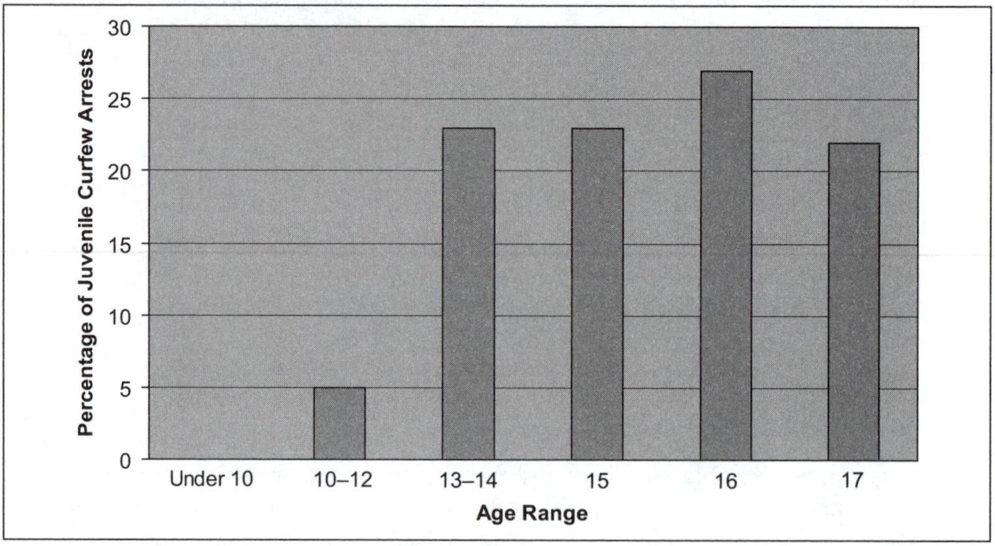

Source: Data from *Crime in the United States—2005* by Federal Bureau of Investigation, 2006, Washington, DC: U.S. Department of Justice, Author.

popular in American cities during the past 2 decades. They have been and continue to be overwhelmingly supported by the public, police departments, and governmental officials (Fried, 2001).

RUNAWAYS

According to National Incidence Studies of Missing, Abducted, Runaway, and Thrownaway Children (NISMART), a runaway episode meets any one of the following criteria (Hammer, Finkelhor, & Sedlack, 2002):

- A child leaves home without permission and stays away overnight.
- A child 14-years-old or younger who is away from home chooses not to come home when expected to and stays away overnight.
- A child 15-years-old or older who is away from home chooses not to come home and stays away two nights.

Many children who run away do so as a result of intense family conflict or physical, sexual, or psychological abuse. Many runaways are really **thrownaways**, who have been pushed out of their homes by parents or other family members (Costello, 2003; see Figure 8–15). It is estimated that about one out of eight American youths runs away at least once before the age of 18 (Meade & Slesnick, 2002; Schaffner, 1998). Moreover, the runaway problem is worldwide. The expanding number of children and adolescents who have left or been forced out of their homes has become a source of concern for policy makers all over the world (Dekel, Peled, & Sprib, 2003). It is estimated that there are about 80 million children across the globe who are living on the streets (Van der Ploeg & Scholte, 1997). Although a majority reside in third world countries, many are also found in industrialized nations. In the United States, it is estimated that there

FIGURE 8–15 Differences Between Runaways and Thrownaways

A runaway meets any one of the following criteria:
- A child leaves home without permission and stays away overnight.
- A child 14-years-old or younger (or older and mentally incompetent) who is away from home chooses not to come home when expected to and stays away overnight.
- A child 15-years-old or older who is away from home chooses not to come home and stays away two nights.

A thrownaway meets either one of the following criteria:
- A child is asked or told to leave home by a parent or other household adult, no adequate alternative care is arranged for the child by a household adult, and the child is out of the household overnight.
- A child who is away from home is prevented from returning home by a parent or other household adult, no adequate alternative care is arranged for the child by a household adult, and the child is out of the household overnight.

Source: From *Runaway/Thrownaway Children: National Estimates and Characteristics* (p. 2) by H. Hammer, D. Finkelhor, and A. J. Sedlak, October 2002, Washington, DC: OJJDP.

are 1.7 million runaway or thrownaway incidents each year (Hammer et al., 2002). Best estimates in Australia are 25,000 (Boss, Edwards, & Pitman, 1995), 40,000 in Germany (Van der Ploeg & Scholte, 1997), 7,000 in the Netherlands (Van der Ploeg & Scholte, 1997), and 77,000 in the United Kingdom (Safe on the Streets Research Team, 1999).

About one out of every four runaways in the United States travels 50 miles or more away from home (Hammer et al., 2002). Most runaway youth (77%) are gone less than a week; 7% are away more than a month (Hammer et al., 2002; see Table 8–5). Approximately 0.4% never return home. Only about one out of five runaways is reported to the police (Hammer et al., 2002). However, police also become involved if a runaway youth is taken into custody for suspicious or criminal activity, regardless of whether or not the parent notified police. Figure 8–16 depicts the ages of runaways taken into custody by police. Although many of these cases are handled informally—for example, returning the youth to parents or referring the youth to community services—others are referred by police to juvenile courts. Youths aged 15 or younger comprise two-thirds of all runaway cases referred to the juvenile courts by law enforcement agencies (Puzzanchera et al., 2004). Although considerable focus and data collection have been directed at those youths who run away from home, the data on runaways also include youths who run away from foster care, shelters, group homes, and residential treatment facilities (Schaffner, 1998). In this section, however, we concentrate on research relating to runaways from homes, particularly those who run away repeatedly or permanently.

Repetitive runaways are at high risk of engaging in delinquent behavior (Baron & Hartnagel, 1998; Kaufman & Widom, 1999; Slesnick & Prestopnik, 2005). Many repetitive runaway youth engage, or are forced to engage, in prostitution, theft, and the sale and distribution of drugs. About one-half of repetitive male and 60% of repetitive female runaways also have a conduct disorder (Booth & Zhang, 1997), and substance

TABLE 8–5: Characteristics and Numbers of Runaway/Thrownaway Episodes

Characteristics of Episode	Estimated Number of Children	Percentage of Total Episodes
Number of miles traveled from home		
1 or less	139,900	8
More than 1 but no more than 10	503,100	30
More than 10 but no more than 50	521,900	31
More than 50 but no more than 100	160,100	10
More than 100	210,600	13
No information	147,300	9
Duration		
6 to less than 7 hours	21,000	1
7 hours to less than 24 hours	307,400	18
24 hours to less than 1 week	975,700	58
1 week to less than 1 month	248,000	15
1 month to less than 6 months	123,000	7
Not returned but located	2,200	<1
Not returned and not located	4,100	<1
No information	1,600	<1
Episode outcome		
Child returned	1,676,200	>99
Child not returned but located	2,200	<1
Child not returned and not located	4,100	<1
No information	400	<1

Source: From *Runaway/Thrownaway Children: National Estimates and Characteristics* by H. Hammer, D. Finkelhor, and A. J. Sedlak, October 2002, Washington, DC: OJJDP.

abuse is very prevalent (Fors & Rojek, 1991; Forst & Crim, 1994; Robertson & Toro, 1999). **Oppositional defiant disorder** is another common diagnosis for runaways (36%; Slesnick & Prestopnik, 2005), and many repetitive runaways demonstrate symptoms of chronic or serious depression (Meade & Slesnick, 2002; Slesnick & Prestopnik, 2005).

According to Schaffner (1998), many runaways are searching for a social connection with others that their families cannot or will not provide, and many are really thrownaways who have been tossed out of the house by a parent or family member. Juvenile courts have not been very tolerant of those youths referred to the courts because of frequent runaway episodes. Frustrated by repeated defiance of court orders to remain at home, judges often hold them in contempt and confine them to secure juvenile facilities as delinquents, frequently with more hard core, violent juvenile offenders.

TRUANCY

School truancy is defined as a pattern of repeated or habitual unauthorized absence from school by any juvenile subject to compulsory education laws.

FIGURE 8–16 Juvenile Arrests for Running Away (2005)

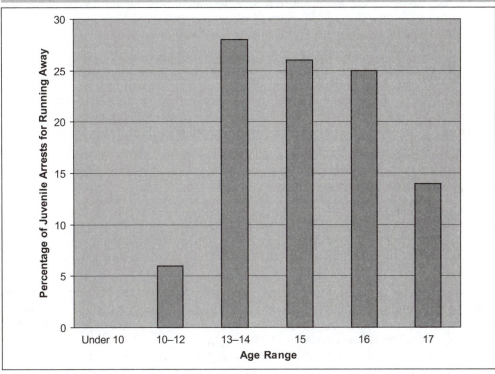

Source: Data from *Crime in the United States—2005* by Federal Bureau of Investigation, 2006, Washington, DC: U.S. Department of Justice, Author.

Research consistently indicates a strong relationship between academic failure, persistent truancy, and delinquency. Truants often have learning disabilities and other school-related problems. Huizinga and Jakob-Chien (1998), in the Denver Youth Survey, found that approximately two-thirds of serious violent delinquents and one-half of serious nonviolent delinquents were frequently truant. The researchers also found that, for males, slightly more than half of the serious violent offenders and slightly less than half of the serious nonviolent offenders had been suspended from school, as compared to less than 20% of nondelinquents. Suspension is an issue different from truancy (although probably related), that also reflects behavioral difficulties in the school setting. The researchers concluded that the vast majority of serious juvenile offenders have some kind of learning or behavioral problem in school.

Policy makers believe truancy should be maintained as a status offense in order to enforce compulsory school attendance and to act as a deterrent to juvenile crime. Juvenile courts formally handled 10% of the truancy cases referred to them by law enforcement agencies between 1985 and 2000. The remaining 90% were handled informally—for example, with warnings or referrals to a diversion program or community agency—or were dismissed without further action. Fifty-four percent of the formally processed cases were males; most were between the ages of 14 and 15. Only 3% of those truant cases formally processed by juvenile courts were securely detained; the other 97% were probably handled through parents and schools. **Secure detention** refers to placement in a restrictive facility under court authority while the individual awaits the outcome of the court process. Usually, a youth in secure detention has been charged with a serious offense or has continually defied the court's authority. Youths can also be placed in nonsecure detention, such as in a group home, with a relative, or in their own home with restrictions on their activity.

Truancy puts juveniles at serious risk in two important ways. First, it damages academic achievement and significantly reduces the opportunity to acquire the verbal skills necessary for higher education or a satisfying employment career. Second, while away from school and home, the juvenile is vulnerable to many of the same risks as those described for runaways.

UNGOVERNABILITY

Ungovernability refers to a parent's or caregiver's belief that a child is unmanageable. In this sense, ungovernability is repeated disregard for lawful and reasonable parental authority. But ungovernability may also pertain to the inability of a juvenile court and other authorities—acting in place of a youth's parents—to control the youth's behavior. Thus, ungovernable children and adolescents express behaviors that not only do not comply with parental or caregiver reasonable demands, but also do not comply with juvenile court expectations. "These youths frequently do not comply with the terms of probation, run away form nonsecure placements, and constantly test whatever rule or authority is asserted" (Costello, 2003, p. 237).

In an unknown percentage of cases youths are ungovernable or incorrigible because their home situations have become intolerable. This may occur as a result of physical, emotional, or sexual victimization or unreasonably restrictive demands on the part of parents or caregivers. As with running away behavior, ungovernability may be a sign of serious problems within the home.

For some children, ungovernability suggests the same behavior patterns as the clinical term **oppositional defiant disorder** (ODD). ODD refers to the recurrent childhood or adolescent pattern of developmentally inappropriate levels of negativistic, defiant, disobedient, and hostile behavior toward authority figures, which persist for at least 6 months. According to the *DSM-IV* (American Psychiatric Association, 1994, p. 91), the diagnosis is based on the occurrence of at least four of the following eight behaviors: (1) losing one's temper, (2) arguing with adults, (3) actively defying or refusing to comply with the requests or rules of adults, (4) deliberately doing things that will annoy other people, (5) blaming others for one's own mistakes or misbehavior, (6) being touchy or easily annoyed by others, (7) being angry and resentful, and (8) being spiteful or vindictive. Critics of the diagnosis maintain that these features characterize virtually every adolescent, but the key word is *persist*. The negativistic and defiant behaviors of ODD refer to *persistent* stubbornness, resistance to directions, and unwillingness to compromise or deal effectively with adults or peers. The prevalence of ODD ranges from 2% to 16%. Prior to adolescence it is chiefly a male phenomenon; during adolescence, male and female rates are about equal. Children with ODD and indicators of depression are at particular risk for conduct disorder (Greene et al., 2004).

Although we draw parallels between ungovernability and ODD, we must caution that many children labeled ungovernable or incorrigible are not defiant because of a behavioral disorder. Instead, for a variety of reasons, their own home situations or alternate placements may have become intolerable. Unfortunately, this status offense category—intended to protect vulnerable children and adolescents—has a history of being abused by adults seeking to control children or to have them removed from the home (Bernard, 1992; I. M. Schwartz, 1989).

Summary and Conclusions

The measurement of juvenile delinquency is a crucial task for criminologists, researchers, and policy makers, but it is not an easy one. Perhaps even more than crimes committed by adults, many crimes committed by juveniles never come to the attention of police. Thus, official data, such as arrest records, provide an incomplete picture. Moreover, juvenile court records do not help us estimate the juvenile crime problem; only about half of those arrested are referred to juvenile court. Many juvenile incidents are handled informally, such as by referral to community agencies. Furthermore, serious juvenile crimes are increasingly handled by criminal courts and thus may never appear in juvenile court data, unless they are formally transferred from juvenile to adult courts.

Primary examples of juvenile statistics include the FBI's UCR program, which produces the predominant official statistics on crime in the United States. UCR data include information on all crimes known to the police as well as on all arrests. UCR data have shown a decade-long trend of declining arrests for juvenile violent crime. Juvenile murder and robbery arrest rates have both declined, and rape and aggravated assault have either decreased or leveled off. Simple assault, though, has increased for both males and females, particularly the latter.

Juvenile court statistics represent those juveniles whose cases have been referred for court processing, such as by police, prosecutors, and sometimes parents. By the turn of this century, juvenile courts nationwide were handling about 1.6 million delinquency cases yearly. Just over a third involved violent offenses. Interestingly, cases involving violence (e.g., criminal homicide, aggravated assault, and burglary) have decreased in recent years, but the number of child delinquents between the ages of 7 and 12 has increased 30% over the past decade. Other relevant statistics include juvenile probation and parole data and the statistics on children in residential placement.

Another form of official data is the government's National Crime Victimization Survey, which polls members of the public to determine the extent to which they have been victims of crime. Victimization data are extremely helpful because most victims do not report their crimes to police. However, such data are limited for purposes of measuring juvenile crime, particularly because victims may not be able to estimate the age of the individual or persons who victimized them. Even so, victims have reported that nearly one-third of personal crimes were committed by juveniles under age 18; more than half of these incidents involved a group of offenders.

Many criminologists prefer unofficial data collected by researchers to indicate the prevalence and nature of juvenile offending. Self-report data, in which juveniles reveal their own antisocial and law-breaking behavior, provide a very different picture of juvenile crime than official data provide. We learn from self-report data that juveniles from all socioeconomic classes are engaged in crime and that the offenses tend to be minor. However, those individuals who engage in serious crime say they commit numerous offenses—so many, in fact, that some criminologists believe they are inflating their reports.

The chapter covers data obtained from official reports, particularly the UCR, and focuses on property and status offenses. Like arrests for violent crimes, arrests for juvenile property crimes have decreased significantly. Arrests for drug offenses and public order violations (e.g., disturbing the peace, public intoxication) have remained largely the same over the past decade.

According to the statistical data on property crimes for which juveniles are arrested, larceny–theft appears by far to be the favored crime in this group. Nearly half of all juvenile court referrals for property offenses involve theft, consisting primarily of thefts of personal property from others (e.g., from school lockers) and shoplifting. This latter activity is almost a rite of passage for many juveniles; as many as 30% to 40% say they shoplift regularly. Other forms of theft appear to be isolated acts or are limited in number and are not a cause for major concern. However, persistent theft may be an indicator of a path toward more serious delinquency.

Arrest data for burglary indicate that juveniles, particularly males, are active here as well. In 2004 nearly one-third of those arrested for burglary were juveniles. The main targets of burglary are residential homes. Burglaries are often committed by juveniles in the company of older acquaintances, who serve as their mentors or tutors. Burglary appears to be committed for excitement or fun or to obtain goods or money.

Status offenses are behaviors for which only juveniles can be sanctioned. Running away, truancy, incorrigibility or ungovernability, and liquor-related offenses are the four main categories found nationwide. In some jurisdictions, tobacco offenses and curfew violations are also status offenses. Status offenses have long been controversial in the juvenile justice system. They represent adult efforts both to control and to protect juveniles, but critics maintain that taking juveniles into custody for these offenses does neither. Gender differences in the processing of status offense violations have been documented; recent research indicates that, at least in the case of runaways, these differences continue to exist, with girls being significantly more likely than boys to be taken into custody.

Status offenders are not serious delinquents and should not be kept in secure institutions. They are not considered a threat to others. Nevertheless, in recent years many juvenile courts have found ways to "bootstrap" status offenders into delinquency categories—for example, by holding them in contempt for violating a court order. Child advocates concerned about this practice believe this not only deprives status offenders of the freedom that is their due but also exposes them to the influences of more serious delinquents. However, juvenile status offenders, particularly runaways, are also vulnerable on the streets, both to victimization and to their own criminal offending. It is estimated that there are about 1.7 million runaway or thrownaway incidents in the United States every year. Those who qualify as repetitive runaways are especially likely to engage in prostitution, theft, and the sale and distribution of drugs. Thus, supporters of the bootstrapping concept maintain that juvenile courts are preventing more serious offending as well as the exploitation of juveniles.

Compared with runaways, truants are rarely detained or bootstrapped into delinquency. Only 3% of truancy cases referred to juvenile courts were securely detained. Research indicates that persistent truants do participate in delinquent acts; in the Denver Youth Study, for example, two-thirds of serious delinquents were frequently truant.

The status offense category of ungovernability appears to be experiencing a revival. This is the most common way for parents or caretakers to bring juveniles to the attention of a juvenile court and seek orders for the child to obey, observe curfew, or otherwise cooperate. The characteristics of juveniles found ungovernable often resemble the features of oppositional defiant disorder, a clinical diagnosis. Estimates of the prevalence of this disorder range from 2% to 16%. Predominantly a disorder of boys in preadolescence, it is found in approximately equal numbers in girls and boys during adolescence. However, we caution against the assumption that all, or even most, juveniles found incorrigible or ungovernable by the juvenile courts have this psychiatric disorder.

Key Terms and Concepts

aftercare

Census of Juveniles in Residential
  Placement

child delinquent

CHINS

dark figure

deinstitutionalizing

index crimes

informal probation

juvenile probation

kleptomania

larceny–theft

National Crime Victimization
  Survey

nonindex crimes

official statistics

oppositional defiant disorder

panel design

parens patriae

parole

Part I crimes

Part II crimes

PINS

response sets

running away

school truancy

secure detention

self-report method (SR)

status offenses

thrownaways

underage liquor-law violations

ungovernability

Uniform Crime Reports

unofficial statistics

voluntary probation

CHAPTER 9
JUVENILE VIOLENT CRIME
∾

CHAPTER OBJECTIVES

◆ Identify the common forms of violence perpetrated by juveniles

◆ Stress the atypical nature of sensational violence

◆ Discuss school violence in some detail

◆ Identify the various forms of juvenile bullying

◆ Review the research on juvenile sex offenders

◆ Highlight the various aspects of juvenile fire setting

◆ Introduce juvenile hate crimes

- A lone teenager walks into the school principal's office and shoots both the principal and his administrative assistant.
- Two teenage boys enter a home on the pretext of taking a survey and stab to death the residents who invited them in.
- A 15-year-old babysitter sexually assaults the 2-year-old child under her care.

These horrific incidents are highly atypical of juvenile offending; violent juvenile crime constitutes only a small fraction of the offenses youths commit. Liquor-law violations, drug-abuse violations, vandalism, theft, receiving stolen property, disorderly conduct, curfew violations, and loitering make up the majority of juvenile offenses. When violence *does* occur, its onset is usually in late adolescence or early adulthood (Loeber et al., 2005). Although physical aggression is apparent in young children, *violent* aggression requires more force, more trauma to the victim, and often the use of a weapon, particularly a gun.

Although juvenile offenses are typically nonviolent, police reported that juveniles were arrested in about 12.4% of all violent crimes in 2005, so we cannot say that violence among juveniles is rare. UCR data consistently indicate that males account for about 80% of the juvenile violent crime. In addition, juveniles often victimize each other; 52% of offenses on juveniles were committed by 15- to 17-year-olds.

According to the UCR, four index, or Part I, crimes are classified as violent crimes: murder and nonnegligent manslaughter, rape, robbery, and aggravated assault. We discuss these offenses in this chapter and add arson, or juvenile fire setting, because the psychological principles involved are often more similar to those involved in violent offending rather than property offending.

Aggravated assault is the most common violent crime committed by juveniles, accounting for 6 out of every 10 juvenile violent crimes, including arson (see Figure 9–1). Aggravated assault is also the most common violent crime committed by juvenile females,

FIGURE 9–1   Distribution of Juvenile Arrests for Violent Crime (2005)

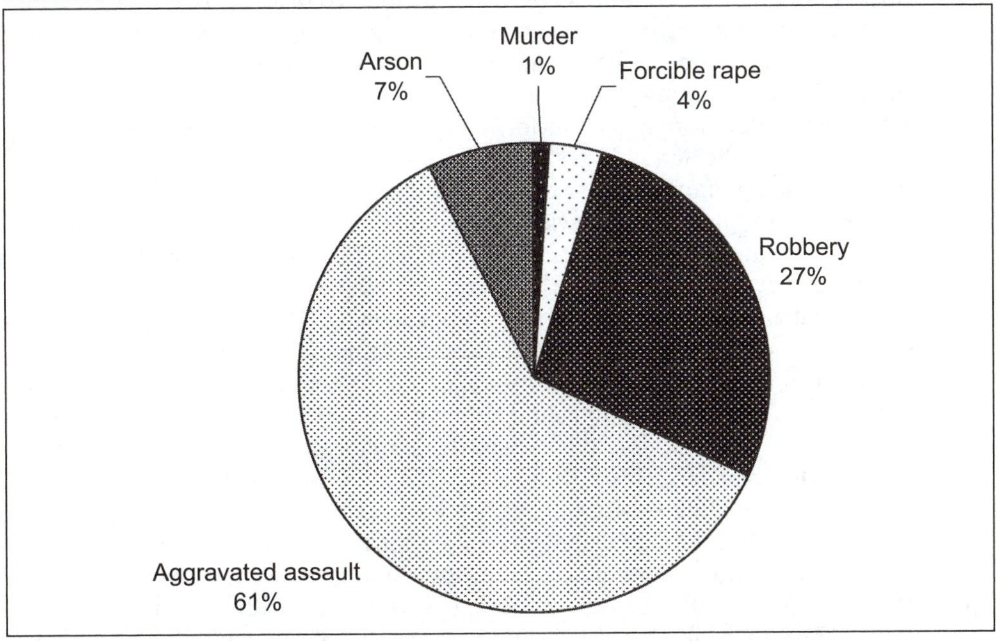

Source: Data from *Crime in the United States—2005* by Federal Bureau of Investigation, 2006, Washington, DC: U.S. Department of Justice, Author.

representing nearly a quarter of the total juvenile aggravated assaults. Interestingly, females also account for 32% of the total simple assault arrests of juveniles. Robbery is the second most common juvenile violent crime, accounting for one out of four of the total juvenile violent crimes. Homicides and nonnegligent manslaughter represent only 1% of the total juvenile violent crime arrests but receive considerable attention from the media. It is important to stress that the overall juvenile arrest rate for violent crimes has declined in recent years, as illustrated by Figure 8–6 in the previous chapter.

SIBLING AND CHILD-TO-PARENT VIOLENCE

Before proceeding to statistics and trends of specific violent offenses, we should briefly discuss youth violence in general. We begin with violence within the family, which is often perpetrated by serious juvenile offenders yet receives little research attention.

SIBLING-TO-SIBLING VIOLENCE

Violence between siblings is believed to be the most common form of intimate violence within families, but surprisingly little is known about it (Gelles, 1997; Wallace, 1996). The violence and abuse a child or adolescent receives from a sibling is often overlooked and trivialized (Simonelli, Mullis, & Rohde, 2005); sibling conflicts are generally seen as a normal part of growing up (Underwood & Patch, 1999). Mothers and fathers display a great tendency to deny the seriousness of the aggressive outbursts of their children in order to perpetuate a "myth of family harmony" (Harbin & Madden, 1979). Yet in many cases, sibling conflict and violence involve punching, choking, beating up, threatening to use a weapon, and actually using a weapon. In addition, sibling violence appears to be linked to violence in dating relationships, family violence in adulthood, and nonfamily adult violence in general (Hoffman, Kiecolt, & Edwards, 2005). More severe forms of child-to-family violence involve murder and have specific terms, such as **siblicide** (sibling killing of a sibling), **patricide** (killing of one's father), **matricide** (killing of one's mother), **sororicide** (killing of one's sister), **fratricide** (killing of one's brother), and **parricide** (killing of one or more of one's parents).

Even though professionals recognize intrafamilial parent-to-child and spouse-to-spouse violence, little systematic research attention has been directed at other forms of intrafamilial violence. Nearly 30 years ago, Steinmetz (1981) reported that almost two-thirds of the adolescent siblings in a family sample characterized by family violence used physical violence to resolve conflict. These findings have been recently supported by Hoffman et al. (2005), who found that 70% of the adolescents in their sample had committed at least one violent act against their closest-age sibling during their senior year of high school. Consistently, families having only boys experience more sibling violence than do families with only girls (Bartol & Bartol, 2005; Hoffman et al., 2005). Hoffman et al. (2005) found that males perpetrated more violent acts against their brothers than against their sisters and more than girls perpetrated against their siblings. In 2002, 72% of murders by siblings involved a brother killing a brother; 14% involved a brother killing a sister (Durose et al., 2005). An additional 14% of siblicide involved a sister killing a brother or sister. Among the 671 intrafamilial murders reported in 2002, 18% (or 119 murders) involved a sibling victim (Durose et al., 2005).

Victims of the more extreme forms of sibling violence tend to be younger siblings. For example, Fehrenbach, Smith, Monastersky, and Deisher (1986) reported that over 40% of the victims of adolescent sexual assault were younger siblings. Available data also suggest that 85% of siblicide offenders and 73% of siblicide victims are male (Dawson & Langan, 1994). If siblings of any age are included, approximately one of every 100 homicides in the United States is a siblicide (Underwood & Patch, 1999). In their analysis, Underwood and Patch (1999) found that the most common circumstance of sibling homicide was some form of argument between the perpetrator and the victim. Interestingly, this same study uncovered in their data set very few incidents involving Asian-Americans or Pacific Islanders. African-Americans, on the other hand, were overrepresented in the data. In addition, firearms predominated as the weapon of choice in siblicides.

CHILD-TO-PARENT VIOLENCE

Child-to-parent violence and abuse has also become an important topic. In one early study (Gelles, 1982), approximately four adolescents (ages 15 to 17) in a hundred were reported to kick, bite, punch, hit with an object, beat up, threaten, or use a gun or knife against a parent. Almost one-third of the restraining orders issued in Massachusetts were requested by parents against their adolescent children (Pagani et al., 2004). In a study using a nationally representative sample of American children, Ullman and Straus (2003) found that 10% of the adolescents (ages 10 to 17) had participated in child-to-parent violence during the previous 12 months. Sixty percent of these youths who used violence had witnessed violence between their parents. In one longitudinal study involving 2,524 Canadian adolescents, Pagani, Larocque, Vitaro, and Tremblay (2003) reported that 13% of the teenagers engaged in physical aggression toward their mothers, ranging from pushing and shoving, punching or kicking, and throwing objects to using a weapon.

In their report for the U.S. Bureau of Juvenile Statistics, Dawson and Langan (1994) estimate that about 2% of murder victims are killed by their children. Like siblicide, the killing of parents is most often committed by sons (Lubenow, 1983; Pagelow, 1989). Mothers are killed far more often than fathers are by both adolescents and adult sons and daughters. Female parricide is exceptionally rare in all countries of the world (d'Orban & O'Connor, 1989). When daughters kill a parent(s), they often secure the help of a male friend or sibling. In Britain, boys most often kill a parent(s) with explosive violence in response to prolonged provocation and parental brutality and abuse (d'Orban & O'Connor, 1989). Heide (1993) identifies three types of youth parricide offenders: the severely abused child, the severely mentally ill child, and the dangerously antisocial child. The complex family dynamics surrounding parricide most often include multiassaultive family patterns, easy access to firearms, alcohol and drug abuse, and a youthful offender's strong feelings of helplessness in coping with the stresses at home. Sometimes the adolescent murderer, as well as other family members, feels a sense of relief that the parent(s) are dead.

Although males predominate in the more extreme forms of juvenile violence toward parents, the gender differences disappear at more moderate levels of violence (Pagani et al., 2004). In addition, the risk of violence toward parents gradually increases during adolescence, peaking at age 15 and diminishing thereafter (Pagani et al., 2004). This pattern corresponds to the peak age of adolescent violence toward nonrelated individuals, noted by Loeber and Stouthamer-Loeber (1998). Most violent incidents between children and parents are associated with conflicts about home responsibilities, money, and privilege (Pagani et al., 2004). Children and adolescents who displayed early and chronic forms of aggression and antisocial behavior are most likely to aggress toward parents (Pagani et al., 2004). "As adolescents, those described as chronically aggressive by their (annually) different primary school teachers were (9 and 4) times at greater risk of engaging in verbal and physical aggression (respectively) toward their mothers in comparison to their persistently nonaggressive peers" (Pagani et al., 2004, p. 534). In fact, violent predispositions during childhood, measured by teachers, are among the best predictors of later violence toward mothers. Pagani et al. (2004) concluded in their study, "Indeed, teacher-rated disruptiveness during early childhood predicted the risk of engaging in physical aggression toward mothers during adolescence" (p. 220).

Multiassaultive families, discussed in some detail in Chapter 2, are characterized by continual cycles of intrafamilial physical aggression and violence. Siblings hit each other, spouses hit each other, parents hit the children, and the older children hit the parents. According to available data, at least 7% of all intact families may be considered multiassaultive (Hotaling & Straus, 1989). Children from these families have an inordinately high rate of assault against nonfamily members (Hotaling & Straus, 1989). These children are also more likely to be involved in a wide variety of property crimes, to have disruptive problems in school, and to be involved with the police (Hotaling & Straus, 1989).

Child-to-parent violence is most likely an interactional process, with each person in the process contributing. Parents may be permissive or inconsistent in their discipline, uncaring in their supervision of the child, and abusive or physical in their forms of punishment. Not surprisingly, parents who use harsh child-rearing techniques are more likely to be assaulted by their children, as compared to parents who use nonaggressive techniques (Pagani et al., 2003). Some studies (e.g., Straus & Stewart, 1999; Ullman & Straus, 2003) report that over 90% of American children, ages 3 to 5, are hit or slapped by their mothers (and about the same percentage is true of fathers). As stressed by Ullman and Straus (2003), this pattern sets into motion a pattern of mutually coercive acts, including child-to-parent violence.

AGGRAVATED ASSAULT

The UCR defines *aggravated assault* as an unlawful attack by one person upon another for the purpose of inflicting severe or aggravated bodily injury. The UCR further specifies that this type of assault is usually accompanied by the use of a weapon or by other means likely to produce death or great bodily harm. Attempted aggravated assault that involves the display of—or threat to use—a gun, knife, or other weapon is included in this crime category. When aggravated assault and larceny–theft occur together, the offense falls in the category of robbery.

Approximately 14% of the total arrests for aggravated assault in 2004 were juveniles. The juvenile arrest rate for aggravated assault, however, was 26% *above* the 1980 level (H. N. Snyder, 2005). Notice in Figure 9–2 that the age bracket of 13–14 has the greatest number of arrests for aggravated assault. Aggravated assault is a frequent

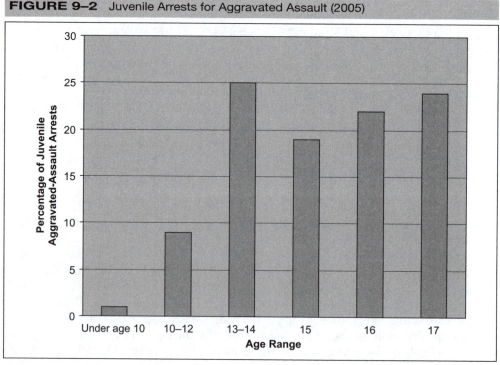

FIGURE 9–2 Juvenile Arrests for Aggravated Assault (2005)

Source: Data from *Crime in the United States—2005* by Federal Bureau of Investigation, 2006, Washington, DC: U.S. Department of Justice, Author.

offense of juveniles regarded as serious and violent offenders (Loeber, Farrington, & Waschbush, 1998). Both aggravated and simple assaults appear to be a distinguishing feature of violent juvenile gangs, accounting for two-thirds of all assaults in some metropolitan areas (Thornberry, 1998).

ROBBERY

According to the definition provided by the UCR, *robbery* is the taking or attempting to take anything of value from the care, custody, or control of a person(s) by force or threat of force or violence and/or by putting the victim in fear. Between 1995 and 2003, the juvenile arrest rate for robbery fell 62%, with similar declines for males and females (H. N. Snyder, 2005). Many of the victims of female juvenile robbery are other girls from whom the offenders take small amounts of cash and occasional jewelry (Chesney-Lind & Paramore, 2001).

More than one-third of the robbery incidents in the United States are "acquaintance robberies," in which the victim knows the offender (Felson, Baumer, & Messner, 2000). In these cases, many of the robbery victims are family members of the perpetrators, often school-aged youths; and the crimes often happen at school, with one student or group of students robbing another. In these acquaintance robberies, the take is usually small, the offenders are less likely to use weapons, and injuries are relatively rare (Felson et al., 2000). Felson et al. note that each of these factors is associated with a lower probability of the victim calling the police; in reality, few youth robberies are actually reported. Figure 9–3 portrays the age range of juvenile arrests for robbery.

FIGURE 9–3 Juvenile Arrests for Robbery (2005)

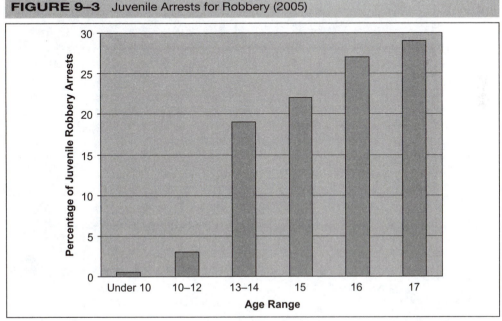

Source: Data from *Crime in the United States—2005* by Federal Bureau of Investigation, 2006, Washington, DC: U.S. Department of Justice, Author.

JUVENILE FIRE SETTING

Arson is defined as "any willful or malicious burning or attempt to burn, with or without intent to defraud, a dwelling house, public building, motor vehicle or aircraft, personal property of another" (FBI, 2005, p. 53). According to the UCR guidelines, only fires that law enforcement investigation determines to have been willfully or maliciously set may be classified as arson. Agencies participating in the UCR program do not report fires of suspicious or unknown origin.

In 2004 complete information was collected for a total of 63,215 arson fires in the United States. In 2005 nearly half (48.6%) of the persons arrested for arson were juveniles, and of those juveniles, nearly 60% were under the age of 15 (FBI, 2006; see Figure 9–4). A large majority (76.3%) of the structures involved were community or public buildings such as churches, jails, or schools. In Australia, by comparison, approximately 20% of the arson fires are set by children and adolescents (Lambie, McCardle, & Coleman, 2002). In a typical year in the United States, fires set by children and youth claim the lives of approximately 300 individuals and destroy more than $300 million worth of property (Putnam & Kirkpatrick, 2005). Children are also often the victims of these fires, accounting for 85% of the lives lost in the United States (U.S. Fire

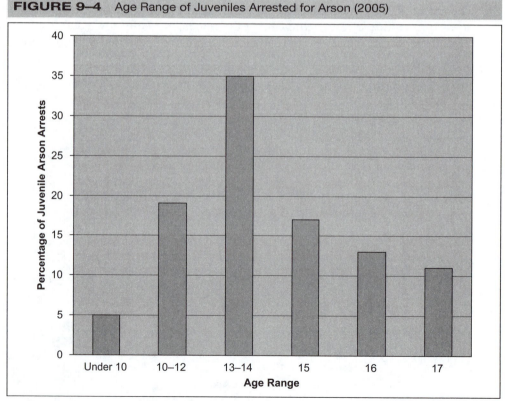

FIGURE 9–4 Age Range of Juveniles Arrested for Arson (2005)

Source: Data from *Crime in the United States—2005* by Federal Bureau of Investigation, 2006, Washington, DC: U.S. Department of Justice, Author.

Administration, 2004a). After deaths caused by motor vehicle accidents, fires are the leading cause of death among young children (Stickle & Blechman, 2002). Not all of these fires, of course, were set with criminal intent or would qualify as arson.

According to UCR data, the total number of arrests for arson in 2004 (both adult and juvenile) was 28.6% lower than the number a decade earlier. The number of arrests of adults for arson declined 22.6%, while the number of juveniles arrested for arson fell 33.7% during this 10-year span. The number of arrests of juvenile males decreased 35.25%; the number of arrests of juvenile females dropped 22.75%.

Most of the known arsonists are young males, often juveniles acting in groups. Some studies have found that between 75% and 85% of all fire setting is done by males, with increasing percentages of females in the 13- to 17-year-old group (FBI, 2003; Stadolnik, 2000). In a comprehensive study of 1,016 juveniles and adults arrested for arson and fire-related crimes, Icove and Estepp (1987) discovered that vandalism was the most frequently identified motive, accounting for 49% of the arsons in the sample. Research (e.g., Robbins & Robbins, 1964) has consistently shown that most fires set by juveniles appear to be motivated by the wish to get back at authority or to gain status or are prompted by a dare or a need for excitement. Therefore, it is not surprising that the Icove-Estepp investigation revealed that the vast majority (96%) of the vandalism fires were set by juveniles, who often set the fire within a 1-mile radius of their homes. About one-half of these juvenile fire setters remained at the scene, presumably for the excitement derived from doing so.

Many fires set by youth go undetected, unreported, or unsolved (Zipper & Wilcox, 2005); it is generally acknowledged that only a small proportion of fires set by juveniles are reported, probably less than 10% (Adler, Nunn, Northam, Lebnan, & Ross, 1994). Zipper and Wilcox (2005) report that, of the 1,241 Massachusetts juveniles referred for counseling services because of arson, only 11% started blazes that were reported. The other incidents were not reported because witnesses or caretakers did not consider the behavior dangerous—no loss of life or significant destruction of property occurred. In such situations, many adults worry that charging juveniles with arson will give them a criminal record that will hamper their future careers. Another study of youth from the third to the eighth grades in 15 school districts in Oregon found that 32% of the students reported having set fires outside their homes, and 29% said they had started fires in their own residences (Zipper & Wilcox, 2005).

DEVELOPMENTAL STAGES OF FIRE SETTING

Arson is the term that specifically defines the setting of fires under certain conditions as a crime. *Fire setting* is the term commonly used in the literature on child psychopathology for essentially the same behavior. It is intentional and willful behavior with an understanding of the potential consequences of that behavior.

Child fire setters have attracted considerable interest among researchers in psychology. Gaynor (1996) outlines three developmental phases related to fire: fire interest, fire play, and fire setting. Fascination and experimentation with fire appears to be a common feature of normal child development. Kafrey (1980) discovered that fascination with fire appears to be nearly universal in children between 5 and 7 years of age. Furthermore, this fascination with fire begins early, with one in five children setting fires before the age of 3. As children get older, fire play (i.e., experimentation) normally takes place between the ages of 5 and 9. At this stage, children experiment with how a fire starts and what it can do. During this phase they are especially vulnerable to the hazards of fire because of their more limited ability to understand its consequences and their lack of effective strategies for extinguishing a fire once it gets out of control (Lambie et al., 2002). Figure 9–5 shows the areas of the home in which children often set fires. By age 10, most children have learned the dangers of fire and its consequences; if they continue to set fires at this point, they have reached the fire-setting phase.

The children who continue to set fires most often demonstrate an intention to use fires to destroy, to gain excitement, or to communicate by drawing attention to themselves and their problems. They also tend to demonstrate poor social skills, inadequate social competence, and impulsiveness, as compared to their peers (Kolko & Kazdin, 1986). In general, persistent fire setters are more likely to demonstrate ADHD and poor impulse control (Forehand, Wierson, Frame, Kemptom, & Armistead, 1991), and many are considered to have "conduct problems" by their teachers. Lambie et al. (2002) report a similar finding from their clinical experiences: Fire setting is just one part of a more comprehensive set of behavior problems, the motives for which are varied but typically include impulse control problems and misdirected anger and boredom. In addition, there is some evidence that children who are consistently cruel to animals and other children tend to engage in repeated fire setting (Slavkin, 2001). And Lambie et al. (2001) point out that adolescent fire setters frequently commit a variety of other crimes, including rape and other sex offenses.

This range of criminal offending has been noted by other researchers as well. A large majority of fire setters known to the juvenile justice system have committed

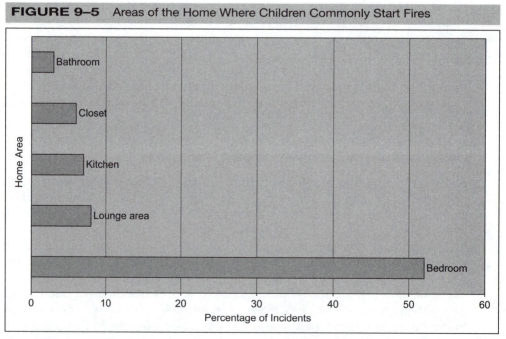

FIGURE 9–5 Areas of the Home Where Children Commonly Start Fires

Source: Data from *Arson and Juveniles: Responding to the Violence* by U.S. Fire Administration, 2004, Washington, DC: Federal Emergency Management Agency, National Fire Data Center.

many other serious juvenile acts besides arson (Ritvo, Shanok, & Lewis, 1983; Stickle & Blechman, 2002). Stickle and Blechman (2002) found that "fire setting juvenile offenders exhibit a pattern of developmentally advanced, serious antisocial behavior consistent with an early starter or life-course-persistent trajectory" (p. 190), a finding also reported by other researchers (Becker, Stuewig, Herrera, & McCloskey, 2004; Forehand et al., 1991). As might be expected, research has revealed that a large proportion of the persistent fire setters are boys, probably at a ratio of 9 to 1 compared to girls (Zipper & Wilcox, 2005).

Nearly all children who set fires beyond the normal fascination and experimental stages tend to have poor relationships with their parents and also appear to be victims of physical abuse (Jackson, Glass, & Hope, 1987). In their comprehensive review, Kolko and Kazdin (1986) suggest that fire setting may be closely associated with parental ineffectiveness and faulty or nonexistent supervision. In a retrospective study by Saunders and Awad (1991), the records of 13 adolescent girls referred to the Toronto Family Court Clinic for setting fires were examined.

> Reading through the 13 charts was a depressing experience even for those of us who have worked for years with families who have many problems and serious difficulties meeting their children's basic needs. These parents had a history of marital problems, separation, violence against the spouse and the children, criminal behaviour, drug and/or alcohol abuse, and inability to take care of the children. (p. 403)

Children who continue to start fires well into adulthood tend to be less intellectually able and less assertive, have limited interpersonal skills and less schooling, are more likely to be underemployed or unemployed, and are more prone toward depression and feelings of helplessness (Murphy & Clare, 1996). In general, research continually finds that as a group, arsonists are inadequate socially and interpersonally, although the exact nature of the inadequacy varies among individuals (Jackson et al., 1987). Research also indicates that fire setting is used by this group as a communicative vehicle in response to conflict and stress (Day & Berney, 2001). Day and Berney also note that fire setting is a common behavioral pattern for mentally retarded individuals, although we must question the degree to which their behavior can be considered intentional. Interestingly, the prevalence rate of fire setting appears to be significantly higher in children referred to a clinic for psychological problems (Kolko & Kazdin, 1989; Lambie et al., 2002).

Research suggests that fire setters (both adolescent and adult) usually have little or no effective means of influencing their environment and find themselves in highly undesirable situations (Jackson et al., 1987). As a result, the arsonist experiences worthlessness and social ineffectiveness. Some suggest that setting fires may allow the person to experience some control or at least some influence over the environment.

FIRE-SETTING TYPOLOGIES

Based on clinical assessments of known fire setters, Kolko (2002) developed a typology that identifies four types of fire setters: (1) curious, (2) pathological, (3) expressive, and (4) delinquent. The typology is based on the assumption of differences in motivation, although it does take into consideration individual and environmental influences. In brief, the curious fire setter uses fire for fascination purposes, the pathological fire setter is driven by psychological or emotional problems, the expressive fire setter is giving a cry for help, and the delinquent fire setter hopes to achieve antisocial or destructive ends (Putnam & Kirkpatrick, 2005). These types are not mutually exclusive; a juvenile could use fire as a cry for help to alleviate psychological distress.

JUVENILE SEX OFFENDERS

Juvenile sex offenders (JSOs) have been subject to considerable psychological research, partly because many adult sex offenders began their sexual offending histories in their youth. Studies have found that over 50% of adult sex offenders committed their first offenses during adolescence or earlier (Cellini, 1995; Cellini, Schwartz, & Readio, 1993). Other disturbing findings include the following: The median age of JSOs is between 14 and 15; more than 90% know their victims; and more than one-third of the offenses have involved the use of force (National Council of Juvenile and Family Court Judges, 1993). The victims are often younger than the juvenile offender, are most often female (75%), and are usually relatives or acquaintances (Righthand & Welch, 2001). Unfortunately, most of the research on JSOs has concentrated on adolescent males, neglecting females and preadolescent males.

Adolescent males commit 20% to 30% of all rapes and 30% to 50% of all child molestations (Becker & Johnson, 2001). However, male JSOs also participate in a much broader variety of sexual activities. In one study, Zolondek, Abel, Northey, and Jordan (2001) found that 10% to 30% of JSOs made obscene phone calls and engaged in phone sex, as well as in a variety of **paraphilias** (i.e., abnormal sexual behavior) such as **exhibitionism, fetishism, frottage**, and **voyeurism** (see Table 9–1). In addition, JSOs tend to commit other crimes, such as shoplifting, burglary, cruelty to animals, fire setting, and physical assaults (Knight & Prentky, 1993).

Although some JSOs attend school and achieve average grades, a significant number are truant, exhibit behavioral problems, and have learning disabilities (Cellini, 1995). Research consistently reveals that most juveniles with sexual behavioral problems have significant deficits in social competence and the ability to get along with others (Becker, 1990; Knight & Prentky, 1993; Prentky, Harris, Frizzell, & Righthand, 2000).

TABLE 9–1: Definitions of Paraphilias

Term	*Definition*
Exhibitionism	• Continual exposure of the genitals to unsuspecting strangers for sexual gratification
Fetishism	• Use of nonsexual object (e.g., shoes, underwear) to arouse sexual excitement in an observer
Partialism	• Use of nonsexual part of the body (e.g., foot, lock of hair, ear) to arouse sexual excitement in an observer
Frottage	• Deliberately and continually rubbing up against other people for sexual excitement (e.g., in a subway)
Voyeurism	• Seeking sexual excitement by observing unsuspecting people who are nude, partially nude, or in the act of sexual activity
Sexual sadism	• Receiving sexual excitement by inflicting physical pain or psychological discomfort on another person
Sexual masochism	• Receiving sexual excitement by being humiliated, bound, beaten, or psychologically abused

Many experts and mental health professionals argue that a juvenile's own sexual victimization as a child is a primary cause of later sex offending. However, these observations have not been uniformly supported by the research (Knight & Prentky, 1993; Prentky et al., 2000; Spaccarelli, Bowden, Coatsworth, & Kim, 1997). In a British study conducted by Salter et al. (2003), only 12% of the 224 JSOs had been sexually abused as children. There is some evidence, however, that a large number of juvenile child molesters may have been sexually abused in early childhood (Prentky et al., 2000), as well as some evidence that persistent, hard-core JSOs have experienced a high incidence of prior sexual abuse and other developmental trauma in their early childhood (Righthand et al., 2005). In these cases the trauma and familial dysfunction are often pervasive and chronic and occur in the absence of environmental protections and supports (Hunter & Figueredo, 1999; Veneziano & Veneziano, 2002). The backgrounds of these JSOs are often characterized by neglectful or rejecting parents, poor self-esteem, an inability to form attachments, and peer rejection.

Many JSOs deny or minimize the sexual offenses they commit and the impact they have on their victims (Ertl & McNamara, 1997). JSOs also tend to distort what has happened in an attempt to avoid full responsibility for their actions. Many high school males have a strong tendency to blame their aggressive and coercive sexual behavior on their victims (Maxwell, Robinson, & Post, 2003). In fact, the rape-related beliefs of high school students tend to be more callous and stereotypical than those of college students (Maxwell et al., 2003; Xenos & Smith, 2001).

JSOs represent a heterogeneous population and defy any unitary profile or simple classification (Becker & Johnson, 2001; van Wijik, van Horn, Bullens, Bijleveld, & Doreleijers, 2005; van Wijik et al., 2006). They come from all ethnic, racial, and socio-economic groups and differ in their psychiatric developmental characteristics, the age and gender of their targeted victims, and the level of violence displayed in the commission of the offenses (Hunter, Figueredo, Malamuth, & Becker, 2003; Hunter, Hazelwood, & Slesinger, 2000). For example, some juvenile offenders seek pubescent female victims, while others prefer prepubescent children (Hunter et al., 2003). The types of sexual offenses committed by juveniles vary widely, ranging from noncontact offenses (such as exhibitionism and voyeurism) to sexual penetration. About half of the contact offenses involve oral-genital contact or attempted or actual vaginal or anal penetration (Righthand & Welch, 2001). JSOs usually use more force when assaulting peers or adults than they do with younger children.

We can divide juvenile sex offenses into three groups, based on the nature of the offense. The first type involves noncontact or hands-off offenses such as voyeurism, obscene phone calls, stalking, and exhibitionism. The second type, forcible rape, is characterized by violence, force, or coercion. The third type, child molestation, involves sexual acts with a victim at least 4 years younger than the offender. Physical force or assaultive behavior is not a dominant feature of this type of sexual offense. We will discuss the last two types here.

FORCIBLE RAPE

According to the 2005 UCR statistics, about 15% of those arrested for forcible rape and 22% of those arrested for all other sex offenses (excluding prostitution) were younger than age 18. Six percent of the total arrests for forcible rape and 11% of the total arrests for other sex offenses were under age 15. The percentage of juvenile arrests for rape has been largely the same for years. As defined in the UCR program, *forcible rape* is the carnal knowledge of a female forcibly and against her will (FBI, 2006). Sexual attacks on males are counted as aggravated assaults or sex offenses, depending on the circumstances and the extent of any injuries. Assaults and attempts to commit rape by force or threat of force are also included, but statutory rape (without force) and other sex offenses are excluded.

The UCR data represent an underestimation, however. Some studies indicate that at least 30% of the rapes in the United State are committed by juveniles (Cellini, 1995). In a survey of high school students, nearly half (48%) of the females reported experiencing sexual aggression, and one-third (34%) of the males admitted committing this type of offending (Maxwell et al., 2003).

An analysis of the total number of arrests for forcible rape and the arrests of juveniles for forcible rape reveals similar racial patterns. Approximately 65.3% of all arrestees were white, 32.2% were black, and the remainder were of other races. Of juveniles arrested for forcible rape, 63.1% were white, 34.7% were black, and the remainder were of other races. Figure 9–6 shows the age distribution for juvenile rape arrests.

Juvenile sex offenders who rape and sexually assault frequently engage in a wide range of other criminal and antisocial but nonsexual behaviors. JSOs tend to shoplift, steal, engage in fire setting, bully and intimidate, display cruelty to animals, and physically

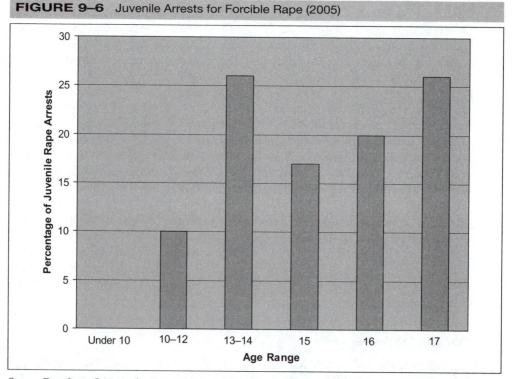

FIGURE 9–6 Juvenile Arrests for Forcible Rape (2005)

Source: Data from *Crime in the United States—2005* by Federal Bureau of Investigation, 2006, Washington, DC: U.S. Department of Justice, Author.

assault others. In one study, for example, more than half of violent JSOs were abnormally cruel to animals, including their own pets (Tingle, Barnard, Robbins, Newman, & Hutchinson, 1986). In addition, JSOs who rape are more likely to commit the sexual offense along with a co-offender, commit a nonsexual offense in conjunction with the sexual assault, and have a previous arrest record (Hunter et al., 2003). Most can be regarded as LCP or chronic juvenile offenders.

Date Rape

Date or acquaintance rape is far more common among juveniles than is generally recognized. **Date rape** refers specifically to a sexual assault that occurs within the context of a dating relationship—a broad term that can include two juveniles just "hanging" together. Some data suggest that up to one-third of young adults between the ages of 16 and 24 report having been involved in at least one dating incident involving a sexual assault (Lingren, 2001). Frintner and Rubinson (1993) conducted a survey of 925 college women, which found that over one-fourth of the respondents had experienced sexual assault or attempted sexual assault. Nearly 83% of these college women who had been sexually assaulted said that the attacker was someone they knew and that most of these incidents had happened during their freshman year. Most relevant for our discussion, Schubot (2001) learned that 15% of his sample of female high school students reported being forced to have sexual intercourse while on a date. Because juveniles are rarely arrested or processed in court for these incidents, date rape statistics are not available from official sources. It is believed, though, that alcohol and other drugs are prominently associated with incidences of date rape.

JUVENILE CHILD MOLESTERS

As mentioned earlier, 30% to 50% of child molestation offenses may be committed by adolescents (Cellini, 1995). Van Wijik et al. (2005) discovered that juvenile child molesters represent a very different group when compared to juvenile rapists. These researchers found that juvenile child molesters demonstrate significantly more social isolation because of poorly developed social skills and very limited interactions with peers. These youngsters were introverted and rejected by peers at an early age. More than 60% of their victims—who, by definition, must be at least 4 or 5 years younger than the perpetrator—are younger than 12, and two-thirds are younger than age 6 (Veneziano & Veneziano, 2002). Ryan, Miyoshi, Metzner, Krugmann, and Fryer (1996) found that 63% of the victims of juvenile molesters were younger than age 9. According to the National Council of Juvenile and Family Court Judges (1993), the median age of victims of molestation is 7 years. A study investigating incest cases reported that sibling offenders are more likely to have molested younger children than are nonsibling offenders (Worling, 1995). In contrast, adolescent rapists are more likely to select victims their own age or older (Veneziano & Veneziano, 2002). Figure 9–7 shows the age range of JSOs, excluding arrests for forcible rape.

As mentioned earlier, juvenile sex molesters are more likely to have been sexually abused themselves in early childhood (Prentky et al., 2000). Juveniles who sexually offend children display lower self-efficacy and self-esteem and higher levels of depression, anxiety, and pessimism than are found for other juveniles (Hunter & Figueredo, 2000; Hunter et al., 2003). Juvenile molesters view themselves as socially inadequate and anticipate peer ridicule and rejection (Hunter et al., 2003). They also show greater

FIGURE 9–7 Juvenile Arrests for Sexual Offenses, Excluding Forcible Rape (2005)

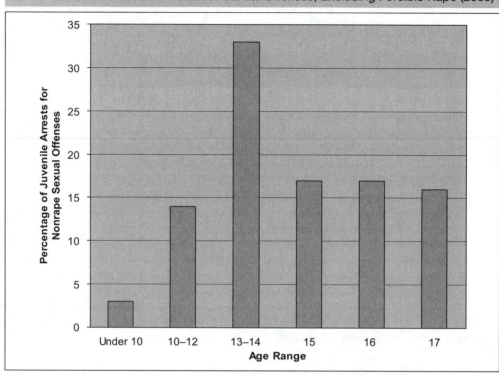

Source: Data from *Crime in the United States—2005* by Federal Bureau of Investigation, 2006, Washington, DC: U.S. Department of Justice, Author.

deficits in psychosocial functioning than other JSOs show, are less aggressive, and are more likely to offend victims to whom they are related (Hunter et al., 2003).

FEMALE JUVENILE SEX OFFENDERS

According to the latest UCR statistics, juvenile females accounted for only 5.5% of all juveniles arrested for sex offenses (excluding forcible rape and prostitution; FBI, 2005). However, the prevalence of female juvenile sexual offending is probably underreported. In addition, research on girls who have committed sex offenses has been sparse, and existing investigations have been limited by small sample size and other methodological shortcomings (Becker, Hall, & Stinson, 2001; Righthand & Welch, 2001). Most of the research on female sex offenders has focused on adult offenders (Bumby & Bumby, 1997).

Fehrenbach and Monastersky (1988) found that most adolescent girls who sexually victimized young children did so while engaged in child care or babysitting. The victims of the 28 female JSOs they studied were 12 years old or younger and were mostly acquaintances (57%), followed by siblings (29%) and other relatives (14%). Matthews, Hunter, and Vuz (1997) provided data on 67 female sex offenders who ranged in age from 11 to 18. More than 90% of their victims were acquaintances or relatives. Both of these studies also found that a high percentage of the abusers (50% and 77.65%, respectively) had a history of being sexually abused themselves. These findings suggest that female JSOs are far more likely to have been sexually abused themselves than are male JSOs. Similar to the findings about male molesters, Bumby and Bumby (1997) found that female JSOs tend to be depressed, have a poor self-concept, have a suicide ideation, and have most often been sexually abused during childhood.

RECIDIVISM OF JUVENILE SEX OFFENDERS

In general, studies have reported that the recidivism rate for juvenile sex offenses ranges between 2% and 14% (Reitzel, 2003; Rubinstein, Yeager, Goodstein, & Lewis, 1993; Sipe, Jensen, & Everett, 1998; Waite et al., 2005). Alexander (1999) found an overall sexual recidivism rate (based on rearrest) of 7%, with juvenile rapists having the highest reoffending rate of all JSOs. However, some investigators (Alexander, 1999; Hunter & Becker, 1999) have reported that JSOs are significantly less likely to reoffend than are adult offenders. There is also considerable evidence that JSOs who are highly impulsive are far more likely to reoffend than are those JSOs who are evaluated as less impulsive (Waite et al., 2005).

In light of concerns about recidivism, psychologists engaged in treating JSOs have developed clinical instruments to evaluate their risk of reoffending. The **J-SOAP** (Prentky & Righthand, 2003) is a 26-item checklist that is usually completed by a clinician to evaluate the risk factors identified in the professional literature as predictive of sexual offending and criminal reoffending (Righthand et al., 2005). The checklist is specifically designed for use with males aged 12 to 18. Although the research on the instrument is extremely promising, so far the available data are insufficient to provide empirically guided cutoff scores (Righthand et al., 2005).

JUVENILE MURDER

Nationwide, the 2005 UCR data yielded an estimated rate of 5.6 murders per 100,000 inhabitants, a 3.4% increase from the 2004 rate but a 33% decrease from the 1995 rate (FBI, 2006). The UCR data further revealed that 94.2% of the offenders were adults; 5.8% were juveniles. A breakdown of the overall data by gender showed that 89.9% of the offenders were male, and 10.1% were female. However, girls accounted for about 20% of the alleged juvenile asssailants. Twelve percent of the juveniles arrested for murder were under age 15 (see Figure 9–8). From 1985 through 2000, juvenile courts handled 1,700 juvenile murders, but the annual number of cases has steadily decreased since 1996 (Puzzanchera et al., 2004). To some extent this reflects nationwide trends to transfer juveniles charged with serious crimes to criminal courts rather than process them in the juvenile system.

Nonetheless, regardless of the courts in which they are processed, the number of juveniles aged 15 or younger who are involved in murder is relatively small (H. N. Snyder, 2001). Between 1980 and 1997, about 2% (or 600 cases) of all murders involved child delinquents (ages 7 to 12), and the annual rate of these homicides has been relatively stable, averaging about 30 homicides per year (Loeber et al., 2003). Nearly all of the homicides committed by children under the age of 15 (94%) involved a single victim, mostly male (70%). Further, more than half (58%) of the murder victims of child delinquents were juveniles under the age of 18, and more than a third (38%) of the victims

FIGURE 9–8 Juvenile Arrests for Murder (2005)

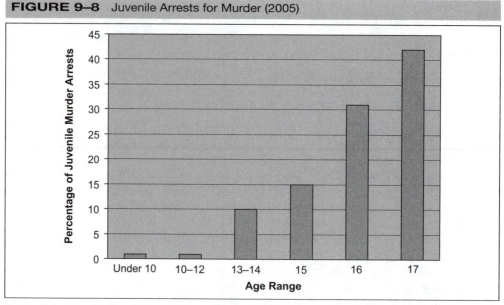

Source: Data from *Crime in the United States—2005* by Federal Bureau of Investigation, 2006, Washington, DC: U.S. Department of Justice, Author.

were under 13 (H. N. Snyder, 2001). Rarely was the victim a parent. More than half (54%) of the victims of child delinquents were killed with firearms; gun play is often a contributing factor when children kill other children (Goetting, 1993). Sexual homicides by child offenders are very uncommon (Myers & Blashfield, 1997).

DEMOGRAPHICS AND PSYCHOLOGICAL CHARACTERISTICS OF JUVENILE MURDERERS

In recent years, researchers have conducted studies with small samples of juvenile murderers in order to obtain more detailed information both about the crimes and about the backgrounds of the offenders. A study by Myers and Scott (1998) examined 18 male juvenile murderers between the ages of 14 and 17 who met the criteria for conduct disorder at the time of their crimes. Of these offenders, 33% were white and 67% were black. Their homicides were committed either in relation to criminal activities (72%) or during interpersonal conflict (28%). The victims were male in eight cases (45%) and females in ten cases (55%). Half of the victims were strangers; the other half were acquaintances (39%) or family members (11%).

The results of the study revealed that 16 of the 18 juvenile murderers (89%) had histories of one or more psychotic episodes (especially paranoid ideation) and other forms of mental disorder. These results were remarkably similar to the prevalence rate in other studies that examined the psychological characteristics of juvenile murderers (e.g., Lewis et al., 1985; Lewis et al., 1988).

Juvenile murderers—and those juveniles who commit violent crimes in general—are more apt to have a history of severe educational difficulties, as compared to the experience of nonviolent juveniles (Heckel & Shumaker, 2001). Myers et al. (1995) report that within their sample of 25 juvenile murderers, 76% demonstrated a learning disability, and 86% had failed at least one grade. Significant language handicaps appear to be the most prominent learning problem among juvenile murderers (Heckel & Shumaker, 2001; Myers & Mutch, 1992).

Many juvenile murderers also appear to have a variety of neurological abnormalities (Heckel & Shumaker, 2001), as has been reported in the medical histories of LCP offenders. Myers and his colleagues (e.g., Myers & Mutch, 1992; Myers, 1994; Myers et al., 1995) have continually noted the high incidence of conduct disorders in their samples of juvenile murderers, ranging from 84% to 88%. ADHD has also been identified with some regularity in juvenile murderers (Heckel & Shumaker, 2001).

Within their sample of 72 adolescent murderers, Benedek and Cornell (1989) identified three groups. One had indicators of mental disorders before and during the crime. A second group was experiencing severe interpersonal conflict with someone, most often a family member. The third group killed in the course of committing another crime, most often robbery or rape.

Loeber et al. (2006) note that virtually all the studies of the causes or factors involved in juvenile homicide have relied on case studies or have examined the background of the offender after the homicide was committed. Loeber and his colleagues describe some of the findings of the **Pittsburgh Youth Study**, a longitudinal study in which three samples of schoolboys were followed from childhood to early adulthood. Thirty-three of the schoolboys were convicted of homicide during the study. The longitudinal data on these schoolboys revealed that almost all of them (93.3%) had been violent prior to the homicide. In addition, these juvenile homicide offenders were more likely to carry a weapon, to qualify for a diagnosis of conduct disorder, and to sell hard drugs. They were also more likely to have been held back in school. "What the study clearly demonstrates is that most homicide and index violent offenders are individuals on developmental trajectories that are already present in early adolescence" (Loeber et al., 2005, p. 213). The researchers also concluded that individual factors (e.g., cognitive, biological, and social skills) were especially powerful in predicting who would commit murder.

Serial murder by children and adolescents is an exceedingly rare phenomenon, and scientific information is extremely sparse (Myers, 2004). Serial murder refers to instances in which an individuals kill a number of victims (usually a minimum of three) over a period of time. The time interval—sometimes referred to as the cooling off period—may be days or weeks but is more likely to be months or years. To qualify as a serial juvenile murder, the killing of two or more individuals would take place before the age of 18.

According to Myers (2004), most serial murders by juveniles are prompted by sexual desires, although the sexual element of the crime may be overt or symbolic. Myers (2002) studied 16 juveniles who had committed a sexual homicide (although not serial) and noted some common characteristics. All 16 had a history of serious school problems, and a majority (94%) came from families considered dysfunctional and abusive. Eighty-eight percent of the families were evaluated as violent. Most of the offenders (88%) exhibited a history of serious interpersonal violence and criminal offenses and displayed the behaviors typical of juvenile psychopaths.

WEAPONS AND VIOLENCE

Year after year, about two-thirds of all murder victims are killed with a firearm. In addition, about 60% of all juvenile suicides involve a firearm (Joyce, 2003/2004).

According to the latest UCR date (FBI, 2006), approximately half of the 1,446 juvenile homicides involved firearms. Hands, fists, or feet were used in about 21% of the murders; knives or cutting instuments, in 8%; and blunt objects, in 4%. The remaining murders involved a variety of other methods (e.g., drowning, poisining, explosives).

According to the 2004 UCR data, 24% of the total arrests for carrying or possessing a firearm were of juveniles, and 9% of the total arrestees were under age 15. Males were four times more likely than females to report carrying a weapon (H. N. Snyder & Sickmund, 1995); the weapons most often carried were knives or razors (55%), followed by clubs (24%), and firearms (21%). In a more recent national survey of more than 16,000 students in Grades 9 to 12, 18% said they had carried a weapon outside the home in the previous 30-day period (Lizotte & Sheppard, 2001). The percentages were higher (22%) for youths living in inner-city neighborhoods. A recent PRIDE survey (2003) reported that approximately 2% of middle school youths (Grades 6 to 8) carried a gun to school on a regular basis during 2002–2003. Available data (e.g., Decker, Pennel, & Caldwell, 1997) report that more than two-thirds of juveniles who carry weapons say they do so primarily for self-protection.

Gun ownership by gang members appears to be a standard feature of many youth gangs (Lizotte & Sheppard, 2001). Gun ownership by juveniles is also related to a wide range of antisocial behaviors, including gun-related crimes, gang membership, and drug selling (Lizotte & Sheppard, 2001). For example, the amount of serious violent crime these juveniles committed during periods of carrying a gun was more than five times the amount they committed while not carrying a gun.

Firearms appear to be especially troublesome for juveniles in minority groups. Research has consistently shown that African-Americans are greatly overrepresented in homicide cases, both as victims and as offenders, and that three-quarters of these deaths are a result of firearms (Berkowitz, 1994). Unfortunately, the use of high-caliber automatic or semiautomatic weapons is growing.

The Violent Crime Control and Law Enforcement Act of 1974 made it a federal offense for any person to sell or transfer a handgun to a person under age 18; it is even a crime for a juvenile to possess ammunition for a handgun. Yet there are multiple ways for juveniles to obtain firearms, and they report being able to do so with ease. Some juveniles (about 28%) ask others, such as older siblings or friends, to buy guns for them (Braga & Kennedy, 2001); about 11% of juveniles buy them from a gun shop or pawnshop. Theft is also an important source of firearms for juveniles; an estimated 500,000 guns are stolen each year, mostly from residences (Braga & Kennedy, 2001), and about 70% of the firearms used by juvenile offenders are obtained through theft (Wright & Rossi, 1994). As pointed out by Braga and Kennedy (2001), juveniles obtain guns through corrupt licensed dealers, unregulated dealers, gun shows, organized gun rings and fences, and criminal firearms trafficking; and most of these firearms have been stolen.

A research project in Boston was able to reduce firearm-related homicides by youths by 75% by utilizing gun-tracing technologies to reduce the flow of guns to juveniles and by administering severe penalties for carrying illegal firearms (Kennedy, 1998; Kennedy, Piehl, & Braga, 1996). Another program, known as the Youth Firearms Violence Initiative, developed by the U.S. Department of Justice's Office of Community Oriented Services, has also demonstrated success in reducing firearm-related youth violence (Dunworth, 2000). Many other gun violence reduction programs involving community participation have begun throughout the United States (Lizotte & Sheppard, 2001).

SCHOOL VIOLENCE

During the last quarter of the 20th century, considerable public attention was directed at school violence. Anecdotal and media accounts of children being victimized at school by other children prompted researchers to study the issue to document the magnitude of the problem. In 1974 the U.S. Congress funded a 3-year study to evaluate the nature and extent of crime, violence, and disruption in the nation's schools. The National Institute of Education, which conducted the study, released its findings in 1977, and the Safe School Study (National Center for Education Statistics, 2006) remains the most comprehensive study available.

In the 2004–2005 school year, an estimated 54.9 million students in prekindergarten through Grade 12 were enrolled in about 125,000 U.S. elementary or secondary schools (National Center for Education Statistics, 2006). In that student population, serious violent crime generally occurred at a rate of about 6 incidents per 1,000. From July 2004 through June 2005, there were 21 homicides and 7 suicides of school-age youth (ages 5 to 18) at school (National Center for Education Statistics, 2006). These data correspond to one homicide or suicide of a school-age youth while at school per 2 million students. Students were far more likely to be victims of serious violence or homicide away from school, where violent crimes occurred at a rate of 12 per 1,000 students. For example, in each school year from 1992 to 2002, youths aged 5 to 19 were over 70 times more likely to be murdered away from school than at school. Still, national statistics indicate that about 1 out of 10 students in secondary schools fear that they will be attacked or harmed while at school (Verlinden, Hersen, & Thomas, 2000).

The topic of school violence took on a more chilling urgency in the later 1990s when a rash of school shootings made headlines. The most infamous case was the mass murder of 12 students and 1 teacher at Columbine High School in Littleton, Colorado, in April 1999. The two teenage boys who did the shootings committed suicide during the incident, during which 20 other students were injured. Although there had been a number of school shootings prior to Columbine—at least 10 between 1996 and 1999—the Columbine shooting prompted a great deal of alarm and concern nationwide. Unfortunately, the media and some experts were quick to make gross generalizations about the school violence problem. O'Toole (2000) lists the usual inaccurate or unverified impressions of school shooters that are often promoted by the news media, including the following:

- School violence is an epidemic.
- All school shooters are alike.
- The school shooter is always a loner.
- School shootings are motivated exclusively by revenge.
- Easy access to weapons is the most significant factor.
- Unusual or aberrant behaviors, interests, or hobbies are hallmarks of the student destined to become violent.

News reports of such incidents may engender a **contagion**, or **copycat, effect**, a tendency in some people to model or copy an activity portrayed in the entertainment or news media. A contagion effect is said to occur when action depicted in the media is assessed as a good idea and then mimicked. School shootings seem to be particularly susceptible to this phenomenon because of the widespread publicity they engender.

Investigations of school shooters have repeatedly found that the two characteristics that consistently emerge are peer rejection and societal rejection. A vast majority of shooters have poor social and coping skills and feel picked on or persecuted (Verlinden et al., 2000). They have expressed anger about being teased or ridiculed and have vowed revenge against particular individuals or groups, Moreover, as a group, school shooters have "lacked social support and prosocial relationships that might have served as protective factors" (Verlinden et al., 2000, p. 44). Cruelty to animals was prominent in the backgrounds of at least half of the shooters (Verlinden et al., 2000). In addition, they revealed a keen interest in guns and other weaponry and often had easy access to firearms. Most of these assailants expected to be killed or planned suicide during or immediately after their attacks, all of which seemed to be carefully planned and thought out beforehand.

In virtually all school shootings, investigators have discovered that the violent intentions of the assailants were repeatedly made clear to others—particularly peers—and often included the time and the place. However, peers rarely reported these threats to the authorities, for reasons that are not well understood, but fear seems to play a major role. A survey by the Safe Schools Coalition of Washington State (1999; cited in Verlinden et al., 2000) revealed that fear of not being believed, fear of retribution, and fear of what might happen to the youth threatening the school violence were the most frequently reported concerns of peers. Verlinden et al. (2000) concluded that the risk for school violence is high when there are multiple warning signs and risk factors. "The more signs there are and the greater the opportunity, motivation, and access to weapons, the greater the possibility that the child may commit a violent act" (Verlinden et al., 2000, p. 47).

In a national study of school violence, Gottfredson, Gottfredson, Payne, and Gottfredson (2005) report that schools in which students find the rules fair and in which discipline is managed consistently experience less violence and disorder—regardless of the type of school or community. The researchers also found that schools characterized by high teacher morale, focus, strong leadership, and high teacher involvement are protected from school crime and violence. The conclusion: School climate makes a significant difference in reducing the overall crime, disorder, and violence that occur within a school building.

JUVENILE BULLYING

School bullying came under intense public and media scrutiny after the shootings at Columbine High School in 1999 and Santana High School in Santee, California, in early 2001 (Ericson, 2001). Over the past 10 years, considerable research-based literature on the topic has emerged, much of it prompted by the information that school shooters were often rejected and bullied and took their revenge through violent actions. The individual who killed 31 students and professors at Virginia Tech in April 2007 was said to have been bullied in high school and ridiculed about his accent, to the point that he resisted speaking. Bullying is a common and significant problem for a large number of children throughout the world. It commonly occurs on playgrounds, in school hallways, neighborhoods, homes, and workplaces. It is also a very common phenomenon in correctional facilities, especially in juvenile ones. It is clear from the research that bullying is good neither for the victim nor for the perpetrator: Both bully victims and bullies themselves are highly disliked (Veenestra et al., 2005) and socially rejected by peers (Eslea et al., 2003).

Bullying is commonly defined as a form of peer aggression in which one or more individuals physically, verbally, and/or psychologically harass a weaker victim (Olweus, 1997; Vijoen, O'Neill, & Sidhu, 2005). In most cases, the bullying is repetitive in nature. Examples of **physical bullying** are hitting, spitting, kicking, punching, pushing, and taking personal belongings. **Verbal bullying** includes name calling, taunting, malicious teasing, and verbal threats. **Psychological bullying** includes spreading rumors and engaging in social exclusion, extortion, or intimidation. For males, physical and verbal bullying is the most common. For girls, verbal bullying (both taunting and making insults of a sexual nature), taking personal belongings, and spreading rumors are most common (Vijoen et al., 2005).

Bullying is most likely to occur as a function of power relationships. It involves a real or perceived imbalance of power, with the more powerful child or group attacking those who are less powerful (Ericson, 2001). There is a widespread belief that being bullied is character building and a necessary part of growing up. Most children can probably expect to experience some bullying or teasing in their early school years, but victims who experience *long-term* bullying often suffer humiliation, insecurity, and loss of self-esteem and develop a fear of going to school (Ericson, 2001). Depression is common, and in rare cases, bullied individuals may commit suicide. About half of bullies report being bullied themselves (Espelage & Swearer, 2003). Studies have shown with some consistency that bullies are at increased risk of becoming involved in serious delinquency and crime (Ericson, 2001; Veenestra et al., 2005). If the bullying is frequent and begins at an early age, early-onset delinquency is a good possibility.

JUVENILE HATE CRIMES

Hate crimes—also called bias crimes—are criminal offenses motivated by an offender's bias against a group to which the victim either belongs or is believed to belong. There must be an underlying criminal offense to qualify as a hate crime—for example, an assault, vandalism, arson, or murder. In this case the criminal conduct is motivated by hatred or prejudice.

The groupings, or protected categories, most commonly identified are race, religion, gender, disability, sexual orientation, and ethnicity. These categories are inclusive; that is, bias crime statutes protect all members of all races (not just blacks or whites) and persons of all sexual orientations (not just gays and lesbians). Statutes in some states also provide penalties for bias crimes against certain age groups (e.g., the elderly) or members of the military. The **Hate Crime Statistics Act** of 1990 requires the FBI to collect data and provide information on the nature and prevalence of violent attacks, intimidation, arson, or property damage directed at persons or groups because of bias against their race, religion, sexual orientation, or ethnicity. In September 1994 the Violent Crime and Control and Law Enforcement Act amended the hate crime act to include physical and mental disabilities in the data collection. Note that the statute does not include gender.

Based on national statistics, hate crimes account for a relatively small percentage of all criminal violence. However, the available data may underrepresent the actual prevalence. Documenting hate or bias crimes is difficult because the intentions of the offender are not always obvious or clear-cut. Law enforcement agencies record hate crimes only when the investigation reveals facts sufficient to conclude that the offender's actions were bias motivated. Available data indicate that the largest number of hate crimes are motivated by racial bias (44.9%), especially against African-Americans, followed by ethnic/national origin bias (21.6%), religious bias (14.3%), sexual orientation bias (14.3%), and disability bias (0.3%; FBI, 2005). Examples of a disability include AIDS, a mental disorder, and mental retardation. Hate crimes, compared to reported crimes in general, are seven times more likely to involve attacks against persons and are most likely committed by multiple offenders (Steinberg, Brooks, & Remtulla, 2003). According to Steinberg et al. (2003), many hate crimes are carried out by juveniles who have no prior involvement with juvenile justice but who see little wrong with their actions.

Unfortunately, up-to-date data on juvenile involvement in hate crimes are somewhat limited but do indicate that adolescents account for a significant proportion of the nation's hate crime, both as perpetrators and as victims. NIBRS data indicate that more than a third of persons arrested for hate crimes are younger than 18. Furthermore, juveniles are more likely to be arrested for property-related hate crimes, such as vandalism, whereas older persons are more likely to be arrested for violent hate crimes. About one-third of the known hate crimes involve juvenile offenders attacking juvenile victims. By far the most common bias crime committed by juveniles involves race; a distant second involves ethnicity, followed by sexual orientation and religion. Hate-motivated behavior—whether in the form of ethnic conflict, harassment, intimidation, or graffiti—is often apparent on school grounds. In the United States, approximately 40% of bias crimes occur in schools (Steinberg et al., 2003).

Summary and Conclusions

The great majority of offenses committed by juveniles are nonviolent. Nevertheless, the four index violent crimes—murder and nonnegligent manslaughter, forcible rape, robbery, and aggravated assault—are not foreign to young offenders. They were involved in 12% of all of those violent crimes solved by police. We discuss both index and nonindex violent offenses in this chapter, including the most common nonindex violent crime of simple assault. We also include the crime of arson.

A considerable amount of juvenile violence never comes to the attention of police and is not recorded in either victimization statistics or self-report data. Violence within families is a good example. Researchers note that little is known about this behavior, although self-report data do provide some insight. In a recent study, for example, 70% of high school seniors admitted committing at least one violent act against their closest-age sibling during their senior year. On the whole, though, sibling-to-sibling violence is often overlooked, trivialized, and considered normal. It may also be covered up in order to preserve the outward appearance of a harmonious family. Nonetheless, juvenile sibling violence has been linked to violence in dating relationships and in both family and nonfamily relationships in adulthood. It is not, therefore, a trivial matter. The victims of the most extreme forms of sibling violence, including sexual assault, are younger siblings.

Children's violence directed at their parents has received increasing research attention in recent years. Like sibling violence, this conduct is generally not recorded in official data. Self-report data, however, suggest that somewhere between 10% and 15%

of adolescents harm their parents with behavior ranging from pushing and shoving to using a weapon. Parental death at the hands of children is rare; approximately 2% of murder victims are killed by their children, usually their sons. This figure applies to perpetrators of all ages, however, and does not specify how many of them were juveniles. When youth do kill their parents (parricide), there is most often a family pattern of violence.

Gender differences are less apparent at moderate levels of violence, with both boys and girls aggressing about equally, and typically against their mothers. Violent incidents peak at age 15 and diminish thereafter, corresponding to the peak age of violence directed outside the family as well. Interestingly, violence during the primary school years, as reported by teachers, is predictive of violence toward a parent during adolescence. Studies indicate strong interaction effects in this type of family violence: Parents who are abusive, permissive, or harsh in their child-rearing techniques are the most likely to be recipients of violence from their children.

Robberies by juveniles are typically perpetrated against acquaintances, including other school-aged youths. These crimes rarely come to the attention of police. Aggravated assaults account for 6 of every 10 juvenile crimes known to police. Data indicate that these crimes are on the increase, with the female rate increasing more than the male rate. Males still make up the majority of juveniles arrested for aggravated assault, however. Aggravated assault—and simple assault—are often associated with violent juvenile gangs. Aggravated assault is the most frequent crime committed by serious and persistent violent offenders.

Juveniles are responsible for a large number of fires set in the United States—approximately 43%. However, the total number of both adult and juvenile arrests for arson has decreased over a 10-year span. On the other hand, it is believed that most fires set by youth are undetected, unreported, or unsolved. Fire setting by children often comes to light in the course of psychiatric or psychological treatment and counseling sessions or when parents, caretakers, or neighbors raise concerns. In one study, nearly a third of primary-grade students reported setting fires in their communities and in their own homes.

Psychologists have identified developmental stages in fire-setting behavior, with the late stages being particularly problematic and symbolic of serious juvenile offending. Many children are fascinated with fires and express interest, sometimes as early as age 3. Fire play—such as playing with matches and experimenting with small fires—occurs in many children between the ages of 5 and 9. Fire play is obviously of concern but does not seem to be indicative of future serious delinquency. Children who continue to set fires at age 10 and beyond are believed to represent the most problematic behavior. Researchers have found these youths to demonstrate poor social skills, impulsiveness, and inadequate social competence. They are more likely than peers to demonstrate ADHD, conduct problems, and poor impulse control. Juvenile fire setting at this stage and into adolescence represents only one behavior in a pattern of many other offenses, including rape and other sex offenses.

Much psychological research has been directed at both juvenile and adult sex offenders. It is estimated that just over half of adult sexual offenders began their offending in their youth; thus, early detection is a crucial consideration. Victims of juvenile sex offenders are typically younger than the offender and are usually female relatives or acquaintances. However, one type of sex offender—the juvenile rapist—typically chooses victims the same age or older. Almost all of the research focuses on male offenders, but some studies have begun to focus on female offenders. Victims of female

JSOs tend to be younger and are often children in the perpetrator's care. The female offender is more likely than the male offender to have been a victim of sexual assault.

Juvenile sex offenders come from a variety of racial, ethnic, and socioeconomic groups and differ widely in the crimes they commit as well as their level of violence. A significant number of sex offenders have learning difficulties and exhibit behavioral problems in school as well as in the home. JSOs have marked deficits in social and interpersonal skills, but research is mixed regarding the offender's own sexual victimization. Although there is evidence that a large number of offenders were themselves victimized, this is not as true for juvenile rapists. However, persistent, hard-core JSOs have a high incidence of prior sexual abuse and other developmental trauma during childhood. Their backgrounds are also characterized by parental and peer rejection, poor self-esteem, and an inability to form attachments.

Recent official data indicate that juveniles are responsible for a relatively small percentage—11%—of murders or nonnegligent manslaughter; only 2% are under age 15. Child delinquents (aged 7 to 12) are responsible for a small number of homicides, about 30 a year; the victims are typically younger than the perpetrators. These killings commonly involve gun play and thus do not reflect an intent to kill. In fact, access to weapons appears to be a major contributing factor to juvenile violence. Older juveniles who commit murder often have a history of severe educational difficulty, language handicaps, conduct disorders, and neurological abnormalities.

School violence, which appeared to be on the increase in the 1990s, has leveled off, but a high percentage of juveniles still report carrying weapons to school. Schools in which students find rules fair, discipline well managed, and teachers with high morale are generally protected from violence. However, the association between bullying and subsequent violent behavior is disturbing. Occasionally, children who are bullied decide to seek revenge by perpetrating violence on others. More typically, the child who is a persistent bullier moves on to become seriously antisocial.

Juvenile hate or bias crimes are an extremely disturbing trend among juveniles. According to NIBRS data, more than a third of persons arrested for hate crimes are younger than 18. However, the hate crimes of juveniles are more likely to be property offenses (e.g., vandalism), whereas those of adults are more likely to be violent. The most common hate crimes of juveniles indicate bias against race or ethnicity, followed by sexual orientation and religion. Almost half of all bias crimes committed by juveniles occur in schools.

Key Terms and Concepts

contagion effect

copycat effect

date rape

exhibitionism

fetishism

fratricide

frottage

Hate Crime Statistics Act

J-SOAP

matricide

multiassaultive families

paraphilias

parricide

patricide

physical bullying

Pittsburgh Youth Study

psychological bullying

siblicide

sororicide

verbal bullying

voyeurism

CHAPTER 10
SUBSTANCE AND ALCOHOL ABUSE

❧

CHAPTER OBJECTIVES

◆ Explore the extent of illicit drug use among the young in the United States

◆ Identify the illicit drugs most abused by juveniles

◆ Review the characteristics and circumstances of adolescents who sell drugs

◆ Identify the various sources of information on drug abuse

◆ Introduce the classification system of psychoactive drugs

◆ Discuss the relationship between drug and alcohol use and juvenile delinquency

Adolescent illicit drug use is widely regarded as one of today's most important social concerns (Ramirez et al., 2004). Although recent surveys in the United States (e.g., Johnston, O'Malley, Bachman, & Schulenberg, 2007; Substance Abuse and Mental Health Administration, 2005) indicate an overall decline or leveling off in the use of drugs and alcohol nationwide, a significant proportion of youth continues to be exposed to the deleterious effects of substance abuse. In 2004, 19.1 million Americans, or 7.9% of the population aged 12 or older, were current illicit drug users who had used the drug within the past month (Substance Abuse, 2005). Among all youths aged 12 to 17, 10.6% were illicit drug users in 2004. Marijuana was, by far, the most commonly used drug among this age group (Substance Abuse, 2005).

Drug use in early adolescence is associated with serious health problems, deviant behavior, high-risk behaviors, and poor academic performance. High-level chronic juvenile offenders are far more likely to use drugs and alcohol excessively, as compared to other juveniles (Wiesner et al., 2005). Figure 10–1 shows the age range of juveniles arrested by law enforcement for drug offenses in 2005.

EXTENT OF USE

A special report from the U.S. Department of Justice (FBI, 2005) reveals that juvenile arrests for drug-abuse violations—involving all drugs—increased 22.9% from 1994 to 2003. However, the data also reveal that in 1994, persons under 18 accounted for 11.8% of the arrests for drug abuse. Ten years later, the juvenile proportion of arrests for drug-abuse violations remained virtually identical at 11.6%. Thus, even though the number of juvenile arrests increased, the percentage of those arrests remained the same. The FBI Special Report defines *drug abuse* as including the sale/manufacturing or possession of an illegal drug. The report finds that most of the arrests of juveniles for

FIGURE 10–1   Juvenile Arrests for Drug Offenses (2005)

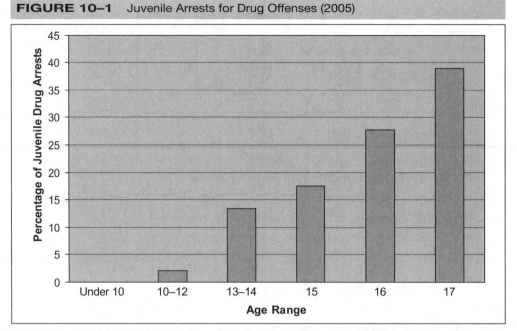

Source: Data from *Crime in the United States—2005* by Federal Bureau of Investigation, 2006, Washington, DC: U.S. Department of Justice, Author.

the period studied were for possession of drugs rather than for the sale or manufacturing of illegal substances.

When an individual is arrested for a drug-abuse violation in the United States, the arresting agency reports to the Department of Justice the type of drug. The types fall into four categories: (1) **opium** or **cocaine** and their derivatives (e.g., morphine, heroine, codeine), (2) **marijuana**, (3) **synthetic narcotics**, and (4) **dangerous nonnarcotic drugs**, such as Demerol and methadone. Between 1994 and 2003, the number of arrests of juveniles for violations involving opium or cocaine declined, while arrests involving marijuana increased. Marijuana remains the drug associated with the highest percentage of juveniles arrested for drug abuse. For example, male juveniles arrested for the sale/manufacturing and possession of marijuana increased from 55.1% of the drug arrests of male juveniles in 1994 to 74.0% in 2003. Arrests of juveniles for violations involving synthetic narcotics and dangerous nonnarcotics consistently accounted for the lowest percentage of juveniles arrested for drug-abuse violations during the 10-year period—and showed a downward trend. The percentage of arrests for violations involving opium or cocaine showed a decline during the 10-year period; arrests of male juveniles for violations involving opium or cocaine fell from 34.2% of the drug arrests of male juveniles in 1994 to 13.4% in 2003.

In 1994, 60.6% of juveniles arrested for drug-abuse violations were white. By 2003, however, that number had increased to 74.9%. Male juveniles were more frequently arrested for drug-abuse violations than female juveniles were, by an average ratio of 6 to 1. The data for the 10 years covered in the FBI Special Report showed that of the arrests in 1994 for drug-abuse violations involving juveniles under age 10, 83.0% were males and 17.0% were females. A decade later, the percentage of males under age 10 dropped to 78.9%, and the percentage of females increased to 21.1%, indicating that there may be a trend of more female juveniles being arrested at a younger age for drug-abuse violations.

Most research on drug and alcohol abuse and dependence has concentrated on males. The few studies that have focused on gender differences among adolescents have consistently shown that males consume alcohol and drugs of various kinds more frequently and in greater quantities than females do and are prone to experience more drug- and alcohol-related problems (Fothergill & Ensminger, 2006; Webb et al., 2002). In addition, there is increasing evidence that males and females experience different substance abuse trajectories and consequences (Fothergill & Ensminger, 2006). Girls who show little commitment to school and academic achievement are at increased risk for later substance-abuse problems (Fothergill & Ensminger, 2006).

There is little evidence that alcohol or drug use *causes* violence in adolescent offenders (H. R. White, Loeber, Stouthamer-Loeber, & Farrington, 1999). Research indicates that aggressive and violent behavior in childhood generally *precedes* the initiation into drug and alcohol abuse, at least in boys. Aggressive behavior in the early school grades and poor school achievement are two of the best predictors of substance abuse later in adolescence and adulthood (Fothergill & Ensminger, 2006). Serious male delinquents (including the most violent offenders) show by far the highest rates of consumption of alcohol, marijuana, and other drugs. On the other hand, girls who are considered shy in early grades are more likely to have high levels of educational attainment and are at low risk for substance or alcohol abuse in adolescence or adulthood (Fothergill & Ensminger, 2006).

ADOLESCENTS WHO SELL DRUGS

In a recent survey, one in nine high school students reported selling drugs during the past year, and most said they sold the drugs at school (Steinman, 2005). About 10% of the juveniles who bought marijuana said they purchased it at school (Substance Abuse, 2005). Students most likely to sell drugs on a regular basis are also more likely to engage in a variety of delinquent acts, including violence, heavy marijuana use, and other risky behaviors. These youths are often hired by older dealers, particularly in cities and larger metropolitan areas. Moreover, regular juvenile sellers generally do not have a strong relationship with their families and prefer to associate with other deviant peers who use and sell drugs. Many are members of gangs. However, for the purposes of explaining delinquency, students who *occasionally* sell drugs to friends and relatives should not be placed in the same category as the more routine seller who distributes a variety of substances. Occasional, friend-based sellers rarely are detected by the authorities and do not usually become involved in serious delinquency.

Little and Steinberg (2006) identified five factors that are significantly related to the tendency of adolescents to sell drugs on a regular and profitable basis: (1) low parental monitoring, (2) poor neighborhood conditions, (3) low neighborhood job opportunity, (4) parental substance use or abuse, and (5) high levels of association with peers involved in serious delinquency and substance abuse. As these researchers note, adolescents who report deriving substantial income from drug dealing also report very low levels of parental monitoring. In fact, the parents of drug-selling adolescents are often frequent drug users themselves. In addition, social scientists find that rising poverty rates in urban centers are closely associated with increased drug selling by disadvantaged youth, for whom the opportunity to make significant income legally is severely restricted by conditions that limit opportunities for education and jobs.

Little and Steinberg (2006) point out that adolescents who participate in the illicit drug market must also be willing to accept the enormous risk of violence, injury, legal sanction, and even death. The Little-Steinberg data support their hypothesis that individual differences in maturity affect adolescents' willingness to accept the risks and demands of drug dealing. Specifically, the researchers found some support for the observation that nonmarijuana drug dealing requires greater initiative, independence, and risk tolerance than dealing marijuana. "Maturity" is necessary because nonmarijuana drugs are more difficult for adolescents to obtain and protect.

THE PATH TO DRUG USE

Many developmental psychologists contend that substance abuse often takes place in an orderly sequence, starting with tobacco use, followed by marijuana, and then hard drug use as a last step (Kandel, Yamaguchi, & Chen, 1992; H. R. White et al., 1999). This observation gives some credence to the idea that marijuana is a "gateway drug," for which society should have zero tolerance, even for its possession in small amounts. **Gateway drugs** are believed to lead to the use of and experimentation with more varied substances, especially "hard drugs." However, before adolescents become dependent on alcohol, tobacco, or any illicit substance, they pass through a stage of **experimental substance use** (ESU; Petraitis, Flay, & Miller, 1995). An unknown number of youth experiment but do not continue with regular use; they try it, don't like it, and don't try it again. Events and variables that determine who experiments with substances and alcohol during adolescence and who continues to use them are multiple, including the availability of drugs, family history, peer pressure, social attitudes concerning drug use, the social and economic context, and individual differences in biopsychological/ psychological makeup. In addition, drug use and experimentation are strongly correlated with cognitions (i.e., attitudes and beliefs) about drugs. Adolescent substance and alcohol abuse is not a passive, one-dimensional process caused exclusively by social influence but is strongly influenced by subjective choices made by the youths (Getz & Bray, 2005). For example, rates of drug use are much higher in populations that do not perceive great risk of harm than in populations that do perceive great risk of harm. Thus, explanations for the sustained heavy use of marijuana in adolescents center partly around the belief that there is very little harm in the use of the drug. Many theories have been proposed to explain the phenomenon of ESU. However, most of these theories have not been empirically tested and do not offer convincing explanations of why some youth experiment with drugs while others do not.

SOURCES OF INFORMATION

Much of this information on the frequency of use by adolescents is found in the publication *Monitoring the Future* (MTF), which reports on an ongoing research project funded by the National Institute of Drug Abuse (NIDA) and administered and analyzed at the Institute for Social Research of the University of Michigan. The data are based on surveys of representative samples of American 8th-, 10th-, and 12th-grade students in both public and private secondary schools across the country. The surveys were started in 1975 and have continued through 2006, with a sample size in 2006 of nearly 48,500 students from 410 schools (Johnston et al., 2007). The surveys are administered to students by University of Michigan staff during regular class periods; participation is voluntary. In the 2006 survey, the proportions that reported *ever* having tried any illicit substance (excluding alcohol) were 21%, 36%, and 48% in Grades 8, 10, and 12, respectively (Johnston et al., 2007). In other words, just under half of American secondary school students today have tried an illicit drug by the time they reach high school graduation. Table 10–1 shows other results for high school seniors.

The 2006 MTF surveys found that a number of drugs showed declines in use, but the declines were modest, not statistically significant, and were usually confined to one grade. Four drugs—OxyContin, Vicodin, Ecstasy, and inhalants—showed an increase in use.

A second source of information about drug abuse is the **National Survey on Drug Use and Health (NSDUH)**. The survey, formerly called the National Household Survey on Drug Abuse (NHSDA), is a project of the Substance Abuse and Mental Health Services Administration. The survey was initiated in 1971 and is considered the primary source of information on the use of illicit drugs, alcohol, and tobacco by the civilian, noninstitutionalized population of the United States aged 12 years or older. Approximately 67,500 persons are interviewed each year.

Still another source of information is the **Drug Abuse Warning Network (DAWN)** report (Office of Applied Studies, 2004). DAWN is a public health surveillance system that monitors drug-related visits to hospital emergency departments (EDs) and drug-related deaths investigated by medical examiners and coroners. DAWN includes ED visits associated with substance abuse and drug misuse, both intentional and accidental.

It is important to keep in mind throughout this chapter that drug and alcohol abuse among children and adolescents is extremely transient and often geographically confined. The prevalence of any drug depends heavily on the preference, accessibility,

TABLE 10–1: Percentages of High School Seniors Reporting Drug Use (2001–2006)

	2001	*2003*	*2006*
Lifetime marijuana	49.0	46.1	42.3
Lifetime inhalants	56.0	52.8	51.2
Lifetime hallucinogens	14.7	10.6	8.3
Lifetime cocaine	8.2	7.7	8.5
Lifetime crack	3.7	3.6	3.5
Lifetime heroin	1.8	1.5	1.4
Lifetime methamphetamine	16.2	14.4	12.4
Any illicit drug	53.9	51.1	48.2
Any illicit drug other than marijuana	30.7	27.7	26.9

Source: Data from *Monitoring the Future: National Results on Adolescent Drug Use: Overview of Key Findings, 2006* by L. D. Johnston, P. M. O'Malley, J. G. Bachman, and J. E. Schulenberg, 2007, Bethesda, MD: National Institute on Drug Abuse.

and perception of whatever is "fashionable" in the area at a particular time. Consequently, prevalence of abuse is constantly in a state of flux among the young, and percentages reported by any survey are highly susceptible to change within a short period of time.

CLASSIFICATION OF PSYCHOACTIVE DRUGS

The term **psychoactive drugs** refers to a group of drugs that affect psychological processes, including thought, emotions, and perceptions. Four major categories of psychoactive drugs will be covered here, although we will deviate slightly from the four categories typically used by government publications. We will follow instead the classification system traditionally used by the medical community and pharmacological researchers (see Table 10–2). To keep the chapter within manageable limits, within each group we will focus on only one or a few representative drugs that are most commonly used by juveniles.

The **hallucinogens**, or **psychedelics**—which include LSD (lysergic acid diethylamine), mescaline, psilocybin, phencyclidine, ketamine, marijuana, and hashish—are our first category. The hallucinogens are chemicals that lead to a change in consciousness involving an alteration of reality, sometimes generating hallucinations. In some respects, these drugs replace the present world with an alternative one, although persons using them can generally attend to their altered state and to reality simultaneously. Because of its widespread use by juveniles, marijuana is the main drug we will cover in the hallucinogens category. We will also touch briefly on phencyclidine (PCP), a powerful drug that goes in cycles of juvenile use. In addition, we will give some attention to ketamine, because of its association with teen parties and acquaintance rape.

Next, we will discuss the **stimulants**, so called because they appear to stimulate central nervous system functions. They include amphetamines (including methamphetamine), methylphenidate (Ritalin), clinical antidepressants, cocaine, caffeine, and nicotine. Again, because of an alleged relationship with juvenile use and offending, the amphetamines and cocaine will be highlighted.

The third group includes the **opiate narcotics**, which generally have sedative (sleep-inducing) and analgesic (pain-relieving) effects. Heroin will be featured in this section. The heroin addict appears frequently in crime statistics, since it is believed that

TABLE 10–2: Four Categories of Psychoactive Drugs

Category	Effects
Hallucinogens	• Changes in consciousness involving alteration of perceptions, sometimes generating hallucinations
Stimulants	• Increase in alertness, excitation, euphoria; enhanced ability to think and function
Opiate narcotics	• Like sedatives (sleep-inducing) or analgesic compounds (pain relieving); effective in cough suppression
Sedative-hypnotic compounds	• Depression of central nervous system functioning; slowing of mental and physical functioning (interference with self-regulation and judgment, reflexes, muscular coordination)

he or she often turns to crime—particularly property crime—to finance this expensive habit. In recent years heroin has become increasingly available to juveniles.

Finally, alcohol will represent the **sedative-hypnotic compounds**. These compounds depress central nervous system functions. In most instances, the sedative-hypnotics are capable of sedating the nervous system and reducing anxiety and tension.

The relationship between drugs and delinquency can be viewed from three perspectives: (1) the sale, manufacture, and distribution of illegal substances and alcohol; (2) the use and possession of illegal substances; and (3) the pharmacological effects of certain drugs on behavior, particularly in promoting antisocial and violent actions. The four-category classification system covered in this chapter is based on the last perspective. Specifically, we are most concerned about the effects the drugs have on the neurophysiology and behavior of the individual.

RELATIONSHIP AMONG DRUGS, ALCOHOL, AND DELINQUENT BEHAVIOR2

The relationship between drugs and antisocial behavior is a complex one. A threefold interaction must be considered: (1) the pharmacological effects of the drug, that is, the chemical impact of the drug on the body; (2) the psychological characteristics of the individual using the drug; and (3) the psychosocial conditions under which the drug is taken. Each of these factors influences the behavior of the individual who is using the drug.

Pharmacological effects are determined by various components of the nervous system (e.g., the amount of neurotransmitter substances within neurons), body weight, blood composition, and other neurophysiological features that significantly influence the chemical effects of the drug. Psychological variables include the mood of the person at the time the drug is consumed, previous experience with the drug, and the person's expectations about the drug's effects. Psychosocial variables include the social atmosphere under which the drug is taken. For example, the people who are present and their expectations, moods, and behavior may all influence an individual's reactions to a drug.

Given all of these variables and the fact that antisocial behavior is highly complex to begin with, deciphering the delinquency–drug connection becomes very difficult, and conclusions tend to be elusive and tentative. The relationship between drugs and delinquency is likely to be further complicated by the cultural and subcultural aspects of drug consumption. Unfortunately, very little research has focused on the contributions of gender or ethnicity to the use of alcohol or drugs (Fothergill & Ensminger, 2006; Petraitis, Flay, & Miller, 1995). In addition, substance preferences shift and change depending on drug availability, law enforcement priorities, and changes in cultural attitudes.

DRUG TOLERANCE AND DEPENDENCE

These two terms are consistently used in the drug literature: tolerance and dependence. **Drug tolerance** is the "state of progressively decreased responsiveness to a drug" (Julien, 1975, p. 29). Tolerance is indicated if an individual requires a larger dose of a drug to reach the same effects previously experienced. In other words, the person has become psychologically and physiologically used to, or habituated to, the drug.

Dependence may be physical, psychological, or both. In simple terms, **physical dependence** refers to the physiological distress and physical pain a person suffers by going without a drug for any length of time. The entertainment media often portray a person going through withdrawal as enduring increasingly severe tremors, headaches, sweating, vomiting, and/or hallucinations. **Psychological dependence** is difficult to distinguish from physical dependence but is characterized by an overwhelming desire to use a drug for its favorable effect. A dependent person is convinced that he or she needs the drug to maintain an optimal sense of well-being. The degree of both physical and psychological dependence varies widely from person to person and drug to drug. In its extreme form, a person's life may be permeated with thoughts of procuring and using the drug, and the user may resort to crime to obtain it. In common parlance, a person who is extremely psychologically and/or physically dependent is an addict.

Secondary psychological dependence may also develop. While primary dependence is associated with the reward of the drug experience (positive reinforcement), secondary dependence refers to expectancies about aversive withdrawal or the painful effects that will accompany the absence of the drug. Thus, to avoid the anticipated pain and discomfort associated with withdrawal, an individual continues to take the drug (negative reinforcement).

The **Controlled Substances Act** (CSA), which is Title II of the Comprehensive Drug Abuse Prevention and Control Act of 1970, places all substances of potential abuse into one of five schedules, based on the substance's medical use, potential for abuse, and dependence potential (see Table 10–3). The purpose of the act is to control the distribution, classification, sale, and use of psychoactive drugs that have the potential for abuse. Although the term *potential for abuse* is not specifically defined in the CSA, classifications are based on available evidence that these drugs can create a hazard to health or can jeopardize the safety of other persons or that there is a significant diversion of the drugs from legitimate drug channels.

TABLE 10–3: Drug Schedules Outlined in the Controlled Substances Act

Schedule	Potential for Abuse	Accepted Medical Use in U.S.	Physical Dependence	Psychological Dependence	Examples
I	High	No	High	High	Heroin, LSD, marijuana
II	High	Yes	High	High	PCP, cocaine, morphine, methamphetamine
III	Medium	Yes	Moderate	High	Codeine, steroids, barbiturates
IV	Low	Yes	Low	Low	Darvon, Talwin, Valium, Xanax
V	Low	Yes	Low	Low	Cough medicines with codeine

Source: Based on *Drugs of Abuse* by Drug Enforcement Administration, 2000, Washington, DC: U.S. Department of Justice.

HALLUCINOGENS AND DISSOCIATIVE DRUGS

As described earlier, hallucinogens are drugs that engender hallucinations, which are distortions in a person's perceptions and interpretations of reality. Under the influence of these drugs, individuals see images, hear sounds, and feel sensations that may seem real to them but do not exist. These drugs also cause delusions, which are strong beliefs that misrepresent reality. Both are temporary and normally dissipate after the drug's effects wear off. Hallucinogens have been used for thousands of years, by many cultures, and in various socially approved ways, including religious ceremonies to instill mystical insights and visions. Various plant compounds, such as mescaline and psilocybin, have been commonly used. Although LSD is the drug most commonly identified with the term *hallucinogen* in this country, marijuana can also be classified in this category.

MARIJUANA

Marijuana (*Cannabis sativa*), which apparently originated in Asia, is among the oldest and most frequently used intoxicants. It is the most popular illegal drug used in the United States (Substance Abuse, 2005), although there are surveys showing a slight decline in use over the past 5 years (Johnston, O'Malley, Bachman, & Schulenberg, 2006). In 2004 there were 14.6 million current users in the United States (Substance Abuse, 2005), and 40% of the U.S. population aged 12 and older reported having tried marijuana at least once. Approximately 3.2 million Americans use marijuana on a daily or almost-daily basis (Department of Health and Human Services, 2005; Office of National Drug Control Policy, 2005). In 2003 about one in five drug-related visits to emergency departments across the country were related to the effects of marijuana (Substance Abuse and Mental Health Services Administration, 2004), and 15% of the marijuana-related visits were by youths under age 18.

Marijuana is also one of the most popular illegal drugs used by juveniles (Department of Health and Human Services, 2003; FBI, 2005; Johnston et al., 2007), third only to alcohol and tobacco in terms of prevalence of use (Windle & Wiesner, 2004). Almost all youths who report using any substance indicate that they have used marijuana (McClelland, Teplin, & Abram, 2004). According to the 2006 *Monitoring the Future* study, 11.7% of 8th graders, 25.2% of 10th graders, and 31.5% of 12th graders have tried marijuana at least once during the past 12 months (Johnston et al., 2007). In that same national study, 6.5% of 8th graders, 14.2% of 10th graders, and 18.3% of 12th graders said they had used marijuana in the previous month. That survey also found that 42.3% of high school students had used marijuana at least once during their lifetimes. In those surveys, a substantial majority of the middle school, high school, and college students all indicated that marijuana is "fairly easy" or "very easy" to obtain. In 2005, for example, 85% of 12th graders and 71% of 10th graders indicated that it was "fairly easy" or "very easy" to get marijuana (Johnston et al., 2007). Perhaps even more startling, in 2006, 40% of 8th graders said marijuana was relatively easy to get. The average age of first use of marijuana is about 13.5 years of age.

Most marijuana users get the drug from friends, either free or by purchase (see Figure 10–2). More than half who bought their marijuana purchased it inside a home,

FIGURE 10–2 Sources of Marijuana for Adolescents (Ages 12–17)

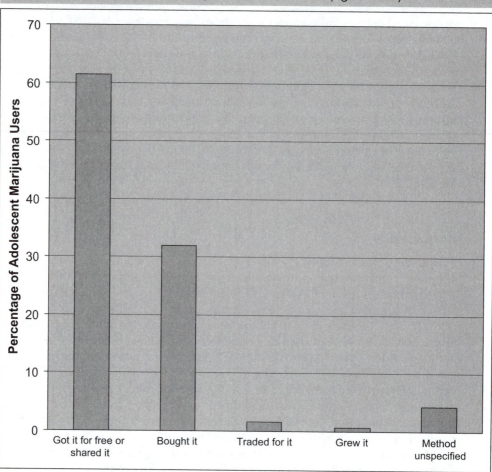

Source: Data from *Monitoring the Future: National Results on Adolescent Drug Use: Overview of Key Findings, 2006* by L. D. Johnston, P. M. O'Malley, J. G. Bachman, and J. E. Schulenberg, 2007, Bethesda, MD: National Institute on Drug Abuse.

apartment, or dorm. About 9% of youths bought their marijuana inside a school building.

Of all the arrests made in 2004, 39% were for marijuana possession and another 5% were for marijuana sale, production, or trafficking (Office of National Drug Control Policy, 2005). Although marijuana is usually not considered a "hard" and dangerous drug, it is illegal and can lead to conviction and incarceration. In addition, heavy use has been linked to a range of poor health outcomes similar to those of heavy cigarette smoking (Windle & Wiesner, 2004). Incarceration for possession, however, is rare, especially for a first offense.

Marijuana and its natural derivatives are classified as Schedule I of the **Controlled Substances Act** because they have generally no medical use in the United States (Drug Enforcement Administration, 2005). In *United States v. Oakland Cannabis Buyers*

Cooperative (2000), this classification was challenged, but the U.S. Supreme Court agreed that marijuana has no medical value and should continue as a Schedule I substance. Nevertheless, many in the medical profession recognize its ability to manage pain in individuals suffering severe illness, such as cancer. Moreover, although some degree of tolerance, dependence, and mild withdrawal symptoms have been reported by heavy smokers, marijuana is generally not considered an addictive or habit-forming drug (Hollister, 1998). Thus, although it remains a Schedule I substance, a number of states do allow marijuana to be prescribed in controlled amounts for palliative care.

Background and Description

The earliest reference to marijuana was found in a book on pharmacy written by the Chinese emperor Shen Nung in 2737 B.C. (Ray, 1972). It was called the "Liberator of Sin" and recommended for such ailments as "female weakness," constipation, and absentmindedness. The word *marijuana* is commonly believed to have derived from *mary jane,* Mexican slang for cheap tobacco, or from the Portuguese word *mariguano*, meaning "intoxicant."

The drug is prepared from the plant *Cannabis*, an annual that is cultivated or grows freely as a weed in both tropical and temperate climates. Canada is fast becoming a primary source for indoor-grown, high-potency marijuana (15% to 25% THC, sometimes called "BC bud") bound for the United States (Office of National Drug Control Policy, 2005). There are at least three species of *Cannabis*—*sativa*, *indica*, and *ruderalis*—each differing in psychoactive potency. The psychoactive (i.e., intoxicating) properties of the plant reside principally in the chemical Delta-9 tetrahydrocannabinol **(THC)**, found mainly in its resin. Thus, the concentration and quality of THC within parts of the plant determine the potency or psychoactive power of the drug. In recent years, research has resulted in the development and marketing of a synthetic THC product, called Marinol®, to control nausea and vomiting caused by chemotherapy and to stimulate appetite in AIDS patients.

THC content varies from one preparation to another, partly because of the quality of the plant itself, but also because of its environment. The strain of the plant (there are over 200), the climate, and the soil conditions all affect THC content. For example, the resin is believed to retard the dehydration of the flowering elements and thus is produced in greater quantities in hot, tropical climates (Hofmann, 1975). Consequently, marijuana grown in the tropics (Mexico, Columbia, Jamaica, and North Africa) presumably has greater psychoactive potential than does American-grown hemp. However, THC potency appears to be more a feature of the species of the plant than of geographic area or climatic conditions.

Enterprising horticulturists in the 1990s were able to develop cannabis strains that easily contained 15% or more THC. Marijuana growers have also been able to breed cannabis strains that have a set of particular psychological and physiological effects, in much the same way that winemakers breed grapes that produce a particular flavor or bouquet in wine (Weisheit, 1992).

Marijuana is usually prepared by cutting the stem beneath the lowest branches, air drying, and stripping seeds, bracts, flowers, leaves, and small stems from the plant. This procedure results in a green, brown, or gray mixture of dried material. The female cannabis plant produces more resin than the larger male plant but slows down resin production once it is fertilized. Therefore, knowledgeable marijuana growers usually separate the male and female plants before pollination occurs, thereby allowing the female plant to continue producing higher levels of THC (although it remains seedless). The higher THC content in the female plant is not found in the leaves or stems but in the buds. *Sinsemilla*, which is Spanish for "without seeds," is a potent form of marijuana produced by harvesting the resinous buds from the unpollinated female plant.

Along with marijuana, hashish—another cannabis extract—is also commonly used in the United States. *Hashish*, the Arabic word for "dry grass," is produced by scraping or in some other way extracting the resin secreted by the flowers. Therefore, hashish—which is usually sold in this country in small cubes, cakes, or even cookie-like shapes—has more THC content than marijuana, with a range as high as 28%.

Both hashish and hash oil (red oil) are produced by repeated extractions of cannabis plant materials, a process that results in a dark, viscous liquid with an average THC content of 16% and a range as high as 43% (Drug Enforcement Administration, 2000). A drop or two on a regular cigarette usually has the effect of one marijuana cigarette.

When exposed to air over a period of time, marijuana appears to lose its psychoactive potency, as THC is converted to cannabinol and other inactive compounds (Mechoulam, 1970). One study found that marijuana exposed to light and air over the course of a year lost more than half of its THC (Weisheit, 1992). Moreover, marijuana with higher levels of THC appears to deteriorate more rapidly than marijuana with lower THC. In the United States, marijuana and hashish are usually smoked, most often in hand-rolled cigarettes (commonly called a "joint" or a "nail") or in a pipe, or "bong." A common practice in some countries is to consume cannabis as "tea" or mixed with other beverages or food. In recent years some youths have developed a method of slicing open a cigar, replacing the tobacco with marijuana, and thus making what they call a "blunt."

There are a wide variety of slang names for marijuana (at last count, over 200), with some of them changing almost monthly. Some terms from the mid-20th century and even before are still used—pot, herb, grass, Mary Jane, weed, reefer. More recent names include boom, gangster, kif, ganja, skunk, and Aunt Mary. There are also an assortment of street names for the different strains, such as Texas tea, Maui wowie, and chronic.

Effects

The psychological effects of cannabis are so subjective and so dependent on such a wide range of variables that any generalizations must be accompanied by the warning that there are numerous exceptions. The strong influence of extrapharmacological factors, together with the widespread variation in THC content in any sample of cannabis, makes it exceedingly difficult to obtain comparable research data. Essentially, the effects of cannabis are unique to each individual. Except for increases in heart rate and peripheral blood flow and the reddening of the membranes around the eyes, there are few consistent physiological changes reported for all persons.

Whoever uses marijuana must *learn* to use it to reach a euphoric "stoned" or "high" state. Ray (1983) reported that a three-stage learning process is involved: First, users must inhale the smoke deeply and hold it in their lungs for 20 to 40 seconds. Then, they must learn to identify and control the effects. Finally, they must learn to label the effects as pleasant. Some users, even experienced ones, may suffer acute anxiety and paranoid thoughts with high levels of THC, but these reactions wear off within a few hours.

Although the psychoactive effects last only 4 to 6 hours (Hollister, 1998), traces of THC (metabolites) may remain in the body for up to 6 months after smoking a single joint. These long-term traces are absorbed by the fatty tissues of the body and consequently can rarely be detected by standard urine testing, since they are usually eliminated by the digestive system through the feces. Because experienced marijuana smokers customarily inhale the smoke deeply and retain it for as long as possible, chronic marijuana users suffer the same health problems (e.g., bronchitis, emphysema, and bronchial asthma) that heavy cigarette smokers experience (Hollister, 1998). In fact, there is some evidence that smoking marijuana in heavy amounts may be more toxic to the lungs than smoking an equal amount of tobacco (Wu, Tashkin, Jiahed, & Rose, 1988). However, the great majority of marijuana users do not consume the equivalent of an average smoker's daily portion of tobacco. Other long-term health hazards of using marijuana are complicated and inconclusive (Hollister, 1998; Mechoulam & Golan, 1998).

Relationship with Delinquency

Marijuana certainly promotes relaxation and interferes with judgment, and it probably makes people more daring and more prone to risk taking. The drug is used extensively as a recreation enhancer. Although it is illegal to produce, possess, sell, or consume marijuana in most jurisdictions in the United States, there is little evidence that the drug propels nonviolent people to become violent or antisocial or to engage in serious criminal behavior. People who act violently under the influence of the drug have had a history of violence *before* using the drug.

Several studies (e.g., Flory, Lynam, Milch, Leukefeld, & Clayton, 2004; Gou et al., 2002) have indicated that marijuana use by adolescents varies in terms of who uses it, how frequently, and for how long. An important study by Windle and Wiesner (2004) is based on the reasonable assumption that juvenile marijuana use continually changes across a youth's developmental years. In their 2-year longitudinal study of 1,205 adolescents, these researchers were able to identify five different developmental trajectories of marijuana use (and nonuse): abstainers, experimental users, decreasers, increasers, and high chronics. Abstainers, those who never reported marijuana use *during the study period*, were the largest group identified, making up 82.4% of the sample. Note that this percentage looks suspiciously high, considering the MTF data. The experimental users (8.8%) were those adolescents who rarely used marijuana. The increasers (3.6%) began using marijuana at a relatively low level but continuously increased their consumption during the study. Two other groups began with a relatively high level of marijuana consumption: The decreasers (3.4%) gradually reduced their use of the drug during the study period, but the high chronics (1.8%) remained high throughout the study. There were no significant gender differences in these groupings. Table 10–4 summarizes these findings.

Compared to the other trajectory groups, the high chronics had higher levels of delinquency, lower academic performance, more drug-using friends, and more stressful life events. The high chronics reported using marijuana an average of 20 days a month during the 2 years of the study. Abstainers, on the other hand, had the lowest levels of involvement with delinquency and the highest levels on protective factors such as perceived family support and better academic achievement. A similar finding was reported by Flory et al. (2004), and H. R. White et al. (1999) reported that *early* marijuana use was

TABLE 10–4: Research Findings of Windle and Wiesner

Developmental Trajectory	Percentage of Sample	Extent of Marijuana Use
Abstainers	82.4	No usage during study period
Experimental users	8.8	Rarely used marijuana
Increasers	3.6	Started low but increased use continuously
Decreasers	3.4	Started high but gradually decreased use
Chronics	1.8	Started high and continued at that level

Source: Based on "Trajectories of Marijuana Use from Adolescence to Young Adulthood: Predictors and Outcomes" by M. Windle and M. Wiesner, 2004, *Development and Psychopathology, 16*, pp. 1007–1027.

associated with *later* violence in adolescence. These data underscore the observation that high and early use of marijuana is associated with serious delinquency, criminal behavior, and other substance abuse during adolescence and young adulthood.

Both independent research and investigations conducted by government-sponsored commissions, however, strongly indicate that marijuana does not *directly* contribute to or cause criminal behavior. The studies do indicate that early and consistent heavy marijuana use by youth goes hand in hand with other drug abuse and with antisocial and delinquency behavior. For example, frequent marijuana users are believed to be six times more likely to become frequent cocaine users than those who do not smoke marijuana (Office of National Drug Control Policy, 2004). But for those juveniles who engage in violence and other antisocial behavior, their behavior *preceded* their initiation into drug and alcohol use (H. R. White et al., 1999). White et al. (1999) further point out that the association between early and heavy marijuana use and increases in serious antisocial behavior may reflect a selection effect. That is, those who use marijuana are usually those who use alcohol and other illegal substances heavily also, and they tend to have been more antisocial and violent before their marijuana use.

Years ago, after an extensive review of available literature, the National Commission on Marijuana and Drug Abuse (1972) came to this conclusion:

> There is no systematic empirical evidence, at least that is drawn from the American experience, to support the thesis that the use of marijuana either inevitably or generally causes, leads to or precipitates criminal, violent, aggressive or delinquent behavior of a sexual or nonsexual nature. If anything, the effects observed suggest that marijuana may be more likely to neutralize criminal behavior and to militate against the commission of aggressive acts. (p. 470)

This conclusion can be explained by the fact that one of the predominant effects of THC is relaxation, resulting in a marked decrease in physical activity. THC induces muscular weakness and an inability to sustain physical effort, so that the user wishes to stay relatively motionless. As Tinklenberg and Stillman (1970) note, "'Being stoned' summarizes these sensations of demobilizing lethargy" (p. 341). It is difficult to imagine "stoned" users engaging in assaultive or violent activity. If anything, THC should reduce the likelihood of criminal activity, particularly aggressive conduct, at least while the individual is under the influence of the drug.

Although the empirical evidence so far indicates that cannabis does not, as a rule, stimulate aggressive behavior or other criminal actions, whenever we deal with human behavior, there will be exceptions. Individuals familiar with the effects of cannabis have heard of occasional negative experiences produced by THC. Although rare, some people do report feelings of panic, hypersensitivity, feelings of being out of contact with surroundings, and bizarre behavior. Some individuals have also experienced rapid, disorganized intrusions of irrelevant thoughts, which prompted them to feel that they were losing control of their minds. Under these conditions, it is plausible that users would interpret the actions of others as threatening and possible that these panicked individuals might attack those around them. In addition, marijuana does have adverse effects on many of the skills needed to drive a car and may lead to reckless or impaired driving, resulting in serious and fatal car accidents. These accidents can then lead to criminal charges, particularly in the case of fatalities. As for the mistaken notion that marijuana is a gateway drug, recent research (e.g., Simons, Gaher, Correia, & Bush, 2005) does indicate that marijuana use is closely connected to club drug use (discussed later in the chapter). However, the researchers emphasize that their finding does not suggest that people who use marijuana *will* progress to use club drugs or any other drugs. Only a small minority of people who use marijuana progress to other drugs (Glantz, Weinberg, Miner, & Colliver, 1999).

In summary, there is no solid evidence to indicate that cannabis contributes to or encourages violent or property crime, in spite of continuing beliefs that this relationship exists. In fact, there is evidence to suggest that cannabis users are less criminally or violently inclined *under the influence of the drug* than are users of other drugs, such as alcohol and amphetamines. There are also no data to support that cannabis is habit forming to the point that a user must get a "fix" and will resort to crime to purchase the drug.

Delinquent or antisocial youth do appear to be more inclined than other youth to use marijuana and its derivatives. However, the primary reason is that marijuana provides a quick, relatively cheap, easy, and certain short-term pleasure for those adolescents looking for immediate gratification. The use of the substance also represents a form of rebellion against the strictures of the adult world. In addition, these youth are more likely to come into contact with peers and young adults, even older adults, who present drug use as the normative thing to do.

PHENCYCLIDINE (PCP)

PCP may be classified as a central nervous system depressant, anesthetic, tranquilizer, or hallucinogen. It has many effects, but most pronounced are its barbiturate-like downer effect, its perceptual distortions and hallucinations, and its amphetamine-like upper effects (such as excitation and hyperactivity). An overdosed person might show signs of moving from upper to downer effects while having hallucinations.

PCP was first synthesized in 1957 but, because of its psychotic and hallucinogenic reactions, was taken off the market for human consumption in 1965 and was limited to veterinary medicine as an animal immobilizing agent. Between 1973 and 1979 the popularity of PCP increased but then declined briefly between 1979 and 1981. It then showed a resurgence in popularity between 1982 and 1990 but has shown a strong decrease in recent years (Substance Abuse and Mental Health Services Administration, 1995). The 2006 MTF indicates that only 2.2% of high school seniors have tried PCP at least once in their lifetimes.

The behavior of some individuals under the influence of PCP is highly unpredictable and may lead to life-threatening situations. The drug is marketed under a number of other names—including Angel Dust, Supergrass, Killer Weed, Embalming Fluid, and Rocket Fuel—because of its range of bizarre and volatile effects (Drug Enforcement Administration, 2005). Under the spell of a PCP psychosis, delusions of superhuman strength, persecution, and grandiosity are not uncommon. On occasion, individuals might use weapons to defend themselves and commit other acts of violence. However, the incidence of violence caused by PCP influence is unknown.

There is wide variation in the degree of purity and in dosage forms of PCP manufactured in clandestine laboratories. It comes in capsules, tablets, liquids, or powders and can be administered orally, by inhalation, and by intravenous injection. Users usually combine PCP with other drugs, particularly marijuana and alcohol. PCP can cause death, although the majority of fatal doses have been combined with alcohol (Brunet, Reiffenstein, Williams, & Wong, 1985–1986). In light of its adverse and negative effects, the reasons for its popularity remain obscure.

Available evidence clearly indicates that PCP users, including juveniles, tend to be multiple illicit drug users, or **polydrug users**. Polydrug users abuse a number of drugs, often at the same time. The extent to which PCP propels a person toward a life of crime is largely unknown, but it does not seem likely that a PCP user would regularly engage in crime to support a PCP habit because the drug is cheap and readily available. Nonetheless, PCP users are generally polydrug users who have demonstrated a variety of antisocial behaviors prior to PCP usage. Polydrug usage is more likely to be one symptom within a complicated matrix of many symptoms found in certain individuals habitually "going against" their cultural and social environments.

LYSERGIC ACID DIETHYLAMIDE (LSD)

LSD, commonly referred to as "acid," was first discovered in 1938 at the Sandoz Laboratories in Switzerland. It was marketed initially as a circulatory and respiratory stimulant but was later used as a research drug in investigating the causes of schizophrenia. The drug is manufactured from lysergic acid, which is found in a fungus that grows on rye and other grains. LSD is usually clear white, odorless, and water soluble and is typically produced in crystalline form. LSD begins to degrade and discolor soon after it is manufactured; it is sold on the street in capsule, tablet, or liquid form. LSD has been manufactured in the form of small tablets (microdots), thin squares of gelatin (window panes), and sugar cubes. At this writing, the most common form of LSD is called "blotter acid," which is sheets of paper soaked in LSD and perforated into ¼-inch-square, individual-dosage units (National Institute on Drug Abuse, 2005). Often the paper used is colored paper so that a buyer may have difficulty determining the drug's purity or age. According to the Drug Enforcement Administration (2003), LSD is the most potent hallucinogen known to science.

The effects of LSD are highly unpredictable and, similar to those of marijuana, depend on the amount taken, the social environment during ingestion, and the user's expectations and mood. The user most commonly has vivid and intense hallucinations. In some instances, the senses seem to reverse, with the user seeing sounds and hearing or feeling colors. "Bad trips" are not uncommon, such as when the user has terrifying images and thoughts, or feelings of despair and hopelessness. LSD is not considered an addictive drug since it does not produce compulsive drug-seeking behavior and cravings. Users do, however, develop a high degree of tolerance for the drug's effects rather quickly.

Although LSD use among juveniles has decreased since reaching a peak in 1996, about 2% of high school students continue to use the drug on a regular basis (Johnston et al., 2007). The use of LSD moves in cycles, becoming popular during some years but then waning in others. Recently, there has been a sharp decrease in its use, probably due in part to its reduced availability to adolescents.

KETAMINE

Ketamine—also called K, Special K, Super Acid, LA Coke, or cat valium—is a dissociative anesthetic with analgesic and amnesic (i.e., conducive to forgetfulness) properties. It was developed in 1962 to replace PCP in veterinary medicine and was first manufactured in the United States as Ketalar (Copeland & Dillon, 2005). Use of ketamine as a surgical anesthetic gained significant popularity on the battlefields of Vietnam (Copeland & Dillon, 2005). Much of the ketamine sold on U.S. streets today is probably intended for veterinary clinics or is imported from overseas. When sold illicitly, it is often converted from a liquid to a powder—similar in appearance to cocaine and heroin—or tablets. Reports indicate that ketamine is being increasingly used in social rather than medical and scientific settings in many parts of the world, especially the United Kingdom and Australia (Copeland & Dillon, 2005). It is often considered a club drug, or "dance drug," because it is used at "raves," or dance parties, a popular scene for teenagers. Ketamine is also frequently used as a key component in fake MDMA (Ecstasy) tablets.

Chemically, Ketamine is similar to PCP but is much less potent and produces less confusion, irrationality, and violent behavior (Drug Enforcement Administration, 2005). As a drug of abuse, ketamine can be administered orally, snorted, or injected. It is also sometimes sprinkled on marijuana and smoked. High doses produce analgesia, amnesia, and coma.

Users report sensations ranging from a pleasant feeling of floating to being separated from their bodies (National Institute on Drug Abuse, 2005). Approximately 50% of ketamine users have had a bad experience with the drug, which is called a "K-hole" (Copeland & Dillon, 2005).

Because ketamine is odorless and tasteless, it can be added to beverages or food without being detected. Along with GHB, ketamine is considered a "date rape" drug because it can be given to unsuspecting victims, inducing amnesia and a helpless physical state. Under these conditions, sexual assault can be carried out without the victim's being able to remember the incident.

According to the 2006 MTF survey, 1.4% of 12th graders, 1.0% of 10th graders, and 0.9% of 8th graders reported having used the drug within the past year (Johnston et al., 2007). The drug has lost popularity since reaching its peak several years ago.

THE STIMULANTS

AMPHETAMINES

Amphetamines and cocaine are classified as central nervous system stimulants and have highly similar effects. Amphetamines are part of a group of synthetic drugs known collectively as amines. The amines, in particular, produce effects in the sympathetic nervous system, a subdivision of the autonomic nervous system, that arouse a person to action, which might include fighting or fleeing from a frightening situation.

Amphetamines are traditionally classified in three major categories: **amphetamine** (e.g., Benzedrine), **dextroamphetamine** (e.g., Dexedrine), and **methamphetamine** (e.g., Methedrine or Desoxyn). Of the three, Benzedrine is the least potent. All may be taken orally, inhaled, or injected, and all act directly on the central nervous system, particularly the reticular activating system. Once the drug is taken, it is rapidly assimilated into the bloodstream but is metabolized and eliminated from the body relatively slowly. Both psychological and physiological reactions vary dramatically with the dose. In addition, the effects of massive quantities intravenously injected differ substantially from low doses administered orally. Reactions to the drugs also vary widely among individuals.

Methamphetamine is our focus here because it is the amphetamine most preferred by juvenile drug users. Methamphetamine's chemical structure is similar to that of amphetamine, but it has more powerful effects on the central nervous system. It is a Schedule II stimulant because it has a high potential for abuse and is available only through a prescription that cannot be refilled (National Institute on Drug Abuse, 2002). Methamphetamine has traditionally been the drug of preference when a user injects a substance directly into the bloodstream. More recently, though, the preferred method of consumption has been by smoking, especially the crystallized form of methamphetamine known as "ice" (J. C. Maxwell, 2004). Ice—also known as shard, shabu, tweak, crystal super ice, LA glass, or crystal meth—is methamphetamine that has been washed in a solvent such as alcohol to remove the impurities. Evaporation of the solvent produces crystals that resemble glass shards or ice shavings. Some users prefer snorting the powder form of the drug; snorting affects the user in about 5 minutes, whereas the effects take a bit longer if the drug is smoked. If the user orally ingests the drug, it takes effect in about 20 minutes. The illegal form of the drug is manufactured in clandestine laboratories (known as meth labs or super labs). Methamphetamine is relatively easy to produce because the ingredients can be purchased at local drug stores (Office of National Drug Control Policy, 2003b). Currently, methamphetamine is the primary drug of abuse in rural America (J. C. Maxwell, 2004).

Methamphetamine produces an increase in alertness and a decrease in appetite; these effects may last as long as 12 hours. In high doses, the drug can cause violent behavior, anxiety, insomnia, and symptoms of paranoia, including delusions, hallucinations, and mood swings. Some chronic users develop sores on their bodies from scratching "crank bugs," bugs that are believed to be crawling under the skin during the user's delusional state.

A form of methamphetamine that has appeared recently in the United States is **methcathionone**, known on the streets as "cat." This was classified as a Schedule I drug in 1993. The drug is usually snorted, although it can be taken orally by mixing it with a drink or can be injected intravenously. Its psychoactive effects are identical to those of methamphetamine.

Methylphenidate, a stimulant known as Ritalin, also has a high potential for abuse and produces many of the same effects as methamphetamine. Many children who were diagnosed with attention-deficit/hyperactivity disorder take Ritalin to stabilize their behavior. Thus, Ritalin is considered easily accessible for children and adolescents who can obtain the drug from classmates or friends with a prescription for it.

COCAINE AND ITS DERIVATIVES

Cocaine is the second most commonly used illicit drug (following marijuana) in the United States (Drug Enforcement Administration, 2005). In 2003 an estimated 2.3 million persons (1% of the U.S. population) were cocaine users, 604,000 of whom used crack. Approximately 1.5 million Americans could be classified as dependent on cocaine use (National Institute on Drug Abuse, 2004). According to DAWN (Office of Applied Studies, 2004), one of every five drug-related visits to emergency rooms in the United States are for the effects of cocaine, mostly for detox or for unanticipated effects. Adults 18 to 25 years old have a higher rate of cocaine use than does any other age group, and males are more likely to use the drug than are females.

In general, there has been little change in adolescent use of powder or crack cocaine since 2001 (Johnston et al., 2007). In 2006, 5.7% of 12th graders, 3.2% of 10th graders, and 2.0% of 8th graders had used powdered cocaine over the previous 12 months. During that same year, 2.1% of 12th graders, 1.3% of 10th graders, and 1.3% of 8th graders had used crack. The two drugs most prevalent among detained juveniles in recent years have consistently been marijuana and cocaine (McClelland et al., 2004).

Cocaine—also called coke, snow, candy—is a chemical extracted from the coca plant (*Erythroxylon coca*), an extremely hardy plant native to Peru. Cocaine has traditionally been much more expensive than amphetamines, partly because it is a natural organic substance that cannot be produced synthetically. Cocaine is considered the most potent stimulant of natural origin (Drug Enforcement Administration, 2005). The coca plant thrives at elevations of 2,000 to 8,000 feet with heavy rainfall (100 inches per year). It is an evergreen shrub, growing to about 3 feet high and generally found on the eastern slopes of the Andes. It has long been used by Peruvians living in or near the Andes; indigenous populations in the region have traditionally chewed coca leaves almost continuously and have commonly kept them tucked in their cheeks. Coca leaves are also used for tea. There are at least 200 strains of coca plants, but the vast majority contain little if any cocaine. However, because of the increasing appetite of North Americans for cocaine, South American growers and entrepreneurs have developed not only vast new areas for the cultivation of coca but also new, more vigorous strains of the plant (Inciardi, 1986).

In the United States and Canada, cocaine is usually administered nasally (sniffing) or intravenously or by inhaling (smoking). Cocaine taken orally is poorly absorbed because it is hydrolyzed (neutralized) by gastrointestinal secretions. Smoking cocaine was first tried in America around 1914, but the high temperature required to burn the chemical (198°C) resulted in the destruction of most of its psychoactive properties (Inaba & Cohen, 1993). As a consequence, cocaine smoking did not become popular in the United States until the mid-1970s, with the arrival of "crack." Crack is produced in such a way that the cocaine can be smoked without destroying its potency. Light users normally sniff powder cocaine to obtain their "high," although chronic sniffing can result in nasal irritation and inflammation. The common unit in the black market is the "spoon," which approximates 1 gram of the diluted drug. In most cases, cocaine is diluted 20 to 30 times its weight. There is no safe way to use cocaine. Any route of administration can lead to toxic amounts, resulting in acute cardiovascular or cerebrovascular emergencies that could lead to sudden death (National Institute on Drug Abuse, 2004).

Background and Description

Around the turn of the century, cocaine was used in soft drinks (such as Kos-Kola, Wiseola, and Care-Cola), cigarettes, cigars, various tonics, foods, sprays, and ointments, including hemorrhoid salves (Smart, 1986). It is often thought that Coca Cola contained cocaine as an active ingredient until 1903, when caffeine was substituted (Kleber, 1988), but this assertion is vigorously denied by representatives of the company, who insist that there is no evidence for it. The famous drink Vin Mariani, so popular among the wealthy at the time, was a combination of French wine and cocaine. However, cocaine began to fall into disfavor when people became concerned about its dangerous and undesirable effects. By 1910 cocaine had become the most hated and feared drug in North America (Kleber, 1988). The Harrison Narcotics Act of 1914 in the United States and the Propriety and Patent Medicines Act of 1908 in Canada sharply curtailed or terminated its usage, and the popularity of cocaine declined until the 1960s.

In national surveys conducted in the early 1980s in Canada, about 4% of college students and 3% of adults said they had used cocaine at least once during the year (Smart, 1986). More recent research suggests that the high level of cocaine use in Canada was declining during the early 1990s (Smart & Adlaf, 1992). In the United States, the incidence remains high, with about 16% to 20% of college students using cocaine at least once during the year (Substance Abuse and Mental Health Services Administration, 1995).

Adolescents and young adults who report a significant amount of illegal income are more than twice as likely to become heavy cocaine users as those who do not (Office of National Drug Control Policy, 2004). Also, adolescents who sell hard drugs are two times more likely to become heavy cocaine users than are those who do not sell hard drugs (Office of National Drug Control Policy, 2004). These findings underscore the fact that young heavy drug users tend to be already engaged in a variety of criminal activities.

Psychological Effects

Both amphetamines and cocaine increase wakefulness, alertness, and vigilance; improve concentration; and produce a feeling of clear thinking. There is generally an elevation of mood, mild euphoria, increased sociability, and a belief that one can do just about anything. In large doses, the effects may be irritability, hypersensitivity, delirium, panic aggression, hallucinations, and psychosis. Injected at chronically high doses, these drugs may precipitate **toxic psychosis**, a syndrome with many of the psychotic features of paranoid schizophrenia. With the metabolization and elimination of the drug, the psychotic episode usually dissipates.

Crack

The most common form of cocaine smoking in the United States involves a process called **freebasing**. There are two popular methods used to produce freebase cocaine, or crack. In one method the freebase is prepared by dissolving cocaine hydrochloride in water and then adding a strong base, such as ammonia or baking soda, to the solution (Weiss & Mirin, 1987). The solution is then heated to crystallize it. This method, sometimes referred to as "cheap basing" or "dirty basing," does not remove many of the impurities or residues, such as the baking soda. The second method involves dissolving cocaine hydrochloride in highly flammable chemicals, such as ether, to extract the cocaine. The ether is then removed by drying the solution, leaving crystals of freebase cocaine. This method creates a purer form of the drug because any additives are filtered out. The result is a product ranging from 37% to 96% purity (Weiss & Mirin, 1987).

Crack has two chemical properties sought by users. First, crystallized cocaine has a lower melting point than the powdered form has, so it can be heated easily in a glass pipe and vaporized to form smoke at a lower temperature (Inaba & Cohen, 1993). The drug is called "crack" because it has a crackling sound when smoked (Abadinsky, 1993; Gold, 1984). The second property is that it is more fat soluble than powdered cocaine and therefore is more readily absorbed by the fatty brain tissue, causing a more immediate and intense reaction (Inaba & Cohen, 1993).

According to Howard Abadinsky (1993), crack is the drug abuser's answer to fast food. Several times more pure than ordinary street cocaine, crack generates a very rapid and intense state of euphoria, which peaks in about 5 minutes. The psychological and physical effects of crack are as powerful as any intravenously injected cocaine. However, the euphoria is short-lived, ending in about 10 to 20 minutes after inhalation, and is followed by depression, irritability, and often an intense craving for more. Although most users limit themselves to one or two "hits," some users seek multiple hits. In order to stay high, crack smokers often find a place where crack can be safely smoked, such as a "crack house," because the smoke and smell are difficult to hide. An overdose of freebase cocaine usually results in very rapid heartbeat and hyperventilation, often accompanied by an overwhelming feeling of impending death. Experts agree that crack is extremely dangerous to the user and may result in a number of life-threatening neurophysiological reactions, such as rapid, irregular heartbeat, respiratory failure, seizures, or a cerebral hemorrhage.

It is estimated that there are about 500,000 regular crack users in the United States, most of whom are 18 to 25 years old (Substance Abuse and Mental Health Services Administration, 1995). One of the major reasons that youth are more drawn to crack than to cocaine involves economics. Although crack is no less expensive than cocaine when sold by weight alone, crack is sold in smaller units, such as small fractions of a gram, making the price more manageable for teenagers.

Some experts regard crack as the most addictive drug currently available on the street (Weiss & Mirin, 1987). The craving for the drug may become so severe that a user will lie, steal, or commit acts of violence in order to obtain more of the drug (Rosecan, Spitz, & Gross, 1987). The popularity of crack probably resides in its instantaneous psychological effects, its inexpensiveness, and its wide availability throughout most major U.S. cities. The drug also provides tremendous profit for its sellers. For example, $20 worth of cocaine powder can easily return a profit of $60 (Ratner, 1993). At one point, about one-third of all arrests made by the New York City Narcotics Division involved cocaine, and over half of them involved crack (Cohn, 1986). Because it is so inexpensive and available, it has become a very popular drug for the young—including preteenagers.

STIMULANTS AND DELINQUENCY

The relationship between stimulants and delinquency has many facets. One thing that emerges clearly from the research literature is that heavy users of stimulants, especially those who use crack cocaine heavily, are often polydrug users (National Institute on Drug Abuse, 2004). Furthermore, persistent offenders tend to be polydrug users.

Although it is difficult at this point in our knowledge to determine which comes first, drug use or involvement in delinquency or crime, the evidence strongly suggests that persistent juvenile offenders have engaged in a variety of illegal activities and troublesome conduct throughout their lifetimes, most probably beginning before the onset of drug or alcohol abuse.

NARCOTIC DRUGS

The word *narcotics* usually provokes intense negative reactions and is often quickly associated with crime. Like the word *dope*, it is widely misused to denote all illegal drugs. In this text, *narcotic drugs* refer only to the derivatives of the opium or poppy plant, *Papaver sominferum*, or to products pharmacologically similar to those derivatives.

Narcotic drugs can be divided into three major categories on the basis of the kind of preparation they require: (1) **narcotics of natural origin**, which include the grown opium and the naturally occurring morphine, codeine, and thebaine; (2) **semisynthetic narcotics**, which include the chemically prepared heroin and oxycodone (OxyContin); and (3) **synthetic narcotics**, which are wholly prepared chemically and include fentanyl, meperidine (Demerol), and hydrocodone (Vicodin). All are narcotics because they produce similar effects: relief of pain, relaxation, peacefulness, and sleep (*narco*, of Greek origin, means "to sleep"). In fact, the opium poppy was named after Somnis, the Roman god of sleep.

Narcotic drugs are highly addictive for some individuals, to the point that they develop a relentless, strong craving. Many heavy narcotic users, however, lead productive lives, without significant interference in their daily routine. There does not appear to be a single type of opium user; a wide variety of people use the drug for various purposes.

HEROIN

The most heavily used illegal narcotic in this country is heroin. Overall, approximately 3.7 million Americans reported using heroin at least once in their lifetime (Drug Enforcement Administration, 2005). In 2005 the percentage of heroin users among 8th, 10th, and 12th graders ranged from 0.8% to 0.9% (Johnston et al., 2007), a pattern that has remained unchanged over the past 5 years. Although these numbers seem extremely low, they nevertheless represent an increase in use by juveniles over the past 20 years.

Heroin is a white, crystalline material, characterized by the bitter taste of alkaloid. Its appearance is largely dictated by its diluents, which in most cases make up 95% to 98% of its total weight. Heroin is rarely taken orally, not only because of its bitter taste, but also because the absorption process is slow and incomplete. Instead, it can be administered intramuscularly, subcutaneously ("skin popping"), or intravenously ("mainlining"), or it can be inhaled ("snorted") or smoked.

The sustained popularity of heroin use among children and adolescents may be due to the increase in its purity, allowing it to be sniffed or smoked (Hopfer, Khuri, Crowley, & Hooks, 2002). In the past, heroin in the United States was usually injected, because this method was the most practical and efficient way to administer low-purity heroin. Currently, however, about 60% of the youths who use the drug do not inject it (Drug Enforcement Administration, 2005; National Institute on Drug Abuse, 2005).

Another reason for the increased use of smoked heroin by American youth may be the mistaken notion that smoking or sniffing heroin is less prone to addiction than using it intravenously.

The effects of heroin depend on the quantity taken, the method of administration, the interval between administrations, the tolerance and dependence of the user, the setting, and the user's expectations. The experienced heavy user of heroin prefers mainlining (i.e., injecting the drug intravenously) because of the sensational thrill, splash, rush, or kick it provides. Moreover, the effects of mainlining are immediate (15 to 30 seconds). The effects usually wear off in 5 to 8 hours, depending on the user's tolerance.

Like all narcotics, heroin is a central nervous system depressant. For many users, it promotes mental clouding, dreamlike states, light sleep punctuated by vivid dreams, and a general feeling of sublime contentment. The body may become permeated with a feeling of warmth, and the extremities may feel heavy. There is little inclination toward physical activity; the user prefers to sit motionless and in a fog.

Relationship with Crime and Delinquency

No other drug group is as closely associated with crime as are the narcotics, particularly heroin. The image of the desperate "junkie" looking for a fix is familiar to everyone. Because of the adverse effects of the drug, it is assumed that the heroin user is bizarre, unpredictable, and therefore dangerous. However, high doses of narcotics produce sleep. Therefore, narcotics users rarely become violent or dangerous. Early research strongly indicated that addicts do *not*, as a general rule, participate in violent crimes such as assault, rape, or homicide (National Institute on Drug Abuse, 1978; Canadian Government's Commission of Inquiry, 1971; National Commission on Marijuana and Drug Abuse, 1973; Tinklenberg & Stillman, 1970). However, there is research evidence that suggests a relationship between heroin addiction and money-producing crime, including prostitution, drug dealing, and larceny. A study in Miami of 573 narcotics users found that they were responsible for almost 6,000 robberies, 6,700 burglaries, 900 stolen vehicles, 25,000 instances of shoplifting, and 46,000 other events of larceny and fraud (Inciardi, 1986). Self-report surveys also find that heroin users report financing their habits largely through "acquisitive crime" (Jarvis & Parker, 1989; Mott, 1986).

Parker and Newcombe (1987), who studied crime patterns and heroin use in the English community of Wirral, located in northwest England, found that many heroin users were from poor sections of the community and were young. The researchers divided their sample into three groups: (1) young offenders who were not known to be using heroin but were highly criminally active; (2) heroin users who engaged in considerable acquisitive crime but were involved in this type of crime prior to their heroin addiction; and (3) heroin users who started engaging in acquisitive crime after beginning drug use in order to support their habit. The Parker-Newcombe investigation suggests that some heroin addicts do support their habit through crime. Furthermore, Ball, Shaffer, and Nurco (1983) found that heroin addicts committed more money-producing crime when they were addicted than when they were not.

It may be misleading to examine the heroin–crime relationship in isolation, without considering the possible interaction between polydrug use and crime. All we can say with some confidence at this point is that those who use heroin also seem to be deeply involved in money-producing crime. Heroin users may not be driven to crime by the needs of their addiction but may, particularly as polydrug users, represent a segment of society that runs counter to society's rules and expectations in multiple ways, drug use and larceny among them. It may well be that most heroin-addicted offenders were involved in crime and antisocial behavior before they became addicted. Research by Faupel (1991) does support this hypothesis. However, studies also suggest that criminal activity increases substantially during periods of heavy drug consumption (Faupel, 1991). Polydrug users tend to switch from drug to drug, depending on what is available and inexpensive at the time, and do not seem physiologically desperate for any one particular drug. Thus, the relationship between heroin use and criminal behavior is complex and varies throughout an addict's career.

OXYCONTIN

Abuse of **OxyContin** and **Vicodin** has been significant and steady in the United States. Vicodin is especially prevalent among juveniles (see Table 10–5). Both drugs are also being used by a significant number of college students as well.

OxyContin (oxycodone) and Vicodin are narcotics that have the properties of a powerful analgesic for pain control. OxyContin is classified as an opioid analgesic that is available through prescription. It was approved in 1995 by the Food and Drug Administration for use in persons with moderate to severe pain, requiring several days or more of relief (Cicero, Inciardi, & Muñoz, 2005). The drug is synthesized from thebaine, a minor constituent of opium. OxyContin comes generally in tablet form, but some abusers crush the tablets and sniff the powder or dissolve the tablets in water for injection.

Overall, OxyContin abuse is by far the most prevalent and widespread abuse of all the opioids and prescription drugs in the United States, and it shows no signs of declining at this time (Cicero et al., 2005). The abuse of this drug is found almost exclusively among white persons (91%), especially those living in rural and suburban areas (Cicero et al., 2005). Interestingly, studies have discovered an overall increase across the country in the abuse of prescription drugs in general (Cicero et al., 2005), probably because prescription drugs are relatively easy to obtain, as compared to other illicit drugs, especially in rural areas.

COLD MEDICINES

An emerging trend among juveniles is the use of over-the-counter cold remedies for the purpose of "getting high" (sometimes referred to as "Robo tripping"). The psychoactive ingredient in this class of drugs is usually dextromethorphan (DXM), a

TABLE 10–5: Percentage of Students Using OxyContin and Vicodin (2006)

	8th Grade	10th Grade	12th Grade
OxyContin	2.6	3.8	4.3
Vicodin	3.0	7.0	9.7

Source: Data from *Monitoring the Future: National Results on Adolescent Drug Use: Overview of Key Findings, 2006* (p. 53) by L. D. Johnston, P. M. O'Malley, J. G. Bachman, and J. E. Schulenberg, 2007, Bethesda, MD: National Institute on Drug Abuse.

cough suppressant that causes alterations of consciousness and mood when taken in high doses. Its effects are similar to those of PCP and ketamine. Common effects include dizziness, blurred vision, mental confusion, slurred speech, abdominal pain, nausea and vomiting, rapid heart beat, and numbness of fingers and toes. Approximately 6% of high school students reported having used the drug within the past year (Johnston et al., 2007). When used in combination with alcohol, cold medicines can become dangerous.

SEDATIVE HYPNOTIC COMPOUNDS

CLUB DRUGS: GHB AND ROHYPNOL

Gamma-hydroxybutryrate (GHB), Rohypnol, Ecstasy (MDMA), ketamine, LSD, and methamphetamine have been considered the "club drugs" in recent years (J. C. Maxwell, 2004). They are called club drugs because they are most often consumed at teenage and young-adult nightclubs, raves, or parties. Although club drugs have attracted considerable national attention, they constitute a relatively small proportion of the drug problem in the United States (see Table 10–6 for the use of club drugs in 2006).

GHB and Rohypnol are nervous system depressants. **GHB** (also known as liquid ecstasy, scoop, liquid X, grievous bodily harm, or Georgia home boy) is a powerful and fast-acting drug most often taken by youths as a pleasure enhancer that produces a rapid state of intoxication. It is usually consumed orally, either as a grainy, white- or sandy-colored powder that is often dissolved in alcohol or as a liquid sold in small bottles. GHB is produced primarily in clandestine laboratories and consequently has no guarantee of quality or purity, making its psychoactive effects unpredictable. The drug can be easily produced by combining gamma-butyrolactone (GBL) with either potassium hydroxide or sodium hydroxide in a container.

The psychoactive effects of GHB begin within 15 to 30 minutes after consumption and, depending on the purity and the dosage, may last as long as 6 hours. It is typically used in combination with other drugs, especially alcohol. GHB has many severe and unpredictable side effects, such as nausea, drowsiness, vomiting, delusions, depression, vertigo (dizziness), hallucinations, seizures, respiratory distress, loss of consciousness, slow heart rate, lowered blood pressure, amnesia, and coma. It also interferes with

TABLE 10–6: Percentage of Students Using Club Drugs (2006)

	8th Grade	*10th Grade*	*12th Grade*
GHB	0.8	0.7	1.1
Rohypnol	0.5	0.5	1.1
Ecstasy	1.4	2.8	4.1
Ketamine	0.9	1.0	1.4
LSD	0.9	1.7	1.7
Methamphetamine	1.8	1.8	2.5

Source: Data from *Monitoring the Future: National Results on Adolescent Drug Use: Overview of Key Findings, 2006* by L. D. Johnston, P. M. O'Malley, J. G. Bachman, and J. E. Schulenberg, 2007, Bethesda, MD: National Institute on Drug Abuse.

circulation, motor coordination, and balance; and at higher doses (2 to 4 grams), it produces significant problems in motor and speech control. At these high doses GHB usually produces a very deep sleep, resembling a coma.

GHB is tasteless and odorless and mixes easily with alcohol or any nonalcoholic drink. Because it can be mixed with food and drinks without detection and because of its ability to sedate and intoxicate unsuspecting victims, GHB has been connected to crime. It is sometimes used in the commission of sexual assaults and often plays a role in date rape. It is also used in some instances to pave the way for robbing heavily sedated or unconscious victims.

Rohypnol (generic: flunitrazepam) is a club drug that has been used to facilitate a sexual assault on individuals who have been physically and mentally incapacitated by the drug. It is popular among youths because of its low cost. Lower doses of Rohypnol typically produce muscle relaxation; higher doses can cause loss of muscle control and consciousness. When combined with alcohol, Rohypnol can cause anterograde amnesia and can also be deadly. The drug is similar to Valium in its chemical components but is 10 times more powerful.

Like GHB, Rohypnol is tasteless and odorless and can be dissolved in liquids, although not as easily as GHB. Rohypnol can also be snorted or injected. It is legally manufactured in over 80 countries as a prescribed sedative for the short-term treatment of severe sleep disorders, but it is not manufactured or approved for sale in the United States, where penalties for possession and distribution can be severe. Since 1999, Rohypnol tablets have been manufactured to turn blue in a drink in order to be more delectable, but colorless tablets are still on the market.

ECSTASY

Ecstasy, or **MDMA**, is a synthetic drug (completely manufactured rather than grown or occurring naturally) that is considered a stimulant but that also has some strong psychedelic properties, similar to those of methamphetamine and mescaline. MDMA is an abbreviation for 3-4 methylenedioxy-methamphetamine. It is sometimes confused with a similar compound—3, 4-methylenedioxyamphetamine, abbreviated MDA. The effects and pharmacological actions of MDA are similar but not identical to those of MDMA (J. C. Maxwell, 2004). Both MDMA and MDA are classified as Schedule I drugs. Other drugs confused with Ecstasy include paramethoxyamphetamine (PMA) and p-methylthioamphetamine (MTA). These are substances packaged as Ecstasy, with similar psychoactive properties, and associated with several deaths, especially in Europe (J. C. Maxwell, 2004).

The use of Ecstasy (also known as Adam, E, X, eccie) increased sharply among teenagers during the late 1990s, reaching its peak in 2001. Since that time, there has been a steady, moderate decease in popularity, but its use still remains high (see Table 10–6). The availability of Ecstasy and other club drugs has decreased considerably from peak levels in 1997 (Johnston et al., 2007).

MDMA is the abbreviation for methylenedioxymethamphetamine. The drug was first manufactured by a German company in 1912 to be used as a possible appetite depressant. It then acquired some popularity in the 1990s as the rave culture swept over Europe's youth. MDMA is often referred to as a club drug because it is commonly used at all-night dance parties known as raves. Being under the drug's effects is often referred to as "rolling" because of the up-and-down rolling of emotions it engenders. In this sense, the drug produces a unique sense of well-being, affection, and love (Strote, Lee, & Wechsler, 2002). It is normally taken in tablet, capsule, or powder form; depending on the dosage, the drug's effects usually last between 4 and 6 hours.

The common psychological effects of MDMA include confusion, depression, anxiety, sleeplessness, drug cravings, and paranoia (Office of National Drug Control Policy, 2000). Its adverse physical side effects include muscle tension, involuntary clenching of the teeth, nausea, blurred vision, faintness, tremors, sweating, and chills. Baby pacifiers are often used by Ecstasy users to prevent danger to or excessive grinding of the teeth. Inhalation of Vick's Vapor Rub is also sometimes used to enhance the drug's psychedelic effects. MDMA can also predispose users to participate in high-risk behavior (Moreland, 2000).

The drug's stimulation properties provide an energy rush that encourages users to stay physically active for long periods of time, such as dancing all night at rave parties. Although the drug is considered safer than many other illicit drugs, there are physical risks. At very high doses, MDMA can cause the body temperature to rise as high as 110 degrees, leading to muscle breakdown and kidney or cardiovascular failure (National Institute on Drug Abuse, 2000). In addition, all-night raves and extensive dancing in crowded and overheated rooms pose the danger of producing not only high body temperatures but also dangerous levels of dehydration. Other adverse side effects of MDMA include hearing and liver damage, strokes, and long-term brain injury (National Institutes of Health, 1999).

Most MDMA found in the United States comes from clandestine laboratories in Western Europe (primarily the Netherlands and Belgium). MDMA is usually consumed in tablet form and takes effect within 30 to 45 minutes. It is estimated that 2 million tablets are smuggled into the United States every week (Drug Enforcement Administration, 2005).

ALCOHOL

Despite the public concern over all of these drugs, the number one drug of abuse has been, and continues to be, alcohol (including ethanol, ethyl alcohol, grain alcohol). All 50 states have a legal drinking age of 21, but most underage persons obtain and drink alcohol illegally at some point. According to the Substance Abuse and Mental Health Administration (2005), 121 million Americans, aged 12 and older, were current drinkers of alcohol in 2004, representing 50% of the population. About 55 million (22.8%) participated in binge drinking, defined as five or more drinks on at least one occasion in the 30 days prior to the survey (Substance Abuse and Mental Health Administration, 2005). And 16.7 million (6.9%) were considered heavy drinkers, defined as participating in binge drinking on 5 or more days in the past month. Most of the binge and heavy drinkers were young adults between the ages of 18 and 25. Overall, teenagers prefer alcohol over other drugs by a significant margin.

About 10.8 million youths, aged 12 to 20, reported drinking alcohol within the month prior to the survey, representing 28.7% of this age group (Substance Abuse and Mental Health Administration, 2005). (Table 10–7 shows the 30-day percentages of use among 8th, 10th, and 12th graders.) Approximately 19.6% of this 12- to -20 age group of drinkers were binge drinkers, and 6.3% were classified as heavy drinkers. In a study involving 930 high school students, Arata, Stafford, and Tims (2003) found that two-fifths

TABLE 10–7: Prevalence of Alcohol Use Among 8th, 10th, and 12th Grade Students (within previous 30 days)

	Percentage of Any Use	*Percentage of Having Been Drunk*
8th graders	17.2	6.2
10th graders	33.8	18.8
12th graders	45.3	30.0

Source: Data from *Monitoring the Future: National Results on Adolescent Drug Use: Overview of Key Findings, 2006* by L. D. Johnston, P. M. O'Malley, J. G. Bachman, and J. E. Schulenberg, 2007, Bethesda, MD: National Institute on Drug Abuse.

TABLE 10–8: Possible Effects of Alcohol Consumption, Based on Blood-Alcohol Concentration (BAC)

BAC	*Possible Effects*
.010–.030	• Slight change in feelings
0.31–.070	• Feelings of warmth, relaxation, friendship
.071–.150	• Talkative, noisy, rowdy behavior; impaired performance on complex tasks, such as driving (.08 usually defined as legally drunk)
.151–.300	• Mental confusion, disorientation, slurred speech, staggering, loss of critical judgment, unstable emotional states, probable appearance as drunk
.301–.400	• Severe intoxication, impairment of circulation and respiration, marked lack of muscular coordination, nausea, vomiting, incontinence, usually passing out
.401 and above	• Coma, death from respiratory and cardiovascular dysfunction

of the males and one-fifth of the females reported frequent binge drinking. Other studies of gender differences in alcohol use among adolescents have consistently reported that males consume alcohol more frequently and in higher quantities than females do and are susceptible to more alcohol-related problems (Webb et al., 2002).

According to DAWN (Office of Applied Studies, 2004), 23% of all drug-related emergency department visits in 2003 involved the effects of alcohol in persons under age 21. Nearly a third of the alcohol-related visits were the result of a youth—especially between the ages of 12 and 17—combining alcohol with other drugs. Marijuana (49%) and cocaine (22%) were the drugs most frequently found in combination with alcohol. Methamphetamine (8%) was also found with some frequency in these visits. There were no gender differences in alcohol-related visits to emergency departments in 2003.

Alcohol is responsible for more deaths and violence than all other drugs combined; it is the third major cause of death. According to the National Highway Traffic Safety Administration (2005), approximately 25% of drivers aged 16 to 20 who were involved in fatal motor vehicle crashes in 2003 had been drinking alcohol. The usual way to determine if an individual is intoxicated is by measuring the person's **blood-alcohol concentration (BAC)**. A blood-alcohol concentration of .10% means there are 100 milligrams of alcohol per 100 milliliters of blood (see Table 10–8 for corresponding effects). A 165-pound man would reach a BAC of .10% if he drank about five drinks within 1 hour on an empty stomach. (A drink is defined as one-and-a-half ounces of liquor, a 12-ounce beer, or a five-ounce glass of wine.) Drivers are generally considered intoxicated with a BAC of .08%.

Psychological Effects

The social, psychological, and psychobiological effects of excessive alcohol use can be just as destructive to the individual, the family, and society in general as addictive substance abuse. Like the heroin addict, the alcoholic can develop a strong psychological and physical dependence on the drug. However, society's attitudes toward alcohol are dramatically different from its attitudes toward other drugs of abuse. In virtually every part of the United States, it is legal and socially acceptable for adults to consume this drug In public, drinking behavior is generally unregulated unless it involves heavy intoxication and correspondingly unacceptable conduct (e.g., disturbing the peace or operating a motor vehicle). In private, one can get as drunk as one wishes, a privilege not granted to other drugs.

The psychoactive effects of alcohol are extremely complex. Miczek and his colleagues (1994) write that the effects of alcohol depend on "a host of interacting pharmacologic, endocrinologic, neurobiologic, genetic, situational, environmental, social, and cultural determinants" (p. 382). Consequently, we can provide only a cursory review of this complicated topic here. At low doses (e.g., 2 or 4 ounces of whiskey), alcohol seems to act as a stimulant on the central nervous system. Initially alcohol appears to affect the inhibitory chemical process of nervous system transmission, producing feelings of euphoria, good cheer, and social and physical warmth. In moderate or high quantities, however, alcohol begins to depress the excitatory processes of the central nervous system, as well as its inhibitory processes. Consequently, the individual's neuromuscular coordination and visual acuity are reduced, and the person feels tired and perceives pain. The ability to concentrate is also impaired. Very often, self-confidence increases, and the drinker becomes more daring, sometimes foolishly so. It is believed that alcohol at moderate levels begins to "numb" the higher brain centers, which process cognitive information, especially judgment and abstract thought. At this point the levels of intoxication are not necessarily dependent on the amount of alcohol ingested; the effects depend on a myriad of interacting variables.

Relationship with Delinquency

There are two ways to look at alcohol and delinquency. One way is to examine violations of liquor laws, such as age restrictions (see Figure 10–3). The second way is to approach alcohol as an instigating chemical prompting violence and delinquent acts. Many studies of adolescents have concluded that alcohol use and violent behavior are linked (Swahn & Donovan, 2004). Several studies also indicate that alcohol use is more common among violent delinquents than among nonviolent delinquents (Ellickson, Saner, & McGuigan, 1997; Huizinga & Jakob-Chien, 1998). On the basis of data collected on 312 youthful offenders at a public juvenile facility, Dawkins (1997) reports that alcohol use is more strongly and consistently related to both violent and nonviolent offenses than is marijuana or other drugs. One study found that even after antecedent peer and family risk factors were adjusted for, young people who abused alcohol were much more likely to engage in violent offenses than were those who did not misuse alcohol (Ferguson, Lynskey, & Horwood, 1996). According to Webb et al. (2002), alcohol use and serious

FIGURE 10–3 Juvenile Arrests for Violation of Liquor Laws (2005)

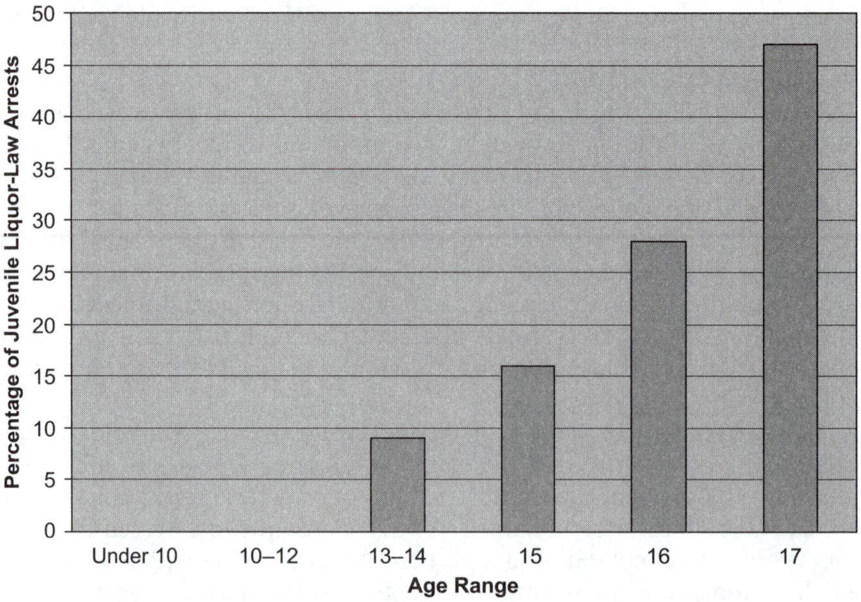

Source: Data from *Crime in the United States—2005* by Federal Bureau of Investigation, 2006, Washington, DC: U.S. Department of Justice, Author.

delinquency are strongly associated, yet the direction of causality is unclear. Does alcohol cause violence, or do violent adolescents drink alcohol?

Numerous other factors must also be taken into account. For example, cultural differences may play a significant role in the alcohol–aggression relationship. In addition, cognitive factors, such as expectations or cognitions, influence how a person responds to alcohol. Alcohol may serve as a cue for acting intoxicated and doing things one normally would not do. In other words, a person may act the way he or she believes alcohol makes one act. Furthermore not all adolescents who drink heavily engage in violence and aggression. Many adolescents use alcohol experimentally, sometimes frequently, and may binge drink without engaging in antisocial, violent, or delinquent behavior.

INHALANTS

The term **inhalant** refers to 1,000 or more different household and commercial products that can be abused by sniffing or "huffing" (i.e., inhaling through the mouth) for an intoxicating effect. These effects can be produced by organic solvents and volatile substances commonly found in adhesives, lighter fluids, cleaning solutions, paint products, nail polish remover, rubber glue, and even Wite-Out. The unwelcome effects of inhalants are usually highly similar to those of alcohol intoxication: slurred speech, loss of motor coordination, distortion of perceptions, headache, vomiting, and nausea. Wheezing may also be apparent, and in some instances, a rash around the nose and mouth may be evident.

Studies have estimated (and probably greatly underestimated) that 5% to 15% of children in the United States have tried inhalants. The 2006 MTF reports that 51.2% of high school seniors have tried inhalants at least once, compared to 29% of 8th graders (Johnston et al., 2007). The easy accessibility, low cost, and ease of transport and concealment make inhalants one of the first substances abused by children (Drug Enforcement Administration, 2005). According to the National Survey on Drug Abuse and Health, there were over 1 million new chronic inhalant users in 2002; the highest incidence is among 10- to 12-year-old children, with rates of use declining as they get older (Drug Enforcement Administration, 2005). Inhalants are not considered gateway drugs that lead to chronic abuse of other illegal substances. The real danger of inhalants is their dangerous side effects. Chronic use of inhalants can produce kidney abnormalities and liver damage and, in rare cases, heart failure or fatal breathing difficulties.

PREDICTORS OF HEAVY DRUG ABUSE

Childhood aggression is highly predictive of later substance abuse (O'Donnell, Hawkins, & Abbott, 1995; Swaim, Deffenbacher, & Wayman, 2004). Specifically, aggressiveness in boys, as early as 5 to 7 years of age, is predictive of frequent drug use in adolescence and drug problems in adulthood. Furthermore, children who are highly aggressive and demonstrate many antisocial behaviors in childhood often become polydrug users. It appears, therefore, that drugs do not usually cause aggression, violence, or serious, persistent delinquency; rather, individuals prone to be antisocial often abuse drugs. McClelland et al. (2004) discovered that virtually all of the youths entering detention in Cook County, Illinois (94%), had used drugs during their lifetimes, and about 85% had used drugs in the previous 6 months. Drugs provide immediate, easy, and predictable short-term pleasure that antisocial individuals often seek (Gottfredson & Hirschi, 1990). Another way of looking at this, however, is that children and adolescents who are exposed to numerous risk factors in their lives and who do not have sufficient protective factors to ameliorate the effects of these risk factors may turn to drugs to obtain short-term pleasure.

According to a study by Kaplow, Curran, Dodge, and the Conduct Problems Prevention Research Group (2002), children who eventually engage in substance abuse as adolescents tend to have the following risk factors: poor social problem-solving skills, hyperactivity, cognitive problems, a parent who abuses substances, and low levels of parental verbal ability. That study, which followed 295 children from kindergarten until age 12, showed that 21% of the children initiated substance use by age 12. In addition, the researchers found that children who had two or more of the identified risk factors had a greater than 50% chance of being included in that statistic. The researchers recommended that prevention efforts be focused on this high-risk group.

Other research indicates that those who have been suspended from school or who demonstrate poor academic performance are far more likely to engage in substance abuse than are those youths who remain in school and do well (McClusky, Krohn, Lizotte, & Rodriguez, 2002). Strong involvement in school is a buffering factor against adolescent use of drugs (Jessor et al., 1995).

Substance abuse among parents and siblings also increases a child's or adolescent's risk for abusing drugs (Andrews, Hops, & Duncan, 1997), but one of the most robust predictors of the onset and maintenance of adolescent drug use is an individual's affiliation with drug-using peers (Ozechowski & Liddle, 2000). Peer influences may be even stronger than family relationships for some youth (Duncan, Duncan, Biglan, & Ary,

1998; Farrell & White, 1998; Wills & Cleary, 1999). Numerous studies report that adolescents who associate with substance-using peers are far more likely to use substances themselves than are those adolescents who affiliate with peers who do not use drugs (Hussong & Hicks, 2003). Substance use by a close or best friend appears to be especially powerful (Urberg, Değirmencioğlu, & Pilgram, 1997). Gang involvement appears to be another risk factor (McClelland et al., 2004), although it is not as influential as substance use by close friends.

Summary and Conclusions

Although recent data indicate an overall decline or leveling off in the use of illegal drugs and alcohol by juveniles, substantial problems remain. Ten percent of youth between the ages of 12 and 17 reported using illegal drugs—excluding alcohol—in 2004, with marijuana being the most common illegal substance. Early adolescent drug use is associated with health problems, deviant behavior, high-risk behaviors, and poor academic performance.

Whereas most high school students who sell drugs report selling them at school, only 10% of the juveniles who admitted buying marijuana said they obtained it at school. Males apparently consume drugs more than females do and have more problems associated with substance abuse. Boys and girls may also have different trajectories, or paths, to drug abuse. For example, the influence of peer groups, including gangs, is a strong risk factor for boys. Girls who have little commitment to school and academic achievement are at increased risk for later substance abuse. Many youths go through a period of experimentation with drugs and do not continue with regular use. Multiple variables influence whether or not they continue, including the availability of drugs, peer pressure, family history, and individual biological and psychological differences. For many juveniles, continued use seems to be correlated with their cognition that such use is not harmful.

Information about drug use can be derived from three main sources. *Monitoring the Future* is an extensive self-report survey of students in secondary school. Like the results of all self-report surveys, these results must be approached cautiously. Nonetheless, over the years this carefully planned and conducted survey has revealed credible patterns and has earned the respect of most criminologists. In addition, the *National Survey on Drug Abuse and Health* polls persons aged 12 or older nationwide, and DAWN, a public health surveillance system, records data on drug-related visits to hospital emergency rooms and drug-related deaths. We have also included information on juvenile drug-related arrests as reported in the UCR.

Four categories of drugs include hallucinogens, stimulants, opiate narcotics, and sedative-hypnotic compounds. Within each category, we focused on the one or two drugs that are believed to be the most heavily used by juveniles or that represent a particular danger to that age group (e.g., club drugs). We are most concerned about the effect of the drugs on the neurophysiology and behavior of the individual. The chemical impact of the drug, the psychological characteristics of the individual, and the psychosocial conditions under which the drug is consumed must all be taken into consideration.

Marijuana is by far the most widely used hallucinogen. About 16% of youth between 12 and 17 admit being current users; the average age at first use is 13.5 years. Marijuana is not considered a hard, dangerous drug, nor is it believed to be addictive at moderate use. Heavy users, though, sometimes report tolerance, dependence, and withdrawal symptoms. Furthermore, heavy use can produce poor health outcomes similar to those of heavy cigarette smoking.

Marijuana does not lead to violent behavior; users report a relaxed, calm state. There are exceptions, however, with some users reporting bad experiences based on the THC content of the drug. In addition, heavy and early use of marijuana is associated with serious delinquency and other substance abuse during adolescence and early adulthood. For juveniles who are not heavy users, though, there is no evidence that marijuana is a gateway drug.

Juvenile use of PCP goes in cycles. It is a relatively cheap drug, can facilitate violent behavior, and is easily obtained. PCP users are typically polydrug users. Ketamine—one of the club drugs—is similar to PCP in chemical content but is less potent and produces less confusion, irritability, and violence. Ketamine is odorless and tasteless and can easily be added to food or beverages—hence its reputation as one of the date rape drugs. It is not widely used, with 1.6% of 12th graders reporting its use in 2004.

Among the stimulant drugs, amphetamines and cocaine are the most likely to be associated with juveniles. Both increase wakefulness and alertness, elevate mood, and increase sociability. In large doses, however, they can produce irritability, hypersensitivity, panic, hallucinations, and aggressive behavior. Amphetamines are synthetic drugs that act directly on the central nervous system and are rapidly assimilated into the bloodstream. Methamphetamine is not difficult to manufacture and can be injected or smoked. Another drug in this category—methylphenidate (commonly known as Ritalin)—has been widely prescribed for ADHD and has been abused in some communities as a result.

The stimulant cocaine is the single most frequently used illicit drug after marijuana. Recent use seems to have leveled off, but about 5% of 12th graders and 2.2% of 8th graders still report having used it over a 12-month period. The smoked version of cocaine—crack—is particularly potent and highly addictive.

Stimulants as a group have a close connection with delinquency in that persistent offenders, who are often polydrug users, make extensive use of these drugs. In persistent juvenile offenders, antisocial behavior usually precedes the use of most drugs; nevertheless, some drug use does facilitate some crime. For example, as just mentioned, stimulants at high doses can produce panic and, consequently, aggressive behavior.

Narcotic drugs provide relief from pain and produce relaxation, a feeling of peace, and sleep. Narcotics are highly addictive for some people. Heroin, the most heavily used narcotic, was formerly available only in injection form. But it can now be sniffed and smoked, making it more accessible and appealing to juveniles. OxyContin, a prescription analgesic for pain control, is one of the newest drugs of choice. Like Ritalin, it is subject to considerable prescription abuse.

The sedative-hypnotics, also referred to as depressants, include alcohol as well as two popular club drugs, GHB and rohypnol. Although the club drugs are believed to make up a small percentage of the total drug problem among juveniles, they are obviously still a cause for concern. They are pleasure enhancers that produce rapid intoxication, and they are typically used in combination with alcohol. They can produce severe, unpredictable side effects.

The number one drug of abuse among juveniles—and the one most preferred and most widely available—is alcohol. Some research indicates that close to 20% of those in the 12–20 age group who report alcohol use could be classified as binge drinkers. Alcohol use and violent behavior are linked, because in many individuals alcohol at moderate levels facilitates aggression. (At low levels it relaxes and disinhibits; at high levels people pass out.) Heavy alcohol use is more common among violent than among nonviolent delinquents.

Inhalants—available in many common household products—can produce effects similar to those of alcohol intoxication, and they can have dangerous side effects. Inhalants are easily accessible and appear to have high use among children 10 to 12 years of age, who may be using them primarily for experimentation. Little research is available on this group of drugs, but at this point they are not considered gateway drugs.

On the whole, it appears that—among delinquents—problem behaviors are predictors of drug abuse; as a general rule, drug abuse does not precede antisocial behavior. The dominant risk factors for substance abuse include poor social skills, high aggression, cognitive problems, poor academic records, lack of involvement in school, parents who abuse drugs, drug-using peers, and gang membership. Not enough information is available on gender, race, and ethnicity to draw conclusions about differences according to these characteristics. Ecological family therapy, whereby the family group and its various social systems are all included in the treatment, along with individualized treatment for the substance abuser appears to hold the greatest promise for successful intervention.

Key Terms and Concepts

amphetamine
blood-alcohol concentration (BAC)
cocaine
controlled Substances Act
crack
dependence
dextroamphetamine
Drug Abuse Warning Network (DAWN)
drug tolerance
Ecstasy
experimental substance use
freebasing
gateway drugs
GHB
hallucinogens
inhalant
ketamine
LSD
marijuana
MDMA
methamphetamine

methcathionone
methylphenidate
Monitoring the Future (MTF)
narcotics of natural origin
National Survey on Drug Use and Health (NSDUH)
opiate narcotics
OxyContin
PCP
physical dependence
polydrug users
proactive drugs
psychedelics
psychoactive drugs
psychological dependence
sedative-hypnotic compounds
semisynthetic narcotics
stimulants
synthetic narcotics
THC
toxic psychosis
Vicodin

CHAPTER 11
YOUTH GANGS

❧

CHAPTER OBJECTIVES

◆ Define youth gangs

◆ Review early theoretical work on youth gangs

◆ Review the demographics of gang members

◆ Identify the various types of youth gangs

◆ Review the various kinds of crimes youth gangs usually commit

◆ Explore the reasons that youths join gangs

In most American cities—and even in some small towns and rural areas—the reality of juvenile gangs or the threat of such gangs evokes anxiety in parents and fear in many residents. In neighborhoods or communities in which gangs are not already established, signs that a gang may have infiltrated—for example, graffiti, the wearing of gang colors, violence as a result of turf battles—usually prompt media attention and some form of community action. In the collective public mind, gangs contaminate the young and contribute substantially to the crime problem, particularly violence and drug-related crimes. The law enforcement community is often involved in programs directed at discouraging children and adolescents from joining gangs, as well as in efforts to suppress crime-related drug activity.

Interestingly, few national-level data are available on the numbers of gangs or gang members, nor is there national information on the characteristics of gangs. Although an increasing number of local and state agencies are collecting juvenile gang statistics, this collection has very little consistency in criteria or uniformity in procedures. Even the definition of a gang has not been firmly established. Therefore, estimates of gang crime are very rough, are subject to considerable error, and may differ substantially from one study to another. For the same reasons, many estimates of gang membership are suspect. Some gangs may brag and inflate their membership, whereas other youths are more likely to hide their affiliation. Researchers not perceived to be working for the government are best able to gather membership information. Esbensen and his associates (Esbensen, Winfree, & Taylor, 2001) say the common, perhaps most valid measure of gang membership is self-nomination, that is, asking someone if he or she is or has ever been a gang member.

DEFINITION

What is a youth gang? Irving Spergel (1995) points out that the definition of youth gangs proposed by Malcolm Klein over 30 years ago is still in common usage today. Klein (1971) defined a *youth gang* as any denotable adolescent group of youngsters who (a) are generally perceived as a distinct aggregation of others in the neighborhood, (b) recognize themselves as a denotable group (almost invariably with a group name), and (c) have been involved in a sufficient number of delinquent incidents to call forth a consistent negative response from neighborhood residents and/or law enforcement agencies. (p. 111)

Howell (1997) expands the definition, saying that a youth gang "is commonly thought of as a self-formed association of peers having the following characteristics: a gang name and recognizable symbols, identifiable leadership, a geographic territory, a regular meeting pattern, and collective actions to carry out illegal activities" (p. 1). Yet many researchers and criminologists find these to be vague definitions that do not provide meaningful information. According to Esbensen et al. (2001), "There is little, if any, consensus to what constitutes a gang and who is a gang member, let alone what gangs do, either inside or outside the law" (p. 106). Esbensen and his colleagues posit that most criminologists or experts employ two widely used benchmarks: (1) youth status, defined as being between the ages of 10 and the early 20s, and (2) the involvement of group members in law-violating or deviant behavior. However, these cannot be the only benchmarks because they would encompass a good percentage of the middle school and high school youth, as well as young adults, in the United States today.

For our purposes here, elements of both the Klein and the Howell definitions will be used. Participation in serious and sustained criminal activity will be a key element that distinguishes youth *gangs* from other youth *groups*. In addition, some level of organization should be present, as indicated by such things as initiation rites, established leaders, and symbols or colors.

EARLY YOUTH GANG THEORIES: A BRIEF OVERVIEW

There has been exceedingly little gang-focused literature of a psychological nature until very recently. In criminology, gangs were typically considered a sociological phenomenon, characterized by group rather than individualized behavior. Thus, theory on youth gangs springs largely from a sociological perspective, most of it coming before the 1980s. All intellectual paths on group delinquency originated with the pioneering efforts of Frederick M. Thrasher in Chicago (Geis, 1965), who published his observations in the well-received classic *The Gang* (1927). At a time when psychiatrically oriented criminologists treated gang behavior as a throwback to primitive man roaming in herds, Thrasher dramatically shifted the discussion. Gang behavior, he said, was one way for youths to react to economic and social conditions. Although his colleagues at the Chicago School of Criminology were drawing similar conclusions about delinquency in general, Thrasher focused exclusively on gangs. He observed that gangs emerged and thrived in the interstitial areas of cities, particularly those areas lying between adjacent commercial and residential neighborhoods. Thrasher essentially equated gangs with group delinquency, since virtually all of the gangs that he studied engaged in criminal activities and apparently all the youths who engaged in criminal activities belonged to gangs.

Thrasher wrote that gangs represented the spontaneous effort of young people to create a society for themselves that offered excitement and adventure in the company of peers. Gangs provided the medium for stimulation, thrills, and togetherness that were not readily available in impoverished neighborhoods. Of the 1,313 gangs Thrasher studied, 530 could be classified as delinquent, and another 609 as "often delinquent." Unfortunately, he did not explain the criteria for these classifications.

Thrasher concluded that faulty social controls were at the root of gang delinquency. Specifically, the youths who violated norms had been ineffectively or weakly socialized by their families, churches, and schools. The social void created by these ineffectual social institutions had thus prompted the youths to seek each other's company and form groups. Free of traditional social controls, youth gangs did what they wanted, subject only to the constraints of their own subculture. Thrasher also observed that female gangs were exceedingly rare (he could locate only six that were independent of male gangs). He attributed the rarity of female gangs to the closer supervision that families, including single-parent families, gave to girls.

Following Thrasher's pioneering work, interest in gang delinquency ebbed, peaked, and ebbed once again. Interest was high in the 1950s and the 1960s, and several provocative theories were proposed. However, since the mid-1960s, few new theories of gang delinquency have been advanced. Mark Stafford (1984) cited two primary reasons for the lost interest: First, the study of gang delinquency was hampered by its parochialism. Researchers and theorists focused almost exclusively on urban boys from the lower-socioeconomic class, which limited the scope of any potential theory. A notable exception is the work of Anne Campbell (1984a), who studied group delinquency among girls. Second, there was considerable disagreement over the use of the word *gang*. For example, what are the social boundaries of a gang? Where does it begin, and where does it end? Members are not always easy to identify, and membership often fluctuates. Furthermore, it is not clear how a gang differs from a group of individuals who associate on a regular basis and occasionally participate in law-violating behavior. Many such groups have their own symbols and manners of dress, but theorists and researchers do not all agree that they qualify as gangs.

SHAW AND McKAY'S CONTRIBUTIONS

While Thrasher was studying youth gangs, researchers at the Chicago Institute for Juvenile Research were working on a systematic study of the ecological distribution of gang delinquency. Clifford R. Shaw and Henry D. McKay were the leaders of this group. The Shaw-McKay research supported Thrasher's contention that delinquency is principally a group activity, since 82% of the juveniles brought before the juvenile court had committed their offenses in the company of others. Shaw and McKay (1931) noted, however, that delinquent acts are typically committed by a few partners who were members of the same gang, but not by the gang as a whole. Furthermore, like Thrasher, they were careful to say that gangs did not "cause" illegal actions but rather facilitated them. Moreover, according to Shaw and McKay, traditions of delinquency are transmitted through successive generations in much the same way that language, social roles, and attitudes are transmitted.

Although members of a gang helped and encouraged one another to engage in unconventional actions, these researchers found that a major factor contributing to delinquency was a lack of parental control. According to Shaw and McKay (1931), when parental influence and control over children were weakened or hampered, delinquent behavior increased dramatically. In crowded urban areas like Chicago, newly arrived immigrants found themselves living partly with their own old-world traditions and partly among new-world expectations. Many children, sensing the confusion, were drawn more to their peer world and less to the traditional lifestyle, which peers rejected. Under these conditions, parents lost much of their influence over their children. In addition, the youths had little respect for parentally supported conventional institutions, such as the church or the school.

Shaw and McKay (1931) observed that many of the alienated youths developed their own splintered subcultures, in which certain forms of conduct were expected and particular symbols took on group-specific meanings. Shaw and McKay stressed that the deviant subcultures were not independent of the ethnic cultural context in which they developed, nor were they autonomous within mainstream American society. Rather, these youth subcultures interacted with several cultural and social contexts simultaneously, adopting some aspects of one, some of another. In essence, Shaw and McKay saw the deviant subculture as one system within many systems.

Shaw and McKay (1931) found that most delinquents they studied had internalized the central values of mainstream society but had difficulty reconciling them with their present predicament. Youths in deprived areas wanted what society advertised that everyone should have, including material goods, education, and prestige. Yet these youths did not have legitimate avenues to obtain what society valued. Gang delinquency provided a means of securing some of these valued aspects of mainstream society.

SOCIAL ABILITY VERSUS SOCIAL DISABILITY MODELS

In 1981 Hansell and Wiatrowski called attention to a major theoretical disagreement about the nature of delinquent gangs and the youths who join them. Some criminologists believe that most gang members have average social and interpersonal skills and generally belong to strong, cohesive groups. Group solidarity, close friendships, and loyalties are assumed to be features of the delinquent gang. In this sense, delinquent groups are not unlike nondelinquent groups, but they become *socialized* to the gang norms and expectations. Other criminologists—a larger group—perceive delinquents as loners, peer rejected and socially isolated, with below-average interpersonal skills. These are social outcasts who gravitate to other deviant and socially inept peers, eventually forming gangs. Because the members comprising them are socially inadequate, the gangs remain unstable, chaotic, disorganized bands of youths who cannot establish close, intimate relationships with one another.

Early theories that viewed delinquent gang members as socially normal and their groups as cohesive and close-knit have traditionally been called **social ability models**. On the other hand, those theories that consider delinquent gang members to be outcasts and socially inept adolescents who make little attempt to develop cohesive groups have been called **social disability models**. Examples of social ability models are the classic theories of Albert K. Cohen, Walter B. Miller, Richard Cloward and Lloyd Ohlin, and Herbert Bloch and Arthur Niederhoffer. Social disability models are best represented in the works of James Short, Jr., Fred Strodbeck, and later by Gerald Patterson.

CONTEMPORARY GANG DEMOGRAPHICS

As suggested earlier, we can provide only rough estimates of the numbers of gangs and gang members and their characteristics. These data are typically derived from

TABLE 11–1: Percentage of Jurisdictions Reporting the Onset of Gang Problems

	Before 1981	*1986–1990*	*1993–1994*	*1995–1996*
Large city	9	38	18	6
Small city	5	20	32	19
Suburban	6	28	32	9
Rural	2	16	46	19

Source: Data from "Modern-Day Youth Gangs" by J. C. Howell, A. Egley, Jr., and D. K. Gleason, June 2002, *Juvenile Justice Bulletin*, Washington, DC: U.S. Department of Justice, OJJDP.

government-sponsored surveys or from the work of individual researchers. Surveys of law enforcement agencies across the country indicate that their significant gang problems began quite recently—1994 is the most frequently cited year (Howell, 1998). Some cities, however, such as Chicago and Los Angeles, have had chronic, serious youth gang problems for a long time. In fact, most of the early information on gangs has been derived almost exclusively from studies focusing on well-known gangs located in those two cities. The names of some of those gangs are universally recognized: Crips, Bloods, Latin Kings, Black Gangster Disciplines, and El Ruk'n. During the 1980s and 1990s, members of Chicago's four largest and most criminally active gangs—Black Gangster Disciples Nation, the Latin Disciples, the Latin Kings, and the Vice Lords—accounted for two-thirds of all gang-related crimes in Chicago and for more than half of the city's gang-related homicides (Block & Block, 1993).

Traditionally, youth gangs have been most prevalent in the central cities of large metropolitan areas, but this pattern seems to be changing (Howell, Egley, & Gleason, 2002). Today, there is a discernible shift to more suburban areas, small cities, towns, and rural areas. Table 11–1 shows this trend.

NUMBER AND SIZE OF YOUTH GANGS

The first systematic study of gangs in the United States was conducted by Frederick M. Thrasher, discussed earlier, who estimated that there were about 1,313 gangs in Chicago alone at the turn of the century (1900). He was convinced that about one-tenth of Chicago's 350,000 boys between the ages of 10 and 20 were influenced by gangs.

The United States has seen a rapid proliferation of youth gangs since 1980 (Howell, 1998). Based on national surveys of urban youth, it is estimated that from 14% to 30% of urban adolescents join gangs at some point (Howell, 1997). Estimates of gang membership in the United States in the mid-1990s ranged from 660,000 to as many as 1.5 million, depending on the definition of *gang* used in the survey (Esbensen et al., 2001). As noted earlier, statistics on membership are not easy to come by. Gang membership is in continual flux, depending on the social, economic, and political climate of a particular geographical region at any given time. The best estimate at this writing indicates that there were approximately 760,000 gang members in 24,000 gangs active in the United States during 2004 (Egley & Ritz, 2006).

Gangs vary in size, often according to whether they are traditional or specialized. Traditional gangs are described as large, enduring, and territorial, averaging about 180 members, whereas more specialized gangs, such as those involved in drug trafficking, average about 25 members (Howell, 1998). In large cities, some gangs of both types are known to number in the thousands (Spergel, 1995). Gang size is also the result of several other interacting factors, including the size of the youth population within a given area, the presence or absence of police and community pressure, and the nature and visibility of the group.

ACTIVE VERSUS TRANSIENT GANG MEMBERSHIP

While a few make the gang a lifelong association, most studies find that one-half to two-thirds of adolescents are members for 1 year or less (Esbensen, 2000; Gatti, Tremblay, Vitaro, & McDuff, 2005; Lacourse et al., 2002; Walker-Barnes & Mason, 2001). This finding seems to defy the conventional wisdom that gangs have a hold on their members throughout their lives (see Figure 11–1). Short-time members are referred to by criminologists as **transient gang members**. There is evidence, also, that some gang-involved members do not participate in delinquent gang activities, suggesting that researchers should look at both gang-involved members and gang-delinquent members (Walker-Barnes & Mason, 2001). Gordon et al. (2004) assert, however, that even a brief spell of gang participation may expose a youth to a substantially heightened risk of sustained delinquency.

ETHNIC AND RACIAL COMPOSITION

Traditionally, youth gangs have been racially or ethnically segregated (Howell et al., 2002). In the early 19th century, gangs in the United States were primarily or exclusively Irish, Jewish, or Italian (Howell, 1997). Today, gangs are increasingly more multiethnic or multiracial in their membership. Approximately 50% of the youth gangs today are racially mixed (Howell et al., 2002).

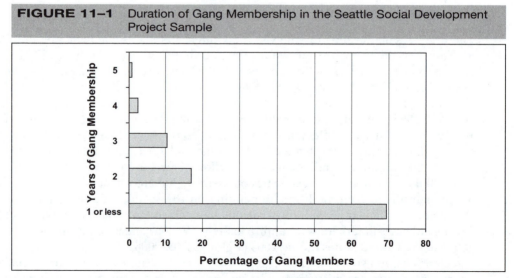

FIGURE 11–1 Duration of Gang Membership in the Seattle Social Development Project Sample

Source: Data from *Early Precursors of Gang Membership: A Study of Seattle Youth* (p. 3) by K. G. Hill, C. Lui, and J. D. Hawkins, December 2001, Washington, DC: U.S. Department of Justice, OJJDP.

Smaller cities have the greatest mixture of ethnic/minority youth gang members, while large cities' gangs are more likely to have more homogeneous ethnic/minority composition (Howell et al., 2002). In Europe youth gangs are composed primarily of a mixture of ethnic or national minorities, often reflecting the immigration and refugee patterns of various countries (Klein, Weerman, & Thornberry, 2006). In Canada youth gangs are mostly made up of some combination of African Canadians, First Nationals, and Caucasians (Astwood Strategy Corporation, 2003).

Overall, approximately 40% of gang members in the United States are white, 36% are black, 16% are Latino and Latina, and 3 percent are Asian (Howell et al., 2002). In one survey of nearly 6,000 eighth graders in 11 different geographical areas across the country (Esbensen & Osgood, 1997), 31% of the students who said they were gang members were black, 25% were Latino, 25% were white, 5% were Asian, and 15% were of other racial and ethnic groups. Asian gangs—especially Vietnamese, Cambodian, and Laotian gangs—seem to be expanding rapidly, particularly in California. Youth gangs among Native Americans and Alaska Natives have also increased and expanded in recent years (Major et al., 2004). It should be emphasized again, however, that percentages gained from surveys change annually, sometimes significantly, depending on when, how, and where the survey is given.

AGE

Until the mid-1970s, juvenile gangs consisted primarily of members ranging in age from 12 to 21 years. Currently, the age range has expanded at both ends, with members now as young as 9 and as old as 30 and older (Curry & Decker, 1998; Goldstein, 1991; Howell, 1998). Young members are often used in capacities such as runners, weapon carriers, and lookouts. If they are caught, the criminal justice system is likely to respond with considerable leniency. The average age of gang members tends to be older in cities in which gangs have been in existence longer, such as Chicago and Los Angeles (Howell, 1998; Klein, 1995; Spergel, 1995). Older members frequently remain in the gang because employment opportunities for disadvantaged populations remain low in the legitimate economy.

A recent national survey of juvenile gang members (National Gang Crime Research Center, 2001) reveals that nearly half (48.5%) joined at or before the age of 12, over two-thirds (69.2%) joined at or before the age 13, and 83.2% joined at or before the age of 14. A very small number (7.6%) joined after the age of 16. Over two-thirds (72.1%) of juvenile gang members reported that violence was involved in their initiation into the gang. Initiation rites are seen as a way for new members to demonstrate commitment to the gang.

GENDER COMPOSITION

Historical Overview

Gang researchers did not take female gangs seriously until the 1980s, when Campbell's 1984 book, *The Girls in the Gang*, and her article on gangs appeared (Moore & Hagedorn, 2001). As noted earlier, Campbell had spent 6 months observing and talking with female members of three gangs in New York City. She reported her results, often in the girls' own words.

The gangs Campbell observed had a traditional pyramidal power structure with males as the head and female members as subordinates. Gang members—both male and female—spent many hours a day in front of television sets, watching game shows, soap operas, and other supposed depictions of American life. The girls almost worshipped clothes and makeup and took particular care of the clothes they had. Despite their failure to fit into mainstream society, gang members were conservative and displayed an American-capitalistic-society-is-all-right attitude. Certain illegal acts, such as selling soft drugs, were not considered wrong by the gang, but burglary, robbery, rape, or assault generally were. When the gang was warring with another gang, however, any criminal activities against that gang were acceptable. Gang members claimed to keep the streets safe and the neighborhood clean. At the same time, they did not seem to mind being portrayed to the public as rebellious, tough, and persecuted.

Campbell found that the female members most generally came from backgrounds of poverty, minority status, unemployment, and unfinished educations. Their homes were characterized by geographical and emotional instability, a pattern she discovered that was more typical of girls than of boys. During their childhoods, these families had moved frequently, and the girls had attended a series of schools. Family life had been consistently stormy and unhappy, and physical violence was common. In addition, physical aggression between parents was particularly frequent, and the girls often grew up fearing physical abuse and, in some cases, sexual abuse themselves. Alone and alienated, the girls gravitated to the gang, hoping to find "sisters" who were like them and who were willing to treat them with respect.

In sum, Campbell found the girls in the gangs neither violent nor overly aggressive nor independent. Their main reason for belonging to the gang was to have companionship and security. Gang members had dreams but believed that these dreams would probably never be fulfilled, in light of their current skills, education, and living arrangements. The girls accepted the traditional double standard with respect to gender: They believed that men were naturally aggressive and dominant, and the girls tolerated this behavior without question in the males in their lives. The roving, unfaithful nature of men was expected and tolerated.

Contemporary Studies

For decades male gang members have outnumbered females by a ratio of nearly 20 to 1 (Goldstein, 1991). This ratio, though, appears to be changing significantly. There is growing evidence that girls are joining gangs in increasing numbers (2% to 4% higher) in recent years (Howell et al., 2002). Some recent surveys suggest that girls and women represent about 10% to 14% of total gang membership in the United States (Howell et al., 2002; Miller, 1992; National Youth Gang Center, 2000). However, L. A. Hughes (2005) suggests that female gang membership may be substantially higher than is commonly reported. Some self-report surveys have indicated that a range of 9% to 38% may be more accurate (Esbensen, 2000; Moore & Hagedorn, 2001). In some localities, girls represent one-fourth to one-third of active gang members (Howell & Egley, 2005).

It is important to keep in mind that girls and young women can participate in gang activity in three different ways: (1) by forming an autonomous, independent gang; (2) by participating as a female auxiliary—that is, the female branch—of a male gang; or (3) by being part of a gender-integrated gang. Esbensen, Deschenes, and Winfree (1999) report that gender mixing in youth gangs is becoming very common. For example, 92% of eighth-grade gang members said that both boys and girls belong to their gangs. These data probably represent some combination of both auxiliary members and gender-integrated gangs. Auxiliary gang membership was by far the most common form of female gang membership during the 1960s and 1970s (W. B. Miller, 1975). Girls were used as weapon carriers and lookouts, and some were presumably used as "sex objects." Group sex as an initiation ritual for female gang members was one of the early stereotypes of female gang members, but the validity of this image is highly questionable (Moore & Hagedorn, 2001).

Although some of these expectations continue to exist in some gangs located in large cities, the responsibilities of female gang members are evolving. Female members are taking more active roles, such as moving drugs and weapons, and are gathering intelligence on rival gangs. Other females are involved in drug sales, robberies, assaults, and drive-by shootings (National Alliance of Crime Investigators Associations, 2005). Youth surveys continually document that the delinquency rates of female gang members are higher than those reported for nongang females and males but lower than those reported for male gang members. In general, female gang members commit fewer violent crimes than male gang members do and are more inclined to commit property and status offenses (Moore & Hagedorn, 2001; see Table 11–2. Drug offenses and liquor-law violations are among the most common crimes committed by female gang members (Moore & Hagedorn, 2001). Chesney-Lind and Shelden (2004) point out that the world the female gang members inhabit does not afford many legitimate opportunities to succeed. "It is a world filled with poverty on the one hand and the ready availability of drugs on the other hand" (p. 72). This state of affairs is especially relevant to many African-American girls.

There are also increasing numbers of independent or unaffiliated female gangs developing around the country, particularly in small towns and rural communities (Moore & Hagedorn, 2001). Many all-girl gangs appear quite involved in property crimes, drug pushing, and violence (Hughes, 2005). Most of their assaults and fights

TABLE 11–2: Gang-Related Charges for Female Arrestees in Chicago (1996)

Offense	*Percentage of Total*
Homicide	0.1
Simple battery	14.9
Mob action	4.8
Other violent offenses	18.7
Total violent offenses	**38.5**
Cocaine possession	2.6
Crack possession	15.6
Other drug offenses	19.6
Total drug offenses	**37.7**
Prostitution	**9.8**
Property	**5.1**
Liquor	**3.5**
Weapons	**2.8**
Other	**2.3**

Source: Data from *Female Gangs: A Focus on Research* by J. W. Moore and J. Hagedorn, 2001, Washington, DC: U.S. Department of Justice, OJJDP.

occur within a school setting and without weapons (National Alliance of Crime Investigators Associations, 2005).

A majority of all-female gangs are either African-American or Latina, although there are also small but increasing numbers of Asian and white female gangs. According to Moore and Hagedorn (2001), Latina gangs have been studied more than African-American female gangs have been—Mexican-Americans in the Southwest and Puerto Ricans in New York City.

GANG MIGRATION

Gang migration refers to the movement of gang members from one region of the country to another. The National Gang Survey (National Gang Crime Research Center, 1997) estimates that approximately 18% of gang members are migrants. Rural regions experience the highest number of gang members who are outsiders, whereas large cities have the fewest outsiders. Most of the gang members moving into rural and suburban regions come from large cities. Many of the migrants are African-American or Latino males who remain connected to their original gang roots.

The reasons for such migration are multiple. Among agencies that reported high levels of gang migration in 2004, social reasons (e.g., members moving with families, pursuit of legitimate opportunities) were offered as the main explanation, but drug market opportunities, avoidance of law enforcement crackdowns, and participation in other illegal ventures were also instrumental in the migration of many gang members (Egley & Ritz, 2006).

GANG DELINQUENCY

Repeatedly, research has documented that members of youth gangs engage in far more crime than nongang youths do, at least in North America (see Figure 11–2). In Europe the criminal activity of youth gangs appears to be more modest, especially in terms of violence (Klein et al., 2006). Some recent studies have indicated that gang members in large American cities account for 86% of serious delinquent acts, 69% of violent delinquent acts, and 70% of drug sales (Thornberry & Burch, 1997). The criminal patterns of youth gangs vary according to the type of gang (Sheldon, Tracy, & Brown, 2001) and the location. Some commit very little crime—a fact that is rarely stated in the media or confirmed by the law enforcement community. Others are heavily involved in serious crimes. For both genders, engaging in serious violence is the delinquent behavior that best distinguishes gang from nongang youth in the United States (Klein et al., 2006). However, contemporary youth gangs that engage in serious delinquency are increasingly involved in burglary and larceny–theft and individual drug sales (Howell et al., 2002). The reasons for this shift to property crimes instead of violent crimes may be that many modern youth gangs are still in the early stages of development in terms of criminal involvement (Howell et al., 2002), which could also explain why some gangs are involved in very little crime. Gangs may move through patterns of offending as they mature, moving from property crimes to more violent acts.

Youth gangs in small communities and rural areas usually do not fit the stereotype of traditional gangs in large cities with chronic gang problems (Howell et al., 2002). A community's gang problems may begin with school-centered gangs, which tend not to be extensively involved in criminal activity in their beginning stages (Howell & Lynch,

FIGURE 11–2   Delinquency Rates Among Gang and Nongang Youth in the Seattle Social Development Project Sample

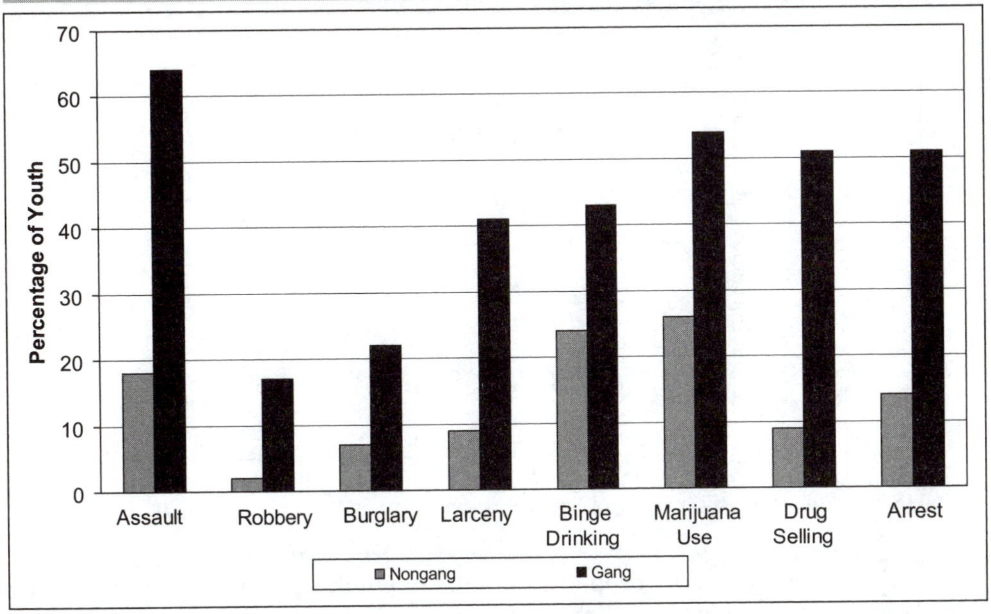

Source: Data from *Early Precursors of Gang Membership: A Study of Seattle Youth* (p. 2) by K. G. Hill, C. Lui, and J. D. Hawkins, December 2001, Washington, DC: U.S. Department of Justice, OJJDP.

2000). Their law-breaking behavior tends to center around altercations with rival gangs, usually in other schools or neighborhoods. In addition, most rural gangs represent local or "homegrown" problems and are not the result of social migration of urban gang youth (Esbensen, 2000).

VIOLENCE

Although there have been peaks and valleys in gang violence over the years, the amount of violence perpetrated by gangs that engage in serious criminal activity has increased in recent years in some cities and has declined in others. During the 1990s, the total number of gang homicides reported in more than 400 cities decreased 15% (Curry, Maxson, & Howell, 2001), but the rate went up in some cities. As noted by Howell (1998), levels of gang violence differ from one city to another, from one community to another, from one gang to another, and even among cliques within the same gang. For example, in two cities, Los Angeles and Chicago, more than half of the nearly 1,000 homicides appear to be gang related (Egley & Major, 2004; Egley & Ritz, 2006); but in another 171 cities, approximately one-fourth of all homicides are estimated to be gang related (Egley & Ritz, 2006). The homicides of individual gangs are characterized by periodic peaks:

Each homicide peak tends to correspond to a series of escalating confrontations, usually over gang member recruitment, impulsive and emotional defense of one's identity as a gang member, turf protection and expansion, defending the honor of the gang, drug wars, and trivial events of a confrontational nature. (Howell, 1997, p. 2)

FIGURE 11–3 Rate of Gang-Related Violent Crime in the United States, According to the Victims (1993–2003)

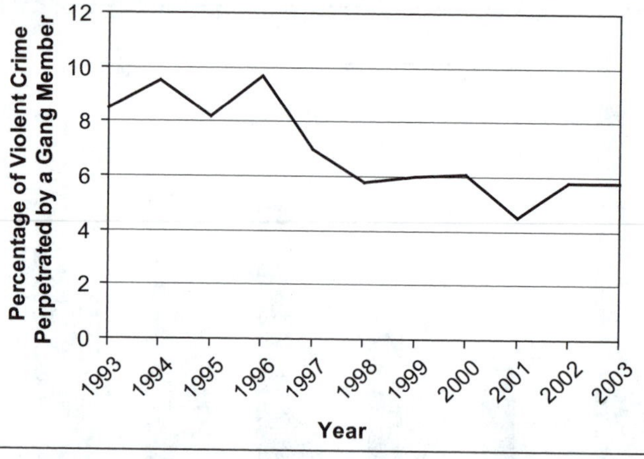

Source: Data from *Violence by Gang Members, 1993–2003* (p. 1) by E. Harrell, June 2005, Washington, DC: U.S. Department of Justice, Office of Justice Programs.

Most of the overall drop in gang-related homicides across the nation during the 1990s is attributable to the 30% drop in gang-related homicides in Los Angeles (Curry et al., 2001; see Figure 11–3). If the decline in Los Angeles is factored out, the homicide rate has remained largely the same across the country. Curry et al. (2001) conclude from their analysis that "gang homicides remained a serious problem in most U.S. cities during the first part of the decade, increasing and decreasing in almost the same proportion of cities" (p. 2).

Most gang violence is directed at other gangs (Howell, 1998). Of the nearly 1,000 gang-related homicides in Chicago from 1987 to 1994, 75% were *between* gangs, 11% were *within* the gang itself, and 14% involved nongang victims murdered by gang members (Block et al., 1996). Howell (1998, 1999) notes that gang homicides have characteristics that differ from those of nongang homicides. Homicides by gang members are more likely to take place in public settings (particularly on the street), to involve multiple participants, to be directed at strangers (who are usually other gang members they do not know), and to be carried out via drive-by shootings. From 1989 through 1993, for example, 22% of Los Angeles gang-related homicides were drive-by, resulting in 590 murders (Hutson, Anglin, & Eckstein, 1996). In a survey of gang members held in juvenile correctional facilities, the National Gang Crime Research Center (2001) discovered that nearly one-half of the gang members admitted they may have killed someone intentionally or unintentionally. Many times they are not sure because they often flee the scene. In some gangs, new membership requires the prospective member to commit a drive-by shooting or some other form of violence.

Studies of urban youth show that gang members are responsible for a large proportion of violent offenses and commit serious and violent crimes at a rate several times higher than that for nongang adolescents (Howell, 1997). Studies have also shown that individuals who affiliate with delinquent gangs during preadolescence commit, as a group, more violent acts than those who affiliate with a gang during later adolescence

(Lacourse, Nagin, Tremblay, Vitaro, & Claes, 2003). In addition, delinquent groups clearly facilitate and encourage aggressive behavior and violence in those adolescents who are already prone to be violent. Research demonstrates that those who were on a trajectory of worsening antisocial behavior are far more likely to join antisocial gangs (Lahey, Gordon, Loeber, Stouthamer-Loeber, & Farrington, 1999). Both male and female gang members acknowledge that gang participation increases their vulnerability to other problems, such as greater contact with the criminal justice system and violent victimization by rival groups (L. A. Hughes, 2005).

DRUG-RELATED OFFENDING AND OTHER ILLEGAL ACTIVITIES

According to government documents (e.g., National Alliance of Crime Investigators Associations, 2005), gangs are the primary distributors of drugs throughout the United States. Serious forms of drug use, drug dealing, and drug-related violence are far more frequent among gang members than among nongang members (Gatti et al., 2005; Esbensen, Peterson, Freng, & Taylor, 2002). In addition, the research evidence indicates that drug use and dealing increases during active membership in a gang and continues at a high level even after leaving the gang (Gatti et al., 2005). Gangs, both adult and juvenile, use drug trafficking—particularly in powder and crack cocaine—as their primary means of financial support.

Drug dealing among Canadian youth gangs appears to concentrate on marijuana and cocaine sales. It is estimated that Canadian youth gang members are responsible for more than one-third (36%) of the street sales of marijuana, followed by 17% of the street sales of crack cocaine, and 11% of powder cocaine (Astwood Strategy Corporation, 2003). They are responsible for a negligible percentage of other drugs—such as heroin (5%), Ecstasy (7%), MDA (5%), and other club drugs (3%)—a pattern that is similar to that of American youth gangs.

The relationships among gang membership, drug use, drug selling, and violence are unclear (Spergel, 1995). The news media and law enforcement agencies have for years claimed a close connection between violence and gang involvement in drugs. The research evidence, however, does not support these claims (Institute for Law and Justice, 1994; Klein, Maxson, & Cunningham, 1988; Spergel, 1995). The relationships appear to be much more complicated than commonly assumed. Although many gang members do engage in drug use and/or trafficking, the link between gang-related *violence* and the drug trade does not seem to be strong.

Some gangs today are becoming involved in more sophisticated enterprises, such as currency counterfeiting or manufacturing and distributing "bootleg" copies of newly released motion pictures (National Gang Crime Research Center, 2001). Youth gangs are also increasing their international contacts and communications, which may involve terrorist activities. In a recent survey, over half of male gang members and one-third of the females indicated that they had used an incendiary device or explosives on a property or person (National Gang Crime Research Center, 2001).

Certain offenses are related to different racial/ethnic youth gangs. In general, African-American gangs tend to be more involved in drug offenses, Latino gangs in turf-related violence, and Asian and white gangs in property crimes (Howell, 1998). In the Los Angeles area, for example, much of the violence of Latino gangs is related to defense of their neighborhood turf, or barrio, from other gangs, whereas African-American gangs tend to be involved in entrepreneurial activities, such as drug selling and distribution, or burglary-related activities.

As noted by Thornberry and his colleagues (Thornberry et al., 1993), "Criminological research has clearly demonstrated that gang members are more likely than nongang members to commit offenses, especially serious and violent offenses, and to do so with high frequency" (p. 55). These researchers further report that the relationship is very strong and is reported in just about every study of American gang behavior. From the time their presence was first noted in the United States, youth gangs have been actively involved in a variety of criminal activities (Howell et al., 2002).

GANGS AND GUNS

Gang members are more than twice as likely as nongang members to own a gun for protection and are more likely to associate with peers who also own guns. Gangs are also more likely to recruit adolescents who own firearms (Howell, 1998). In addition, active gang members are much more likely than other juveniles to *carry* guns most of the time (Decker et al., 1997; Howell & Decker, 1999). In a study of youth gang members in St. Louis, 81% indicated that they owned guns, and two-thirds of them had used their guns at least once (Decker & Van Winkle, 1996). In the St. Louis study, the situations in which guns were used most often were gang fights; they were used less frequently in drive-bys and in defending gang members from strangers or drug buyers who tried to rob them.

Gang members who perceive a threat from rival gangs carry guns to protect themselves. They believe their rivals have guns and they need better and more sophisticated ones—such as AK-47s, Tech-9s, Uzis, and other high-powered weapons—to gain an advantage. Gang members also use guns to protect or enhance their reputation or reclaim respect (Stretesky & Pogrebin, 2007). In fact, one-third of youth gang members thought it was acceptable to shoot someone who disrespected them (Decker et al., 1997). Guns provide a sense of power and intimidation for some gang members. Stretesky and Pogrebin (2007) point out that guns are very important symbols for identity and impression management. Overall, "guns are probably far more important to the daily lives and identities of gang members than most policy makers might imagine, precisely because they help project a reputation and create respect" (Stretesky & Pogrebin, 2007, p. 109). It should also be noted that only a small number of gang members commit most of the serious crimes with guns.

THE SUPER PREDATOR CONCEPT

The concept of a **super predator** can probably be traced back to an article in *The Weekly Standard* by John Dilulio (1995), who claimed among other things that certain juvenile gang members are committing homicidal violence in "wolf packs." These super predators, according to Dilulio, spring from conditions of "moral poverty," characterized by growing up without loving, capable, responsible adults in social settings and neighborhoods that are deviant, criminal, and violent. Whether the term *super predator* is a valid term that depicts an unusual group of gang members is highly questionable.

The concept of a super predator was put to the test by the National Gang Crime Research Center. It identified the super predator as someone (1) who has joined a gang, (2) who remains an active gang member, (3) who comes from a dysfunctional family, and (4) whose criminal and violent behavior distinguishes this offender from other offenders by its severity (National Gang Crime Research Center, 1997). The super predator begins his career in violence at an early age and remains active in serious crime across his lifetime. According to the National Gang Crime Research Center (1997), super predators account for approximately 6% of the gang members in the United States but account for a disproportionately high amount of crime and violence.

The so-called super predator is highly similar, if not identical, to the LCP offender discussed in previous chapters, except that he or she is a member of a youth gang. Creating another label for this LCP offender adds little to our knowledge and simply adds a sensational element to the serious juvenile offender. Furthermore, the term encourages fear of crime because of its emphasis on the vulnerability of victims.

YOUTH GANG TYPOLOGIES

A number of youth gang typologies have been proposed over the years. Among the more popular in contemporary thinking is the Maxson-Klein typology (Maxson & Klein, 1995; Klein & Maxson, 1996), which consists of five different gang types or structures: traditional, neotraditional, compressed, collective, and specialty gangs.

- **Traditional gangs** have usually been in existence for 20 or more years, although they keep regenerating themselves. They contain relatively clear subgroups, generally separated by age but sometimes divided on the basis of neighborhood. Compared to other gangs, these tend to have a wide age range—from 9 or 10 years of age to the 30s. Traditional gangs tend to be very large, numbering 100 or more members.
- **Neotraditional gangs** resemble traditional gangs, except that the neotraditional gangs have not been in existence as long (probably less than 10 years). They are usually medium in size, ranging from 50 to 100 members. Neotraditional gangs are very territorial, claiming turf and defending it. In many instances, they have a goal of becoming well-established and powerful traditional gangs.
- **Compressed gangs** are small, usually having fewer than 50 members. The age range is narrow, with 10 years or less between the youngest and the oldest members. Some compressed gangs are territorial, but many are not. Compressed gangs have a short history, and it is often unclear whether they will grow and solidify into more traditional forms or simply remain small or disband. This type of youth gang is the most common, representing about 40% of known gangs in the United States.
- **Collective gangs** are similar to compressed gangs, except that they are bigger and have a wider age range between the youngest and the oldest members. In general, a collective gang "resembles a kind of shapeless mass of adolescents and young adult members that has not developed the distinguishing characteristics of other gangs" (Klein & Maxson, 1996, p. 21).
- **Specialty gangs** focus on specific criminal activity, such as motor vehicle theft, burglary, or drug dealing. They tend to be small and usually have a history of less than 10 years. Normally, specialty gangs have a well-defined territory within which they practice their criminal activity. Basically, these gangs are formed almost exclusively to pursue their criminal intentions rather than for social reasons.

An interesting typology that reflects the wide spectrum of antisocial involvement in youth gangs is outlined in a report by the Canadian Research Institute for Law and the Family (Mellor, MacRae, Pauls, & Hornick, 2005). The typology is very similar to one presented by the Australian Institute of Criminology (R. White, 2002). The authors identify five discrete gang categories that illustrate an increasing level of criminal activity, organizational structure, and recruitment strategies:

- Type A (**groups of friends**) are based largely on interest and usually do not involve criminal activity. These young people usually hang out together in public places such as shopping malls.
- Type B (**spontaneous criminal activity/gangs**) are formed by youth who share some commonality in their interests, values, and probably their antisocial behavior. Some scholars refer to these groups as "wannabe groups" (R. White, 2002), because they are a loose band of young people who get together primarily to engage in spontaneous social activity and exciting, impulsive criminal activity. The antisocial behavior of this group is "situationally motivated and much of this type of gang/group activity can be categorized as gratuitous violence and bullying by misdirected and unsupervised youth" (Mellor et al., 2005, p. vi). Most members are not that committed to the gang or its culture and are often transient members.
- Type C (**purposive gangs**) come together for a specific purpose or intention. For example, stealing motor vehicles, burglary, shoplifting, or vigilante-type violence might be the primary goal of a group. Such a group may emerge from a larger gang and may disband once the primary goal of the group is disrupted or changed.
- Type D (**youth street gangs**) are highly visible hard-core groups that come together primarily for profit-driven criminal activity, power/protection, or organized violence against rival street gangs. These groups are generally described as a semistructured organization. Type D gangs identify themselves by adopting a gang name, colors, clothing, jewelry, styles, and/or tattoos. They generally stake out definite territory or turf.
- Type E (**structured criminal organizations**) are highly organized and structured criminal networks that are usually led by criminally experienced adults for the purpose of illegal economic or financial gain. Youths are used primarily for specific activities designed to further the gang's criminal activities.

WHY DO YOUTHS JOIN GANGS?

Over the years, researchers have identified a large assortment of potential risk factors for youth gang involvement, which tend to be the same risk factors identified for juvenile offending that we discussed in Chapters 2 and 3. In recent years, scholars, researchers, and practitioners have proposed three broad hypotheses to explain why youths join gangs. These hypotheses should help us organize the extensive theory and research on why children and adolescents join gangs, but we will quickly find that they tend to overlap a great deal. In addition, the three hypotheses do not always fit the reasons perfectly.

The first hypothesis is known as the selection hypothesis. The **selection hypothesis** contends that gang members are individuals who are delinquent and violent prior to joining the group. Thus, gang members are individuals prone to engage in serious and violent delinquent acts *prior* to joining the gang. Deviant friends are attracted to one another because of similarities in attitudes and behavior, but their association does not cause delinquent behavior (Bagwell, 2004; Tremblay, Masse, Vitaro, & Dobkin, 1995). Gang members invite these youths whom they perceive as similar in attitudes and values to themselves. In effect, gang entry for already-violent youth might be thought of as the next developmental step in the escalating antisocial behavior of some boys (Lahey et al., 1999).

The second hypothesis is known as the **social facilitation hypothesis**. This hypothesis argues that gang members are no different from nongang members *prior* to joining the gang and *after* leaving the gang. This perspective contends that the gang actually facilitates and encourages antisocial and violent behavior in its active members. Thus, the influence of the gang causes children and adolescents to engage in antisocial behavior; the gang provides the social setting for crime and violence to flourish (Stretesky & Pogrebin, 2007). This hypothesis is compatible with socialization theories and social learning theories, discussed in Chapter 5.

The third hypothesis, called the **enhancement hypothesis**, accommodates both selection and social facilitation perspectives (Thornberry et al., 1993). In this model, gangs are believed to recruit their members from adolescents who are already delinquent and violent. The gangs then provide the social setting to facilitate and encourage their members' antisocial and violent behavior.

REASONS THAT BOYS JOIN GANGS

There are many compelling reasons that youths join gangs—the enhanced prestige or status that a gang affords, opportunities to make money and to be economically taken care of, protection from other gangs. A few juveniles, perhaps many, are virtually born into gangs as a result of neighborhood traditions and their parents' or siblings' earlier gang involvement (Howell, 1998). Many others report that family conflict and school problems are major reasons for joining (Wyrick, 2000). One major reason for antisocial boys to join gangs is the powerful attraction to others like themselves.

Similarities in Attitudes and Behavior

One of the repetitive themes in developmental psychology is that children and adolescents are attracted to others like themselves who will accept them. This is especially true for the adolescent years, when peers become increasingly influential. Substance-abusing boys, for example, seek out similar friends once their substance-abusing behaviors are developed (Dobkin, Tremblay, Masse, & Vitaro, 1995). Peer friends become confidants with whom they can share ideas, values, and attitudes. As we documented in earlier chapters, peer rejection in the early school years often has a substantial impact on prosocial peer relationships in the later school years. This is particularly true for those children who are both aggressive and peer rejected. In many instances, these children migrate to peers who are also aggressive and have been similarly socially rejected. Finding outcasts like themselves is probably very reinforcing.

As noted in earlier chapters, LCP or early-onset offenders often have difficulty with prosocial peers and consequently have limited opportunity for association with conventional, normal peers. Because human beings are naturally social creatures, these LCPs or early starters most often gravitate toward similarly antisocial peers *early* in their development. Contemporary developmental research clearly indicates that boys who are rejected by their prosocial peer group are more likely to be involved in delinquent gangs in adolescence (Bagwell, 2004). As described earlier, peer rejection in first grade usually predicts antisocial behavior in fourth grade and delinquent gang involvement in adolescence (Cowan & Cowan, 2004).

Most studies of gang membership show that gang involvement begins around age 13 and increases up to age 18 (Lahey et al., 1999). The dynamics of early gang involvement may be different from those of gang involvement later in adolescence. In other words, the reasons for preadolescents joining gangs are likely to be significantly different from the reasons for adolescents joining gangs. For example, the child who becomes involved with a gang early in development is more likely to have had serious peer-relationship problems or to have been exposed to a seriously dysfunctional family.

Gang members do not typically encourage active members to have close friends outside the gang (Craig, Vitaro, Gagnon, & Tremblay, 2002). In effect, gangs often remain socially isolated from prosocial and socially competent peers. "As a result, their socialization experiences are imbalanced in the direction of negative interactions and they are at continued risk for learning aggressive behaviours" (Craig et al., 2002, p. 55). Thus, antisocial groups or gangs are likely to provide a high degree of reinforcement for antisocial behavior and very little reinforcement for prosocial behavior (Bagwell 2004; Jessor & Jessor, 1977).

Dysfunctional Families

One recurrent theme in the youth gang literature is that adolescents are attracted to gangs because their families fail to provide the basic needs and demands that families typically provide (Eitle, Gunkel, & Van Gundy, 2004). Eitle et al. point out that these "surrogate families" are attractive to adolescents because they can provide a sense of belonging, emotional support, and resources for material needs.

Studies also show that early association with deviant peers is especially prevalent among youth who are from dysfunctional families that provide little supervision or monitoring of the child's activities (Bagwell, 2004). Many of these dysfunctional families also use inappropriate control and discipline and show a negative emotional relationship between parent and child. Most of the time, antisocial boys spend time together in neighborhood and community settings outside close adult monitoring and supervision (Bagwell, 2004).

Ethnic and cultural differences in parenting may also be critical in gang involvement. In fact, some of the inconsistencies reported in the research literature on the effects of dysfunctional families may be due to ethnic differences in parenting (Walker-Barnes & Mason, 2001). Walker-Barnes and Mason (2001) found that for African-American youth, parenting was especially important in gang involvement. They discovered that higher levels of behavioral control (supervision and monitoring) and lower levels of lax and psychological control (coercive, guilt-based control) were related to *decreases* in gang delinquency for these youth. In contrast, lax control had no effect on Hispanic youth, and neither lax nor psychological control had an effect on white youth. However, higher levels of parental *warmth* were significantly effective in decreasing gang involvement for all ethnic and cultural youths who participated in the study. These results highlight both the need for prevention strategies based on ethnic and cultural differences and the importance of parental warmth, regardless of ethnic or cultural origin.

In addition, homeless and runaway youth often seek gangs for companionship, protection, acceptance, social support, and tutelage for surviving on their own (Yoder, Whitbeck, & Hoyt, 2003). These youths are usually homeless or have run away because of serious problems within the home. Yoder et al. (2003) report that a significant number of 602 homeless or runaway youths had become either gang involved (32.2%) or active gang members (15.4%).

REASONS THAT GIRLS JOIN GANGS

As mentioned previously, female gang members are more likely than male gang members to come from troubled families and are far more likely to have run away from home. Many seek refuge from the physical, emotional, and sexual abuse occurring in their dysfunctional families (Moore & Hagedorn, 2001). Friendship, solidarity, self-affirmation, and a sense of new possibilities have been found to motivate young inner-city females to join and remain in gangs (Moore & Hagedorn, 2001). Gangs frequently offer a family-like setting that is lacking in the lives of female gang members. Chesney-Lind and Shelden (2004) posit that the gang imparts a sort of haven for sexually abused and battered girls who have no genuine sense of safety elsewhere.

Protection also appears to be a very important motivation for girls. Gangs provide girls a means of protecting themselves from violence from other men in their lives (J. Miller, 2001). However, when a girl joins a gang, she remains at risk for personal injury and even death from rival gangs (or from her own gang in rare instances), and she may have much more exposure to the criminal justice system than she would otherwise have. In many communities, law enforcement officials watch known or suspected gang members very closely.

Some girls and young women join gangs for economic reasons: they are unemployed or have lost other financial resources. In addition, many girls join gangs because at least one other member of their family is a member of a gang (J. Miller, 2001). Overall, many of the reasons that girls join gangs are the same reasons that boys join gangs—specifically, "a sense of belonging (familylike), power, protection, respect, fear, and, sometimes, paranoia" (Chesney-Lind & Shelden, 2004, p. 79).

Females, like males, generally go through some form of initiation. "Some of these initiations may include being beaten, kicked by gang members, participating in a robbery or drive-by shooting, getting tattoos, having to fight 5 to 12 gang members at once, or having sex with multiple gang members" (Chesney-Lind & Shelden, 2004, p. 81). According to Chesney-Lind and Shelden, a small number of gangs have what are called "roll-ins"—situations in which a female rolls a pair of dice to determine how many males will have sex with her. However, the stereotype of sex-based initiation ceremonies is less widespread than is often believed.

CONCLUSIONS

Social and behavioral scientists have discovered that the easy generalizations and firm conclusions about why youth join gangs are unwarranted; the reasons are extremely elusive and overlapping. And although they have found evidence to support all three hypotheses to some extent, other hypotheses may be worth pursuing as well.

The perspective with the strongest support at this point is the enhancement hypothesis. Contemporary research (e.g., Bendixen, Endresen, & Olweus, 2006;

Stretesky & Pogrebin, 2007; Thornberry et al., 1993) does confirm that the influence of antisocial friends, groups, or gangs facilitates antisocial behavior in children or adolescents *already prone* to engage in such behavior. This influence is probably especially powerful for aggressive preteens, who may use the gang as a training ground for engaging in more serious and violent behavior. Aggressive children who experience peer rejection at an early age seek out and associate with other socially rejected and aggressive peers, who in turn amplify the tendency to be antisocial and delinquent. Friendships, groups, and gangs "have the potential to promote the maintenance and regulation of existing antisocial tendencies and even to foster the development and expression of more severe antisocial responding to the external world" (Bagwell, 2004, p. 53). Coie (2004) further asserts that "the impact of deviant peer group influences on the crystallization of an antisocial developmental trajectory has been solidly documented" (p. 257). Therefore, it appears clear that for *some* youth in *some* gangs, delinquent behavior and violence increase during periods of active membership in the gang and decrease after they leave the gang.

However, the ability of the social facilitation hypothesis to stand on its own is questionable. Although this hypothesis is compatible with the social learning perspective, there is little empirical evidence to date that convinces us that delinquent, antisocial gangs will transform a prosocial, well-adjusted child into an antisocial, troubled youth (Bagwell, 2004). It is conceivable, although unlikely, that such a child would join a gang because his friends belong or because he needs protection from members of other gangs, but many such youths do not participate in the antisocial behavior promoted by the group (Walker-Barnes & Mason, 2001). Again, it is possible that gang involvement might encourage some adjusted, prosocial youth to engage in minor forms of delinquent actions (e.g., graffiti, vandalism), but gang involvement is unlikely to lead *many* to commit serious, violent crimes.

The selection hypothesis contends that gangs recruit individuals who are already delinquent or are at least antisocial and aggressive. To what extent gang members *recruit* others like themselves remains unknown, but it is certainly clear that children and adolescents seek out and associate with peers similar to themselves in deviant attitudes, values, experiences, and aggressive behavior. It has been documented that this occurs quite early, at least before 10 years of age (Cairns & Cairns, 1991; Craig et al., 2002).

But as we have noted, children and adolescents join gangs for many other reasons as well. Some become involved in gangs because some of their family members (siblings, parents, relatives) or neighbors are gang members. Others join for protection from abuse from others in their lives. Serious marital discord, poor family or child management, financial strain, low achievement in school all play important roles in influencing gang involvement. The three hypotheses presented here help organize these factors, but they do not portray completely the matrix of reasons for joining or participating in gangs, nor the situations and experiences that lead to gang participation.

Summary and Conclusions

According to the definition adopted in this text, juvenile gangs engage in substantial illegal activity, although the individual members within them do not necessarily do so. To distinguish gangs from other groupings of juveniles, we indicate that gangs must be involved in crime on a regular basis and must include some of the rituals associated with gangs, such as initiation rites for new members and specified symbols and colors. Although the illegal activity is well documented, gangs vary in the amount of such activity they pursue, as well as in the forms it takes. Not all gangs engage in violence; many that do use violence primarily to settle turf battles or to avenge an assault against one of their members. Although fear of drive-by shootings and attacks often overtakes a community or neighborhood, such random violence is not typical of most gangs. Furthermore, although gangs and gang members often engage in drug-related crime, there is little evidence of a connection between drug crime and violence among gangs.

It is extremely difficult to obtain statistics on both the number of gangs operating in the United States at any given time and the extent and prevalence of gang membership. Data on gangs are usually obtained on a piecemeal basis, and few are available on a national scale. Gang membership may be approaching 1 million, but that figure should be accepted with caution. Both the law enforcement community and gangs themselves may inflate estimates of membership, which is often in flux and dependent upon economic conditions, mobility of residents in a geographical area, gang suppression programs, and opportunities for participating in criminal activities.

We can point with confidence to some trends in membership, however. Specifically, membership appears to be expanding at both ends of the age spectrum, with young children (under 10) increasingly joining gangs and older members in their 20s remaining in the group. Children who join gangs during preadolescence are especially likely to progress to serious, persistent delinquency in adolescence. Gangs are also becoming more racially and ethnically diverse, particularly in smaller cities, where the likelihood of having sufficient numbers of any one group is smaller. Gender trends are also apparent; gangs on the whole are becoming more gender inclusive, although girls continue to take on subservient roles and lower-status tasks. Female-only gangs are rarely independent and are typically attached to a male gang.

Theories of gang behavior, as well as explanations of why juveniles join gangs, have been proposed primarily by sociologists. Frederick Thrasher wrote the classic sociological treatise on gangs, specifically on gangs in Chicago. Thrasher saw gangs as a normative way for lower-class juveniles in urban areas to bond together in the face of social disorganization and the inability of parents to socialize their children in the proper way. Shaw and McKay, who also studied delinquency in Chicago, took a similar approach, noting that delinquency was transmitted through successive generations. When parents experienced diminished control over their children, gang membership and subsequent delinquency were likely to result. Gangs established their own subcultures and tried to obtain the material acquisitions promoted by mainstream society. In general, early theories saw gangs as either socially able, developing cohesiveness and a close-knit spirit among their members, or socially disabled, consisting primarily of outcasts and socially inept adolescents.

There continue to be various theories on why gangs exist and why youths join them. An estimated 24,000 gangs are active in the United States today, comprised of some 760,000 gang members. Gang members seem to be joining earlier and remaining in the gang longer. However, one-half to two-thirds of gang members are short-termers, or transient members. Even a brief period of membership may expose an individual youth to heightened risk of delinquency, however.

Our focus on research on female gangs reflects a renewed scholarly interest in this area. The autonomous female gang remains the exception: Most female gang members belong to the auxiliary of a male gang or, as is increasingly common, to a gender-integrated gang. Female gang members have lower delinquency rates than male gang members; their most common offense is drug related. Autonomous female gangs tend to appear in small towns and rural communities rather than in urban areas. Girls in these gangs are primarily involved in property crimes, drug dealing, and assaults, particularly in the school setting.

Gang violence is a serious problem but is directed most at other gangs. Although not all gang members commit violent offenses, as a group they are responsible for a large percentage of offenses and commit serious and violent crime at a much higher rate than nongang adolescents do. Likewise, gangs and gang members are disproportionately involved in drug offending. Recent data confirm that gangs are the primary distributors of drugs throughout the United States. Nevertheless, the link between drug offending and violence is not as strong as has been assumed. In other words, while some gang violence is associated with the drug trade, other forms of violence represent factors independent of drug distribution (e.g., turf battles, initiation rituals, revenge shootings). Gang members are also far more likely than nongang members to carry guns on a daily basis. In sum, the relation between violence and drugs is a complex one.

Typologies range from Thrasher's very early division to approaches based on contemporary research. In the United States, the most common type of gang, representing about 40% of all gangs, is the compressed gang of fewer than 50 members. The gang that tends to receive the most media attention, the traditional gang, is very large but is less common on a nationwide basis.

Contemporary theory on why youths join and remain in gangs reflects several perspectives. Some youths are vulnerable to joining during preadolescence, while others are more vulnerable during their adolescent period. Life-course-persistent offenders, for example, begin their antisocial behavior very early and gravitate toward like-minded antisocial peers early in their development. Peer rejection, even in first grade, predicts delinquent gang involvement in adolescence. Because gangs do not encourage their members to have friends outside the gang, the youths have little opportunity to interact with prosocial peers, placing gang members at continuing risk for more antisocial behavior. While many gang members come from troubled families, girls are even more likely than boys to have these dysfunctional backgrounds. There are many reasons that a youth joins a gang. However, the enhancement hypothesis—which posits that gang activities facilitate a youth's already-established interest in antisocial behavior—seems to have the strongest support.

Key Terms and Concepts

collective gangs

compressed gangs

enhancement hypothesis

gang migration

groups of friends

neotraditional gangs

purposive gangs

selection hypothesis

social ability models

social disability models

social facilitation hypothesis

specialty gangs

spontaneous criminal activity gangs

structured criminal organizations

super predator

traditional gangs

transient gang members

youth street gangs

CHAPTER 12
PREVENTION AND EARLY INTERVENTION

❧

CHAPTER OBJECTIVES

◆ Describe ingredients necessary for successful prevention programs

◆ Introduce classification of prevention and intervention programs

◆ Revisit resilience and the role it plays in prevention

◆ Describe primary and secondary prevention goals and strategies

◆ Provide examples of successful prevention programs

◆ Describe selective prevention programs

The number of prevention, early intervention, and treatment programs that have been tried over the past three decades with both delinquents and children at risk is overwhelming. Unfortunately, few programs designed to reduce delinquent or pre-delinquent behavior have been effective or have shown lasting effects (Tarolla, Wagner, Rabinowitz, & Tubman, 2002; Zigler, Taussig, & Black, 1992). Many have never been evaluated scientifically in keeping with sound research principles.

Serious forms of antisocial behavior in school-aged children and adolescents have been found to be particularly resistant to change (Borduin et al., 1995; Shaw et al., 2003). Serious juvenile offenders are especially prone to have low motivation for altering their antisocial behaviors and to display noncompliance, a lack of trust, and high levels of anger and impulsiveness (Tarolla et al., 2002). Although programs aimed at such conduct abound, "by the time children reach these programs, often after referral by court personnel, they are already entrenched in a long history of antisocial interaction with parents, schools, and community that is not easily reversed" (Zigler et al., 1992, p. 997).

Even though these conclusions are discouraging, positive changes have been occurring. Some programs are emerging as highly successful in eliminating antisocial behavior and reducing delinquent behavior, even in children with serious behavior problems and even in institutionalized delinquents. Other programs show considerable promise.

CHARACTERISTICS OF SUCCESSFUL PROGRAMS

Effective programs share common features. Zigler et al. (1992) concluded in their review that delinquency can be prevented by *early* childhood intervention programs that promote competence (social, interpersonal, and academic) and resilience across multiple systems in which children are embedded (i.e., family, school, peers, and community). In contrast, crisis-oriented programs emphasizing counseling or social casework to deal with a presenting problem have been ineffective, largely because they focus on a single setting or competency and often are applied too late. Successful and promising prevention and treatment programs have the following characteristics.

THEY BEGIN EARLY

As we learned in earlier chapters, seriously antisocial children can be identified when they are as young as 4 or 5 years old on the basis of their aggressive, disruptive, and non-compliant behaviors across home and preschool or school settings. In fact, Terrie Moffitt (1993; Moffitt et al., 1996) presents convincing evidence that the LCP delinquent manifests discernible indicators of antisocial behavior as early as age 3. Thus, some researchers (e.g., Guerra et al., 1995) recommend that prevention begin no later than the first grade and definitely before age 8. Because seriously antisocial children are likely to progress in a spiral of escalating and more severe antisocial and violent behaviors, early intervention is critical if it is to be effective (Conduct Problems Prevention Research Group, 2004). In addition, there appears to be a puzzling jump in antisocial behavior between the first and second grades for many children. Therefore, prevention programs enacted later than the first grade will probably need to be more intensive. Guerra, Huesmann, Tolan, Van Acker, and Eron (1995) have observed that aggressive and antisocial behavior begins to develop earlier in children living in the most economically deprived urban neighborhoods, an observation that appears to hold for both boys and girls (Tolan & Thomas, 1995). In addition, as we learned earlier, considerable evidence suggests that the earlier the signs of antisocial behavior appear, the more serious or violent the antisocial or criminal behavior will be later on (Tolan & Thomas, 1995).

Early antisocial indicators often forecast a life of crime. As noted by Rolf Loeber (1990, p. 6), "There is considerable continuity among disruptive and antisocial behaviors over time, even though they may manifest themselves differently at different ages." Loeber further finds that as children and adolescents progress toward more serious delinquent behavior, they tend to move toward diversification, rather than from one specific deviant behavior to another. For example, rather than moving from stealing *to* assault, youths move from stealing to stealing *and* assaultive behavior. Thus, it is clear that without early intervention many children who are at risk for delinquency are more likely to engage in increasing levels of serious, chronic offending as they grow older.

THEY FOLLOW DEVELOPMENTAL PRINCIPLES

Prevention programs that are effective are soundly based on child developmental principles obtained from well-designed research (Dodge, 2001). As has been noted throughout this book, different developmental pathways can lead to serious violence and delinquency, and the age of onset of these behaviors can vary considerably. In designing programs to prevent violence and chronic antisocial behavior, it is critical to understand the factors that place youths on a developmental trajectory of serious delinquency.

It is equally important to understand how these factors interact with the social environment. As persons move through life, they enter and exit a series of developmental stages (Dahlberg & Potter, 2001). Data from the Rochester project (Thornberry, Huizinga, & Loeber, 1995) indicate that protective factors must be *constantly present* during transition from early to late adolescence and must not simply be in place at a single point in childhood or adolescence (Conduct Problems, 2004). "Although the negative impact of early risk factors may be buffered by the provision of protective support services during the grade school years, the risk factors themselves may continue to influence developmental trajectories during adolescence" (Conduct Problems, 2004, p. 193). This point is especially relevant when a child or adolescent continues to live in a dangerous social, physical, and emotional environment.

In an extensive review, Tremblay, LeMarquand, and Vitaro (1999) examined 50 prevention programs and discovered that 20 of them had been evaluated under carefully designed test conditions. Those programs that were most effective were based on sound child developmental research (Dodge, 2001). Linking the appropriate prevention program with the developmental stage of the youth is critical for significant, long-term success in delinquency prevention.

THEY FOCUS ON MULTIPLE SETTINGS AND SYSTEMS

Successful intervention programs must not only begin as early as possible, but must also be skillfully directed at as many causes and negative influences as possible. Targeting multiple potential risk or protective factors rather than one or two in isolation greatly increases the likelihood of positive adjustment and the significant reduction of antisocial and violent behavior (Tedeschi & Kilmer, 2005). Programs that have shown long-term success have utilized multipronged approaches concentrating on treating children through their broad social environments, including improving their relationships with family and peers and helping the youths develop better academic skills.

In addition, effective intervention programs include prenatal and perinatal medical care and intensive health education for pregnant women and mothers with young children (Coordinating Council, 1996). For example, the Early Childhood Nurse Home Visitation program, supported by the Office of Juvenile Justice and Delinquency Prevention (OJJDP), focuses on prenatal and early postnatal prevention. Research indicates that the program can significantly reduce the risk factors that contribute to the development of antisocial behavior in childhood (Olds, Hill, & Rumsey, 1998). Such services reduce the risk factors of head and neurological injuries, exposure to toxins, maternal substance abuse, nutritional deficiencies, and perinatal difficulties. Recent research (Dietrich et al., 2001; Needleman et al., 2002) has discovered a strong relationship between high levels of lead in the bones of children and violence and delinquency in adolescence.

There is little doubt that living conditions in the poorest inner-city neighborhoods are extremely harsh and that a daily onslaught of violence, substance abuse, child abuse, and hopelessness is highly disruptive to normal development, even if such conditions are experienced only indirectly. For children who are *directly* exposed to an adverse family life and inadequate living arrangements—with little opportunity to develop the social, interpersonal, and academic skills to deal effectively with their environment—the damage may be almost irreparable. Clearly, the longer children are exposed to an adverse environment, the more difficult it will be to direct their life course away from crime and delinquency.

THEY ACKNOWLEDGE AND RESPECT CULTURAL BACKGROUNDS

Although some urban neighborhoods contain numerous risk factors, these same neighborhoods may also be rich in values and traditions that, if acknowledged, would qualify as crucial protective factors. For example, various ethnic and racial groups place great value on the extended family, a particular style of music, or certain holiday traditions and celebrations. Effective programs are sensitive to a family's cultural background and heritage. Even ways of communicating can vary among groups; some cultures stress the importance of eye contact, for example, while others consider it disrespectful. Such cultural markers can affect the development of antisocial behavior, sometimes promoting it but often suppressing it.

Even poverty can affect individuals differently because of their ethnicity and the *meaning* of poverty within a given cultural context (Guerra et al., 1995). For example, whereas one group may regard being poor as something to be expected, albeit something to be overcome, another group may view it as a sign of oppression by a dominant group in society. Moreover, in some cultural groups, stealing brings shame upon one's family; in others, stealing may be the norm, as long as the target of the theft is limited to those outside the group. Of course, individual members of these groups may not necessarily act in accordance with the group's values and expectations. But effective treatment providers must constantly be aware of the cultural background of the juveniles they deal with, as well as the realization that the culture may not regulate the juveniles' behavior.

THEY FOCUS ON THE FAMILY FIRST

Research has continually shown that the most successful interventions concentrate first on improving parenting and the family system in general and *then* on improving peer relations and academic skills. Certain family relationships and parenting practices strongly promote serious and violent delinquency regardless of ethnic or socioeconomic status (Gorman-Smith, Tolan, Huesmann, & Zelli, 1996). The family characteristics most closely connected to serious delinquency are poor parental monitoring and supervision of children's activities, poor and inconsistent discipline, and a lack of family closeness or cohesion. According to Dishion and Andrews (1995), studies have consistently revealed that negative, coercive exchanges between parents and children are predictive of child antisocial behavior (e.g., Patterson, 1986a), delinquent behavior (e.g., Bank & Patterson, 1992), and adolescent substance abuse (e.g., Dishion & Loeber, 1985). Research also indicates that emotional closeness and family cohesion—which provide emotional support, adequate communication, and warmth and love—are essential in the prevention of antisocial behavior and delinquency (Gorman-Smith et al., 1996).

Peer systems are critically important, too, and research has shown that negative peer associations are significant predictors of both substance abuse and delinquency (O'Donnell et al., 1995). Thus far, though, intervention programs have been unsuccessful in utilizing peer groups as effective change agents to modify antisocial behaviors. Interventions that are peer focused can actually have unintended negative effects if they require increased contact with antisocial peers (Vitaro & Tremblay, 1994). For example, Dishion and Andrews (1995) found that placing high-risk teens together in groups encouraged escalations in tobacco use and problem behaviors in school and may have actually increased contact with deviant peers and, in the long run, exacerbated the teens' antisocial involvement. Dishion and Andrews recommend that intervention programs using antisocial peers as change agents be discouraged unless the programs are very carefully designed. Similarly, research indicates that group homes for delinquents may increase delinquent behavior (Chamberlain, 1996); antisocial peers tend to model and encourage other antisocial peers.

CLASSIFICATION OF PREVENTION AND TREATMENT PROGRAMS

As mentioned earlier, many prevention, intervention, and treatment programs have been tried with children and adolescents over the past 35 years, but few have been submitted to rigorous evaluation. Of those that have been evaluated, most have failed if we use future offending or long-term positive outcomes as criteria. Because of the large number of programs, we will cover only a small sample of those programs that are well known or that have been notably successful or promising.

Research on prevention identifies three main approaches: (1) primary prevention (also called universal prevention in the literature); (2) selective prevention (also called secondary prevention); and (3) treatment or intervention (also called tertiary prevention). Although this classification organizes discussion, there is often overlap among these approaches because many programs target a mixture of populations. For example, Project Head Start—which was originally designed to provide a catch-up educational program for economically disadvantaged families and was considered a primary prevention program—has evolved into a broader program that helps a wider socioeconomic spectrum. Because some of the children in Head Start may qualify as seriously at-risk children, the program could be considered a selective program for them.

Primary, or **universal, prevention** is designed to prevent delinquent behavior before any signs of that behavioral pattern emerge. Primary prevention programs are most often implemented early in children's developmental sequence, preferably before the ages of 7 or 8. Typically, these programs are conducted in the school or preschool setting and focus on large groups of children, *regardless of possible differences in their risk for delinquency*. In most instances, primary prevention programs target all children within a particular geographical area or setting (e.g., a school or school grade) without any further selection criteria (Offord, Chmura Kraemeer, Kazdin, Jensen, & Harrington, 1998). Many of these programs require the promulgation of far-reaching policies and procedures, which often involve legislative authorization and funding. Examples include widespread programs to enhance prenatal care, maternal and infant care and nutrition, and family management (Committee on Preventive Psychiatry, 1999). Another excellent example of this approach is the development of resilience or protective factors in young children before school entry or soon after entry. We will discuss this powerful approach in more detail shortly.

Selective, or **secondary, prevention** consists of working with *specific* children and adolescents who are at high risk and who display some early signs of antisocial behavior but have not yet been classified or adjudicated delinquent.

> In violence prevention programs, secondary prevention efforts are often aimed at children who are deemed at-risk based on numerous indicators including the following: earlier aggressive behavior, poor social skills, low child intellect, ineffective parenting style, neighborhood deterioration, poverty, access to firearms or drugs, and deviant peer groups. (Fields & McNamara, 2003, p. 74).

Pharmacotherapy (mostly for ADHD) and individual therapy are routinely utilized as part of secondary prevention (Fields & McNamara, 2003).

The basic assumption in selective prevention is that early detection and early intervention will prevent youngsters from graduating into more serious, habitual offending. A good example of this type of prevention is the Perry Preschool Project, started in 1962. The project was an organized educational program directed at the cognitive and social development of young children considered at high risk for delinquency and school failure (Berrueta-Clement, Schweinhart, Barnett, & Weikart, 1987). Another well-known example is juvenile diversion, which diverts some offenders from formal court processing—typically first-time offenders charged with nonserious crimes—but places them in short-term programs to discourage them from reoffending. An advantage of selective prevention programs is that they focus on those youths who should benefit most from the services.

The third approach is generally referred to as **treatment** (or intervention) in the delinquency literature. We prefer to use the term *treatment*, because it can be argued that primary and selective prevention are also forms of intervention. Furthermore, although there is some overlap between selective prevention and treatment—juveniles in selective prevention programs also often receive treatment—we use *treatment* to apply to those programs designed to reduce serious, habitual delinquent or antisocial behavior by adjudicated delinquents. Treatment, or tertiary prevention, is designed for children and adolescents who have already offended. Thus, tertiary prevention targets individuals who already exhibit delinquent or serious antisocial behavior and violence. The goal is to decrease further delinquency, psychological problems, and violence in the future. Many of these youths are referred for psychological care in the community or are placed in residential correctional facilities, training schools, or rehabilitation centers. Figure 12–1 illustrates the three approaches.

Unfortunately, tertiary prevention programs have a high failure rate. One reason, Felner (1999) notes, is that they are often after-the-fact and are inadequately funded or poorly applied. Consequently, primary and secondary prevention efforts appear to

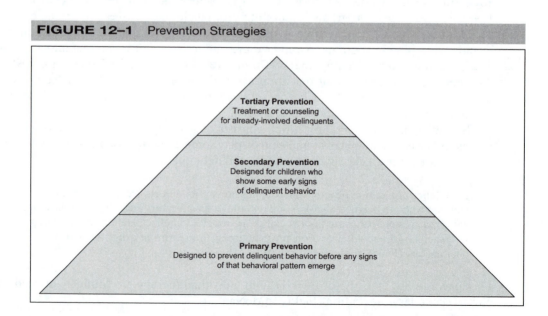

FIGURE 12–1   Prevention Strategies

Tertiary Prevention
Treatment or counseling
for already-involved delinquents

Secondary Prevention
Designed for children who
show some early signs
of delinquent behavior

Primary Prevention
Designed to prevent delinquent behavior before any signs
of that behavioral pattern emerge

hold far more promise for altering antisocial behavior (Fields & McNamara, 2003). For one thing, primary and secondary prevention programs can be administered in groups, whereas tertiary approaches often require a more individualized strategy. In their review of the research literature on the prevention and treatment of violent behavior in youths, Fields and McNamara (2003) found that the vast majority of primary and secondary prevention programs had at least one significant positive outcome. Although many of the changes were modest and short-term, the partial successes are promising and should lead to greater advancement in the near future. This chapter concentrates on primary and selective prevention approaches; Chapter 13 focuses on treatment.

PROTECTIVE FACTORS

In the past, prevention and treatment programs tried to reduce or eliminate *risk* factors that children and adolescents face during their formative years. In recent years, however, a discernible shift has taken place that emphasizes the development and enhancement of **protective factors**. Although both approaches are important, this chapter will focus on protective factors through the development of resilience. We contend that the development of resilience is an extremely effective method of primary and selective prevention of delinquency in children and adolescents and has enormous potential as an effective treatment strategy.

PROMOTING RESILIENCE

Humans vary a great deal in their ability to cope and adapt to negative, traumatic, and adverse experiences. High levels of resilience exist at one end of the continuum and maladjustment, at the other end. With increasing awareness of the protective factors that promote resilience in children and adolescence, theorists, researchers, and policy makers are now attempting to apply this knowledge to the prevention of antisocial behavior, particularly in children considered at moderate to high risk. Prevention and treatment programs designed to foster and maintain resilience in youth are also known as **strength-based programs**. These programs attempt to build certain skills or strengths in children or adolescents so that they can better resist antisocial behaviors and be more positive in their daily lives. In short, the goal is to foster adaptive and prosocial behavior that will last a lifetime. As we learned in Chapter 4, the accumulating evidence reveals that resilient children and adolescents (and adults) exhibit positive social, interpersonal, and cognitive competencies that help them survive and succeed even in high-stress and adverse environments.

It should be emphasized again that resilience is made up of ordinary rather than extraordinary processes and that the *average* child can be taught to become resilient (E. J. Smith, 2006). Prevention programs that promote cognitive and social competencies in children or adolescents, improve child-rearing practices in the family, and foster the development and maintenance of effective social support systems are most likely to be effective in the long run. As Masten (2001) writes, "The great threats to human development are those that jeopardize the systems underlying these adaptive processes, including brain development and cognition, caregiver–child relationships, regulation of emotion and behavior, and the motivation for learning and engaging in the environment" (p. 234).

Strategies for developing resilience include the enhancement of a child's strengths and interests, as well as the reduction of risks or stressors and the facilitation of protective processes. Overall, the rallying cry for many programs focusing on enhancing resilience has become this: "Every child has talents, strengths, and interests that offer the child potential for a bright future" (Damon, 2004, p. 13). Such attitudes reflect a major transformation over the past few decades in conceptualizing the prevention of antisocial behavior and other childhood problems.

Children who are at risk of engaging in serious antisocial behavior have been exposed to aversive events. These can include, alone or in combination, dire economic situations, abuse (physical or emotional), rejection by peers, trauma (e.g., the sudden loss of a parent or sibling). There is no single means of maintaining equilibrium following highly aversive events; rather there are multiple pathways to resilience (Bonanno, 2004), just as there are multiple pathways to delinquency. For example, as we mentioned in Chapter 4, McKnight and Loper (2002) found that the most prominent resilience factors in adolescent girls at risk for delinquency were an academic motivation and a desire to go to college, an absence of substance abuse, feeling loved and wanted, a belief that teachers treat students fairly, parental trust of adolescent children, and religiosity.

Waaktaar et al. (2004) conducted a study to explore how resilience or protective factors could be used to help at-risk youths. The youths averaged 12.3 years of age, and a little over a third were girls. The participants represented a medley of cultural and ethnic backgrounds, including the West Indies, Far East, Central Asia, the Arab world, and northeast Africa. All had experienced serious and/or multiple life stresses and, at the time of the study, were not receiving satisfactory help through psychiatric intervention.

The researchers targeted four resilience factors for therapeutic intervention: positive peer relations, self-efficacy, creativity, and coherence. **Positive peer relations** were defined as prosocial interactions, peer acceptance, and support. **Self-efficacy** is the belief that one can achieve desired goals through one's own actions (Bandura, 1989, 1997). Hundreds of studies have supported the observation that self-efficacy leads to a range of positive outcomes; it is regarded as central to resilience (Lightsey, 2006). **Creativity** in this context refers to individual talent to create an artistic or other communicative product, such as a song, dance, film, play, poem, or short story. A creative approach encourages children to express themselves and their experiences symbolically. **Coherence** refers to the ways in which people evaluate themselves and their circumstances, both cognitively and emotionally. This factor involves "helping young people to find a coherent meaning to their past, present, and future life through positive thinking, accepting the reality of their bad experiences, avoiding self-blame for uncontrollable circumstances and finding adaptive paths forward" (Waaktaar et al., 2004, p. 173). The researchers discovered that child therapy focusing on these four concepts has the potential to enhance resilience significantly.

An excellent illustration of a culturally sensitive program designed to develop resilience is **Project SELF**, a school curriculum that attempts to promote self-esteem, self-efficacy, confidence, and improved problem-solving skills in inner-city fourth-grade African-American children through a culturally based curriculum (Hampson, Rahman, Brown, Taylor, & Donaldson, 1998). The researchers write, "Using a pre/post evaluation design with a control group, we demonstrated that students who received the program exhibited greater improved knowledge of the curriculum, elevated self-esteem, a greater sense of self-efficacy, and improved long-term consequential thinking skills as compared to controls" (Hampson et al., 1998, p. 24). What really made the difference, the researchers concluded, was the program's focus on "the students' own ancestral history, biology, beliefs and values, choices and potential" throughout the curriculum (Hampson et al., 1998, p. 27). In order to improve resilience, the researchers reasoned, children must engage their cultural or ethnic identity.

Notably lacking in existing research on resilience is the role played by biology and genetic factors (Luthar et al., 2000). It is clear that biological factors affect psychological processes and that psychological processes, in turn, affect biological factors. It may be that resilience is strongly affected by genetic or biological predispositions even though it is more strongly affected by the social environment. If so, effective prevention programs should certainly include prenatal and perinatal medical care and intensive health education for pregnant women and mothers with young children. These services can reduce the delinquency risk factors of head and neurological injuries, exposure to toxins, maternal substance abuse, nutritional deficiencies, and perinatal difficulties.

UNDERSTANDING PROTECTIVE PROCESSES

Over the past few years, research has begun to shift away from simply *identifying* protective factors and has focused more on trying to understand the underlying protective *processes* (Luthar et al., 2000). We often read about highly successful people or well-known historical figures who experience stressful and adverse conditions during childhood but who manage to adapt and excel. But we do not know precisely what processes contributed to this adaptation. As researchers have identified the characteristics of resilience and determined the forces of the social environment that contribute to resilience, there has been a growth in programs that build and strengthen protective mechanisms. However, the knowledge of exactly how these factors work is still lacking (Waaktaar et al., 2004). Perhaps even more challenging is how these systems can be most effectively implemented in working with at-risk children.

One of the many questions that need to be answered revolves around the multidimensional nature of resilience. For example, can we expect at-risk children who demonstrate resilience in one area to show a comparable resilience in other areas? If an at-risk child does well in school, can we expect that same child to demonstrate similarly positive outcomes in his or her social or emotional life? So far, the research suggests a tentative yes to both questions. When effective intervention improves one resilience characteristic of a child, this is likely to also affect other resilience factors in that child, creating what are called "positive chain reactions" by clinicians (Waaktaar et al., 2004).

PRIMARY PREVENTION

Mulvey, Arthur, and Reppucci (1993) divide primary prevention approaches into three major strategies, depending on where the focus is placed within the youth's systems: **family-based prevention, school-based prevention**, and **community-based prevention**. As we have learned, research studies have consistently shown that the most promising strategies for preventing antisocial and delinquent behavior in juveniles should concentrate on the cognitive and interpersonal skills of the children and the parenting skills of primary caretakers. Programs should begin early, be multisystemic, and be based on sound research of child development. Programs that skillfully incorporate these elements have the best chance to show positive, stable, and long-term effects.

FAMILY-BASED PREVENTION

The most logical place to begin in preventing delinquency is the family. Family-based prevention is designed to help families cope with the stresses of child rearing by either training the caregivers in family management techniques or developing a supportive network for the family. The latter approach provides a broad range of services to the family, such as day care, medical care, counseling, casework, and appropriate referrals to other agencies. A classic misstep of this approach is illustrated by the **Cambridge–Somerville Youth Study** (see McCord, McCord, & Zola, 1959). The program was launched in 1936 to prevent delinquency and develop character by means of friendly guidance. It was believed that delinquency could be prevented if a close and caring friendship was developed between a youngster and an adult counselor. The fundamental reasoning was that if intensive family and individual counseling was provided—buttressed by proper medical care, recreational facilities, and other social services—delinquency could be prevented. The project focused on 650 boys, aged 6 to 12 and attending schools in the factory-dominated cities of Cambridge and Somerville, Massachusetts.

According to Dodge (2001), this program was innocently based on the well-intentioned but flawed assumption that *public identification* of youth as at risk, *indiscriminate application of resources* to the targeted population, and *random placement of these children in summer camps* could prevent crime. Dodge asserts that since the time of the Cambridge–Somerville program, developmental research has discovered that such approaches have the effect of accelerating rather than dampening delinquent behavior. Boys who had been in the program were more likely to commit crime than was a comparable group of boys who had not been in the program. The Cambridge–Somerville experiment did, however, set the stage for more sophisticated, family-based prevention programs that are research based and that have shown significantly more positive short-term outcomes.

The **Yale Child Welfare Research Program** was an intervention program that provided "a coordinated set of social work, pediatric, child care, and psychological services for 30 months following birth to low income mothers and their firstborn children" (Mulvey et al., 1993, p. 137). Each family interacted with a small team of persons: a home visitor (social worker or psychologist), a pediatrician, a primary day-care worker, and a developmental examiner (Seitz, Rosenbaum, & Apfel, 1985). The primary goal of the project was to reduce the negative impact of the many stressors experienced by economically disadvantaged mothers. Thus, in contrast to the Cambridge–Somerville project, intervention occurred on a number of levels, and each family worked intensely with a team of professionals over an extended period of time.

In a 10-year follow-up, boys who were in the Yale program had better school attendance, demonstrated fewer conduct problems in the classroom, and generally exhibited less predelinquent behavior than a comparison group of boys. However, we must be cautious in generalizing the results to children of other disadvantaged mothers. Participants (mothers and firstborns) were screened so thoroughly that any indications of physical problems at birth for the infant or any signs of serious psychological or cognitive problems in the mother were sufficient reasons to eliminate the family from further consideration in the project. Furthermore, there were only 18 children in both the intervention group and the control group. In addition, the children were still preadolescent at the time of the 10-year follow-up and, therefore, somewhat young to be evaluated for delinquent behaviors. Ongoing follow-up studies are likely scheduled. Nonetheless, the results of the Yale study suggest some promising leads in the development of effective strategies for dealing with possible determinants of delinquency.

Development of Family Resilience

As discussed throughout this book, there is a growing interest among researchers and practitioners in discovering how to foster and maintain family resilience, as well as individual resilience in children (Simon et al., 2005). Research has consistently reported that the ability of the family to overcome the risk factors of adverse environments is one of the core factors of any prevention program designed to reduce or eliminate antisocial or delinquency behavior. The central aim of prevention programs focused on family resilience is to discover each family's unique resources and to encourage family members to acknowledge, adapt, and apply those resources to their current and future challenges and problems (Simon et al., 2005).

As defined in Chapter 4, *family resilience* is "the ability of a family to respond positively to an adverse situation and emerge from the situation feeling strengthened, more resourceful, and more confident than its prior state" (Simon et al., 2005, p. 427). The concept of family resilience extends beyond individuals functioning independently of each other (Walsh, 2003). Rather, family resilience can best be seen as the response of a functioning unit in which the risk and resilience of one or more family members affects the entire group. Whereas stresses, severe crises, and persistent adversity affect the overall dynamic of a family, programs that develop the resilience of the family strengthen the ability of all family members to deal with multiple risks, both individually and collectively. Resilience building enables the family to rally in times of crisis, to buffer stress, to reduce the risk of family emotional problems, and to support optimal adaptation (Walsh, 2003).

Walsh (2003) identifies three key factors that must be addressed by professionals if a family is to develop and maintain resilience: family belief system, organizational patterns, and communication. A family's **belief system** strongly influences how it views crises, distress, and the options available. Resilience is fostered by shared beliefs that increase options for problem resolution, healing, and growth. Shared beliefs can help members find meaning in crisis events and facilitate hope. Walsh notes that high-functioning families hold a more optimistic view of life. In contrast, hopelessness and a pessimistic view of life rob a family and its members of meaning, purpose, and a sense of future possibilities. Hopelessness breeds discouragement, antisocial behavior, violence, and psychological disorders such as depression. A positive family belief system encourages perseverance, confidence, and a can-do spirit.

The second major factor, **organizational patterns**, involves flexibility, connectedness, and identification of available resources. Walsh identifies flexibility as one of the core processes in resilience. It is not simply "bouncing back" but is more like "bouncing ahead." In the aftermath of most major transitions and crisis events, families cannot simply return to normal life as they knew it; resilient families bounce forward, changing to meet new challenges. Connectedness refers to the ability of family members to rely on each other in times of crisis and challenge, and identification of community resources refers to the knowledge of where to go for community help and financial support as necessary. Thus, in the face of a crisis, members of a resilient family adapt to that crisis by relying on each other for support and seeking out help within their surrounding community if needed.

The third factor crucial to family resilience is **open communication** within the family. Communication processes foster resilience by bringing clarity to crisis situations, encouraging emotional expression, and developing collaborative problem solving. Walsh (2003) states that ambiguity or secrecy can block understanding, closeness, and mastery, whereas clarifying and sharing crucial information facilitates family closeness. In addition, open communication—supported by mutual trust, empathy, and tolerance of differences—helps family members share the wide range of feelings prompted by crises or stressful events. Moreover, collaborative problem solving leads to shared decision making and the negotiation of differences with fairness and reciprocity over time.

It is well known that many serious and violent delinquents come from an adverse family milieu, characterized by numerous stress-inducing factors such as economic hardship or health problems. However, if at least one parent or caretaker in an otherwise multistressed, disadvantaged family is resilient, that person is better able to foster resilience and competence in the children. Parents with appropriate parenting skills can provide a structured, predictable, regulated environment that contributes to healthy social, emotional, and cognitive development (Lösel & Bender, 2003). According to Garmezy (1991), multistressed families that nonetheless produce resilient children engage more frequently in joint activities and possess many of the characteristics discussed here. Mature and resilient parents and other competent caregivers (e.g., grandparents, older siblings, and other family relatives) are able to buffer the onslaught and accumulating effects of risk factors inherent in any adverse environment.

One good example of a family-based prevention program is the **Strengthening Families Program** (SFP; Kumpfer & Tait, 2000). The program began in 1983 as a 4-year prevention project designed to reduce drug abuse in drug-abusing parents and their high-risk children (aged 6 to 10). "SFP was designed to reduce environmental risk factors with the ultimate objective of increasing personal resiliency and minimizing susceptibility to drug abuse in high-risk youth" (Kumpfer & Tait, 2000, p. 2). Family climate and parenting skills are major determinants of self-efficacy and resilience development, as well as the second major determinant, after peer pressure, of alcohol and drug use. Thus, the strategies were to improve parenting skills, improve the family environment, and train parents to nurture and provide appropriate learning opportunities for their children. The mission was to involve the *whole* family instead of the parents or the children alone. In general, research results of the program indicate that the *combination* of building all three skills—parental, child, and family—was the most successful, compared to a focus on single skills. "SFP increased children's positive behavior and prosocial skills, improved adults' parenting skills, and enhanced the family environment by improving communication, clarifying family rules, and decreasing family conflict" (Kumpfer & Tait, 2000, pp. 1–2). SFP has been tested, evaluated and replicated in a variety of ethnic and cultural settings.

SCHOOL-BASED PREVENTION

As we learned earlier, negative school experiences and academic failure are closely associated with serious delinquency (Lösel & Bender, 2003; Hawkins et al., 1998). The great majority of youths in detention and treatment facilities are performing below grade level, and many have histories of truancy. It is estimated that 82% of the inmates in American correctional facilities are high school dropouts (Hamburg, 1998; E. J. Smith, 2006). In contrast, positive school experiences and academic achievement provide protection against delinquency (Gottfredson, 2001; Lösel & Bender, 2003). High academic achievement, motivation, and an education beyond high school are often characteristic of resilient individuals and of low involvement in antisocial behavior. Good school achievement and school bonding seem to exercise a protective function against antisocial behavior even when they are not accompanied by above-average intelligence (Lösel & Bender, 2003). In other words, a child can be of average or below-average intelligence and still have positive experiences in school. This may seem to be an obvious statement, but it has relevance for the continuation of school-based activities that appeal to a wide range of children.

Motivation is a major concern of school-based prevention programs, especially intrinsic as opposed to extrinsic motivation, both of which were discussed in Chapter 4. Recall that resilient people tend to demonstrate significant amounts of intrinsic motivation, which seems to be encouraged and enhanced by praise that encourages competency and efficacy. Children should be praised for attempts at mastery over something, rather than for comparing favorably to other children.

School-based prevention programs focus on working with youth within the school environment, including preschool, although family and community systems are also often included in the program. Programs that begin in the early years of formal schooling, such as the first grade, have a captive audience (i.e., all children must attend school under the law or be home schooled) as compared to preschool programs, in which participation is usually voluntary. Therefore, schools have been a popular setting for universal and primary programs of prevention (Tolan & Guerra, 1994). However, there are two noteworthy illustrations of school-based prevention programs focused on the preschool population, Project Head Start and the Perry Preschool Project. We discuss the Perry project later in the chapter as an example of selective prevention.

Project Head Start

This program began in 1965 as a 6- to 8-week summer program for 3- to 5-year-olds from economically disadvantaged families. Because professionals involved quickly realized that a longer educational program was necessary, Head Start was lengthened to 2 years. By 1992, Head Start enrolled approximately 600,000 preschoolers at a cost of $2.2 billion (Zigler, 1994).

The fundamental assumption underlying **Project Head Start** is that disadvantaged children are at risk for low academic achievement, which ultimately leads to persistent poverty and unfulfilled, unproductive lives. The program has four major components: education (including a creative preschool program), health (both physical and mental), parent involvement (in all planning and administrative aspects of each program), and a broad range of social services. However, the 2,000 or more Head Start programs vary significantly in the type and quality of the services they render (Zigler & Stevenson,

1993). For example, some are center based, while others are home based. In addition, many have been extended to include children who could benefit from the program but are not necessarily economically disadvantaged.

Project Head Start does appear to produce significant and meaningful gains in intellectual performance and socioeconomic development by the end of the 2 years of intervention. Furthermore, this improvement seems to last for at least 2 to 3 years thereafter. However, it is debatable how long these gains continue from that point. Some effects seem to disappear by elementary school, although these findings may reflect variations in the quality of the Head Start programs and differences in the outcome measures used in the evaluations (Gamble & Zigler, 1989; Mulvey et al., 1993). Unfortunately, evaluations of Head Start's effectiveness at preventing delinquency remain sparse and inconclusive (Mulvey et al., 1993), but some Head Start programs have shown impressive results. On balance, Head Start results do suggest that many children get a jump on their academic and social lives and that these effects significantly reduce the risk for later delinquency.

First and Best Teacher Project

One preschool primary prevention experiment that seems promising—but is too new for long-term evaluation—is the **First and Best Teacher** (F&BT) project, which targets a population of preschool-aged children (ages 3 to 5) receiving subsidized child care at sites located in low-income neighborhoods in inner-city Jacksonville, Florida. The project attempts to reduce risk factors while concurrently enhancing protective factors relevant to high-crime neighborhoods (G. D. Evans et al., 2001). F&BT attempts to apply ecologically sensitive prevention programs within both the home and the child-care-center settings (G. D. Evans et al., 2001). Nineteen child-care centers were randomly selected from more than 100 comparable centers. The project consists of an intensive, 60-hour program followed by weekly, individual mentoring sessions between professional child-care educators and child-care-center staff. The program also includes in-home family sessions that provide instruction to strengthen parenting and supervisory skills. Child-care staff reinforce prosocial behavior among children and work with them to improve problem solving and conflict resolution.

Other Promising School-Based Programs

Because school-based programs focus on children within the school setting, they often do not extend to other developmental contexts, such as the family (Tolan & Guerra, 1994). Furthermore, rarely do school-based programs specifically assess their long-term effects on delinquency. Occasionally, the evaluations do examine some related antisocial behaviors—such as aggression or truancy—but in their analyses, the researchers make only tangential connections to delinquency. Consequently, it is difficult to evaluate properly the effectiveness of many school-based programs as prevention approaches to delinquency. As we have repeatedly emphasized, delinquency prevention strategies that focus on multiple systems show greater promise than single-system prevention programs, such as those that focus exclusively on the school.

One exception to this single-system focus is a program developed by Hawkins and his colleagues (Hawkins, Von Cleve, & Catalano, 1991) and described by Tolan and Guerra (1994). First- and second-grade school children from low-income urban schools were taught social problem-solving skills. In addition, teachers were trained in classroom management and interactive teaching skills, and parents were trained in family management skills. Thus, the program encompassed both the school and the family systems. The program's underlying premise was that aggressive and antisocial behaviors in the early elementary school grades are precursors of delinquency in adolescence, and if these behaviors can be substantially reduced or eliminated early, the chances for later involvement in delinquency are correspondingly reduced.

The program was evaluated at the end of the second grade. Lower rates of aggressiveness were found for boys in the classrooms utilizing the intervention strategies, as compared with boys in classrooms that did not receive any intervention strategies. In addition, boys who received the intervention were less likely to be extremely antisocial. Children in the intervention classrooms showed increased interest in school, and their families improved their management skills. Most troubling, however, is the finding that the intervention strategies had virtually no effect on the classroom behavior of the African-American children, a result that may have been due to differences in parental participation. Parents and caretakers of the African-American children often were unable to participate because of other occupational or family commitments. They may also have been discouraged from participating by a perception that the program was not sensitive to their African-American culture. Overall, the study does provide a limited demonstration that a combination of improved instructional methods and improved family management skills can reduce antisocial behavior in young children of a particular cultural background. However, when a program does not seem to work well with a distinct group of participants, it merits a closer look to see how it could be adapted to better fit their needs.

In another school-based project, Tremblay and his colleagues (Tremblay, Pagani-Kurtz, Masse, Vitaro, & Pihl, 1995) developed an intervention program that concentrated on disruptive kindergarten boys from inner-city low-socioeconomic neighborhood schools in Montreal. Teachers used the Social Behavior Questionnaire (SBQ) to assess disruptive behavior; boys who scored above the 70th percentile on the SBQ were considered to be at risk for later antisocial behavior and delinquency. The 2-year program included home-based parent training and school-based social skills training. Both training strategies were implemented by a multidisciplinary team consisting of child-care workers, a psychologist, and a social worker.

The parental training involved (a) teaching parents to monitor their children's behavior and to give positive reinforcement for socially appropriate behaviors, (b) training parents to discipline appropriately, and (c) teaching parents crisis-management techniques. The control group consisted of disruptive boys who did not receive any of the interventions given the treatment groups. Delinquency was assessed by self-reports of the youths and by court records. The latter did not reveal any significant differences between the groups. On self-reports, though, the treated boys reported fewer delinquent behaviors at yearly assessments from 10 to 15 years of age. Overall, the preventive intervention appeared to have a significant long-term impact on the social development of the disruptive kindergarten boys, although the effects appeared to decrease with time. The researchers recommended that young adolescents be given "booster" sessions of similar treatments to reduce the risk for delinquency during the teen years. Thus, periodic follow-up sessions would be added to help maintain the effects of the initial intervention.

One promising school program that is also too young for long-term evaluation is **Early Alliance**. This program focuses on children in first grade in 12 schools located primarily in socioeconomically disadvantaged neighborhoods. The program is really an experiment to determine whether a combination of family, peer, and school strategies can promote competence and reduce the risk for delinquency, substance abuse, and school failure (Dumas, Lynch, Laughlin, Smith, & Prinz, 2001). The program has a family component and three school-based components.

As described by Ikeda, Simon, and Swahn (2001), the school-based components are (a) a classroom program in first and second grades to encourage prosocial coping skills and to enhance positive school–home communications, (b) a peer-coping-skills program delivered in small groups during first grade, and (c) an after-school reading–mentoring program designed to strengthen reading skills and encourage interest in academic endeavors. The family component couples the promotion of parenting skills with support and advocacy for unmet family needs (Ikeda et al., 2001). As with the F&BT program, it remains too early to make conclusions about the long-term effectiveness of Early Alliance. And like the Montreal program described by Tremblay et al. (1995), this program may need booster sessions to maintain positive effects.

COMMUNITY-BASED PREVENTION

To increase the probability of success, prevention programs may have to draw other social systems into their approach. Vera and Shin (2006) emphasize that while middle-class youth have access to community-building opportunities, such as sports or clubs, many families residing in low-income neighborhoods have few options for community activities. In fact, some parents find themselves discouraging children from becoming too involved in the community because of the chronic violence, drug activity, and gang conflicts within their neighborhoods. According to Vera and Shin (2006), "A parent's warning that the neighborhood is too dangerous for playing reinforces the notion that the world is a threatening place" (p. 82). Unfortunately, for many children it *is* threatening.

Vera and Shin (2006) suggest a number of approaches that can be taken to improve family involvement in the community and, at the same time, enhance resilience. For example, they point out that many lower-income parents work in jobs that do not allow for adequate sick leave, vacation time, or day-care services. Consequently, if extended family networks are unavailable and child care is too expensive, children are often left unsupervised. But study after study finds that lack of parental supervision and monitoring is a strong predictor of delinquency, drug abuse, and unwanted pregnancy. Vera and Shin recommend lobbying politicians to enact legislation granting parents better benefits, vacation time, and affordable, *quality* day-care opportunities. A partnership between parents and school administrators focused on expanding after-school programs is another potential solution.

These suggestions are broad-based interventions. Most criminologists believe that, if achieved, they would make a significant dent in the delinquency problem. However, most criminologists also believe that we are a long way from attaining these goals. As a result, many communities turn to more narrow-based prevention programs, including those focusing on youth recreation or after-school drop-in centers. One of the earliest programs in community-based prevention was the **Chicago Area Project** (CAP), discussed in Chapter 5. Although there was some evidence that delinquency rates in the project neighborhoods decreased by almost 50% during the 1930s, the project was never empirically evaluated or researched (Mulvey et al., 1993). Consequently, while the spirit of the CAP is often admired, its overall effectiveness remains in doubt.

Many youth recreation programs (e.g., Police Athletic League, Boys' and Girls' Clubs, supervised intramural sports, and the Fresh Air Fund) have been introduced over the years to offer constructive activities for children and teens, in an attempt to reduce their involvement in antisocial activity (Mulvey et al., 1993). According to Mulvey and his colleagues, more than 20 million youths aged 6 to 15 participated in some form of organized recreational activity during the early 1990s. However, whether these activities actually reduce delinquency to any significant extent is unknown since there have been no methodologically sound evaluations of the programs.

The problem with any community-based or organized recreation program is that neighborhood organizing by itself does not reduce delinquency significantly (Mulvey et al., 1993). This is especially the case for LCP delinquents. Any effective community-based program needs to fully encompass the family system, the school system, and peer influences, with particular emphasis directed at the family. Prevention and treatment strategies must be directed at strengthening the resilience of *both* the child and the family.

Despite this pessimistic appraisal of community-based programs, they should continue to be used, and more are needed. They may be needed particularly for the vast majority of young people who do not engage in persistent antisocial behavior but who need adult monitoring to help them negotiate the developmental hurdles of late childhood and early adolescence—and in some cases to keep them physically safe. All young people need structured activities, places to go, and adult mentors. When these are unavailable through the family or the school, the community can play a crucial supplementary role.

The Positive Youth Development Movement

Within the past 10 years, American psychologists have begun to subscribe to the concept of positive youth development (E. J. Smith, 2006) and to support the project that bears its name. **Positive Youth Development** (PYD) is a community-driven project designed to foster competence in multiple domains (e.g., social, emotional, academic) of all youth, irrespective of the degree of risk present at the community level (Meschke & Patterson, 2003). Implicit in this approach is an understanding that there are universal protective factors that all youth need in order to succeed, such as connectedness to positive, caring adults at home, at school, and in the community (Luthar et al., 2000; Meschke & Patterson, 2003). PYD focuses on each child's unique talents, interests, strengths, and future potential and views young people as a resource rather than a problem for society (Damon, 2004). Not only does the program strive to prevent children and adolescents from engaging in delinquent behaviors; it also tries to build their abilities and competencies.

The ultimate goals of PYD programs are to develop and enhance the five Cs in youth: competence, confidence, connection, character, and compassion (Lerner et al., 2005). As outlined by Lerner et al. (2005), competence refers to a positive view of one's actions in social, academic, cognitive, and vocational realms. Confidence is an internal sense of overall self-worth and self-efficacy. Connection is represented by positive bonds with people and institutions, such as peers, family, school, and community. Character is reflected in respect for societal and cultural rules, adherence to standards of correct behavior, a sense of right and wrong, and integrity. Compassion is seen in a sense of sympathy and empathy for others. PYD attempts to achieve these goals by increasing participants' exposure to supportive and empowering environments in which activities create multiple opportunities for the development of the 5 Cs (Roth & Brooks-Gunn, 2003).

Although there are relatively few data on the overall effectiveness of PYD programs, Lerner et al. (2005) conducted a longitudinal study (the 4-H Study of Positive Youth Development) that investigated the individual and ecological bases of healthy, positive development among diverse adolescents. According to the authors, the results were very promising. But like several other programs discussed here, PYD must await further study, including long-term evaluation of youths who have been exposed to the program. Further descriptions of precisely how the program works are also needed.

SELECTIVE PREVENTION

As noted earlier, selective (or secondary) prevention is directed at children and adolescents who are believed to be at risk of engaging in delinquency, as predicted by any number of risk factors (e.g., low self-concept, highly dysfunctional family situation, conduct disorder). Furthermore, these children and adolescents are likely to have taken a step into delinquency, such as by being truant, possessing malt beverages, joining a delinquent gang, or engaging in other problem behaviors. In a comprehensive review of the research literature, Tremblay and Craig (1995) concluded that selective prevention programs with at-risk youths tend to be successful mainly when the intervention aims at more than one risk factor, lasts for relatively long periods of time (at least 1 year), and is implemented before adolescence. In addition, the time must be quality time, and the more intensive the intervention the better. The successful programs identified by Tremblay and Craig were especially effective when implemented during the preschool or early elementary school years.

Selective prevention programs are increasingly provided primarily to those children identified as showing *early* signs of developing serious and persistent antisocial behavior; high-risk children can be identified with reasonable accuracy in early life, at least by the beginning of elementary school (Dodge & Pettit, 2003; Hill, Lochman, Coie, & Greenberg, 2004; Lochman & Conduct Problems Prevention Research Group, 1995). As noted by Dodge and Pettit (2003), the effectiveness of early screening has major consequences for public policy. Schools can play a more active role than they have played in the past in identifying young children who could benefit from a prevention program. In addition, selective prevention programs can be more focused, more efficient, and more intensive than universal prevention programs (Hill et al., 2004). Prevention with young children offers far more hope than prevention with adolescents, who may already be down the path of persistent antisocial behavior. However, prevention methods must span childhood and adolescence, because new risk factors emerge at each new developmental stage (Dodge & Pettit, 2003).

According to the Carnegie Council on Adolescent Development (1995), approximately 25% of American youth aged 10 to 17 are *highly* vulnerable to the negative consequences of multiple high-risk behaviors, such as substance abuse, school failure, and delinquency. About 7 million youth are particularly vulnerable to delinquency, gang activity, criminal activities, and violence (see E. J. Smith, 2006). An additional 7 million adolescents are at moderate risk for dropping out of school, bullying or being bullied in school, and/or committing suicide (Carnegie Council on Adolescent Development, 1995). We do not know, of course, how many of these children would have been identified as high risk in their preschool years.

THE FAST TRACK EXPERIMENT

The **Fast Track Project** is a multisite, multicomponent prevention program for young children at high risk for long-term antisocial behavior (Conduct Problems Prevention Research Group, 1999). It is based on developmental pathway theory (e.g., Moffitt, 1993) and is longitudinal in design. Fast Track is a two-pronged project: Participants in the program included both high-risk children (selective or secondary prevention) and all children in Grades 1 to 5 (primary or universal prevention) within a particular school. The children in the high-risk group began to show persistent and serious antisocial behavior in early childhood (before first grade), as reported by parents and teachers. The Fast Track program is guided by developmental theory that posits that multiple influences interact in the development of antisocial behavior (Conduct Problems, 2004).

Fast Track is divided into two major phases: the elementary school (Grades 1 to 5) and the adolescent periods (Grades 6 to 10). The elementary school phase addresses six areas of risk and protective factors: parenting, social problem solving and emotional coping skills, peer relations, classroom atmosphere and curriculum, academic achievement with a focus on reading, and home–school relations (Conduct Problems, 2004). The families of the children were invited to participate in weekly parent–child groups, plus home visits, tutoring, and school follow-up. The adolescent phase focuses on four areas associated with successful adolescent adjustment: peer affiliation and peer influence, academic orientation and achievement, social cognition and identity development, and parent and family relationships (Conduct Problems, 2004). The protective role of parental supervision and monitoring was also emphasized.

Children in the program were compared to a group of similar high-risk children who did not participate in the program (the control group). Evaluations of the program's effectiveness were taken at the end of first and third grades. Early results indicated that the participating children, relative to the children in the control condition, progressed significantly in their acquisition of most of the skills deemed to be critical protective factors (Conduct Problems, 1999). The high-risk experimental-group children exhibited improvements in their social, emotional, and academic skills, especially their reading skills. Their peer relationships also improved significantly, and results were equally effective for both boys and girls. In addition, parents who participated in the program displayed more warmth, appropriate and consistent discipline, self-efficacy, and positive school involvement.

The primary prevention effects of Fast Track were equally impressive. Classrooms that participated in the program were found to have lower peer-rated aggression and lower peer-related hyperactive-disruptive behaviors than those classrooms had that did not participate in the program (the control groups). Furthermore, ratings by research observers in the prevention classrooms indicated that the classroom atmosphere was better, students were better able to express their feelings appropriately (i.e., self-regulated), and the classroom as a whole was better able to stay focused and on task.

Fast Track provides an effective example of a carefully articulated developmental model that accounts for the change and accumulation of risk and protective factors throughout the developmental period, starting with children at school entry and continuing through adolescence in high school (Conduct Problems, 2004). However, designers of Fast Track faced many challenges and discovered how difficult it is to overcome the effects of dangerous, crime-ridden neighborhoods and the influences of impoverished families in which parental psychopathology and substance abuse are too familiar.

THE HIGH/SCOPE PERRY PRESCHOOL PROJECT

The **High/Scope Perry Preschool Project** (PPP) is a well-established early-childhood secondary prevention program that began in 1962 and was designed to target specific age-related factors in high-risk children. Actually, the original Perry Preschool no longer exists, but the High/Scope Educational Research Foundation continues to collect follow-up data from the original participants of the study—123 high-risk African-American children (Parks, 2000). The participants were 3- and 4-year-olds at the time who were from low-socioeconomic environments, had low IQ scores (between 75 and 85), and were at high risk of failing school. Fifty-eight of these children were assigned to the program group, and 65 were assigned to a control that did not go through the program. The participants were followed until their 27th birthdays. The program was based on an active-learning model that emphasized age-related intellectual and social development. As described by Parks (2000), the children attended the preschool for 2.5 hours per day for 2 years. Parents participated in small monthly meetings with other parents in the program, and teachers made weekly home visits.

Teacher and self-report data indicate that the program group had lower misconduct scores, fewer incidences of fighting or other violent behavior, and fewer incidences of property damage. The group also had a lower incidence of teenage pregnancy, a higher level of educational attainment and success, and less likelihood of using illicit drugs. In addition, data collected from police and court records show that, compared to the control group, the program resulted in a significantly lower rate of crime and delinquency. Only 31% of the program group had ever been arrested, compared with 51% of the control group. For example, when the participants were 19 years old, researchers discovered that the program group had fewer arrests overall (1.3 arrests per person as compared to 2.3 arrests per person for the control group) and fewer arrests for serious offenses (0.7 arrests compared to 2.0 arrests per person). At age 27 the control group had twice the number of arrests that the program group had (4.0 arrests per person compared to 1.8 arrests per person). Perhaps more revealing is that 35% of the control group were considered frequent offenders (defined as having had five or more arrests) as compared to only 7% of the program group.

The Perry Preschool program clearly demonstrated that early childhood intervention can stop or at least reduce the developmental trajectory toward antisocial behavior and delinquency. This model, when combined with other parental-skills and family training, holds enormous promise. As asserted by Parks (2000), "A multicomponent approach to enhancing child development promotes protective factors and reduces risk factors by addressing many systems and influences that affect a child's development" (p. 4).

JUVENILE DIVERSION

Juvenile **diversion** has long been an integral, and largely unstudied, part of the juvenile justice system (Austin, Johnson, & Weitzer, 2005). The selective prevention programs discussed thus far are aimed at early childhood years; diversion, by contrast, typically involves adolescents or preadolescents. Diversion is essentially a steering away of youth from the formal system of court processing—most typically youth accused of a first-time nonserious crime. For example, youth in diversion have often been accused of (and have admitted) possession of malt beverages, minor vandalism, or shoplifting. As it most commonly occurs, diversion also provides alternative programs and services. It is useful, therefore, to make a distinction between the diversion process and a diversion program (Rutherford & McDermott, 1976). The process of diverting the youth away can occur in a very short span of time. Depending on the jurisdiction, a referral decision is made by police, an intake worker, a prosecutor, or a juvenile court judge. The further along in the system when the decision is made, however, the less it represents the true diversion process.

Diversion as a program offers services to youth in the hope that intervention will prevent recidivism. It is rare today to see diversion occurring without an accompanying program, but the programs vary widely in the extent, type, and quality of services they offer. This variation makes it very difficult to assess their effectiveness. Diversion ideally should be an option only for juveniles who would otherwise be sent to juvenile court for more formal processing. Some critics charge that it is increasingly used for juveniles who would otherwise have been diverted informally by police, perhaps given warnings or referred to other community services.

Diversion programs are operated under different auspices, including private groups, probation offices, social services, or the juvenile courts themselves. One typical model involves a board of community volunteers (often including other youths) who interview a youth and decide what will be required to make amends. Youths under diversion may be required to write letters of apology to their victims, rake leaves in the town park, work to give restitution, provide volunteer tutoring services, enroll in a mediation program, tour correctional facilities, even attend week-long boot camps. Some programs also include job training or referral to community agencies for family counseling, group therapy, or substance abuse treatment. In agreeing to participate in a diversion program, a youth admits his or her culpability for the offense charged, signs a contract, and is left with no record upon completion of the terms of the contract.

As pointed out by Austin et al. (2005), empirical studies of diversion in the 1970s produced mixed results. Some studies reported recidivism was reduced, others found no reduction in recidivism, and still others revealed mixed results. More recently, however, researchers have focused on the specific programs offered by diversion and have been more likely to find significant effects in reducing recidivism.

TEEN COURTS

Many states have experimented with **teen courts**, sometimes called peer courts, usually as part of a diversion program. They are often seen as a cost-effective alternative to a traditional juvenile court for some offenders. It is estimated that there are about 675 teen courts operating in the United States (Butts & Buck, 2000). Teen courts are generally used for younger juveniles (aged 10 to 15), those with no prior arrest records, and those charged with less serious offenses (Butts & Buck, 2000). Figure 12–2 shows the types of offenses usually handled by teen courts. A teen court is most often offered as a voluntary alternative to the more formal processing of the juvenile court.

The typical teen court is comprised of high school students who serve as a jury. As a rule, teen courts do not serve as triers of fact, deciding on the issue of guilt. Rather they are a sentencing tribunal, fashioning an appropriate punishment for a juvenile who has admitted committing a criminal act (see Figure 12–3). In some jurisdictions, however, an adversarial model is used, whereby a "prosecutor" represents the community and a "defense lawyer" forces the "state" to prove its case beyond a reasonable doubt. A "judge" is then the neutral arbiter, and a "jury" decides the defendant's fate.

Teen courts have received broad community support, primarily because of the high levels of satisfaction that have been expressed by parents, teachers, and the youths involved. Although some studies have indicated promising results, little research has been conducted on outcomes in reducing further involvement with the justice system (Butts & Buck, 2000). It should be noted, though, that teen courts have features that are highly likely to promote resilience, increase self-confidence, and offer positive encouragement to youths who participate.

FIGURE 12–2 Offenses Handled by Teen Courts

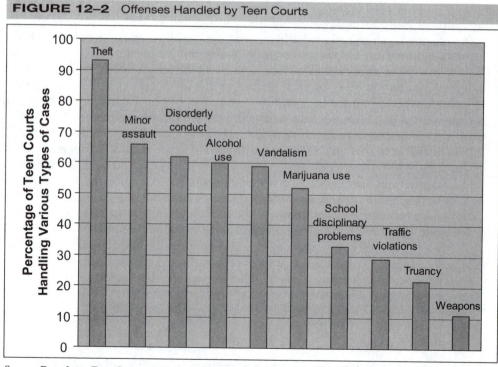

Source: Data from *Teen Courts: A Focus on Research* (p. 5) by J. A. Butts and J. Buck, October 2000, Washington, DC: U.S. Department of Justice, OJJDP.

FIGURE 12–3   Sanctions Imposed by Teen Courts

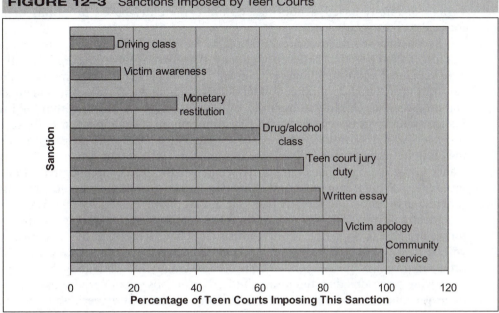

Source: Data from *Teen Courts: A Focus on Research* by J. A. Butts and J. Buck, October 2000, Washington, DC: U.S. Department of Justice, OJJDP.

Summary and Conclusions

Despite the fact that few prevention and treatment programs have been evaluated and few of those have been shown to have lasting effects, we suggest that there is reason to hope. The chapter has reviewed a number of very promising approaches to prevention and early intervention, some of which have produced favorable research results. We have also reviewed key features of successful programs, which should begin early, follow sound developmental principles, respect cultural backgrounds, focus on multiple settings, and focus on the family first.

For organizational purposes we adopt the widely used tripartite division into primary (or universal), secondary (or selective), and tertiary prevention (or intervention or treatment). The terms *intervention* and *treatment* are often used in the first two contexts as well; thus, we refer to early intervention or to treatment associated with secondary prevention. Even though the terminology may overlap the divisions, primary programs are typically directed at all children; secondary programs, at children at risk of engaging in delinquency, including children who may have taken initial steps; and tertiary programs, at children or adolescents who are fully engaged.

Many contemporary primary and secondary prevention programs have shifted their emphasis from reducing risk factors to promoting protective factors, including competence and resilience. Increasing children's self-esteem, promoting positive peer relations, and strengthening family cohesion hold promise for the future of all children, including those at risk of serious antisocial behavior. Recent innovations in this area are the positive youth development programs sanctioned by many psychologists as a way of fostering competence in all children across multiple domains. We discussed a variety of family-based, school-based, and community-based programs that have focused on these goals.

Secondary, or selective, prevention is increasingly focusing on protective factors but also recognizes that children who may already have taken a step into antisocial behavior need additional intervention. We reviewed several programs, including the carefully articulated developmental model provided by Fast Track, which includes special programs for children at high risk of delinquency. In addition, within the juvenile justice system, youths charged with first-time, minor offending are often referred to diversion, which is considered a form of secondary prevention. The diversion approach may require that juveniles participate in some form of treatment, such as that for substance abuse or anger management. To gauge whether this is an effective strategy, we must evaluate the treatment, not the diversion itself. Moreover, it should be recognized that not all diverted youth really need the intervention.

Ideally, all prevention programs would be primary or secondary in nature; the better we are able to approach youths' antisocial behavior early on, the less these youths will be involved in full-blown delinquency. Consequently, those who work with children and juveniles have expended considerable energy in formulating, evaluating, and improving programs directed at all children or at those with early signs of antisocial behavior. One-time intervention may not always be the answer; because of the changes that occur during the developmental process, many children need booster intervention as they approach adolescence. Thus, early intervention is best considered an ongoing process, and some youths—even if provided with early intervention—will continue on the delinquency pathway and will eventually be in need of tertiary intervention, the topic of the next chapter.

Key Terms and Concepts

belief system
Cambridge–Somerville Youth Study
Chicago Area Project
coherence
community-based prevention
creativity
diversion
Early Alliance
family-based prevention
Fast Track Project
First and Best Teacher
High/Scope Perry Preschool
  Project
open communication
organizational patterns
positive peer relations

Positive Youth Development
primary prevention
Project Head Start
Project SELF
protective factors
school-based prevention
secondary prevention
selective prevention
self-efficacy
strength-based programs
Strengthening Families Program
teen courts
treatment
universal prevention
Yale Child Welfare Research
  Program

CHAPTER 13
TREATMENT APPROACHES

*

CHAPTER OBJECTIVES

◆ Review challenges to the successful treatment of serious juvenile offenders

◆ Sketch the history of juvenile courts

◆ Review the philosophy, procedures, and options of the juvenile justice system

◆ Describe secure detention and confinement

◆ Highlight treatment programs with favorable research results

◆ Discuss treatment of specific categories of offenders

Children and adolescents who are already highly involved in antisocial and delinquent behavior present a considerable challenge to those who must care for them. This chapter examines what works with these children or adolescents, many of whom are under the supervision of the juvenile justice system. Because of their age, the nature of their offense, or their repetitive offending, many of these youths have been placed away from their homes and in institutional or other group settings. Approximately one-fourth of adjudicated delinquency cases result in a judicial disposition of out-of-home placement, perhaps in a residential treatment center, juvenile corrections facility, foster home, or group home (Puzzanchera, 2003a). Juveniles adjudicated for drug or property offenses are less likely to be placed outside the home than are those adjudicated for person or public order offenses. A relatively high percentage of public order offenses result in out-of-home placement; this category includes escapes from institutions and probation and parole violations. Even when kept in their own homes, however, adjudicated delinquents are usually on probation or on a conditional release. Juveniles on probation often receive treatment services in the community, some of which may be highly similar to those received by youths in institutions or in foster or group homes.

The task of altering the antisocial behavior of persistent, chronic juvenile offenders is not an easy one, and the track record is littered with failures, if *failure* is defined as repeat offending. As pointed out throughout the text, juveniles who commit serious and violent offenses most often have shown persistent antisocial behaviors beginning in early childhood and have generally continued to commit criminal actions throughout their lives. As emphasized in the previous chapter, interventions that do not begin early have a discouragingly low probability of success, and the most effective interventions for young children also focus on parents and are home or school or community based (Burns et al., 2003).

Despite these challenges, professionals who work with adjudicated delinquents keep trying. Researchers have identified over 230 different treatment programs that have been used for children and adolescents who engage in serious antisocial behavior (Kazdin, 1994). The effectiveness of a vast majority of these approaches has yet to be evaluated or empirically investigated, but the research that *has* been conducted strongly indicates the following: Treatment programs that concentrate on changing thought processes (i.e., cognitions) and self-regulation hold considerable promise if the treatment programs include the family, school, peers, and community. In other words, treatments that have been shown to be most effective have targeted multiple systems at various levels.

Furthermore, as research has continually demonstrated, individual-based psychotherapy is not effective when used in isolation (Committee on Preventive Psychiatry, 1999; Tarolla et al., 2002). Simply applying a form of psychotherapy to a child or adolescent already on a developmental path leading to serious delinquency, *without involving the family and the social environment*, is a waste of time, money, and energy in most cases. As Letourneau and Miner (2005) observe,

> The developmental literature suggests that treatments that focus primarily on changing the individual characteristics (e.g., cognitions and behaviors) of youthful offenders, without also targeting relevant factors with caregivers (e.g., monitoring), peers (e.g., improving ties with prosocial peers), and school (e.g., increasing and improving caregiver–teacher communications) might be of limited usefulness. (p. 306)

Any prevention or treatment program that focuses on only one risk factor is unlikely to lead to long-lasting change in delinquency, because multiple other forces act to support antisocial development (Dodge & Pettit, 2003).

Restrictive interventions, such as residential treatment and incarceration, have not been effective for serious juvenile offenders and are extremely expensive (Henggeler, 1996). The juvenile justice system has little choice other than to incarcerate some juveniles, but it is difficult to argue that the primary purpose is to rehabilitate them. According to Henggeler (1996), "Restrictive out-of-home placements neither address the known determinants of serious antisocial behavior nor alter the natural ecology to which the youth will eventually return. Indeed, data show that incarceration may not even serve a community protection function" (p. 139).

To do justice to those who provide services in restrictive settings, we need to acknowledge that a number of obstacles are in their paths, beginning with the setting itself. In addition, juveniles who receive treatment while confined in an institution differ from those who receive treatment in a noninstitutional setting, chiefly in the nature and seriousness of their offending. For example, those offenders who are in an institution are likely to be considered dangerous or at high risk to reoffend. They are also likely to be older—the average age is 15 to 16—and, thus, more entrenched in their offending patterns.

It is difficult to draw conclusions about the overall effectiveness of intervention programs under the auspices of juvenile corrections because there are so many different treatment programs with different policies, procedures, staff training, and outcome measures. Krisberg and Howell (1998) remarked that in juvenile corrections "there are training schools, detention centers, camps, ranches, wagon trains, environmental institutes, group homes, boot camps, residential programs for emotionally disturbed youths, chemical dependency programs, correctional sailing shills [passenger ships], and independent living arrangements" (p. 347). Juvenile corrections also involve a wide range in size, locations, and security levels.

When it comes to the LCP offender, traditional treatment programs have had little success historically, whether provided in community or residential settings (Borduin, 1994). That is, even when LCPs remain in the community, treatment is problematic. Programs that have been effective with mild or adolescent-limited offenders have been unsuccessful when applied to LCPs or serious delinquents. In most instances, as soon as youths leave the therapeutic milieu and return to their natural social environments, the chronic antisocial behavior reemerges. In fact, the poor track record with LCPs has prompted some professionals and policy makers to resist providing rehabilitative or treatment services to these serious offenders (Borduin, 1994).

An examination of these treatment failures reveals that rehabilitation and treatment services have often been too simplistic, individually based, or narrowly focused. Many programs do not include or even recognize the many influences that unwittingly promote and contribute to antisocial behavior. Not only must effective treatment approaches be multisystemic and address the multidimensional causes of juvenile offending; they must also be intensive and long-lasting because these juvenile offenders have already become deeply entrenched in their antisocial behavioral patterns. The behaviors of hard-core juvenile offenders are often severe, pervasive, and well learned. While treatment for them is by no means hopeless, LCP delinquents require innovation and extreme patience for the many frustrating setbacks that will certainly occur over the long haul.

With these cautions in mind, we discuss here some of the treatment approaches that have been used with delinquents. Before we do, however, it is important to become somewhat familiar with the juvenile justice system. Understanding some of the underlying philosophy of the system, its procedures, and the options available to a juvenile court is critical in determining what has worked and why.

THE JUVENILE JUSTICE SYSTEM

The juvenile justice system in the United States is just over 100 years old; its birth date is usually set at 1899, with the passage of the **Juvenile Court Act** in Illinois. This comprehensive child welfare law created a juvenile court and gave it jurisdiction over delinquent, dependent, or neglected children. The Juvenile Court Act set the stage for and the philosophy of the contemporary juvenile justice system, one based on rehabilitation rather than punishment, and by 1925 all but two states (Maine and Wyoming) had established juvenile courts (Tappan, 1949). Today, juvenile courts exist in some form in every state, either separately or as part of a family court system.

Before juvenile courts existed, children in need of care, at risk of delinquency, or charged with crimes were routinely handled by criminal courts. If judges believed they could not remain with their own families, the children could be placed in private homes or in homes for wayward youth. Some were apprenticed to work at low or nonexistent wages. Juveniles aged 16 or older could also be sent to reformatories.

The Illinois juvenile statute—and the laws of other states that followed its model— circumvented the usual formalities of the criminal process and provided new options for intervening in the lives of a child, in addition to incarceration. The law provided for nonadversarial proceedings that focused more on the child and the child's protection than on the nature of the offense. Court proceedings were to be conducted informally, whereby an intimate, friendly relationship would presumably be established between the judge and the child. Even the physical layout of the court was to reflect a benevolent philosophy. Hearings were usually conducted in a small, private room, often in the judge's chambers, with a simple table arranged so that the judge would appear less intimidating and authoritative. Uniformed officers were excluded from the hearings, and no record was kept of the proceedings or of the disposition of the cases.

The statute encouraged the court to try to understand and help the child rather than to blame or condemn. With the help of probation officers, the court investigated the social background, psychological makeup, and level of maturity of the child and recommended strategies for reducing or eliminating the antisocial behavior. Children were to remain with their parents if at all possible, but in some cases parental surrogates who maintained contact with the courts were assigned as guardians. Thus, under this new law, juvenile courts could use their authority to reach into homes they considered undesirable and intervene before children developed chronic delinquent behavior. The court hearing and all collateral investigations were meant to focus on the needs of the child, not on guilt or innocence. Ostensibly, the court's purpose was not to punish but to "save" the child. In short, the underlying intent of legislators was to encourage the juvenile court to function as the primary institution and mediator for the treatment and resocialization of a delinquent or wayward child.

Critics of the juvenile courts have argued that many judges and other court officials abused their power, operated without sufficient outside scrutiny, and were not as benevolent as they were apparently intended to be (Bernard, 1992). As such abuses and shortcomings of the courts came to light, they were accompanied by calls for reform. In the 1960s, the U.S. Supreme Court responded with landmark rulings—*Kent v. U.S.* (1966) and *In re Gault* (1967)—declaring that juveniles were entitled to certain constitutional rights. We cover some of these in our discussion of juvenile hearings shortly.

Today, some of the principles associated with the earlier juvenile courts still exist. Juvenile courts are rehabilitative rather than punitive in orientation. However, they are also less informal and more adversarial. The juvenile justice system of today assumes that juveniles are accountable for their offenses but not as accountable as adults, given the age and developmental differences. The age of juveniles eligible for today's courts varies, with the modal upper limit being 16. However, even if age eligible, some juveniles are transferred to adult courts because they are approaching the cut-off age or because their crimes are so heinous. Nonetheless, juveniles charged with very serious offenses, including murder, are not uncommonly processed in juvenile courts. Juveniles are still seen as more likely than adults to be rehabilitated, presumably because their antisocial behavior is not as entrenched.

THE JUVENILE JUSTICE AND DELINQUENCY PREVENTION ACT

In 1974, following more than a decade of hearings on juvenile crime and the state of juvenile courts and institutions, Congress passed the **Juvenile Justice and Delinquency Prevention Act** (JJDPA). This significant federal law altered the course of juvenile justice more than any other legislative action since the passage in 1899 of the Chicago Juvenile Court Act. As the statute's name suggests, its philosophy was preventive.

The 1974 statute contains a broad mandate for reform and qualifies as the most comprehensive federal juvenile justice legislation ever enacted (Krisberg, Schwartz, Litsky, & Austin, 1986). The legislation had broad-based support from juvenile justice and child welfare professionals, public interest groups, and Congress itself (Krisberg et al., 1986). It boosted efforts at juvenile justice reform already in progress at the state level and stimulated nationwide reforms. It was intended to deinstitutionalize status offenders (e.g., incorrigibles, truants, runaways); provide alternatives to incarceration for nonserious youthful offenders; provide additional funds to localities to improve delinquency prevention programs; establish a federal assistance program to deal with the problems of runaway youth; and ensure that juveniles would not be detained in the same facilities as adults. The JJDPA is often thought of as promoting the four *D*s:

- **Decriminalization**: Status offenses should not be considered delinquency.
- **Deinstitutionalization**: Juveniles should be sent to institutions only as a last resort; status offenders should not be institutionalized; and juveniles in adult jails and correctional facilities should be separated from adults by sight and sound.
- **Diversion**: Alternatives to juvenile court should be considered and used.
- **Due process**: The constitutional rights of juveniles should be recognized.

Note that the concept of deinstitutionalization, as addressed in the JJDPA, referred to several groups of juveniles. First, and perhaps most prominently featured, were status offenders, who until that time had been commonly placed in training schools with youths who had committed criminal offenses. Second, many members of Congress felt that nonserious delinquents—those found to have committed nonviolent offenses, for example—should not be institutionalized. The JJDPA, therefore, strongly encouraged the development of alternatives to incarceration for dealing with delin-quent youth (Krisberg & Schwartz, 1983). Finally, the JJDPA reflected concern about the problem of juveniles held in adult jails. It initially called on states to keep juveniles "out of sight and sound" of adult offenders but eventually mandated that they be kept out of adult facilities altogether. Thus, although the deinstitutionalization of status offenders (DSOs) is a crucial component of overall deinstitutionalization efforts, the term applies to other juveniles as well.

Proponents of the JJDPA assumed that juveniles, because of their age and experi-ence, are less culpable than adult offenders and are more amenable to treatment and rehabilitation, both of which are difficult, if not impossible, to achieve in punitive or coer-cive institutional settings (Smith, Alexander, Kemp, & Lamert, 1980). Despite the good intentions of the early juvenile courts, it had been widely documented that juveniles were being institutionalized more than was necessary. In addition, institutions were believed to encourage brutality and inhumane treatment, and the social systems that developed among the juveniles promoted recalcitrance and resistance to treatment (Smith et al., 1980). It was thought that deinstitutionalization would bypass these group systems.

The JJDPA also created the Office of Juvenile Justice and Delinquency Prevention (OJJDP), which had four major functions: (1) information collection and dissemination, (2) research and evaluation, (3) development and review of standards, and (4) training through National Training Institutes. Also established were an independent Runaway Youth Program (to be administered by the Department of Health, Education, and Welfare, now defunct) and a National Institute of Corrections within the Justice Department. To this day, the OJJDP provides grants to researchers for the evaluation of a variety of prevention and treatment programs. But it is now only one of a wide variety of funding agencies, including many private ones, that fund research in juvenile justice. Over the years, Congress has made significant revisions to the original JJDPA.

JUVENILE DETENTION AND CONFINEMENT

A youth who is well entrenched in a pattern of antisocial behavior may not necessarily have attained the label *delinquent* from the official juvenile justice system. Many antisocial youths escape the detection of police, and many who are taken into official custody are processed informally, without ever reaching a court proceeding. Nonetheless, the youths who are typically the subject of research are those who have been brought into the justice system.

SECURE DETENTION AND SECURE CONFINEMENT

After a juvenile has been taken into custody or arrested by police, the first major decision is whether he or she should be detained. The term *juvenile detention* is widely used to refer to any form of residential placement for juveniles, both before and after an adjudication of delinquency. Technically, however, **detention** is a temporary disposition pending further court proceedings, and the decision to detain a juvenile is made early in the process.

For our purposes, we will distinguish between secure detention and secure confinement. **Secure detention** refers "to the holding of youth, upon arrest, in a juvenile facility (e.g., juvenile hall) for two main purposes: to insure that the youth appears for all court hearings and to protect the community from future offending" (Austin et al., 2005, p. 1). **Secure confinement**, by contrast, refers "to youth who *have been adjudicated delinquent* and are committed to the custody of correctional facilities for periods generally ranging from a few months to several years" (p. 1). In most cases, secure confinement is reserved for the small number of juvenile offenders who pose a threat to public safety, account for a disproportionate number of all serious offenses committed by juveniles, or are unsuitable for other programs, such as those offered in the community (Zavlek, 2005). There are exceptions, however. For example, juvenile offenders may be placed in secure confinement if community resources are lacking (e.g., if programs for substance abusers are in short supply).

The detention decision may be made by a juvenile court officer, such as an intake worker, a probation officer, or another authorized agency. It is at this point that first-time, nonserious offenders may be referred to diversion, as discussed in Chapter 12. If the initial decision is to detain the youth, it is reviewed and finalized in a formal detention hearing conducted shortly after the youth's admission to a detention facility (usually within 72 hours; see Figure 13–1). If a judge or authorized agent decides that continued detention is in order, the youth remains in the juvenile hall, sometimes until the adjudicatory hearing, which is the equivalent of an adult trial. Available data suggest that on a typical day, 750 juveniles, or 1 in 10 juvenile arrestees, are placed in secure detention (H. N. Snyder & Sickmund, 1995). In most cases, youth are held in detention for a short period of time and are then released to the custody of their parents or caretakers until final disposition of their cases.

Juvenile courts also have the option of placing youths in nonsecure detention, which is placement in their own homes or a group or foster home with a variety of restrictions

FIGURE 13–1 Key Decision Points in the Juvenile Justice System with Illustrative Intervention Options and Strategies

Prearrest (Primary Prevention)	Arrest (Arrest/Referral, Intake/Detention)	Adjudication (Case Filing Pretrial Release/Detention) (Trail/Adjudication Sentencing/Disposition)		Disposition (Sanction,Sentence Modification)	Postdisposition (Aftercare)
Intervention options/strategies • Early interventions by child care professionals (health care, education, social services) based on risk factors for delinquency • Social services agency interventions to address problematic child-rearing practices in community home • Interventions to change community norms about violence (public information campaigns)	*Intervention options/strategies* • Emergency mental health/delox services • Crisis intervention services • Law enforcement diversion programs • Intake and assessment services	*Intervention options/strategies:* • Intake release screening • Community supervision • Electronic monitoring • Day reporting • Home detention • Attendant care • Pretrial residential programs (emergency foster or shelter care, staff secure detention, secure detention) • Mental health and substance abuse services	*Intervention options/strategies:* • Youth and family evaluation services • Diversion programs • Dispute resolution/mediation programs • Continued out-of-home care during adjudication (emergency foster or shelter care, staff secure detention, secure detention) • Continued access to mental health and substance abuse services during adjudication	*Intervention options/strategies:* • Restitution/community service • Community supervision/case management • Intensive community supervision • Electronic monitoring • Day reporting • Alternative education programs • Job training/placement services • Mediation/victim reconciliation • Counseling • Mentoring • Substance abuse treatment • Family support services • Work programs • Residential program as a dispositional placement (halfway houses, foster and group homes, residential treatment) • Independent living services	*Intervention options/strategies:* • Reentry services and programs (disposition options/strategies configured for successful reentry on release from secure facility)

Use of intervention options and strategies can reduce reliance on secure confinement. This model reserves secure placement for the small number of offenders who pose a threat to public safety or who are unsuitable for alternative settings or programs

All youth coming in contact with the juvenile justice system

Small Community-Based Secure Facility

Aftercare Programs

Source: From *Planning Community-Based Facilities for Violent Juvenile Offenders as Part of a System of Graduated Sanctions* (p. 12) by S. Zavlek, August 2005, Washington, DC: U.S. Department of Justice, OJJDP.

on their coming and going. These may include intensive supervision, electronic monitoring, curfews, or alternative forms of careful monitoring. Youths who have already been adjudicated delinquent may also be subjected to these specialized programs.

Youths charged with more serious offenses or those with complicated cases may remain in secure detention for weeks or months. The juvenile court has wide discretion over who shall be confined and, in certain cases, over the length of that confinement. Because juvenile detention centers are often very crowded and may lack sufficient programming, decisions to detain youths in this manner should not be made lightly.

Psychologists and other mental health practitioners are often consulted in the decision about whether to detain a youth, particularly when there is concern about danger to the community. This process involves making a **risk assessment**, that is, estimating the probability that the juvenile will commit another offense. Risk assessment also refers to the process of determining an offender's risk of committing technical violations (e.g., probation or parole failures), failing to appear before the court, or engaging in other negative outcomes (Austin et al., 2005). Such predictions may be clinical or actuarial. **Clinical predictions** are based on a decision maker's subjective interpretation of the situation and may or may not include an interview with the individual. **Actuarial predictions**—often referred to as objective risk assessments—are based on demonstrated statistical relationships between a characteristic and an outcome. For example, a history of violence is a good predictor of future violence.

JUVENILE HEARINGS

A juvenile hearing is the equivalent of an adult criminal trial, and juveniles are entitled to most of the same due process rights that adults enjoy (*In re Gault*, 1967)—the right to an attorney, the right not to incriminate themselves (i.e., they do not have to testify), the right to confront and cross-examine the witnesses against them. However, researchers have found that many juveniles are not represented by lawyers in their delinquency proceedings, primarily because they have waived (or have been persuaded to waive) this right (Feld, 1998). In most jurisdictions, juveniles do *not* have the right to an open proceeding; thus, most juvenile delinquency hearings are closed to the public and the media. In addition, juveniles do not have the right to a trial by jury, although some jurisdictions do provide them. If a juvenile challenges the charges and does not wish to plead guilty, the offense must be proved beyond a reasonable doubt.

We are most concerned with a juvenile's fate after a finding of delinquency. When a juvenile admits guilt or is found guilty by the presiding judge, a sentencing decision (usually called a disposition) is made. The typical juvenile proceeding results in probation, or a conditional release, frequently accompanied by mandated treatment, such as for substance abuse or anger management. However, as mentioned earlier, about one-fourth of proceedings result in out-of-home placement, some of these in institutional settings. In these cases, too, the sentencing judge may recommend that the youth receive specific treatment services.

COMMUNITY TREATMENT

Advocates for juveniles clearly prefer a community sanction for juveniles found to have committed an offense. Institutions are not pleasant settings, and research on traditional, secure confinement in correctional facilities has found it linked to high recidivism rates.

Studies commonly report that as many as 50% to 70% of previously incarcerated youths are rearrested within 1 or 2 years after release (Wiebush, Wagner, McNulty, Wang, & Le, 2005). Even if a violent, repetitive offender is willing and able to change and rehabilitation seems to have been achieved within an institutional setting, the youth generally returns to the social systems from whence he or she came. In other words, juveniles discharged from institutions usually go back to the same home, the same neighborhood, the same community, the same peer network, and the same systems that teach, encourage, and support the same deviant behaviors.

The growing recognition that traditional institutional settings leave much to be desired has led to innovative attempts to treat even serious delinquents in the community. A significant amount of research indicates that well-structured, properly implemented, community-based or family-based programs are far more effective than secure correctional programs in reducing recidivism (Austin et al., 2005). Programs such as intensive supervision, group homes, day reporting centers, or probation allow for a greater connection between youths and their families, schools, and other community-based support agencies. Youths remaining in the community can also benefit from specific programs, including treatment for anger management, substance abuse, or sex offenses.

Some community programs fall under the general rubric of "family preservation programs," so named because of their emphasis on providing services to the whole family and keeping family members together as much as possible. Although some families simply will not survive, all efforts should be made to offer support. One such program in particular—multisystemic therapy—has gained considerable research attention.

Multisystemic Therapy

Scott Henggeler and his colleagues have designed a nonresidential treatment approach called **multisystemic therapy** (MST), which has been found to be highly effective for serious and chronic juvenile offenders (Cullen & Gendreau, 2000; Henggeler & Borduin, 1990; Henggeler, Melton, & Smith, 1992; Krisberg & Howell, 1998; Scherer, Brondino, Henggeler, Melton, & Hanley, 1994). The focus of MST is the family, and the family must be actively involved in the program. However, the program also pays attention to other systems in an offender's life, such as the school and the neighborhood. In other words, MST addresses the cognitive and systemic factors that are considered to be risk factors for antisocial behavior (Schaeffer & Borduin, 2005). Together, counselors and family members collaborate to develop pertinent treatment goals as well as appropriate plans to meet these goals (Henggeler, 1996). Barriers and impediments to the plan—such as uncooperative family members, teachers, and school administrators—are worked with directly and actively. MST is an action-based treatment program—it tries to get the involved family members to take "action" (i.e., behaviorally do something) rather than just talking. The overriding purpose of MST is to help parents deal effectively with their children's behavioral problems and help the children cope with family, peer, school, and neighborhood problems.

MST is an intensive, time-limited form of intervention. Trained therapists have daily contact with the adolescent and the family, totaling approximately 60 hours over 4 months. The caseload of the therapist is small, averaging four to six families per counselor. MST therapists identify both strengths and problem areas within the individual, the family, and other social systems, such as peers, school, social service agencies, and parents' workplace. For example, a strength in the school could be an especially supportive teacher; a problem could be extensive bullying by the youth.

MST focuses primarily on the strengths of the family, identifying positive aspects and providing the parent(s) with the resources needed for effective parenting and for developing a better-functioning and cohesive family unit. A family's strength might be its musical abilities, its sense of humor, its supportive grandparent, and/or its religious faith. On the other hand, parents might need help communicating effectively with their children, solving problems, or being less susceptible to manipulation by the child. Other parents might need ways to reduce stress or their own dependency on alcohol, or they might need referral to community services.

MST therapists also help the targeted youth remediate deficits in interpersonal skills that hinder acceptance by prosocial peers. The youth and the therapist might work on modifying thought processes and coping mechanisms that interfere with the family, peer, school, and neighborhood microsystems. Other MST strategies include decreasing a teenager's antisocial peer contacts and increasing affiliation with prosocial peers and activities, as well as developing ways to monitor and promote the youth's school performance. Sometimes youth are helped to find jobs or engage in after-school recreational activities.

One of the first studies of the effectiveness of MST was conducted with a population of youths from Simpsonville, South Carolina, each of whom had at least three nonviolent arrests or one violent arrest and lived with at least one parent. The participants in the study averaged 3.5 arrests and had spent an average of 9.5 weeks in lockup in a correctional facility. Their average age was 15.2 years. The results showed that, compared to a control group of youths who received the usual community services (court-ordered curfew and/or referral to a community agency), those youths receiving MST were less likely to be arrested. Incarceration was reduced by 64% during a 59-week follow-up. The MST youths were also reportedly less aggressive with peers, as compared to the control group. Significantly, the lower rearrest rates held for at least 2.5 years after treatment (Henggeler, Melton, Smith, Schoenweld, & Henley, 1993). This is a relatively long follow-up, compared to that of most intervention studies, and demonstrates that the program has considerable promise.

In another study, Borduin et al. (1995) examined the long-term effects of MST, as compared to those of individual therapy, on the prevention of criminal behavior and violent offending among 176 juvenile offenders at high risk of committing more serious crimes. A 4-year follow-up of rearrest data revealed that MST was more effective than individual therapy in preventing future criminal behavior, including violent behavior. The MST program reduced rearrests for violent and other serious crime by 63% over the 4-year period.

In a more recent follow-up of the Borduin et al. (1995) study, Schaeffer and Borduin (2005) followed the original 176 participants for nearly 14 years. The data showed that MST participants had significantly lower recidivism rates during follow-up than did those participants who received individual therapy—50% versus 81%, respectively. (Depending on the study, recidivism refers to rearrest, reconviction, or incarceration after an initial juvenile arrest, conviction, or incarceration.) Furthermore, MST offenders, when compared to individually treated offenders, had 54% fewer arrests and 57% fewer days of confinement in adult correctional facilities.

Other studies of MST have shown between 25% and 70% reductions in rates of rearrest, decreases in an offender's need for mental health programs, and improvements in family functioning (Austin et al., 2005; Mihalic, Irwin, Elliott, Fagan, & Hansen, 2001). MST has also reduced out-of-home placements by 47% to 64%. Positive results were maintained for at least 4 years for most programs.

SECURE CONFINEMENT

Although community treatment may be the preferred option for juveniles, even for those who have committed violent and other serious offenses, it is not a realistic option for all. Juveniles placed in institutional settings, such as training schools or rehabilitation centers, are typically the most hard-core delinquents or those who have committed a particularly heinous offense but have not been transferred to criminal courts. For these youths, secure confinement is usually looked at as the last option, when all else has failed. However, in some jurisdictions, a lack of alternative community programs leaves juvenile judges with few options for placing youths with substance abuse or mental health problems. Consequently, secure juvenile correctional facilities are not necessarily filled with the most serious LCP offenders or juveniles who have committed a one-time brutal crime.

When juveniles first arrive at these settings, they are subjected to classification, a process of determining the level of custody they should be assigned. This process is especially important for determining the risk that these juveniles present to the staff, themselves, and other youths in the facility. Thus, classification also occurs in detention centers, where youths are often in crisis and must be watched closely for possible suicidal behavior. Classification also determines the extent to which these youths might try to escape or engage in other institutional misconduct. Basically, the classification rating determines the section of the facility to which an offender is assigned, as well as the level of security. (In very small facilities, of course, there may be few options.) Usually, youths are reclassified after 60 to 90 days in the facility. If they do not demonstrate misconduct and do not appear a danger to themselves or to others, they may be placed in a lower custody level.

Classification is not only for custody purposes, however; it is also a crucial process for determining treatment needs. Staff and mental health consultants typically administer a battery of tests for placement in educational and treatment programs. Thus, youths who have been heavily involved in alcohol or drug abuse might be placed in a residential substance abuse treatment wing or program.

Not all projections of the success of institutional treatment are gloomy. On the basis of an extensive study of the effects of residential treatment programs, Grietens and Hellinckx (2004) report that we should be moderately optimistic about the future effects of treatment, or tertiary prevention. In their analysis of American and European residential treatment programs designed for juvenile offenders, they found that, on average, recidivism was reduced by 9%. Nine percent may not seem very promising, but when we consider that we are dealing with juveniles who have a long history of deeply entrenched antisocial behavior, it is significant.

Lipsey and Wilson (1998) examined the effectiveness of 200 treatment programs for serious juvenile offenders. The analysis included 83 studies of the effects of treatment with *institutionalized* offenders, 74 of which involved juveniles in the custody of juvenile justice institutions and 9 that involved residential institutions administered by mental health or private agencies. The analysis also included 117 treatment programs for *noninstitutionalized* juveniles, most of whom were on probation or parole. Although the results were mixed and confusing, with no one particular treatment program showing superiority, the average program for both institutionalized and noninstitutionalized offenders produced a 12% reduction in reoffense rates. The most effective programs (e.g., teaching-family homes, interpersonal skills development, and other broad-based interventions) were able to produce a 40% reduction rate, a very promising result, while some other traditional programs (e.g., Wilderness/Challenge, vocational programs, milieu therapy) were largely ineffective by most measures. The most effective programs included key components—such as social skills training, parent management, and family support—*in combination*. One-dimensional programs—for example, anger management alone—were not successful.

TREATMENT OF SPECIFIC GROUPS OF OFFENDERS

To date, little systematic research has focused on the effectiveness of treatment with distinct types of offenders (Lipsey, Wilson, & Cothern, 2000), but this is clearly warranted. For example, we do not know which specific treatment approaches work best with juvenile sex offenders, murderers, juveniles with psychopathic tendencies, or substance abusers.

JUVENILE SEX OFFENDERS

Juvenile sex offenders (JSOs) are sometimes treated in community settings, but we focus here on the serious offenders who are most likely to be held in restrictive institutional settings. Juvenile sex offenders, like adult sex offenders, are often viewed as a homogeneous group of individuals, even though research shows that they vary widely in the frequency and type of sexual activity they engage in and in their personal attributes, such as age, background, personality, race, religion, beliefs, attitudes, and social skills. Researchers are beginning to pay more attention to female JSOs (e.g., Becker et al., 2001; Righthand & Welch, 2001), but we know little about effective treatment approaches, particularly for those held in institutional settings.

JSO treatment is grounded on the premise that deviant sexual behaviors are associated with distorted thought patterns that serve to deny, justify, minimize, and rationalize the offender's actions (Eastman, 2004). Research reveals that sexually aggressive male juveniles subscribe to attitudes and ideology that encourage them to be dominant, controlling, and powerful, whereas females are expected to be submissive, permissive, and compliant. Such a cognitive orientation seems to have a particularly strong disinhibitory effect on sexually aggressive juveniles, prompting them to interpret ambiguous behaviors of girls or women as come-ons, to believe that females are not really offended by coercive sexual behavior, and to perceive victims as deriving gratification from being sexually assaulted (Lipton, McDonel, & McFall, 1987). It is not clear whether female JSOs hold similar distorted thought patterns, but research does indicate that they tend to be depressed, have suicidal ideation, and have been victims of sexual abuse themselves (Bumby & Bumby, 1997).

Malamuth has discovered that sexually aggressive males have information-processing deficits in their ability to separate friendly from seductive behavior, or assertive from hostile behavior (Malamuth & Brown, 1994; Murphy, Coleman, & Haynes, 1986). For example, sexually aggressive males are significantly less accurate in reading a female's cues in first-date interactions. This cognitive deficit is especially apparent when the female's communication is direct, clear, and strong. If she protests "too much," it means—to the sexually aggressive male—that she really wants the opposite. This information-processing deficiency may be the result of a lack of opportunity during early childhood to develop the social and interpersonal skills needed to detect correct cues from others.

Treatment approaches with JSOs have traditionally addressed attitudes and values, social skills, arousal patterns, denial, and past victimization (Kahn & LaFond, 1988; Sciarra, 1999). However, these treatment programs were modeled after treatment programs designed for adult sex offenders, and few studies examined whether these same programs were effective in the treatment of JSOs. In 1988 a task force known as the National Adolescent Perpetrator Network was commissioned to study JSOs and propose treatment strategies and goals. The group identified several characteristics of JSOs and recommended that treatment plans include these corresponding components:

- Help offenders accept responsibility for their antisocial sexual actions
- Challenge cognitive distortions and rationalizations that support or trigger the offending behaviors
- Develop empathy in the offenders for their victims and enhance the management of emotions
- Teach social and interpersonal skills (including dating skills)
- Instill a positive self-identity and improve self-esteem (Eastman, 2004)

Unfortunately, the number of studies examining the effectiveness of treatment in reaching these goals remains small (Sciarra, 1999), although there is currently considerable ongoing research evaluating treatment programs for juveniles (Veneziano & Veneziano, 2002).

The more contemporary programs designed for JSOs are different from those that target adult sexual offenders, primarily because contemporary research suggests that juveniles are far more changeable than adults, are more influenced by the social environment, and appear to be at lower risk for sexual recidivism (Veneziano & Veneziano, 2002). However, Eastman (2004) points out that a majority of studies concentrate on the recidivism rates of JSOs rather than on the goals of treatment. The outcome measure of recidivism, she notes, is used in different ways by different researchers in different contexts. This is a common problem with studies of recidivism for other crimes as well, as we mentioned earlier. For example, some studies define *recidivism* as the arrest of a juvenile offender after completion of treatment, while others define the term as rearrest and conviction after the completion of treatment. In some other cases, *recidivism* is defined as rearrest for *any* crime, not just a crime related to the behavior for which the juvenile was treated. Eastman (2004) notes that the scarcity of empirical research on treatment efficacy "has left professionals in the field making decisions on treatment and program effectiveness based on a small number of studies using outcome measures that professionals in the field have not uniformly defined or that are subject to debate about whether their use is ethical" (p. 475).

JUVENILES WHO KILL

Most of the treatment information on juvenile murderers is from clinical reports of a few cases referred for treatment (Heide, 2003). Juveniles who commit homicide generally are placed in a juvenile facility in which they rarely receive treatment tailored to their needs. Mental health care in juvenile facilities is typically minimal because of financial constraints and limited awareness of the psychological needs of this population (Heide, 2003). In addition, the likelihood of juvenile murderers receiving intensive psychological treatment and intervention decreases as they enter adolescence (Heide, 2003; Myers, 1992). Older adolescent murderers are often placed in adult prisons or are held in a juvenile institution until they are age-eligible for transfer to an adult prison. Psychiatric hospitalization, although commonly used for young children who kill, is rarely used for adolescent murderers (Heide, 2003).

Overall, young killers appear to make a satisfactory adjustment in a correctional facility and in the community after release from custody (Heide, 2003); youths held in juvenile facilities must be released upon reaching adulthood, typically age 18. A satisfactory adjustment is especially true for those youths who have killed family members in an isolated act of violence (Hillbrand, Alexandre, Young, & Spitz, 1999). However, hard-core, persistent, violent delinquents who killed in the course of committing other crimes do not make a good adjustment and often continue offending after release.

Although many treatment programs target juveniles who have committed violent crimes, few specifically target those who have murdered. One exception is the capital offender program at the Giddings State Home and School in Texas. Initially limited to juvenile murderers, the program was expanded in 1999 to include some youths who have committed other serious violent offenses. The program is intended to help these juveniles understand what makes them act violently and criminally and help them identify ways to cope with the feelings that trigger dangerous behavior. Among other things, youths are required to reenact their crimes while role-playing both the perpetrator and the victim. The Texas Youth Commission (2005) reported that this specialized treatment program reduced the recidivism (i.e., rearrest) of capital offenders by 46% during the 5-year period from 1999 to 2003. The Texas Youth Commission also evaluated personality and behavioral changes in the youths while in the program and again after release. According to the commission, the youths in the program became significantly less hostile and aggressive, assumed more responsibility, and developed more empathy for their victims (Heide, 2003).

JUVENILE OFFENDERS WITH PSYCHOPATHIC FEATURES

A long line of research documents that *adult* psychopaths are not responsive to treatment, whether in prisons, psychiatric treatment centers, or the community (e.g., Alterman, Rutherford, Cacciola, McKay, & Boardman, 1998; Hare et al., 2000; Hill, Rogers, & Bickford, 1996). Not surprisingly, then, some commentary has indicated that psychotherapy or intervention with psychopaths is basically a waste of time. Gacono, Nieberding, Owen, Rubal, and Bodholt (2001) concluded from their review that "simply stated, at this time there is no empirical evidence to suggest that psychopathy is treatable" (p. 111). O'Neill, Lidz, and Heilbrun (2003) concurred: "To date, there is no treatment for psychopathy that has been established as effective" (p. 300). In fact, some forms of treatment (e.g., milieu therapy) have been linked to higher rates of violent recidivism in psychopaths (Rice, Harris, & Cormier, 1992). Several studies indicate that psychopaths are either completely nonresponsive to treatment or they play the treatment game well, pretending to cooperate but in actuality "conning" the treatment provider (Hare, 1996; Porter et al., 2000; Rice et al., 1992). Farrington (2005) states:

> It seems to be generally believed that psychopaths are difficult to treat because (a) they are an extreme, qualitatively distinct category; (b) psychopathy is extremely persistent throughout life; (c) psychopathy has biological causes which cannot be changed by psychosocial interventions; and (d) the lying, conning, and manipulativeness of psychopaths make them treatment resistant. (pp. 494–495)

However, with advancing knowledge and theoretical development, the clinical lore that psychopathy is untreatable may instead conclude that some and perhaps even most psychopaths can be effectively treated (Salekin, 2002). Some studies have already indicated that intensive and lengthy treatment can yield positive results (Salekin, 2002; Skeem, Monahan, & Mulvey, 2002). While stating that there is no known effective treatment program for psychopaths, Hare (1996) adds that psychopathic features are not immutable. And if they are not immutable, there is hope for treating juveniles who fall into this category of offenders.

Unfortunately, little is known about the effectiveness of prevention and treatment methods for child and adolescent psychopathy (Farrington, 2005, p. 494), or youth with psychopathic features. (Remember that many theorists and researchers resist calling juveniles psychopaths but prefer to discuss their psychopathic features or characteristics.) Logically, it makes sense to hypothesize that children and adolescents with psychopathic features would respond more positively than adults to prevention and treatment strategies because of their youthful malleability. Consequently, researchers have begun to evaluate the effectiveness of (a) treatment programs designed specifically for juveniles with psychopathic characteristics and (b) programs for youthful offenders that include those with psychopathic characteristics, identified by their scores on instruments like the PCL:YV, the APSD, or other measures (discussed in Chapter 7).

Studies have underscored the observations that children and adolescents with psychopathic features show distinct sets of emotional and cognitive deficits that lead to their violent and antisocial behavior. According to Salekin and Frick (2005), knowledge about these areas may be important for designing more individualized interventions for youths with psychopathic traits. For example, laboratory studies have revealed that children with conduct problems and high levels of callous-unemotional (CU) traits tend to respond better to reward-driven interventions and poorly to punishment-driven or fear-induced forms of intervention (Hawes & Dadds, 2005). These findings imply that such children would respond well to reward-based strategies for changing behavior but would remain insensitive to other disciplinary practices. "The assessment of CU traits in addition to other established risk factors may allow such children to be targeted with more individualized intervention" (Hawes & Dadds, 2005, p. 740).

However, juveniles with psychopathic characteristics did not fare well in an outpatient substance abuse treatment program based on a cognitive-behavioral model, in which the adolescents set goals and learned coping skills (O'Neill et al., 2003). In this program the youths had daily group therapy sessions and twice-weekly 1-hour sessions of individual therapy. And while the youths who scored low on the PCL:YV did benefit from the program, those with high scores did not. The youths with higher scores were more likely to be rearrested and demonstrated higher attrition from the program, lower quality of participation, and more frequent use of alcohol and drugs while in the treatment program. The reasons for their failure in this program are unknown.

On a more promising note, in their survey of over 500 child clinical psychologists, Salekin et al. (2001) discovered that many of these clinicians reported that they were moderately to significantly successful in treating children and adolescents with psychopathic features. The treatment duration for these psychopathic youth averaged about 12 months. "After nearly 1 year of treatment these youths reportedly made marked improvement on such criteria as violence and recidivism" (Salekin et al., 2001, p. 192). The clinicians estimated that approximately 42% of the boys and 45% of the girls made moderate to marked improvement in reducing their psychopathic symptomatology overall. "These findings are important," Salekin et al. conclude, "and indicate that psychopathy, at least in youth, may be less recalcitrant to treatment than previously thought" (p. 192).

Salekin (2002) also published a comprehensive review of 42 studies specifically directed at treating psychopathy. Despite some methodological shortcomings with many of the studies (e.g., small sample size, diverse definitions of psychopathy), cognitive-behavioral, psychodynamic, and eclectic interventions were shown to be effective. The most notable benefits included a reduction in psychopathic characteristics, such as a decrease in lying, an increase in remorse or empathy, and improved relations with others. Salekin specifically noted that one intensive action-oriented program was highly successful (88%) with youngsters showing psychopathic tendencies. Ingram, Gerard, Quay, and Levison (1970) devised that program to specifically address psychopathic behaviors in youth. The program was based on the sensation-seeking model, which kept the 20 young participants interested in treatment throughout the sessions. The program was able to decrease institutional aggressive behavior and to improve overall adjustment in the community.

Those psychotherapies that proved most effective tended to be more intensive and were often combined with other programs, such as group psychotherapy, pharmacotherapy, or the involvement of family members. "These results indicate, at least preliminarily, that for complex problems such as psychopathy, more elaborate and intensive intervention programs involving individual psychotherapy, treatment of family members, and input from groups (other patients/inmates) are beneficial and may enhance their overall effectiveness" (Salekin, 2002, p. 105). The key to success with psychopaths may be the scope, type, intensity, and duration of the treatment as well as the training of the staff applying the intervention. Salekin (2002) points out that those intervention programs that were less successful were characterized by little input from trained mental health professionals and extremely little one-to-one patient–psychologist contact. He further stated that early intervention is particularly important in working with children exhibiting psychopathic traits. Salekin concludes that the therapeutic pessimism that surrounds the treatment of psychopathy and undermines the motivation to search for effective modes of intervention is unwarranted.

JUVENILE DRUG OFFENDERS

Juvenile substance abusers are treated in the community or in a noncorrectional treatment facility more often than in juvenile training schools or rehabilitation centers.

In the community, family-based therapy is often used. According to Ozechowski and Liddle (2000), family-based therapy is one of the most thoroughly studied treatments for adolescent drug abuse and often is the core of effective therapy. Basically, family therapy tries to orchestrate emotional and cognitive change within individuals and interactional changes among family members (Ozechowski & Liddle, 2000). For youths in institutional settings, family-based therapy is a far less realistic option because the family must come to the institution. Furthermore, institutional staff are often of the opinion that youths in their care are better off if they have minimal contact with their deviant families.

Regardless of its modest effectiveness, focusing exclusively on the family—the traditional approach in family-based therapy—is not enough. In general, programs that focus on only one potential influence on youth substance use have not been found to be effective (Meschke & Patterson, 2003). Many variables are involved in the creation and maintenance of adolescent drug abuse, and as many as possible should be addressed in effective prevention and treatment programs. More recently, *ecological* family-based therapy has broadened the boundaries of prevention and treatment well beyond the family. This approach targets not only the individual and the family, but also the interactions the child or adolescent has with the school, peers, and the community. The ultimate goal is to reduce the multiple developmental risk factors that impinge on a child or adolescent and to enhance the available protective factors within the individual, family, and extrafamilial systems.

Research on ecological family-based therapy demonstrates that it is impressive in reducing alcohol, marijuana, and hard drug use, including cocaine, heroin, and other narcotics (Ozechowski & Liddle, 2000). In their comprehensive review of the research and theoretical literature, Ozechowski and Liddle (2000) conclude that strong and consistent empirical support exists for the efficacy of ecological family-based therapy in reducing adolescent drug use. Furthermore, the approach has been found effective over considerable periods after treatment has terminated. To some extent, ecological family-based treatment also appears to reduce antisocial behavior and delinquency beyond drug abuse.

At the individual level, male and female adolescent drug abusers differ in ways that must be considered in any effective family-based treatment. Specifically, female adolescent drug abusers appear to be more depressed and to have higher levels of anxiety, as compared to their male counterparts (Dakof, 2000; Hops, Davis, & Lewin, 1999; Opland, Winters, & Stinchfield, 1995). Thus, some clinicians believe that ecological family-based therapy for female adolescent drug abusers demands a particular focus on their emotional and psychological distress as well as their substance abuse. Furthermore, clinicians and researchers have found that particular types of prevention strategies work better for different age groups (Meschke & Patterson, 2003). For example, preventing drug use between 6th and 9th grades is most effective if older adolescents teach refusal skills to children and younger adolescents (Newcomb & Bentler, 1989).

Juvenile Drug Courts

Beginning in the mid-1980s, some state courts began experimenting with the idea of dedicating special courtrooms to drug cases, primarily to speed up the processing of cases (Belenko & Dumanovsky, 1993; Belenko & Logan, 2003). The role of these courts then expanded to include monitoring of treatment, drug testing, and other services to drug-involved offenders. The first **juvenile drug court** began in Key West in October

1993 (American University, 2001), in response to a perceived need to intervene more effectively in the substance abuse problems of juveniles.

Although juvenile drug courts "have become quite popular, they have generally neither been empirically nor theoretically based, nor guided by sound evaluations" (Belenko & Logan, 2003, p. 205). So far, the data are inconclusive; drug courts have not successfully demonstrated that they can divert drug-involved juveniles from a life of substance abuse. If drug courts do not provide wider services to juveniles and their families, they may not achieve what their supporters had hoped to accomplish. On the other hand, if drug courts can succeed in providing effective treatment and other services—not just drug testing and monitoring behavior—they may be a good alternative to incarcerating juveniles whose major problem is substance abuse.

MENTALLY DISORDERED JUVENILE OFFENDERS

Earlier in the book we noted that, as a group, juvenile offenders are not mentally disordered or mentally ill in the clinical sense. However, many *early-onset* juvenile offenders do exhibit a variety of mental disorders or behavioral and/or emotional problems, particularly ADHD, and unfortunately, many of them are not identified until they have had some contact with the police or juvenile court.

Researchers have found that schools are the place where most early child delinquents (younger than 13) receive some form of counseling, treatment, or intervention (Burns et al., 2003). In this sense, they are receiving a form of primary or secondary prevention, and several school intervention programs have yielded encouraging results. Their approaches include classroom- and schoolwide behavior management, social-competence curriculums, conflict-resolution and violence-prevention curriculums, bullying prevention, and multicomponent classroom-based efforts that help teachers and parents manage, socialize, and educate students and improve their cognitive, social, and emotional competencies (Burns et al., 2003). Social-competence programs that have sufficient intensity and duration have been found to be especially effective for children younger than age 13. Note that all of these programs should be beneficial for all children, not just those at risk for engaging in antisocial behavior.

Research has also found that mental and behavioral disorders are pervasive among *incarcerated* juveniles, ranging as high as 80% (Burns et al., 2003). Although it is likely that some overdiagnosis inflates these statistics, it is clear that a significant number of juveniles in these settings do have mental health problems, which may or may not be addressed sufficiently by program staff, depending upon the quality of the setting. Within the juvenile justice system, however, a number of specialized treatment facilities are available for youths with serious problems. These are typically private facilities that accept adjudicated youth, sometimes from other states, for intensive treatment.

NONTRADITIONAL RESIDENTIAL TREATMENT

Thus far we have discussed community services and treatment in restrictive institutional settings. However, many nontraditional residential treatment programs are available in less-restrictive physical settings, such as juvenile boot camps, wilderness camps, or other adventure and survival programs. Such settings typically may include youths who have committed serious crimes, but their offenses are more likely to have been nonviolent ones. Still, a highly aggressive youth might be sent to one of these non-traditional settings, and it is not unusual for sex-offending juveniles to be included as well, probably assigned to a special unit in which sex-offender treatment is available. Research on the effectiveness of JSO treatment in a wilderness setting is virtually non-existent, however.

BOOT CAMPS

In the 1980s, many states developed a system of "shock incarceration"—commonly called **boot camps**—for adult offenders. Initially based on a military model, shock incarceration was intended to provide an intensively structured, short-term alternative to prison. By the end of the 1980s, the "model" boot-camp programs included military-style discipline, a rehabilitative component (such as substance abuse treatment), and community follow-up, or "aftershock." Although there continue to be serious questions raised about the success of the boot-camp model, shock incarceration seems destined to remain an intermediate sanction for some adult offenders (MacKenzie & Hebert, 1995).

Boot camps were not immediately adopted in the juvenile justice system, primarily because there were questions about their appropriateness. Faced with increased over-crowding in juvenile facilities, however, policy makers began to consider the possibility of a boot-camp alternative for less-serious juvenile offenders who were believed to need more structure than typical community probation but less structure than an institution. The first juvenile boot camp was established in 1985 in Orleans Parish, Louisiana (Tyler, Darville, & Stalnaker, 2001). Then, in the early 1990s, OJJDP funded demonstration projects at three sites to develop a model boot-camp program for male juveniles, aged 13 to 18.

The ambitious goals of the model boot-camp programs, as reported by Bourque et al. (1996), were as follows:

- Serve as a cost-effective alternative to institutionalization
- Promote discipline through physical conditioning and teamwork
- Instill moral values and a work ethic
- Promote literacy and increase academic achievement
- Reduce drug and alcohol abuse
- Encourage participants to become productive, law-abiding citizens
- Ensure that offenders are held accountable for their actions

The boot-camp experience included a 90-day residential program heavily focused on military drills, discipline, and physical conditioning. The regimen included uniforms, military jargon, and an exhausting daily routine from 5:30 or 6:00 A.M. until 9:00 or 10:00 P.M. Rehabilitation activities—such as remedial education, life-skills education and counseling, and substance abuse education—were included to a lesser extent.

The boys in the model programs had committed a wide range of offenses, including property, drug, and other felonies but excluding violent offenses. At all three sites, the programs demonstrated short-term success during the residential phase, and at least 80% of the boys graduated from boot camp, having improved in educational performance, physical fitness, and behavior. The staff noted their improvements in respect for authority, self-discipline, teamwork, and physical appearance. The youths themselves rated their experience positively, noting that they believed they had significantly changed the direction of their lives.

A variety of aftercare services were made available, depending on the site. These included specially created aftercare centers, mainstreaming into local boys' clubs, academic instruction, drug counseling, and support services. However, the aftercare results were discouraging and began to raise important questions about the effectiveness of boot camps for juvenile offenders. In a 1-year follow-up, all three sites reported high rates of noncompliance, absenteeism, and new arrests. "No site graduated more than 50 percent of its aftercare participants, and terminations were most commonly caused by new arrests in two sites" (Bourque et al., 1996).

In assessing what went wrong, Bourque and his colleagues suggested, among other things, that a more appropriate balance between militaristic and rehabilitative elements was needed. Although discipline could be an important motivating tool, they posited, the educational, psychological, and emotional needs of the youths should be better addressed. The researchers also suggested fine-tuning the selection of youths, noting in particular that youths with prior incarceration experience were less likely to survive the aftercare component. In addition two of the programs seemed to include too many serious offenders, whereas a third was overly restrictive for youths who could have done just as well or better in another probation alternative.

Despite these shortcomings, the growth of juvenile boot camps continued in many states (Tyler et al., 2001). In Texas alone, the board of Texas Juvenile Probation, in 1998, approved 18 proposals to construct juvenile boot-camp facilities across the state. Over the years, three identifiable styles of boot camp have evolved—the military-drill style, the rehabilitative approach, and the educational/vocational model—but a majority of boot camps still concentrate on the military drill, which focuses on strict discipline as the central theme (Tyler et al., 2001). It appears that the military style is popular with the public and politicians because it projects the image of getting tough with juvenile crime. However, documented instances of extreme abuse have led to the closure of juvenile boot camps in Arizona, Georgia, and Maryland (Bottcher & Ezell, 2005), and this trend could continue. In 2000 Maryland disbanded its juvenile boot camps and fired top juvenile justice officials after publicity surrounding allegations of physical and emotional abuse of juveniles. One news story recounted split lips and bloody noses inflicted by staff who slammed the teens to the ground (Nelson, 2003).

Today's juvenile boot camps vary in cost, staff-to-inmate ratios, size, and style. Most are intended for male juveniles, but boot camps for female offenders are also available. The overall evaluation of juvenile boot camps is extremely disappointing. The research literature has continually reported that juvenile boot camps are ineffective in reducing recidivism (MacKenzie, Layton, Souryal, Sealock, & Bin Kashem, 2001), even when intensive aftercare is provided (Bottcher & Ezell, 2005). In addition, juvenile boot camps are far more costly (at least 10 times more) than juvenile probation, which includes supervised intensive probation (Tyler et al., 2001). In their incisive review, Tyler and his associates (2001) assert, "The overall conclusion we must draw from this study is that juvenile boot camps are unlikely to be effective both in terms of costs and recidivism unless they incorporate a program to give a delinquent the skills, the motivation, and the resources to avoid the environment and lifestyle that contributed to the delinquency in the first place" (p. 456). We would add that what happens during the aftercare component—when the juvenile is back in the community and interacting with family, school, and peers—is crucial.

WILDERNESS AND ADVENTURE PROGRAMS

Wilderness and adventure programs are different from boot camps and seem to offer more hope as an effective strategy for some youth. A wide range of camps, ranches, and outdoor programs—mostly privately operated—are offered to juvenile offenders. Among the most well known are those supported by the Eckerd Foundation, a private organization based in Florida. Associated Marine Industries (AMI) is another such enterprise.

Wilderness and adventure programs accept both juveniles who are at risk of committing criminal acts and those who are already adjudicated delinquent; thus, they operate as both selective and tertiary prevention programs. In these programs, the at-risk juveniles are usually status offenders who are runaways or are otherwise considered incorrigible and difficult to manage by their parents or guardians. Often, substance abuse or acting-out sexual behaviors are part of the pattern. The offenses of the adjudicated delinquents range from drug offenses to violent crime. Some programs accept JSOs but many do not. Those that do are likely to offer specialized treatment for these offenders, but as noted earlier, research on the effectiveness of this treatment is not available. Wilderness camps are often considered the "last chance" for juveniles before being sent to a secure juvenile facility.

Descriptions of these programs suggest that, although they do not subscribe to a common model, they do have some things in common. For example, they de-emphasize traditional classroom education and emphasize the progressive development of physical skills, which are believed to improve self-efficacy. The programs also try to develop a positive peer culture, wherein youth support one another's prosocial behavior and confront one another when antisocial behavior is displayed. Wilderness camps are more likely than boot camps to include therapeutic components, such as drama therapy, development of communication and problem-solving skills, or individual counseling. However, it is unknown to what extent psychologists or trained clinicians provide treatment services.

Wilderness and adventure programs have received some favorable research support, but unfortunately, the studies are generally methodologically flawed and almost never use a control group for comparison purposes (Brown, Borduin, & Henggeler, 2001). Consequently, their overall effectiveness is largely unknown.

As a group, nontraditional residential programs may be philosophically appealing as alternatives to institutional treatment of juvenile offenders. Like many drug-treatment facilities, nontraditional residential programs are often privately operated and thus accept not only adjudicated delinquents on a contract basis but also youths who are voluntarily placed there by their parents or caretakers. Consequently, both youths with behavioral problems and youths adjudicated delinquent may be in these programs. Regardless of their offenses, however, all of these youths must eventually return to a community setting and to families, peers, and school or work obligations. If the intervention approach does not take these systems into consideration, significant successful treatment is unlikely.

Summary and Conclusions

Juveniles who are already deeply entrenched in delinquency or serious antisocial behaviors present major challenges to treatment providers. Tertiary prevention includes a wide variety of rehabilitative options that have been tried with these juveniles, many in residential settings. With some exceptions, the research evaluating these options does not demonstrate widespread effectiveness. Virtually all experts believe that early intervention programs are the best approach. Realistically, however, some children, preadolescents, and adolescents are not provided with or do not benefit sufficiently from early intervention and thus remain in need of treatment.

The first juvenile court was established in 1899, and by the end of the first quarter of the 20th century, juvenile courts had been established in nearly every state. These early courts were informal and rehabilitative in orientation but did not necessarily produce successful outcomes. In the 1960s and 1970s, both juvenile courts and the juvenile justice system as a whole changed dramatically. Juveniles were provided with legal rights, and there was a shift to finding community alternatives to training schools whenever possible. With the passage of the JJDPA, Congress funded a wide range of programs aimed at diverting youths from court and preventing delinquency.

Once juveniles are taken into custody, secure detention is warranted if they are believed to be a danger to themselves or others, but some courts also allow juveniles to be detained temporarily for their own protection from continuing criminal activity. Although secure detention is typically short-term, some juveniles are kept for longer periods, until their juvenile hearings. Once a juvenile has pleaded guilty or has been found by the judge to have committed the alleged crime, a disposition decision is made.

Probation, or conditional release, is the most common disposition given to juvenile offenders as a group, but about 1 in 4 juveniles receive out-of-home placement. Representatives of juvenile corrections, often in consultation with juvenile court officials, decide whether a youth will go to a group home, residential treatment center, or nontraditional residential program. Because the juvenile system is rehabilitative in orientation, judges, probation officers, social service workers, and even a child's own lawyers attempt to fashion an effective treatment package for the youth, either in the community or in residential settings. The juvenile justice system has a wide range of options for juveniles, including small private facilities, wilderness experiences, intensive supervision, training schools, boot camps, and specialized programs for violent juveniles, sex offenders, and substance abusers. The great majority of these programs have not been sufficiently evaluated with respect to their effectiveness at reducing recidivism or bringing about significant behavioral change.

In recent years, community treatment programs for serious offenders have received increasing attention, particularly because the shortcomings of traditional residential programs have been apparent. Multisystemic therapy (MST) provides intensive, short-term treatment to serious juvenile offenders and their families, with impressive results. Other family-based treatment approaches, particularly those that are ecologically oriented, are also promising. Nontraditional residential programs, such as boot camps and wilderness camps, are popular approaches but have little research support. Boot camps in particular have been highly criticized by scholars and researchers who emphasize, among other deficiencies, their ineffective militaristic orientation and their lack of attention to educational programming. Abuses of power in boot camps have also come to public attention, resulting in their closure in some states.

Although there is no lack of attention in the literature about what does not work for juveniles as a group, there is far less information available regarding what does work for specific categories of juveniles. Fortunately, this is beginning to change, with increasingly more studies becoming available on the treatment of sex offenders, substance abusers, violent juveniles, and juveniles who are mentally disordered. Treatment of serious juvenile offenders, although extremely challenging, is nonetheless possible, even in institutional settings. It is highly likely, however, that the chances for success are greater if juveniles can be kept in community settings that are tied to their social support systems.

Key Terms and Concepts

actuarial predictions
boot camps
clinical predictions
decriminalization
deinstitutionalization
detention
diversion
due process
Juvenile Court Act

juvenile drug court
Juvenile Justice and Delinquency
  Prevention Act
multisystemic therapy (MST)
risk assessment
secure confinement
secure detention
wilderness and adventure programs

REFERENCES

Abadinsky, H. (1993). *Drug abuse* (2nd ed.). Chicago: Nelson-Hall.

Ackerman, B. P., Brown, E., & Izard, C. E. (2003). Continuity and change in levels of externalizing behavior in school children from economically disadvantaged families. *Child Development, 74,* 694–709.

Adler, J. (2002, February 25). The "thrill" of theft: It's not just movie stars. *Newsweek,* p. 52.

Adler, R., Nunn, R., Northam, E., Lebnan, V., & Ross, R. (1994). Secondary prevention of childhood fire-setting. *Journal of the American Academy of Child and Adolescent Psychiatry, 33,* 1194–1202.

Agnew, R. (1992). Foundation for a general strain theory of crime and delinquency. *Criminology, 30,* 47–88.

Agnew, R. (1999). A general strain theory of community differences in crime rates. *Journal of Research in Crime & Delinquency, 36,* 123–155.

Agnew, R. (2001). Building on the foundation of general strain theory: Specifying the type of strain most likely to lead to crime and delinquency. *Journal of Research in Crime & Delinquency, 38,* 319–361.

Agnew, R. (2003). An integrated theory of the adolescent peak in offending. *Youth & Society, 34,* 263–299.

Akers, R. L. (1977). *Deviant behavior: A social learning approach* (2nd ed.). Belmont, CA: Wadsworth.

Akers, R. L. (1985). *Deviant behavior: A social learning approach* (3rd ed.). Belmont, CA: Wadsworth.

Akers, R. L. (1997). *Criminological theories: Introduction and evaluation* (2nd ed.). Los Angeles: Roxbury.

Akers, R. L., & Cochran, J. K. (1985). Adolescent marijuana use: A test of three theories of deviant behavior. *Deviant Behavior, 6,* 323–346.

Akers, R. L., & Lee, G. (1996). A longitudinal test of social learning theory: Adolescent smoking. *Journal of Drug Issues, 26,* 317–343.

Aldwin, C. M. (1994). *Stress, coping, and development: An integrative perspective.* New York: Guilford.

Alexander, K. L., & Entwisle, D. R. (1988). Achievement in the first 2 years of school: Patterns and processes. *Monographs of the Society for Research in Child Development, 53* (3, Serial No. 218).

Alexander, M. A. (1999). Sexual offender treatment efficacy revisited. *Sexual Abuse: A Journal of Research and Treatment, 11,* 101–116.

Allport, G. (1961). *Pattern and growth in personality.* New York: Holt, Rinehart & Winston.

Alterman, A. I., Rutherford, M. J., Cacciola, J. S., McKay, J. R., & Boardman, C. R. (1998). Prediction of 7 months methadone maintenance treatment responses by four measures of antisociality. *Drug and Alcohol Dependence, 49,* 217–223.

Alvord, M. K., & Grados, J. J. (2005). Enhancing resilience in children: A protective approach. *Professional Psychology: Research and Practice, 36,* 238–245.

American Psychiatric Association. (1994). *Diagnostic and statistical manual of mental disorders* (4th ed.). Washington, DC: Author.

American Psychological Association. (1996). Basic behavioral science research for mental health: Vulnerability and resilience. *American Psychologist, 51,* 22–28.

American University. (2001). *Drug court activity update: Summary.* Washington, DC: U.S. Department of Justice, Office of Justice Programs.

Andershed, H., Kerr, M., Stattin, H., Levander, S. (2002). Psychopathic traits in non-referred youths: A new assessment tool. In E. Blauuw & L. Sheridan (Eds.), *Psychopaths: Current international perspectives.* The Hague, Netherlands: Elsevier.

Andrews, J. A., Hops, H., & Duncan, S. C. (1997). Adolescent modeling of parent substance abuse: The moderating effect of the relationship with parent. *Journal of Family Psychology, 11,* 259–270.

Arata, C. M., Stafford, J., & Tims, M. S. (2003). High school drinking and its consequences. *Adolescence, 38,* 567–579.

Arkow, P. (1998). The correlations between cruelty to animals and child abuse and the implications for veterinary medicine. In R. Lockwood & F. R. Ascione (Eds.), *Cruelty to animals and interpersonal violence: Readings in research and application.* West Lafayette, IN: Purdue University Press.

Arluke, A., Levin, J., Luke, C., & Ascione, F. (1999). The relationship of animal abuse to violence and other forms of antisocial behavior. *Journal of Interpersonal Violence, 14,* 963–975.

Armstrong, T. D., & Costello, E. J. (2002). Community studies of adolescent substance use, abuse, or dependence and psychiatric comorbidity. *Journal of Consulting and Clinical Psychology, 70*, 1224–1239.

Arseneault, L., Tremblay, R. E., Boulerice, B., & Saucier, J-F. (2002). Obstetrical complications and violent delinquency: Testing two developmental pathways. *Child Development, 73*, 496–508.

Arseneault, L., Tremblay, R. E., Boulerice, B., Séguin, J. R., & Saucier, J-F. (2000). Minor physical anomalies and family adversity as risk factors for violent delinquency in adolescence. *American Journal of Psychiatry, 157*, 917–923.

Ascione, F. R., Thompson, T. M., & Black, T. (1997). Childhood cruelty to animals: Assessing cruelty dimensions and motivations. *Anthrozoos, 10*, 170–177.

Asquith, J. L., & Bristow, D. N. (2000). To catch a thief: A pedagogical study of retail shoplifting. *Journal of Education for Business, 75*, 271–277.

Astwood Strategy Corporation. (2003, December). *Results of the 2002 Canadian police survey on youth gangs.* Toronto: Author.

Austin, J., Johnson, K. D., & Weitzer, R. (2005, September). *Alternatives to the secure detention and confinement of juvenile offenders.* Washington, DC: U.S. Department of Justice, Office of Juvenile Justice and Delinquency Prevention.

Bagwell, C. L. (2004). Friendships, peer networks, and antisocial behavior. In J. B. Kupersmidt & K. A. Dodge (Eds.), *Children's peer relations: From development to intervention.* Washington, DC: American Psychological Association.

Bagwell, C. L., & Coie, J. D. (1999, April). *The friendship relations of antisocial boys.* Paper presented at the biennial meeting of the Society for Research on Child Development, Albuquerque, NM.

Ball, J. C., Shaffer, J. W., & Nurco, D. N. (1983). The day-to-day criminality of heroin addicts in Baltimore—A study in the continuity of offense rates. *Drug and Alcohol Dependence, 12*, 119–142.

Bandstra, E. S., Morrow, C. E., Vogel, A. L., Fifer, R. C., Ofir, A. Y., Dausa, A. T., et al. (2002). Longitudinal influence of prenatal cocaine exposure on child language functioning. *Neurotoxicology and Teratology, 24*, 297–308.

Bandstra, E. S., Vogel, A. I., Morrow, C. E., Xue, L., & Anthony, J. C. (2004). Severity of prenatal cocaine exposure and child language functioning through age 7: A longitudinal latent growth curve analysis. *Substance Use and Misuse, 39*, 25–29.

Bandura, A. (1965). Influence of models' reinforcement contingencies on the acquisition of imitative responses. *Journal of Personality and Social Psychology, 1*, 589–595.

Bandura, A. (1977). *Social learning theory* (2nd ed.). Englewood Cliffs, NJ: Prentice Hall.

Bandura, A. (1989). Human agency in social cognitive theory. *American Psychologist, 44*, 1175–1184.

Bandura, A. (1997). *Self-efficacy: The exercise of control.* New York: Freeman.

Bandura, A., & Walters, R. H. (1963). *Social learning and personality development.* New York: Holt, Rinehart.

Bank, L., & Patterson, G. R. (1992). The use of structural equation modeling in combining data from different types of assessment. In J. C. Rosen & P. McReynolds (Eds.), *Advances in psychological assessment* (Vol. 8). New York: Plenum.

Barbarin, O. A. (1993). Coping and resilience: Exploring the inner lives of African American children. *Journal of Black Psychology, 19*, 478–492.

Barkley, R. A. (1999). Theories of attention-deficit/hyperactivity disorder. In H. C. Quay & A. E. Hogan (Eds.), *Handbook of disruptive behavior disorders.* New York: Academic/Plenum.

Baron, R. A. (1977). *Human aggression.* New York: Plenum.

Baron, S. W., & Hartnagel, T. F. (1998). Street youth and criminal violence. *Journal of Research in Crime & Delinquency, 35*, 166–192.

Barry, C. T., Frick, P. J., DeShazo, T. M., McCoy, M. G., Ellis, M., & Loney, B. R. (2000). The importance of callous-unemotional traits for extending the concept of psychopathy to children. *Journal of Abnormal Psychology, 109*, 335–340.

Bartol, C. R., & Bartol, A. M. (2004). *Introduction to forensic psychology.* Thousand Oaks, CA: Sage.

Bartol, C. R., & Bartol, A. M. (2005). *Criminal behavior: A psychosocial approach* (7th ed.). Upper Saddle River, NJ: Prentice Hall.

Bates, J. E. (1980). The concept of difficult temperament. *Merrill-Palmer Quarterly, 26*, 299–319.

Bates, J. E. (2000). Temperament as an emotion construct: Theoretical and practical issues. In M. Lewis & J. M. Haviland-Jones (Eds.), *Handbook of emotions* (2nd ed.). New York: Guilford.

Bates, J. E., Marvinney, D., Kelly, T., Dodge, K. A., Bennett, D. S., & Pettit, G. (1994). *Developmental Psychology, 30*, 690–700.

Bates, J. E., Pettit, G. S., Dodge, K. A., & Ridge, B. (1998). Interaction of temperamental resistance to control and restrictive parenting in the development of externalizing behavior. *Developmental Psychology, 34*, 982–995.

Baum, K. (2005, August). *Juvenile victimization and offending, 1993–2003.* U.S. Department of Justice, Bureau of Justice Statistics.

Baumeister, R. F., DeWall, C. N., Ciarocco, N. J., & Twenge, J. M. (2005). Social exclusion impairs self-regulation. *Journal of Personality and Social Psychology, 88,* 589–604.

Baumrind, D. (1967). Authoritarian vs. authoritative parental control. *Adolescence, 3,* 255–272.

Baumrind, D. (1971). Current patterns of parental authority. *Developmental Psychology Monograph, 4,* 1–103.

Baumrind, D. (1991). Parenting styles and adolescent development. In J. Brooks-Gunn, R. Lerner, & A. C. Petersen (Eds.), *The encyclopedia of adolescence.* New York: Garland.

Becker, H. S. (1963). *Outsiders: Studies in the sociology of deviance.* New York: Free Press.

Becker, J. V. (1990). Treating adolescent sexual offenders. *Professional Psychology: Research and Practice, 21,* 362–365.

Becker, J. V., Hall, S. R., & Stinson, J. D. (2001). Female sexual offenders: Clinical, legal and policy issues. *Journal of Forensic Psychology Practice, 1,* 29–50.

Becker, J. V., & Johnson, B. R. (2001). Treating juvenile sex offenders. In J. B. Ashford, B. D. Sales, & W. H. Reid (Eds.), *Treating adult and juvenile offenders with special needs.* Washington, DC: American Psychological Association.

Becker, K. D., Stuewig, J., Herrera, V. M., & McCloskey, L. A. (2004). A study of firesetting and animal cruelty in children: Family influences and adolescent outcomes. *Journal of the American Academy of Child and Adolescent Psychiatry, 43,* 905–913.

Belenko, S., & Dumanovsky, T. (1993). *Special drug courts: Program brief.* Washington, DC: U.S. Department of Justice, Bureau of Justice Assistance.

Belenko, S., & Logan, T. K. (2003). Delivering more effective treatment to adolescents: Improving the juvenile court model. *Journal of Substance Abuse Treatment, 25,* 189–211.

Belsky, J. (1999). Interactional and contextual determinants of attachment security. In J. Cassidy & P. R. Shaver (Eds.), *Handbook of attachment: Theory, research, and clinical applications.* New York: Guilford.

Belsky, J., Lerner, R. M., & Spanier, G. B. (1984). *The child in the family.* New York: Random House.

Belsky, J., Woodworth, S., & Crnic, K. (1996). Trouble in the second year: Three questions about family interaction. *Child Development, 67,* 556–578.

Bendixen, M., Endresen, I. M., & Olweus, D. (2006). Joining and leaving gangs: Selection and facilitation effects on self-reported antisocial behaviour in early adolescence. *European Journal of Criminology, 3,* 85–114.

Benedek, E., & Cornell, D. (Eds.) (1989). *Juvenile homicide.* Washington, DC: American Psychiatric Press.

Bennett, D. S., Bendersky, M., & Lewis, M. (2002). Children's intellectual and emotional-behavioral adjustment at 4 years as a function of cocaine exposure, maternal characteristics, and environmental risk. *Developmental Psychology, 38,* 648–658.

Berkowitz, L. (1994). Guns and youth. In L. E. Eron, J. H. Gentry, & P. Schlegel (Eds.), *Reason to hope: A psychosocial perspective on violence and youth.* Washington, DC: American Psychological Association.

Bernard, T. J. (1992). *The cycle of juvenile justice.* New York: Oxford University Press.

Berrueta-Clement, J. R., Schweinhart, L. J., Barnett, W. S., & Weikart, D. P. (1987). The effects of early educational intervention in adolescence and early adulthood. In J. D. Burchard & S. N. Burchard (Eds.), *Prevention of delinquent behavior.* Newbury Park, CA: Sage.

Bierman, K. L., Smoot, D. L., & Aumiller, K. (1993). Characteristics of aggressive-rejected, aggressive (nonrejected), and rejected (nonaggressive) boys. *Child Development, 64,* 139–151.

Bierman, K. L., & Wargo, J. B. (1995). Predicting the longitudinal course associated with aggressive-rejected, aggressive (nonrejected), and rejected (nonaggressive) status. *Developmental and Psychopathology, 7,* 669–682.

Bijou, S. W., & Baer, D. M. (1961). *Child development.* New York: Appleton-Century-Crofts.

Blair, R. J. R. (1995). A cognitive developmental approach to morality: Integrating the psychopath. *Cognition, 57,* 1–29.

Blair, R. J. R. (1997). Moral reasoning in the child with psychopathic tendencies. *Personality and Individual Differences, 22,* 731–739.

Blair, R. J. R. (1999). Responsiveness to distress cues in the child with psychopathic tendencies. *Personality and Individual Differences, 27,* 135–145.

Blair, R. J. R. (2001). Neuro-cognitive models of aggression, the antisocial personality disorders and psychopathy. *Journal of Neurology, Neurosurgery & Psychiatry, 71,* 727–731.

Blair, R. J. R., & Coles, M. (2000). Expression recognition and behavioural problems in early adolescence. *Cognitive Development, 15,* 421–434.

Blair, R. J. R., Colledge, E., Murray, L., & Mitchell, D. G. V. (2001). A selective impairment in the processing of sad and fearful expressions in children with psychopathic tendencies. *Journal of Abnormal Child Psychology, 29,* 491–498.

Blair, R. J. R., & Firth, U. (2000). Neurocognitive explanations of the antisocial personality disorders. *Criminal Behaviour and Mental Health, 10,* S66–S82.

Blair, R. J. R., Mitchell, D. G. V., Perschardt, K. S., Colledge, E., Leonard, R. A., Shine, J. H., Murray, L. K., & Perrett, D. I. (2004). Reduced sensitivity to others' fearful expressions in psychopathic individuals. *Personality and Individual Differences, 37*, 111–122.

Blechman, E. A. (1982). Are children with one parent at psychological risk? A methodological review. *Journal of Marriage and the Family, 44*, 179–195.

Blitstein, J. L., Murray, D. M., Lytle, L. A., Birnbaum, A. S., & Perry, C. L. (2005). Predictors of violent behavior in an early adolescent cohort: Similarities and differences across genders. *Health Education and Behavior, 32*, 175–194.

Block, C. R., Christakos, A., Jacob, A., & Prszbylski, R. (1996). *Street gangs and crime: Patterns and trends in Chicago* (Research bulletin). Chicago: Illinois Justice Information Authority.

Block, R., & Block, C. R. (1993). *Street gang crime in Chicago.* Washington, DC: U.S. Department of Justice, National Institute of Justice.

Bonanno, G. A. (2004). Loss, trauma, and human resilience: Have we underestimated the human capacity to thrive after extremely aversive events? *American Psychologist, 59*, 20–28.

Bongers, I. L., Koot, H. M., van der Ende, J., & Verhulst, F. C. (2003). The normative development of child and adolescent problem behavior. *Journal of Abnormal Psychology, 112*, 179–192.

Bongers, I. L., Koot, H. M., van der Ende, J., & Verhulst, F. C. (2004). Developmental trajectories of externalizing behaviors in childhood and adolescence. *Child Development, 75*, 1523–1537.

Bono, K., Sheinberg, N., Scott, K., & Claussen, A. (2007). Early intervention for children prenatally exposed to cocaine. *Infants & Young Children, 20*, 26–37.

Booth, R. E., & Zhang, Y. (1997). Conduct disorder and HIV risk behaviors among runaway and homeless adolescents. *Drug and Alcohol Dependency, 48*, 69–76.

Borduin, C. M. (1994). Innovative models of treatment and service delivery in the juvenile justice system. *Journal of Clinical Child Psychology, 23*, 19–25.

Borduin, C. M., Mann, B. J., Cone, L. T., Henggeler, S. W., Fucci, B. R., Blaske, D. M., et al. (1995). Multisystemic treatment of serious juvenile offenders: Long-term prevention of criminality and violence. *Journal of Consulting and Clinical Psychology, 63*, 569–578.

Born, M., Chevalier, V., & Humblet, I. (1997). Resilience, desistance and delinquent career of adolescent offenders. *Journal of Adolescence, 20*, 679–694.

Boss, P., Edwards, S., & Pitman, S. (1995). *Profile of young Australians: Facts, figures, and issues.* South Melbourne, Australia: Churchill Livingstone.

Bottcher, J., & Ezell, M. E. (2005). Examining the effectiveness of boot camps: A randomized experiment with a long-term follow up. *Journal of Research in Crime & Delinquency, 42*, 309–332.

Bourque, B. B., Cronin, R. C., Felker, D. B., Pearson, F. R., Han, M., & Hill, S. M. (1996). *Boot camps for juvenile offenders: An implementation evaluation of three demonstration programs* (Research in Brief). Washington, DC: National Institute of Justice.

Boyle, M. H., & Offord, D. R. (1991). Psychiatric disorders and substance use in adolescence. *Canadian Journal of Psychiatry, 36*, 699–705.

Braga, A. A., & Kennedy, D. M. (2001). The illicit acquisition of firearms by youth and juveniles. *Journal of Criminal Justice, 29*, 379–388.

Braithwaite, J. (1997). Charles Tittle's control balance and criminological theory. *Theoretical Criminology, 1*, 77–97.

Brame, B., Nagin, D. S., & Tremblay, R. E. (2001). Developmental trajectories of physical aggression from school entry to late adolescence. *Journal of Child Psychology and Psychiatry, 42*, 503–512.

Brandt, J. R., Kennedy, W. A., Patrick, C. J., & Curtain, J. J. (1997). Assessment of psychopathy in a population of incarcerated adolescent offenders. *Psychological Assessment, 9*, 429–435.

Brendgen, M., Vitaro, F., Bukowski, W. M., Doyle, A. B., & Markiewicz, D. (2001). Developmental profiles of peer social preference over the course of elementary school: Associations with trajectories of externalizing and internalizing behavior. *Developmental Psychology, 37*, 308–320.

Brennan, P. A., Grekin, E. R., & Mednick, S. A. (1999). Maternal smoking during pregnancy and adult male criminal outcomes. *Archives of General Psychiatry, 56*, 215–219.

Brennan, P. A., Hall, J., Bor, W., Najman, J. M., & Williams, G. (2003). Integrating biological and social processes in relation to early-onset persistent aggression in boys and girls. *Developmental Psychology, 39*, 309–323.

Brennan, P. A., Hamman, C., Andersen, M. J., Bor, W., Najman, J. M., & Williams, G. M. (2000). Chronicity, severity, and timing of maternal depressive symptoms: Relationships with child outcomes at age 5. *Developmental Psychology, 36*, 759–766.

Brennan, P. A., Mednick, S. A., & Kandel, E. (1993). Congenital determinants of violent and property offending. In D. J. Pepler & K. H. Rubins (Eds.),

The development and treatment of childhood aggression. Hillsdale, NJ: Erlbaum.

Brennan, P. A., Mednick, S. A., & Raine, A. (1997). Biosocial interactions and violence: A focus on perinatal factors. In R. A. Raine, P. A. Brennan, D. Farrington, & S. A. Mednick (Eds.), *Biosocial bases of violence.* New York: Plenum.

Brezina, T., Piquero, A. R., & Mazerolle, P. (2001). Student anger and aggressive behavior in school: An initial test of Agnew's macro-level strain theory. *Journal of Research in Crime & Delinquency, 38,* 362–386.

Brody, D. J., Pirkle, J., Kramer, R., Flegal, K., Matte, T. D., Gunter, E., & Pascal, D. (1994). Blood levels in the U.S. population: Phase I of the Third National Health and Nutrition Examination Survey. *Journal of the American Medical Association, 272,* 277–283.

Broidy, L. M., & Agnew, R. (1997). Gender and crime: A general strain theory perspective. *Journal of Research in Crime & Delinquency, 34,* 275–306.

Broidy, L. M., Nagin, D. S., Tremblay, R. E., Bates, J. E., Brame, B., Dodge, K. A., et al. (2003). Developmental trajectories of childhood disruptive behaviors and adolescent delinquency: A six-site cross-national study. *Developmental Psychology, 39,* 222–245.

Bronfenbrenner, U. (1979). *The ecology of human development.* Cambridge, MA: Harvard University Press.

Bronfenbrenner, U. (1986a). Ecology of the family as a context for human development: Research perspectives. *Developmental Psychology, 22,* 723–742.

Bronfenbrenner, U. (1986b). Recent advances in research on the ecology of human development. In R. K. Silbereisen, K. Eyferth, & G. Rudinger (Eds.), *Development as action in context.* Berlin: Springer-Verlag.

Brook, J. S., Cohen, P., & Brook, D. W. (1998). Longitudinal study of co-occurring psychiatric disorders and substance use. *Journal of the American Academy of Child and Adolescent Psychiatry, 37,* 322–330.

Brown, T. L., Borduin, C. M., & Henggeler, S. W. (2001). Treating juvenile offenders in community settings. In J. B. Ashford, B. D. Sales, & W. H. Reid (Eds.), *Treating adult and juvenile offenders with special needs.* Washington, DC: American Psychological Association.

Browning, K., & Huizinga, D. (1999, April). Highlights of findings from the Denver Youth Survey. *OJJDP Fact Sheet.* Washington, DC: U.S. Department of Justice, Office of Juvenile Justice and Delinquency Prevention.

Browning, K., & Loeber, R. (1999, February). Highlights of findings from the Pittsburgh Youth Study. *OJJDP Fact Sheet.* Washington, DC: U.S. Department of Justice, Office of Juvenile Justice and Delinquency Prevention.

Browning, K., Thornberry, T., & Porter, P. K. (1999, April). Highlights of findings from the Rochester Youth Development Study. *OJJDP Fact Sheet.* Washington, DC: U.S. Department of Justice, Office of Juvenile Justice and Delinquency Prevention.

Brownlie, E. B., Beitchman, J. J., Escobar, M., Young, A., Atkinson, L., Johnson, C., Wilson, B., & Douglas, L. (2004). Early language impairment and young adult delinquent and aggressive behavior. *Journal of Abnormal Child Psychology, 32,* 453–467.

Brunet, B. L., Reiffenstein, R. J., Williams, T., & Wong, L. (1985–1986). Toxicity of phencyclidine and ethanol in combination. *Alcohol and Drug Research, 6,* 341–349.

Buckner, J. C., Mezzacappa, E., & Beardslee, W. R. (2003). Characteristics of resilient youths living in poverty: The role of self-regulatory processes. *Development and Psychopathology, 15,* 139–162.

Buh, E. S., & Ladd, G. W. (2001). Peer rejection as an antecedent of young children's school adjustment: An examination of mediating processes. *Developmental Psychology, 37,* 550–560.

Bullard, R. D., & Wright, B. (1993). Environmental justice for all: Current perspectives on health and research needs. *Toxicology and Industrial Health, 9,* 821–841.

Bumby, K. M., & Bumby, N. H. (1997). Adolescent female sexual offenders. In J. R. Cellini & B. Schwartz (Eds.), *The sex offender: New insights, treatment innovations and legal developments* (Vol. 2). Kingston, NJ: Civil Research Institute.

Bureau of Justice Statistics. (2005, November). *School violence rate stable: Lowest level in a decade.* Washington, DC: U.S. Department of Justice, Bureau of Statistics.

Burgess, E. W., & Akers, R. L. (1966). A differential association–reinforcement theory of criminal behavior. *Social Problems, 14,* 128–147.

Burns, B. J., Howell, J. C., Wiig, J. K., Augimeri, L. K., Welsh, B. C., Loeber, R., & Petechuk, D. (2003, March). *Treatment, services, and intervention programs for child delinquents.* Washington, DC: U.S. Department of Justice.

Burt, S. A., Krueger, R. F., McGue, M., & Iacono, W. G. (2001). Sources of covariation among attention-deficit/hyperactivity disorder, oppositional defiant disorder, and conduct disorder: The importance of shared environment. *Journal of Abnormal Psychology, 110*, 516–525.

Burton, V. S., Jr., Evans, T. D., Cullen, F. T., Olivares, K. M., & Dunaway, R. G. (1999). Age, self-control, and adults' offending behaviors: A research note assessing a general theory of crime. *Journal of Criminal Justice, 27*, 45–54.

Bussey, K. (1992). Lying and truthfulness: Children's definitions, standards, and evaluative reactions. *Child Development, 63*, 129–137.

Butts. J. A., & Buck, J. (2000, October). *Teen courts: A focus on research.* Washington, DC: U.S. Department of Justice, Office of Juvenile Justice and Delinquency Prevention.

Butts, J., Snyder, H., Finnegan, T., Aughenbaugh, A., Tierney, N., Sullivan, D., et al. (1995). *Juvenile court statistics, 1992.* Washington, DC: U.S. Department of Justice, OJJDP.

Cairns, R. B. (1983). The emergence of developmental psychology. In P. H. Mussen (Ed.), *Handbook of child psychology* (Vol. 1, 4th ed.). New York: Wiley.

Cairns, R., & Cairns, B. (1991). Social cognition and social networks: A developmental perspective. In D. Pepler & K. Rubin (Eds.), *The development and treatment of childhood aggression.* Hillsdale, NJ: Erlbaum.

Caldwell, M., Skeem, J., Salekin, R., & Van Rybroek, G. (2006). Treatment response of adolescent offenders with psychopathy features: A 2-year follow-up. *Criminal Justice and Behavior, 33*, 571–596.

Calkins, S. D., & Fox, N. A. (2002). Self-regulatory processes in early personality development: A multilevel approach to the study of childhood social withdrawal and aggression. *Development and Psychopathology, 14*, 477–498.

Campbell, A. (1984a). *The girls in the gang.* Oxford, England: Basil Blackwell.

Campbell, A. (1984b). Girls' talk: The social representation of aggression by female gang members. *Criminal Justice and Behavior, 11*, 139–156.

Campbell, M. A., Porter, S., & Santor, D. (2004). Psychopathic traits in adolescent offenders: An evaluation of criminal history, clinical, and psychosocial correlates. *Behavioral Sciences & the Law, 22*, 23–47.

Campbell, S. B. (1994). Hard-to-manage preschool boys: Externalizing behaviour, social competence, and family context at two-year follow-up. *Journal of Abnormal Child Psychology, 22*, 147–157.

Campbell, S. B. (1995). Behavior problems in preschool children: A review of recent research. *Journal of Child Psychology and Psychiatry, 36*, 113–149.

Campbell, S. B. (2000). Attention-deficit/hyperactivity disorder: A developmental view. In A. J. Sameroff,

M. Lewis, & S. M. Miller (Eds.), *Handbook of developmental psychopathology* (2nd ed.). New York: Kluwer Academic/Plenum.

Canadian Government's Commission of Inquiry. (1971). *The non-medical use of drugs: Interim report.* London: Penguin Books.

Capaldi, D. M., Dishion, T. J., Stoolmiller, M., & Yoerger, K. (2001). Aggression toward female partners by at-risk young men: The contribution of male adolescent friendships. *Developmental Psychology, 37*, 61–73.

Caputo, A. A., Frick, P. J., & Brodsky, S. L. (1999). Family violence and juvenile sex offenders: The potential mediating role of psychopathic traits and negative attitudes toward women. *Criminal Justice and Behavior, 26*, 338–356.

Carey, J. T. (1975). *Sociology and public affairs: The Chicago School.* Beverly Hills, CA: Sage.

Carnegie Council on Adolescent Development. (1995). *Great transitions: Preparing American youth for a new century.* New York: Carnegie Corporation of New York.

Carraher, T. N., Carraher, D., & Schliemann, A. D. (1985). Mathematics in the streets and schools. *British Journal of Developmental Psychology, 3*, 21–29.

Caspi, A. (2000). The child is father of the man: Personality continuities from childhood to adulthood. *Journal of Personality and Social Psychology, 78*, 158–172.

Caspi, A., & Silva, P. A. (1995). Temperament qualities at age three predict personality traits in young adulthood: Longitudinal evidence from birth cohort. *Child Development, 66*, 486–498.

Caspi, A., Wright, B. R. E., Moffitt, T. E., & Silva, P. A. (1998). Early failure in the labor market: Childhood and adolescent predictors of unemployment in the transition to adulthood. *American Sociological Review, 63*, 424–451.

Catalano, S. M. (2005, September). *Criminal victimization, 2004.* U.S. Department of Justice, Bureau of Justice Statistics.

Ceci, S. J., Leichtman, M. D., & Putnick, M. E. (1992). *Cognitive and social factors in early deception.* Hillsdale, NJ: Erlbaum.

Cellini, H. R. (1995). Assessment and treatment of the adolescent sexual offender. In B. Schwartz & H. R. Cellini (Eds.), *The sex offender: Corrections, treatment and legal practice* (Vol. 1). Kingston, NJ: Civil Research Institute.

Cellini, H. R., Schwartz, H., & Readio, S. (1993, December). *Child sexual abuse: An administrator's nightmare.* Washington, DC: National School Safety Center.

Chamberlain, P. (1996). Treatment foster care for adolescents with conduct disorders and delinquency.

In P. S. Jensen & D. Hibbs (Eds.), *Psychological treatment research with children and adolescents.* Rockville, MD: National Institute of Mental Health.

Chang L., Schwartz, D., Dodge, K. A., & McBride-Chang, C. (2003). Harsh parenting in relation to child emotion regulation and aggression. *Journal of Family Psychology, 17,* 598–606.

Chen, J. D., & George, R. A. (2005). Cultivating resilience in children from divorced families. *The Family Journal: Counseling and Therapy for Couples and Families, 13,* 452–455.

Chen, Y.-H., Arria, A., & Anthony, J. C. (2003). Firesetting in adolescents and being aggressive, shy, and rejected by peers: New epidemiological evidence from a national sample survey. *Journal of the American Academy of Psychiatry and Law, 31,* 44–52.

Chesney-Lind, M., & Paramore, V. V. (2001). Are girls getting more violent? Exploring juvenile robbery trends. *Journal of Contemporary Criminal Justice, 17,* 142–166.

Chesney-Lind, M., & Shelden, R. (1998). *Girls, delinquency, and juvenile justice* (2nd ed). Belmont, CA: West/Wadsworth.

Chesney-Lind, M., & Shelden, R. G. (2004). *Girls, delinquency, and juvenile justice* (3rd ed.). Belmont, CA: Thomson/Wadsworth.

Chilcoat, H. D., Dishion, T. J., & Anthony, J. C. (1995). Parent monitoring and the incidence of drug sampling in urban elementary school children. *American Journal of Epidemiology, 14,* 25–31.

Chung, I-J, Hill, K. G., Hawkins, J. D., Gilchrist, L. D., & Nagin, D. S. (2002). Childhood predictors of offense trajectories. *Journal of Research in Crime & Delinquency, 39,* 60–90.

Cicchetti, D. (1987). Developmental psychopathology in infancy: Illustration from the study of maltreated youngsters. *Journal of Consulting and Clinical Psychology, 55,* 837–845.

Cicchetti, D., & Rogosch, F. A. (1997). The role of self-organization in the promotion of resilience in maltreated children. *Development and Psychopathology, 9,* 797–815.

Cicchetti, D., & Rogosch, F. A. (2002). A developmental psychopathology perspective on adolescence. *Journal of Clinical and Consulting Psychology, 70,* 6–20.

Cicero, T. J., Inciardi, J. A., & Muñoz, A. (2005). Trends in abuse of OxyContin® and other opioid analgesics in the United States: 2002–2004. *The Journal of Pain, 6,* 662–672.

Cillessen, A. H. N., & Mayeux, L. (2004). Sociometric status and peer group behavior: Previous findings and current directions. In J. B. Kupersmidt & K. A. Dodge (Eds.), *Children's peer relations:* *From development to intervention.* Washington, DC: American Psychological Association.

Cillessen, A. H. N., van IJzendoorn, H. W., Van Lieshout, C. F. M., & Hartup, W. W. (1992). Heterogeneity among peer-rejected boys: Subtypes and stabilities. *Child Development, 63,* 893–905.

Clark, C., Prior, M., Kinsella, G. (2000). Do executive function deficits differentiate between adolescents with ADHD and oppositional defiant disorder/conduct disorder? A neuropsychological study using the Six Elements Test and Hayling Sentence Completion Test. *Journal of Abnormal Child Psychology, 28,* 403–414.

Clark, C., Prior, M., Kinsella, G. (2002). The relationship between executive function abilities, adaptive behaviour, and academic achievement in children with externalizing behaviour problems. *Journal of Child Psychology and Psychiatry, 43,* 785–796.

Cleckley, H. (1941). *The mask of sanity.* St. Louis, MO: C. V. Mosby.

Cleckley, H. (1976). *The mask of sanity* (5th ed.). St. Louis, MO: C. V. Mosby.

Clements, C. B., Althouse, R., Ax, R. K., Magaletta, P. R., Fagan, T. J., & Wormith, J. S. (2007). Systemic issues and correctional outcomes: Expanding the scope of correctional psychology. *Criminal Justice and Behavior, 34,* 919–932.

Cloward, R. A., & Ohlin, L. E. (1960). *Delinquency and opportunity: A theory of delinquent gangs.* Glencoe, IL: Free Press.

Cohen, A. K. (1955). *Delinquent boys: The culture of the gang.* Glencoe, IL: Free Press.

Cohen, D., & Strayer, J. (1996). Empathy in conduct-disordered and comparison youth. *Developmental Psychology, 32,* 988–998.

Cohen, N. J., Menna, R., Vallance, D. D., Barwick, M., Im, N., & Horodezky, N. B. (1998). Language, social cognitive processing, and behavioral characteristics of psychiatrically disturbed children with previously identified and suspected language impairments. *Journal of Child Psychology and Psychiatry, 39,* 853–864.

Cohn, V. (1986). Crack use. *NIDA Notes, 1,* 6.

Coie, J. D. (1990). Toward a theory of peer rejection. In S. R. Asher & J. D. Coie (Eds.), *Peer rejection in childhood.* New York: Cambridge University Press.

Coie, J. D. (2004). The impact of negative social experience on the development of antisocial behavior. In J. B. Kupersmidt & K. A. Dodge (Eds.), *Children's peer relations: From development to intervention.* Washington, DC: American Psychological Association.

Coie, J. D., Belding, M., & Underwood, M. (1988). Aggression and peer rejection in childhood.

In B. Lahey & A. Kazdin (Eds.), *Advances in clinical child psychology* (Vol. 2). New York: Plenum.

Coie, J. D., Dodge, K., & Kupersmith, J. (1990). Peer group behavior and social status. In S. R. Asher & J. D. Coie (Eds.), *Peer rejection in childhood.* Cambridge, England: Cambridge University Press.

Coie, J. D., & Miller-Johnson, S. (2001). Peer factors and interventions. In R. Loeber & D. P. Farrington (Eds.), *Child delinquents: Development, intervention, and service needs.* Thousand Oaks, CA: Sage.

Coie, J. D., Underwood, M., & Lochman, J. E. (1991). Programmatic intervention with aggressive children in the school setting. In D. J. Pepler & K. H. Rubin (Eds.), *The development and treatment of childhood aggression.* Hillsdale, NJ: Erlbaum.

Coie, J. D., Watt, N. F., West, S. G., Hawkins, D., Asarmpw, J. R., Markman, H. J., Ramey, S. L., Shure, M. B., & Long, B. (1993). The science of prevention: A conceptual framework and some directions for a national research program. *American Psychologist, 48,* 1013–1022.

Coley, R. J. (2002). *An uneven start: Indicators of inequality in school readiness.* Princeton, NJ: Educational Testing Service.

Colwell, M. J., Pettit, G. S., Meece, D., Bates, J. E., & Dodge, K. A. (2001). Cumulative risk and continuity in nonparental care from infancy to early adolescence. *Merrill-Palmer Quarterly, 47,* 207–234.

Committee on Preventive Psychiatry. (1999). Violent behavior in children and youth: Preventive intervention from a psychiatric perspective. *Journal of the American Academy of Child & Adolescent Psychiatry, 38,* 235–241.

Conduct Problems Prevention Research Group. (1999). Initial impact of the Fast Track prevention trial for conduct problems: I. The high-risk sample. *Journal of Consulting and Clinical Psychology, 67,* 631–647.

Conduct Problems Prevention Research Group. (2004). The fast track experiment: Translating the developmental model into a prevention design. In J. B. Kupersmidt & K. A. Dodge (Eds.), *Children's peer relations: From development to intervention.* Washington, DC: American Psychological Association.

Constantine, N., Benard, B., & Diaz, M. (1999). *Measuring protective factors and resilient traits in youth: The Healthy Kids Resilience Assessment.* Paper presented at the seventh annual meeting of the Society of Prevention Research, New Orleans, LA.

Conway, A. M. (2005). Girls, aggression, and emotion regulation. *American Journal of Orthopsychiatry, 75,* 334–339.

Cooke, D. J., & Michie, C. (2001). Refining the construct of psychopathy: Towards a hierarchical model. *Psychological Assessment, 13,* 171–188.

Cooke, D. J., Michie, C., Hart, S. D., & Clark, D. A. (2004). Reconstructing psychopathy: Clarifying the significance of antisocial and socially deviant behavior in the diagnosis of psychopathic personality disorder. *Journal of Personality Disorders, 18,* 337–357.

Coordinating Council on Juvenile Justice and Delinquency Prevention. (1996). *Combating violence and delinquency: The national juvenile justice action plan.* Washington, DC: U.S. Government Printing Office.

Copeland, J., & Dillon, P. (2005). The health and psychosocial consequences of ketamine use. *International Journal of Drug Policy, 16,* 122–131.

Corrado, R. R., Vincent, G. M., Hart, S. D., & Cohen, I. M. (2004). Predictive validity of the Psychopathy Checklist: Youth Version for general and violent recidivism. *Behavioral Sciences & the Law, 22,* 5–22.

Cortes, J. B., & Gatti, F. M. (1972). *Delinquency and crime: A biopsychological approach.* New York: Seminar Press.

Costa, P. T., & Widiger, T. A. (2002). Introduction: Personality disorders and the five-factor model of personality. In P. T. Costa & T. A. Widiger (Eds.), *Personality disorders and the five factor model* (2nd ed.). Washington, DC: American Psychological Association.

Costello, J. C. (2003). "Wayward and noncompliant" people with mental disability: What advocates of involuntary outpatient commitment can learn from the juvenile court experience with status offense jurisdiction. *Psychology, Public Policy, and Law, 9,* 233–257.

Côté, S. M., Vaillancourt, T., Barker, E. D., Nagin, D., & Tremblay, R. E. (2007). The joint development of physical and indirect aggression: Predictors of continuity and change during childhood. *Development and Psychopathology, 9,* 37–55.

Côté, S., Zoccolillo, M., Tremblay, R. E., Nagin, D., & Vitaro, F. (2001). Predicting girls' conduct disorder in adolescence from childhood trajectories of disruptive behaviors. *Journal of the American Academy of Child and Adolescent Psychiatry, 40,* 678–684.

Cowan, P. A., & Cowan, C. P. (2004). From family relationships to peer rejection to antisocial behavior in middle childhood. In J. B. Kupersmidt & K. A. Dodge (Eds.), *Children's peer relations: From development to intervention.* Washington, DC: American Psychological Association.

Cowen, E. L., Wyman, P. A., Work, W. C., & Parker, G. R. (1990). The Rochester Child Resilience Project: Overview and summary of first year findings. *Development and Psychopathology, 2,* 193–212.

Cox, A. D., Cox, D., Anderson, R. D., & Moschis, G. P. (1993). Social influences on adolescent shoplifting—Theory, evidence, and implications for the retail industry. *Journal of Retailing, 69,* 234–246.

Cox, D., Cox, A. D., & Moschis, G. P. (1990). When consumer behavior goes bad: An investigation of adolescent shoplifting. *Journal of Consumer Research, 17,* 149–159.

Craig, W., Vitaro, F., Gagnon, C., & Tremblay, R. E. (2002). The road to gang membership: Characteristics of male gang and nongang members from ages 10 to 14. *Social Development, 11,* 53–68.

Cressey, D. R. (1960). The theory of differential association: An introduction. *Social Problems, 8,* 2–5.

Crick, N. R. (1995). Relational aggression: The role of intent attributions, feelings of distress, and provocation type. *Development and Psychopathology, 7,* 313–327.

Crick, N. R., Casa, J. F., & Ku, H. C. (1999). Relational and physical forms of peer victimization in preschool. *Developmental Psychology, 35,* 376–385.

Crick, N. R., Casa, J. F., & Mosher, M. (1997). Relational and overt aggression in preschool. *Developmental Psychology, 33,* 579–588.

Crick, N. R., & Grotpeter, J. K. (1995). Relational aggression, gender, and social psychological adjustment. *Child Development, 66,* 710–722.

Cromwell, P. F. (1994). Juvenile burglars. *Juvenile and Family Court Journal, 45,* 85–91.

Cromwell, P. F., Olson, J. F., & Avary, D. W. (1994). *Juvenile burglars* (NCJ#149488). Washington, DC: U.S. Department of Justice.

Cruise, K. R., Colwell, L. H., Lyons, P. M., & Baker, M. D. (2003). Prototypical analysis of adolescent psychopathy: Investigating the juvenile justice perspective. *Behavioral Sciences & the Law, 21,* 829–846.

Cullen, F., & Gendreau, P. (2000). Assessing correctional rehabilitation: Policy, practice, and prospects. In J. Horney (Ed.), *Criminal Justice 2000* (Vol. 3). Washington, DC: U.S. Department of Justice, National Institute of Justice.

Curry, G. D., & Decker, S. H. (1998). *Confronting gangs: Crime and community.* Los Angeles: Roxbury.

Curry, G. D., Maxson, C. L., & Howell, J. C. (2001, March). *Youth gang homicides in the 1990s.* Washington, DC: U.S. Department of Justice, Office of Juvenile Justice and Delinquency Prevention.

Curtis, W. J., & Cicchetti, D. (2003). Moving research on resilience into the 21st century: Theoretical and methodological considerations in examining the biological contributors to resilience. *Development and Psychopathology, 15,* 773–810.

Dadds, M. R., Whiting, C., Bunn, P., Fraser, J. A., Charlson, H. H., & Pirola-Merlo, A. (2004). Measurement of cruelty in children: The Cruelty to Animals Inventory. *Journal of Abnormal Child Psychology, 32,* 321–334.

Dåderman, A. M., & Kristiansson, M. (2003). Degree of psychopathy: Implications for treatment in male juvenile delinquents. *International Journal of Law and Psychiatry, 26,* 310–315.

Dahlberg, L. L., & Potter, L. B. (2001). Youth violence: Developmental pathways and prevention challenges. *American Journal of Preventive Medicine, 20*(1), 3–14.

Dakof, G. A. (2000). Understanding gender differences in adolescent drug abuse: Issues of comorbidity and family functioning. *Journal of Psychoactive Drugs, 32,* 25–32.

Damon, W. (2004). What is positive youth development? *Annals, AAPSS, 591,* 13–24.

Darling, N., & Steinberg, L. (1993). Parenting style as context: An integrative model. *Psychological Bulletin, 113,* 487–496.

Datesman, S. K., & Scarpitti, F. R. (1975). Female delinquency and broken homes: A reassessment. *Criminology, 13,* 33–54.

Davey, M., Eaker, D. G., & Walters, L. H. (2003). Resilience processes in adolescents: Personality profiles, self-worth, and coping. *Journal of Adolescent Research, 18,* 347–362.

Davidson, R. J. (2000). Affective style, psychopathology, and resilience: Brain mechanisms and plasticity. *American Psychologist, 55,* 1196–1214.

Dawkins, M. P. (1997). Drug use and violent crime among adolescents. *Adolescence, 32,* 395–405.

Dawson, J. M., & Langan, P. A. (1994). *Murder in families* (NCJ 143498). Washington, DC: U.S. Department of Justice, Bureau of Justice Statistics.

Day, K., & Berney, T. (2001). Treatment and care for offenders with mental retardation. In J. B. Ashford, B. D. Sales, & W. H. Reid (Eds.), *Treating adult and juvenile offenders with special needs.* Washington, DC: American Psychological Association.

Deater-Deckard, K., & Dodge, K. A. (1997). Externalizing behavior problems and discipline revisited: Nonlinear effects and variation by culture, context, and gender. *Psychological Inquiry, 8,* 161–175.

Deater-Deckard, K., Dodge, K. A., Bates, J. E., & Pettit, G. S. (1996). Physical discipline among African-American and European-American mothers: Links to children's externalizing behaviors. *Developmental Psychology, 32,* 1065–1072.

Deater-Deckard, K., Lansford, J. E., Dodge, K. A., Pettit, G. S., & Bates, J. E. (2003). The development of attitudes about physical punishment: An 8-year longitudinal study. *Journal of Family Psychology, 17,* 351–360.

De Boo, G. M., & Prins, P. J. M. (2007). Social incompetence in children with ADHD: Possible moderators and mediators in social-skills training. *Clinical Psychology Review, 27,* 78–97.

Decker, S. H., Pennel, S., & Caldwell, A. (1997). *Illegal firearms: Access and use by arrestees.* Washington, DC: U.S. Department of Justice, National Institute of Justice.

Decker, S. H., & Van Winkle, B. (1996). *Life in the gang: Family, friends, and violence.* New York: Cambridge University Press.

Dekel, R., Peled, E., & Sprio, S. E. (2003). Shelters for houseless youth: A follow-up evaluation. *Journal of Adolescence, 26,* 201–212.

Delaney-Black, V., Covington, C., Templin, T., Ager, J., Nordstrom-Klee, B., Martier, S., et al. (2000). Teacher-assessed behavior of children prenatally exposed to cocaine. *Pediatrics, 106,* 782–791.

Department of Health and Human Services. (2003, September). *Overview of findings from the 2002 national survey on drug use and health.* Rockville, MD: Substance Abuse and Mental Health Services, Office of Applied Studies.

Diamond, T., & Muller, R. T. (2004). The relationship between witnessing parental conflict during childhood and later psychological adjustment among university students: Disentangling confounding risk factors. *Canadian Journal of Behavioural Science, 36,* 295–309.

Dietrich, K. N., Ris, M. D., Succop, P. A., Berger, O. G., & Bornschein, R. L. (2001). Early exposure to lead and juvenile delinquency. *Neurotoxicology and Teratology, 23,* 511–518.

Dilulio, J. J. (1995, November 27). The coming of the super-predators. *The Weekly Standard,* pp. 23–26.

Dionne, G., Tremblay, R., Boivin, M., Laplante, D., & Pérusse, D. (2003). Physical aggression and expressive vocabulary in 19-month-old twins. *Developmental Psychology, 39,* 261–273.

Dishion, T. J., & Andrews, D. W. (1995). Preventing escalation in problem behaviors with high-risk young adolescents: Immediate and 1-year outcomes. *Journal of Consulting and Clinical Psychology, 63,* 538–548.

Dishion, T. J., Andrews, D. W., & Crosby, L. (1995). Preventing escalation in problem behavior with high-risk adolescents: Immediate and one-year

outcomes. *Journal of Consulting and Clinical Psychology, 63,* 538–548.

Dishion, T. J., & Loeber, R. (1985). Male adolescent marijuana and alcohol use: The role of parents and peers revisited. *American Journal of Drug and Alcohol Abuse, 11,* 11–25.

Dishion, T. J., Nelson, S. E., & Yasui, M. (2005). Predicting early adolescent gang involvement from middle school adaptation. *Journal of Clinical Child and Adolescent Psychology, 34,* 62–73.

Dobkin, P. L., Tremblay, R. E., Masse, L. C., & Vitaro, F. (1995). Individual and peer characteristics in predicting boys' early onset of substance abuse: A seven-year longitudinal study. *Child Development, 66,* 1198–1214.

Dodge, K. A. (1986). A social-information-processing model of social competence in children. In M. Perlmutter (Ed.), *Minnesota symposium on child psychology* (Vol. 18). Hillsdale, NJ: Erlbaum.

Dodge, K. A. (1993). Social-cognitive mechanisms in the development of conduct disorder and depression. *Annual Review of Psychology, 44,* 559–584.

Dodge, K. A. (2001). The science of youth violence prevention: Progressing from developmental epidemiology to efficacy to effectiveness in public policy. *American Journal of Preventive Medicine, 20*(1), 63–70.

Dodge, K. A. (2002). Mediation, moderation, and mechanisms of how parenting affects children's aggressive behavior. In J. G. Borkowksi, S. L. Ramey, & M. Bristol-Power (Eds.), *Parenting and the child's world: Influences on academic, intellectual and social development.* Mahwah, NJ: Erlbaum.

Dodge, K. A. (2003). Do social information-processing patterns mediate aggressive behavior? In B. B. Lahey, T. E. Moffitt, & A. Caspi (Eds.), *Causes of conduct disorder and juvenile delinquency.* New York: Guilford.

Dodge, K. A. (2006). Translational science in action: Hostile attribution style and the development of aggressive behavior problems. *Developmental and Psychopathology, 18,* 791–814.

Dodge, K. A., Bates, J. E., & Pettit, G. S. (1990). Mechanisms in the cycle of violence. *Science, 250,* 1678–1683.

Dodge, K. A., Coie, J. D., Pettit, G. S., & Price, J. M. (1990). Peer status and aggression in boys' groups: Developmental and contextual analyses. *Child Development, 61,* 1289–1309.

Dodge, K. A., Laird, R., Lochman, J. E., Zelli, A., & Conduct Problems Prevention Research Group. (2002). Multi-dimensional latent construct analysis of children's social information-processing patterns: Correlations with aggressive behavior problems. *Psychological Assessment, 14,* 60–73.

Dodge, K. A., Lansford, J. E., Burks, V. S., Bates, J. E., Pettit, G. S., Fontaine, R., & Price, J. M. (2003). Peer rejection and social information-processing factors in the development of aggressive behavior problems in children. *Child Development, 74*, 374–393.

Dodge, K. A., & Pettit, G. S. (2003). A biopsychosocial model of the development of chronic conduct problems in adolescence. *Developmental Psychology, 39*, 349–371.

Doll, B., & Lyon, M. A. (1998). Risk and resilience: Implications for the delivery of educational and mental health services in schools. *School Psychology Review, 27*, 348–363.

Donnerstein, E., Slaby, R. G., & Eron, L. D. (1994). The mass media and youth aggression. In E. Eron, J. H. Gentry, & P. Schlegel (Eds.), *Reason to hope: A psychosocial perspective on violence and youth*. Washington, DC: American Psychological Association.

d'Orban, P. T., & O'Connor, A. (1989). Women who kill their parents. *British Journal of Psychiatry, 154*, 27–33.

Dornbusch, S. M., Carlsmith, J. M., Buschwall, S. J., Ritter, P. L., Leiderman, H., Hastorf, C., & Ross, R. T. (1985). Single parents, extended households, and the control of adolescents. *Child Development, 56*, 326–341.

Douglas, J. W. B., Ross, J. M., & Simpson, H. R. (1968). *All our future*. London: Peter Davies.

Downes, D., & Rock, P. (1982). *Understanding deviance*. Oxford, England: Clarendon Press.

Drug Enforcement Administration. (2000). *Drugs of abuse*. Washington, DC: U.S. Department of Justice.

Drug Enforcement Administration. (2003). *Lysergic acid diethylamide (LSD)*. Washington, DC: U.S. Department of Justice.

Drug Enforcement Administration. (2005). *Drugs of abuse*. Washington, DC: U.S. Department of Justice.

Dubrow, E. F., Edwards, S., & Ippolito, M. F. (1997). Life stressors, neighborhood disadvantage, and resources: A focus on inner-city children's adjustment. *Journal of Clinical Child Psychology, 26*, 130–144.

Dumas, J. E., Lynch, A. M., Laughlin, J. E., Smith, E. P., & Prinz, R. J. (2001). Promoting intervention fidelity: Conceptual issues, methods, and preliminary results from the early alliance prevention trial. *American Journal of Preventive Medicine, 20*(1), 38–47.

Duncan, S. C., Duncan, T. E., Biglan, A., & Ary, D. (1998). Contribution of the social context to the development of adolescent substance abuse: A multivariate latent growth modeling approach. *Drug and Alcohol Dependence, 50*, 57–71.

D'Unger, A. V., Land, K. C., McCall, P. L., & Nagin, D. S. (1998). How many latent classes of delinquent/criminal careers? *American Journal of Sociology, 103*, 1593–1630.

Dunworth, T. (2000). *National evaluation of the Youth Firearms Violence Initiative* (Research in Brief). Washington, DC: U.S. Department of Justice, National Institute of Justice.

Durose, M. R., Harlow, C. W., Langan, P. A., Motivans, M., Rantala, R. R., & Smith, E. L. (2005, June). *Family violence statistics: Including statistics on strangers and acquaintances*. Washington, DC: U.S. Department of Justice, Bureau of Justice Statistics.

Eastman, B. J. (2004). Assessing the efficacy of treatment for adolescent sex offenders: A cross-over longitudinal study. *The Prison Journal, 84*, 472–485.

Eddy, J. M. (2003). *Conduct disorders: The latest assessment and treatment strategies*. Kansas City, MO: Compact Clinicals.

Edens, J. F., & Cahill, M. A. (2007). Psychopathy in adolescence and criminal recidivism in young adulthood: Longitudinal results from a multiethnic sample of youthful offenders. *Assessment, 14*, 57–64.

Edens, J. F., Guy, L. S., & Fernandez, K. (2003). Psychopathic traits predict attitudes toward a juvenile capital murderer. *Behavioral Sciences & the Law, 21*, 807–828.

Edens, J. F., Skeem, J. L., Cruise, K. R., & Cauffman, E. (2001). Assessment of 'juvenile psychopathy' and its association with violence: A critical review. *Behavioral Sciences & the Law, 19*, 53–80.

Edleson, J. L. (1999). The overlap between child maltreatment and woman battering. *Violence Against Women, 5*, 134–154.

Egley, A., Jr., & Major, A. K. (2004, April). *Highlights of the 2002 National Youth Gang Survey*. Washington, DC: U.S. Department of Justice, Office of Juvenile Justice and Delinquency Prevention.

Egley, A., Jr., & Ritz, C. (2006, April). *Highlights of the 2004 National Youth Gang Survey*. Washington, DC: U.S. Department of Justice, Office of Juvenile Justice and Delinquency Prevention.

Ehringer, M. A., Rhee, S. H., Young, S., Corley, R., & Hewitt, J. K. (2006). Genetic and environmental contribution to common psychopathologies of childhood and adolescence: A study of twins and their siblings. *Journal of Abnormal Child Psychology, 34*, 1–17.

Eisenberg, N. (1998). *Social, emotional, and personality development* (5th ed., Vol. 3). New York: Wiley.

Eisenberg, N., & Fabes, R. A. (1998). Prosocial development. In W. Damon (Series Ed.) & N. Eisenberg (Vol. Ed.), *Handbook of child psychology: Vol. 3. Social, emotional, and personality development* (5th ed.). New York: Wiley.

Eisenberg, N., Gabes, R. A., Shepard, S. A., Guthrie, I. K., Murphy, B. C., & Reiser, M. (1999). Parental reactions to children's negative emotions: Longitudinal relations to quality of child social functioning. *Child Development, 70,* 513–534.

Eisenberg, N., Gershoff, E. T., Fabes, R. A., Shepard, S. A., Cumberland, A. J., Losoya, S. H., Guthrie, I. K., & Murphy, B. C. (2001). Mothers' emotional expressivity and children's behavior problems and social competence: Mediation through children's regulation. *Developmental Psychology, 37,* 475–490.

Eisenberg, N., Spinrad, T. L., Fabes, R. A., Reiser, M., Cumberland, A., Shepard, S. A., et al. (2004). The relations of effortful control and impulsivity to children's resiliency and adjustment. *Child Development, 75,* 25–46.

Eisenberg, N., & Strayer, J. (Eds.). (1987). *Empathy and its development.* Cambridge, UK: Cambridge University Press.

Eitle, D., Gunkel, S., & Van Gundy, K. (2004). Cumulative exposure to stressful life events and male gang membership. *Journal of Criminal Justice, 32,* 93–111.

Eley, T. C., Lichtenstein, P., & Moffitt, T. E. (2003). A longitudinal behavior genetic analysis of the etiology of aggressive and nonaggressive antisocial behavior. *Developmental Psychology, 15,* 383–402.

Ellickson, P. L., Bui, K., Bell, R., & McGuigan, K. A. (1998). Does early drug use increase the risk of dropping out of high school? *Journal of Drug Issues, 28,* 357–380.

Ellickson, P., Saner, H., & McGuigan, K. A. (1997). Profiles of violent youth: Substance use and other concurrent problems. *American Journal of Public Health, 87,* 985–991.

Elliott, D. S. (1994). Serious violent offenders: Onset, developmental course, and termination—The American Society of Criminology 1993 presidential address. *Criminology, 32,* 1–21.

Elliott, D. S., Dunford, T. W., & Huizinga, D. (1987). The identification and prediction of career offenders utilizing self-reported and official data. In J. D. Burchard & S. N. Burchard (Eds.), *Prevention of delinquent behavior.* Newbury Park, CA: Sage.

Elliott, D. S., & Menard, S. (1996). Delinquent friends and delinquent behavior: Temporal and developmental patterns. In J. D. Hawkins (Ed.), *Delinquency and crime: Current theories.* New York: Cambridge University Press.

Elliott, D. S., Wilson, W. J., Huizinga, D., Sampson, R. J., Elliott, A., & Rankin, B. (1996). The effects of neighborhood disadvantage on adolescent development. *Journal of Research in Crime & Delinquency, 33,* 389–426.

Else-Quest, N. M., Hyde, J. S., Goldsmith, H. H., & Van Hulle, C. A. (2006). Gender differences in temperament: A meta-analysis. *Psychological Bulletin, 132,* 33–72.

Emery, R. E. (1982). Interparental conflict and the children of discord and divorce. *Psychological Bulletin, 92,* 310–330.

Epps, P., & Parnell, R. W. (1952). Physique and temperament of women delinquents compared with women undergraduates. *British Journal of Medical Psychology, 25,* 249–255.

Epstein, M. J., & Sharma, J. (1998). *Behavioral and Emotional Rating Scale: A strength-based approach to assessment.* Austin, TX: Pro-Ed.

Erel, O., & Burman, B. (1995). Interrelatedness of marital relations and parent–child relations: A meta-analytic review. *Psychological Bulletin, 118,* 108–132.

Erhardt, D., & Hinshaw, S. P. (1994). Initial sociometric impressions of attention-deficit hyperactivity disorder and comparison boys: Predictions from social behaviors and from nonbehavioral variables. *Journal of Consulting and Clinical Psychology, 62,* 833–842.

Ericson, N. (2001, June). *Addressing the problem of juvenile bullying.* Washington, DC: U.S. Department of Justice, Office of Juvenile Justice and Delinquency Prevention.

Ernst, C., & Angst, J. (1983). *Birth order: Its influence on personality.* Berlin: Springer-Verlag.

Eron, L. D., Huesmann, L. R., & Zelli, A. (1991). The role of parental variables in the learning of aggression. In D. J. Pepler & K. H. Rubin (Eds.), *The development and treatment of childhood aggression.* Hillsdale, NJ: Erlbaum.

Eron, L. D., & Slaby, R. G. (1994). Introduction. In L. D. Eron, J. H. Gentry, & P. Schlegel (Eds.), *Reason to hope: A psychosocial perspective on violence and youth.* Washington, DC: American Psychological Association.

Ertl, M. A., & McNamara, J. R. (1997). Treatment of juvenile sex offenders: A review of the literature. *Child and Adolescent Social Work Journal, 14,* 199–221.

Esbensen, F.-A. (2000, September). *Preventing adolescent gang involvement.* Washington, DC: U.S. Department of Justice, Office of Juvenile Justice and Delinquency Prevention.

Esbensen, F.-A., Deschenes, E. P., & Winfree, L. T. (1999). Differences between gang girls and gang boys: Results from a multi-site survey. *Youth and Society, 31,* 27–53.

Esbensen, F.-A., & Osgood, D. W. (1997). *National evaluation of G.R.E.A.T.* Washington, DC: U.S. Department of Justice, National Institute of Justice.

Esbensen, F.-A., Peterson, D., Freng, A., & Taylor, T. J. (2002). Initiation of drug use, drug sales, and violent offending among a sample of gang and non-gang youth. In C. R. Huff (Ed.), *Gangs in America* (3rd ed). Beverly Hills, CA: Sage.

Esbensen, F.-A., & Weerman, F. M. (2005). Youth gangs and troublesome youth groups in the United States and the Netherlands. *European Journal of Criminology, 2*, 5–37.

Esbensen, F.-A., Winfree, L. T., Jr., & Taylor, T. J. (2001). Youth gangs and definitional issues: When is a gang a gang, and why does it matter? *Crime & Delinquency, 47*, 105–130.

Eslea, M., Menesini, E., Morita, Y., O'Moore, M., Mora-Merchán, J. A., Pereira, B., & Smith, P. K. (2003). Friendship and loneliness among bullies and victims: Data from seven countries. *Aggressive Behavior, 30*, 71–83.

Espelage, D. L., & Swearer, S. M. (2003). Research on school bullying and victimization: What have we learned and where do we go from here? *School Psychology Review, 32*, 365–383.

Evans, G. D., Rey, J., Hemphill, M. M., Perskins, D. F., Austin, W., & Racine, P. (2001). Academic-community collaboration: An ecology for early childhood violence prevention. *American Journal of Preventive Medicine, 20*(1), 22–30.

Evans, G. W. (2004). The environment of childhood poverty. *American Psychologist, 59*, 77–92.

Ewing, C. P. (1990). *When children kill: The dynamics of juvenile homicide.* Lexington, MA: D. C. Heath.

Eysenck, H. J., & Gudjonsson, G. H. (1989). *The causes and cures of criminality.* New York: Plenum.

Falkenbach, D. M., Poythress, N. G., & Heide, K. M. (2003). Psychopathic features in a juvenile diversion population: Reliability and predictive validity of two self-report measures. *Behavioral Sciences & the Law, 21*, 787–805.

Farmer, E. M. Z., Compton, S. N., Burns, B. J., & Robertson, E. (2002). Review of the evidence base for treatment of childhood psychopathology externalizing disorders. *Journal of Consulting and Clinical Psychology, 70*, 1267–1302.

Farrell, A. D., & White, K. S. (1998). Peer influence and drug use among urban adolescents: Family structure and parent–adolescent relationship as protective factors. *Journal of Consulting and Clinical Psychology, 66*, 248–258.

Farrington, D. P. (1979). Environmental stress, delinquent behavior, and conviction. In I. G. Sarason & C. D. Spielberger (Eds.), *Stress and anxiety* (Vol. 6). Washington, DC: Hemisphere.

Farrington, D. P. (1989). Early predictors of adolescent aggression and adult violence. *Violence and Victims, 4*, 79–100.

Farrington, D. P. (1991). Childhood aggression and adult violence: Early precursors and later life outcomes. In D. J. Pepler & K. H. Rubin (Eds.), *The development and treatment of childhood aggression.* Hillsdale, NJ: Erlbaum.

Farrington, D. P. (1995). Crime and physical health: Illnesses, injuries, accidents and offending in the Cambridge Study. *Criminal Behaviour and Mental Health, 5*, 278–286.

Farrington, D. P. (2005). The importance of child and adolescent psychopathy. *Journal of Abnormal Child Psychology, 33*, 489–497.

Farrington, D. P. (2006). Family background and psychopathy. In C. J. Patrick (Ed.), *Handbook of psychopathy.* New York: Guilford.

Farrington, D. P., & Burrows, J. N. (1993). Did shoplifting really decrease? *British Journal of Criminology, 33*, 57–59.

Farrington, D. P., Gundry, G., & West, D. J. (1975). The familial transmission of criminality. *Medicine, Science and the Law, 15*, 177–186.

Farrington, D. P., & Hawkins, J. D. (1991). Predicting participation, early onset, and later persistence in officially recorded offending. *Criminal Behaviour and Mental Health, 1*, 1–33.

Farrington, D. P., Ohlin, L. E., & Wilson, J. Q. (1986). *Understanding and controlling crime.* New York: Springer-Verlag.

Faupel, C. E. (1991). *Shooting dope: Career patterns of hard-core heroin users.* Gainesville: University of Florida Press.

Federal Bureau of Investigation. (2003). *Uniform Crime Reports—2002.* Washington, DC: U.S. Department of Justice.

Federal Bureau of Investigation. (2004). *National incident-based reporting system.* Washington, DC: U.S. Department of Justice.

Federal Bureau of Investigation. (2005). *Uniform Crime Reports—2004.* Washington, DC: U.S. Department of Justice.

Federal Bureau of Investigation. (2006). *Crime in the United States—2005.* Washington, DC: U.S. Department of Justice, Author.

Federal Interagency Forum on Child and Family Statistics. (2000). *America's children: Key national indicators.* Washington, DC: Author.

Federal Interagency Forum on Child and Family Statistics. (2005). *America's children: Key national indicators of well-being 2005.* Washington, DC: Author.

Federle, K. H., & Chesney-Lind, M. (1992). Special issues in juvenile justice: Gender, race, and ethnicity. In I. M. Schwartz (Ed.), *Juvenile justice and public policy.* New York: Lexington Books.

Fehrenbach, P. A., & Monastersky, C. (1988). Characteristics of female sexual offenders. *American Journal of Orthopsychiatry, 58,* 148–151.

Fehrenbach, P. A., Smith, W., Monastersky, C., & Deisher, R. W. (1986). Adolescent sexual offenders: Offender and offense characteristics. *American Journal of Orthopsychiatry, 56,* 225–233.

Feld, B. C. (1998). Juvenile and criminal justice systems' responses to youth violence. In M. Tonry & M. H. Moore (Eds.), *Youth violence. Crime and justice: A review of research* (Vol. 24). Chicago: University of Chicago Press.

Feldman, R., & Klein, P. S. (2003). Toddlers' self-regulated compliance to mothers, caregivers, and fathers: Implications for theories of socialization. *Developmental Psychology, 39,* 680–692.

Felner, R. D. (1999). An ecological perspective on pathways of risk, vulnerability, and adaptation. In S. W. Russ & T. H. Ollendick (Eds.), *Handbook of psychotherapies with children and families.* New York: Kluwer Academic/Plenum.

Felson, R. B., Baumer, E. P., & Messner, S. F. (2000). Acquaintance robbery. *Journal of Research in Crime & Delinquency, 37,* 284–305.

Felthous, A. R., & Kellert, S. R. (1986). Violence against animals and people: Is aggression against living creatures generalized? *Bulletin of the American Academy of Psychiatry and Law, 14,* 55–59.

Felthous, A. R., & Kellert, S. R. (1987). Childhood cruelty to animals and later aggression against people: A review. *American Journal of Psychiatry, 144,* 710–717.

Ferguson, D. M., Lynskey, M. T., & Horwood, L. J. (1996). Alcohol misuse and juvenile offending in adolescence. *Addiction, 91,* 483–494.

Fergusson, D. (1998). Stability and change in externalizing disorders. *European Archives of Psychiatry and Clinical Neuroscience, 248,* 4–13.

Fergusson, D. M., Horwood, L. J., & Nagin, D. S. (2000). Offending trajectories in a New Zealand birth cohort. *Criminology, 38,* 525–552.

Fields, S. A., & McNamara, J. R. (2003). The prevention of child and adolescent violence: A review. *Aggression and Violent Behavior, 8,* 61–91.

Filstead, W. J. (1970). *Qualitative methodology: First-hand involvement in the social world.* Chicago: Markham.

Finestone, H. (1975). The delinquent and society: The Shaw and McKay tradition. In J. F. Short, Jr. (Ed.), *Delinquency, crime and society.* Chicago: University of Chicago Press.

Finkelhor, D., Ormrod, R., Turner, H., & Hamby, S. L. (2005). The victimization of children and youth: A comprehensive national survey. *Child Maltreatment, 10,* 5–25.

Finnegan, T. A., Puzzanchera, C., Snyder, H. N., Stahl, A. L., & Tierney, N. (2004, December). *Juvenile Court Statistics* (NCJ 209736). Washington, DC: U.S. Department of Justice, Office of Juvenile Justice and Delinquency Prevention.

Fishbein, D. (2001). *Biobehavioral perspectives in criminology.* Belmont, CA: Wadsworth/Thomson Learning.

Flannery, D. J., Williams, L. L., & Vazsonyi, A. T. (1999). Who are they with and what are they doing? Delinquent behavior, substance abuse, and early adolescents' after-school time. *American Journal of Orthopsychiatry, 69,* 247–253.

Flory, K., Lynam, D., Milch, R., Leukefeld, C., & Clayton, R. (2004). Early adolescent through young adult alcohol and marijuana use trajectories: Early predictors, young adult outcomes, and predictive utility. *Development and Psychopathology, 16,* 193–213.

Folkman, S., & Moskowitz, J. T. (2000). Positive affect and the other side of coping. *American Psychologist, 55,* 647–654.

Forehand, R., Wierson, M., Frame, C. L., Kemptom, T., & Armistead, L. (1991). Juvenile firesetting: A unique syndrome or an advanced level of antisocial behavior? *Behavioral Research and Therapy, 29,* 125–128.

Forney, W. S., Forney, J. C., & Crutsinger, C. (2005). Developmental stages of age and moral reasoning as predictors of juvenile delinquents' behavioral intention to steal clothing. *Family and Consumer Sciences Research Journal, 34,* 110–126.

Fors, S. W., & Rojek, D. G. (1991). A comparison of drug involvement between runaways and school youths. *Journal of Drug Education, 21,* 13–25.

Forst, M. L., & Crim, D. (1994). A substance abuse profile of delinquent and homeless youths. *Journal of Drug Education, 24,* 219–231.

Forth, A. E., & Burke, H. C. (1998). Psychopathy in adolescence: Assessment, violence, and developmental precursors. In D. J. Cooke, A. E. Forth, & R. D. Hare (Eds.), *Psychopathy: Theory, research and implications for society.* Boston: Kluwer Academic.

Forth, A. E., Kosson, D. S., & Hare, R. D. (1997). *Hare Psychopathy Checklist: Youth Version.* Toronto, Canada: Multi-Health Systems.

Forth, A. E., Kosson, D. S., Hare, R. D. (2003). *Psychopathy Checklist–Youth Version: Technical manual.* Toronto: Multi-Health Systems.

Fothergill, K. E., & Ensminger, M. E. (2006). Childhood and adolescent antecedents of drug and alcohol problems: A longitudinal study. *Drug and Alcohol Dependence, 82*, 61–76.

Fox, J. A., & Zawitz, M. A. (2004, November). *Homicide trends in the United States: 2002 update.* Washington, DC: U.S. Department of Justice, Bureau of Justice Statistics.

Fox, S. J. (1970). Juvenile justice reform: An historical perspective. *Stanford Law Review, 22*, 1187–1239.

Frank, D. A., Augustyn, M., Grant Knight, W., Pell, T., & Zuckerman, B. (2001). Growth, development, and behavior in early childhood following prenatal cocaine exposure. *JAMA, 285*, 1613–1625.

Frederickson, B. L. (2001). The role of positive emotions in positive psychology: The broaden-and-build theory of positive emotions. *American Psychologist, 56*, 218–226.

Frick, P. J. (1998). Callous-unemotional traits and conduct problems: Applying the two-factor model of psychopathy to children. In D. J. Cooke, A. E. Forth, & R. D. Hare (Eds.), *Psychopathy: Theory, research and implications for society.* Boston: Kluwer Academic.

Frick, P. J. (2002). Juvenile psychopathy from a developmental perspective: Implications for construct development and use in forensic assessments. *Law and Human Behavior, 26*, 247–253.

Frick, P. J. (2004). Developmental pathways to conduct disorder: Implications for servicing youth who show severe and aggressive antisocial behavior. *Psychology in the Schools, 41*, 823–834.

Frick, P. J., Barry, C. T., & Bodin, S. D. (2000). Applying the concept of psychopathy to children: Implications for the assessment of antisocial youth. In C. B. Gacono (Ed.), *The clinical and forensic assessment of psychopathy.* Mahwah, NJ: Erlbaum.

Frick, P. J., & Dantagnan, A. L. (2005). Predicting the stability of conduct problems in children with and without callous-unemotional traits. *Journal of Child and Family Studies, 14*, 469–485.

Frick, P. J., & Hare, R. D. (2001). *The Antisocial Process Screening Device.* Toronto: Multi-Health Systems.

Frick, P. J., O'Brien, B. S., Wootton, J. M., & McBurnett, K. (1994). Psychopathy and conduct problems in children. *Journal of Abnormal Psychology, 103*, 700–707.

Fried, C. S. (2001). Juvenile curfews: Are they an effective and constitutional means of combating juvenile violence? *Behavioral Sciences & the Law, 19*, 127–141.

Frintner, M., & Rubinson, L. (1993). Acquaintance rape: The influence of alcohol, fraternity membership and sports team membership. *Journal of Sex Education and Therapy, 19*, 272–284.

Fuligni, A. J., & Eccles, J. S. (1993). Perceived parent–child relationships and early adolescents' orientation toward peers. *Developmental Psychology, 29*, 622–632.

Gacono, C. B., Nieberding, R. J., Owen, A., Rubel, J., & Bodholt, K. (2001). Treating conduct disorder, antisocial, and psychopathic personalities. In J. B. Ashford, B. D. Sales, & W. H. Reid (Eds.), *Treating adult and juvenile offenders with special needs.* Washington, DC: American Psychological Association.

Gamble, T. J., & Zigler, E. (1989). The Head Start synthesis project: A critique. *Journal of Applied Developmental Psychology, 10*, 267–274.

Ganger, J., & Brent, M. R. (2004). Reexamining the vocabulary spurt. *Developmental Psychology, 40*, 621–632.

Garbarino, J. (1976). A preliminary study of some ecological correlates of child abuse: The impact of socioeconomic stress on mothers. *Child Development, 47*, 178–185.

Garbarino, J. (1982). Sociocultural risk: Dangers to competence. In C. B. Kopp & J. B. Krakow (Eds.), *The child: Development in a social context.* Reading, MA: Addison-Wesley.

Garbarino, J., & Asp, C. E. (1981). *Successful schools and competent students.* Lexington, MA: Lexington Books.

Garbarino, J., & Kostelny, K. (1992). Child maltreatment as a community problem. *Child Abuse and Neglect, 16*, 455–464.

Garbarino, J., Kostelny, K. E., & Dubrow, N. (1991). What children can tell us about living in danger. *American Psychologist, 46*, 376–383.

Garcia, M. M., Shaw, D. S., Winslow, E. B., & Yaggi, K. E. (2000). Destructive sibling conflict and the development of conduct problems in young boys. *Developmental Psychology, 36*, 44–53.

Gardner, H. (1983). *Frames of mind: The theory of multiple intelligences.* New York: Basic Books.

Gardner, H. (1998). Are there additional intelligences: The case for naturalist, spiritual, and existential intelligences. In K. Kane (Ed.), *Education, information, and transformation.* Englewood Cliffs, NJ: Prentice Hall.

Gardner, H. (2000). *Intelligence reframed: Multiple intelligences for the 21st century.* New York: Basic Books.

Gardner, M., & Steinberg, L. (2005). Peer influence on risk taking, risk preference, and risky decision making in adolescence and adulthood: An experimental study. *Developmental Psychology, 41*, 625–635.

Garmezy, N. (1983). Stressors of childhood. In N. Garmezy & M. Rutter (Eds.), *Stress, coping & development in children.* New York: McGraw-Hill.

Garmezy, N. (1985). Stress-resistant children: The search for protective factors. In J. E. Stevenson (Ed.),

Recent research in developmental psychopathology. Journal of Child Psychology and Psychiatry Book Supplement No. 4. Oxford, UK: Pergamon Press.

Garmezy, N. (1991). Resiliency and vulnerability to adverse developmental outcomes associated with poverty. *American Behavioral Scientist, 34,* 416–430.

Gatti, U., Tremblay, R. E., Vitaro, F., & McDuff, P. (2005). Youth gangs, delinquency, and drug use: A test of the selection, facilitation, and enhancement hypotheses. *Journal of Child Psychology and Psychiatry, 46,* 1178–1190.

Gaynor, J. (1996). Firesetting. In M. Lewis (Ed.), *Child and adolescent psychiatry: A comprehensive textbook.* Baltimore: Williams & Wilkins.

Geis, G. (1965). *Juvenile gangs.* Washington, DC: U.S. Government Printing Office.

Geis, G. (2000). On the absence of self-control as the basis for a general theory of crime: A critique. *Theoretical Criminology, 4,* 35–53.

Gelles, R. J. (1982). Domestic criminal violence. In M. E. Wolfgang & N. A. Weiner (Eds.), *Criminal violence.* Thousand Oaks, CA: Sage.

Gelles, R. J. (1997). *Intimate violence in families.* Thousand Oaks, CA: Sage.

Gendreau, P. (1996). Offender rehabilitation: What we know and what needs to be done. *Criminal Justice and Behavior, 23,* 144–161.

Gerbner, G., & Gross, L. (1976). Living with television: The violence profile. *Journal of Communications, 26,* 173–199.

Gerwitz, J. L. (1961). A learning analysis of the effects of normal stimulation, privation, and deprivation on the acquisition of social motivation and attachment. In B. M. Foss (Ed.), *Determinants of infant behavior.* New York: Wiley.

Getz, J. G., & Bray, J. H. (2005). Predicting heavy alcohol use among adolescents. *American Journal of Orthopsychiatry, 75,* 102–116.

Giddan, J. J., Milling, L., & Campbell, N. B. (1996). Unrecognized language and speech deficits in preadolescent psychiatric patients. *American Journal of Orthopsychiatry, 66,* 85–92.

Glantz, M. D., Weinberg, N. S., Miner, L. L., & Colliver, J. D. (1999). The etiology of drug abuse: Mapping paths. In M. D. Glantz & C. R. Hartel (Eds.), *Drug abuse: Origins and interventions.* Washington, DC: American Psychological Association.

Gleason, J. B., & Ely, R. (2002). Gender differences in language development. In A. M. De Lisi & R. De Lisi (Eds.), *Biology, society, and behavior: The development of sex differences in cognition.* Westport, CT: Ablex.

Glueck, S., & Glueck, E. T. (1950). *Unraveling juvenile delinquency.* Cambridge, MA: Harvard University Press.

Glueck, S., & Glueck, E. T. (1956). *Physique and delinquency.* New York: Harper.

Goetting, A. (1993). Patterns of homicide among children. In A. V. Wilson (Ed.), *Homicide: The victim/ offender connection.* Cincinnati, OH: Anderson.

Gold, M. S. (1984). *800-cocaine.* New York: Bantam.

Goldstein, A. P. (1991). *Delinquent gangs: A psychological perspective.* Champaign, IL: Research Press.

Goldstein, A. P., & Soriano, F. I. (1994). Juvenile gangs. In L. D. Eron, J. J. Gentry, & P. Schlegal (Eds.), *Reason to hope: A psychosocial perspective on violence and youth.* Washington, DC: American Psychological Association.

Goldstein, N. E., Arnold, D. H., Rosenberg, J. L., Stowe, R. M., & Ortiz, C. (2001). Contagion of aggression in day care classrooms as a function of peer and toddler responses. *Journal of Educational Psychology, 93,* 708–719.

Goldstein, S. E., Davis-Kean, P. E., & Eccles, J. S. (2005). Parents, peers, and problem behavior: A longitudinal investigation of the impact of relationship perceptions and characteristics on the development of adolescent problem behavior. *Developmental Psychology, 41,* 401–413.

Goodman, R. (1999). The extended version of the Strengths and Difficulties Questionnaire as a guide to child psychiatric cases and consequent burden. *Journal of Child Psychology and Psychiatry and Allied Disciplines, 40,* 791–799.

Gordon, R. A., Lahey, B. B., Kawai, E., Loeber, R., Stouthamer-Loeber, M., & Farrington, D. P. (2004). Antisocial behavior and youth gang membership: Selection and socialization. *Criminology, 42,* 55–87.

Gorman-Smith, D., & Loeber, R. (2005). Are developmental pathways in disruptive behaviors the same for girls and boys? *Journal of Child and Family Studies, 14,* 15–27.

Gorman-Smith, D., Tolan, P. H., Huesmann, L. R., & Zelli, A. (1996). The relation of family functioning to violence among inner-city minority youths. *Journal of Family Psychology, 10,* 115–129.

Gottfredson, D. C. (2001). *Schools and delinquency.* Cambridge, UK: Cambridge University Press.

Gottfredson, G. D., Gottfredson, D. C., Payne, A. A., & Gottfredson, N. C. (2005). School climate predictors of school disorder: Results from a national study of delinquency prevention in schools. *Journal of Research in Crime & Delinquency, 42,* 412–444.

Gottfredson, M., & Hirschi, T. (1987). The methodological adequacy of longitudinal research on crime. *Criminology, 25,* 581–614.

Gottfredson, M., & Hirschi, T. (1990). *A general theory of crime.* Stanford, CA: Stanford University Press.

Gottman, J. M. (2001). Crime, hostility, wife battering, and the heart: On the Meehan et al. (2001) failure to replicate the Gottman et al. (1995) typology. *Journal of Family Psychology, 15,* 409–414.

Gove, W., & Crutchfield, R. D. (1982). The family and delinquency. *The Sociological Quarterly, 23,* 301–319.

Granic, I., & Patterson, G. R. (2006). Toward a comprehensive model of antisocial development: A dynamic systems approach. *Psychological Review, 113,* 101–131.

Greenberg, D. F. (1985). Age, crime and social explanation. *American Journal of Sociology, 91,* 1–21.

Greenberg, D. F. (1991). Modeling criminal careers. *Criminology, 25,* 17–46.

Greenberg, D. F. (1992). Comparing criminal career models. *Criminology, 30,* 141–147.

Greenberg, D. F. (1999). The weak strength of social control theory. *Crime & Delinquency, 45,* 66–81.

Greene, R. W., Ablon, J. S., Monuteaux, M. C., Goring, J. C., Henin, A., Raezeer-Blakely, L., Edwards, G., Markey, J., & Rabbitt, S. (2004). Effectiveness of collaborative problem solving in affectively dysregulated children with oppositional-defiant disorder: Initial findings. *Journal of Consulting and Clinical Psychology, 72,* 1157–1164.

Gresham, F. M., Lane, K. L., & Lambros, K. M. (2000). Comorbidity of conduct problems and ADHD: Identification of "fledgling psychopaths." *Journal of Emotional and Behavioral Disorders, 8,* 83–93.

Gretton, H. M., Hare, R. D., & Catchpole, R. E. H. (2004). Psychopathy and offending from adolescence to adulthood: A 10-year follow-up. *Journal of Consulting and Clinical Psychology, 73,* 636–645.

Gretton, H. M., McBride, M., Hare, R. D., O'Shaughnessy, R., & Kumka, G. (2001). Psychopathy and recidivism in adolescent sex offenders. *Criminal Justice and Behavior, 28,* 427–449.

Grietens, H., & Hellinckx, W. (2004). Evaluating effects of residential treatment for juvenile offenders by statistical metaanalysis: A review. *Aggression and Violent Behavior, 9,* 401–415.

Grotpeter, J. K., & Crick, N. R. (1996). Relational aggression, overt aggression, and friendship. *Child Development, 67,* 2328–2338.

Guerra, N. G., Huesmann, L. R., Tolan, P. H., Van Acker, R., & Eron, L. D. (1995). Stressful events and individual beliefs as correlates of economic disadvantage and aggression among urban children. *Journal of Consulting and Clinical Psycology, 63,* 518–528.

Guo, J., Chung, I. J., Hill, K. G., Hawkins, J. D., Catalano, R. F., & Abbott, R. D. (2002). Developmental relationships between adolescent substance use and risky sexual behavior in young adulthood. *Journal of Adolescent Health, 31,* 354–362.

Guy, S. M., Smith, G. M., & Bentler, P. M. (1994). The influence of adolescent substance use and socialization on deviant behavior in young adulthood. *Criminal Justice and Behavior, 21,* 236–255.

Guymer, A. C., Mellor, D., Luk, E. S., & Pearse, V. (2001). The development of a screening questionnaire for childhood cruelty to animals. *Journal of Child Psychology and Psychiatry, 42,* 1057–1063.

Haapassalo, J., & Tremblay, R. E. (1994). Physically aggressive boys from ages 6 to 12: Family background, parenting behavior, and prediction of delinquency. *Journal of Consulting and Clinical Psychology, 62,* 1044–1052.

Hall, C. L. (1997). Cultural malpractice: The growing obsolescence of psychology with the changing U.S. population. *American Psychologist, 52,* 642–651.

Hamburg, M. A. (1998). Youth violence is a public health concern. In D. S. Elliott, B. A. Hamburg, & K. R. Williams (Eds.), *Violence in American schools: A new perspective.* Cambridge, UK: Cambridge University Press.

Hammer, H., Finkelhor, D., & Sedlak, A. J. (2002, October). *Runaway/thrownaway children: National estimates and characteristics.* Washington, DC: Office of Juvenile Justice and Delinquency Prevention.

Hamparian, D. M., Esters, L. K., Munteen, S. M., Priestino, R. R., Swisher, R. G., Wallace, P. L., & White, J. L. (1982). *Youth in adult courts: Between two worlds.* Washington, DC: U.S. Government Printing Office.

Hamparian, D. M., Schuster, R., Dinitz, S., & Conrad, J. D. (1978). *The violent few.* Lexington, MA: Lexington Books.

Hampson, J. E., Rahman, M. A., Brown, B., Taylor, M. E., & Donaldson, C. J. (1998). Project SELF: Beyond resilience. *Urban Education, 33,* 6–33.

Hansell, S., & Wiatrowski, M. D. (1981). Competing conceptions of delinquent peer relations. In G. G. Jensen (Ed.), *Sociology of delinquency: Current issues.* Beverly Hills, CA: Sage.

Harbin, H. T., & Madden, D. J. (1979). Battered parents: A new syndrome. *American Journal of Psychiatry, 136,* 1288–1291.

Hare, R. D. (1965a). A conflict and learning theory analysis of psychopathic behavior. *Journal of Research in Crime and Delinquency, 2,* 12–19.

Hare, R. D. (1965b). Acquisition and generalization of a conditioned-fear response in psychopathic and nonpsychopathic criminals. *Journal of Psychology, 59,* 367–370.

Hare, R. D. (1970). *Psychopathy: Theory and research.* New York: Wiley.

Hare, R. D. (1980). A research scale for the assessment of psychopathy in criminal populations. *Personality and Individual Differences, 1,* 111–119.

Hare, R. D. (1985). *The Hare Psychopathy Checklist.* Toronto: Multi-Health Systems.

Hare, R. D. (1986). Criminal psychopaths. In J. C. Yuille (Ed.), *Selection and training: The role of psychology.* Boston: Martinus Nijhoff.

Hare, R. D. (1991). *The Hare Psychopathy Checklist—Revised.* Toronto: Multi-Health Systems.

Hare, R. D. (1996). Psychopathy: A clinical construct whose time has come. *Criminal Justice and Behavior, 23,* 25–54.

Hare, R. D. (1998). Emotional processing in psychopaths. In D. J. Cooke, R. D. Hare, & A. Forth (Eds.), *Psychopathy: Theory, research, and implications for society.* Dordrecht, Netherlands: Kluwer Academic.

Hare, R. D. (2003). *The Hare Psychopathy Checklist—Revised* (2nd ed.). Toronto: Multi-Health Systems.

Hare, R. D., Clark, D., Grann, M., & Thornton, D. (2000). Psychopathy and the predictive validity of the PCL-R: An international perspective. *Behavioral Sciences & the Law, 18,* 623–645.

Hare, R. D., & Hervé, H. F. (1999). *Hare P-Scan: Research version.* Toronto: Multi-Health Systems.

Hare, R. D., McPherson, L. M., & Forth, A. E. (1988). Male psychopaths and their criminal careers. *Journal of Consulting and Clinical Psychology, 56,* 710–714.

Harlow, C. W. (2005, November). *Hate crime reported by victims and police.* U.S. Department of Justice, Bureau of Justice Statistics.

Harms, P. (2002, February). *Robbery cases in juvenile court, 1989–1998.* Washington, DC: U.S. Department of Justice, Office of Juvenile Justice and Delinquency Prevention.

Harpur, J. T., & Hare, R. D. (1994). The assessment of psychopathy as a function of age. *Journal of Abnormal Psychology, 103,* 604–609.

Harrell, E. (2005, June). *Violence by gang members, 1993–2003.* Washington, DC: U.S. Department of Justice, Office of Justice Programs.

Harrison-Hale, A. O., McLoyd, V. C., & Smedley, B. (2004). Racial and ethnic status: Risk and protective processes among African American families. In K. L. Maton, C. J. Schellenbach, B. J. Leadbetter, & A. L. Solarz (Eds.), *Investing in children, youth, families, and communities: Strengths-based research and policy.* Washington, DC: American Psychological Association.

Hart, B., & Risley, T. R. (1995). *Meaningful differences in the everyday experience of young American children.* Baltimore: Brookes.

Hart, B., & Risley, T. R. (1999). *The social world of children learning to talk.* Baltimore: Brookes.

Hart, C. H., Nelson, A. A., Robinson, C. C., Olsen, S. F., & McNeilly-Choque, M. K. (1998). Overt and relational aggression in Russian nursery-school-age children: Parenting style and marital linkages. *Developmental Psychology, 34,* 687–697.

Hart, D., Hofmann, V., Edelstein, W., & Keller, M. (1997). The relation of childhood personality types to adolescent behavior and development: A longitudinal study of Icelandic children. *Developmental Psychology, 33,* 195–205.

Hart, E. L. O., Lahey, B. B., Loeber, R., Applegate, B., Green, S. M., & Frick, P. J. (1995). Developmental change in attention-deficit hyperactivity in boys: A four-year longitudinal study. *Journal of Abnormal Child Psychology, 23,* 729–749.

Hart, S. D., & Dempster, R. J. (1997). Impulsivity and psychopathy. In C. D. Webster & M. A. Jackson (Eds.), *Impulsivity: Theory, assessment and treatment.* New York: Guilford.

Hart, S. D., & Hare, R. D. (1997). Psychopathy: Assessment and association with criminal conduct. In D. M. Stoff & J. Breiling (Eds.), *Handbook of antisocial behavior.* New York: Wiley.

Hart, S. D., Hare, R. D., & Forth, A. E. (1993). Psychopathy as a risk marker for violence: Development and validation of a screening version of the Revised Psychopathy Checklist. In J. Monahan & H. Steadman (Eds.), *Violence and mental disorder: Development in risk assessment.* Chicago: University of Chicago Press.

Hart, S. D., Watt, K. A., & Vincent, G. M. (2002). Commentary on Seagrave and Grisso: Impressions of the state of the art. *Law and Human Behavior, 26,* 241–245.

Hartley, C. C. (2002). The co-occurrence of child maltreatment and domestic violence: Examining both neglect and child physical abuse. *Child Maltreatment, 7,* 349–358.

Hartup, W. W. (1983). Peer relations. In P. H. Mussen (Ed.), *Handbook of child psychology* (Vol. 4, 4th ed.). New York: Wiley.

Haselager, G. J. T., Cillessen, A. H. N., Van Lieshout, C. F. M., Riksen-Walraven, J. M. A., & Hartup, W. W. (2002). Heterogeneity among peer-rejected boys across middle childhood: Developmental pathways of social behavior. *Developmental Psychology, 38,* 446–456.

Hastings, P. D., Zahn-Waxler, C., Usher, B., Robinson, J., & Bridges, D. (2000). The development of concern for others in children with behavior problems. *Developmental Psychology, 36,* 531–546.

Hawes, D. J., & Dadds, M. R. (2005). The treatment of conduct problems in children with callous-unemotional traits. *Journal of Consulting and Clinical Psychology, 73,* 737–741.

Hawkins, J. D., Herrenkohl, T., Farrington, D. P., Brewer, D., Catalano, R. F., & Harachi, T. W. (1998).

A review of predictors of youth violence. In R. Loeber & D. P. Farrington (Eds.), *Serious & violent juvenile offenders: Risk factors and successful interventions*. Thousand Oaks, CA: Sage.

Hawkins, J. D., Von Cleve, E., & Catalano, R. F. (1991). Reducing early childhood aggression: Results of a primary prevention program. *Journal of the American Academy of Child and Adolescent Psychiatry, 30*, 208–217.

Heck, C., & Walsh, A. (2000). The effects of maltreatment and family structure on minor and serious delinquency. *International Journal of Offender Therapy and Comparative Criminology, 44*, 178–193.

Heckel, R. V., & Shumaker, D. M. (2001). *Children who murder: A psychological perspective*. Westport, CT: Praeger.

Heide, K. M. (1993). Adolescent parricide offenders: Synthesis, illustration and future directions. In A. V. Wilson (Ed.), *Homicide: The victim/offender connection*. Cincinnati, OH: Anderson.

Heide, K. M. (1999). *Young killers: The challenge of juvenile homicide*. Thousand Oaks, CA: Sage.

Heide, K. M. (2003). Youth homicide: A review of the literature and blueprint for action. *International Journal of Offender Therapy and Comparative Criminology, 47*, 6–36.

Hemphill, J. F., & Hare, R. D. (2004). Some misconceptions about the Hare PCL-R and risk assessment: A reply to Gendreau, Goggin, and Smith. *Criminal Justice and Behavior, 31*, 203–243.

Hemphill, J. F., Hare, R. D., & Wong, S. (1998). Psychopathy and recidivism: A review. *Legal and Criminological Psychology, 3*, 139–170.

Henderlong, J., & Lepper, M. R. (2002). The effects of praise on children's intrinsic motivation: A review and synthesis. *Psychological Bulletin, 128*, 774–795.

Henggeler, S. W. (1996). Treatment of violent juvenile offenders—we have the knowledge. *Journal of Family Psychology, 10*, 1371–141.

Henggeler, S. W., & Borduin, C. M. (1990). *Family therapy and beyond: A multisystemic approach to treating the behavior problems of children and adolescents*. Pacific Grove, CA: Brooks/Cole.

Henggeler, S. W., Melton, G. B., & Smith, L. A. (1992). Family preservation using multisystemic therapy—An effective alternative to incarcerating serious juvenile offenders. *Journal of Consulting and Clinical Psychology, 60*, 953–961.

Henggeler, S. W., Melton, G. B., Smith, L. A., Schoenwald, S. K., & Hanley, J. (1993). Family preservation using multisystemic therapy: Long-term follow-up to a clinical trial with serious juvenile offenders. *Journal of Child and Family Studies, 2*, 283–293.

Henker, B., & Whalen, C. K. (1989). Hyperactivity and attention deficits. *American Psychologist, 44*, 216–224.

Henry, B., Caspi, A., Moffitt, T. E., & Silva, P. A. (1996). Temperament and familial predictors of violent and nonviolent criminal conviction: Age 3 to age 18. *Developmental Psychology, 32*, 614–623.

Hensley, C., & Tallichet, S. E. (2005). Learning to be cruel?: Exploring the onset and frequency of animal cruelty. *International Journal of Offender Therapy and Comparative Criminology, 49*, 37–47.

Hernández, P. (2002). Resilience in families and communities: Latin American contributions from the psychology of liberation. *The Family Journal: Counseling and Therapy for Couples and Families, 10*, 334–343.

Herpertz, S. C., Werth, U., Lukas, G., Qunaibi, M., Schuerkens, A., Kunert, H. J., et al. (2001). Emotion in criminal offenders with psychopathy and borderline personality disorder. *Archives of General Psychiatry, 58*, 737–745.

Herrenkohl, T. L., Hawkins, J. D., Chung, I., Hill, K. G., & Battin-Pearson, S. (2001). School and community risk factors and interventions. In R. Loeber & D. P. Farrington (Eds.), *Child delinquents: Development, intervention, and service needs*. Thousand Oaks, CA: Sage.

Herrenkohl, T. L., Huang, B., Tajima, E. A., & Whitney, S. D. (2003). Examining the link between child abuse and youth violence: An analysis of mediating mechanisms. *Journal of Interpersonal Violence, 18*, 1189–1208.

Herrenkohl, T. L., Maguin, E., Hill, K. G., Hawkins, J. D., Abbott, R. D., & Catalano, R. F. (2000). Developmental risk factors for youth violence. *Journal of Adolescent Health, 26*, 176–186.

Hetherington, E. M., Cox, M., & Cox, R. (1979). Family interaction and the social, emotional, and cognitive development of children following divorce. In V. Vaughn & T. Brazelton (Eds.), *The family: Setting priorities*. New York: Science & Medicine.

Hicks, B. M., Markon, K. E., Patrick, C. J., Krueger, R. F., & Newman, J. P. (2004). Identifying psychopathy subtypes on the basis of personality structure. *Psychological Assessment, 16*, 276–288.

Hill, A. L., Degnan, K. A., Calkins, S. D., & Keane, S. P. (2006). Profiles of externalizing behavior problems for boys and girls across preschool: The roles of emotional regulation and inattention. *Developmental Psychology, 42*, 913–928.

Hill, C. D., Rogers, R., & Bickford, M. E. (1996). Predicting aggressive and social disruptive behavior in a maximum security forensic psychiatric hospital. *Journal of Forensic Sciences, 41*, 56–69.

Hill, K. G., Howell, J. C., Hawkins, J. D., & Battin-Pearson, S. R. (1999). Childhood risk factors for adolescent gang membership: Results from the Seattle Social Development Project. *Journal of Research in Crime & Delinquency, 36*, 300–322.

Hill, K. G., Lui, C., & Hawkins, J. D. (2001, December). *Early precursors of gang membership: A study of Seattle youth*. Washington, DC: U.S. Department of Justice, Office of Juvenile Justice and Delinquency Prevention.

Hill, L. G., Lochman, J. E., Coie, J. D., & Geenberg, M. T. (2004). Effectiveness of early screening for externalizing problems: Issues of screening accuracy and utility. *Journal of Consulting and Clinical Psychology, 72*, 809–820.

Hillbrand, M., Alexandre, J. W., Young, J. L., & Spitz, R. T. (1999). Parricide: Characteristics of offenders and victims, legal factors, and treatment issues. *Aggression and Violent Behavior, 4*, 179–190.

Hindelang, M. J. (1973). Causes of delinquency: A partial replication and extension. *Social Problems, 20*, 471–487.

Hindelang, M. J., Hirschi, T., & Weis, J. G. (1981). *Measuring delinquency*. Beverly Hills, CA: Sage.

Hinshaw, S. P. (1992). Externalizing behavior problems and academic underachievement in childhood and adolescence: Causal relationships and underlying mechanisms. *Psychological Bulletin, 111*, 127–155.

Hinshaw, S. P., & Anderson, C. A. (1996). Conduct and oppositional defiant disorders. In E. J. Mash (Ed.), *Child psychopathology*. New York: Guilford.

Hirschi, T. (1969). *Causes of delinquency*. Berkeley: University of California Press.

Hirschi, T., & Gottfredson, M. (1993). Commentary: Testing the general theory of crime. *Journal of Research in Crime & Delinquency, 30*, 47–54.

Hirschi, T., & Hindelang, M. J. (1977). Intelligence and delinquency. *American Sociological Review, 42*, 571–587.

Hoffman, K. L., Kiecolt, K. J., & Edwards, J. N. (2005). Physical violence between siblings: A theoretical and empirical analysis. *Journal of Family Issues, 26*, 1103–1130.

Hofmann, F. G. (1975). *A handbook on drug and alcohol abuse: The biomedical aspects*. New York: Oxford University Press.

Hogan, R., & Jones, W. H. (1983). A role-theoretical model of criminal conduct. In W. S. Laufer & J. M. Day (Eds.), *Personality theory, moral development and criminal behavior*. Lexington, MA: Lexington Books.

Hollister, L. F. (1998). Health aspects of cannabis: Revisited. *International Journal of Neuropsychopharmacology, 1*, 71–80.

Hollister-Wagner, G. H., Foshee, V. A., & Jackson, C. (2001). Adolescent aggression: Models of resilience. *Journal of Applied Social Psychology, 31*, 445–466.

Holmes, C. T. (1989). Grade level retention effects: A meta-analysis of research studies. In L. A. Shepard & M. L. Smith (Eds.), *Flunking grades: Research and policies on retention*. Philadelphia: Falmer Press.

Holtzworth-Munroe, A., Smulter, N., & Sandin, E. (1997). A brief review of the research on husband violence: Part II—The psychological effects of husband violence on battered women and their children. *Aggression and Violent Behavior, 2*, 179–213.

Hopfer, C. J., Khuri, E., Crowley, T. J., & Hooks, S. (2002). Adolescent heroin use: A review of the descriptive and treatment literature. *Journal of Substance Abuse Treatment, 23*, 231–237.

Hops, H., Davis, B., & Lewin, L. M. (1999). The development of alcohol and other substance use: A gender study of family and peer context. *Journal of Studies on Alcohol, 13*, 22–31.

Horowitz, L., Jannson, L., Ljungberg, T., & Hedenbro, M. (2005). Behavioural patterns of conflict resolution strategies in preschool boys with language impairment in comparison with boys with typical language development. *International Journal of Language and Communication Disorders, 40*, 431–454.

Hotaling, G. T., & Straus, M. A. (1989). Intrafamily violence, and crime and violence outside the family. In L. Ohlin & M. Tonry (Eds.), *Family violence* (Vol. 11). Chicago: University of Chicago Press.

Howell, J. C. (1997, December). Youth gangs. *OJJDP Fact Sheet*. Washington, DC: U.S. Department of Justice, Office of Juvenile Justice and Delinquency Prevention.

Howell, J. C. (1998, August). *Youth gangs: An overview*. Washington, DC: U.S. Department of Justice, Office of Juvenile Justice and Delinquency Prevention.

Howell, J. C. (1999). Youth gang homicides: A literature review. *Crime & Delinquency, 45*, 208–241.

Howell, J. C., & Decker, S. H. (1999, January). *The youth gangs, drugs, and violence connection*. Washington, DC: U.S. Department of Justice, OJJDP.

Howell, J. C., & Egley, A., Jr. (2005). Moving risk factors into developmental theories of gang membership. *Youth Violence and Juvenile Justice, 3*, 334–354.

Howell, J. C., Egley, A., Jr., & Gleason, D. K. (2002, June). Modern-day youth gangs. *Juvenile Justice Bulletin*. Washington, DC: U.S. Department of Justice, Office of Juvenile Justice and Delinquency Prevention.

Howell, J. C., & Lynch, J. P. (2000). *Youth gangs in schools* (Youth Gang Series bulletin). Washington, DC: U.S. Department of Justice, Office of Juvenile Justice and Delinquency Prevention.

Howes, C., & Olenick, M. (1986). Family and child care influences on toddlers' compliance. *Child Development, 57*, 202–216.

Hoza, B., Mrug, S., Gerdes, A. C., Bukowski, W. M., Kraemer, H. C., Wigal, T., et al. (2005). What aspects of peer relationships are impaired in children with attention deficit/hyperactivity disorder? *Journal of Consulting and Clinical Psychology, 73*, 411–423.

Hubbard, J. A., Dodge, K. A., Cillessen, A. H. N., Coie, J. D., & Schwartz, D. (2001). The dyadic nature of social information processing in boys' reactive and proactive aggression. *Journal of Personality and Social Psychology, 80*, 268–280.

Huebner, A. J., & Betts, S. C. (2002). Exploring the utility of social control theory for youth development: Issues of attachment, involvement, and gender. *Youth & Society, 34*, 123–145.

Huesmann, L. R. (1988). An information processing model for the development of aggression. *Aggressive Behavior, 14*, 13–24.

Huesmann, L. R., & Eron, L. D. (Eds.). (1986). *Television and the aggressive child: A cross-national comparison.* Hillsdale, NJ: Erlbaum.

Hughes, C., Dunn, J., & White, A. (1998). Trick or treat? Uneven understanding of mind and emotion and executive dysfunction in "hard-to-manage" preschoolers. *Journal of Child Psychology and Psychiatry, 39*, 981–994.

Hughes, C., White, A., Sharpen, J., & Dunn, J. (2000). Antisocial, angry, and unsympathetic: "Hard to manage" preschoolers' peer problems, and possible cognitive influences. *Journal of Child Psychology and Psychiatry, 41*, 169–179.

Hughes, L. A. (2005). Studying youth gangs: Alternative methods and conclusions. *Journal of Contemporary Criminal Justice, 21*, 98–119.

Huizinga, D., & Jakob-Chien, C. (1998). The contemporaneous co-occurrence of serious and violent juvenile offending and other problem behaviors. In R. Loeber & D. P. Farrington (Eds.), *Serious & violent juvenile offenders: Risk factors and successful interventions.* Thousand Oaks, CA: Sage.

Hunter, A. J. (2001). A cross-cultural comparison of resilience in adolescents. *Journal of Pediatric Nursing, 16*, 172–179.

Hunter, J. A., & Becker, J. V. (1999). Motivators of adolescent sex offenders and treatment perspectives. In J. Shaw (Ed.), *Sexual aggression.* Washington, DC: American Psychiatric Press.

Hunter, J. A., & Figueredo, A. J. (1999). Factors associated with treatment compliance in a population of juvenile sexual offenders. *Sexual Abuse: A Journal of Research and Treatment, 11*, 49–67.

Hunter, J. A., & Figueredo, A. J. (2000). The influence of personality and history of sexual victimization in the prediction of offense characteristics of juvenile sex offenders. *Behavior Modification, 24*, 241–263.

Hunter, J. A., Figueredo, A. J., Malamuth, N. M., & Becker, J. V. (2003). Juvenile sex offenders: Toward the development of a typology. *Sexual Abuse: A Journal of Research and Treatment, 15*, 27–48.

Hunter, J. A., Hazelwood, R. R., & Slesinger, D. (2000). Juvenile-perpetrated sex crimes: Patterns of offending and predictors of violence. *Journal of Family Violence, 15*, 81–93.

Hussong, A. M., & Hicks, R. E. (2003). Affect and peer context interactively impact adolescent substance abuse. *Journal of Abnormal Child Psychology, 31*, 413–426.

Huston, A. C., Donnerstein, E., Fairchild, H., Feshbach, N. D., Katz, P. A., & Murray, J. P. (1992). *Big world, small screen: The role of television in American society.* Lincoln: University of Nebraska Press.

Hutson, H., Anglin, D., & Eckstein, M. (1996). Drive-by shootings by violent street gangs in Los Angeles: A five-year review from 1989 to 1993, *Academic Emergency Medicine, 3*, 300–303.

Hutson, H. R., Anglin, D., & Pratts, M. J. (1994). Adolescents and children injured or killed in drive-by shootings in Los Angeles. *New England Journal of Medicine, 330*, 324–327.

Icove, D. J., & Estepp, M. H. (1987, April). Motive-based offender profiles of arson and fire-related crime. *FBI Law Enforcement Bulletin*, 17–23.

Ikeda, R. M., Simon, T. R., & Swahn, M. (2001). The prevention of youth violence: The rationale for and characteristics of four evaluation projects. *American Journal of Preventive Medicine, 20*, 15–21.

Inaba, D. S., & Cohen, W. E. (1993). *Uppers, downers, all arounders: Physical and mental effects of psychoactive drugs* (2nd ed.). Ashland, OR: CNS Productions.

Inciardi, J. A. (1986). *The war on drugs: Heroin, cocaine, crime and public policy.* Palo Alto, CA: Mayfield.

Ingoldsby, E. M., & Shaw, D. S. (2002). Neighborhood contextual factors and early-starting antisocial pathways. *Clinical Child and Family Psychology Review, 5*, 21–55.

Ingram, G. L., Gerard, R. E., Quay, H. C., & Levison, R. B. (1970). An experimental program for the psychopathic delinquent: Looking in the "correctional wastebasket." *Journal of Research in Crime & Delinquency, 7*, 24–30.

In re Gault, 387 U.S. 1 (1967).

Institute for Law and Justice. (1994). *Gang prosecution in the United States*. Washington, DC: U.S. Government Printing Office.

Ishikawa, S. S., & Raine, A. (2004). Prefrontal deficits and antisocial behavior: A causal model. In B. B. Lahey, T. E. Moffitt, & A. Caspi (Eds.), *Causes of conduct disorder and juvenile delinquency*. New York: Guilford.

Ishikawa, S. S., Raine, A., Lencz, T., Bihrle, S., & Lacasse, L. (2001). Autonomic stress reactivity and executive functions in successful and unsuccessful criminal psychopaths from the community. *Journal of Abnormal Psychology, 110*, 423–432.

Jackson, H. F., Glass, C., & Hope, S. (1987). A functional analysis of recidivistic arson. *British Journal of Clinical Psychology, 26*, 175–185.

Jaffee, S. R., Caspi, A., Moffitt, T. E., Dodge, K. A., Rutter, M., Taylor, A., & Tully, L. A. (2005). Nature × nurture: Genetic vulnerabilities interact with physical maltreatment to promote conduct problems. *Development and Psychopathology, 17*, 67–84.

Jarvis, G., & Parker, H. (1989). Young heroin users and crime. *British Journal of Criminology, 29*, 175–185.

Jensen, G. (1999). A critique of control balance theory. *Theoretical Criminology, 3*, 339–343.

Jesness, C. F. (1987). Early identification of delinquent-prone children: An overview. In J. D. Burchard & S. N. Burchard (Eds.), *Prevention of delinquent behavior*. Newbury Park, CA: Sage.

Jessor, R., & Jessor, S. L. (1977). *Problem behavior and psychosocial development*. New York: Academic Press.

Jessor, R., Van den Bos, J., Vanderryn, J., Costa, F. M., & Turbin, M. S. (1995). Protective factors in adolescent problem behavior: Moderator effects on developmental change. *Developmental Psychology, 31*, 923–933.

Jester, J. M., Nigg, J. T., Adams, K., Fitzgerald, H. E., Puttler, L. I., Wong, M. M., & Zucker, R. A. (2005). Inattention/hyperactivity and aggression from early childhood to adolescence: Heterogeneity of trajectories and differential influence of family environment characteristics. *Development and Psychopathology, 17*, 99–125.

Johnson, R. E. (1986). Family structure and delinquency: General patterns and gender differences. *Criminology, 24*, 64–80.

Johnston, L. D., O'Malley, P. M., & Bachman, J. G. (2000). *Monitoring the future: National results on adolescent drug use: Overview of key findings, 1999*. University of Michigan Institute for Social Research, National Institute on Drug Abuse, and U.S. Department of Health and Human Services.

Johnston, L. D., O'Malley, P. M., Bachman, J. G., & Schulenberg, J. E. (2006). *Monitoring the future: National results on adolescent drug use: Overview of key findings, 2005*. Bethesda, MD: National Institute on Drug Abuse.

Johnston, L. D., O'Malley, P. M., Bachman, J. G., & Schulenberg, J. E. (2007). *Monitoring the future: National results on adolescent drug use: Overview of key findings, 2006*. Bethesda, MD: National Institute on Drug Abuse.

Johnstone, L., & Cooke, D. J. (2004). Psychopathic-like traits in childhood: Conceptual and measurement concerns. *Behavioral Sciences & the Law, 22*, 103–125.

Jolly, M. K. (1979). Young, female and outside the law: A call for justice for the girl "delinquent." In R. Crown & G. McCarthy (Eds.), *Teenage women in the juvenile justice system: Changing values*. Tucson, AZ: New Directions for Young Women.

Joyce, E. (2003/2004). Teen dating violence: Facing the epidemic. *National Center for Victims of Crime*, pp. 1–9.

Julien, R. M. (1975). *A primer of drug action*. San Francisco, CA: W. H. Freeman.

Junger, M., & Marshall, I. H. (1997). The interethnic generalizability of social control theory: An empirical test. *Journal of Research in Crime & Delinquency, 34*, 79–112.

Kaczmarek, P. (2006). Counseling psychology and strength-based counseling: A promise yet to fully materialize. *The Counseling Psychologist, 34*, 90–95.

Kafrey, D. (1980). Playing with matches: Children and fire. In D. Canter (Ed.), *Fires and human behaviour*. Chichester, UK: Wiley.

Kahn, T. J., & LaFond, M. A. (1988). Treatment of the adolescent sex offender. *Child and Adolescent Social Work, 5*, 135–148.

Kandel, D. B., Johnson, J. G., Bird, H. R., Canino, G., Goodman, S. H., Lahey, B. B., Regler, D. A., & Schwab-Stone, M. (1997). Psychiatric disorders associated with substance abuse among children and adolescents: Findings from the Methods for the Epidemiology of Child and Adolescent Mental Disorders (MECA) Study. *Journal of Abnormal Child Psychology, 25*, 121–132.

Kandel, D., Yamaguchi, K., & Chen, K. (1992). Stages of drug involvement from adolescence to adulthood: Further evidence for the gateway theory. *Journal of Studies on Alcohol, 53*, 447–457.

Kaplow, J. B., Curran, P. J., Dodge, K. A., & Conduct Problems Prevention Research Group. (2002). Child, parent, and peer predictors of early-onset substance use: A multisite longitudinal study. *Journal of Abnormal Child Psychology, 30*, 199–216.

Kaufman, J. G., & Widom, C. S. (1999). Childhood victimization, running away, and delinquency. *Journal of Research in Crime & Delinquency, 36*, 347–370.

Kazdin, A. E. (1989). Developmental psychopathology: Current research, issues, and directions. *American Psychologist, 44*, 180–187.

Kazdin, A. E. (1994). Psychotherapy for children and adolescents. In A. E. Bergin & S. L. O, Garfield (Eds.), *Handbook of psychotherapy and behavior change* (4th ed.). New York: Wiley.

Keenan, K. (2001). Uncovering preschool precursors to problem behavior. In R. Loeber & D. P. Farrington (Eds.), *Child delinquents: Development, intervention, and service needs*. Thousand Oaks, CA: Sage.

Keenan, K., & Shaw, D. (1997). Developmental and social influences on young girls' early problem behavior. *Psychological Bulletin, 121*, 95–113.

Keenan, K., & Shaw, D. (2003). Starting at the beginning: Exploring the etiology of antisocial behavior in the first years of life. In B. B. Lahey, T. E. Moffitt, & A. Caspi (Eds.), *Causes of conduct disorder and juvenile delinquency*. New York: Guilford.

Keenan, K., & Wakeschlag, L. (2000). More than the terrible twos: The nature and severity of behavior problems in clinic-referred preschool children. *Journal of Abnormal Child Psychology, 28*, 33–46.

Keiley, K., Howe, T. R., Dodge, K. A., Bates, J. E., & Pettit, G. S. (2001). The timing of child physical maltreatment: A cross-domain growth analysis of impact of adolescent externalizing and internalizing problems. *Development and Psychopathology, 13*, 891–912.

Keiley, M. K., Bates, J. E., Dodge, K. A., & Pettit, G. S. (2000). A cross-domain growth analysis: Externalizing and internalizing behaviors during 8 years of childhood. *Journal of Abnormal Child Psychology, 28*, 161–179.

Kellam, S. G., Adams, R. G., Brown, H. C., & Ensminger, M. E. (1982). The long-term evolution of the family structure of teenage and older mothers. *Journal of Marriage and the Family, 44*, 539–554.

Kellert, S. R., & Felthous, A. R. (1985). Childhood cruelty to animals among criminals and noncriminals. *Human Relations, 38*, 1113–1129.

Kelley, T. M., Kennedy, D. B., & Homant, R. J. (2003). Evaluation of an individualized treatment program for adolescent shoplifters. *Adolescence, 38*, 725–733.

Kempf, K. L. (1993). The empirical status of Hirschi's social control theory. In F. Adler & W. S. Lauder (Eds.), *Directions in criminological research* (Vol. 4). New Brunswick, NJ: Transaction.

Kennedy, D. M. (1998). Pulling levers: Getting deterrence right. *National Institute of Justice Journal, 236*, 2–8.

Kennedy, D. M., Piehl, A. M., & Braga, A. A. (1996). *Youth gun violence in Boston: Gun markets, serious youth offenders, and a use reduction strategy* (Research in Brief). Washington, DC: U.S. Department of Justice, National Institute of Justice.

Kent v. U.S., 383 U.S. 541 (1966).

Kerns, K. A., Aspelmeier, J. E., Gentzler, A. L., & Grabill, C. M. (2001). Parent–child attachment and monitoring in middle childhood. *Journal of Family Psychology, 15*, 69–81.

Kiang, L., Moreno, A. J., & Robinson, J. L. (2004). Maternal preconceptions about parenting predict child temperament, maternal sensitivity, and children's empathy. *Developmental Psychology, 40*, 1081–1092.

Kilgore, K., Snyder, J., & Lentz, C. (2000). The contribution of parental discipline, parental monitoring, and school risk to early-onset conduct problems in African American boys and girls. *Developmental Psychology, 36*, 835–845.

Kim-Cohen, J., Moffitt, T. E., Caspi, A., & Taylor, A. (2004). Genetic and environmental processes in young children's resilience and vulnerability to socioeconomic deprivation. *Child Development, 75*, 651–668.

King, C. H. (1975). The ego and the integration of violence in homicidal youth. *American Journal of Orthopsychiatry, 45*, 134–144.

Kitzmann, K. M., Gaylord, N. K., Holt, A. R., & Kenney, E. D. (2003). Child witness to domestic violence: A meta-analytic review. *Journal of Consulting and Clinical Psychology, 71*, 339–352.

Kleber, H. D. (1988). Epidemic cocaine abuse: America's present, Britain's future. *British Journal of Addiction, 83*, 1359–1371.

Klein, M. (1971). *Street gangs and street workers*. Englewood Cliffs, NJ: Prentice Hall.

Klein, M. W. (1995). *The American street gang*. New York: Oxford University Press.

Klein, M. W., & Maxson, C. L. (1996, April). *Gang structures, crime patterns, and police responses* (Document #188511). Washington, DC: U.S. Department of Justice.

Klein, M. W., & Maxson, C. L. (2006). *Street gang patterns and policies*. Oxford, UK: Oxford University Press.

Klein, M., Maxson, C. L., & Cunningham, L. C. (1988). *Gang involvement in cocaine 'rock' trafficking*. Project Summary/Final Report, Center for Research and Crime Control, Social Science

Research Institute, University of Southern California, Los Angeles.

Klein, M. W., Weerman, F. M., & Thornberry, T. (2006). Street gang violence in Europe. *European Journal of Criminology, 3*, 413–437.

Klemke, L. W. (1978). Does apprehension for shoplifting amplify or terminate shoplifting activity? *Law & Society Review, 12*, 391–403.

Klemke, L. W. (1982). Exploring adolescent shoplifting. *Sociology and Social Research, 67*, 59–75.

Klemke, L. W. (1992). *The sociology of shoplifting: Boosters and snitches today*. Wesport, CT: Praeger.

Knight, R. A., & Prentky, R. A. (1993). Exploring characteristics for classifying juvenile offenders. In H. E. Barbaree, W. I. Marshall, & S. M. Hudson (Eds.), *The juvenile sex offender*. New York: Guilford.

Kochanska, G. (1998). Mother–child relationship, child fearfulness, and emerging attachment: A short-term longitudinal study. *Developmental Psychology, 34*, 480–490.

Kochanska, G., & Aksan, N. (1995). Mother–child mutually positive affect, the quality of child compliance to requests and prohibitions, and maternal control as correlates of early internalization. *Child Development, 66*, 236–254.

Kochanska, G., Aksan, N., & Carlson, J. J. (2005). Temperament, relationships, and young children's receptive cooperation with their parents. *Developmental Psychology, 41*, 648–660.

Kochanska, G., Coy, K. C., & Murray, K. T. (2001). The development of self-regulation in the first four years of life. *Child Development, 72*, 1091–1111.

Kochanska, G., Friesenborg, A. E., Lange, L. A., & Martel, M. M. (2004). Parents' personality and infants' temperament as contributors to their emerging relationship. *Journal of Personality and Social Psychology, 86*, 744–759.

Kochanska, G., Murray, K., & Coy, K. (1997). Inhibitory control as a contributor to conscience in childhood: From toddler to early school age. *Child Development, 68*, 263–277.

Kohn, M. L. (1977). *Class and conformity: A study in values* (2nd ed.). Chicago: University of Chicago Press.

Koivisto, H., & Haapasalo, J. (1996). Childhood maltreatment and adulthood in psychopathy in light of file-based assessments among mental state examinees. *Studies on Crime and Crime Prevention, 5*, 91–104.

Kolko, D. (Ed.). (2002). *Handbook on firesetting in children and youth*. Boston, MA: Academic Press.

Kolko, D. J., & Kazdin, A. E. (1986). A conceptualization of firesetting in children and adolescents. *Journal of Abnormal Child Psychology, 14*, 49–62.

Kolko, D. J., & Kazdin, A. E. (1989). The children's firesetting interview with psychiatrically referred and nonreferred children. *Journal of Abnormal Child Psychology, 17*, 609–624.

Kornhauser, R. R. (1978). *Social sources of delinquency: An appraisal of analytic models*. Chicago: University of Chicago Press.

Kosson, D. S., Cyterski, T. D., Steverwald, B. L., Neuman, C. S., & Walker-Matthes, S. (2002). The reliability and validity of the Psychopathy Checklist: Youth Version (PCL:YV) in nonincarcerated adolescent males. *Psychological Assessment, 14*, 97–109.

Kraemer, H. C., Yesavage, J. A., Taylor, J. L., & Kupfer, D. (2000). How can we learn about developmental processes from cross-sectional studies, or can we? *American Journal of Psychiatry, 157*, 163–171.

Krasnovsky, T., & Lane, R. (1998). Shoplifting: A review of the literature. *Aggression and Violent Behavior, 3*, 219–235.

Kratcoski, P. C., & Kratcoski, L. D. (1996). *Juvenile delinquency* (4th ed.). Upper Saddle River, NJ: Prentice Hall.

Kratzer, L., & Hodgins, S. (1999). A typology of offenders: A test of Moffitt's theory among males and females from childhood to age 30. *Criminal Behaviour and Mental Health, 9*, 57–73.

Krisberg, B., & Howell, J. C. (1998). The impact of the juvenile justice system and prospects for graduated sanctions in a comprehensive strategy. In R. Loeber & D. P. Farrington (Eds.), *Serious & violent juvenile offenders: Risk factors and successful interventions*. Thousand Oaks, CA: Sage.

Krisberg, B., & Schwartz, I. (1983). Rethinking juvenile justice. *Crime and Delinquency, 29*, 333–364.

Krisberg, B., Schwartz, I. M., Litsky, P., & Austin, J. (1986). The watershed of juvenile justice reform. *Crime & Delinquency, 32*, 5–38.

Krohn, M. D., Akers, R. L., Radosevich, M. J., & Lanza-Kaduce, L. (1982). Norm qualities and adolescent drinking and drug behavior: The effects of norm quality and reference group on using and abusing alcohol and marijuana. *Journal of Drug Issues, 4*, 343–360.

Krohn, M. D., Thornberry, T. P., Rivera, C., & Le Blanc, M. (2001). Later delinquency careers. In R. Loeber & D. P. Farrington (Eds.), *Child delinquents: Development, intervention, and service needs*. Thousand Oaks, CA: Sage.

Kruh, I. P., Frick, P. J., & Clements, C. B. (2005). Historical and personality correlates to the violence patterns of juveniles tried as adults. *Criminal Justice and Behavior, 32*, 69–96.

Kuby, R. W., & Csikszentmihalyi, M. (1990). *Television and the quality of life: How viewing shapes everyday experience*. Hillsdale, NJ: Erlbaum.

Kumpfer, K. L., & Tait, C. M. (2000, April). *Family skills training for parents and children.* Washington, DC: U.S. Department of Justice, Office of Juvenile Justice and Delinquency Prevention.

Kuperman, S., Schlosser, S. S., Lidral, J., & Reich, W. (1999). Relationship of child psychopathology to parental alcoholism and antisocial personality disorder. *Journal of the American Academy of Child and Adolescent Psychiatry, 38,* 686–692.

Lacourse, E., Côté, S., Nagin, D. S., Vitaro, F., Brendgen, M., & Tremblay, R. E. (2002). A longitudinal-experimental approach to testing theories of antisocial behavior development. *Development and Psychopathology, 14,* 909–924.

Lacourse, E., Nagin, D., Tremblay, R. E., Vitaro, F., & Claes, M. (2003). Developmental trajectories of boys' delinquent group membership and facilitation of violent behaviors during adolescence. *Development and Psychopathology, 15,* 183–197.

Ladd, G. W., Birch, S. H., & Buhs, E. S. (1999). Children's social and scholastic lives in kindergarten: Related spheres of influence? *Child Development, 70,* 1373–1400.

Lagattuta, K. H., & Wellman, H. M. (2002). Differences in early parent–child conversations among negative versus positive emotions: Implications for the development of psychological understanding. *Developmental Psychology, 38,* 564–580.

Lahey, B. B., Gordon, R. A., Loeber, R., Stouthamer-Loeber, M., & Farrington, D. P. (1999). Boys who join gangs: A prospective study of predictors of first gang entry. *Journal of Abnormal Child Psychology, 27,* 261–276.

Lahey, B. B., Loeber, R., Hart, E. L., Frick, P. J., Applegate, B., Zhang, Q., Green, S. M., & Russo, M. (1995). Four-year longitudinal study of conduct disorder in boys: Patterns and predictors of persistence. *Journal of Abnormal Psychology, 104,* 83–93.

Lahey, B. B., Schwab-Stone, M., Goodman, S. H., Waldman, I. D., Canino, G., Rathouz, P. J., et al. (2000). Age and gender differences in oppositional behavior and conduct problems: A cross-sectional household study of middle childhood and adolescence. *Journal of Abnormal Psychology, 109,* 488–503.

Lahey, B. B., & Waldman, I. D. (2003). A developmental propensity model of the origins of conduct problems during childhood and adolescence. In B. B. Lahey, T. E. Moffitt, & A. Caspi (Eds.), *Causes of conduct disorder and juvenile delinquency.* New York: Guilford.

Laird, R. D., Jordan, K., Dodge, K. A., Pettit, G. S., & Bates, J. E. (2001). Peer rejection in childhood, involvement with antisocial peers in early adolescence, and the development of externalizing problems. *Development and Psychopathology, 13,* 337–354.

Laird, R. D., Pettit, G. S., Bates, J. E., & Dodge, K. A. (2003). Parents' monitoring—Relevant knowledge and adolescents' delinquent behavior: Evidence of correlated developmental changes and reciprocal influences. *Child Development, 74,* 752–768.

Laird, R. D., Pettit, G. S., Dodge, K. A., & Bates, J. E. (2005). Peer relationship antecedents of delinquent behavior in late adolescence: Is there evidence of demographic group differences in developmental processes? *Development and Psychopathology, 17,* 127–144.

Lamb, M. E. (1977). The effects of divorce on children's personality development. *Journal of Divorce, 2,* 163–174.

Lambie, I., McCardle, S., & Coleman, R. (2002). Where there's smoke there's fire: Firesetting behaviour in children and adolescents. *New Zealand Journal of Psychology, 31,* 73–79.

Lamontagne, Y., Boyer, R., Hetu, C., & Lacerate-Lamontagne, C. (2000). Anxiety, significant losses, depression, and irrational beliefs in first-offence shoplifters. *Canadian Journal of Psychiatry, 45,* 63–66.

Lang, S., af Klinteberg, B., & Alm, P.-O. (2002). Adult psychopathy and violent behavior in males with early neglect and abuse. *Acta Psychiatrica Scandinavica, 106,* 93–100.

Langsford, J. E., Dodge, K. A., Pettit, G. S., Bates, J. E., Crozier, I., & Kaplow, J. (2002). Long-term effects of early child physical maltreatment on psychological, behavioral, and academic problems in adolescence: A 12-year prospective study. *Archives of Pediatrics and Adolescent Medicine, 156,* 824–830.

Larson, R. W., & Verma, S. (1999). How children and adolescents spend time around the world: Work, play, and developmental opportunities. *Psychological Bulletin, 125,* 701–736.

Laub, J. H., Nagin, D. S., & Sampson, R. J. (1998). Trajectories of change in criminal offending: Good marriages and the desistance process. *American Sociological Review, 63,* 225–238.

Laucht, M., Esser, G., Baving, L., Gerhold, M., Hoesch, I., Ihle, W., Steigleider, P., et al. (2000). Behavioral sequelae of perinatal insults and early family adversity at 8 years of age. *Journal of the American Academy of Child and Adolescent Psychiatry, 39,* 1229–1237.

Lawrence, R. (1998). *School crime and juvenile justice.* New York: Oxford University Press.

Leaper, C., & Smith, T. E. (2004). A meta-analytic review of gender variations in children's language use: Talkativeness, affiliative speech, and assertive speech. *Developmental Psychology, 40*, 993–1027.

Le Blanc, M., McDuff P., Charlebois, P., & Gagnon, C. (1991). Social and psychological consequences, at 10 years old, of an earlier onset of self-reported delinquency, *Psychiatry: Journal for the Study of Interpersonal Processes, 54*, 133–147.

Lees, J. P., & Newson, L. J. (1954). Family or sibship position of some aspects of juvenile delinquency. *British Journal of Delinquency, 5*, 46–55.

Lemert, E. M. (1951). *Social pathology*. New York: McGraw-Hill.

Lemert, E. M. (1983). Interview with E. M. Lemert, March 16, 1979. In J. H. Laub (Ed.), *Criminology in the making: An oral history*. Boston: Northeastern University Press.

Lengua, L. J., Wolchik, S. A., Sandler, I. N., & West, S. G. (2000). The additive and interactive effects of parenting and temperament in predicting problems of children in divorce. *Journal of Clinical Child Psychology, 29*, 232–244.

Lerner, R. M., Lerner, J. V., Almerigi, J. B., Theokas, C., Phelps, E., et al. (2005). Positive youth development, participation in community youth development programs, and community contributions of fifth-grade adolescents: Findings from the first wave of the 4-H study of positive youth development. *Journal of Early Adolescence, 25*, 17–71.

Letourneau, E. J., & Miner, M. H. (2005). Juvenile sex offenders: A case against the legal and clinical status quo. *Sexual Abuse: A Journal of Research and Treatment, 17*, 293–312.

Leve, L. D., & Chamberlain, P. (2004). Female juvenile offenders: Defining an early-onset pathway for delinquency. *Journal of Child and Family Studies, 13*, 439–452.

Leve, L. D., Kim, H. K., & Pears, K. C. (2005). Childhood temperament and family environment as predictors of internalizing and externalizing trajectories from ages 5 to 17. *Journal of Abnormal Psychology, 33*, 505–520.

Lewis, D. O., Lovely, R., Yeager, C., Ferguson, G., Friedman, M., Sloane, G., Friedman, H., & Pincus, J. H. (1988). Intrinsic and environmental characteristics of juvenile murderers. *Journal of the American Academy of Child and Adolescent Psychiatry, 27*, 582–587.

Lewis, D. O., Moy, E., Jackson, L. D., Aaronson, R., Restifo, N., Serra, S., & Simos, A. (1985). Biopsychological characteristics of children who later murder: A prospective study. *American Journal of Psychiatry, 142*, 1161–1167.

Lewis, M. (1993). The emergence of human emotions. In M. Lewis & J. M. Haviland (Eds.), *Handbook of emotions*. New York: Guilford.

Lexcen, F. J., Vincent, G. M., & Grisso, T. (2004). Validity and structure of a self-report measure of youth psychopathy. *Behavioral Sciences & the Law, 22*, 69–84.

Li, X., Stanton, B., & Feigelman, S. (2000). Impact of perceived parental monitoring on adolescent risk behavior over 4 years. *Journal of Adolescent Health, 27*, 49–56.

Lightsey, O. R., Jr. (2006). Resilience, meaning, and well-being. *The Counseling Psychologist, 34*, 96–107.

Lingren, H. G. (2001). *Dating violence and acquaintance assault*. Lincoln: Nebraska Cooperative Extension, University of Nebraska.

Linver, M. R., Brooks-Gunn, J., & Kohen, D. E. (2002). Family processes as pathways from income to young children's development. *Developmental Psychology, 38*, 719–734.

Lipsey, M. E., & Wilson, D. B. (1998). Effective intervention for serious juvenile offenders: A synthesis of research. In R. Loeber & D. P. Farrington (Eds.), *Serious & violent juvenile offenders: Risk factors and successful interventions*. Thousand Oaks, CA: Sage.

Lipsey, M. E., Wilson, D. B., & Cothern, L. (2000). *Effective intervention for serious juvenile offenders*. Washington, DC: U.S. Department of Justice, Office of Juvenile Justice and Delinquency Prevention.

Lipton, D. N., McDonel, E. C., & McFall, R. M. (1987). Heterosocial perception in rapists. *Journal of Consulting and Clinical Psychology, 55*, 17–21.

Little, M., & Steinberg, L. (2006). Psychosocial correlates of adolescent drug dealing in the inner city: Potential roles of opportunity, conventional commitments, and maturity. *Journal of Research in Crime & Delinquency, 43*, 357–386.

Liu, J., Raine, A., Venables, P. H., & Mednick, S. A. (2004). Malnutrition at age 3 years and externalizing behavior at ages 8, 11, and 17 years. *American Journal of Psychiatry, 161*, 2005–2013.

Liu, J., & Wuerker, A. (2005). Biosocial bases of aggressive and violent behavior—Implications for nursing studies. *International Journal of Nursing Studies, 42*, 229–241.

Lizotte, A., & Sheppard, D. (2001, July). *Gun use by male juveniles: Research and prevention*. Washington, DC: U.S. Department of Justice, Office of Juvenile Justice and Delinquency Prevention.

Lo, L. (1994). Exploring teenage shoplifting behavior: A choice and constraint approach. *Environment and Behavior, 26*, 613–639.

Lochman, J. G., & Conduct Problems Prevention Research Group. (1995). Screening of child behavior problems for prevention programs at school entry. *Journal of Consulting and Clinical Psychology, 63*, 549–559.

Loeber, R. (1988). Natural histories of conduct problems, delinquency, and associated substance use:

Evidence for developmental progressions. In B. B. Lahey & A. E. Kazdin (Eds.), *Advances in clinical child psychology* (Vol. 11). New York: Plenum Press.

Loeber, R. (1990). Development and risk factors of juvenile antisocial behavior and delinquency. *Clinical Psychology Review, 10,* 1–41.

Loeber, R., Burke, J. D., Lahey, B. B., Winters, A., & Zera, M. (2000). Oppositional defiant and conduct disorder: A review of the past ten years, Part I. *Journal of the American Academy of Child and Adolescent Psychiatry, 39,* 1468–1484.

Loeber, R., & Farrington, D. P. (2000). Young children who commit crime: Epidemiology, development origins, risk factors, early interventions, and policy implications. *Development and Psychopathology, 12,* 737–762.

Loeber, R., & Farrington, D. P. (2001). The significance of child delinquency. In R. Loeber & D. P. Farrington (Eds.), *Child delinquents: Development, intervention, and service needs.* Thousand Oaks, CA: Sage.

Loeber, R., Farrington, D. P., & Petechuk, D. (2003, May). Child delinquency: Early intervention and prevention. *Child Delinquency Bulletin Series.* Washington, DC: U.S. Department of Justice, Office of Juvenile Justice and Delinquency Prevention.

Loeber, R., Farrington, D. P., Stouthamer-Loeber, M., & Van Kammen, W. B. (1998). *Antisocial behavior and mental health problems: Explanatory factors in childhood and adolescence.* Mahwah, NJ: Erlbaum.

Loeber, R., Farrington, D. P., & Waschbush, D. A. (1998). Serious and violent juvenile offenders. In R. Loeber & D. P. Farrington (Eds.), *Serious & violent juvenile offenders: Risk factors and successful interventions.* Thousand Oaks, CA: Sage.

Loeber, R., Lacourse, E., & Homish, D. L. (2005). Homicide, violence, and developmental trajectories. In R. E. Tremblay, W. W. Hartup, & J. Archer (Eds.), *Developmental origins of aggression.* New York: Guilford.

Loeber, R., Slot, N. W., & Stouthamer-Loeber, M. (2006). A three-dimensional, cumulative development model of serious delinquency. In P.-O. H. Wikström & R. J. Sampson (Eds.), *The explanation of crime: Context, mechanisms and development.* New York: Cambridge University Press.

Loeber, R., & Stouthamer-Loeber, M. (1986). Family factors as correlates and predictors of juvenile conduct problems and delinquency. In N. Morris & M. Tonry (Eds.), *Crime and justice: An annual review of research* (Vol. 7). Chicago: University of Chicago Press.

Loeber, R., & Stouthamer-Loeber, M. (1998). Development of juvenile aggression and violence: Some common misconceptions and controversies. *American Psychologist, 53,* 242–259.

Loney, B. R., Frick, P. J., Clements, C. B., Ellis, M. L., & Kerlin, K. (2003). Callous-unemotional traits, impulsivity, and emotional processing in antisocial adolescents. *Journal of Clinical Child and Adolescent Psychology, 32,* 66–80.

Longshore, D., Chang, E., Hsieh, S., & Messina, N. (2004). Social control and social bonds: A combined control perspective on deviance. *Crime & Delinquency, 50,* 542–564.

Longshore, D., & Turner, S. (1998). Self-control and criminal opportunity: Cross-sectional tests of the general theory of crime. *Criminal Justice and Behavior, 25,* 81–98.

Lorber, M. F. (2004). Psychophysiology of aggression, psychopathy, and conduct problems: A meta-analysis. *Psychological Bulletin, 130,* 531–552.

Lösel, F., & Bender, D. (2003). Protective factors and resilience. In D. P. Farrington & J. W. Coid (Eds.), *Early prevention of adult antisocial behaviour.* Cambridge, UK: Cambridge University Press.

Loth, E. A., & Heggen, K. (2003). A study of resilience in young Ethiopian famine survivors. *Journal of Transcultural Nursing, 14,* 313–320.

Lou, H. H. (1927). *Juvenile courts in the United States.* New York: Arno.

Loukas, A., Zucker, R. A., Fitzgerald, H. F., & Krull, J. L. (2003). Developmental trajectories of descriptive behavior problems among sons of alcoholics: Effects of parent psychopathology, family conflict, and child undercontrol. *Journal of Abnormal Psychology, 112,* 119–131.

Lovett, B. J., & Sheffield, R. A. (2007). Affective empathy deficits in aggressive children and adolescents: A critical review. *Clinical Psychology Review, 27,* 1–13.

Lubenow, G. (1983, June 27). When kids kill their parents. *Newsweek,* pp. 35–36.

Luk, E. S. L., Staiger, P. K., Wong, L., & Mathai, J. (1999). Children who are cruel to animals—a revisit. *Australian and New Zealand Journal of Psychiatry, 33,* 29–36.

Luthar, S. S., Cicchetti, D., & Becker, B. (2000). The construct of resilience: A critical evaluation and guidelines for future work. *Child Development, 71,* 543–562.

Lykken, D. T. (1957). A study of anxiety in the sociopathic personality. *Journal of Abnormal and Social Psychology, 55,* 6–10.

Lykken, D. T. (1995). *The antisocial personalities.* Hillsdale, NJ: Erlbaum.

Lynam, D. R. (1996). The early identification of chronic offenders: Who is the fledgling psychopath? *Psychological Bulletin, 120,* 209–234.

Lynam, D. R. (1997). Pursuing the psychopath: Capturing the fledgling psychopath in a nomological net. *Journal of Abnormal Psychology, 106*, 425–438.

Lynam, D. R. (1998). Early identification of the fledgling psychopath: Locating the psychopathic child in the current nomenclature. *Journal of Abnormal Psychology, 107*, 566–575.

Lynam, D. R. (2002). Fledging psychopathy: A view from personality theory. *Law and Human Behavior, 26*, 255–259.

Lynam, D. R., Capi, A., Moffitt, T. E., Raine, A., Loeber, R., & Stouthamer-Loeber, M. (2005). Adolescent psychopathy and the big five: Results from two samples. *Journal of Abnormal Psychology, 33*, 431–443.

Lyons, J. S., Uziel-Miller, N. D., Reyes, F., & Sokol, P. T. (2000). Strengths of children and adolescents in residential settings: Prevalence and associations with psychopathology and discharge placement. *Journal of the American Academy of Child & Adolescent Psychiatry, 39*, 176–181.

Lyubomirsky, S. (2001). Why are some people happier than others? The role of cognitive and motivational processes in well-being. *American Psychologist, 56*, 239–249.

Maccoby, E. E., & Martin, J. A. (1983). Socialization in the context of the family: Parent-child interaction. In P. H. Mussen (Ed.), *Handbook of child psychology: Vol. 4. Socialization, personality, and social development*. New York: Wiley.

MacKenzie, D. L., & Hebert, E. (Eds.). (1995). *Correctional boot camps: A tough intermediate sanction*. Washington, DC: National Institute of Justice.

MacKenzie, D. L., Layton, D., Souryal, C., Sealock, M., & Bin Kashem, M. (2001). Effects of correctional boot camps on offending. *The Annals of the American Academy of Political and Social Sciences, 578*, 126–143.

Magnusson, D. (1981). *Toward a psychology of situations: An interactional perspective*. Hillsdale, NJ: Erlbaum.

Magnusson, D., & Allen, V. L. (1983). Implications and applications of an interactional perspective for human development. In D. Magnusson & V. L. Allen (Eds.), *Human development: An interactional perspective*. New York: Academic Press.

Major, A. K., Egley, A., Jr., Howell, J. C., Mendenhall, B., & Armstrong, T. (2004, March). *Youth gangs in Indian country*. Washington, DC: U.S. Department of Justice, Office of Juvenile Justice and Delinquency Prevention.

Malamuth, N. M., & Brown, L. M. (1994). Sexually aggressive men's perceptions of women's communications: Testing three explanations. *Journal of Personality and Social Psychology, 67*, 699–712.

Males, M. A., & Maccallair, D. (1999). An analysis of curfew enforcement and juvenile crime in California. *Western Criminology Review, 28*, 33–40.

Manian, N., Strauman, T. J., & Denney, N. (1998). Temperament, recalled parental style, and self-regulation: Testing the developmental postulates of self-discrepancy theory. *Journal of Personality and Social Psychology, 75*, 1321–1332.

Marcus, B. (2004). Self-control in the general theory of crime: Theoretical implications of a measurement problem. *Theoretical Criminology, 8*, 33–55.

Marcus, R. F. (1999). A gender-linked exploratory factor analysis of anti-social behavior in young adolescents. *Adolescence, 34*, 33–46.

Marshal, M. P., & Chassin, L. (2000). Peer influence on adolescent alcohol use: The moderating role of parental support and discipline. *Applied Developmental Science, 4*, 80–88.

Marshall, L. A., & Cooke, D. J. (1999). The childhood experiences of psychopaths: A retrospective study of familial and societal factors. *Journal of Personality Disorders, 13*, 211–225.

Masten, A. S. (1994). Resilience in individual development: Successful adaptation despite risk and adversity. In M. C. Wang & E. W. Gordon (Eds.), *Educational resilience in inner-city America: Challenges and prospects*. Hillsdale, NJ: Erlbaum.

Masten, A. S. (2001). Ordinary magic: Resilience processes in development. *American Psychologist, 56*, 227–238.

Masten, A. S., Best, K. M., & Garmezy, N. (1990). Resilience and development: Contributions from the study of children who overcome adversity. *Development and Psychopathology, 2*, 425–444.

Masten, A. S., Burt, K. B., Roisman, G. I., Obradović, J., Long, J. D., & Tellegen, A. (2004). Resources and resilience in the transition to adulthood: Continuity and change. *Development and Psychopathology, 16*, 1071–1094.

Masten, A. S., & Coatsworth, J. D. (1998). The development of competence in favorable and unfavorable environments. *American Psychologist, 53*, 205–220.

Masten, A. S., & Curtis, W. J. (2000). Integrating competence and psychopathology: Pathways toward a comprehensive science of adaptation in development. *Development and Psychopathology, 12*, 529–550.

Masten, A. S., Hubbard, J. J., Gest, S. D., Tellegren, A., Garmezy, N., & Ramirez, M. (1999). Competence in the context of adversity: Pathways to resilience and maladaptation from childhood to late adolescence. *Development and Psychopathology, 11*, 143–169.

Matsueda, R. (1982). Testing control theory and differential association: A causal modeling approach. *American Sociological Review, 47*, 489–504.

Matthews, J. K., Hunter, J. A., & Vuz, I. (1997). Juvenile female sexual offenders: Clinical characteristics and treatment issues. *Sexual Abuse: A Journal of Research and Treatment, 9*, 187–199.

Maughan, B., Pickles, A., Rowe, R., Costello, E. J., & Angold, A. (2000). Developmental trajectories of aggressive and non-aggressive conduct disorder. *Journal of Quantitative Criminology, 16*, 199–221.

Maxson, C., & Klein, M. W. (1995). Investigating gang structures. *Journal of Gang Research, 3*, 33–40.

Maxwell, C. D., Robinson, A. L., & Post, L. A. (2003). The nature and predictors of sexual victimization and offending among adolescents. *Journal of Youth and Adolescence, 32*, 465–478.

Maxwell, J. C. (2004). *Patterns of club drug use in the U.S., 2004.* Austin, TX: Center for Excellence in Drug Epidemiology, Gulf Coast Addiction Technology Transfer Center, University of Texas.

Mayfield, M. G., & Widom, C. S. (1996). The cycle of violence. *Archives of Pediatric and Adolescent Medicine, 150*, 390–395.

Mazerolle, P., Brame, R., Paternoster, R., Piquero, A., & Dean, C. (2000). Onset age, persistence, and offending versatility: Comparisons across gender. *Criminology, 38*, 1143–1172.

Mazerolle, P., Piquero, A. R., & Capowich, G. E. (2003). Examining the links between strain, situational and dispositional anger, and crime: Further specifying and testing general strain theory. *Youth & Society, 35*, 131–157.

Mazulis, A. H., Hyde, J. S., & Clark, R. (2004). Father involvement moderates the effect of maternal depression during a child's infancy on child behavior problems in kindergarten. *Journal of Family Psychology, 18*, 575–588.

McCabe, K. M., Rodgers, C., Yeh, M., & Hough, R. (2004). Gender differences in childhood onset conduct disorder. *Development and Psychopathology, 16*, 179–192.

McClelland, G. M., Teplin, L. A., & Abram, K. M. (2004, June). Detection and prevalence of substance abuse among juvenile detainees. *Juvenile Justice Bulletin.* Washington, DC: Office of Justice Programs, Office of Juvenile Justice and Delinquency Prevention.

McCluskey, C. P., Krohn, M. D., Lizotte, A. J., & Rodriguez, M. L. (2002). Early substance use and school achievement: An examination of Latino, White, and African American youth. *Journal of Drug Issues, 32*, 921–944.

McCord, W., & McCord, J. (1959/1964). *The psychopath: An essay on the criminal mind.* Princeton, NJ: Van Nostrand.

McCord, W., McCord, J., & Zola, I, K. (1959). *Origins of crime: A new evaluation of the Cambridge-Somerville Youth Study.* New York: Columbia University Press.

McCrae, R. R., & Costa, P. T. (1990). *Personality in adulthood.* New York: Guilford.

McDermott, P. A. (1996). A nationwide study of developmental and gender prevalence for psychopathology in childhood and adolescence. *Journal of Abnormal Child Psychology, 24*, 53–66.

McDougall, P., Hymel, S., Vaillancourt, T., & Mercer, L. (2001). The consequences of childhood peer rejection. In M. R. Leary (Ed.), *Interpersonal rejection.* London: Oxford University Press.

McDowall, D., Loftin, C., & Wiersema, B. (2000). The impact of youth curfew laws on juvenile crime rates. *Crime & Delinquency, 46*, 76–91.

McFadyen-Ketchum, S. A., Bates, J. E., Dodge, K. A., & Pettit, G. S. (1996). Patterns of change in early childhood aggressive-disruptive behavior: Gender differences in predictions from early coercive and affectionate mother–child interactions. *Child Development, 67*, 2417–2433.

McGloin, J. M., & Widom, C. S. (2001). Resilience among abused and neglected children grown up. *Development and Psychopathology, 13*, 1021–1038.

McKnight, L. R., & Loper, A. B. (2002). The effect of risk and resilience factors on the prediction of delinquency in adolescent girls. *School Psychology International, 23*, 186–198.

McLoyd, V. C. (1998). Socioeconomic disadvantage and child development. *American Psychologist, 53*, 185–204.

Meade, M. A., & Slesnick, N. (2002). Ethical considerations for research and treatment with runaway and homeless adolescents. *The Journal of Psychology, 136*, 449–464.

Meaney, M. J. (2001). Maternal care, gene expression, and the transmission of individual differences in stress reactivity across generations. *Annual Review of Neuroscience, 24*, 1161–1192.

Mechoulam, R. (1970). Marihuana chemistry. *Science, 168*, 1159–1166.

Mechoulam, R., & Golan, D. (1998). Comment on "Health Aspects of Cannabis: Revisited" (Hollister). *International Journal of Neuropsychopharmacology, 1*, 83–85.

Mednick, S. A., & Kandel, E. S. (1988). Congenital determinants of violence. *Bulletin of the*

American Academy of Psychiatry and the Law, 16, 101–109.

Meisels, S. J. (1992). Doing harm by doing good: Iatrogenic effects of early childhood enrollment and promotion policies. *Early Childhood Research Quarterly, 7*, 155–174.

Mellor, B., MacRae, L., Pauls, M., & Hornick, J. P. (2005, September). *Youth gangs in Canada: A preliminary review of programs and services.* Calgary, Alberta: Canadian Research Institute for Law and the Family.

Melnick, S. M., & Hinshaw, S. P. (1996). What they want and what they get: The social goals of boys with ADHD and comparison boys. *Journal of Abnormal Child Psychology, 24*, 169–185.

Merton, R. K. (1938). Social structure and anomie. *American Sociological Review, 3*, 672–682.

Merz-Perez, L., Heide, K. M., & Silverman, I. J. (2001). Childhood cruelty to animals and subsequent violence against humans. *International Journal of Offender Therapy and Comparative Criminology, 45*, 556–573.

Meschke, L. L., & Patterson, J. M. (2003). Resilience as a theoretical basis for substance abuse prevention. *The Journal of Primary Prevention, 23*, 483–514.

Messinger, D. S., & Lester, B. M. (2007). Prenatal substance exposure and human development. In A. Fogel, B. J. King, & S. Shanker (Eds.), *Council on Human Development, Bethesda, MD.* Cambridge, UK: Cambridge University Press.

Miczek, K. A., DeBold, J. F., Haney, M., Tidey, J., Vivian, J., & Weerts, E. M. (1994). Alcohol, drugs of abuse, aggression, and violence. In A. J. Reiss & J. A. Roth (Eds.), *Understanding and preventing violence: Vol. 3. Social influences.* Washington, DC: National Academy Press.

Mihalic, S., Irwin, K., Elliott, D., Fagan, A., & Hansen, D. (2001). *Blueprints for violence prevention.* Washington, DC: U.S. Department of Justice, Office of Juvenile Justice and Delinquency Prevention.

Mikami, A. Y., & Hinshaw, S. P. (2006). Resilient adolescent adjustment among girls: Buffers of childhood peer rejection and attention-deficit/hyperactivity disorder. *Journal of Abnormal Child Psychology, 34*, 825–839.

Miller, J. (2001). *One of the guys: Girls, gangs, and gender.* New York: Oxford University Press.

Miller, J. D., Lynam, D. R., Widiger, T. A., & Leukefeld, C. (2001). Personality disorders as extreme variants of common personality dimensions. Can the five-factor model of personality adequately represent psychopath? *Journal of Personality, 69*, 253–276.

Miller, P. A., & Eisenberg, N. (1988). The relation of empathy to aggressive and externalizing/antisocial behavior. *Psychological Bulletin, 103*, 324–344.

Miller, W. B. (1975). *Violence by youth gangs and youth groups as a crime problem in major American cities.* Washington, DC: U.S. Department of Justice, Office of Juvenile Justice and Delinquency Prevention.

Miller, W. B. (1992). *Crime by youth gangs and groups in the United States.* Washington, DC: Department of Justice, Office of Justice Programs, Office of Juvenile Justice and Delinquency Prevention.

Miller-Johnson, S., Coie, J. D., Maumary-Gremaud, A., Bierman, K., & Conduct Problems Prevention Research Group. (2002). Peer rejection and aggression and early starter models of conduct disorder. *Journal of Abnormal Child Psychology, 3*, 217–230.

Moffitt, T. E. (1990). Juvenile delinquency and attention deficit disorder: Boys' developmental trajectories from age 13 to age 15. *Child Development, 61*, 893–910.

Moffitt, T. E. (1993a). Adolescent-limited and life-course-persistent antisocial behavior: A developmental taxonomy. *Psychological Review, 100*, 674–701.

Moffitt, T. E. (1993b). The neuropsychology of conduct disorder. *Development and Psychopathology, 5*, 135–151.

Moffitt, T. E. (1994). Natural histories of delinquency. In E. Weitekamp & H. J. Kerner (Eds.), *Cross-national longitudinal research on human development and criminal behavior.* Dordrecht, The Netherlands: Kluwer Academic Press.

Moffitt, T. E. (1997). Adolescent-limited and life-course-persistent offending: A complementary pair of developmental theories. In T. Thornberry (Ed.), *Advances in criminological theory: Developmental theories of crime and delinquency.* London: Transaction Press.

Moffitt, T. E. (2003). Life-course-persistent and adolescent-limited antisocial behavior: A 10-year research review and research agenda. In B. B. Lahey, T. E. Moffitt, & A. Caspi (Eds.), *Causes of conduct disorder and juvenile delinquency.* New York: Guilford.

Moffitt, T. E. (2005). The new look of behavioral genetics in developmental psychopathology: Gene–environment interplay in antisocial behaviors. *Psychological Bulletin, 131*, 533–534.

Moffitt, T. E., & Caspi, A. S. (2001). Childhood predictors differentiate life-course-persistent and adolescent-limited pathways among males and females. *Development and Psychopathology, 13*, 355–375.

Moffitt, T. E., & Caspi, A. S. (2006). Evidence from behavioral genetics for environmental contributions to antisocial conduct. In P.-O. H. Wikström & R. J. Sampson (Eds.), *The explanation of crime: Context, mechanisms and development*. New York: Cambridge University Press.

Moffitt, T. E., Caspi, A., Dickson, N., Silva, P., & Stanton, W. (1996). Childhood-onset versus adolescent-onset antisocial conduct problems in males: Natural history from ages 3 to 18. *Development and Psychopathology, 8*, 399–424.

Moffitt, T. E., Caspi, A., Harrington, H., & Milne, B. J. (2002). Males on the life-course-persistent and adolescent-limited antisocial pathways: Follow-up at age 26 years. *Development and Psychopathology, 14*, 179–207.

Moffitt, T. E., Caspi, A., Rutter, M., & Silva, P. A. (2001). *Sex differences in antisocial behaviour: Conduct disorder, delinquency, and violence in the Dunedin Longitudinal Study*. Cambridge, UK: Cambridge University Press.

Moffitt, T. E., Gabrielli, W. F., Mednick, S. A., & Schulsinger, F. (1981). Socioeconomic status, IQ, and delinquency. *Journal of Abnormal Psychology, 90*, 152–156.

Moffitt, T. E., Lynam, D. R., & Silva, P. A. (1994). Neuropsychological tests predicting persistent male delinquency. *Criminology, 33*, 111–139.

Moffitt, T. E., & Silva, P. A. (1988). Self-reported delinquency, neuropsychological deficit, and history of attention deficit disorder. *Journal of Abnormal Child Psychology, 16*, 553–569.

Montagne, B., van Honk, J., Kessles, R. P. C., Frigerio, E., Burt, M., van Zandvoort, M. J. E., Perrett, D. I., & de Haan, E. H. F. (2005). Reduced efficiency in recognizing fear in subjects scoring high on psychopathic personality characteristics. *Personality and Individual Differences, 38*, 5–11.

Montemayor, R. (1978). Men and their bodies: The relationships between body types and behavior. *Journal of Social Issues, 34*, 48–64.

Montgomery, D., Miville, M. L., Winterowd, C., Jeffires, B., & Baysden, M. F. (2000). American Indian college students: An exploration into resiliency factors revealed through personal histories. *Cultural Diversity and Ethnic Minority Psychology, 6*, 387–398.

Moore, J. W., & Hagedorn, J, (2001). *Female gangs: A focus on research*. Washington, DC: U.S. Department of Justice, OJJDP.

Moreland, J. (2000). Toxicity of drug abuse— amphetamine designer drugs (ecstasy): Mental effects and consequences of a single dose. *Tox Letters*, 147–152.

Morgan, A. B., & Lilienfeld, S. O. (2000). A meta-analytic review of the relation between antisocial behavior and neuropsychological measures of executive functions. *Clinical Psychology Review, 20*, 113–136.

Mott, J. (1986). Opioid use and burglary. *British Journal of Addiction, 81*, 671–677.

Mounts, N. S. (2002). Parental management of adolescent peer relationships in context: The role of parenting style. *Journal of Family Psychology, 16*, 58–69.

Mounts, N. S., & Steinberg, L. (1995). An ecological analysis of peer influence on adolescent grade point average and drug use. *Developmental Psychology, 31*, 915–922.

Mulder, R. T., Wells, J. E., Joyce, P. R., Bushnell, J. A. (1994). Antisocial women. *Journal of Personality Disorders, 8*, 279–287.

Mulvey, E. P., Arthur, M. W., & Reppucci, N. D. (1993). The prevention and treatment of juvenile delinquency: A review of the research. *Clinical Psychology Review, 13*, 133–167.

Murphy, G. H., & Clare, C. H. (1996). Analysis of motivation in people with mild learning disabilities (mental handicap) who set fires. *Psychology, Crime, & Law, 2*, 153–164.

Murphy, W. D., Coleman, E. M., & Haynes, M. R. (1986). Factors related to coercive sexual behavior with a nonclinical sample of males. *Violence and Victims, 1*, 255–278.

Murray, J., Janson, C. E., & Farrington, D. P. (2007). Crime in adult offspring of prisoners: A cross-national comparison of two longitudinal samples. *Criminal Justice and Behavior, 34*, 133–149.

Murrie, D. C., & Cornell, D. G. (2000). The Millon Adolescent Clinical Inventory and psychopathy. *Journal of Personality Assessment, 75*, 110–125.

Murrie, D. C., & Cornell, D. G. (2002). Psychopathy screening of incarcerated juveniles: A comparison of measures. *Psychological Assessment, 75*, 110–125.

Murrie, D. C., Cornell, D. G., Kaplan, S., McConville, D., & Levy-Elkon, A. (2004). Psychopathy scores and violence among juvenile offenders: A multi-measure study. *Behavioral Sciences & the Law, 22*, 49–67.

Myers, W. C. (1992). What treatments do we have for children and adolescents who have killed? *Bulletin of the American Academy of Psychiatry and Law, 20*, 47–58.

Myers, W. C. (1994). Sexual homicide by adolescents. *Journal of the American Academy of Child and Adolescent Psychiatry, 33*, 962–969.

Myers, W. C. (2002). *Juvenile sexual homicide*. London: Academic Press.

Myers, W. C. (2004). Serial murder by children and adolescents. *Behavioral Sciences & the Law, 22*, 357–374.

Myers, W. C., & Blashfield, R. (1997). Psychopathology and personality in juvenile sexual homicide offenders. *Journal of the American Academy of Psychiatry and Law, 25*, 497–508.

Myers, W. C., & Mutch, P. J. (1992). Language disorders in disruptive behaviour disordered homicidal youth. *Journal of Forensic Sciences, 37*, 919–922.

Myers, W. C., & Scott, K. (1998). Psychotic and conduct disorder symptoms in juvenile murderers. *Homicide Studies, 2*, 160–175.

Myers, W. C., Scott, K., Burgess, A. W., & Burgess, A. G. (1995). Psychopathology, biopsychosocial factors, crime characteristics, and classification of 25 homicidal youths. *Journal of the American Academy of Child and Adolescent Psychiatry, 34*, 1483–1489.

Nagin, D. S., Farrington, D. P., & Moffitt, T. E. (1995). Life-course trajectories of different types of offenders. *Criminology, 33*, 111–139.

Nagin, D. S., & Land, K. C. (1993). Age, criminal careers, and population heterogeneity: Specification and estimation of a nonparametric, mixed Poisson model. *Criminology, 31*, 163–189.

Nagin, D., & Tremblay, R. E. (1999). Trajectories of boys' physical aggression, opposition, and hyperactivity on the path to physically violent and nonviolent juvenile delinquency. *Child Development, 70*, 1181–1196.

Nasby, W., Hayden, B., & DePaulo, B. M. (1979). Attributional bias among aggressive boys to interpret unambiguous social stimuli as displays of hostility. *Journal of Abnormal Psychology, 89*, 459–468.

National Alliance of Crime Investigators Associations. (2005). *National gang threat assessment.* Washington, DC: U.S. Department of Justice, Bureau of Justice Assistance.

National Center for Education Statistics. (2006). *Executive summary: Indicators of school crime and safety, 2006.* Available at http://www.ojp. usdoj/bjs/absract/iscs05.htm.

National Center for Juvenile Justice. (2003, July). *Juvenile court statistics 1999.* Washington, DC: U.S. Department of Justice, Office of Juvenile Justice and Delinquency Prevention.

National Commission on Marihuana and Drug Abuse. (1972). *Marihuana: A signal of misunderstanding* (Appendix, Vol. 1). Washington, DC: U.S. Government Printing Office.

National Commission on Marihuana and Drug Abuse. (1973). *Drug use in America: Problem in perspective* (2nd report). Washington, DC: U.S. Government Printing Office.

National Council of Juvenile and Family Court Judges. (1993). The revised report from the National Task Force on Juvenile Sexual Offending. *Juvenile and Family Court Journal, 44*, 1–120.

National Gang Crime Research Center. (1997). *Bomb and arson crimes among American gang members: A behavioral science profile.* Peotone, IL: Author.

National Gang Crime Research Center. (2001). *The facts about gang life in America today: A national study of over 4,000 gang members.* Peotone, IL: Author.

National Highway Traffic Safety Administration. (2005, March). *Alcohol involvement in fatal motor vehicle traffic crashes, 2003.* Springfield, VA: Author.

National Institute of Education. (1977). *Violent schools—Safe school: The safe school study report to the Congress—Executive summary.* Washington, DC: U.S. Department of Health, Education, and Welfare.

National Institute of Mental Health. (1982). *Television and behavior: Ten years of scientific progress and implications for the eighties. Summary Report* (Vol. 1). Washington, DC: U.S. Government Printing Office.

National Institute on Drug Abuse. (1978). Drug abuse and crime. In L. D. Savitz & N. Johnson (Eds.), *Crime in society.* New York: Wiley.

National Institute on Drug Abuse. (2000, June). *Epidemiologic trends in drug abuse.* Rockville, MD: U. S. Government Printing Office.

National Institute on Drug Abuse. (2002). *Methamphetamine: Abuse and Addiction.* Rockville, MD: U.S. Department of Health and Human Services.

National Institute on Drug Abuse. (2004, November). *Cocaine: Abuse and addiction.* Rockville, MD: U.S. Department of Health and Human Services.

National Institute on Drug Abuse. (2005). *Hallucinogens and dissociative drugs.* Rockville, MD: U.S. Department of Health and Human Services.

National Institute on Drug Abuse and University of Michigan. (2005a, December). *Monitoring the Future: 2004 data from in-school surveys of 8th-, 10th-, and 12th-grade students.* Washington, DC: National Institute on Drug Abuse.

National Institute on Drug Abuse and University of Michigan. (2005b, December). *Monitoring the Future national survey results on drug use, 1975–2003: Volume 2. College students & adults ages 19–45.* Washington, DC: National Institute on Drug Abuse.

National Institutes of Health. (1999, June). *NIDA news release: Long-term brain injury from use of ecstasy.* Rockville, MD: National Institute on Drug Abuse.

National Youth Gang Center. (1997). *The facts about gang life in America today: A national study of over 4,000 gang members*. Pestone, IL: Author.

National Youth Gang Center. (2000). *1998 National Youth Gang Survey*. Washington, DC: U.S. Department of Justice, Office of Juvenile Justice and Delinquency Prevention.

National Youth Gang Center. (2001). *Special report of the NGCRC: Preliminary results of project GANGMILL*. Pestone, IL: Author.

National Youth Gang Center. (2002). *Bomb and arson crimes among American gang members: A behavioral science profile*. Pestone, IL: Author.

Needleman, H. L., McFarland, C., Ness, R. B., Fienberg, S. E., & Tobin, M. J. (2002). Bone lead levels in adjudicated delinquents: A case control study. *Neurotoxicology and Teratology, 24*, 711–717.

Neilsen, A., & Gerber, D. (1979). Psychological aspects of truancy in early adolescence. *Adolescence, 41*, 313–326.

Neisser, U., Boodoo, G., Bouchard, T., Boykin, A. W., Brody, N., Ceci, S. J., et al. (1996). Intelligence: Knowns and unknowns. *American Psychologist, 51*, 77–101.

Nelson, C. A., & Bloom, F. E. (1997). Child development and neuroscience. *Child Development, 68*, 970–987.

Nelson, D. R., Hammen, C., Brennan, P. A., & Ullman, J. B. (2003). The impact of maternal depression in adolescent adjustment: The role of expressed emotion. *Journal of Consulting and Clinical Psychology, 71*, 935–944.

Nelson, D. W. (2003). *On adolescent crime: Trend to end fad justice (newsletter)*. Baltimore: Annie E. Casey Foundation.

Nettler, G. (1984). *Explaining crime* (3rd ed.). New York: McGraw-Hill.

Neugebauer, R., Hoek, H. W., & Susser, E. (1999). Prenatal exposure to wartime famine and development of antisocial personality disorder in early adulthood. *Journal of the American Medical Association, 4*, 479–481.

Neumann, C. S., Kosson, D. S., Forth, A. E., & Hare, R. D. (2006). Factor structure of the Hare Psychopathy Checklist: Youth Version (PCL:YV) in incarcerated adolescents. *Psychological Assessment, 18*, 142–154.

Newcomb, A. F., Bukowksi, W. M., & Pattee, L. (1993). Children's peer relations: A meta-analytic review of popular, rejected, neglected, controversial and average sociometric status. *Psychological Bulletin, 113*, 99–128.

Newcomb, M. D., & Bentler, P. M. (1989). Substance use and abuse among children and teenagers. *American Psychologist, 44*, 242–248.

Newman, J. P., MacCoon, D. G., Vaughn, L. J., & Sadeh, N. (2005). Validating a distinction between primary and secondary psychopathy with measures of Gray's BIS and BAS constructs. *Journal of Abnormal Psychology, 114*, 319–323.

Newman, J. P., Schmitt, W. A., & Voss, W. D. (1997). The impact of motivationally neutral cues on psychopathic individuals: Assessing the generality of the response modulation hypothesis. *Journal of Abnormal Psychology, 106*, 563–575.

NICHD Early Child Care Research Network. (2006). Child-care effect sizes for the NICHD study of early child care and youth development. *American Psychologist, 61*, 99–116.

Nigg, J. T. (2001). Is ADHD an inhibitory disorder? *Psychological Bulletin, 127*, 571–598.

Nigg, J. T., & Huang-Pollock, C. L. (2003). An early–onset model of the role of executive functions and intelligence in conduct disorder/delinquency. In B. B. Lahey, T. E. Moffitt, and A. Caspi (Eds.), *Causes of conduct disorder and juvenile delinquency*. New York: Guilford.

Nigg, J. T., Quamma, J. P., Greenberg, M. T., & Kusche, C. A. (1999). A two-year longitudinal study of neuropsychological and cognitive performance in relation to behavioral problems and competencies in elementary school children. *Journal of Abnormal Child Psychology, 27*, 51–63.

Nix, R. L., Pinderhughes, E. E., Dodge, K. A., Bates, J. E., Pettit, G. S., & McFadyen-Ketchum, S. A. (1999). The relation between mothers' hostile attribution tendencies and children's externalizing behavior problems: The mediating role of mothers' harsh discipline practices. *Child Development, 70*, 896–909.

Norland, S., Shover, N., Thornton, W., & James, J. (1979). Intrafamily conflict and delinquency. *Pacific Sociological Review, 22*, 233–237.

Nye, F. I. (1958). *Family relationships and delinquent behavior*. New York: Wiley.

O'Brien, B. S., & Frick, P. J. (1996). Reward dominance: Associations with anxiety, conduct problems, and psychopathy in children. *Journal of Abnormal Child Psychology, 24*, 223–240.

O'Donnell, J., Hawkins, J. D., & Abbott, R. D. (1995). Predicting serious delinquency and substance abuse among aggressive boys. *Journal of Consulting and Clinical Psychology, 63*, 529–537.

Office of Applied Studies. (2004). *Drug abuse warning network, 2003*. Rockville, MD: U.S. Department of Health and Human Services.

Office of National Drug Control Policy. (2000, June). *MDMA*. Washington, DC: Author.

Office of National Drug Control Policy. (2003a, October). *Marijuana*. Washington, DC: Author.

Office of National Drug Control Policy. (2003b, November). *Methamphetamine*. Washington, DC: Author.

Office of National Drug Control Policy. (2004). *Predicting heavy drug use*. Washington, DC: Author.

Office of National Drug Control Policy. (2005, November). *Marijuana*. Washington, DC: Author.

Offord, D. R., Boyle, M. H., & Racine, Y. A. (1991). The epidemiology of antisocial behavior in childhood and adolescence. In D. J. Pepler & K. H. Rubin (Eds.), *The development and treatment of childhood aggression*. Hillsdale, NJ: Erlbaum.

Offord, D. R., Chmura Kraemeer, H., Kazdin, A. E., Jensen, P. S., & Harrington, R. (1998). Lowering the burden of suffering from child psychiatric disorder: Trade-offs among clinical, targeted, and universal interventions. *Journal of the American Academy of Child & Adolescent Psychiatry, 37,* 686–694.

Offord, D. R., Lipman, E. L., & Duku, E. K. (2001). Epidemiology of problem behavior up to age 12 years. In R. Loeber & D. P. Farrington (Eds.), *Child delinquents: Development, intervention, and service needs*. Thousand Oaks, CA: Sage.

Ogloff, J. R., & Wong, S. (1990). Electrodermal and cardiovascular evidence of a coping response in psychopaths. *Criminal Justice and Behavior, 17,* 231–245.

OJJDP. (2005, September 13). Juveniles on probation. *OJJDP Statistical Briefing Book*. Washington, DC: U.S. Department of Justice, Office of Juvenile Justice and Delinquency Prevention.

Olds, D., Hill, P., & Rumsey, E. (1998). *Prenatal and early childhood nurse home visitation*. Washington, DC: U.S. Department of Justice, Office of Juvenile Justice and Delinquency Prevention.

Olson, S. L., Sameroff, A. J., Kerr, D. C. R., Lopez, N. L., & Wellman, H. M. (2005). Developmental foundations of externalizing problems in young children: The role of effortful control. *Development and Psychopathology, 17,* 25–45.

Olsson, C. A., Bond, L., Burns, J. M., Vella-Broderick, D. A., & Sawyer, S. M. (2003). Adolescence resilience: A concept analysis. *Journal of Adolescence, 26,* 1–11.

Olweus, D. (1997). Bully/victim problems in school: Facts and intervention. *European Journal of Psychology of Education, 12,* 495–510.

O'Neill, M. L., Lidz, V., & Heilbrun, K. (2003). Adolescents with psychopathic characteristics in a substance abusing cohort: Treatment process and outcomes. *Law and Human Behavior, 27,* 299–313.

Opland, G. A., Winters, K C., & Stinchfield, R. D. (1995). Examining gender differences in drug-abusing adolescents. *Psychology of Addictive Behaviors, 9,* 167–175.

Ortiz, J., & Raine, A. (2004). Heart rate level and antisocial behavior in children and adolescents: A meta-analysis. *Journal of the American Academy of Child and Adolescent Psychiatry, 43,* 154–162.

Osgood, W. D., O'Malley, P. M., Bachman, G. G., & Johnstone, L. D. (1989). Time trends and urge trends in arrests and self-reported illegal behavior. *Criminology, 27,* 389–415.

O'Toole, M. E. (2000). *The school shooter: A threat assessment perspective*. Quantico, VA: National Center for the Analysis of Violent Crime, Critical Incident Response Group.

Owens, L., Slee, P., & Shute, R. (2000). "It hurts a hell of a lot ..." The effects of indirect aggression on teenage girls. *School Psychology International, 21,* 359–376.

Ozechowski, T. J., & Liddle, H. A. (2000). Family-based therapy for adolescent drug abuse: Knowns and unknowns. *Clinical Child and Family Psychology Review, 3,* 269–298.

Ozer, E. J. (2005). The impact of violence on urban adolescents: Longitudinal effects of perceived school connection and family support. *Journal of Adolescent Research, 20,* 167–192.

Pagani, L., Larocque, D., Vitaro, F., & Tremblay, R. E. (2003). Verbal and physical abuse toward mothers: The role of family configuration, environment, and coping strategies. *Journal of Youth and Adolescence, 32,* 215–222.

Pagani, L. S., Tremblay, R. E., Nagin, D., Zoccolillo, M., Vitaro, F., & McDuff, P. (2004). Risk factor models for adolescent verbal and physical aggression toward mothers. *International Journal of Behavioral Development, 28,* 528–537.

Pagelow, M. D. (1989). The incidence and prevalence of criminal abuse of other family members. In L. Ohlin & M. Tonry (Eds.), *Family violence* (Vol. 11). Chicago: University of Chicago Press.

Park, R. E. K., Burgess, E. W., & McKenzie, R. D. (1928). *The city*. Chicago: University of Chicago Press.

Parker, H., & Newcombe, R. (1987). Heroin use and acquisitive crime in an English community. *British Journal of Sociology, 38,* 331–350.

Parker, J. G., & Asher, S. R. (1987). Peer relations and later personal adjustment: Are low-accepted children at risk? *Psychological Bulletin, 102,* 357–389.

Parks, G. (2000, October). *The High/Scope Perry Preschool Project*. Washington, DC: U.S. Department of Justice, Office of Juvenile Justice and Delinquency Prevention.

Paternoster, R., & Mazerolle, P. (1994). General strain theory and delinquency: A replication and extension. *Journal of Research in Crime & Delinquency, 31*, 235–263.

Patrick, C. J., Zempolich, K. A., & Levenston, G. K. (1997). Emotionality and violent behavior in psychopaths: A biosocial analysis. In A. Raine, P. A. Brennan, D. P. Farrington, & S. A. Mednick (Eds.), *Biosocial bases of violence*. New York: Plenum.

Patterson, G. R. (1982). *Coercive family process*. Eugene, OR: Castalia.

Patterson, G. R. (1986a). The contribution of siblings to training for fighting: A microsocial analysis. In D. Olweus, J. Block, & M. Radke-Yarrow (Eds.), *Development of antisocial and prosocial behavior*. Orlando, FL: Academic Press.

Patterson, G. R. (1986b). Performance models for antisocial boys. *American Psychologist, 41*, 432–444.

Patterson, G. R., DeBaryshe, B. D., & Ramsey, E. (1989). A developmental perspective on antisocial behavior. *American Psychologist, 44*, 329–335.

Patterson, G. R., DeGarmo, D., & Knutson, N. (2000). Hyperactive and antisocial behaviors: Comorbid or two points in the same process? *Developmental and Psychopathology, 12*, 91–106.

Patterson, G. R., Dishion, T. J., & Bank, L. (1984). Family interaction: A process model of deviance training. *Aggressive Behavior, 10*, 253–267.

Patterson, G. R., Reid, J. B., & Dishion, T. J. (1992). *Antisocial boys: A social interactional approach*. Eugene, OR: Castalia.

Patterson, G. R., & Yoerger, K. (2002). A developmental model for early- and late-onset delinquency. In J. B. Reid, G. R. Patterson, & J. J. Snyder (Eds.), *Antisocial behavior in children and adults: A developmental analysis and the Oregon model for intervention*. Washington, DC: American Psychological Association.

Peirce, B. K. (1969/1869). *A half century with juvenile delinquents*. Montclair, NJ: Patterson Smith.

Pennington, B., & Ozonoff, S. (1996). Executive functions and developmental psychopathology. *Journal of Child Psychology and Psychiatry, 37*, 51–87.

Pepler, D. J., Byrd, W., & King, G. (1991). A social-cognitively based social skills training program for aggressive children. In D. J. Pepler & K. H. Rubin (Eds.), *The development and treatment of childhood aggression*. Hillsdale, NJ: Erlbaum.

Pepler, D. J., & Slaby, R. G. (1994). Theoretical and developmental perspectives on youth and violence. In L. D. Eron, J. H. Gentry, & P. Schlegel (Eds.), *Reason to hope: A psychosocial perspective on violence and youth*. Washington, DC: American Psychological Association.

Perkins, D. F., Luster, T., & Jank, W. (2002). Protective factors, physical abuse, and purging from community-wide surveys of female adolescents. *Journal of Adolescent Research, 17*, 377–400.

Peterson, J. B., & Flanders, J. L. (2005). Play and the regulation of aggression. In R. E. Tremblay, W. H. Hartup, & J. Archer (Eds.), *Developmental origins of aggression*. New York: Guilford.

Petraitis, J., Flay, B. R., & Miller, T. Q. (1995). Reviewing theories of adolescent substance abuse: Organizing pieces in the puzzle. *Psychological Bulletin, 117*, 67–86.

Petras, H., Schaeffer, C. M., Ialongo, N., Hubbard, S., Muthén, B., Lambert, S. F., Poduska, J., & Kellam, S. (2004). When the course of aggressive behavior in childhood does not predict antisocial behavior outcomes in adolescence and young adulthood: An examination of potential explanatory variables. *Development and Psychopathology, 16*, 919–941.

Petrila, J., & Skeem, J. L. (2003). Juvenile psychopathy: The debate. *Behavioral Sciences & the Law, 21*, 689–694.

Pettit, G. S., Laird, R. D., Bates, J. E., & Dodge, K. A. (1997). Patterns of after-school care in middle childhood: Risk factors and developmental outcomes. *Merrill-Palmer Quarterly, 43*, 515–538.

Pfiffner, L. J., McBurnett, K., Rathouz, P. J., & Judice, S. (2005). Family correlates of oppositional and conduct disorders in children with attention deficit/hyperactivity disorder. *Journal of Abnormal Child Psychology, 33*, 551–563.

Phillips, D., Voran, M., Kisker, E., Howes, C., & Whitbook, M. (1994). Childcare for children in poverty: Opportunity or inequity? *Child Development, 65*, 472–492.

Pine, D. S., Shaffer, D., Schonfeld, I. S., & Davies, M. (1997). Minor physical anomalies: Modifiers of environmental risk for psychiatric impairment? *Journal of the American Academy of Child and Adolescent Psychiatry, 36*, 1187–1194.

Piquero, A. R., & Hickman, M. (2003). Extending Tittle's control balance theory to account for victimization. *Criminal Justice and Behavior, 30*, 282–301.

Plomin, R. (2004). Genetics and developmental psychology. *Merrill-Palmer Quarterly, 50*, 341–352.

Plummer, D. L., & Graziano, W. G. (1987). Impact of grade retention on the social development of elementary school children. *Developmental Psychology, 23*, 267–275.

Pollard, J. A., Hawkins, D., & Arthur, M. W. (1999). Risk and protection: Are both necessary to understand diverse behavioral outcomes in adolescence? *Social Work Research, 23*, 145–158.

Porter, S., Birt, A. R., & Boer, D. P. (2001). Investigation of the criminal and conditional release histories of Canadian federal offenders as a function of psychopathy and age. *Law and Human Behavior, 25,* 647–661.

Porter, S., Fairweather, D., Drugge, J., Herve, H., Birt, A. R., & Boer, D. (2000). Profiles of psychopathy in incarcerated sexual offenders. *Criminal Justice and Behavior, 27,* 216–233.

Posner, J. K., & Rothbart, M. K. (2000). Developing mechanisms of self-regulation. *Development and Psychopathology, 15,* 185–205.

Posner, J. K., & Vandell, D. L. (1999). After-school activities and the development of low-income urban children: A longitudinal study. *Developmental Psychology, 35,* 868–879.

Prentky, R. A., Harris, B., Frizzell, K., & Righthand, S. (2000). An actuarial procedure of assessing risk in juvenile sex offenders. *Sexual Abuse: A Journal of Research and Treatment, 12,* 71–93.

Prentky, R. A., & Righthand, S. (2003). *Juvenile Sex Offender Assessment Protocol: Manual.* Bridgewater, MA: Justice Resource Institute.

Price, C., & Kunz, J. (2003). Rethinking the paradigm of juvenile delinquency as related to divorce. *Journal of Divorce and Remarriage, 39,* 109–133.

PRIDE Surveys. (2003). *2002–2003 PRIDE surveys national summary, grades 6 through 12.* Bowling Green, KY: Author.

Prinstein, M. J., & La Greca, A. M. (2004). Childhood peer rejection and aggression predictors of adolescent girls' externalizing and health risk behaviors: A 6-year longitudinal study. *Journal of Consulting and Clinical Psychology, 72,* 103–112.

Putnam, C. T., & Kirkpatrick, J. T. (2005, May). Juvenile firesetting: A research overview. *Juvenile Justice Bulletin* (NCJ 207606). Washington, DC: U.S. Department of Justice, Office of Juvenile Justice and Delinquency Prevention.

Puura, K., Almqvist, F., Tamminen, T., Piha, J., Kumpulainen, K., Rasanen, E., Moilanen, I., & Koivisto, A. M. (1998). Children with symptoms of depression—What do adults see? *Journal of Child Psychology and Psychiatry, 29,* 577–585.

Puzzanchera, C. M. (2003a, September). Juvenile court placement of adjudicated youth, 1990–1999. *OJJDP Fact Sheet.* Washington, DC: U.S. Department of Justice, Office of Juvenile Justice and Delinquency Prevention.

Puzzanchera, C. M. (2003b, September). Juvenile delinquency probation caseload, 1990–1999. *OJJDP Fact Sheet.* Washington, DC: U.S. Department of Justice, Office of Juvenile Justice and Delinquency Prevention.

Puzzanchera, C. M., Stahl, A. L., Finnegan, T. A., Tierney, N., & Snyder, H. N. (2004, December). *Juvenile court statistics 2000.* Washington, DC: Office of Juvenile Justice and Delinquency Prevention, National Center for Juvenile Justice.

Quay, H. C. (1965). Psychopathic personality: Pathological stimulation-seeking. *American Journal of Psychiatry, 122,* 180–183.

Quinsey, V. L., Skilling, T. A., Lalumière, M. L., & Craig, W. M. (2004). *Juvenile delinquency: Understanding the origins of individual differences.* Washington, DC: American Psychological Association.

Raine, A. (1993). *The psychopathology of crime: Criminal behavior as a clinical disorder.* San Diego, CA: Academic Press.

Raine, A. (1996). Autonomic nervous system activity and violence. In D. M. Stoff & R. B. Cairns (Eds.), *Aggression and violence: Genetic neurobiological and biological perspectives.* Mahwah, NJ: Erlbaum.

Raine, A. (2002). Biosocial studies of antisocial and violent behavior in children and adults: A review. *Journal of Abnormal Child Psychology, 30,* 311–326.

Raine, A., Brennan, P., & Mednick, S. A. (1997). Interaction between birth complications and early maternal rejection in predisposing individuals to adult violence: Specificity to serious, early-onset violence. *American Journal of Psychiatry, 134,* 1265–1271.

Raine, A., Reynolds, C., Mednick, S. A., Venables, P. H., & Farrington, D. P. (1999). "Is large body size during childhood a risk factor for later aggression?" Reply. *Archives of General Psychiatry, 56,* 284.

Raine, A., Reynolds, C., Venables, P. H., Mednick, S. A., & Farrington, D. P. (1998). Fearlessness, stimulation-seeking, and large body size at age 3 as early predispositions to childhood aggression at age 11 years. *Archives of General Psychiatry, 55,* 745–751.

Raine, A., Venables, P. H., & Williams, M. (1995). High autonomic arousal and electrodermal orienting at age 15 years as protective factors against criminal behavior at age 29 years. *American Journal of Psychiatry, 152,* 1595–1600.

Raine, A., Venables, P. H., & Williams, M. (1996). Better autonomic arousal and faster electrodermal half-recovery time at age 15 years as possible protective factors against crime at age 29 years. *Developmental Psychology, 32,* 624–630.

Ramirez, J. R., Crano, W. D., Quist, R., Burgoon, M., Alvaro, E. M., & Grandpre, J. (2004). Acculturation, familism, parental monitoring, and knowledge as predictors of marijuana and inhalant use in adolescents. *Psychology of Addictive Behavior, 18,* 3–11.

Rankin, J. H. (1983). The family context of delinquency. *Social Problems, 30,* 466–479.

Räsänen, P., Hakiko, H., Isohanni, M., Hodgins, S., Järvelin, M.-R., & Tiihonen, J. (1999). Maternal smoking during pregnancy and risk of criminal behavior among adult male offspring in the Northern Finland 1966 birth cohort. *American Journal of Psychiatry, 156*, 857–862.

Ratner, M. S. (1993). Sex, drugs, and public policy: Studying and understanding the sex-for-crack phenomenon. In M. S. Ratner (Ed.), *Crack pipe as pimp: An ethnographic investigation of sex-for-crack exchanges.* New York: Lexington Books.

Ray, O. (1972). *Drugs, society and human behavior.* St. Louis, MO: C. V. Mosby.

Ray, O. (1983). *Drugs, society and human behavior* (3rd ed.). St. Louis, MO: C. V. Mosby.

Reckless, W. C. (1961). *The crime problem* (2nd ed.). New York: Appleton-Century-Crofts.

Reckless, W. C. (1973). *The crime problem* (5th ed.). New York: Appleton-Century-Crofts.

Reckless, W. C., & Dinitz, S. (1967). Pioneering with self-concept as a vulnerability factor in delinquency. *Journal of Criminal Law, Criminology and Police Science, 63*, 515–523.

Reid, J. B. (1993). Prevention of conduct disorder before and after school entry: Relating interventions to developmental findings. *Development and Psychopathology, 5*, 243–262.

Reiss, A. J., Jr. (1986). Why are communities important in understanding crime? In A. J. Reiss, Jr., & M. Tonry (Eds.), *Communities and crime.* Chicago: University of Chicago Press.

Reiss, A. J., & Rhodes, A. L. (1961). The distribution of juvenile delinquency in the social class structure. *American Sociological Review, 26*, 720–732.

Reitzel, L. R. (2003, January). Sexual offender update: Juvenile sexual offender recidivism and treatment effectiveness. *Correctional Psychologist, 35*(1), 3–4.

Reivich, K., & Shatté, A. (2002). *The resilience factor.* New York: Broadway Books.

Reynolds, K. M., Seydlitz, R., & Jenkins, P. (2000). Do juvenile curfew laws work? A time-series analysis of the New Orleans law. *Justice Quarterly, 17*, 205–230.

Rhee, S. H., & Waldman, I. D. (2002). Genetic and environmental influences on antisocial behavior: A meta-analysis of twin and adoption studies. *Psychological Bulletin, 128*, 490–529.

Rice, M. E., Harris, G. T., Cormier, C. (1992). An evaluation of a maximum security therapeutic community for psychopaths and other mentally disordered offenders. *Law and Human Behavior, 16*, 399–412.

Rick, P. J., Lahey, B. B., Loeber, R., Tannenbaum, L., Van Horn, Y., Christt, M. A. G., et al. (1993). Oppositional defiant disorder and conduct disorder: A meta-analytical review of factor analyses and cross-validation in a clinic sample. *Clinical Psychological Review, 13*, 319–340.

Righthand, S., Prentky, R., Knight, R., Carpenter, E., Hecker, J. E., & Nangle, D. (2005). Factor structure and validation of the Juvenile Sex Offender Assessment Protocol (J-SOAP). *Sexual Abuse: A Journal of Research and Treatment, 17*, 13–30.

Righthand, S., & Welch, C. (2001, March). *Juveniles who have sexually offended: A review of the professional literature.* Washington, DC: U.S. Department of Justice, Office of Juvenile Justice and Delinquency Prevention.

Ritvo, E., Shanok, S. S., & Lewis, D. O. (1983). Firesetting and nonfiresetting delinquents. *Child Psychiatry and Human Development, 13*, 259–267.

Rivera, B., & Widom, C. S. (1990). Childhood victimization and violent offending. *Violence and Victims, 5*, 19–35.

Robbins, E., & Robbins, L. (1964). Arson with special reference to pyromania. *New York State Journal of Medicine, 2*, 795–798.

Robertson, M. J., & Toro, P. A. (1999). Homeless youth: Research, intervention and policy. In L. B. Forsburg & D. L. Dennis (Eds.), *Practical lessons: The 1998 national symposium on homelessness research.* Washington, DC: U.S. Department of Housing and Urban Development, U.S. Department of Health and Human Services.

Robins, C. A., & Martin, S. S. (1993). Gender, styles of deviance, and drinking problems. *Journal of Health and Social Behavior, 34*, 302–321.

Robinson, J. A. L. (2000). Are there implications for prevention research from studies of resilience? *Child Development, 71*, 570–572.

Robinson, J. L., Zahn-Waxler, C., & Emde, R. N. (1994). Patterns of development in early empathic behavior: Environmental and child constitutional influences. *Social Development, 3*, 125–145.

Robinson, J. L., Zahn-Waxler, C., & Emde, R. N. (2001). Relationship context as a moderator of sources of individual differences in empathic development. In R. N. Emde & J. K. Hewitt (Eds.), *Infancy to early childhood: Genetic and environmental influences on development change.* London: Oxford University Press.

Rodman, H., & Grams, P. (1967). Juvenile delinquency and the family: A review and discussion. *Task force report: Juvenile delinquency and youth crime.* Washington, DC: U.S. Government Printing Office.

Roebuck, T. M., Mattson, S. N., & Riley, E. P. (1999). Behavioral and psychosocial profiles of alcohol-exposed children. *Alcoholism, Clinical and Experimental Research, 23*, 1070–1076.

Roeser, R. W., & Eccles, J. S. (2000). Schooling and mental health. In A. J. Sameroff & M. Lewis (Eds.), *Handbook of developmental psychopathology* (2nd ed.). New York: Kluwer Academic/Plenum Press.

Rogers, R. (1996). *Survey of Attitudes and Life Experiences (SALE)*. Unpublished test. University of North Texas, Denton.

Rogers, R., Salekin, R. T., Hill, C., Sewall, K. W., Murdock, M. E., & Neumann, C. S. (2000). The Psychopathy Checklist—Screening Version: An examination of criteria in three forensic samples. *Assessment, 7*, 1–15.

Rogers, R., Vitacco, M. J., Jackson, R. L., Martin, M., Collins, M., & Sewell, K. W. (2002). Faking psychopathy? An examination of response styles with antisocial youth. *Journal of Personality Assessment, 78*, 31–46.

Romano, E., Tremblay, R. E., Boulerice, B., & Swisher, R. (2005). Multilevel correlates of childhood physical aggression and prosocial behavior. *Journal of Abnormal Child Psychology, 33*, 565–578.

Rose, A. J., Swenson, L. P., & Waller, E. M. (2004). Overt and relational aggression and perceived popularity: Developmental differences in concurrent and prospective relations. *Developmental Psychology, 40*, 378–387.

Rosecan, J. S., Spitz, H. I., & Gross, B. (1987). Contemporary issues in the treatment of cocaine abuse. In H. I. Spitz & J. S. Rosecan (Eds.), *Cocaine abuse: New directions in treatment and research*. New York: Brunner/Mazel.

Roth, J. L., & Brooks-Gunn, J. (2003). What exactly is a youth development program? Answers from research and practice. *Applied Developmental Science, 7*, 94–111.

Rothbart, M. K. (1989). Temperament and development. In G. A. Kohnstamm, J. E. Bates, & M. K. Rothbart (Eds.), *Temperament in childhood*. New York: Wiley.

Rothbart, M. K., Ahadi, S. A., & Evans, D. E. (2000). Temperament and personality: Origins and outcomes. *Journal of Personality and Social Psychology, 78*, 122–135.

Rothbart, M. K., & Bates, J. E. (1998). Temperament. In W. Damon & N. Eisenberg (Eds.), *Handbook of child psychology: Vol. 3. Social, emotional, and personality development* (5th ed.). New York: Wiley.

Rothbart, M. K., Derryberry, D., & Posner, M. I. (1994). A psychobiological approach to the development of temperament. In J. E. Bates & T. D. Wachs (Eds.), *Temperament: Individual differences at the interface of biology and behavior*. Washington, DC: American Psychological Association.

Rothman, D. (1971). *The discovery of the asylum*. Boston: Little, Brown.

Rowe, D. C., & Gulley, B. (1992). Sibling effects on substance abuse and delinquency. *Criminology, 35*, 217–233.

Rowe, D. C., Rodgers, D. C., & Meseck-Bushey, S. (1992). Sibling delinquency and the family environment: Shared and unshared influences. *Child Development, 63*, 57–67.

Rubin, K. H., Bukowksi, W., & Parker, J. G. (1998). Peer interactions, relationships, and groups. In W. Damon (Series Ed.) & N. Eisenberg (Vol. Ed.), *Handbook of child psychology: Vol. 3. Social, emotional, and personality development* (5th ed.). New York: Wiley.

Rubin, K. H., Burgess, K. B., Dwyer, K. M., & Hastings, P. D. (2003). Predicting preschoolers' externalizing behaviors from toddler temperament, conflict, and maternal negativity. *Developmental Psychology, 39*, 164–176.

Rubin, K. H., Hastings, P., Chen, X., Stewart, S., & McNichol, K. (1998). Intrapersonal and maternal correlates of aggression, conflict, and externalizing problems in toddlers. *Child Development, 69*, 1614–1629.

Rubin, J. Z., Provenzano, F. J., & Luria, A. (1974). The eye of the beholder: Parents' views on sex of newborns. *American Journal of Orthopsychiatry, 44*, 512–519.

Rubinstein, M., Yeager, C. A., Goodstein, C., & Lewis, D. O. (1993). Sexually assaultive male juveniles: A follow-up. *American Journal of Psychiatry, 150*, 262–265.

Ruchkin, V. (2002). Family impact on violent youth. In R. R. Corrado, R. Roesch, S. D. Hart, & J. K. Gierowski (Eds.), *Multi-problem violent youth: A foundation for comparative research on needs, interventions, and outcomes*. Amsterdam: IOS Press.

Rutherford, A., & McDermott, R. (1976). *National evaluation program: Phase I summary report*. Washington, DC: U.S. Department of Justice.

Rutter, M. (1979). Protective factors in children's responses to stress and disadvantage. In M. W. Kent & J. E. Rolf (Eds.), *Primary prevention of psychopathology: Vol. 3. Social competence in children*. Hanover, NH: University Press of New England.

Rutter, M. (1997). Individual differences and levels of antisocial behavior. In A. Raine & P. A. Brennan (Eds.), *Biological bases of violence*. New York: Plenum.

Rutter, M. (1999). Resilience concepts and findings: Implications for family therapy. *Journal of Family Therapy, 21*, 119–144.

Rutter, M. (2003). Crucial paths from risk indicator to causal mechanism. In B. B. Lahey, T. E. Moffitt, & A. Caspi (Eds.), *Causes of conduct disorder and juvenile delinquency*. New York: Guilford.

Rutter, M. (2005). Commentary: What is the meaning and utility of the psychopathy concept? *Journal of Abnormal Child Psychology, 33*, 499–503.

Rutter, M., & English and Romanian Adoptees (ERA) Study Team. (1998). Developmental catch-up and deficit, following adoption after severe early privation. *Journal of Child Psychology and Psychiatry, 39*, 465–476.

Rutter, M., Giller, H., & Hagell, A. (1998). *Antisocial behavior by young people.* Cambridge, UK: Cambridge University Press.

Ryan, G., Miyoshi, T. J., Metzner, J. L., Krugman, R. D., & Fryer, G. E. (1996). Trends in a national sample of sexually abusive youths. *Journal of the American Academy of Child and Adolescent Psychiatry, 33*, 17–25.

Safe on the Streets Research Team. (1999). *Still running.* London, UK: The Children's Society.

Safe Schools Coalition of Washington State. (1999, January). *Understanding harassment and violence in the schools: A report on the five year violence research project.* Available at http://www.safeschoolscoalition.org.

Salekin, R. T. (2002). Psychopathy and therapeutic pessimism: Clinical lore or clinical reality? *Clinical Psychology Review, 22*, 79–112.

Salekin, R. T. (2006). Psychopathy in children and adolescents: Key issues in conceptualization and assessment. In C. T. Patrick (Ed.), *Handbook of psychopathy.* New York: Guilford.

Salekin, R. T., Brannen, D. N., Zalot, A. A., Leistico, A.-M., & Neumann, C. S. (2006). Factor structure of psychopathy in youth: Testing the applicability of the new four-factor model. *Criminal Justice and Behavior, 33*, 135–157.

Salekin, R. T., & Frick, P. J. (2005). Psychopathy in children and adolescents: The need for a developmental perspective. *Journal of Abnormal Child Psychology, 33*, 403–409.

Salekin, R. T., Leistico, A.-M. R., Trobst, K. K., Schrum, C. L., & Lochman, J. E. (2005). Adolescent psychopathy and personality theory—the interpersonal circumplex: Expanding evidence of a nomological net. *Journal of Abnormal Child Psychology, 33*, 445–460.

Salekin, R. T., Rogers, R., & Machin, D. (2001). Psychopathy in youth: Pursuing diagnostic clarity. *Journal of Youth and Adolescence, 30*, 173–195.

Salekin, R. T., Rogers, R., & Sewell, K. W. (1997). Construct validity of psychopathy in a female offender sample: A multitrait-multimethod evaluation. *Journal of Abnormal Psychology, 106*, 576–585.

Salekin, R. T., Rogers, R., Ustad, K. L., & Sewell, K. W. (1998). Psychopathy and recidivism among female inmates. *Law and Human Behavior, 22*, 109–128.

Salekin, R. T., Ziegler, T. A., Larrea, M. A., Anthony, V. L., & Bennett, A. D. (2003). Predicting psychopathy with two Millon Adolescent psychopathy scales: The importance of egocentric and callous traits. *Journal of Personality Assessment, 80*, 154–163.

Saltaris, C. (2002). Psychopathy in juvenile offenders: Can temperament and attachment be considered as robust developmental precursors? *Clinical Psychology Review, 22*, 729–752.

Salter, D., McMillan, D., Richards, M., Talbot, T., Hodges, J., Arnon, B., et al. (2003). Development of sexually abusive behaviour in sexually victimised males: A longitudinal study. *The Lancet, 361*, 108–115.

Sameroff, A. J., Peck, S. C., & Eccles, J. S. (2004). Changing ecological determinants of conduct problems from early adolescence to early childhood. *Development and Psychopathology, 16*, 873–896.

Sampson, R. J., Raudenbush, S. W., & Earls, F. (1997). Neighborhoods and violent crime: A multilevel study of collective efficacy. *Science, 277*, 918–924.

Sandstrom, M. J., & Zakriski, A. L. (2004). Understanding the experience of peer rejection. In J. B. Kupersmidt & K. A. Dodge (Eds.), *Children's peer relations: From development to intervention.* Washington, DC: American Psychological Association.

Satterfield, J., Swanson, J., Schell, A., & Lee, F. (1994). Prediction of antisocial behavior in attention-deficit hyperactivity disorder boys from aggression/defiance scores. *Journal of the American Academy of Child and Adolescent Psychiatry, 33*, 185–191.

Saunders, E. B., & Awad, G. A. (1991). Adolescent female firesetters. *Canadian Journal of Psychiatry, 36*, 401–404.

Savelsberg, J. J. (1999). Human nature and social control in complex society: A critique of Charles Tittle's control balance. *Theoretical Criminology, 3*, 331–338.

Scarr, S. (1998). American child care today. *American Psychologist, 53*, 95–108.

Schaeffer, C. M., & Borduin, C. M. (2005). Long-term follow-up to a randomized clinical trial of multisystemic therapy with serious and violent juvenile offenders. *Journal of Consulting and Clinical Psychology, 73*, 445–453.

Schaeffer, C. M., Petras, H., Ialongo, N., Poduska, J., & Kellam, S. (2003). Modeling growth in boys' aggressive behavior across elementary school links to later criminal involvement, conduct disorder, and antisocial personality disorder. *Developmental Psychology, 39*, 1020–1035.

Schaffner, L. (1998). Searching for connection: A new look at teenaged runaways. *Adolescence, 33*, 619–626.

Scherer, D. G., Brondino, M. J., Henggeler, S. W., Melton, G. B., & Hanley, J. H. (1994). Multisystemic family preservation therapy: Preliminary findings from a study of rural and minority serious adolescent offenders. *Journal of Emotional and Behavioral Disorders, 2,* 198–206.

Schubot, D. (2001). Date rape prevalence among female high school students in a rural Midwestern state during 1993, 1995, and 1997. *Journal of Interpersonal Violence, 16,* 291–296.

Schwartz, D., & Proctor, L. J. (2000). Community violence exposure and children's social adjustment in the school peer group: The mediating roles of emotion regulation and social cognition. *Journal of Consulting and Clinical Psychology, 68,* 670–683.

Schwartz, H., & Jacobs, J. (1979). *Qualitative sociology: A method to the madness.* New York: Free Press.

Schwartz, I. M. (1989). *(In)justice for juveniles: Rethinking the best interests of the child.* Lexington, MA: Lexington Books.

Schwartz, I. M., & Jackson-Beeck, M., & Anderson, R. (1984). The "hidden" system of juvenile control. *Crime & Delinquency, 30,* 371–385.

Sciarra, D. (1999). Assessment and treatment of adolescent sex offenders: A review from a cross-cultural perspective. *Journal of Offender Rehabilitation, 28,* 103–118.

Seagrave, D., & Grisso, T. (2002). Adolescent development and measurement of juvenile psychopathy. *Law and Human Behavior, 26,* 219–239.

Séguin, J. R., Nagin, D., Asaad, J. M., & Tremblay, R. E. (2004). Cognitive-neuropsychological function in chronic physical aggression and hyperactivity. *Journal of Abnormal Psychology, 113,* 603–613.

Séguin, J., Tremblay, R. E., Boulerice, B., Pihl, R. O., & Harden, P. (1999). Executive functions and physical aggression after controlling for attention deficit hyperactivity disorder, general memory, and IQ. *Journal of Child Psychology and Psychiatry, 40,* 1197–1208.

Seitz, V., Rosenbaum, L. K., & Apfel, N. H. (1985). Effects of family support intervention: A ten-year follow-up. *Child Development, 56,* 376–391.

Serin, R. C., & Preston, D. L. (2001). Managing and treating violent offenders. In J. B. Ashford & B. D. Sales (Eds.), *Treating adult and juvenile offenders with special needs.* Washington, DC: American Psychological Association.

Seto, M. C., & Barbaree, H. E. (1999). Predictors of psychopathy and release outcome in a criminal population. *Psychological Assessment, 2,* 419–442.

Shaw, C. R., & McKay, H. D. (1931). Social factors in juvenile delinquency. In *Report on the causes of crime* (Vol. 2). Washington, DC: National Commission on Law Observance and Enforcement.

Shaw, C. R., & McKay, H. D. (1942). *Juvenile delinquency and urban areas.* Chicago: University of Chicago Press.

Shaw, D. S., Gilliom, M., Ingoldsby, E. M., & Nagin, D. S. (2003). Trajectories leading to school-age conduct problems. *Developmental Psychology, 39,* 189–200.

Shaw, D. S., Owens, E. B., Giovannelli, J., & Winslow, E. B. (2001). Infant and toddler pathways leading to early externalizing disorders. *Journal of the American Academy of Child and Adolescent Psychiatry, 40,* 36–43.

Sheldon, R. G., Tracy, S. K., & Brown, W. B. (2001). *Youth gangs in American society* (2nd ed.). Belmont, CA: Wadsworth/Thomson Learning.

Sheldon, W. H., Hartl, E. M., & McDermott, E. (1949). *Varieties of delinquent youth: An introduction to constitutional psychiatry.* New York: Harper.

Sickmund, M. (2004, June). *Juveniles in corrections* (NCJ 202885). Washington, DC: U.S. Department of Justice, Office of Juvenile Justice and Delinquency Prevention.

Sickmund, M. (2006, June). *Juvenile residential facility census, 2002: Selected findings.* Washington, DC: U.S. Department of Justice, Office of Juvenile Justice and Delinquency Prevention.

Sickmund, M., Sladky, T. J., & Kang, W. (2004, May). *Census of juveniles in residential placement databook.* Washington, DC: Department of Justice.

Silva, P. A. (1990). The Dunedin Multidisciplinary Health and Development Study: A fifteen year longitudinal study. *Pediatric and Perinatal Epidemiology, 4,* 96–127.

Silverthorn, P., & Frick, P. J. (1999). Developmental pathways to antisocial behavior: The delayed-onset pathway in girls. *Development and Psychopathology, 11,* 101–126.

Silverthorn, P., Frick, P. J., & Reynolds, R. (2001). Timing of onset and correlates of severe conduct problems in adjudicated girls and boys. *Journal of Psychopathology and Behavioral Assessment, 23,* 171–181.

Simon, J. B., Murphy, J. J., & Smith, S. M. (2005). Understanding and fostering family resilience. *The Family Journal: Counseling and Therapy for Couples and Families, 13,* 427–436.

Simonelli, C. J., Mullis, T., & Rohde, C. (2005). Scale of negative family interactions: A measure of parental and sibling aggression. *Journal of Interpersonal Violence, 20,* 792–803.

Simons, J. S., Gaher, R. M., Correia, C. J., & Bush, J. A. (2005). Club drug use among college students. *Addictive Behaviors, 30,* 1619–1624.

Sinclair, J. J., Pettit, G. S., Harrist, A. W., Dodge, K. A., & Bates, J. E. (1994). Encounters with aggressive peers in early childhood: Frequency, age differences, and correlates of risk for behaviour problems. *International Journal of Behavioural Development, 17,* 675–696.

Singer, M. I., Miller, D. B., Guo, S., Flannery, D. J., Frierson, T., & Slovack, K. (1999). Contributors to violent behavior among elementary and middle school children. *Pediatrics, 104,* 878–884.

Sipe, R., Jensen, E. L., & Everett, R. S. (1988). Adolescent sexual offenders grown up: Recidivism in young adulthood. *Criminal Justice and Behavior, 25,* 109–124.

Skeem, J. L., & Cauffman, E. (2003). Views of the downward extension: Comparing the youth version of the Psychopathy Checklist with the Youth Psychopathic Traits Inventory. *Behavioral Sciences & the Law, 21,* 737–770.

Skeem, J. L., Monahan, J., & Mulvey, E. P. (2002). Psychopathy, treatment involvement, and subsequent violence among civil psychiatric patients. *Law and Human Behavior, 26,* 577–603.

Skilling, T. A., Quinsey, V. L., & Craig, W. M. (2001). Evidence of a taxon underlying serious antisocial behavior in boys. *Criminal Justice and Behavior, 28,* 450–470.

Slavkin, M. L. (2001). Enuresis, firesetting, and cruelty to animals: Does the ego triad show predictive validity? *Adolescence, 36,* 461–467.

Slep, A. M. S., & O'Leary, S. G. (2005). Parent and partner violence in families with young children: Rates, patterns, and connections. *Journal of Consulting and Clinical Psychology, 73,* 435–444.

Slesnick, N., & Prestopnik, J. (2005). Dual and multiple diagnosis among substance abuse runaway youth. *American Journal of Drug and Alcohol Abuse, 31,* 179–202.

Smart, R. G. (1986). Cocaine use and problems in North America. *British Journal of Criminology, 28,* 109–128.

Smart, R. G., & Adlaf, E. M. (1992). Recent studies of cocaine use and abuse in Canada. *Canadian Journal of Criminology, 34,* 1–13.

Smith, C. P., Alexander, P. S., Kemp, G. L., & Lemert, E. N. (1980). *The national assessment of serious juvenile crime and the juvenile justice system: The need for a rational response* (Vol. 3). Washington, DC: U.S. Government Printing Office.

Smith, D. (1995). *Criminology for social work.* Hampshire, UK: Macmillan.

Smith, E. J. (2006). The strength-based counseling model. *The Counseling Psychologist, 34,* 13–79.

Smith, G. (1999). Resilience concepts and findings: Implications for family therapy. *Journal of Family Therapy, 21,* 154–158.

Smith, T. R. (2004). Low self-control, staged opportunity, and subsequent fraudulent behavior. *Criminal Justice and Behavior, 31,* 542–563.

Snyder, H. N. (2000). *Juvenile arrests 1999.* Washington, DC: U.S. Department of Justice, Office of Juvenile Justice and Delinquency Prevention.

Snyder, H. N. (2001). Epidemiology of official offending. In R. Loeber & D. P. Farrington (Eds.), *Child delinquents: Development, intervention, and service needs.* Thousand Oaks, CA: Sage.

Snyder, H. N. (2005, August). *Juvenile arrests 2003.* Washington, DC: U.S. Department of Justice, Office of Juvenile Justice and Delinquency Prevention.

Snyder, H. N. (2006, December). *Juvenile arrests 2004.* Washington, DC: U.S. Department of Justice, Office of Juvenile Justice and Delinquency Prevention.

Snyder, H. N., Espiritu, R. C., Huizinga, D., Loeber, R., & Petechuk, D. (2003, March). Prevalence and development of child delinquency. *Child Delinquency Bulletin Series* (NCJ193411). Washington, DC: U.S. Department of Justice, Office of Juvenile Justice and Delinquency Prevention.

Snyder, H. N., & Sickmund, M. (1995). *Juvenile offenders and victims: A focus on violence.* Pittsburgh, PA: National Center for Juvenile Justice.

Snyder, J., Cramer, A., Afrank, J., & Patterson, G. R. (2005). The contributions of ineffective discipline and parental hostile attributions of child misbehavior to the development of conduct problems at home and school. *Developmental Psychology, 41,* 30–41.

Snyder, J., & Patterson, G. (1987). Family interaction and delinquent behavior. In H. C. Quay (Ed.), *Handbook of juvenile delinquency.* New York: Wiley.

Snyder, J., Reid, J., & Patterson, G. (2003). A social learning model of child and adolescent antisocial behavior. In B. B. Lahey, T. E. Moffitt, & A. Caspi (Eds.), *Causes of conduct disorder and juvenile delinquency.* New York: Guilford.

Spaccarelli, S., Bowden, B., Coatsworth, J. D., & Kim, S. (1997). Psychosocial correlates of male sexual aggression in a chronic delinquent sample. *Criminal Justice and Behavior, 24,* 71–95.

Spain, S. E., Douglas, K. S., Poythress, N. G., & Epstein, M. (2004). The relationship between psychopathic features, violence and treatment outcomes: The comparison of three youth measures of psychopathic features. *Behavioral Sciences & the Law, 22,* 85–102.

Speltz, M. L., DeKlyen, M., Calderon, R., Greenberg, M. T., & Fisher, P. A. (1999). Neuropsychological characteristics and test behaviors of boys with early onset conduct problems. *Journal of Abnormal Psychology, 108*, 315–325.

Spergel, I. A. (1995). *The youth gang problem.* New York: Oxford University Press.

Stadolnik, R. F. (2000). *Drawn to the flame: Assessment and treatment of juvenile firesetting behavior.* Sarasota, FL: Professional Resources Press.

Stafford, M. (1984). Gang delinquency. In R. F. Meier (Ed.), *Major forms of crime.* Beverly Hills, CA: Sage.

Stahl, A. L. (2006, November). *Delinquency cases in juvenile court, 2002.* Washington, DC: U.S. Department of Justice, Office of Justice Programs.

Stahl, A., Puzzanchera, C., Sladky, A., Finnegan, T., Tierney, N., & Snyder, H. (2006, December). *Juvenile Court Statistics 2001–2002.* Washington, DC: Office of Juvenile Justice and Delinquency Prevention.

Stanger, C., Achenbach, T. M., & Verhulst, F. C. (1997). Accelerated longitudinal comparisons of aggressive versus delinquency syndromes. *Development and Psychopathology, 9*, 43–58.

Stansbury, K., & Zimmermann, L. K. (1999). Relations among child language skills, maternal socialization of emotion regulation, and child behavior problems. *Child Psychiatry and Human Development, 30*, 121–142.

Stattin, H., & Kerr, M. (2000). Parental monitoring: A reinterpretation. *Child Development, 71*, 1072–1085.

Stattin, H., & Klackenberg-Larsson, I. (1993). Early language and intelligence development and their relationship to future criminal behavior. *Journal of Abnormal Psychology, 102*, 369–378.

Stattin, H., & Magnusson, D. (1991). Stability and change in criminal behaviour up to age 30. *The British Journal of Criminology, 31*, 327–346.

Steinberg, A., Brooks, J., & Remtulla, T. (2003). Youth hate crimes: Identification, prevention, and intervention. *American Journal of Psychiatry, 160*, 979–989.

Steinberg, L., Fletcher, A., & Darling, N. (1994). Parental monitoring and peer influences on adolescent substance use. *Pediatrics, 93*, 1060–1064.

Steinberg, L., Len Chung, H., & Little, M. (2004). Reentry of young offenders from the justice system: A developmental perspective. *Youth Violence and Juvenile Justice, 2*, 21–38.

Steinhart, D. J. (1996). Status offenses. *The Juvenile Court, 6*(3), 86–99.

Steinman, K. J. (2005). Drug selling among high school students: Related risk behaviors and psychosocial characteristics. *Journal of Adolescent Health, 36*, 71–79.

Steinmetz, S. K. (1981). A cross-cultural comparison of sibling violence. *International Journal of Family Psychiatry, 2*, 337–351.

Stern, K. R. (2001, May). A treatment study of children with attention deficit hyperactivity disorder. *OJJDP Fact Sheet.* Washington, DC: U.S. Department of Justice, Office of Juvenile Justice and Delinquency Prevention.

Stern, M., & Karaker, K. H. (1989). Sex stereotyping of infants: A review of gender labeling studies. *Sex Roles, 20*, 501–522.

Sternberg, R. J. (1985). *Beyond IQ.* New York: Cambridge University Press.

Sternberg, R. J. (1988). *The triarchic mind: A new theory of human intelligence.* New York: Viking.

Stevens, D., Charman, T., & Blair, R. J. R. (2001). Recognition of emotion in facial expressions and vocal tones in children with psychopathic tendencies. *Journal of Genetic Psychology, 162*, 201–211.

Stickel, T., & Blechman, E. (2002). Aggression and fire: Antisocial behavior in firesetting and non-firesetting juvenile offenders. *Journal of Psychopathology and Behavioral Assessment, 24*, 177–193.

Stone, M. H. (1998). Sadistic personality in murderers. In T. Millon, E. Simonsen, M. Burket-Smith, & R. Davis (Eds.), *Psychopathy: Antisocial, criminal, and violent behavior.* New York: Guilford.

Stouthamer-Loeber, M., Loeber, R., Farrington, D. P., Zhang, Q., van Kammen, W., & Maguin, E. (1993). The double edge of protective and risk factors for delinquency: Interrelations and developmental patterns. *Development and Psychopathology, 5*, 683–701.

Stouthamer-Loeber, M., Loeber, R., Homish, D. L., & Wei, E. (2001). Maltreatment of boys and the development of disruptive and delinquent behavior. *Development and Psychopathology, 13*, 941–955.

Stouthamer-Loeber, M., Wei, E., Loeber, R., & Masten, A. S. (2004). Desistence from persistent serious delinquency in the transition to adulthood. *Development and Psychopathology, 16*, 897–918.

Stowe, R. M., Arnold, D. H., & Ortiz, C. (2000). Gender differences in the relationship of language development to disruptive behavior and peer relationships in preschoolers. *Journal of Applied Developmental Psychology, 20*, 521–536.

Straus, M. A., & Stewart, J. H. (1999). Corporal punishment by American parents: National data on prevalence, chronicity, severity, and duration in relation to child and family characteristics. *Clinical Child and Family Psychology Review, 2*, 55–70.

Stretesky, P. B., & Pogrebin, M. R. (2007). Gang-related gun violence: Socialization, identity, and self. *Journal of Contemporary Ethnography, 36,* 85–114.

Strote, J., Lee, J. E., & Wechsler, H. (2002). Increasing MDMA use among college students: Results of a national survey. *Journal of Adolescent Health, 30,* 64–72.

Substance Abuse and Mental Health Services Administration. (1995, September). *Preliminary estimates from the 1994 national household survey on drug abuse* (Advance Report Number 10). Washington, DC: U.S. Government Printing Office.

Substance Abuse and Mental Health Services Administration. (2005, September). *2004 National Survey on Drug Abuse and Mental Health.* Rockville, MD: U.S. Department of Health and Human Services.

Sullivan, M. L. (2005). Maybe we shouldn't study "gangs": Does reification obscure youth violence? *Journal of Contemporary Criminal Justice, 21,* 170–190.

Surgeon General's Scientific Advisory Committee on Television and Social Behavior. (1972). *Television and growing up: The impact of television violence.* Washington, DC: U.S. Government Printing Office.

Sutherland, E. H. (1973). *On analyzing crime.* Chicago: University of Chicago Press.

Sutherland, E. H., & Cressey, D. R. (1974). *Criminology* (9th ed.). Philadelphia: Lippincott.

Sutton, S. K., Vitale, J. E., & Newman, J. P. (2002). Emotion among women with psychopathy during picture perception. *Journal of Abnormal Psychology, 111,* 610–619.

Swahn, M. H., & Donovan, J. E. (2004). Correlates and predictors of violent behavior among adolescent drinkers. *Journal of Adolescent Health, 34,* 480–492.

Swaim, R. C., Deffenbacher, J. L., & Wayman, J. C. (2004). Concurrent and prospective effects of multi-dimensional aggression and anger on adolescent alcohol abuse. *Aggressive Behavior, 30,* 356–372.

Sykes, G. M., & Matza, D. (1957). Techniques of neutralization: A theory of delinquency. *American Sociological Review, 22,* 664–670.

Szatmari, P., Boyle, M., & Offord, D. R. (1989). ADHD and CD: Degree of diagnostic overlap and difference among correlates. *Journal of the American Academy of Child and Adolescent Psychiatry, 28,* 865–872.

Tannenbaum, F. (1938). *Crime and the community.* Boston: Ginn.

Tappan, P. W. (1949). *Juvenile delinquency.* New York: McGraw-Hill.

Tarolla, S. M., Wagner, E. F., Rabinowitz, J., & Tubman, J. G. (2002). Understanding and treating juvenile offenders: A review of current knowledge and future directions. *Aggression and Violent Behavior, 7,* 125–143.

Taylor, C. (2001). The relationship between social and self-control: Tracing Hirschi's criminological career. *Theoretical Criminology, 5,* 369–388.

Taylor, E. R., Kelly, J., Valescu, S., Reynolds, G. S., Sherman, J., & German, V. (2001). Is stealing a gateway crime? *Community Mental Health Journal, 37,* 347–358.

Tedeschi, R. G., & Kilmer, R. P. (2005). Assessing strengths, resilience, and growth to guide clinical interventions. *Professional Psychology: Research and Practice, 36,* 230–237.

Texas Youth Commission. (2005, January 12). *Agency treatment effectiveness 2004.* Austin, TX: Author.

Thomas, A., & Chess, S. (1977). *Temperament and development.* New York: Brunner/Mazel.

Thomas, B. S. (1996). A path analysis of gender differences in adolescent onset of alcohol, tobacco and other drug use (ATOD): Reported ATOD use and adverse consequences of ATOD use. *Journal of Addictive Disease, 15,* 33–52.

Thomas, W. I., & Znaniecki, F. (1927). *The Polish peasant in Europe and America.* New York: Knopf.

Thompson, K. M., & Braaten-Antrim, R. (1998). Youth maltreatment and gang involvement. *Journal of Interpersonal Violence, 13,* 328–345.

Thompson, R. A., & Nelson, C. A. (2001). Developmental science and the media: Early brain development. *American Psychologist, 56,* 5–15.

Thornberry, T. P. (1987). Toward an interactional theory of delinquency. *Criminology, 25,* 863–891.

Thornberry, T. P. (1998). Membership in youth gangs and involvement in serious and violent offending. In R. Loeber & D. P. Farrington (Eds.), *Serious & violent juvenile offenders: Risk factors and successful interventions.* Thousand Oaks, CA: Sage.

Thornberry, T. P., & Burch, J. H. II. (1997). *Gang members and delinquent behavior.* Washington, DC: U.S. Department of Justice, Office of Juvenile Justice and Delinquency Prevention.

Thornberry, T. P., Huizinga, D., & Loeber, R. (1995). The prevention of serious delinquency and violence: Implication from the program of research on the causes and correlates of delinquency. In J. C. Howell, B. Krisberg, J. D. Hawkins, & J. Wilson (Eds.), *Sourcebook on serious violent and chronic juvenile offenders.* Thousand Oaks, CA: Sage.

Thornberry, T. P., Ireland, T. O., & Smith, C. A. (2001). The importance of timing: The varying impact of childhood and adolescent maltreatment on multiple problem outcomes. *Development and Psychopathology, 13*, 957–979.

Thornberry, T. P., & Krohn, M. (1997). Peers, drug use, and delinquency. In D. M. Stoff, J. Breiling, & J. D. Maser (Eds.), Handbook of antisocial behavior. New York: Wiley.

Thornberry, T. P., & Krohn, M. D. (2001). The development of delinquency: An interactional perspective. In S. O. White (Ed.), *Handbook of law and social science: Youth and justice*. New York: Plenum.

Thornberry, T. P., Krohn, M., Lizotte, A. J., & Chard-Wierschem, D. (1993). The role of juvenile gangs in facilitating delinquent behavior. *Journal of Research in Crime & Delinquency, 30*, 55–87.

Thrasher, F. M. (1927). *The gang: A study of 1,313 gangs in Chicago*. Chicago: University of Chicago Press.

Tiết, Q. Q., & Huizinga, D. (2002). Dimensions of the construct of resilience and adaptation among inner-city youth. *Journal of Adolescent Research, 17*, 260–276.

Tiihonen, J., Hodgins, S., Vaurio, O., Laakso, M., Repo, E., Soininen, H., et al. (2000). Amygdaloid volume loss in psychopathy. *Society for Neuroscience Abstracts, 2017*, 135–144.

Tingle, D., Barnard, G. W., Robbins, L., Newman, G., & Hutchinson, D. (1986). Childhood and adolescent characteristics of pedophiles and rapists. *International Journal of Law and Psychiatry, 9*, 103–116.

Tinklenberg, J. R., & Stillman, R. C. (1970). Drug use and violence. In D. Daniels, M. Gilula, & F. Ochberg (Eds.), *Violence and the struggle for existence*. Boston, MA: Little, Brown.

Tittle, C. R. (1995). *Control balance: Toward a general theory of deviance*. Boulder, CO: Westview.

Tittle, C. R. (2004). Refining control balance theory. *Theoretical Criminology, 8*, 395–428.

Toby, J. (1957). The differential impact of family disorganization. *American Sociological Review, 22*, 505–512.

Tolan, P. H., Gorman-Smith, D., & Henry, D. B. (2003). On developmental ecology of urban males' youth violence. *Developmental Psychology, 39*, 274–279.

Tolan, P. H., & Guerra, N. G. (1994). Prevention of delinquency: Current status and issues. *Applied & Preventive Psychology, 3*, 251–273.

Tolan, P. H., & Thomas, P. (1995). The implications of age of onset for delinquency: II. Longitudinal data. *Journal of Abnormal Child Psychology, 23*, 157–169.

Tolan, P. T. (1966). How resilient is the concept of resilience? *The Community Psychologist, 29*, 12–15.

Tonglet, M. (2002). Consumer misbehavior: An exploratory study of shoplifting. *Journal of Consumer Behaviour, 1*, 336–355.

Tremblay, R. E. (2000). The development of aggressive behaviour during childhood: What have we learned in the past century? *International Journal of Behavioral Development, 24*, 129–141.

Tremblay, R. E. (2003). Why socialization fails: The case of chronic physical aggression. In B. B. Lahey, T. E. Moffitt, & A. Caspi (Eds.), *Causes of conduct disorder and juvenile delinquency*. New York: Guilford.

Tremblay, R. E. (2004). The development of human physical aggression: How important is early childhood? In L. A. Leavitt & D. M. B. Hall (Eds.), *Social and moral development: Emerging evidence on the toddler years*. New Brunswick, NJ: Johnson and Johnson Pediatric Institute.

Tremblay, R. E. (2006). Prevention of youth violence: Why not start at the beginning? *Journal of Abnormal Child Psychology, 34*, 481–487.

Tremblay, R. E., & Craig, W. (1995). Developmental crime prevention. In M. Tonry & D. P. Farrington (Eds.), *Building a safer society: Strategic approaches to crime prevention* (Vol. 19). Chicago: University of Chicago Press.

Tremblay, R. E., Japel, C., Perusse, D., McDuff, P., Boivin, M., Zoccolillo, M., & Montplaisir, J. (1999). The search for the age of "onset" of physical aggression: Rosseau and Bandura revisited. *Criminal Behaviour and Mental Health, 9*, 8–23.

Tremblay, R. E., & LeMarquand, D. (2001). Individual risk and protective factors. In R. Loeber & D. P. Farrington (Eds.), *Child delinquents: Development, intervention, and service needs*. Thousand Oaks, CA: Sage.

Tremblay, R. E., LeMarquand, D., & Vitaro, F. (1999). The prevention of oppositional defiant disorder and conduct disorder. In H. C. Quay & A. F. Hogan (Eds.), *Handbook of disruptive behavior disorders*. New York: Kluwer Academic/Plenum.

Tremblay. R. E., Masse, B., Perron, D., & Leblanc, M. (1992). Early disruptive behavior, poor school achievement, delinquent behavior, and delinquent personality: Longitudinal analyses. *Journal of Consulting and Clinical Psychology, 60*, 64–72.

Tremblay, R. E., Masse, B., Vitaro, F., & Dobkin, P. L. (1995). The impact of friends' deviant behavior on early onset of delinquency: Longitudinal data from 6 to 13 years of age. *Development and Psychopathology, 7*, 649–667.

Tremblay, R. E., Nagin, D. S., Séguin, J. R., Zoccolillo, M., Zelazo, P., Boivin, M., et al. (2004). Physical aggression during early childhood: Trajectories and predictors. *Pediatrics, 114* (1), e43–e50.

Tremblay, R. E., Pagani-Kurtz, L., Masse, L. C., Vitaro, F., & Pihl, R. O. (1995). A bimodal preventive intervention for disruptive kindergarten boys: Its impact through mid-adolescence, *Journal of Consulting and Clinical Psychology, 63*, 560–568.

Tremblay, R. E., Pihl, R. O., Vitaro, F., & Dobkin, P. L. (1994). Predicting early onset of male antisocial behavior from preschool behavior. *Archives of General Psychiatry, 51*, 732–739.

Tremblay, R. E., Vitaro, F., Gagnon, C., Piche, C., & Royer, N. (1992). A prosocial scale for the preschool behaviour questionnaire: Concurrent and predictive correlates. *International Journal of Behavioral Development, 15*, 227–245.

Tugade, M. M., & Frederickson, B. L. (2004). Resilient individuals use positive emotions to bounce back from negative emotional expressions. *Journal of Personality and Social Psychology, 86*, 320–333.

Twenge, J. M., Baumeister, R. F., Tice, D. M., & Stucke, T. S. (2001). If you can't join them, beat them: Effects of social exclusion on aggressive behavior. *Journal of Personality and Social Psychology, 81*, 1058–1069.

Tyler, J., Darville, R., & Stalnaker, K. (2001). Juvenile boot camps: A descriptive analysis of program diversity and effectiveness. *The Social Science Journal, 38*, 445–460.

Ullman, A., & Straus, M. A. (2003). Violence by children against mothers in relation to violence between parents and corporal punishment by parents. *Journal of Comparative Family Studies, 34*, 41–64.

Underwood, R. C., & Patch, P. C. (1999). Siblicide: A descriptive analysis of sibling homicide. *Homicide Studies, 3*, 333–348.

United States v. Oakland Cannabis Buyers Cooperative, 121 S. Ct. 21 (2000).

Urberg, K. A., Değirmencioğlu, S. M., & Pilgram, C. (1997). Close friend and group influences on adolescent cigarette smoking and alcohol use. *Developmental Psychology, 33*, 834–844.

U.S. Department of Justice. (1988). *Report to the nation on crime and justice: The data* (2nd ed.). Washington, DC: U.S. Government Printing Office.

U.S. Fire Administration. (2004a) *Arson and juveniles: Responding to the violence.* Washington, DC: Federal Emergency Management Agency, National Fire Data Center.

U.S. Fire Administration. (2004b). *Juvenile firesetting—youth firesetting facts.* Washington, DC: Federal Emergency Management Agency, U.S. Fire Administration.

Vandell, D. L. (2004). Early child care: The known and the unknown. *Merrill-Palmer Quarterly, 50*, 387–414.

Vandell, D. L., & Posner, J. K. (1999). Conceptualization and measurement of children's after-school environments. In S. L. Freidman & T. D. Wachs (Eds.), *Measuring environment across the life-span: Emerging methods and concepts.* Washington, DC: American Psychological Association.

Van der Ploeg, J., & Scholte, E. (1997). *Homeless youth.* London: Sage.

Vandersall, T. A., & Wiener, J. M. (1970). Children who set fires. *Archives of General Psychology, 22*, 63–71.

van Goozen, S. H. M., Fairchild, G., Snoek, H., & Harold, G. T. (2007). The evidence for a neurobiological model of childhood antisocial behavior. *Psychological Bulletin, 133*, 149–182.

van IJzendoorn, M. H., Juffer, F., Klein Poelhuis, C. W. (2005). Adoption and cognitive development: A meta-analytic comparison of adopted and nonadopted children's IQ and school performance. *Psychological Bulletin, 131*, 301–316.

van Lier, P. A. C., Vitaro, F., Wanner, B., Vuijk, P., & Crijnen, A. A. M. (2005). Gender differences in developmental links among antisocial behavior, friends' antisocial behavior, and peer rejection in childhood: Results from two cultures. *Child Development, 76*, 841–855.

van Lier, P. A. C., Vuijk, P., & Crijen, A. M. (2005). Understanding mechanisms of change in the development of antisocial behavior: The impact of a universal intervention. *Journal of Abnormal Psychology, 33*, 521–533.

van Wijik, A., van Horn, J., Bullens, R., Bijleveld, C., & Doreleijers, T. (2005). Juvenile sex offenders: A group on its own? *International Journal of Offender Therapy and Comparative Criminology, 49*, 25–36.

van Wijik, A., Vermeirten, R., Loeber, R., Hart-Kerkhoffs, L., Doreleijers, T., & Bullens, R. (2006). Juvenile sex offenders compared to non-sex offenders: A review of the literature 1995–2005. *Trauma, Violence, & Abuse, 7*, 227–243.

Veenestra, R., Lindenberg, S., Oldehinkel, A. J., De Winter, A. F., Verhulst, F. C., & Ormel, J. (2005). Bullying and victimization in elementary schools: A comparison of bullies, victims, bully/victims, and uninvolved preadolescents. *Developmental Psychology, 41*, 672–682.

Veneziano, C., & Veneziano, L. (2002). Adolescent sex offenders: A review of the literature. *Trauma, Violence, & Abuse, 3*, 247–260.

Vera, E. M., & Shin, R. Q. (2006). Promoting strengths in a socially toxic world: Supporting resilience with systemic interventions. *The Counseling Psychologist, 34,* 80–89.

Verlinden, S., Hersen, M., & Thomas, J. (2000). Risk factors in school shootings. *Clinical Psychology Review, 20,* 3–56.

Viding, E. (2004). Understanding the development of psychopathy. *Journal of Child Psychology and Psychiatry, 45,* 1329–1337.

Viding, E., Blair, R. J. R., Moffitt, T. E., & Plomin, R. (2004). Evidence for substantial genetic risk for psychopathy in 7-year-olds. *Journal of Child Psychology and Psychiatry, 45,* 1–6.

Vijoen, J. L., O'Neill, M. L., & Sidhu, A. (2005). Bullying behaviors in female and male adolescent offenders: Prevalence, types, and association with psychosocial adjustment. *Aggressive Behavior, 31,* 521–536.

Vitacco, M. J., Neumann, C. S., & Jackson, R. L. (2005). Testing a four-factor model of psychopathy and its association with ethnicity, gender, intelligence, and violence. *Journal of Consulting and Clinical Psychology, 73,* 466–476.

Vitacco, M. J., Rogers, R., & Neumann, C. S. (2003). The Antisocial Process Screening Device: An examination of its construct and criterion-related validity. *Assessment, 10,* 143–150.

Vitale, J. E., Smith, S. S., Brinkley, C. A., & Newman, J. P. (2002). The reliability and validity of the Psychopathy Checklist—Revised in a sample of female offenders. *Criminal Justice and Behavior, 29,* 202–231.

Vitaro, F., Brendgen, M., & Barker, E. D. (2006). Subtypes of aggressive behaviors: A developmental perspective. *International Journal of Behavioral Development, 30,* 12–19.

Vitaro, F., & Tremblay, R. E. (1994). Impact of a prevention program on aggressive children's friendships and social adjustment. *Journal of Abnormal Child Psychology, 22,* 457–476.

Vold, G. B. (1979). *Theoretical criminology* (2nd ed.). New York: Oxford University Press.

von Bertalanffy, L. (1968). *General systems theory.* New York: George Braziller.

von Eye, A., & Schuster, C. (2000). The road to freedom: Quantitative developmental methodology in the third millennium. *International Journal of Behavioral Development, 24,* 35–43.

Waaktaar, T., Christie, H. J., Borge, A. I. H., & Torgerson, S. (2004). How can young people's resilience be enhanced? Experiences from a clinical intervention project. *Clinical Child Psychology and Psychiatry, 9,* 167–183.

Wadsworth, M. E. J. (1975). Delinquency in a national sample of children. *British Journal of Criminology, 15,* 167–174.

Wadsworth, M. (1979). *Roots of delinquency: Infancy, adolescence and crime.* Oxford, UK: Martin Robertson.

Waite, D., Keller, A., McGarvey, E. L., Wieckowski, E., Pinkerton, R., & Brown, G. L. (2005). *Sexual Abuse: A Journal of Research and Treatment, 17,* 313–331.

Wald, J., & Losen, D. (2003). *Defining and redirecting a school-to-prison pipeline.* Cambridge, MA: Civil Rights Project at Harvard University. Available at http://www.civilrightsproject.harvard.edu/research/pipeline03/research03all.php.

Walker-Barnes, C. J., & Mason, C. A. (2001). Ethnic differences in the effect of parenting on gang involvement and gang delinquency: A longitudinal, hierarchical linear modeling perspective. *Child Development, 72,* 1814–1831.

Wallace, H. (1996). *Family violence: Legal, medical, and social perspectives.* Boston: Allyn & Bacon.

Waller, M. A. (2001). Resilience in ecosystemic context: Evolution of the concept. *American Journal of Orthopsychiatry, 71,* 290–297.

Walsh, F. (1998). *Strengthening family resilience.* New York: Guilford.

Walsh, F. (2003). Family resilience: A framework for clinical practice. *Family Process, 42,* 1–18.

Walters, G. D. (2002a). *Criminal belief systems: An integrated-interactive theory of lifestyle.* Westport, CT: Praeger.

Walters, G. D. (2002b). Developmental trajectories, transitions, and nonlinear dynamic systems: A model of crime deceleration and desistance. *International Journal of Offender Therapy and Comparative Criminology, 46,* 30–44.

Wandersman, A., & Nation, M. (1998). Urban neighborhoods and mental health: Psychological contributions to understanding toxicity, resilience, and interventions. *American Psychologist, 53,* 647–656.

Wang, M. C. (1997). Next steps in inner-city education: Focusing on resilience development and learning success. *Education and Urban Society, 29,* 255–276.

Wang, M. C., Reynolds, M. C., & Walberg, H. J. (1986). Rethinking special education. *Educational Leadership, 44,* 26–31.

Wasik, B. A., Bond, M. A., & Hindman, A. (2006). The effects of a language and literacy intervention of Head Start children and teachers. *Journal of Educational Psychology, 98,* 63–74.

Wasserman, G. A., & Miller, L. S. (1999). The prevention of serious and violent juvenile offending. In R. Loeber & D. P. Farrington (Eds.), *Serious & violent juvenile offenders: Risk factors and successful interventions.* Thousand Oaks, CA: Sage.

Wasserman, G. A., & Seracini, A. M. (2001). Family risk factors and interventions. In R. Loeber &

D. P. Farrington (Eds.), *Child delinquents: Development, intervention, and service needs.* Thousand Oaks, CA: Sage.

Webb, J. A., Bray, J. H., Getz, J. G., & Adams, G. (2002). Gender, perceived parental monitoring, and behavioral adjustment: Influences on adolescent alcohol use. *American Journal of Orthopsychiatry, 72*, 392–400.

Webster-Stratton, C., Reid, J., & Hammond, M. (2001). Social skills and problem-solving training for children with early-onset conduct problems: Who benefits? *Journal of Child Psychology and Psychiatry and Allied Disciplines, 42*, 943–952.

Weiler, B. L., & Widom, C. S. (1996). Psychopathy and violent behavior in abused and neglected young adults. *Criminal Behavior and Mental Health, 6*, 253–271.

Weinberg, M. K., Tronick, E. Z., Cohn, J. F., & Olson, K. L. (1999). Gender differences in emotional expressivity and self-regulation during early infancy. *Developmental Psychology, 35*, 175–188.

Weinberg, N. Z., & Glantz, M. D. (1999). Child psychopathology risk factors for drug abuse: Overview. *Journal of Clinical Child Psychology, 28*, 290–297.

Weis, J. G., & Sederstrom, J. (1981). *The prevention of serious delinquency. What to do?* Washington, DC: U.S. Department of Justice.

Weisheit, R. A. (1992). *Domestic marijuana: A neglected industry.* New York: Greenwood Press.

Weiss, R. D., & Mirin, S. M. (1987). *Cocaine.* Washington, DC: American Psychiatric Press.

Weisz, J. R., Chaiyasit, W., Weiss, B., Eastman, K., Eastman, C. L., & Jackson, A. (1995). A multimethod study of problem behavior among Thai and American children in school: Teacher reports versus direct observations. *Child Development, 66*, 402–415.

Weithorn, L. A. (1988). Mental hospitalization of troublesome youth: An analysis of skyrocketing admission rates. *Stanford Law Review, 40*, 773–838.

Wellford, C. F. (1987, May). Towards an integrated theory of criminal behavior. *Albany conference on theoretical integration in the study of deviance and crime.* State University of New York at Albany.

Wells, L. E., & Rankin, J. H. (1985). Broken homes and juvenile delinquency: An empirical review. *Criminal Justice Abstracts, 17*, 249–272.

Wells, L. E., & Rankin, J. H. (1986). The broken homes model of delinquency: Analytic issues. *Journal of Research in Crime and Delinquency, 23*, 68–93.

Werner, E. E. (1987). Vulnerability and resiliency in children at risk for delinquency: A longitudinal study from birth to young adulthood. In J. D. Burchard & S. N. Burchard (Eds.), *Prevention of delinquency.* Newbury Park, CA: Sage.

Werner, E. E. (1993). Risk, resilience, and recovery: Perspectives from the Kauai longitudinal study. *Development and Psychopathology, 5*, 503–515.

Werner, E. E. (1995). Resilience in development. *Current Directions in Psychological Science, 4*, 81–85.

Werner, E. E., Bierman, J. M., & French, F. E. (1971). *The children of Kauai: A longitudinal study from the prenatal period to age ten.* Honolulu: University of Hawaii Press.

Werner, E. E., & Smith, R. S. (1977). *Kauai's children come of age.* Honolulu: University of Hawaii Press.

Werner, E. E., & Smith, R. S. (1982). *Vulnerable, but invincible: A longitudinal study of resilient children and youth.* New York: McGraw-Hill.

West, D. J. (1982). *Delinquency: Its roots, careers and prospects.* Cambridge, MA: Harvard University Press.

West, D. J., & Farrington, D. P. (1973). *Who becomes delinquent?* London: Heinemann Educational.

West, D. J., & Farrington, D. P. (1977). *The delinquent way of life.* London: Heinemann.

West, J., Denton, K., & Germino-Hausken, E. (2000). *America's kindergartners.* Washington, DC: National Center for Educational Statistics.

Whitcomb, D. (2001). Child victimization. In G. Coleman, M. Gaboury, M. Murray, & A. Seymour (Eds.), *National Victim Assistance Academy.* Washington, DC: U.S. Department of Justice.

White, H. R., Loeber, R., Stouthamer-Loeber, M., & Farrington, D. P. (1999). Developmental associations between substance abuse and violence. *Development and Psychopathology, 11*, 785–803.

White, J. L., Moffitt, T. E., Earls, F., Robins, L., & Silva, P. A. (1990). How early can we tell? Predictors of childhood conduct disorder and delinquency. *Criminology, 28*, 507–533.

White, R. (2002, August). *Understanding youth gangs.* Canberra: Australian Institute of Criminology.

Wicks-Nelson, R., & Israel, A. C. (1991). *Behavior disorders of childhood* (2nd ed). Upper Saddle River, NJ: Prentice Hall.

Wicks-Nelson, R., & Israel, A. C. (2003). *Behavior disorders in children* (5th ed). Upper Saddle River, NJ: Prentice Hall.

Widom, C. S. (2000, January). Childhood victimization: Early adversity, later psychopathology. *The National Institute of Justice Journal, 3–9*.

Widom, C. S., & Maxfield, M. G. (2001). *An update on the "cycle of violence"* (NCJ 184894). Washington, DC: National Institute of Justice.

Wiebush, R., Wagner, D., McNulty, B., Wang, Y., & Le, T. (2005). *Implementation and outcome evaluation of the intensive aftercare program.*

Washington, DC: U.S. Department of Justice, Office of Juvenile Justice and Delinquency Prevention.

Wiesner, M., & Kim, H. K. (2006). Co-occuring delinquency and depressive symptoms of adolescent boys and girls: A dual trajectory modeling approach. *Developmental Psychology, 42*, 1220–1235.

Wiesner, M., Kim, H. K., & Capaldi, D. M. (2005). Developmental trajectories of offending: Validation and prediction to young adult alcohol use, drug use, and depressive symptoms. *Development and Psychopathology, 17*, 251–270.

Wiesner, M., & Windle, M. (2004). Assessing covariates of adolescent delinquency trajectories: A latent growth mixture modeling approach. *Journal of Youth and Adolescence, 33*, 431–442.

Wilgosh, L, & Paitich, D. (1982). Ratings of parent behaviors for delinquents from two-parent and single-parent homes. *International Journal of Social Psychiatry, 28*, 141–143.

Wills, T. A., & Cleary, S. D. (1999). Peer and adolescent substance use among 6th–9th graders: Latent growth analyses of influence versus selection mechanism. *Health Psychology, 18*, 453–463.

Wills, T. A., & Stoolmiller, M. (2002). The role of self-control in early escalation of substance abuse: A time-varying analysis. *Journal of Consulting and Clinical Psychology, 70*, 986–997.

Wills, T. A., Walker, C., Mendoza, D., & Ainette, M. G. (2006). Behavioral and emotional self-control: Relations to substance use in samples of middle and high school students. *Psychology of Addictive Behaviors, 20*, 265–278.

Wilson, H. (1975). Juvenile delinquency, parent criminality and social handicap. *British Journal of Criminology, 15*, 241–250.

Wilson, J. Q., & Herrnstein, R. J. (1985). *Crime and human nature.* New York: Simon & Schuster.

Wilson, W. J. (1996). *When work disappears.* Chicago: University of Chicago Press.

Windle, M., & Wiesner, M. (2004). Trajectories of marijuana use from adolescence to young adulthood: Predictors and outcomes. *Development and Psychopathology, 16*, 1007–1027.

Wolfgang, M. E. (1983). Delinquency in two birth cohorts. *American Behavioral Scientist, 27*, 75–86.

Wolfgang, M. E., Figlio, R. M., & Sellin, T. (1972). *Delinquency in a birth cohort.* Chicago: University of Chicago Press.

Wood, P. B., Pfefferbaum, B., & Arneklev, B. J. (1993). Risk-taking and self-control: Social psychological correlates of delinquency. *Journal of Crime and Justice, 16*, 111–130.

Woodworth, M., & Porter, S. (2002). In cold blood: Characteristics of criminal homicides as function of psychopathy. *Journal of Abnormal Psychology, 111*, 436–445.

Worling, J. R. (1995). Adolescent sibling incest offenders: Differences in family and individual functioning when compared to adolescent nonsibling sex offenders. *Child Abuse & Neglect, 19*, 633–643.

Wright, B. R. E., Caspi, A., Moffitt, T. E., & Silva, P. A. (1999). Low self-control, social bonds, and crime: Social causation, social selection, or both? *Criminology, 37*, 479–514.

Wright, J. D., & Rossi, P. H. (1994). *Armed and considered dangerous: A survey of felons and their firearms.* New York: Aldine De Gruyter.

Wu, T. C., Tashkin, D. P., Jiahed, B., & Rose, J. E. (1988). Pulmonary hazards of smoking marijuana as compared with tobacco. *New England Journal of Medicine, 318*, 347–351.

Wyrick, P. A. (2000). *Vietnamese youth gang involvement.* Washington, DC: U.S. Department of Justice, Office of Juvenile Justice and Delinquency Prevention.

Xenos, S., & Smith, D. (2001). Perceptions of rape and sexual assault among Australian adolescents and young adults. *Journal of Interpersonal Violence, 16*, 1103–1119.

Yates, A., Beutler, L. E., & Crago, M. (1983). Characteristics of young violent offenders. *Journal of Psychiatry and Law, 11*, 139–149.

Yoder, K. A., Whitbeck, L. B., & Hoyt, D. R. (2003). Gang involvement and membership among homeless and runaway youth. *Youth and Society, 34*, 441–467.

Young, S., Fox, N. A., & Zahn-Waxler, C. (1999). Relations between temperament and empathy. *Developmental Psychology, 35*, 1189–1197.

Zahn-Waxler, C., Radke-Yarrow, M., Wagner, E., & Chapman, M. (1992). Development of concern for others. *Developmental Psychology, 28*, 126–136.

Zahn-Waxler, C., Robinson, J. L., & Emde, R. N. (1992). The development of empathy in twins. *Developmental Psychology, 28*, 1038–1047.

Zahn-Waxler, C., Schiro, K., Robinson, J. L., Emde, R. N., & Schmitz, S. (2001). Empathy and prosocial patterns in young MZ and DZ twins: Development and genetic and environmental influences. In R. N. Emde & J. K. Hewitt (Eds.), *Infancy to early childhood: Genetic and environmental influences on development change.* London: Oxford University Press.

Zavlek, S. (2005, August). *Planning community-based facilities for violent juvenile offenders as part of a system of graduated sanctions.* Washington,

DC: U.S. Department of Justice, Office of Juvenile Justice and Delinquency Prevention.

Zelazo, P. D., Carter, A., Resnick, J. S., Frye, D. (1997). Early development of executive functions: A problem-solving framework. *Review of General Psychology, 1*, 198–226.

Zigler, E. (1994). Reshaping early childhood interventions to be a more effective weapon against poverty. *American Journal of Community Psychology, 22*, 37–47.

Zigler, E. F., & Stevenson, M. F. (1993). *Children in a changing world: Development and social issues* (2nd ed.). Pacific Grove, CA: Brooks/Cole.

Zigler, E., Taussig, C., & Black, K. (1992). Early childhood intervention: A promising prevention for juvenile delinquency. *American Psychologist, 47*, 997–1006.

Zipper, P., & Wilcox, D. K. (2005, April). The importance of early intervention. *FBI Law Enforcement Bulletin, 74*, 3–9.

Zolondek, S. C., Abel, G. G., Northey, W. F., Jr., & Jordan, A. D. (2001). The self-reported behaviors of juvenile sexual offenders. *Journal of Interpersonal Violence, 16*, 73–85.

Zucker, R. A., Fitzgerald, H. E., Refior, S. K., Puttler, L. I., Pallas, D. M., & Ellis, D. A. (2000). The clinical and social ecology of childhood for children of alcoholics: Description of a study and implications for a differentiated social policy. In H. E. Fitzgerald, B. M. Lester, & B. S. Zuckerman (Eds.), *Children of addiction: Research, health, and public policy issues* (pp. 109–141). New York: RoutledgeFalmer.

AUTHOR INDEX

SUBJECT INDEX

❧